THE CAMBRIDGE TRANSLATIONS OF
MEDIEVAL PHILOSOPHICAL TEXTS

The long-awaited second volume of *The Cambridge Translations of Medieval Philosophical Texts* will allow scholars and students access, for the first time in English, to major texts in ethics and political thought from one of the most fruitful periods of speculation and analysis in the history of western thought.

Beginning with Albert the Great, who introduced to the Latin west the challenging moral philosophy and natural science of Aristotle, and concluding with the first substantial presentation in English of the revolutionary ideas on property and political power of John Wyclif, the seventeen texts in this anthology offer late medieval treatments of fundamental issues in human conduct that are both conceptually subtle and of direct practical import.

The volume includes editorial introductions, an analytical index, and suggestions for further reading.

This is an important resource for scholars and students of medieval philosophy, history, political science, theology, and literature.

D0219693

THE CAMBRIDGE TRANSLATIONS OF MEDIEVAL PHILOSOPHICAL TEXTS

GENERAL EDITOR: ELEONORE STUMP, ST. LOUIS UNIVERSITY

FOUNDING EDITOR: NORMAN KRETZMANN

Also in the series:

Forthcoming volumes:

The Cambridge Translations of Medieval Philosophical Texts

VOLUME TWO
ETHICS AND POLITICAL PHILOSOPHY

EDITORS

ARTHUR STEPHEN McGRADE
UNIVERSITY OF CONNECTICUT

JOHN KILCULLEN
MACQUARIE UNIVERSITY

MATTHEW KEMPSHALL
UNIVERSITY OF OXFORD

CAMBRIDGE UNIVERSITY PRESS

PUBLISHED BY THE PRESS SYNDICATE OF THE UNIVERSITY OF CAMBRIDGE
The Pitt Building, Trumpington Street, Cambridge, United Kingdom

CAMBRIDGE UNIVERSITY PRESS
The Edinburgh Building, Cambridge CB2 2RU, UK
40 West 20th Street, New York, NY 10011-4211, USA
10 Stamford Road, Oakleigh, VIC 3166, Australia
Ruiz de Alarcón 13, 28014 Madrid, Spain
Dock House, The Waterfront, Cape Town 8001, South Africa

http://www.cambridge.org

First published 2001

Printed in the United States of America

Typeface Bembo 11/13 pt.   *System* DeskTopPro$_{/UX}$ [BV]

A catalog record for this book is available from the British Library.

Library of Congress Cataloging in Publication Data
Ethics and political philosophy / editors, Arthur Stephen McGrade, John Kilcullen,
Matthew Kempshall.
p. cm. – (The Cambridge translations of medieval philosophical texts ; v. 2)
Includes bibliographical references and index.
ISBN 0-521-23625-8 (hb) – ISBN 0-521-28082-6 (pbk.)
1. Ethics, Medieval.   2. Political science – Philosophy.   I. McGrade, Arthur Stephen.
II. Kilcullen, John, 1938–   III. Kempshall, M. S.   IV. Series.

BJ231 .E84 2000
172'.0902 – dc21
99-087118

ISBN   0 521 23625 8   hardback
ISBN   0 521 28082 6   paperback

*This volume is dedicated to the memory of Michael Wilks,
generous model for a generation of scholars in his field.*

CONTENTS

PREFACE

The idea of a series of volumes to be known as *The Cambridge Translations of Medieval Philosophical Texts* originated in the Cambridge University Press almost as soon as work on *The Cambridge History of Later Medieval Philosophy* had begun. The first volume in the series, *Logic and the Philosophy of Language*, edited by Norman Kretzmann and Eleonore Stump, appeared in 1988. Work on the present volume began in 1991 with the selection of texts to be translated and the gathering of a team to do the translating. We are now happy to present a body of texts in moral philosophy which we have come to appreciate increasingly while working with them. A. S. McGrade, who is primarily responsible for Translations 1–2 and 13–14 and for editing the volume as a whole, was able to devote full time to the project in early 1991, thanks to a sabbatical leave from teaching granted by the University of Connecticut and a Visiting Fellowship from Clare Hall, Cambridge, and in 1994–95, thanks to a grant from the Translations Program of The National Endowment for the Humanities and the further hospitality of Clare Hall. Supplementary grants from the University of Connecticut Research Foundation and the encouragement of its director, Thomas G. Giolas, have been a great help to him. He is also grateful to the staffs of libraries at the University of Cambridge; the Episcopal Divinity School in Cambridge, Massachusetts; Harvard University; Yale University; the University of Connecticut; and St. John's College and Merton College, Oxford. He is grateful above all to his wife for her continuing civilizing influence on his English and for saving him from many misrenderings of Latin. John Kilcullen, who is primarily responsible for Translations 15–17, wishes to thank John Scott for his work in establishing corrected texts of Ockham's *Dialogus* and Wyclif's *De civili dominio* and Professor Oliver O'Donovan for a number of corrections and improvements to the translation from Wyclif. Matthew Kempshall, who is primarily responsible for Translations 3–12, wishes to thank the Trustees of Canon Robert Murray for the award of the Murray Research Fellowship.

Evidence of indebtedness to the exemplary inaugural volume in this series is to be found on almost every page of our translations. We owe additional thanks to Professor Stump for her oversight of the present volume.

We join with all students of medieval philosophy in regretting the death of Norman Kretzmann, to whom another volume in this series will fittingly be dedicated.

GENERAL INTRODUCTION

The aim of this volume is the same as that of *The Cambridge History of Later Medieval Philosophy* (CHLMP), to which it is a companion: to help make the activity of contemporary philosophy intellectually continuous with medieval philosophy. Direct acquaintance with medieval philosophical texts, or acquaintance as close to direct as translation from one language to another can provide, is crucial for this end. Philosophy is peculiarly resistant to summary. Even the best scholarly discourse about an Albert the Great or William of Ockham cannot provide the historical insight and incitement to further reflection that comes from reading the philosopher's own work. Our hope, then, is that this volume may both stimulate current philosophical discussion of normative issues and significantly broaden the understanding of earlier discussions.

Modern scholarship has recovered much that is philosophically illuminating from the Middle Ages. In particular, by focusing on late medieval problems and approaches that are intelligible from within the mind-set of Anglophone analytic philosophy, CHLMP has elicited increased engagement with medieval thought even from those who are not especially sympathetic to the period's dominant religious and metaphysical presuppositions. Yet at the same time as medieval thought has become more congenial to contemporary philosophers, doubts have been raised in various quarters about the intellectual and moral values of modernity and Enlightenment on the basis of which contemporary philosophy itself has developed. Few would wish to return to the thirteenth century – certainly not the editors of this volume – but the combination of resonance with contemporary philosophical method and challenge to current assumptions offered by our late medieval predecessors gives special point to the study of their contributions to moral philosophy.

In selecting texts to translate, we were guided by the philosophical and historical considerations represented in the relevant chapters of CHLMP and modified by our own research, especially by the recent work of one of us on scholastic discussions of self-sacrifice (as in Translations 5–8) and resistance (Translations 9–11), topics of current philosophical interest not treated in detail in CHLMP. We were also constrained by several formal considerations. As far as practicable, we wanted the translated texts to be complete works or at least topically complete segments of longer works, and we wanted to present texts that were not already available in English. We also wanted to provide examples of the major genres of philosophical writing in the later Middle Ages: commentary (both 'literal' or phrase by phrase commentary and commentary-with-questions, the forms in which traditional theological texts received analytic scrutiny and usually the first written forms of encounter with the challenging body of Aristotelian texts entering the Latin west in our period), quodlibetic and disputed questions (edited transcripts of formal academic exercises in which issues of particular speculative or practical importance received concentrated attention, often from leading thinkers in contention with one another), systematic summas, and the Mirror for Princes form (manuals of advice for rulers that could also contain statements of political principles and arguments of general philosophical significance). Because of these constraints and limited space, we have not been able to present the full range of medieval views on any topic. For example, although the section of Peter of Auvergne's commentary on Aristotle's *Politics* that we translate was important for later discussions of constitutional or mixed government, it gives little hint of the wealth of late medieval material on this subject studied in James M. Blythe's *Ideal Government and the Mixed Constitution in the Middle Ages* (Princeton: Princeton University Press, 1992). Again, our translation of five questions from Augustine of Ancona's *Summa on Ecclesiastical Power* is a sample from one of the best medieval models for theorizing about the nature of sovereignty, but we provide little that is directly relevant to the complementary topic of individual rights, aside from Ockham's arguments against the obligation to give up a religious belief at the bare rebuke of a superior. For the extensive late medieval literature on rights, briefly discussed in CHLMP X.39, 'Rights, Natural Rights, and the Philosophy of Law,' the reader is referred to already translated works of Thomas Aquinas, John of Paris, Marsilius of Padua, and William of Ockham and to the studies of Brian Tierney (*The Idea of Natural Rights*, Atlanta: Scholars Press, 1997) and Annabel S. Brett (*Liberty, Right and Nature: Individual Rights in Later Scholastic Thought*, Cambridge: Cambridge University Press, 1997). Aquinas and Duns Scotus, preeminent figures of the period, are missing from this volume because their work in moral philosophy is to some extent available in translation – to a great extent in the case of Aquinas, in the case of Scotus to a far lesser extent than is merited by his stature and influence. Only lack of space explains the omission of selections from the writings of such acute thinkers as Boethius of Dacia, Durand of St Pour-çain, Robert Holkot, Adam Wodeham, Gregory of Rimini, Thomas Bradwardine, Jean Gerson, and Nicole Oresme.

We have arranged the contents of the volume in a loosely historical order. Thematic groupings of some selections within this framework suggest the dialogical character of philosophy in the period from which the texts are drawn. A further indication of this is the extent to which, as recorded in the Index, the same concepts and theses play important roles in selections throughout the volume.

These translations can be approached in a number of ways. They can be read as responses by philosophically trained thinkers to the possibilities and problems of the world in which they lived. In some selections, engagement with practical issues is quite direct. In almost every case, there is a fresh concern with the conscience, virtues, and ultimate fulfillment of individuals or with the rational organization of communal life. The import of these contributions in relation to other factors in later medieval society is not always easy to assess. Philosophical attention to personal life in this period produced subtle analyses of the interactions of thought, will, and emotion in human conduct, analyses which both reflected and enhanced individual self-awareness – but they also gave support to the individualism involved in dissent and heresy, the gravest of all problems from a medieval point of view. Discussions of who should rule, and with what accountability, arguably contributed to the growth of responsible government, but the rationalization of political life in the thirteenth and fourteenth centuries which some of these discussions supported has also been seen as a source of what could later be described as oppression by state power. Judgments about the spirit of the age will benefit (in quality if not in simplicity) from attention to texts such as those presented here.

For philosophical readers not primarily concerned with the culture and politics of the Middle Ages, this volume can fruitfully be read as the response, in moral philosophy, of an intellectual community educated in Christian Platonism to the reintroduction in the west of Aristotelian treatises dealing with every major field of knowledge in a relatively naturalistic way. Engagement with the Philosopher, sometimes highly critical but usually accommodating, is especially evident in the earlier selections but is also present at the end of the volume in the reconverted Platonist, John Wyclif. Aristotle, like the world outside the academy, presented problems and possibilities closely intertwined. For example, the *Nicomachean Ethics* (henceforth simply '*Ethics*') could be assimilated as a source of wise counsel on how to live as a pilgrim or wayfarer in this life while moving toward the final joy of heaven, and Aristotle's reasoned exaltation of the contemplative life in Book X of the *Ethics* could even be used as a model for discussing the vision of God at the heart of that final joy. But the *Ethics* could also be read as setting out a program for happiness in this world that neither required nor allowed an other-worldly supplement. Likewise, the *Politics*, with its analytical discussions of constitutions and political practices, offered a framework for discussing how human beings might achieve well-being in their lives together, but it was far from obvious how even the best Aristotelian polity (if it could be identified) related to the authority and sacramental practices of the church. In light of these examples, it is not surprising that issues of immediate practical importance and issues raised by Aristotle were often dealt with in the same treatise or, indeed, in the same argument.

The first translation in the volume is taken from Albert the Great's *On the Ethics*, written in 1248–52, the first dialectical encounter with the whole text of Aristotle's *Ethics* in the Latin west. We have chosen to present Albert's questions on Book X because of the range of topics treated in the book: the nature and value of pleasure, civic and contemplative happiness, and the need, once an adequate conception of happiness has been achieved, to give it political expression. In Albert's nineteen lessons on Book X, most major propositions of the Philosopher's text are critically examined, with results that greatly influenced subsequent thought about the issues treated, most immediately the thought of Albert's pupil, Thomas Aquinas, but also that of Jean Buridan a century later, whose questions on *Ethics* X are presented in Translation 16.

Another important vehicle for scholastic philosophical analysis, along with commentary on Aristotle, was commentary on the *Sentences* of Peter Lombard, a mid-twelfth-century compilation and discussion of quotations from the church fathers which became the standard theology textbook in the later Middle Ages. It is in their commentaries on the *Sentences* that we find some of the most important philosophizing of Scotus, Ockham, and other later figures, as well as Bonaventure, who lectured on the *Sentences* at Paris at about the same time as Albert was lecturing on the *Ethics* in Cologne. Translation 2, Bonaventure's discussion of conscience and synderesis (the 'spark' of conscience, treated by medieval thinkers as a moral capacity in some way distinct from conscience) serves to introduce a topic that is important in its own right and recurs in several of our later selections.

The next nine selections are specifically political in content, at least in their points of departure. In the first of these, the prologue and selected chapters from Giles of Rome's widely disseminated *On the Rule of Princes*, we find politics built on a foundation of ethics and presented with explicit attention to rhetoric as a necessity for practical effectiveness. Writing primarily for the instruction of a future king of France but incidentally for the enlightenment of the crown's subjects, Giles maintains that rational rule of a kingdom presupposes rational rule of self. In propounding ways of achieving either sort of rule, Giles conveys the results of reflection on a wide variety of sources in an 'easy' method of exposition appealing to the will as well as to the intellect and operating by reference to what is typical and general, a method he defended at the beginning of his work. Both in his method and in his construction of political wisdom on a foundation of personal morality, Giles presented new Aristotelian content in a traditional literary genre – the Mirror for Princes – going back to Augustine and Gregory the Great.

Formal scholastic appropriation of Aristotle's *Politics* began in earnest with the literal commentary commenced by Thomas Aquinas and completed by Peter of Auvergne. Peter's later commentary on the *Politics* in question form was also influential. Translation 4 presents portions of Peter's two treatments of sections of *Politics* III that are significant both for constitutional theory – for discussions of the comparative merits of different forms of political community and the power of the people in each of them – and for debates about urgent practical issues of the day.

Aristotle's systematic analysis in the *Politics* of the various species of human community realizable in this life raised questions that had received comparatively little attention in an earlier tradition predominantly concerned with the contrast between the (ultimately heavenly) city of God and a generic 'earthly city' driven by love of self even to the point of contempt for God. One such issue was the rationality of self-sacrifice for the well-being of one's earthly commonwealth, Henry of Ghent's topic in Translation 5. Henry's conclusion, that choosing to die for such an end is rational even if one has no hope of a future life as a reward, is the implicit basis for a broader investigation of altruism by two of Henry's late thirteenth-century contemporaries, Godfrey of Fontaines and James of Viterbo (in Translations 6–8). Here self-sacrifice in a political context is compared with the love of God above all else, which continued to be the supreme value of later as well as earlier medieval ethics. The debate between Godfrey and James about the logic – or, indeed, the 'natural' possibility – of such devotion is sparked by the clash of Aristotle's assertion that friendliness toward another derives from friendliness toward oneself with the pervasive Augustinian thesis that love of anything beyond oneself requires God's grace. A number of recurrent medieval themes are presented in these texts: the interplay, in discerning the good, between natural rationality and a reason enlightened by divine revelation; dispute about the present condition of the human will as perverse or weak or, on the contrary, robust and responsible; analogical use of the part–whole relation to understand the relations of individual to community and creature to God; and the use of metaphysics as a basis for ethics (in this case the metaphysics of identity and resemblance as a basis for understanding friendship, self-sacrifice for one's community, and devotion to God above all else). The combination of modern-seeming analytic method with medieval content is especially evident in these texts.

Translations 9–11, again from texts of Henry of Ghent, Godfrey of Fontaines, and James of Viterbo, come back to earth. Aristotelian and other classical philosophical sources, along with Roman and canon law in some cases, are here utilized to address urgent practical problems, problems of obedience and resistance occasioned by controversial trends in contemporary government: arbitrariness in legislation and taxation, personal rather than legal rule. Historians of politics and political thought have yet to exploit fully the resources of such discussions.

The final translation in this political group, Translation 12, is a selection from the extensive medieval literature on the just war. The specific question posed by John of Naples, whether a Christian king could rightly use Saracen mercenaries to defend his kingdom against Christian attackers, adds interreligious dimensions to an already difficult problem. In the course of presenting eighteen arguments against employing non-Christians to fight Christians, four arguments in favor of such an expedient, and five theses aimed at adjudicating the question, John touches on many of the circumstances thought relevant to the morality of war in the early fourteenth century. The extent to which morality *was* then thought relevant to war suggests restraint in the use of 'medieval' in military contexts as a synonym for unrestrained brutality.

Translation 13, On Using and Enjoying, is from the beginning of Ockham's commentary on Lombard's *Sentences*. Here Ockham develops further some of the themes introduced in the earlier selections on self-sacrifice and also resumes the discussion of pleasure and happiness begun in this volume with Albert the Great's questions on *Ethics* X. Ockham's point of departure is Augustine's conviction that God and God alone is to be loved as an ultimate end, while all other things are only to be used. Ockham agrees, but by making room for acts of will between enjoying and using he, like most of the authors represented in this volume, allows for the possibility of an authentic moral life without specific religious commitments. In developing his position on these matters, Ockham outlines a moral psychology that is general in scope, thereby providing an example of work in another area where the medieval literature is vast.

The questions from Augustine of Ancona's *Summa on Ecclesiastical Power* making up Translation 14 approach questions of faith, reason, and conscience from a specifically political angle. Augustine's *Summa* is the antithesis of Marsilius of Padua's *Defender of Peace*, which had appeared a few years before it. Where Marsilius had seen the claims to comprehensive secular as well as ecclesiastical authority made by and for the contemporary papacy as the single greatest threat to Europe in his time and had accordingly propounded a political theory that foreshadowed the modern secular state, Augustine of Ancona held that universal papal power was an essential part of God's plan for the world. Yet Augustine also recognized the claims of natural law, conscience, and other sources of direction besides papal judgment, as well as the dangers of papal misgovernment and – at least as a possibility recognized in canon law – doctrinal error. Whether he was consistent in his accommodation of all these normative principles is controversial, but the attempt was important, and the stresses it involved are typical of political thought in this period.

Augustine of Ancona appealed to a traditional, biblically grounded conception of 'fraternal correction' (Matthew 18:15: 'If your brother sins against you, go and correct him privately . . .' – the beginning of a procedure that ends with 'Tell the church') to argue that, notwithstanding the papacy's transcendent authority, every Christian is bound to correct an erring pope (for the pope is every Christian's brother). The chapters from Ockham's massive dialogue on heresy presented in Translation 15 add the requirement that, for any doctrinal correction at all to be legitimate, even the correction of an inferior by a superior, the erring individual must be clearly shown that the view being corrected is indeed erroneous. This adaptation of the traditional idea is theoretically revolutionary, but its exact practical significance is unclear. It is at least another emphatic example of the questioning of authority in medieval scholastic thought.

Translation 16, Jean Buridan's questions on *Ethics* X is nominally concerned with the same Aristotelian text as the selection from Albert the Great which opens the volume. Buridan's treatment of the text is very different, however, in ways characteristic of changes in scholasticism during the intervening century. Most obviously, there are fewer questions in Buridan than in Albert and a more intense pursuit of those few. Buridan quickly sets aside the topic of pleasure, which had occupied Albert for nearly half of his lessons on *Ethics* X, on the ground that he had discussed it enough in his questions on Book VII. He further narrows his inquiry by taking it for granted that happiness, the second main topic of Book X, is to be found in the activity of our best power in accordance with its best virtue and by assuming that the best power is the one that is most free. This narrowing of scope, accomplished in a short paragraph, sets the stage for an intricate discussion of freedom of intellect and freedom of will as primary constituents of human happiness. In the course of this discussion Buridan refines and in places implicitly criticizes the moral psychology set forth by Ockham in Translation 13. A concern with conceptual analysis of natural processes such as Buridan exhibits here with regard to mental processes, rather than with the situation of substances and their properties in a broader metaphysical scheme, is also typical of mid-fourteenth-century Oxford and Paris philosophy.

John Wyclif, known as the Morning Star of the Reformation, can as well be called the Evening Star of Medieval Scholasticism. Wyclif broke with the analytic, nonspeculative style of philosophy just remarked on in Buridan and still prevalent at Oxford when he wrote *On Civil Lordship* in the 1370s or 1380s, but this was a break with what Wyclif saw as superficial current fashion, and it was made with appeals to patristic and earlier medieval tradition. In Translation 17, which concludes the volume, Wyclif seeks to resituate property and political power in the framework of creation and divine providence from which, as he saw it, a too prosperous church had allowed them to fall out. His central idea, also prominent in several other selections in this volume, was charity, i.e., Christian love, love of God above all else and of one's neighbor as oneself, which Wyclif held to be possible only through grace. To have charity, he argued, is to participate in God's lordship of all creation, whereas to be in mortal sin is to be a slave to sin and cut off from all meaningful authority over self or others. In comparison with the spiritual lordship over the whole world enjoyed by those with charity, civil lordship, with its essential coerciveness, is clearly secondary (indeed, relatively unreal) in Wyclif's scheme, but it is unclear what implications he intended this secondary status to have for practical politics. Whatever Wyclif's intentions, his writings were a factor in generating and sustaining a potent and fiercely resisted leveling movement in late medieval England and in the Bohemia of Jan Hus. Among the authors represented in our selections, Wyclif is the clearest example of the impact philosophical reflection could have on events in the medieval Latin west.

In order to include as much translated material as possible, and because *The Cambridge Translations of Medieval Philosophical Texts* are companion volumes to CHLMP, we have kept the introductions to individual selections short and have included no explanatory notes. The relevant chapters of CHLMP listed at the end of each introduction provide discussions of the material in most selections, as well as explanatory and bibliographical notes. The Bibliography, Biographies, and Indexes of CHLMP will also help the reader pursue questions raised by these texts. We provide additional suggestions for reading on topics not treated extensively in CHLMP. The present volume, too, has a detailed Index, the main entries in which are accompanied by the corresponding Latin words whenever appropriate.

We have adopted a number of editorial conventions, including those employed by Norman Kretzmann and Eleonore Stump in the first volume in this series, *Logic and the Philosophy of Language*. When we think that our translation of a Latin expression may be unusual, technical, uncertain, or otherwise noteworthy, we print the Latin in single parentheses immediately after the translated word or phrase. We also use single parentheses around English words, phrases, or sentences as part of our punctuation of the translated text when we think that the medieval author has written something parenthetically. We have adjusted our authors' biblical references to conform to the nomenclature and divisions of the New Revised Standard Version of the Bible. Other bibliographical references supplied by us or taken from those supplied by the editor of the Latin text are printed in single parentheses at the appropriate place in the translation. We usually expand only those references made by our authors which are to works available in English. The editions we have used provide many additional references. Our citations of Aristotle's works conform to the book and chapter divisions of the Revised Oxford Translation edited by Jonathan Barnes (Princeton: Princeton University Press, 1984).

When the edition from which we translated includes section numbers, we have kept these in the translation. Page, folio, or signature numbers of the editions we have used are indicated within curly brackets – e.g., {708A} – at the appropriate places in the translation.

We indicate our own substantive additions to the text by printing the word or phrase in square brackets – e.g., [ordered].

Occasionally we have emended the Latin text from which we translated. Except for Translations 15, 16, and 17, in which the necessary corrections to our copy-texts were so numerous as to require a separate listing at the end of the selection, our emendations are enclosed within double parentheses at the appropriate place in the translation. Most emendations have this form: ((*oportet/valet*)), which indicates that we are replacing the word '*valet*' in the edition with the word '*oportet*' and translating accordingly. When the word or phrase we prefer appears among the textual variants in the Latin edition's critical apparatus, we have indicated this by including '[var.]' within the double parentheses. Similarly, when our emendation is based on another edition or manuscript that we have consulted ourselves, e.g., the 1473 edition of the text for Translation 14, we indicate this within the double parentheses in this way: '[with edn 1473].' When our translation depends on adding or omitting a word or phrase to or from the edition, we indicate this by '*add*' or '*om.*' followed by the word or phrase supplied or deleted.

Our translations are based on the following editions, numbered to correspond with the numbering of the translations:

1 Albert the Great: *Questions on Book X of the Ethics. Super Ethica, Commentum et Quaestiones, Libri VI–X*, ed. Wilhelmus Kübel, in vol. XIV, part 2 of *Alberti Magni Opera Omnia*, pp. 708–92; Monasterii Westfalorum in aedibus Aschendorff, 1987.

2 Bonaventure: *Conscience and Synderesis. In II librum Sententiarum*, Distinction 39, Articles 1–2, in *S. Bonaventurae Commentaria in quatuor libros Sententiarum*, vol. II, pp. 898–915; Ad Claras Aquas (Quaracchi): Ex typographia Collegii S. Bonaventurae, 1885.

3 Giles of Rome: *On the Rule of Princes* (selections). *Egidii Romani . . . de regimine principum*, sigs. air–aiiv; oir–v. Venice: Bernardinus Vercelensis, 1502.

4 Peter of Auvergne: *Commentary and Questions on Book III of Aristotle's Politics* (selections). Latin text of Aristotle, ed. F. Susemihl, *Aristotelis Politicorum libri octo cum vetusta translatione Guilelmi de Moerbeka*, pp. 189–98, 219–26; Leipzig: B. G. Teubner, 1872. *Sententia libri Politicorum*, ed. Robertus Busa, in vol. IV of *S. Thomae Aquinatis Opera omnia*, pp. 413–15, 419–20; Stuttgart-Bad Cannstatt: Frommann-Holzboog, 1980. *Petri de Alvernia Quaestiones supra libros Politicorum*, ed. Christoph Flüeler in vol. I of his *Rezeption und Interpretation der Aristotelischen Politica im späten Mittlelalter*, pp. 214–22; Amsterdam/ Philadelphia: B. R. Grüner, 1992.

5 Henry of Ghent: *Is It Rational for Someone without Hope of a Future Life to Choose to Die for the Commonwealth? Quodlibet XII*, question 13, ed. J. Decorte, pp. 67–79; *Henricus de Gandavo Quodlibet XII*, Leuven University Press, 1987.

6 Godfrey of Fontaines: *Does a Human Being Following the Dictates of Natural Reason Have to Judge that He Ought to Love God More than Himself?* Quodlibet X, question 6, ed. J. Hoffmans, *Les Philosophes Belges* vol. IV, pp. 318–26; Louvain: Institut Supérieur de Philosophie de l'Université, 1924.

7 James of Viterbo: *Does a Human Being Have a Greater Natural Love for God than for Himself, or Vice Versa?* Quodlibet II, question 20, ed. Eelcko Ypma, pp. 202–14; *Jacobi de Viterbo O.E.S.A. Disputatio secunda de quolibet*; Würzburg: Augustinus-Verlag, 1969.

8 Godfrey of Fontaines: *Reply to James of Viterbo on Love of God and Self,* Quodlibet XIII, question 1, ed. J. Hoffmans, pp. 180–83; Louvain: Institut Supérieur de Philosophie de l'Université, 1932.

9 Henry of Ghent: *Is a Subject Bound to Obey a Statute When It Is Not Evident that It Promotes the Common Utility?* Quodlibet XIV, question 8, in *Henrici Goethalis a Gandavo . . . Aurea quodlibeta* vol. II, fol. 352ra–vb; Venice: V. Zuccolius, 1613.

10 Godfrey of Fontaines: *Are Subjects Bound to Pay a Tax When the Need for It Is Not Evident?* Quodlibet XI, question 17, ed. J. Hoffmans, in *Les Philosophes Belges* vol. V, pp. 76–78; Louvain: Institut Supérieur de Philosophie de l'Université, 1932.

11 James of Viterbo: *Is It Better to Be Ruled by the Best Man than by the Best Laws?* Quodlibet IV, question 30, ed. Eelcko Ypma, pp. 107–10; *Jacobi de Viterbo O.E.S.A. Disputatio quarta de quolibet*; Würzburg: Augustinus-Verlag, 1975.

12 John of Naples: *Should a Christian King Use Unbelievers to Defend His Kingdom?* in his *Quaestiones disputatae*, pp. 323–30; Naples: D. Gravina, 1618.

13 William of Ockham: *Using and Enjoying. Scriptum in librum primum Sententiarum ordinatio,* Distinction 1, questions 1–4 and 6, ed. Gedeon Gál with the assistance of Stephen Brown, pp. 371–447, 486–507; St. Bonaventure, N.Y.: Franciscan Institute, 1967.

14 Augustine of Ancona: *Summa on Ecclesiastical Power* (selections). *Summa de ecclesiastica potestate,* pp. 56–67; 129–40; 332–36; Rome: Georgius Ferrarius, 1584 (compared with several manuscripts and other editions).

15 William of Ockham: *Is an Errant Individual Bound to Recant at the Rebuke of a Superior? Dialogus,* Part I, Book 4, chapters 13–15, 20–21, ed. Melchior Goldast in his *Monarchiae S. Romanae Imperii,* vol. II, pp. 454–56, 459–60; Frankfurt: Typis Nicolai Hoffmanni, 1614; repr. Graz: Akademische Druck- u. Verlagsanstalt, 1960 (compared with another edition – ed. J. Trechsel in vol. I of *Guillelmus de Occam, O.F.M., Opera plurima*; Lyons, 1494 – and with several manuscripts; critical apparatus to be found at http://www.britac.ac.uk/pubs/dialogus/ockdial.html).

16 Jean Buridan: *Questions on Book X of the Ethics. Quaestiones Joannis buridani super decem libros ethicorum,* fols 203r–14v; Paris: Ponset Le Preux, 1513 (compared with several manuscripts; critical apparatus to be found at http://www.humanities.mq.edu.au/Ockham/wburlat.html).

17 John Wyclif: *On Civil Lordship* (selections). *Tractatus de civili dominio liber primus,* ed. R. L. Poole, pp. 1–73; London: Trübner, 1885 (compared with two manuscripts, one of which, Paris, B.N. f.l. 15869, was unknown to Poole; the text translated is a conflation of these sources; it can be found at http://www.humanities.mq.edu.au/Ockham/wwyclat.html).

ALBERT THE GREAT
QUESTIONS ON BOOK X OF THE ETHICS

Introduction

Albert the Great (referred to as such from the fourteenth century) was born near Ulm about the year 1200. His first university studies were at Padua, where he joined the Dominican Order around 1220/3. He returned to Germany to study theology and in 1245 became the first German master at the University of Paris. Thomas Aquinas, one of Albert's pupils at Paris, followed him to Cologne, where Albert founded a Dominican house of studies and taught from 1248 to 1252. The following selection, which dates from this period, is taken from the first of Albert's two commentaries on the *Nicomachean Ethics*. There is a tradition that Aquinas was assigned to write down these lectures. Albert was the Dominican Provincial in Germany from 1254 to 1257 and at papal insistence was elected bishop of Regensburg in 1260, but he was allowed to return to teaching at Cologne in 1262. In 1277 he went to Paris in a vain attempt to prevent the condemnation by Bishop Stephen Tempier of 219 propositions in philosophy and theology, many of which were commonly associated with his and Aquinas's teachings. He died at Cologne in 1280.

Albert was the first interpreter in the Latin west of Aristotle's work in its entirety. He distinguished sharply between philosophy and theology, insisting that philosophical problems be solved philosophically and denouncing the enemies of philosophy as 'brute beasts' who 'blaspheme against what they do not know.' The comprehensiveness of Albert's grasp of Aristotle's own synoptic consideration of nature and human affairs shows itself in his easy movement through the physical, psychological, metaphysical, and moral aspects of the topics he investigates. Albert made extensive use of Byzantine and Arabic sources in commending the Philosopher to his contemporaries, and partly because of this his Aristotelianism has a Neoplatonic cast. His presentation of Aristotle nonetheless held its own in the later Middle Ages both against opponents of the intrusion of philosophy into the domain of theology and in contrast with other interpretations of Aristotle.

In writing on the *Ethics*, Albert relied on Robert Grosseteste's translation of the work itself and of several Greek commentaries on it, as well as on his own wide reading. Albert's conception of happiness in this life as achieved through a philosophical ascent from consideration of earthly things to an intellectual intuition of immaterial realities subtly frames his treatment of *Ethics* X. He begins with verses from Boethius contrasting 'the chains of heavy earth' (for Albert, the bodily pleasures discussed with discrimination in the first part of Book X) with 'the shining fountain of good,' the divine understanding, the source of a contemplative happiness imitating it, which is the main subject of the second part of the book. Albert's goal of detachment from earthly things does not inhibit him from making a detailed psycho-physical inquiry into the nature of physical pleasure or, indeed, from offering a positive valuation of it, though a qualified one. Nevertheless, contemplation, or, in a vividly visionary sense of the term, 'speculation,' is for Albert the height of human good.

The following translation includes all of Albert's questions on *Ethics* X. His paraphrases of Aristotle's text at the end of each lesson are omitted.

For further reading, see CHLMP IX.34, 'The Reception and Interpretation of Aristotle's *Ethics*,' and IX.35, 'Happiness: the Perfection of Man'; and Alain de Libera, 'Albert the Great' in Edward Craig, ed. *The Routledge Encyclopedia of Philosophy*, vol. I (London and New York: Routledge, 1998), pp. 828–35.

Questions on Book X of the Ethics

Lesson 1

{708A} 'After these matters [we ought perhaps next to discuss] pleasure' (1172a16).

Boethius says in his book *On the Consolation of Philosophy* (III, poem 12):

> Happy are they who can look into the shining fountain of good,
> Happy are they who can loose the chains of heavy earth.

All the material of this tenth book is drawn together and taken hold of in these words. For the greatest good is that which is good of itself and to which other things are ordered, and this is especially the perfect activity of the speculative understanding, which is called contemplative happiness. Now the fountain of this [activity] is the divine understanding, which pours forth the light of knowledge into all who know and is itself imitated in contemplative happiness. This is because the ultimate perfection of all our contemplation is in him whom it is most desirable to know – and this is a question about the divine understanding, as the Commentator [Averroes] says on *Metaphysics* XI (comm. 51). Now God himself contemplates his own understanding most perfectly, and in understanding himself he understands all other things. For this reason contemplative happiness is a certain imitation of the divine understanding, and so through contemplative happiness one sees the fountain of good, which is called 'shining' because 'there are not any shadows in it' (1 John 1:5). Thus the subject of the second part of this book, which is contemplative happiness, is grasped in the first verse. Now the chains of heavy earth are bodily pleasures, by which we are joined to what is below, drawn downward from the height of our nature to its depths. These chains are perfectly loosed by those who enjoy the true pleasures of understanding. And thus the subject of the first part of the book, which is concerned with the pleasures of understanding, is grasped in the second verse. Accordingly, the book, up to that part where he joins this science to political science (1179a33), is divided into two parts, because he first discusses pleasure and then (beginning at 'Now that we have spoken,' chapter 6 [1176a30]) contemplative happiness. The first part is divided in two. First he shows {708B} that it is necessary to discuss pleasure; then (beginning at 'Eudoxus,' chapter 2 [1172b9]) he discusses it.

Here we have to ask five questions.

[1. Is a Discussion of Pleasure Germane to the Present Inquiry?]

First, whether a discussion of pleasure is germane to the present inquiry.

[1a] It Seems Not

[i] What life is concerned with and what it is ordered to are not the same. But our life is concerned with pleasures and distresses, as can be gathered from the preceding books. Therefore, he ought not to discuss these sub-

jects in this last book, where he intends to discuss the things to which our life is ordered as to an ultimate end.

[ii] Moreover, the [anonymous] Commentator said above that the moral and intellectual virtues differ, in that the former are concerned with pleasures and distresses while the latter are not. But in this tenth book he [Aristotle] intends to discuss the end of the intellectual virtues. Therefore, etc.

[iii] Moreover, just as affection and understanding differ, so also do their perfections differ. But the good is the perfection of affection, part of which is pleasure. Therefore, etc.

[iv] Moreover, defining factors should be discussed with the things they define. But self-control is defined in relation to pleasure, for those are called self-controlled who keep hold of themselves in the face of pleasures. Therefore, etc.

[1b] Against

Everything essential to a topic ought to be discussed along with it. But pleasure is essential to contemplative happiness, which he intends to take up. The Commentator [Michael of Ephesus] proves this on the ground that happiness is unintelligible without pleasure. Therefore he had to discuss it here, too.

Moreover, Anselm says (*On the Fall of the Devil* 4) that blessedness consists of the advantageous. Now pleasant things are advantageous; and so as before.

Moreover, Dionysius [rather, Avicenna, *Metaphysica*, tr. 8 c. 7; *Opera*, Venice 1508, fol. 101rb] says that pleasure arises from being joined with something agreeable (*ex coniunctione convenientis*). But in contemplative happiness the understanding is joined with what is most agreeable to it. In it, therefore, there is the greatest pleasure. Now each subject ought to be discussed in relation to what is best and greatest in it, because {709A} the perfect is the measure of everything in its genus. Therefore, along with contemplative happiness he had to discuss pleasure.

[1c. Responses to the Preceding Arguments]

We concede this [last set of arguments].

[i] We say to the first [of the opening arguments] that moral virtue is concerned with bodily pleasures, with respect to which it holds to the

mean, but it is not [ordered] to them. It is [ordered] to the pleasures of understanding as an ordered disposition. That is why he discusses these [pleasures] here.

[ii] From this the solution to the second is plain.

[iii] To the third we have to say that in contemplative happiness the true is taken not only as true, as the perfection of understanding, but also as the understanding's good, and so from its being joined to the understanding there follows pleasure.

[iv] We have to say to the fourth, as to the first, that it is based on bodily pleasures.

[2. Should Aristotle Have Discussed Pleasure after Happiness?]

[2a. Arguments that He Should Have]

Second, it seems that he ought to have discussed pleasure after happiness.

[i] For the cause is prior to the caused. But the cause of pleasure is activity proper and natural to a thing. Now this is happiness. Therefore, [he ought to have discussed it] before [discussing pleasure].

[ii] Moreover, defining factors are known prior to what they define. But proper activity is posited in the definition of pleasure, which is a flowering of nature arising from proper activity. Therefore, he should first have discussed proper activity, which is happiness.

[iii] Or, on the other hand, it seems he ought to have discussed it at the beginning of the whole work, because the general comes before the specific. But pleasure, as has been said, is found generally, in both moral and intellectual matters. Therefore, etc.

[iv] Moreover, he said above, in the second book (c. 3, 1104b4–5), that pleasure is a sign that a habit has been generated. But habit is common to intellectual and moral matters. Therefore, etc.

[2b] Solution

We have to say that in contemplative happiness proper activity is its matter, so to speak, while the formal [element], the reason it is taken to be happiness, is pleasure. For proper activity does not make a person happy insofar as it is activity and involves motion (in this respect it induces weariness) but insofar as it is pleasant. Hence he needed to discuss pleasure before happiness and after the activities of the intellectual virtues, which are, so to speak, the material [elements] in happiness.

[2c. Replies to the Opening Arguments]

[i, ii] {709B} From this the solution to the first two is plain.

[iii] To the third we have to say that the moral virtues are concerned with bodily pleasures, but in contemplative happiness there are unqualified pleasures, the pleasures of the understanding, and hence they ought to be discussed with it. The first pleasure is caused by the working of virtue, hence the need to discuss it after the virtues, as being caused by them in common.

[iv] We have to say to the fourth that the activity of a habit is pleasant insofar as the habit becomes a sort of nature. With pathological habits, therefore, which are without qualification against nature, there are not true pleasures but qualified ones. Now the habits of the moral virtues do indeed have true pleasures, [but they are] qualified, not unqualified, insofar as they are perfections of the irrational parts [of the soul], which [do, however,] participate in reason, and in this respect they are proper and true. But the habits of understanding have proper and true pleasures that are unqualified, and hence [the true nature of] pleasure should be discussed in connection with them.

[3. Is Pleasure Most Closely Connected to Human Nature?]

[3a. It Seems Not]

Third, it seems that pleasure is not 'most closely connected to our kind' (1172a19–20).

[i] For to every nature there is something agreeable. But pleasure arises from being joined with the agreeable. Therefore, any nature whatever has some pleasure proper to it, as the ass, for example, takes pleasure in bitter vetch. Therefore, [pleasure] is not closely connected only to humans.

[ii] Moreover, he means either bodily or spiritual pleasures. If bodily or

animal [pleasures], these are also found in the brutes. If spiritual, these are found more in the intelligences. Therefore, he speaks falsely.

[iii] Moreover, opposition impedes the intensity of pleasure. For since one power's being active withdraws another from being active [and] pleasure is consequent on activity, pleasure must impede pleasure. But in humans there is a spiritual nature and a bodily, and there is pleasure in both. Therefore, it is reduced in both.

[3b] Against

Something is most properly attributed to that which it belongs to in its whole range. But pleasure belongs in this way to humans but not to others, because we have both animal and intellectual pleasures, while brutes have only the animal {710A} and spiritual substances the intellectual. Therefore, etc.

Moreover, unqualified bodily pleasures relate to touch, as Avicenna says. But among the animals humans have the finest sense of touch, as is said in the *De anima* (II 9, 421a19–20). Therefore, etc.

We grant the preceding.

[3c. Replies to the Opening Arguments]

[i] To the first we have to say that the ass does indeed have a pleasure proper to its own nature, but it is not ordered to the pleasures of understanding, which are unqualified (not having a contrary), as is the case [with bodily pleasures] in humans.

[ii] To the second we have to say that he is talking about both [kinds of pleasure], both generally and as to the order some of them have to others; and the latter is found only in humans.

[iii] To the third we have to say that it is true that certain pleasures diminish others, but diminished bodily pleasures are in order, because intense ones are vicious. But the more intense the [pleasures] of understanding are the nobler they are, because they are not intensified by receding from a contrary but by approaching one [object?]. Hence I gladly concede that these [pleasures] are truer in the intelligences.

[4. Is Pleasure Relevant to This Inquiry Even Granting It Is a Motive in Morals?]

[4a. It Seems Not]

Fourth, it seems that [the discussion of pleasure] is irrelevant here even if it is conceded that pleasures incline us in morals (1172a24).

[i] For he is not considering morals in this book. Therefore, it cannot be argued from this that pleasure ought to be discussed [here].

[ii] Moreover, different factors incline us to different ways of life. But the contemplative life is different from the civic life. If, therefore, pleasure inclines us in the moral life (that is, the civic life), something else will incline us in the contemplative life. So he ought to discuss that here and not pleasure.

[iii] Moreover, the hedonistic (*voluptuosa*) life is different from the civic and the contemplative. But pleasure inclines us to the hedonistic life. Therefore, it pertains to neither the civic nor the contemplative life.

[iv] Moreover, what we should most flee in life is not an inclination in it. But in Book II (9, 1109b7–10) he said that for good morals we must especially flee pleasures. Therefore, etc.

[4b] Solution

{710B} We have to say that pleasure is a measure of human life, because those [lives] that have good pleasures are judged good, and those that have shameful ones shameful. On this account he says that they are an inclination to every life.

[4c. Replies to the Opening Arguments]

[i] To the first we have to say that although he is not concerned here with morals in themselves, nevertheless he is concerned with them as they relate to the ultimate end, namely, contemplative happiness, to which the moral virtues are ordered as dispositions, as he will prove below (in c. 8, 1178a16–23).

[ii] To the second we have to say that the moral life is ordered to the contemplative, and for this reason the same thing can incline us in both.

[iii] To the third we have to say that in the hedonistic life disgraceful

pleasures are inclining factors, pleasures prohibited in the moral life. He is not concerned with these here.

[iv] From this the solution to the last is plain.

[5. Do Actions Nullify Truth?]

[5a. It Seems Not]

Fifth, it seems that a deed does not destroy the truth (1172a35–b1).

For in Book II (4, 1105b2–3) he said that there are many who know [how to act] but do what is contrary. But insofar as they know, they have the truth in mind. Therefore, a contrary deed does not destroy the truth.

Moreover, he said above in Book VII (7, 1150b19–21), regarding those who lack self-control, that they are corrupt in what they do, because they follow their passions, yet their reason is not corrupt. Therefore the same.

Moreover, the Lord says in the Gospel (Matthew 23:3): 'Do what they say [not what they do].' Therefore, etc.

[5b] Solution

We have to say that a contrary deed does not destroy the truth in the mind about what should be done as to its truth but as to the opinion of the crowd. They reckon that no one who was knowledgeable would do bad things except in the belief that they should be done and hence that they do what they do as being good – because deeds reveal more than words, as Anselm says (*On Truth* 9) about the man who eats herbs that he tells others are poisonous and throws away those he says are edible. He shows which are wholesome more by what he does than by what he says.

From this the solution to the objections is plain. . . .

Lesson 2

{712A} 'Eudoxus therefore' (1172b9).

Having shown that pleasure should be discussed, he begins to discuss it. This is divided into two parts. First he discusses it according to the opinion of others, then (at 'What [pleasure] is, or what sort of thing it is' [c. 4, 1174a13]) according to his own opinion. The first is divided into two.

First he sets out the opinion of those who placed pleasure in the genus of the good, then (at 'Yet if [pleasure] is not a quality,' chapter 3 [1173a13]) the opinion of those who [placed it in the genus] of the bad. The [reason for this] order is clear, because evil is the privation of good and is known through it.

About this part I ask five questions.

[1. Is Everything Chosen for the Sake of Pleasure?]

First, is pleasure choice-worthy *per se*, as the reason other things are choice-worthy, i.e., as that for the sake of which everything is chosen? It seems so.

[1a. Arguments that Everything Is Sought for the Sake of Pleasure]

[i] For everything sought is sought insofar as it is agreeable. But being joined with what is agreeable produces pleasure. Therefore, etc.

[ii] Moreover, the Philosopher says in *Physics* I (9, 192a16–25) that everything that seeks something else is, as such, imperfect, and what it desires is its perfection. But every perfection is agreeable and proportioned to what it can perfect. Now joining with such a thing causes pleasure. Therefore, etc.

[iii] If you say that what all desire is a form that gives being (whence it is commonly said that being is the good which all seek), the argument still holds. For form is not desired as giving being in the sense of first being [i.e., the existence of a thing], because this is imperfect and is ordered to something else. But what is ultimately desired is being in the sense of being in activity (*in agere*), to which first being is ordered, since each thing has some activity (*operationem*) that follows from the kind of thing it is. Now activity proper to a thing is the cause of pleasure. Therefore, pleasure will still be the reason for choosing in all cases.

[iv] Moreover, everything sought is sought insofar as it is good. But not by reason of being morally honorable (*honesti*), because what is morally honorable is loved in itself, not so that it may be joined [to us] (which is required in every seeking, namely, a joining with what is sought); nor, similarly, by reason of being useful, because the useful is pursued as means to an end, as he said in Book VIII (3, 1156a10–16). Therefore, since the

good is only of three kinds, the morally honorable, the pleasant, {712B} and the useful, it remains that it is the pleasant that is chosen for itself.

[1b] Against

Since each thing is sought insofar as it is good, that which has the character (*ratione*) of the good more powerfully will be more choice-worthy *per se*. Now the morally honorable is more powerful in this respect than the pleasant. Therefore, etc.

Moreover, what is incidental cannot be the reason for other things. But the pleasant is sought incidentally – that is why he said in Book VIII (3, 1156a17–19) that friendship is pleasant incidentally, because it exists with a relation back to oneself. Therefore, etc.

Moreover, what is of a particular kind of itself is such universally, as all color is visible. But not all pleasure is choice-worthy, as disgraceful and unnatural [pleasures are not].

Moreover, the Philosopher says (1172b15) that this view gained credence, not because of what was said to prove it, but because of its author's good character. It therefore seems that the reasons proving it are not sufficient.

[1c] Solution

We have to say that just as nothing is understood except in virtue of something making it understandable, so also nothing is chosen or sought unless the action of seeking is directed by some reason. Something can therefore be called good and choice-worthy in two ways: either as an object that is good and choice-worthy – a good and natural pleasure is choice-worthy in this way – or as the reason for being choice-worthy, by participation in which all things are choice-worthy. This is the procession of goodness and choice-worthiness according to Dionysius (*On the Divine Names* 4.2), just as by the procession of life all who participate in it are living beings. Pleasure is not choice-worthy in this [second] way, and so neither will it be choice-worthy *per se* in this way. Something can be called good and choice-worthy *per se* in two ways: either through lack of a cause – and in this way only God is good *per se*, because he does not have a cause of his goodness but from thence the procession of goodness itself derives – or else by lack of anything extraneous, and in this way the very nature or essence of goodness is called good *per se*, which as such has nothing mixed [with it] besides what pertains to goodness.

[1d. Replies to the Opening Arguments]

[i] To the first we therefore have to say that each thing is sought insofar as it is good, and its being agreeable follows from this. Hence Eudoxus erred, taking a concomitant feature for something primary. {713A}

[ii] To the second we have to say, similarly, that perfection is desired insofar as it is an end, and thus insofar as it is good, not insofar as it is agreeable. But [being agreeable] follows, although it could be said with respect to the will's seeking that the seeker need not ((*oportet/valet* [var.])) be imperfect, because one can seek something for the sake of another, as friendship is called [good] *per se* without a relation back to oneself.

[iii] We have to answer similarly to the third concerning proper activity.

[iv] To the fourth we have to say that the morally honorable is more of a reason for choice-worthiness than the pleasant, because it is what draws by its own force, and accordingly it is sought in the manner of friendship (*per modum amicitiae*), not as wanting something (*per modum concupiscentiae*).

[2. Is Eudoxus' Second Argument for Pleasure as the Good Really Invalid?]

[2a. It Seems Valid]

Second, it seems that Eudoxus' second argument is entirely valid (1172b17–20)

[i] For if a given thing has a given feature, its opposite will have the opposite feature. But distress, which is the opposite of pleasure, is always of itself something to be fled. Therefore, pleasure is *per se* choice-worthy.

[ii] Moreover, what is desired as an end is not pursued for the sake of something else but for itself. But pleasure is like this, as he said in Book VII (13, 1153b9–24). Therefore, etc.

[iii] Moreover, the Philosopher himself says (VII 13, 1153b1–4) that pleasure is opposed to distress as good to bad. But the choice-worthy and what is to be fled follow the good and the bad. Therefore, it seems that his reasoning follows.

[2b] Against

What is choice-worthy for its own sake, as best, is the end of some good life. Now pleasure is not the end of the civic life, because the end of that life is the good of a people. Nor again is it the end of the contemplative life, because the end of that life is contemplation of theoretical truths. It can, however, be the end of the hedonistic life, but the end of that life is not choice-worthy. Therefore, etc.

Moreover, nothing that can be separated from another thing is the same as it in essence even when they exist together. But [in some cases] pleasure is separated from the morally honorable, although the morally honorable never exists without the pleasant. The morally honorable and the pleasant therefore differ in essence even when they exist together. But the morally honorable is what is chosen *per se*. Therefore, pleasure is never choice-worthy *per se*.

Moreover, in wholes composed of potencies, the perfect character of the whole exists only in the last [potency]. {713B} For example, the perfect character of the soul exists only in the [power of] understanding. But the parts of good are of this sort, as has been said above (in the introduction to Lesson 1). Therefore, perfect good is only the morally honorable, which is the last and includes the others, and it is not in the pleasant.

[2c] Solution

We have to say that pleasure is indeed good as something having goodness, not as the reason everything else is good. And we concede the last arguments.

[2d. Replies to the Opening Arguments]

[i] To the first we have to say that it follows from this that pleasure is choice-worthy as an object of choice, but not as the reason for choosing other things.

[ii] To the second we have to say that pleasure separated from the morally honorable is not an end without qualification or good without qualification, but [the end or good] of a certain [being], namely, of a bodily nature. Now when it has been joined with the morally honorable it is not itself the reason for the end's being an end, but it follows from the

character of the morally honorable, according to which that good [the morally honorable] is an end.

[iii] To the third we have to say that the Philosopher means that [pleasure] is opposed to distress as good to bad, not as best to worst.

[3. Is Eudoxus' Third Argument Invalid?]

[3a. It Seems Valid]

Third, it seems that Eudoxus' third argument holds (1172b23–26).

[i] For he [Aristotle] said in Book I (7, 1097b17–18) that blessedness [if counted as one good among others] is more choice-worthy with the [addition of the] least of goods than by itself. But blessedness is good *per se*. This therefore seems to be a condition of a good *per se*, that it is more choice-worthy when mixed with other things, and so Eudoxus' argument goes through.

[ii] Moreover, when something is said to become a greater good, this is not understood to occur by a quantitative addition but by intensification of its quality. Now a quality is intensified in two ways. One way is by the intensification of its cause, as, for example, white [becomes whiter] by the intensification of color. It cannot be said that pleasure makes the morally honorable a greater good in this way, because it is not its cause (rather the contrary). It must therefore intensify its goodness as something joined to it agreeing with it in form, because this is another mode of intensification, as, for example, the hot by the addition of the hot becomes hotter. But the morally honorable is good *per se*. Therefore, pleasure, agreeing with it in form, will also be good *per se*.

[iii] Moreover, if the morally honorable supervenes upon the pleasant, it supervenes upon it either as the same or as different from it. Not as different, because mixing different things with one another causes dilution of both, and so it follows that the morally honorable {714A} would be less pleasant. Therefore, it supervenes upon it as the same in form, and so the same [conclusion follows] as before.

[3b] For the Opposite

Aristotle himself invalidates this argument in the text.

Moreover, either the morally honorable is the same as the pleasant or it is different from it. If it is the same, it does not add to or mix with the pleasant, because things that have been mixed penetrate one another, but nothing penetrates itself. If the morally honorable is different from the pleasant, then, since the morally honorable is good *per se*, pleasure will not be good *per se*. So it seems that from this argument there follows the contrary of what it is meant to prove.

[3c] Solution

We have to say that one thing is said to be more choice-worthy and better than another in two ways. One is because it is good and choice-worthy for more reasons. In this way, pleasure added to the morally honorable (or to anything else) makes it more choice-worthy, as long as it is not choice-worthy *per se*, as the nature of goodness is, but [only] participates in goodness. One thing can also be more choice-worthy than another by coming closer to what is good *per se* – closer, that is, to the reason for goodness and choice in everything. Pleasure does not make morally honorable things more choice-worthy in this way. If it did so, Eudoxus' reasoning would follow: pleasure would be good *per se*. But because he considered only the first mode, from which a conclusion also follows [but not the conclusion proposed], his reasoning does not follow. We concede the arguments for this.

[3d. Replies to the Opening Arguments]

[i] To the first we therefore have to say that the civic blessedness about which he spoke in Book I is not a separated [i.e., transcendent] good, but a good that is in us and is an object of choice, not the reason everything is choice-worthy. Because of this the least of goods makes it better, by [adding] more reasons it is good, not by coming close to the true reason things are good.

[ii] To the second we have to say that it [pleasure] does make [the morally honorable] better, as has been said, yet not by intensifying the reason for its being good in itself but by setting another reason for goodness alongside it. Hence it does not follow that it is the same in form.

[iii] To the third we have to say that [pleasure] does not add to [the morally honorable] as either completely the same or completely different but as its own power. For the morally honorable has the power to be pleasant, just as sensitivity is a certain power of the intellectual [soul].

[4. Is Aristotle Mistaken in Saying that Every Good Is More Choice-Worthy with Another Good Added?]

[4a. It Seems that This Is Wrong]

Fourth, Aristotle seems to be wrong [in saying that every good is more choice-worthy with another good than taken alone (1172b27–28)].

For if the thousandth part of a millet seed were added to the whole earth, which is most heavy, it would not make it heavier. But the goodness of the first [good], {714B} since it is infinite, is more distant from the goodness of any created good than the weight of the earth from the least weight. Therefore, the least good added to it would not make it better.

[4b] Against

Two are more than one. But by the addition of the least good any good which was good before for one reason becomes good for more reasons. Therefore, it becomes better.

Moreover, adding a number in counting necessarily adds something real, as Boethius says (*De Trinitate* 3). But the addition of good to good is a numerical addition to something numbered. Therefore, it becomes really better.

Moreover, the Commentator's objection [Michael of Ephesus on the millet seed] does not seem valid, because there is only one reason for the earth's heaviness. Therefore, it cannot become heavier by coming to have more reasons for being heavy. There are many reasons things are good, however. Therefore, good and heaviness are not alike.

[4c] Solution

We have to say that 'good' has two senses. It may refer (as Aristotle is using the term here) to something that participates in goodness, which, when joined with another [good], becomes better by having more reasons it is good. There is also a certain good that is good *per se* or as the very nature of goodness. Such is the first cause, which pours forth goodness. It indeed is not better from the joining to it of something else, because there is no reason for goodness in anything except from such a good. That is why no addition can be made to it with respect to reasons for goodness. But when it is mixed with an extraneous nature it becomes less good from the admixture of the extraneous nature. Thus, for example, goodness *per se* is something better than [the goodness] of an angel participating in goodness. Aristotle is not talking about this, however, but about a good that is in us, for we also participate in this.

From this the solution to the whole [question] is clear.

[5. Is Plato Right in Saying that What Is Good of Itself Is Not Mixed with Anything?]

[5a. This Seems Wrong]

Fifth, what Plato says (that the good that is good *per se* is not mixed with anything [cf. 1095a26–28]) seems false.

For everything that increases [something when] added [to it] agrees [with it] in form. But the least good added to the good that is good *per se* increases its goodness. It therefore agrees with it in form. Therefore, it is good *per se*, and so the good that is good *per se* can be joined to another.

Moreover, Anselm says (*Freedom of Choice* 1) that what increases free choice when added to it and diminishes it when subtracted is either freedom of choice or a part of freedom. Similarly, then, what makes a good better {715A} when added to it is either goodness itself or a part of goodness. But there are many such things. Therefore, many things that are good *per se* can be added to something else.

Moreover, an end is good *per se*. Now happiness is the end of human life. Therefore, it is good *per se*. But if something is added to it, it is made more choice-worthy, as was said in Book I (7, 1097b17f). Therefore, a good that is good *per se* can be added to something else.

Moreover, it seems from the text that we do not share in a good that is good *per se*. This seems false, because nothing is good except insofar as it participates in good *per se*. So it would follow that nothing would be good.

[5b] Against

That which is good *per se* is nothing other than the nature of the good. But what is mixed with something else is not only the nature of the good. Therefore, it is not good *per se*.

Moreover, what is shadowy in its goodness is not good of itself. But according to Dionysius (*On the Divine Names* 4.20), in the procession in which [what is good of itself] is mixed with the things that participate in it, it becomes shadowy. Therefore, etc.

Moreover, as Aristotle says (*Physics* II 6, 198a8–9; cf. *Politics* IV 11, 1296b7–9), everything (such as motion and time) that distances a thing from [its] foundation (*principio*) inclines it to the worse. But the mixture of goodness with what is extraneous to the nature of goodness distances it more and more from the foundation of all goodness. That is why certain things become bodily and mutable and fall into other defects. Therefore, the mixture of goodness with other things leads to {715B} the worse. But what has been led to the worse is not good *per se*. Therefore, the good that is good *per se* cannot be joined to something else.

[5c] Solution

We have to say that 'good *per se*' has two senses. It may mean what is good through a nature in which it participates. The morally honorable is good *per se* in this way, just as humans are said to be animals *per se*, even though [being human] adds something over and above the nature of an animal. Aristotle is speaking in this way about the good *per se*. What is good *per se* in this sense can be joined to something else. In another sense 'good *per se*' refers to what is nothing other than the nature of goodness. What is good *per se* in this sense cannot be joined with anything else. For if there is something that is good *per se* as the first cause of goodness, of which there is no other cause, it cannot be mixed with other things either *per se* or incidentally, either as to essence or as to being. If, however, the good *per se* is the very nature of goodness, as Plato used to say that the human *per se* was a separate nature of the human (cf. I 6, 1096a34–b2), in that case it cannot be shared in or mixed [with others] except incidentally, because it is not [shared] essentially but according to the being it has in this [thing] and that.

And from this the solution to the whole [question] is clear. . . .

Lesson 3

{717A} 'Yet if [pleasure] is not [a quality]' (1173a13).

Now that he has set forth the opinions of those who said that pleasure is the chief good, he proceeds here to the opinions of those who deny that it is a good. First he sets forth the opinions of those who [merely] deny that pleasure is good, then (at 'In reply to those who bring forward' [1173b20]) the opinions of those who even assert that it is bad.

About the first I ask five questions.

[1. Is Being Good a Quality?]

First, whether being good is a quality.

[1a] It Seems So

[i] For a quality is that according to which it is said how we are (*quales dicimur*). But by being good we are called good, which is a certain how we are. Therefore, etc.

[ii] Moreover, every predicate says either what or how a thing is, as is said in the *Topics* (I 9, 103b25–26). But 'good' is not predicated in the first way, especially of creatures, whose goodness is not of their own essence. Therefore, etc.

[iii] Moreover, when it is said that an activity is good, 'good' predicates either the nature of activity (and so, since every activity is an activity, every activity will be good, which is false) or it predicates something else. But it cannot predicate anything else except a quality. Therefore, activity, too, is called good by a certain quality, and so his own objection seems invalid.

[1b] Solution

We have to say, as was said in Book I (6, 1096a23–27), that the good encompasses all beings, and for this reason it is found not only in the genus of quality but in other genera.

[1c. Replies to the Opening Arguments]

[i] But to what was said first to the contrary we have to say that 'good' does [indeed] say how we are. It is predicated in this way. Yet it does not follow from this that it is in the genus of quality, because, as Avicenna says (*Logica* I, ed. 1508, f. 5ra), every form is predicated as saying how a thing is. Now form can be considered in two ways: as [it is] form and gives being (in which respect it has the character of a form) and [as] it is turned

to being a principle of activity (in which respect it has the character of a power). If form is considered as form, its 'how' will accord with the substantial being {717B} of that whose form it is, and since form is the end of a thing's coming into being it will also be its goodness and the thing will be called good according to its own substantial being. To be good in this way will be substance in the genus of substance, quantity in [the genus of] quantity, and so on for the other [Aristotelian categories]. Now if form is considered as a principle of activity, something may be called good according to [form] in this way, too. Since activity does not flow from the essence of substantial form except by the mediation of a natural power consequent on it, which is in the genus of quality, to be good in this way will signify how a thing is, but in the genus of quality.

[ii] The solution to the second is clear from this.

[iii] To the third we have to say that if an activity is called good according to its own substantial form, 'good' in this sense does predicate the nature of activity, and in this sense every activity *will* be good. If, however, it is called good in relation to the virtue of which it is the activity, in that case it is called good insofar as it comes up to the measure of the virtue. Thus Aristotle's objection still holds, because the activity will be called good even though it is not a quality itself (but has something of a quality about it).

[iv] To the fourth [which is missing] we have to say that when a virtue is called a good quality, 'good' predicates of it the order of an end [i.e., that it is a quality one should aim at having], according to which it is called good, which is something formal in it. Similarly, when it is said with Augustine (*On the Trinity* VIII 3.4) that 'goodness is good' (although this is not strictly correct, according to the Philosopher) 'goodness' in the abstract stands for what it is to be good, but 'good' in the concrete predicates the order of an end, and because in this way goodness is taken formally, for this reason it can be turned back upon itself so that it names itself.

[2. Is Every Good Determinate?]

[2a. It Seems So]

Second, it seems that every good is determinate, as Pythagoras said (cf. *Metaphysics* I 5, 986a23–26).

[i] For everything that has an end is determinate, because an end is a term. But every good has an end, because it is called good from [its] relation to an end. Therefore, etc.

[ii] Moreover, there is no [actual] seeking except for something determinate, since seeking as such is infinite. But every seeking is for a good insofar as it is good. Therefore, the good insofar as it is good is determinate. {718A}

[iii] Moreover, if a good is sought, it is sought either as good or as best. If as good or by reason of being good, since everything that moves in any order moves in the character of a first mover, then the good as good will be the first mover of the seeking, and so every good will be a best, because this is first. If [a good is sought] by reason of [being] the best, since the best is determinate − because it is not susceptible of more and less − everything sought will be determinate. And so the same [conclusion follows] as before.

[2b] Against

Everything that is moved is indeterminate, because nothing is moved unless it is in a state of potentiality, and every potentiality for motion is, as such, indeterminate. But some good is moved; otherwise, every good would be the first good. Therefore, etc.

Moreover, health is a particular good. But health is not determinate, because there are many conditions [that count as healthy], as Avicenna says (*Liber de anima* II 3), one of which comes closer to true health than another. Therefore, not every good is determinate.

[2c] Solution

We have to say that something can be called determinate in two ways: either as to essence or as to being. Since essence indicates the simple quiddity of a thing [i.e., its defining characteristics], something that meets the terms of its quiddity will be called determinate as to essence. In this sense every good is determinate, for that which does not meet the terms of its quiddity is imperfect, and every such thing is bad. The act of an essence in a composite [entity], however, is according to being. Hence something that attains the best and ultimate mode of participating in its essence is determinate according to being. It is not necessary for every good to be determinate in this way but only that which is best, which attains the most perfect measure of goodness. Now this, speaking without qualification and without restriction to [any] genus, is only one [thing], namely, the highest good; but it is different in different genera. For example, there is a measure of participating in health in humans that human nature does not exceed. Because Pythagoras did not know how to distinguish between these two modes of the determinate he asserted that whatever is indeterminate even according to being is not good, such as woman and motion and everything that can be more or less. Because of this he erred, and from this Aristotle argues against him.

[2d. Replies to the Opening Arguments]

[i] To the first we therefore have to say that [being an] end is a term of the quiddity of goodness, because substantial goodness is so called from [being] an end, which is the term of a coming into being, {718B} namely, [substantial] form. Now the goodness that follows after [substantial being] is also so called from [being] an end, [that] from which the character of that goodness is taken.

[ii] To the second we have to say that that which is desired is something finite in itself as to essence that finishes another thing as to being insofar as it brings it closer to the perfect mode of participating in the goodness of its kind.

[iii] To the third we have to say that what is sought is, as to its subject, a particular good, but it is sought by reason of what is best, which is not in it as to essence but extraneously. Because of this it does not follow that [what is sought] is itself the best.

[3. Is Pleasure Determinate?]

[3a. It Seems So]

Third, it seems that pleasure is something determinate (cf. 1173a16–17).

[i] For everything indeterminate is in motion, because nothing is intensified or abated except by motion. That is why in grammar comparative names are called movables. But pleasure is separate from motion, as the Philosopher himself says (1173a31–64). Therefore, it is determinate.

[ii] Moreover, nothing is moved by way of either intensification or

abatement unless it is mixed or concrete. For whiteness [in the abstract] is
not comparative, but a white [thing in the degree to which it is white is].
Since, therefore, he is inquiring about the comparativeness of pleasure,
whether it is in the concrete or in the abstract seems superfluous, for he is
disputing against philosophers who were proceeding reasonably in their
positions.

[iii] Moreover, it seems that pleasure in the abstract admits of being
more or less. For he said in Book VII (14, 1154b24–25) that if the nature
of something is simple its activity will be most pleasant, but the pleasure
of that whose nature is composite he said was imperfect. Therefore, it
seems that one pleasure will be more a pleasure than another.

[3b] Solution

We have to say that pleasure *per se* is indeed determinate, but as to [its]
cause it is abated or intensified, so that one individual is said to be more
pleased than another. Now the cause of pleasure is the activity of a natural
habit. As a result, the more natural a habit is the more one will be pleased.
For this reason when the very nature [of a thing] is the habit producing
the activity, as it is in God, there is the greatest pleasure. Where a habit is
turned into nature through habituation there is less pleasure than where
the habit is {719A} inborn by nature. To put it simply, the closer a habit
is to nature, the greater will be the pleasure [associated with it], and for
this reason the simpler a nature is, the greater is its pleasure, because the
habit is that much less distant from nature.

[3c. Replies to the Opening Arguments]

[i] To the first we therefore have to say that although every pleasure is
separate from motion as from an essential [=internal, constitutive] principle, yet there is a pleasure that has rather a connection [with motion],
namely, the pleasure of a bodily nature, the activity of which is mixed
with motion and can thus admit of more or less.

[ii] To the second we have to say that something can be intensified in
two ways. One is according to its cause, which is in a subject – and here
intensification occurs with respect to one form, as one thing is called
whiter than another – and in this way only concrete things are intensified.
Something is [also] intensified, however, by comparison to one principle
from which many forms proceed, and then, when comparison is made

among different forms, what comes closer to that principle will be called truer. For example, human intellectuality is said to be less than that of an angel, inasmuch as it does not come as close to the divine intellectuality, which is the principle of all intellectuality. (It should be noted that he makes a distinction about this. So pleasure *does* admit of more and less even in the abstract.)

[iii] From this the solution to the whole [question] is clear.

[4. Is Pleasure a Motion?]

[4a. It Seems So]

Fourth, it seems that pleasure is a motion.

[i] For everything that is induced by motion or ((*sive/suum* [var.])) becoming is a motion, and anything whose becoming is a motion is itself, while it is in process of becoming, a motion. For example, whitening, which is a motion toward whiteness, is whiteness itself flowing, as Avicenna says (*Liber de anima* III 4). Since, then, pleasure is induced by motion (because someone who at one time does not feel pleasure afterwards does), pleasure itself will therefore be a motion.

[ii] Moreover, motion is the act of something in potentiality as such [i.e., as being in potentiality]. But pleasure is of this sort, because it is a transition from potentiality to act, for someone who was only potentially pleased is now actually pleased.

[iii] Moreover, it is certain that it happens for someone to be pleased. But 'being pleased' indicates a sort of being made. Therefore, pleasure is a making. But making is a motion. Therefore, etc.

[iv] Moreover, everything that is expected in the future and passes into the past is a motion, because past and future are parts of time, which is the measure of motion. But pleasure is like this, {719B} for we say that someone was pleased before and is pleased now and is to be pleased in future. Therefore, etc.

[v] Moreover, everything that exists exists either all at once or successively. But one person's pleasure does not exist all at once. Therefore there is succession in it. Therefore, etc.

[vi] Moreover, everything that exists exists in a time or in a moment or in eternity or in an eon [the mode of duration proper to an angel]. But a human being's pleasure is not in eternity or in an eon or even in a

moment, since it often lasts through a day or a year. Therefore, it is in a time, and so it follows that it is a motion.

[4b] Solution

We have to say that pleasure is not a motion but that it is always conse-quent on activity – not, however, always consequent on [an activity] that is a motion but [only] sometimes. For activity differs from motion, in that activity is the act of a natural form, always consequent on it. Lighting, for example, is the act of light, and yet since one part of this act is no more a potentiality than another, but the whole is equally perfectly act, it is certain that it differs from motion, which is more in act the closer it comes to its end point. This activity is not indeed mixed with motion on the side of form, since the essence of a thing (the principles of which are eternal and immovable) is without motion. On the side of what participates in form, however, if it is a composite nature subject to different motions, motion is mixed with it. But motion is not joined in any way to a simple nature, which participates in form without motion. Therefore, considered from the side of form, it [activity] is most noble, nobler and more perfect even than form itself, because form is ordered to it as to an end; and thus also it is pleasant. From that side [of a thing] which is mixed with motion, however, there can also be pain, according as motion induces weariness. This is clear in the activity of our understanding, in which fatigue occurs from excessive heating of the brain due to the dispersion of spirits when intelligible species [i.e., representations] have to be abstracted from phan-tasms. Thus it is clear that pleasure is consequent on activity as its essential cause, but motion is only incidentally concomitant.

[4c. Replies to the Opening Arguments]

[i] To the first we therefore have to say that that which is induced *per se* and immediately by motion is motion in its coming to be, but pleasure is not induced by motion except dispositively (but [it is induced essentially] by activity). So too through motion there is a disposition [of matter] to essential form, which, however, never 'flows,' because it does not have a contrary with which it can be mixed. {720A}

[ii] To the second we have to say that pleasure is the act of something existing in act as such [i.e., as being in act], because it is the ultimate act of something that already has form and is waiting for nothing further [to

complete it]. Similarly, a transition [from not being pleased to being pleased] is said [to occur], not in the sense that there is a flow from one thing into another (because that is motion), but because one thing exists after another, as day comes from morning without motion in between.

[iii] To the third we have to say that being pleased (*delectari*) is called an act in the sense of being, not doing, as if we said the act of humanity is being human (*humanari*). Hence just as one signifies being (*esse*) in the idiom of doing (*agere*), and this is not a motion, so also with being pleased.

[iv] To the fourth we have to say that just as being a human is said with respect to past and future, not on the side of the form itself by which a human exists but on the side of what participates [in the form] according as it is subject to motion, so it is with pleasure. On the side of the form, however, it is all at once and not in time. This is clear from the fact that pleasure exists from being joined with what is agreeable. As a result, there can be pleasure only when the agreeable has already been conjoined, and this is not something successive.

[v, vi] From this the solution to the following two is clear.

[5. Is Pleasure a Coming Into Being?]

[5a. It Seems that It Is]

Fifth, it seems that pleasure is a coming into being (*generatio*).

[i] For a coming into being is the end of motion. Similarly, there is pleasure in the end of motion. Therefore, it seems that they are the same, since there are not several motions of one thing in one respect.

[ii] Moreover, everyone who is pleased comes away from {720B} distress, which is contrary, or from not being pleased, which is intermediate. Therefore, he seems in his reasoning to suppose what is false in denying this with regard to pleasure (1173b5).

[iii] Moreover, everything that ceases to exist has an opposite that is destructive of it, at least incidentally. But pleasure ceases to exist through distress. Therefore, distress is contrary to it, and so it seems that Aristotle's reasoning does not preclude pleasure being a coming into being.

[5b] Solution

We have to say that although coming into being is the way *to* a substance, pleasure is not the way *to* anything. Rather, it is something ultimate consequent on form and activity. Pleasure is in no way a coming into being.

[5c. Replies to the Opening Arguments]

[i] For this reason we have to say to the first, that pleasure is an end *of* motion, as that in which motion rests (as substantial form is also). For this reason it does not follow that it is a coming into being, which is what is last *in* motion.

[ii] To the second we have to say that the pleasures that have a contrary distress are bodily pleasures mixed with motion and are not pleasures without qualification, nor do [even] these have a contrary from the side of their being pleasures but according to their involvement with motion.

[iii] From this the solution to the third is clear. . . .

Lesson 4

{722A} 'In reply to those who bring forward' (1173b20)

After he has set out the reasons of those who deny that pleasure is good (maintaining, however, that they are not good ones), here he sets out the opinions of those who say that all pleasures are bad, although some of them did not believe this but said it to move people away from bad pleasures.

Now here we ask three questions.

[1. Are Any Pleasures Disgraceful?]

First, about this, that he calls certain pleasures disgraceful, which are pleasures to some but not to all (1173b20–25).

[1a] It Seems that No Pleasure Is Disgraceful

[i] For nothing is disgraceful except vice. But since pleasure is a passion, it is not a vice, since there is vice [only] in a habit or an act. Therefore, etc.

[ii] Moreover, nothing agreeable is disgraceful. But every pleasure exists from being joined with what is agreeable. Therefore, etc.

[iii] Moreover, if any pleasures were disgraceful, this would especially

be true of bodily ones. But these are intended by nature, as [for example] animals are aroused to the act of the generative power for the conservation of the species, as the Philosopher says (*The History of Animals* VI 18, 571b8–10). Therefore, etc.

[iv] Moreover, it seems that a pleasure that is a pleasure to one is a pleasure to all. For nothing brings pleasure unless it agrees in form with the one being pleased, because pleasure is a passion, and passion follows the form of its subject and its principle. But that which has a pleasurable form induces pleasure in anyone, as long as there is a capacity for pleasure, just as something hot heats everything capable of being heated. Therefore, this sort of pleasure is pleasant to all.

[v] Moreover, this sort of pleasure (which is [pleasant] to one and not to all) is caused either by the pleasant thing or else by those who are being pleased. If the first, then, since the pleasant thing exists in the same way for everyone, it will be equally [pleasant] to everyone. If the pleasure is caused by those who are pleased, then, since those who are pleased are always present, they will necessarily always be pleased, just as, if [the power of] sight were sufficient for seeing and nothing visible were required, the eye would always see. Now this is false. Therefore, we must assert the first [alternative].

[1b] Solution

We have to say that here he names as disgraceful pleasures the unnatural ones, which he called pathological or bestial in Book VII (5, 1148b15–24). {722B} As was said there, these are indeed not pleasant except to those whose nature has been corrupted by a habit that has overspread it. To those who have a healthy nature, however, they are horrible, as being against nature.

[1b. Replies to the Opening Arguments]

[i] To the first we therefore have to say that although pleasures of this sort are not vices in substance, nevertheless they incline to vice, and it is from this that they are disgraceful.

[ii] To the second we have to say that pleasures like this do not come from being joined with what is agreeable without qualification but from being joined with what is agreeable to a habit that corrupts nature.

[iii] To the third we have to say that nature never intends inordinate

pleasures, since these impede nature's end, but it intends moderate ones, and these must be moderated by laws, as was said in [our discussion of] Book VII.

[iv] To the fourth we have to say that the acts of active [principles] exist in passive ones in the mode of the latter, not in the mode of the former. Because of this the same active [principle] affects different recipients with different passions, as for example [heat] hardens some things and liquefies others. (If, however, the passion followed the form of the agent, then the cause would always have a unique effect, and the same passion would be produced in everything by the same agent.) Hence it is that the same thing produces pleasure in one individual and not in another.

[v] We have to answer similarly to the fifth.

[2. Why Are the Pleasures of Good Persons Not Pleasant for All?]

[2a. It Seems that They Are]

Second, it seems that the pleasures that are choice-worthy for the good are choice-worthy for all.

[i] For what is choice-worthy for the good is choice-worthy without qualification, as he said in Book IX (9, 1170a13–15). But what is choice-worthy without qualification is choice-worthy for anyone in need. Now to be in need means not having something one is naturally constituted to have. But the bad are in such a condition. Therefore, pleasures of this sort are also choice-worthy for the wicked.

[ii] Moreover, he means this either about necessary pleasures – and it cannot be true about these, because he [rather, the anonymous commentator] says that these are chosen by everyone and no one can survive without them – or else about natural but unnecessary pleasures – and holy men too abstain from these – or else he is talking about pleasures that are neither natural nor necessary – and these are not choice-worthy for anyone. It therefore seems that what he says is false in every case.

[iii] Moreover, where the good act {723A} well, the bad [can] engage in good activity, although they do not act well (like those who do things that are just but not *as* the just do them [cf. II 4, 1105b7–9]). Therefore, if the good act well with regard to pleasures, choosing them because of this [i.e., for the sake of acting well?], the activity of the bad regarding pleasure

will be good. Now good activity is choice-worthy for anyone. Therefore, etc.

[iv] Moreover, he seems to put forward an unsuitable example when he says (1173b26–27) that money is not choice-worthy for a traitor to his country [reading *prodenti* as 'for a traitor' instead of 'for being a traitor']. For the rich, who are not so needy, cannot be corrupted to betray their country, especially since betraying a country in which they have many possessions would be harmful to them. So it seems that for those betraying their country having riches would be choice-worthy, because by this means they would desist from their betrayal.

[2c] Solution

We have to say that on this point the Philosopher is talking about pleasures that are not disgraceful and which the good do indeed choose in moderation, in accord with the standard of virtue. But because the wicked are wholly given to the pursuit of pleasure, it is beneficial for them to be held back from pleasures, even from those they could licitly use. For from this they will reach the mean more quickly, as with those who straighten bent sticks [by bending them in the opposite direction], as he said in Book II (9, 1109b6–7), whereas [without such over-compensation] they would because of their corruptness be more stimulated to pursue even disgraceful pleasures and would not observe the mean.

[2d. Replies to the Opening Arguments]

[i] From this the solution to the first is clear.

[ii] To the second we have to say that pleasure is natural, necessary, or neither, depending on whether it follows on an activity that is for the conservation of the species or the individual or is against nature. For this reason he is talking here about pleasure as pleasure and not with respect to any of the other modes.

[iii] To the third we have to say that if pleasure were essential to virtue, as giving to all their own is essential to justice, it would follow that, just as the good act well regarding pleasures themselves, so the activity of the bad regarding them would be good. But pleasure is a material [factor] in virtuous activity and for this reason there can be good and bad activity regarding it, just as there can be prodigality [a vice] and generosity [a virtue] regarding money.

[iv] To the fourth we have to say that there are people to whom treachery is pleasing for its own sake, and the Philosopher is talking about them. If people like this have {723B} riches, they gain confidence for completing the betrayal of their country.

[3. Do the Pleasures of the Good and the Bad Differ in Kind?]

[3a. It Seems that They Do Not]

Third, it seems that the pleasures of the good and the bad do not differ in kind.

[i] For difference in kind among the passions is taken from what is active [in causing them], not from the subject [in which they exist]. Therefore, he ought to have shown differences in kind among pleasures from differences among pleasing things rather than from differences among those pleased.

[ii] Moreover, pleasure follows the nature of the one pleased. But all humans are the same in kind and differ in number. Therefore, etc.

[iii] Moreover, it seems false to say that nonmusicians do not take pleasure in musical activities, because everyone takes pleasure in the harmonies of song, which are musical. Therefore, etc.

[3b. Solution]

We have to say that pleasures do indeed differ in kind according to differences among pleasing things, if ultimate kinds are used [to distinguish them], but they are the same in kind if common kinds are used.

[3c. Replies to the Opening Arguments]

[i] To the first we therefore have to say that there are different habits in different pleasure-takers, according to which they are susceptible to different pleasant things. And thus differences among pleasures can be taken from differences among pleasure-takers because of the proportion of pleasure-taker to pleasant thing (just as sight is receptive to another sense-object than hearing is), and for this reason the experience (*passio*) of each is different.

[ii] To the second we have to say that all humans are the same in essential kind, but they differ in kind in certain accidental respects, through which they are susceptible to different pleasant things according to the different habits imbued in them.

[iii] To the third we have to say that he does not mean by nonmusicians those who lack the habit of music but those who are not [physically] disposed to it. There are some people who care nothing for sounds because of defects in their hearing. . . .

Lesson 5

{724B} 'What [pleasure] is, or what sort of thing it is' (1174a13).

Now that he has discussed pleasure according to the opinion of others, here he begins to discuss it in accordance with his own opinion. First he says what his intention is; second (at 'It seems' [1174a14]), he carries it out. About the first, he undertakes to discuss 'what it is' and 'what sort of thing it is,' so that the discussion of pleasure according to his own opinion may start from the beginning. According to some [authors] these two differ in that we know what a thing is when we know its genus, but we know what sort of thing it is when we know it by its specific differentiae. {725A} On this interpretation the following part, which begins at 'It seems' (1174a12), is divided in two. First he inquires what pleasure is according to its genus, second (at 'Now it perfects [the activity]' [1174b23]) what sort of thing it is according to its differentiae. The first is then divided in two, because first he shows what pleasure is according to its genus, because it is a certain whole which exists all at once, not successively; second (at 'Now [every] sense [is active in relation to its object],' [1174b14]), he shows what it is in, because the subject of an accident also falls within its definition. Another – and better – interpretation is that 'what a thing is' refers to its simple quiddity according as this depends on its own essential principles as these are metaphysical forms, whether substantial or accidental (for example, whiteness, as signified in the abstract), but 'of what sort a thing is' refers to form according to the being it has in a subject named from it, because according to every form something is said to be 'of a sort.' On this interpretation, this part is divided in two. First he shows what pleasure is according to its essence, because it is a certain whole, that is, not something that has being successively. Second (at 'Now [every] sense [is active in relation to its object]'), he shows what sort of thing it is, namely, according as it has being in a subject.

About the first, I ask three questions.

[1. Is Pleasure in Time?]

First, whether pleasure is in time.

[1a] It Seems that It Is

[i] For as the Philosopher says (cf. Alexander of Hales, *Glossa*, 1.1, d. 9; ed. Quarrachi, p. 116.8–10, n. 3), as eternity is to the eternal, so is eon to that whose duration is measured by it and time to the temporal. But time does not measure anything that exists eternally. Neither, therefore, does eternity or eon measure anything in time. But pleasure exists in temporal beings (in humans, for example). Therefore, etc.

[ii] Moreover, to be in time, as the Philosopher says (*Physics* IV 12, 221a7–9), is to be measured by a certain part of time. Now everything that is exceeded by a time is measured by some part of time. Everything that begins and ends is of this sort, however. But pleasure is of this sort. Therefore, etc.

[iii] Moreover, as the Philosopher says in *Physics* IV (12, 221b8–9), rest is in time. But to be at rest is to be unmoved. Therefore, by the same reasoning, although pleasure is in the terminus of motion [rather than in the motion itself], it will be in time.

[iv] Moreover, everything whose duration is not complete all at once exists in time. But pleasure is of this sort. Therefore, etc. {725B}

[v] Moreover, what is not in time is eternal. But pleasure is not eternal, because the eternal always exists, as he said in Book VI (3, 1139b22–24). But pleasure does not always exist. Therefore, etc.

[vi] Moreover, all contingent things are measured by time, as he said in *Physics* IV (12, 221a26–67). But pleasure is of this sort, for my being pleased is not necessary. Therefore, etc.

[vii] Moreover, when there is an activity or motion, there is pleasure. But 'when' does not refer to the duration of eternity or eon or a moment, because there is no motion in these. Therefore, it refers to the duration of time.

[viii] Moreover, he says (VII 12, 1153a13–15) that pleasure coexists –

that is, exists at once with – activity. But it is not understood to exist at once with it because it is in the same subject, because by the same reasoning it would coexist with whiteness. It must therefore be understood to coexist in time.

[1b] Solution

We have to say that to be in time is to be measured by a certain part of time. Now a thing may be measured by a certain part of time either *per se* or incidentally. What is measured by time only because it exists in a temporal thing is measured by time incidentally, as when we say a line and other mathematical [objects] are measured by time, because they are in physical [objects] as to being. Something is measured by time *per se* in two ways, a primary and a posterior. In the first way motion is measured by time, for its parts do not exist at once but [some] are always awaited as future until completion [of the motion], for time measures by before and after. Now time measures in a posterior way that which it numbers only insofar as it has a *relation* to motion. It is in this way that rest is in time. For if rest is taken as a form in which something is at rest, at which a motion is terminated, it is not the case that it is in time, because that form is complete all at once, nor does it await anything in the future to complete it. But as it exists in something that is at rest rest has being in time, for the potentiality of the thing in which it exists (through which it happened for the thing to be moved) is not terminated under that form, and because of this there always remains in it the possibility of [further] motion. And in this way, too, we say that the pleasure that exists in a mobile thing is in time (for it is clear that the pleasures existing in eternal things are not in time in any way).

[1c. Replies to the Opening Arguments]

[i] Hence the first is solved. {726A}

[ii] We have to say to the second, similarly, that pleasure does not begin or come to an end in accordance with its own being (according as it is a form of the agreeable, which pleases), but it begins and comes to an end in a particular individual, and it is temporal from that side, as is also the case with being a human or being at rest in any way whatever.

[iii] To the third, it is clear that pleasure is in time in the same way as rest is.

[iv] We have to say to the fourth that the duration of the existence of pleasure is all at once according as it comes from a pleasing form, because it gets its whole perfection in one moment. But as it is the act of a potency of the individual who is pleased, there is succession in it, as has been said.

[v] To the fifth we have to say that from the side of the potency of the subject in which it exists, pleasure is not eternal but contingent.

[vi] Hence the solution to the sixth is clear.

[vii] To the seventh we have to say that 'when' does indicate duration of time. Yet it does so as being in time is commonly taken as to all the modes that have been determined [in the Solution?]. Nevertheless, it is false that when there is motion there is pleasure. Indeed, the more motion there is, the weaker the pleasure and the more weariness and labor.

[viii] From this the solution to the eighth is clear.

[2. Does Seeing Occur All at Once?]

[2a. It Seems that It Does Not]

Second, it seems that seeing does not occur [all] at once (1174a14).

[i] For a certain philosopher [Alkindi] says in his *Optics* that seeing occurs in time. Now no such thing occurs all at once. Therefore, etc.

[ii] Moreover, Avicenna says (*Liber de anima* III 2; cf. *De anima* II 7, 418b25–26) that the visual ray is at the wall before it is in the west [if, for example, you open your eyes to look at a garden wall and over it to the western sky beyond]. But seeing is consequent on the emission of this ray. Therefore, seeing will not occur all at once.

[iii] Moreover, Euclid proves (*Liber de visu*, ed. Theisen, *Mediaeval Studies* 41, 1979, p. 62) that a thing is not seen all at once, but only as much of a thing as falls within the diameter [the visual cone in Euclid] that is understood to go out from the eye to the thing seen. But there is seeing when a thing is seen. Therefore, seeing does not occur all at once.

[2b] Against

Every spatial motion occurs in time, the time being multiplied as the distance is multiplied. Therefore, if seeing as far as the wall occurred in some [unit of] time, then seeing as far as the east[ern horizon], where one would see the sun rise, would occur in a time {726B} multiplied in proportion to the multiplication of the distance. Now ((*autem/aut*)) that much time could not fail to be perceived. Therefore, since we do not perceive [such a lapse of time], it seems that seeing over any distance whatever does not occur in time.

Moreover, seeing follows the motion of light. But illumination is sudden, since it is the terminus of a motion, as the Commentator [Averroes] says on *Physics* VII (comm. 121). Therefore, seeing occurs all at once.

Moreover, seeing occurs from the reception of species. Therefore if seeing did not occur all at once, the species would need to be received first in a qualified way and afterwards perfectly. Now this cannot be, because then there would be a motion in sight itself from the imperfect to the perfect, as there is in bleaching. Therefore, seeing occurs all at once.

[2c] Solution

We have to say that seeing can be considered in two ways: [i] either as the reception of species or [ii] as the activity of sight. [i] If it is taken in the first way, seeing does not occur in time but is all at once. For what can be sensed is related to the senses in three ways in the various senses. The sensible is joined to certain senses materially, as in taste and touch. On the other hand, certain senses do not receive any of the object's matter but only matter from the medium, as in smell and hearing. In certain cases, however, the sense does not receive anything material but only the intention of the sensible [object], and that is sight. Therefore among all the senses its reception is more formal, and hence too there is no succession in it according to which it would receive what is near more quickly than what is distant. [ii] Now if seeing is taken as the activity of sight, it is twofold, because the activity of sight is either [iia] in its activity concerning the visible, and so again there will be no succession, because it judges and knows the whole visible species at once; or [iib] in a ray going out from the eye, according to the opinion of those who held that sight comes about in this way – and according to them there will thus be a motion of the ray, a motion in space to what is near before what is distant. But this is not the case according to his [Aristotle's] opinion, and for this reason he says without qualification that vision occurs all at once.

[2d. Replies to the Opening Arguments]

[i] To the first we therefore have to say that if what that philosopher says is right, then a succession does occur {727A} in seeing – from the side of the medium, not from the side of the object.

[ii] To the second we have to say that Avicenna is speaking according to the opinion of Plato, who held that sight comes about from extramission [of a visual ray] (*Timaeus* 45B).

[iii] To the third we have to say that Euclid's statement is meant with reference to the quantitative parts of the visible, which are not offered to sight all at once. He does not mean that the species of a thing is [first] received in a qualified way and afterwards perfectly, as happens in bleaching.

[3. Do the Parts of a Motion Differ in Kind?]

[3a. It Seems that They Do Not]

Third, it seems that the parts of a motion do not differ in kind (cf. 1174a22f).

[i] For from the fact that something is in potentiality, it is not determinate as to kind. But motion is an imperfect act, mixed with potentiality. It is not in perfect act except when it is in its terminus. Therefore, it seems that if a motion is divided into parts, it will not take on different kinds according to the different parts.

[ii] Moreover, motion is only specified as to kind by the terminus to which it tends. But this is one in any one motion. Therefore, there are not different kinds in the parts.

[iii] Moreover, it seems that the example of building (1174a19–29) is not to the point, because in building there are many motions, not parts of one motion. For the motion in which stones are carved is different from that in which they are raised up in the building. It therefore seems that it cannot be proved from this that one motion has parts different in kind.

[iv] Moreover, it seems that even in a line different parts have different characteristics (*rationes*), and so it seems that he ought not to have excepted a line (1174b1).

[3b] Solution

We have to say that the 'now' is related to time in two ways, either [i] as its substance or [ii] as its terminus. [i] If the 'now' is considered as what it is, then there is the same 'now' in the subject [motion] in its whole temporal duration, just as the thing in motion (to which the 'now' is attached) is the same in the whole motion. [ii] But as to the being it has inasmuch as earlier and later apply to it, it is different, just as the thing in motion is different according to its different changes of place. Thus a motion is caused according to differences in the moving thing and time according to different {727B} 'nows.' So, then, inasmuch as the 'now' is itself the same in its own substance, it is the substance of time; as it is different, however, it is the terminus of a time, which is terminated at two 'nows,' just as a line is terminated by two points. A 'now' terminates a time, however, according as the 'now' is designated in the time itself, and this happens when time stops numbering a motion – that is, when the motion itself is terminated – and just as time can be designated by reference to the 'nows,' so too can motion be designated by reference to its different parts. If a single motion is designated in its different parts, it is always found to be terminated in one ['now'] and in another, and since a motion gets a specific character from its termini, the parts will differ from one another in kind. For example, if something changes from white to black in at least three hours, it will be something changing in paleness if it is designated by reference to a 'now' of the first hour and something changeable and dark if it is designated by reference to the 'now' terminating the second hour.

[3c. Replies to the Opening Arguments]

[i] To the first we therefore have to say that insofar as an act [i.e., the actualization of a potentiality] is in process it does not make a motion to be of a specific kind, but when the motion is terminated [at different points] by designation of [its] parts, then the act is taken as something completed, and so it makes the motion [i.e., each part of the whole motion] to be of a specific kind.

[ii] To the second we have to say that that toward which there is motion can be taken as pure act, and in this way it is only one, as whiteness or blackness is one; or as act mixed together with a contrary, as the intermediate colors are, and then such a mixed act, if we consider it as stable,

makes the motion to be of a specific kind, although it does not do this insofar as it is in process.

[iii] To the third we have to say that building can be considered in two ways: either as the action of the builder, and so considered it is not one motion; or as the motion of the thing built, and so considered it is one motion and toward one terminus, namely, toward the kind of thing being built.

[iv] To the fourth we have to say that differences of character among the parts of a line occur insofar as motions terminated to them differ from one another in kind from the fact that [each] is situated in such and such a place. This is not due, however, to the character of the line itself insofar as it is mathematical, because in this respect nothing is to be found in it except points dividing and continuing the line, which is of one character everywhere. . . .

Lesson 6

{729A} 'Now a sense [is active in relation to its object]' (1174b14).

Here he shows what sort of thing pleasure is according to his own division [between sense and understanding], discussing it according to the being it has in that in which it exists. There are two parts. First he shows that there is pleasure in the activity of sense and understanding; second (at 'And the pleasure perfects [the activity],' chapter 6 [c. 4, 1174b23]) he shows how it is related to the activity.

About the first part I ask two questions.

[1. Is There Pleasure in the Activity of Sensing?]

First, whether there is pleasure in the activity of sensing (1174b19).

[1a] It Seems Not

[i] For every activity of sense involves labor, as he says in *On Sleeping and Waking* (1, 454a26–29). But where there is labor there is distress, not pleasure.

[ii] Moreover, sense is a passive potency, as he proves in the *De anima* (II 5, 417a6–7). But no passive potency produces its own actualization

(*actum*). Rather, the actualization takes place *in* it. Therefore, sense does not work on what is perceptible, as he says. Rather, what is perceptible works on the sense.

[iii] Moreover, the most beautiful sense-object seems to be that which is the actualization of all sense-objects, namely, light. But light does not please sight but instead offends it. Therefore, it seems false to say that what is most pleasant is the activity of sight in relation to the most beautiful thing seen.

[iv] Moreover, the Commentator [Averroes, *Ethica* X 4], solves [the problem by saying] that undergoing is twofold. Some takes away from a substance, leading to its destruction, and such undergoing is not pleasant but distressful. Some leads to perfection, and this is pleasant; sensing is an undergoing of this sort. But to the contrary: every undergoing involves motion. But motion is punishing, insofar as it makes for separation. Therefore, it seems that no undergoing can be pleasant.

[1b] Solution

We have to say with Avicenna (*Liber de anima* IV 3), that grief is a sensing of something harmful. For this reason, conversely, there is pleasure with the sensing and grasping of the agreeable. Now because that activity of a thing in which its potency is fulfilled to the ultimate degree is most agreeable to it, for this reason the activity of sense and understanding involves pleasure. Even animals take pleasure in those of their activities which have perceptive force.

[1c. Replies to the Opening Arguments]

[i] To the first we therefore have to say that sensing does involve labor insofar as it involves motion, but {729B} according as it is the activity of sight it is pleasant.

[ii] To the second we have to say that according as a sensory power is in a state of potentiality it does not act but rather undergoes. According as it has already been perfected by the species being joined with it, however, it has its own activity.

[iii] To the third we have to say that although light is most beautiful in itself, it is nevertheless not most beautiful as regards sensing. But that is called most beautiful [in this respect] which is proportioned to the arrangement (*harmoniam*) of the sense.

[iv] To the fourth we have to say that for a composite nature pleasure does not occur without undergoing and motion. The pleasure is not derived from the motion, however, but from activity itself, which differs from motion, as has been said before.

[2. Is There Pleasure in Understanding?]

[2a. It Seems Not]

Second, it seems that there is no pleasure in understanding (1174b20–21).

[i] For everything that abstracts from features connected with matter abstracts from the nature of the agreeable and disagreeable. But understanding is like this, as is proved in *De anima* III (c. 4). Therefore, pleasure, which comes from being joined with the agreeable, does not occur in it.

[ii] Moreover, the agreeable and the disagreeable have it in them to arouse appetite. But appetite differs from speculative understanding, because it moves [us] to approach or avoidance. Therefore, the agreeable has no effect on the speculative understanding, and so there is no pleasure in it.

[iii] If you say that there is [pleasure] in [understanding] according as it is practical, [I argue] to the contrary. The speculative [understanding] becomes practical only by engaging in comparisons [of alternative courses of action?], in which it is ordered to a particular, of which it is the act. In theoretical contemplation, however, there is no comparison but a process of analysis. It therefore seems that there can be no pleasure.

[iv] Moreover, the true insofar as it is true is simpler than the true considered as pleasant. But speculative understanding is perfected to a greater extent in what is simpler. Therefore, it is perfected to a greater extent in contemplation of the true without pleasure than with pleasure.

[2b] Solution

We have to say that understanding affords the greatest and truest pleasure, a pleasure to which there is no contrary.

[2c. Replies to the Opening Arguments]

[i] {730A} To the first we therefore have to say that from the very fact that a species is abstracted, it acquires the character of being agreeable to

the understanding, which is separate [from matter] and unmixed [with it]. It is true, however, that it does not have the character of being agreeable to a nature joined with matter.

[ii, iii] From this the solution to the second and third is clear, because what is agreeable in this way does not act on appetite or practical understanding but on the understanding insofar as it is speculative.

[iv] We have to say to the fourth, that when we speak of 'the true as pleasant,' nothing is added in reality but only in the concept of a relation, inasmuch as the true is taken in comparison with the understanding, to which it is agreeable *per se*. For this reason there is no increase in complexity. . . .

Lesson 7

{730A} 'And the pleasure perfects [the activity]' (1174b23).

Here he discusses pleasure in relation to activity, and this is divided in two. First he discusses the relation of pleasure to activity in general; second {730B} (at 'Because [activities are made more precise and enduring],' chapter 8 [c. 5, 1175b13]), its relation to proper and extraneous activities. The first part is further divided in two. First he considers the relation of pleasure to activity in general, then (at '[One might think that all] seek [pleasure]' [1175a10]), he shows that pleasure is something that can be sought.

About the first I ask three questions.

[1. Is Activity Perfected by Pleasure?]

First, whether activity is perfected by pleasure.

[1a] It Seems Not

[i] For what is best in any order is not perfected by anything [else], since a perfection is always more excellent than what it perfects. But activity is what is best in any nature, because it is the ultimate act of the nature itself. Therefore, etc.

[ii] Moreover, as the Philosopher says in *De anima* III (5, 430a18–19), agent and form are nobler than what is acted upon. But pleasure is the

perfection of something passive, because it is [itself] a kind of undergoing, while activity follows on form. Therefore, activity is nobler than pleasure, and it is therefore not perfected by it.

[iii] Moreover, nothing is perfect without its proper activity. But many activities are perfect without pleasure, for example, those of inanimate things. Therefore, pleasure is not the perfection of activity.

[iv] Moreover, everything that acts acts from itself. But pleasure always comes from something extraneous, because it arises from being joined with the agreeable. But what stands in need of something extraneous is less perfect than what is sufficient to itself. Activity is therefore more perfect than pleasure and thus is not perfected by it.

[1b. For the Opposite]

[v] What is said in the text is to the contrary.

[vi] Moreover, that which maintains an activity perfects it, because what perfects a thing is the same in form as what conserves it in being. But pleasure maintains activities in those engaged in them, because as a result of pleasure being added they persist more in the activities proper to them. Therefore, etc.

[1c. An Additional Question]

[vii] I ask further: If [pleasure] perfects, how does it perfect? It seems that it does so as form.

[viii] For 'perfecting' is said either effectively or formally. But the one engaged in an activity, not pleasure, effects it. Therefore, [pleasure] perfects as form.

[ix] Moreover, when what perfects is something joined with a thing, it is always form. But pleasure is joined with activity. Therefore, etc. {731A}

[x] Moreover, if pleasure is not form, then, since it is joined [with activity], it will be an accident. But an accident does not finish anything, and what does not finish does not perfect. Therefore, pleasure does not perfect activity, and this is contrary to what has been assumed.

[xi] Moreover, an accident follows on a thing. But what follows on something does not perfect it. Therefore, the same as before.

[xii] Moreover, the example of youth seems unsuitable, for there are many youths without beauty. Therefore, youth is not perfected by beauty.

[1d. A Further Question]

[xiii] I ask further whether activity is sought because of pleasure or conversely. It seems that activity is sought because of pleasure.

[xiv] For if there is something ultimately intended in an order, everything is sought because of it. But everything has an ultimately intended pleasure, because everything that is by nature capable of participating in pleasure seeks it, as is said in the following section (1175a10). Therefore, activity is sought because of pleasure.

[xv] Moreover, in any order whatever what precedes is ordered to what follows as to an end and not conversely, because motion ceases when the end is reached. But activity precedes pleasure as its cause. Therefore, it occurs for the sake of it and not conversely.

[xvi] Moreover, all human activities are ordered to happiness. But pleasure is formal in happiness. Therefore, pleasure seems to be the end of the activities.

[1e] Against

[xvii] What is best in any genus is its end. But activity is what is best in any nature because it is its ultimate perfection. Therefore, etc.

[xviii] Moreover, in natural things we see that nature has always joined pleasures to activities for the sake of the activities themselves, as is clear in the activities of nutrition and reproduction. It therefore seems that pleasure is naturally ordered to activity.

[1f] Solution

To the first part of the question (i–vi) we have to say that activity can be considered in two ways, either in itself ((*se/esse* [var.])) or as it exists in those who are active. If it is considered in itself ((*se/esse* [var.])) it is what is best, and it is not perfected by pleasure, and thus the first four arguments go through. If activity is considered as it exists in those who are active, then pleasure is said to perfect their activity, insofar as it maintains them in it and they come to persist in it because of the sweetness {731B} of pleasure. This is what it is to be the perfection of something in a qualified sense, and so the fifth and sixth arguments go through.

[vii] To the second part of the question (vii–xii) we have to say that pleasure perfects activity as an end, not that it is the end of the activity in itself but as it exists in the one engaged in it. For this reason he also says in the text (1174b32) that it is 'a kind of end.'

[viii] Hence to the first argument for that part of the question we have to say that it proceeds from an insufficient [division], because not everything that perfects is a form or an efficient [cause], but an end is also something that perfects.

[ix] To the second we have to say that pleasure is indeed a form – not, however, of the activity but of those who are active according as they are active.

[x] To the third we have to say that pleasure is without doubt an accident, nor does it finish or perfect as to substantial being but as to well-being.

[xi] We have to reply similarly to the fourth.

[xii] We have to say to the fifth that the example of youth is suitable, because just as beauty is a certain flower of youth, making it more to be sought, so pleasure is a certain flower of nature, by which it blooms again on its own activity.

[xiii] To the third part of the question we have to say that pleasure is ordered without qualification to activity, but the converse is true according as [activity] exists in those engaged in it, for they order their activity to the sweetness they find in pleasure. And it is also thus with happiness.

[xiv–xviii] Hence the solution to all the [remaining] objections is clear.

[2. Is There Pleasure in All the Senses?]

[2a. It Seems Not]

Second, it seems that there is not pleasure in all the senses (cf. 1174b20–21).

[i] As is said in the book *On Sleeping and Waking* (1, 454a8), wherever there is a potentiality, there is a [corresponding] actuality. But animals have senses other than touch, yet they do not take pleasure in the perception of their objects – for example, odors and colors. Therefore, it does not seem that pleasure follows on the activity of any sense whatever.

[ii] Moreover, whatever has pleasure only as it is directed into something else does not have pleasure of itself. But, as Avicenna says (*Liber de anima* II 3), there is pleasure in the other senses only as they relate to taste or touch. Therefore, they do not have pleasure in themselves. {732A}

[iii] Moreover, pleasure only arises from being joined with the agreeable. But the agreeable thing itself is conjoined only in taste and touch. Therefore, there is pleasure only in these senses.

[iv] Moreover, pleasure is a kind of fruit (*fructus*). But to enjoy (*frui*) pertains to taste. Therefore, etc.

[2b. A Further Question]

[v] I ask further, what he means by 'most powerful in sense' (cf. 1174b22).

[vi] It seems that the greatest pleasure does not occur in what is most powerful in sense, because the most powerful in sense is not in humans, because we fall far short of the other animals in certain senses. Yet the pleasures of these senses are especially agreeable to us – for example, the pleasures of sight and smell. Therefore, etc.

[vii] Moreover, the most powerful in sense [when this means the most powerful sense-object] seems to be that which actualizes other sense-objects, namely, light, and especially sunlight. But things of this sort are not pleasant. Therefore, etc.

[viii] Moreover, labor impedes pleasure. But the treatises of natural scientists attest that seeing and hearing are laborious. Therefore, etc.

[ix] Moreover, in seeing and hearing one is altered in certain ways. Now alteration, since it is a motion, occurs because of a defect. Therefore, it seems that the greatest pleasure does not occur in what is most powerful in these [sensations, i.e., in the greatest alteration].

[2c. A Further Question]

[x] I ask further whether the greatest pleasure is in sight or in touch.

[xi] It seems that it is in touch, for touch is the first sense, that by which an animal is an animal, as is said in *De anima* II (2, 413b4–5). But pleasure follows the activity of sense. Therefore, the greatest pleasure ought to be in it.

[xii] Moreover, just as sense stands to sense and sense-object to sense-object, so pleasure stands to pleasure, because in sensory pleasures there are only these two factors. But the other senses are based on touch. (That

is why when its organ has been immobilized the other senses cannot act, as is clear in sleep.) Similarly, other sense-objects, both odors and colors, are based on the hot and the cold, by which they are caused. Therefore, pleasure [in the other senses] will also [be based] on [the] pleasure [of touch].

[2d. Against]

[xiii] What is said here in the text (1174b25–26) and in the beginning of the *Metaphysics* (I 1, 980a23–24) is to the contrary.

[xiv] Moreover, pleasure follows cognition. But every cognition is ordered to one power, namely, the understanding. Therefore, the {732B} nearer something is to that, the greater the pleasure in it. But among all the senses sight and hearing are nearer to understanding, because they are teachable, and as between these two sight more than hearing, because it serves for discovery. Therefore, the greatest pleasure is in it.

[2e] Solution

To the first part of the question (i–iv) we have to say that sensing can be considered in two ways. [i] One way is in accord with the reception of what is sensed, and here there is motion and a certain alteration, which produces laboring on account of the motion disarranging the organ, and so it does not produce pleasure. [ii] Sensing can also be considered as to the use or exercise of sense, where 'sensing' refers to the activity of a sense already perfected by a species of what is sensed, and since such activity follows on the sense's own perfection it will be pleasant.

[2f. Replies to the Opening Arguments]

[i] To the first we therefore have to say that the other animals do not have the senses in their greatest perfection, which is in an order to intellectual cognition. Because of this they do not participate in the pleasure of sight and other spiritual senses, which is more like spiritual pleasure.

[ii] To the second we have to say that Avicenna is speaking with reference to natural pleasure, not pleasure pertaining to the soul *(delectationem animalem)*.

[iii–iv] The third and fourth arguments go through for natural pleasure, because he means 'enjoying' in the sense in which cattle 'enjoy' fodder.

[2g. Solution to the Second Part of the Question (v–ix)]

[v] To the second part of the question we have to say that 'the most powerful in sense' is not meant either according to [sensory] power or according to sense-object but according to rank in the order to intellectual cognition. In this respect humans have what is most powerful in sense.

[vi–ix] From this the solution to the four objections made there is clear, the first of which took 'most powerful' according to [sensory] power and the second according to sense-object, while the third and fourth were based on sensing as reception of a sense-object.

[2h. Solution to the Third Part of the Question]

[x] To the third part of the question we have to say that certain pleasures are natural and certain pleasures pertain to the soul. In natural pleasure the more material senses prevail – touch, and the others in order of nearness to touch. As to pleasure pertaining to the soul, on the other hand, which is ordered to intellectual cognition, there is greater pleasure in vision and in other senses in order as they approach it in spirituality. {733A} But such pleasure is proper to humans, who perceive the natures of things from odors and sounds, but the other animals do not take pleasure in these except as they are ordered to taste and touch, and this is natural pleasure.

[3. Is It Possible to Be Pleased Continually?]

[3a. It Seems Possible]

Third, it seems that someone could be pleased continually (cf. 1175a3–4).

[i] For any power that is maintained for activity by being in activity can be always active. But every cognitive power is perfected for its activity by habit, which comes from frequent activity. Therefore it seems that, since pleasure follows on activity, one could be pleased continually.

[ii] Moreover, it is said in the text (1175a1f) that there is pleasure as long as [sense and object] remain alike. But since cognition arises from the assimilation of power to object, assimilation increases in the activity. It therefore seems that the more sense or understanding is active, the more one is pleased.

[iii] Moreover, the Philosopher says in De anima III (4, 429b3–4) that

when we understand what is greatest among the things that can be understood, we do not understand other things less but more, although this is not the case in sensing. But pleasure follows on understanding. It therefore seems that, however much the understanding understands, it could be pleased further in understanding.

[3b] To the Contrary

[iv] As we are aware from experience, we cannot be always active. But pleasure follows activity. Therefore, we cannot be continually pleased either.

[v] Moreover, in *Metaphysics* XI (cf. XII 9, 1074b28–29) it is said that an understanding that has a more divine understanding [above it] understands with labor. But our possible understanding has a more divine one [above it], namely, the active understanding, which brings it from potentiality to act. Therefore it understands with labor. Now no power that labors in its action can be active continually. Therefore, it cannot be pleased continually either.

[vi] Moreover, every movement toward form distances a thing from its starting point, as the Philosopher says (*Physics* II 6, 198a8–9; *Politics* IV 11, 1296b7–9). But understanding and sensing are movements of this sort. Therefore, they take [the powers involved] away from [their initial state], and so it follows that they induce weariness.

[3c. A Further Question]

[vii] I ask further, whether we take more pleasure in what is novel. It seems not. (Cf. 1175a6.)

[viii] For the activity of one's own habits is the reason {733B} for pleasure. Now habits arises from habituation. But everything habitual is old. Therefore, there is more pleasure in old things.

[ix] Moreover, the more a power is maintained in activity, the more pleasurably it acts, because with less labor. But a power is maintained by habit and habituation. Therefore, the same as before.

[3d. To the Contrary]

[x] What Aristotle says in the text is to the contrary.

[3e. A Further Question]

[xi] Moreover, I ask: Why do we take more pleasure in new things seen than [in those appearing to] the other senses? (Cf. 1175a7–8.)

[3f] Solution [to the First Part of the Question (i–vi)]

To the first part of the question we have to say that there can be pleasure in a nature that is simple, as the divine nature is, or in a composite nature. In a simple nature (or in one turned to the simple, as an angelic nature is), pleasure is not mixed with motion, because the activity causing it is without motion and because of this does not induce weariness and can be continual. It follows that the pleasure effected by it [can be continual]. In a composite nature, however, such as human nature, activity is joined with motion, either with motion in the active power itself, as in the activity of the senses, or else with motion in preceding powers, as in the motions of imagination ((*imaginationis/imaginis*)), memory, and the other sensory powers joined [as prerequisite] to the activity of understanding. And because bodily motion disarranges and consequently weakens the organs involved, for this reason we cannot understand or sense continually, and thus we cannot be continually pleased either.

[3g. Replies to the Opening Arguments]

[i] To the first we therefore have to say that as a result of habituation one acts with more facility after an interval of rest [than one who is not habituated], but immediately after many activities that have induced weariness, further activity is necessarily faulty.

[ii] To the second we have to say that it follows incidentally that there is not assimilation, insofar as the organ, when exhausted, is not as it was before.

[iii] To the third we have to say the same as to the first.

[iv–vi] We concede the other three.

[3h. Solution to the Second Part of the Question (vii–xi)]

[vii] To the second part of the question we have to say that because of the natural desire to know, our appetite is greater for knowing new things (both things previously wholly unknown and things known ((*nota/nova*))

by habit [in virtue of which one could think about them] but without
{734A} sensory experience. Because of this there arises a more vehement
motion toward them. It is true that after we have become accustomed to
them the activity is stronger, but the reason they please more in the
beginning is because of the vehemence of the motion. And because vision
serves most for cognition and shows the most differences we take the
greatest pleasure in seeing new things. Hence the Commentator (Michael
of Ephesus) says that he has seen people exhausted on a journey flock to
see lions as if they had not been toiling.

[viii–xi] From this the solution to the whole is clear. . . .

Lesson 8

{734B} 'Now [one might think that all] seek pleasure' (1175a10).

Now that he has shown that pleasure perfects activity, he shows from
this that all seek pleasure as a perfection of activities proper to themselves.
{735A}

I ask five questions about this part.

[1. Do All Seek Pleasure?]

First, whether all seek pleasure.

[1a] *It Seems Not*

[i] For those who declare that something is universally bad do not seek it,
because only what is or appears good is sought. But there have been
philosophers who held that pleasure is universally bad. Therefore, etc.

[ii] Moreover, whoever shuns all pleasure without exception does not
seek it. But there exist insensible individuals who shun pleasures, as he said
in Book III (11, 1119a5–7; cf. II 2, 1104a24). Therefore, etc.

[iii] Moreover, pleasure is not the end of any life except the hedonistic.
Not everyone seeks this life, however. Therefore, it does not seem to
follow that if all seek life all seek pleasure.

[iv] Moreover, he said above (c. 3, 1174a4–8), that there are some things
which would be sought even if they were not pleasant, for example, those
that are morally honorable. Therefore, they can be sought and loved

without any pleasure. Therefore, although there is activity with respect to what is loved, it does not follow that pleasure is sought by all, although activity is universally sought.

[1b] Solution

We have to say that although not everyone seeks the pleasures of the soul or even bodily pleasures, nevertheless all look for the pleasures proper to a habit that is itself proper to them. For unless they were pleased in doing such things they would not do them frequently, and so a habit would not be established. As a result, since pleasure arises from a proper habit, whether natural or unnatural, it must be pleasant.

[1c. Replies to the Opening Arguments]

[i] To the first we therefore have to say that those who used to say that pleasure was universally bad had regard to certain disgraceful pleasures and did not seek pleasures of this sort. But they had to seek some pleasure, since they carried on some activities, which they did not engage in without pleasure.

[ii] To the second we have to say that insensible individuals shun the pleasures of taste and touch, which the self-indulgent pursue. But they do not shun all pleasures, since they take pleasure in the very fact that they shun the ones they do.

[iii] To the third we have to say that bodily pleasure is the end of the hedonistic life. It is also necessary that there be some pleasure proper to any other life, since every life whatever has some {735A} activity proper to it.

[iv] To the fourth we have to say that the Philosopher spoke hypothetically above, not meaning to assert that there is [in fact] any activity proper to an individual that is not pleasant. Here, however, he is talking about the real order.

[2. Is Pleasure Connected with Activity?]

[2a. It Seems Not]

Second, it seems that pleasure is not connected with activity.

[i] For pleasure arises from being joined with the agreeable. Now such

conjoining is an undergoing, since it is a kind of receiving. Therefore, it seems that pleasure is connected more with undergoing than with activity.

[ii] Moreover, activity cannot be pleasant unless it is perceived, just as light does not please in lighting but in being perceived. But there is no perception without reception. Therefore, the same.

[iii] Moreover, there is no undergoing without motion. But our activities do not occur without undergoing (hence they are also laborious). Therefore they involve motion. But motion impedes pleasure. Therefore, pleasure is not connected with our acts.

[iv] Moreover, it seems that activity can never exist together with motion in the same subject, for while something is in motion, it is in a state of becoming. But as long as it is in a state of becoming, no habit is achieved. Now activity follows on habit. Therefore, it seems that there cannot be motion and activity in the same thing.

[2b] Solution

We have to say with the Philosopher in *On Generation [and Corruption]* I (cf. 5, 321b16–19) that a growing thing is unlike in the beginning, like in the end. Similarly, I say that something producing pleasure by being joined with a thing can be considered in two ways: either as it is in motion – and so considered it is not yet agreeable – or as it is in the term of the motion – and considered in this way it is now perfectly agreeable and purified. While it is in motion, therefore, the recipient is still receiving and thus is also not pleased, because the thing is not yet agreeable but contrary. But when it is in the term of the motion, it has been purified of contraries [i.e., of things contrary to the recipient], and at that point it is perfectly agreeable. There then follows a proper activity, which is pleasant. And so it is clear that pleasure is connected more with activity than undergoing.

[2c. Replies to the Opening Arguments]

[i] To the first we therefore have to say that being joined with the agreeable is not an undergoing when the conjoining has already been effected and assimilation is complete, because then [the conjoined thing] has been turned into the nature of the thing [to which it has been joined]. For this reason, because {736A} sensing is a certain undergoing, Avicenna says (*Liber de anima* II 3) that the heat of a fever is not sensed, because it has been turned into the nature [of the fevered individual].

[ii] To the second we have to say that where there is no perception of activity, there cannot be unqualified pleasure but only natural pleasure, which is a qualified pleasure – as Isaac [Israeli] also says that plants have natural senses, namely, taste and touch (*De elementis* III; *Opera*, Lyons 1515, f. [Xra]).

[iii] To the third we have to say that motion is an imperfect act and thus has something of the form toward which the motion tends, in which respect there is pleasure in it, and also something of the contrary, in which respect it induces weariness. Eating, for example, is pleasant according as it is a motion of the food toward being joined [with one].

[iv] To the fourth we have to say that motion can be taken either as near its starting point – in which respect, because of the predominance of what is contrary [to its final state], there cannot be activity – or as near to its term – and then, because the form toward which there is motion is in process of conquering, there can be some activity, though not a perfect one.

[3. Can Pleasures Be Differentiated by Activities?]

[3a. It Seems Not]

Third, it seems that pleasures cannot be differentiated on the basis of the activities [with which they are connected].

[i] For an effect takes its differentia only from its own essential cause. But activity is not an essential cause of pleasure, because it is neither its form nor its matter. Therefore, etc.

[ii] Moreover, all pleasure is of one character, because it arises from being conjoined with what is agreeable. Now activities are of various characters. Therefore, pleasure is not differentiated by activity.

[iii] Moreover, for one thing what is agreeable to it can only be one. But pleasure arises from being joined with the agreeable. Therefore, for one thing there is one pleasure. For one thing, however, there are many activities. Therefore, the same.

[3b] Solution

We have to say that [different] activities induce different pleasures, as bodily [activity] bodily [pleasure] and spiritual spiritual. Because of this, pleasures must differ according to the differences among activities.

[3c. Replies to the Opening Arguments]

[i] To the first we therefore have to say that effects are also differentiated by extrinsic causes as long as these act univocally, because human engenders human, and horse horse. Now an activity is a particular sort of univocal agent, insofar, namely, as intellectual activity induces intellectual pleasure and sensible sensible. {736B}

[ii] To the second we have to say that pleasures are of one character in general, but they are of different specific natures, as are activities also.

[iii] To the third we have to say that for one thing in the same respect only one thing is agreeable, but nothing prevents there being different things agreeable to it in different respects. And so there are different pleasures, as there are also [different] activities.

[4. Does Pleasure Always Augment Activity?]

[4a. It Seems Not]

Fourth, it seems that pleasure does not always augment activity.

[i] For an effect does not augment its own cause, rather the contrary. But activity is the cause of pleasure. Therefore, etc.

[ii] Moreover, what augments is always something added to what is augmented. But pleasure is simultaneous with activity, not something added to it. Therefore, it does not augment it.

[iii] Moreover, what augments always precedes the [final] quantity of what is augmented, because it is its cause. But pleasure does not precede the quantity of an activity. Rather, it follows it, because from a great activity there is great pleasure.

[iv] Moreover, the same thing cannot both augment and be augmented by the same thing. But activity augments pleasure. Therefore, pleasure does not augment activity.

[4b] Solution

We have to say, as we said above (Lesson 7, 1f) about perfection, that activity perfects pleasure without qualification, but pleasure perfects activity in relation to us, insofar as it maintains activity. So, too, we have to say about augmenting, that activity augments pleasure essentially, as its cause, but pleasure augments an activity in relation to us, insofar as someone persists more in an activity because of pleasure, and thus activities are multiplied.

[4c. Replies to the Opening Arguments]

[i] To the first we therefore have to say that an effect can augment a cause in a qualified way, as has been said.

[ii] To the second we have to say that that reasoning goes through with regard to something that augments essentially [i.e., adds to the substance of a thing], as food augments the body, but such augmentation is not at issue here.

[iii] To the third we have to say that pleasure follows the quantity of the activity that is its cause. Nonetheless it precedes the quantity of the activities that spring up from the multiplication of activities for the sake of pleasure.

[iv] To the fourth we have to say that the same thing cannot both augment and be augmented in the same way, but {737A} nothing prevents it from doing both in different ways. For one thing may augment *per se* and without qualification and be augmented in a qualified way.

[5. Does an Unrelated Pleasure Impede Activity?]

[5a. It Seems Not]

Fifth, it seems that an extraneous pleasure does not impede activity.

For every homogeneous whole with many parts can act in all its parts. But the soul is a whole of this sort, having many powers as parts. It can therefore be in activity with respect to many powers. Now pleasure follows activity. Therefore, pleasure [from the activity] of one power does not impede pleasure [from the activity of] another power.

Moreover, in the soul there are many powers. But a power is the basis (*principium*) of activity. Therefore, the soul can engage in several activities at once.

Moreover, activity proceeds either from the essence [of the soul] or from its powers. Not from the essence, because, since the essence is only one, there would be only one activity. Therefore from the powers, and since they are many there will be many activities which do not impede one another.

We have to say that an activity does not proceed from the [soul's] essence alone or from a power alone, but from the essence in the power. Because its powers are many, the soul can engage in many activities. Because, however, its essence is one, many activities cannot be engaged in intensely at the same time, but when one power is vigorously active, another is either totally inactive or its activity is greatly abated. For this reason the pleasure {737B} following on an extraneous activity also impedes the pleasure proper to a given one.

And from this the solution to the whole question is clear. . . .

Lesson 9

{738A} 'Because the proper [pleasure]' (1175b13).

In this part he discusses pleasure in relation to proper or extraneous activity, and it is divided into two. First he does what has been said, second (at '[The pleasures involved in activities are] more proper [to them than the desires]' [1175b30]), he shows the difference between pleasure and wanting (*concupiscentia*).

[o. What Does Aristotle Mean by a Proper Pleasure?]

About this part I ask: What should be called {738B} a proper pleasure [1175b13]?

[oa. It Seems that Every Pleasure Is Proper]

For it seems that every pleasure is proper.

[i] For pleasure arises from being joined with what is agreeable. But everything agreeable is proper. Therefore, etc.

[ii] Moreover, opposites have opposite effects. But pleasure and distress are opposites. It therefore seems false to say that an extraneous pleasure may produce the same result as a proper distress.

[iii] Moreover, the common is opposed to the proper. When, therefore, he distinguishes extraneous pleasure in opposition to proper, he seems to divide badly.

[iv] Moreover, destruction, since it is a privation, does not admit of more or less. But extraneous pleasure and proper distress destroy proper activity. Therefore, he ought not to have added that they do 'almost' the same, but the same without qualification.

[v] Moreover, what is necessary on a certain condition is neither good nor bad morally speaking. But when something agreeable is given, pleasure follows necessarily. Therefore, it seems that he divides pleasure badly into debased and morally serious.

[vi] Moreover, no passion is debased or worthy except righteous indignation and modesty. But pleasure is a passion and is neither of these. Therefore, etc.

[ob] Solution

We have to say that a pleasure is not called proper here as distinguished from what is common but from the properness of a habit. For each pleasure or activity related to a habit that has become natural is called proper, whether the habit is without qualification natural or not natural.

[oc. Replies to the Opening Arguments]

[i] And so the solution to the first is clear, because something can be agreeable in some respect that nevertheless is not agreeable in relation to a proper habit, as bodily pleasures to the insensible individual. That is why they do not please if they are joined with someone like this, and nevertheless the pleasures are also proper [to people generally?].

[ii] To the second we have to say that opposites have opposite effects on the same thing, but they can have a single effect on different things. For example, heat solidifies some things, and cold solidifies others. Thus, from the pleasure proper to one [habit] there follows in another [habit], to which that pleasure is extraneous, the same effect as follows in it from the distress [properly] opposed to it, namely, disruption of its proper activity.

[iii] The solution to the third is clear from what has been said. {739A}

[iv] To the fourth we have to say that although privations are not essentially intensified or abated, yet in relation to what causes them they fall away more or less from the habit, and so in a certain way they are

intensified or abated. Thus it is in the case at hand, for [proper?] distress disrupts activity in every respect, namely, both as to its general character as being distress and also as to its specific character as being such a distress as it is, namely, both by reason of the genus in relation to which it is a distress and also by reason of the species in relation to which it is such and such a distress; but an extraneous pleasure destroys activity by reason of its species and not by reason of its genus. He notes this difference when he says 'almost.'

[v] To the fifth we have to say that in morals a consequent is judged to be voluntary if its antecedent is voluntary, as was said in [discussing] Book III. Because it is in our power whether or not something agreeable be joined with us, the pleasure is judged voluntary, both the debased and the worthy.

[vi] From this the solution to the sixth is clear, because a passion is also called voluntary by reason of the action on which it follows. . . .

{739B} Next, when he says 'More proper' (1175b30), he shows the difference between pleasure and wanting by comparison with activity.

And about this part I ask five questions.

[1. Are Wantings Separate from Pleasures in Time and Nature, as Aristotle Says?]

First, whether wantings are separate from pleasures in time and in nature, as he says.

[1a] It Seems Not

[i] For what essentially is an activity is not separate from activity. But wanting is like this, for he is not talking about a wanting that is a power or a habit. Therefore, etc.

[ii] Moreover, theologians distinguish the wanting that exists before an act from that which exists in the act (cf. Peter Lombard, *Libri IV Sententiarum* II, d. 30, c. 9). But that which exists in the act is a single sin with the act, otherwise it would be necessary for every sin to be two sins, since a wanting is joined to every sinful act. Therefore, it is not separate from activity.

[iii] Moreover, he is talking about either inner or outer activities. If about the outer, what he says seems inadequate, since he ignores the inner ones, which have more the character of activity. If he is talking about inner activities, however, it seems wrong to say that wantings are separate from activities, since wantings are a particular kind of inner activity.

[iv] Moreover, whenever things are separate in time, they are also separate by nature, because things that are by nature one are inseparable from one another. Therefore, it seems superfluous to say that they are separate in time *and* nature.

[1b] Solution

We have to say that wanting is said to be separate from activity by nature insofar as it is distinguished from it by having a distinct character. It is separate from it in time, however, insofar as it is marked off from it as its cause, which it is – in the mode of a material cause. {740A} For wanting pertains to an imperfect power, but activity follows from a habit perfecting a power. As a result, wanting and activity are related to one another as matter and form.

[1c. Replies to the Opening Arguments]

[i] To the first we therefore have to say that to want is not without qualification to be active, even if it is a kind of motion.

[ii] To the second we have to say that wanting is not essentially one with activity, but from them there is effected a single sin, which is, so to speak, a composite unity.

[iii] To the third we have to say that inner acts can be considered according as they are perfect, and so considered they have the character of activities, but they are not wantings except when they are imperfect.

[iv] To the fourth we have to say that it happens in many cases that things prior by nature in some particular thing are posterior in time (cf. *Metaphysics* IX 8, 1049b10–12), as potentiality is prior in time to actuality in something that is later moved from potentiality to actuality (although actuality is prior by nature), and it is not prior in time without qualification [in the universe as a whole]. Similarly, wanting, since it is mixed with an imperfect power, is posterior to activity by nature but prior in time. Because of this he asserted both ['separate in time *and* nature'] to mark this double separation.

[2. Is Sight Purer than the Other Senses?]

[2a. It Seems Not]

Second, it seems that sight is not purer than the other senses.

[i] For every particular sense receives what it senses when matter is present. But purity in cognition refers to separation from matter. Therefore, one [sense] is not purer than another.

[ii] Moreover, among cognitive powers some are called purer than others according to their different degrees of abstraction. Thus, understanding is purer than imagination, and the latter is purer than the outer senses. But all the outer senses are at a single degree of abstraction, because they receive the impressions (*intentiones*) of sensibles when matter is present. Therefore, the same.

[iii] Moreover, in all the outer senses there is equally an activity of soul (in which the impressions of sensibles are received in the sense organs) and an activity of nature (in which the medium is changed by the sensibles). Therefore, there is the same degree of purity in all of them.

[iv] Moreover, what is more general seems to be simpler and consequently purer. But among all the senses touch is more general, as is said in *De anima* II (2, 413b4–5). {740B} It therefore seems that it is purer than vision.

[2b] Solution

We have to say that the purity of powers of apprehension is judged from the way they abstract from matter. For this reason it is said that the understanding, which abstracts from matter and from features connected with it, is purer than the inner senses, which do not abstract from features connected with matter when they receive particular forms or impressions, and that the inner senses are purer than the outer senses, which are only in activity when matter is present. Now although all the outer senses agree in this general [characteristic], they are nevertheless distinguished from one another in purity according as one receives more spiritually than another when matter is present. For some senses do not receive the species of a sensible unless it is really joined with them, as is the case for taste and touch; in some, on the other hand, the species is received with something of the medium, although not with anything of the object, as happens in smell and hearing, for sound is brought to hearing by a certain pulsation of the medium. But in sight nothing is received from either the medium or the object except the sensible impression alone. Because of this it is a more spiritual receiver. And that is why sight occurs instantly, whereas the other senses are affected in a time. And that is why the wind carries sounds and odors and does not carry colors to sight. That is also why vision occurs at a point, in that whatever is seen is seen within an angle.

[2c. Replies to the Opening Arguments]

[i–iii] From this the solution is clear to the first three, which proceed according to what is common to all the particular senses.

[iv] To the fourth we have to say that the sense of touch is more general, not by generality of form, but by a generality, as it were, of matter, in that it is the foundation of the others. Hence it does not follow that it is purer but that it is more material.

[3. Is There One Pleasure for Humans More than for Other Animals?]

[3a. It Seems that There Ought to Be]

Third, it seems that for humans more than for other animals there ought to be one pleasure.

[i] For the unity of pleasure in the other animals follows the unity of their makeup. But the human makeup comes back to one thing more than that of other animals. Therefore, its pleasure ought more to be one.

[ii] Moreover, among all the animals, humans are nobler. But to the extent that something is nobler, it comes closer to being one. Therefore, etc.

[iii] Moreover, to the extent that something is nearer to the one first simplest being, it seems to be {741A} more one. But human nature is most like the first being; therefore, etc. And so human pleasure ought to be simple, as God's is.

[iv] If you say that humans have more pleasures, because they have both bodily and intellectual ones, it seems that at least with respect to the body they ought not to have more than the other animals.

[v] Moreover, pleasures follow on activities. But activities are multiplied in accordance with their objects rather than in accordance with those

engaging in them. Therefore, he ought to have taken the diversity of pleasures more from the side of pleasant things than from the side of those taking pleasure.

[3b] Solution

We have to say that the first mover in humans is a manifold one, namely, the soul. Because of this there are many activities in humans, in accordance with the soul's many powers and conceptions. Now although there are sensory activities in the other animals, yet in them the first mover is nature, because in them the senses are more actuated than acting, as Damascene says. Because of this there follows in them, from the unity of nature, one uniform activity (thus every swallow builds its nest in the same way) and also on this account one pleasure.

[3c. Replies to the Opening Arguments]

[i] To the first we therefore have to say that although the human makeup comes back to a greater uniformity (*aequalitatem*) [than that of other animals], it is nevertheless an instrument of the soul. Because of this, in accordance with the manifoldness of its first motor many activities are effected.

[ii] To the second we have to say that humans excel the other animals and are more like God as to the understanding, in accordance with which they have one ultimate and simplest pleasure and activity. Nonetheless they have other activities which are ordered to that one.

[iii] From this the solution to the third is clear.

[iv] To the fourth we have to say just as to the first.

[v] To the fifth we have to say that different pleasure-takers are by nature apt to take pleasure in different pleasant things. Because of this there is a single reason for differentiating pleasures both from the side of pleasant things and from the side of those who take pleasure in them.

[4. Are the Pleasures of the Virtuous More Natural to Humans than Other Pleasures?]

[4a. It Seems Not]

Fourth, it seems that the pleasures of the virtuous are neither more natural to humans nor truer [than other pleasures].

[i] For the more general something is, the simpler and the truer it is. But the pleasures of the virtuous are those of a few, while the other [pleasures] are those of the many. Therefore, the latter seem truer. {741B}

[ii] Moreover, that in which something remains if left to itself seems most natural to it, as being above [is most natural] to fire. But if humans are left to themselves, they will take more pleasure in physically pleasant things than in virtuously pleasant ones. Therefore, the pleasures of the virtues are not most natural to them.

[iii] Moreover, bodily pleasures are ordered to the good maintenance of the body. Therefore, it seems false that pleasures other than those of the virtuous belong to the corrupt.

[iv] Moreover, pleasures are manifold: natural and necessary, natural but unnecessary, and neither natural nor necessary. Only those that are both unnatural and unnecessary belong to corrupt people. Therefore, what he says is insufficient.

[4b] Solution

We have to say that the pleasures of the virtuous are found in the activities of humans as humans – activities proceeding from habits that perfect the part of us that reasons or understands. Because of this they are truer.

[4c. Replies to the Opening Arguments]

[i] We therefore have to say to the first, as was said above, that not everything that is more general is simpler but [only] what follows on form. What is more material is less pure, however, and thus it is with the pleasures in which the many take pleasure.

[ii] To the second we have to say that if humans are left to their own nature perfected by habit, then they will take pleasure in the virtues. They will not be able to have the pleasures of a perfect nature, however, unless their own nature has been perfected by habit.

[iii] To the third we have to say that the pleasures of the virtuous are not only spiritual but also bodily, as long as they are natural and necessary ones. These pertain to them as to *use*, because they use them (or also the natural and unnecessary ones that are in order for them), because they order them to a due end.

[iv] From this the solution to the last is clear.

[5. Is There Only One Pleasure for the Virtuous?]

[5a. It Seems So]

Fifth, it seems that for the virtuous there is [only] one pleasure.

For pleasure does not pertain to [the virtuous] except according to the activity of virtue. Now the best virtue is one, prudence in things to be done and wisdom in speculative matters. Therefore, the pleasure is also one.

Moreover, as Dionysius says, the more virtuous one is, the more unified, whereas he describes others as living a divided life. But for those who are unified there seems to be [only] one pleasure. Therefore, etc.

[5b] Against

{742A} The virtues are many, but the virtuous take pleasure in the activities of all the virtues. Therefore, their pleasures are also many.

Moreover, pleasure relating to the genus of the morally honorable is a formal constituent of happiness. But happiness is twofold. Therefore, there is not only one pleasure.

[5c] Solution

We have to say that there is only one ultimate activity for humans, namely, contemplation of the highest realities (*contemplatio altissimarum substantiarum*), but there are many other activities ordered to that one, some supporting it (as the other cognitive activities do) and some disposing [us] for it (as the activities of the moral virtues do). Similarly, there is only one ultimate pleasure for humans insofar as they are human, but there are many others ordered to that one, because even civic happiness is ordered to contemplative happiness as a disposition [for it].

And from this the solution to the objections is clear. . . .

Lesson 10

{743A} 'Now that we have spoken of [the virtues, the forms of friendship, and the varieties of pleasure]' (1176a31).

In this part he begins to discuss contemplative happiness, and it is divided into three. First he inquires about its genus and shows that it consists in the activity of virtue. Second (at 'If happiness is' [c. 7, 1177a12]), he shows that it is the activity of the most perfect virtue (namely, of wisdom), which is one of its differentiae. Third (at 'Now perfect [happiness]' [1178b7]), he shows that it consists in the best activity possible in accordance with that habit.

About the first I ask three questions.

[1. Does a Separate Book Begin Here?]

First, whether a separate book begins here.

[1a] It Seems So

[i] Because he places this treatise next to the things said above about virtue, friendship, and pleasure. Therefore, it seems to be {743B} distinct from all of them.

[ii] Moreover, the Commentator [Michael of Ephesus] says that the moral virtues are ordered to civic happiness and that both the moral and intellectual virtues are ordered to contemplative happiness. But an end is distinct from the means to it. It therefore seems that the treatise on contemplative happiness should be distinguished from all the preceding.

[iii] Moreover, the Commentator seems to be wrong in saying this. For things that do not depend on one another seem to be ordered to different ends. But the moral and intellectual virtues do not depend on one another, since they can be separated. Therefore, it seems that they are not [ordered] to a single end.

[iv] Moreover, the Commentator [Michael of Ephesus] says that friendship is threefold. One, which exists among contemplatives, accords with the reasoning part [of the soul]. Another, which exists among comrades in arms, accords with the irascible part. The third, pleasant friendship, accords with the wanting part. He says it is on this account that the Philosopher refers to friendships in the plural here.

[1b] Against

Aristotle never divided friendship in this way above [in Books VIII and IX], although he did lay down several other divisions. Therefore, it seems that he uses the plural more because of those types.

Moreover, it seems that there is no division, because according to the Philosopher in the *Topics* (IV 5, 126a11–13), every friendship is in reason, and so there seems to be none based on the irascible and the wanting.

[1c] Solution [in Replies to the Opening Arguments]

[i] To the first we have to say that the treatment of contemplative happiness is distinguished from all the preceding by this, that they are all ordered to it, even civic happiness, all the virtues, and friendship (and consequently pleasure, too, because according to the nature of the thing activity is unqualifiedly best and is the end of pleasure, although conversely as to the one who is active). But because pleasure is mixed with happiness as its form, so to speak, he needed to discuss both in the same book, though in different chapters.

[ii] From this the solution to the second is clear.

[iii] To the third we have to say that one thing is said to be ordered to another 'by order of the thing' (*ordine rei*) when they depend on one another in some way. In this way the intellectual virtues are ordered to contemplative happiness. {744A} In another way one thing is ordered to another 'by an order of disposition' (*ordine dispositionis*). It is in this way that the moral virtues are ordered to the intellectual and consequently to contemplative happiness, insofar as the understanding is left freer for activity when the passions have been calmed. And this is to be the end of a thing in the one who is active rather than the end of the thing in itself.

[iv] To the fourth we have to say that friendship is always in reason as to what it is, but as to what the sharing involved in a friendship is concerned with, it is sometimes the object of reason, sometimes the object of other parts of us. He did not lay that division down above because it is based on what is more material in friendship, not on what is essential in it.

[2. Does Contemplative Happiness Have to Do with Activities?]

[2a. It Seems Not]

Second, it seems that contemplative happiness is not concerned with activities.

[i] For civic and contemplative happiness are not concerned with the

same things. But civic happiness is concerned with activities, as was said in Book I (5, 1095b22–23). Therefore, etc.

[ii] Moreover, a principle is nobler and more perfect than that of which it is a principle. But the principle of activity is habit (and also nature – otherwise a habit could not be acquired from activities). Therefore, since contemplative happiness is most perfect, it will not be an activity but seems rather to be a habit, because a habit is more perfect in nature.

[iii] Moreover, in *Metaphysics* I (2, 982b4–6, 25–27) it is said that all activities are for the sake of something else. But contemplative happiness is most sought after for its own sake. Therefore, it seems that it is not an activity.

[iv] Moreover, he seems to put forward unsuitable examples, for plants have no habit acquired by activity. Therefore, it would not follow that if happiness were a habit a happy life would be like the life of a plant.

[v] Moreover, he said in Book I (13, 1102b10–11) that the dreams of the good are better than those of anyone else. But one is especially happy in accordance with virtue. Therefore, neither is there anything unsuitable in calling someone happy in a life of sleeping.

[vi] Moreover, no one who has what is best can be unfortunate. But the habit of virtue is among the best of things. Therefore, it would not follow that if happiness were a matter of virtuous habit a happy person would be unfortunate, as he says [could be the case].

[2b] Solution

We have to say that there is a happiness to {744B} which human life is ordered (especially the contemplative life) which is not itself ordered to anything else. For this reason happiness must be an activity that is the ultimate perfection of human nature. That is why it is called second act, and habit or form [is called] first act.

[2c. Replies to the Opening Arguments]

[i] To the first we therefore have to say that human activities are twofold. Some are external, as when one is active concerning external things and bodily activities. Mechanical art, moral virtue, and also civic happiness are concerned with such [activities]. Some activities, on the other hand, are inner. These, such as understanding, willing, and the like, are perfections of the powers involved. Both the intellectual and moral virtues are con-

cerned with these. But there is a difference. The passions are bound up with the deeds of the moral virtues, since they [the moral virtues] are perfections of the rational parts [of the soul] only by participation, but the activities of the intellectual virtues are pure and altogether separate from the passions, because they are perfections of the rational parts by essence. And so it is clear how civic and contemplative happiness concern activities in different ways.

[ii] To the second we have to say that an active principle is indeed more perfect and nobler than the effect produced by its action, as an agent is nobler than what it acts on. But a habit is not properly a principle of activity by acting. Rather, activity follows on habit as its perfection and is for this reason nobler than it. Now nature is a principle of activity insofar as it supplies an act which takes its form from habit. For this reason activities before habit are imperfect, and none of them is happiness.

[iii] To the third we have to say that the Philosopher is speaking there about external activities.

[iv] To the fourth we have to say that someone who has a habit [acquired by activity but not exercised] is like a sleeper, in whom there are natural habits of the senses that are not in use. Now in sleep the natural powers [of digestion and growth] are vigorous, while the animal [powers of perception and movement] are abated. For this reason a life of sleeping – and consequently a life of [unexercised] habit – compares with the life of a plant.

[v] To the fifth we have to say that in many cases the dreams of the good are better because of their waking deeds, although sometimes the contrary happens, when the phantasms in sleep follow the turning about of the soul, because the animal powers are bound. {745A} As a result, there is not enough of a difference here to distinguish the happy from the unhappy.

[vi] To the sixth we have to say that someone is called unfortunate with respect to external goods, which are mostly subject to fortune, not in relation to virtuous habits, which should not be committed to fortune. For this reason someone who is unfortunate can be most perfect as to virtuous habit yet will fall short of perfect activity, inasmuch as external goods furnish means for the activity of happiness. For this reason such a person is not happy according to the best and most perfect possible happiness.

[3. Should Aristotle Have Mentioned Play Here?]

[3a. It Seems Not]

Third, it seems that he ought not to have mentioned play here.

[i] For play is not asserted to be the end of any life. But here he is looking for the end of human life. Therefore, etc.

[ii] Moreover, play is more in action than in contemplation. It therefore seems that he ought rather to have mentioned play in his treatment of civic happiness.

[iii] Moreover, he seems to contradict himself. For first he says that playful activities are choice-worthy of themselves. Afterwards he says that play is ordered to what is serious.

[iv] Moreover, a tyrant sins more in terms of injustice than self-indulgence. But like seeks out like. Therefore, since a lover of amusement lacks self-restraint or is self-indulgent, as he said in Book VII (7, 1150b16), it seems that tyrants would not seek out lovers of amusement.

[v] Moreover, being witty is a virtue, as he said in Book IV (8, 1128a10), but a tyrant does not seek out the virtuous. Therefore, it is false to say that tyrants favor those who are witty.

[3b] Solution

We have to say that certain sorts of play are shameful and servile, namely, those that are played for money or involve things that are morally dishonorable. He is not here talking about these but about games of a free character which involve acts like acts of virtue, such as the ancient games of wrestling and running which, as Vitruvius says (*De architectura* V 11), were instituted among citizens for exercise lest their bodies {745B} grow weak from physical inactivity generating thick humors. So it is also clear that such games are ordered to contemplative happiness, because the spirits and humors are refined by such exercises and the spirits are made more agile, with the result that one can speculate with greater refinement.

[3c. Replies to the Opening Arguments]

[i] To the first we therefore have to say that with respect to the activity involved in it play is not asserted to be the end of any life, but through

the effect it has in a person – namely, rest – it is asserted to be the end of the hedonistic life, and it also has some order to contemplation.

[ii] To the second we have to say that the activity of play is a certain action, but in that activity the rational powers rest from serious meditation. For this reason, in the way indicated above, it is ordered more to contemplative than to civic happiness, because in play there is no rest from external activities.

[iii] To the third we have to say that first he speaks according to the opinions of the Epicureans – raising objections – but afterwards in accord with the truth. Or, alternatively, we have to say that playful activities of a liberal character are choice-worthy of themselves because they have in them something that pleases, although they are also ordered to something else. In the same way virtuous activities are chosen for themselves and nevertheless are ordered to happiness, because they are choice-worthy by their own form, although they are ordered to another end.

[iv] To the fourth we have to say that above in Book VII he called 'lovers of amusement' those who engage in lascivious games, such as ring-dancing and games of that sort. He is not talking about these here.

[v] To the fifth we have to say that here he names as witty someone who goes too far in play (who is properly called a buffoon), because in the estimation of a tyrant such an individual is a wit. . . .

Lesson 11

{747B} 'But if happiness is [activity in accordance with virtue]' (c. 7, 1177a12).

Now that he has shown that contemplative happiness lies in an activity that is choice-worthy in itself – which was, as it were, its genus – here he begins to investigate its differentiae. First he shows of which virtue it is the activity, namely, the best virtue. First he shows that ultimate happiness exists in accord with contemplative virtue and the activity of speculative understanding, proving that all the differentiae said by others to be the differentiae of happiness agree with it. Second (at 'But such [a life would be] altogether [too high for humans]' [1177b26]), he shows the differentiae or conditions of the contemplative life in which this sort of activity is found. The first part is divided in two. First he proves by the differentiae of happiness that contemplative happiness exists in accord with the activity of speculative understanding perfected by its proper virtue. Second (at 'Now [the activity] of the practical [virtues]' [1177b6]), he shows that those differentiae do not agree as much with the differentiae of practical understanding as with the virtue of speculative understanding.

About the first part I ask eight questions.

[1. Does Contemplative Happiness Exist in Accord with the Activity of One Virtue?]

First, whether contemplative happiness exists in accord with the activity of one virtue.

[1a] It Seems Not

[i] For as Boethius says (*On the Consolation of Philosophy* III, prose 2), blessedness is a state of all goods, etc. But all goods are gathered together by all the virtues. Therefore, etc.

[ii] Moreover, he himself proves in the text that contemplative happiness is most sufficient. But it cannot be of this sort unless it includes everything necessary for contemplation. It therefore seems that it exists at least in accord with all the intellectual [virtues].

[iii] Moreover, he proved in Book I (7, 1098a7–17) that happiness does not exist except in accord with the activity of perfect virtue. Now there is perfection in virtue only when one has all the virtues. Therefore, etc.

[iv] Moreover, if it exists only in accord with one [virtue], it will only be in accord with wisdom, which is called first philosophy. But that is about universal principles, in which things are known only in potentiality – an imperfect cognition not befitting contemplative happiness. Therefore, it seems that it cannot be in accord with any one virtue.

[1b] Against

Of one habit there is one activity. But happiness is one activity. Therefore, it exists in accord with one virtue. {748A}

Moreover, contemplative happiness is even more unitary than civic [happiness]. But civic happiness exists in accord with the activity of one virtue, namely, prudence. Therefore, etc.

Moreover, he himself suggests in the text that it exists in accord with wisdom. But wisdom is one among the intellectual virtues. Therefore, [contemplative happiness] exists according to one virtue.

[1c] Solution

We have to say that, just as in theorems the cognition of a second is based on cognition of a first and cognition of a third on cognition of the second and the first (and so on successively), and as in definitions too the definition of a posterior presupposes and includes the definition of the prior (as the definition of human being [presupposes and includes] the definition of animal), so it is also in the whole order of what can be known. All knowables are seen in the light of first principles, which are prior without qualification and which wisdom is about. For this reason, when wisdom is given the other particular sciences are not given, although if it is taken away all the others, which rest on it, are undermined, because such is the disposition of principles to the things following from them. So, therefore, I say that with regard to eliciting [knowledge], contemplative happiness is the activity of only one virtue, namely, wisdom, by whose light any contemplation whatever has virtue, but as regards completion, it is [the activity] of many [virtues], because there must be particular sciences, by which universal principles may be brought to particular conclusions, just as civic happiness has also been said to be the activity of one eliciting [virtue], prudence, as regards the eliciting [of its activity], yet with the other moral virtues assisting it.

[1d. Replies to the Opening Arguments]

[i] To the first we therefore have to say that in contemplative happiness there is something that is good as eliciting an act, and this is one, namely, wisdom. To it belongs the contemplation of divine things (cf. Augustine, *On the Trinity* XIV 1), in contemplating which is the summit of this happiness. There are certain things, however, that assist [wisdom], as the other intellectual virtues, which aid the understanding in such activity in coming from the posterior to the prior by way of analysis. And there are certain things that dispose [us for wisdom], as the moral virtues and the things ordered to them, as was said above.

[ii] To the second we have to say that sufficiency with respect to the act is in one virtue eliciting it and in others assisting, but sufficiency with

respect to virtue is in the cognition of principles, which virtually contain everything deduced from them.

[iii] To the third we have to say that perfection as to {748B} every particular conclusion is not required for the existence of contemplative happiness, because this is impossible for humans, but [perfection] as to universal principles and the noblest beings [is required], and in this is perfect wisdom.

[iv] To the fourth we have to say that the contemplation of God is the contemplation of a universal principle, [but] not of a universal predicated of everything, since God is a certain being determinate in his essence. For this reason [contemplative] beholding (*speculatio*) of him, in which this happiness consists most of all, is not in potentiality but is perfect. Now the beholding of other universals that are contemplated to very good effect is completed by the particular assisting sciences, and thus the contemplation that is happiness does not remain imperfect.

We concede the others.

[2. Is Contemplative Happiness Related to the Power of Understanding?]

[2a. It Seems Not]

Second, it seems that contemplative happiness is not related to the power of understanding.

[i] For he distinguished understanding from wisdom in Book VI (3, 1139b15–17). But here he says that contemplative happiness is related to wisdom. Therefore, it is not related to understanding.

[ii] Moreover, what is simpler ought to pertain to a simpler power, as is clear in the whole order of the virtues by which we apprehend things. But the understanding cognizes other intelligibles, all of which are less simple than God, in contemplation of whom there is contemplative happiness. Therefore, it seems that this pertains to a simpler power than the understanding.

[iii] Moreover, he seems to suggest in the text that there is something in us worthier than understanding, when he says, 'whether this understanding or something else' (1177a13). But the noblest thing in us is the activity of contemplative happiness. Therefore, the same.

[iv] Moreover, contemplative happiness pertains to humans as humans.

But in Book VI (1, 1139a11–12) he divided human cognition into the scientific and the calculative (*ratiocinativum*). It therefore seems that contemplative happiness relates to this [division?] and not to understanding.

[v] Moreover, this happiness is according to that which is dominant in humans, as he says in the text. But Augustine says that reason is dominant in humans. Therefore, it is according to reason.

[2b] Against

What is noblest in a lower nature is where it has contact with a higher. For it is said in chapter 7 of *On the Divine Names* that God always joins [the ends] of things that are prior to the beginnings of those that are next. But it is in {749A} intellectuality that human nature reaches the nature of the intelligences. That, therefore, is what is noblest in humans, and so contemplative happiness ought to exist in relation to understanding (*intellectum*).

Moreover, as sense stands to reason, so does reason stand to understanding. But sense at its highest reaches reason, namely, in the estimative [power], which receives, with the senses, spiritual impressions not received from the senses. Therefore, it seems that the ultimate in a reasoning nature is where it reaches the intellectual, and so the same as before.

Moreover, as is said in *De anima* III (11, 434a12–14), the parts of the soul are ordered in the same way as the motive powers in the heavens. But in them what is best in the lower – that is, altitude – is found where it reaches what is lowest in the higher. Therefore, etc.

[2c] Solution

We have to say that every cognition by way of reasoning is a kind of collecting (*collatione*), whether it is of contingent things (which, according to what was said in Book VI [1, 1139a6–12], is called calculative), or whether it is scientific (which is also a process, deducing effects from causes). This [need for a discursive process] occurs because [in a reasoning nature] the ray of the cognitive virtue is overshadowed and directed to the continuous and time, where it does not grasp the quiddities of things in its own simplicity (cf. *De anima* III 6, 430b19–20) but either with quantity alone, as in mathematics, or with quantity and qualities admitting of contraries, as in natural things, which are immersed in time. Because of this the completion of a reasoning nature is when it attains to simple quiddities; for in this it is joined with higher, separate substances, who have such cognition. Because of this, its contemplative happiness is with respect to the understanding, in accordance with which it attains to activity of this sort. We concede the last arguments.

[2d. Replies to the Opening Arguments]

[i] To the first, on the other hand, we have to say that in Book VI he distinguished wisdom from understanding as habit from habit, so to speak, not denying that wisdom is according to the best activity of the power of understanding, as he also said there (c. 7, 1141b2–3).

[ii] To the second we have to say that what is simplest, God, can be considered in two ways. When he is considered in himself God is owed a more simplified power. That is why in order to see God the understanding, according to blessed Dionysius' statements (*On the Celestial Hierarchy* 4.3), is elevated by theophanies coming down to it. For this reason the saints also assert that the intelligence by which God is known in us is simpler than the understanding. God can also {749B} be considered as to the mode of thinking (*cogitandi*), and in this way there is the same mode of cognition in [our] cognition of God and the wise cognition of other things, because in this way he is cognized through their simple quiddities. Hence one power suffices for this.

[iii] To the third we have to say that when the Philosopher speaks in such fashion he does not mean to say that there is another nature in us nobler than the intellectual but because there is another, nobler being of the same nature, according to which that nature can be more elevated from matter and less immersed, as will be said later.

[iv] To the fourth we have to say that that can be called human in which human nature exists, and in this sense the calculative is human; or that can be called human which is noblest in human nature, and this is the understanding. That is why a human being is called an understanding.

[v] To the fifth we have to say that reason is dominant in the activity of a human being, but what is supreme in its nature is the understanding.

[3. Is the Understanding in Us as Part of Our Soul?]

[3a. It Seems Not]

Third, it seems that the understanding is not something that is in us as part of our soul.

[i] For those things of which there is one essential activity seem to be one. But the understanding by which we understand is the same activity as that of the separate intelligences, namely, understanding the simple quiddities of things. Therefore, it seems that it is a certain separate substance and is not in us.

[ii] Moreover, what is separate by its own nature cannot be joined to a body. But the understanding is like this according to its own nature. This is clear from its activity, which is completed without bodily organs. Therefore, etc.

[iii] Moreover, everything that is joined to something and makes it one as form does is [first] in it as potentiality and is brought out from it by the act of a mover. But the understanding is not brought out from the potentiality of matter but comes from without, as is said in chapter 16 of *On [the Generation of] Animals* (II 3, 736a24–b28). Therefore, it seems that it is not part of the soul, because by [the soul] a human is [made] one as by form.

[iv] Moreover, as sense stands to reason, so reason stands to understanding. But there is nothing of reason in sense. Therefore there will be nothing of understanding in the rational soul. Therefore, etc. {750A}

[v] Moreover, as is said in *De anima* II (2, 413b26–27), the understanding is separated from the other parts of the soul as the perpetual from the perishable. But what is like that is not a part of the soul. Therefore, etc.

[vi] Moreover, it is impossible for two contradictories to be true of the same thing. But the soul is the act of the body; the understanding, on the other hand, is not the act of any body, as is said in *De anima* III (4, 429a24–25). Therefore, the being (*esse*) of the understanding is not in the essence of the soul.

[3b] For the Opposite

A mean that is not produced by negation participates essentially in [each] extreme. But our soul is a mean between sensory nature and the pure intellectual nature that is in the intelligences. Therefore, just as sense belongs to the soul, so also does understanding.

Moreover, there cannot be a single activity of things distinct in place. But in spiritual things the Philosopher names as [being in] distinct places things distinct as to subject (*Physics* IV 1, 208b8–25). Therefore, since our soul has the activity of understanding, the understanding is not distinct from our soul as to subject.

Moreover, if the understanding were not in the soul essentially, then intellectuality would be accidental to humans. But it is possible for what is accidental not to exist (or it can at least be understood not to exist) while that to which it is accidental remains. A human being could therefore exist or be understood without an intellectual nature. This is against Aristotle, [who holds] (1178a6–7) that a human, as human, *is* an understanding.

Moreover, nature only comes from one extreme to another through what is between them. It is said, for example, in *On [the History of] Animals* (VIII 1, 588b4–17) that [nature] comes from the marine to the terrestrial through things that are in a certain way marine and in a certain way terrestrial. But we find some forms entirely mixed with matter and others entirely separate, namely, the intelligences. Therefore the soul, which is between them, must be mixed as to something of itself and separate as to something of itself. Therefore, {750B} the understanding is something belonging to the soul.

[3c. A Further Question]

[vii] Moreover, I ask how the five things he says about the understanding are to be taken, namely, that it is principal (*principatur*), that it dominates, that it has intelligence about good and divine things, and that it is the most divine of all that is in us.

[3d] Solution

We have to say, as the Commentator [Michael of Ephesus] says, that there have been different opinions about this. For Plato and some who follow him have held that the understanding is not part of the soul but something separate and divine, namely, the intelligence of the tenth order or some other substance, and that the human soul is illuminated by its light as air is illuminated by the sun – with this difference, that the air only receives light and does not retain it whereas the soul both receives and holds the intellectual light, like a live coal; and so our soul does not understand by a light that it has from itself but by what it receives from a separate substance; and insofar as it retains it it becomes in a certain way natural to it and not entirely accidental. But Aristotle and all the other Peripatetics, as the Commentator says, have wanted to maintain that the understanding is part of the soul. That is why he says in *De anima* III (5, 430a10–17) that in the soul there is an acting (*agens*) and a possible understanding, just as [there is

an active and a potential element] in every other nature whatever. And
their position is supported by this, that it is possible for a single nature to
be mixed [with matter] as to something of itself and to escape mixture as
to something of itself, just as the light of a fire is impure when it is joined
with [something else] and produces a certain redness when joined with
charcoal but retains its own clarity when it is in the air (and it would also
be like this if it were something permanent in it). Similarly, they want to
maintain that by the nature of the soul as it is immersed in the body
powers flow from it that are affixed to organs, as the senses and nutritive
powers. From {751A} that part, however, by which it keeps to itself and
is raised above mixture there flow powers not affixed to organs, as the
powers of understanding. And so the understanding is something of the
soul as a power of it.

Because this latter opinion is more reasonable and more in accord with
the faith, we hold to this way and for this reason we concede the last
arguments.

[3e. Replies to the Opening Arguments]

[i] To the first we say that as to the simple essence that is beheld (*speculan-
tur*) the activity of our understanding is the same activity as the activity of
an intelligence abstracted [from matter] but that it is not the same as to its
being, because our understanding grasps it and joins it with the continuous
and time.

[ii] To the second we have to say that our soul is separated as to
something and conjoined as to something, as has been said.

[iii] To the third we have to say that no form exists according to its
own perfect being in a matter from which it is brought out, because this
would be to posit the latency of forms [in matter], but it is in it only
inchoately. But among forms some hold themselves more on the side of
matter. These are more material and they also *are* more in matter, from
which they are brought out. Other forms come closer to resembling the
first mover, and these are less in matter. Now among all forms the human
soul is most like the first movers. Because of this it is brought out from
matter as to something of itself, namely, as to its sensitive and nutritive
part, and as to something of itself it exists from without and is not brought
out of matter, namely, as to the understanding. And this seems to be the
intention of the Philosopher, who says in chapter 16 of *On* [*the Generation
of*] *Animals* (II 3, 736b27–28) that the vegetative soul and the sensory are

in the seed and that the understanding alone is from without; and this is what certain masters say: that nature does not fashion the human soul but works *to* the soul.

[iv] To the fourth we have to say that sense is only perfect where it exists in the essence of the rational soul, and then it is joined to reason as a power of it and reason is its completion.

[v] To the fifth we have to say that it is not separated essentially but in the manner that has been said.

[vi] To the sixth we have to say that nothing keeps the soul from both being and not being the act of the body in different respects, as has been said.

[3f. Reply to the Further Question (3c)]

To the question at the end we have to say that the understanding that is in us can be considered in three ways: {751B} [i] in its order to the other parts [of our nature], and this either [ia] as to nature, and thus it is said 'to be principal,' or [ib] as to activity, and thus it is said 'to dominate'; or [ii] in comparison with its proper objects, and thus it is said 'to have intelligence,' etc., or [iii] in a third way in comparison with [its] cause, and thus, [iiia] as to the very cause by which an intellectual nature exists in us it is a certain 'divine [thing],' because it exists in us from God, but [iiib] insofar as such a nature has been received, as to this it is said to be 'the most divine' of all that is in us.

[4. Can We Continue the Work of Contemplation?]

[4a. It Seems Not]

Fourth, it seems that we can hardly continue the work of contemplation.

[i] For we cannot continue that for which we are hardly sufficient. But we are most insufficient for wise contemplation (*contemplationem sapientialem*, [the contemplation related to the intellectual virtue of wisdom]), because they [the objects of such contemplation] are above us, and our understanding stands to them as the owl's eye to the light of the sun. Therefore, etc.

[ii] Moreover, that which is most composite is more remote from what is simpler. But humans are most composite of all things, because every

composition is preserved in us. Therefore, we are furthest away from the simple and continuous activity that is the activity of God the most simple, which is wise contemplation.

[iii] Moreover, that for which many things are needed is more easily impeded and consequently continued less. But many things are required for wise contemplation, because everything else is ordered to it. Therefore, etc.

[iv] Moreover, we can continue most that activity which is most proportioned to us. That, however, is contemplation of mathematical knowables, which neither have variability from matter as things in nature do nor are above the capacity of our understanding as divine things are. It therefore seems that we especially cannot continue wise contemplation.

[4b] For the Opposite

A nobler happiness is more continuous, because continuity is one of the conditions of happiness. But contemplative happiness is noblest. Therefore, its activity is most continuous.

Moreover, the nearer something is to that which exists always and eternally, the more continuous it is. But wise contemplation is nearest {752A} to those things which exist always, because it is about the simpler quiddities, which are imperishable. Therefore, etc.

Moreover, the more like God something is, the more continuous it is. But such contemplation is most like the divine activity, as will be said below.

Moreover, that in which the appetite is more rapt and on which it is exercised with less boredom can be continued more. But the contemplation of divine things totally carries away (*rapit*) our appetite into itself because of its loftiness, and it is never boring, because new contemplations are always found therein. Therefore, etc.

These are the Commentator's [Michael of Ephesus'] arguments, and they are sound. Hence we concede them.

[4c. Replies to the Opening Arguments]

[i] We say to the first that according as it is imperfect, the understanding is not sufficient for contemplating divine things, but according as it is perfected by the habit of wisdom, it is sufficient for philosophical contemplation, and according as it is perfected by theophanies descending from God, it is perfected for divine contemplation.

[ii] To the second we have to say that when the components of a composite are mixed together they do not retain their own simplicity, and so the composite is remote from the most simple. But when the components are not mixed, they make a thing nearer to God, because to the extent that something participates in more of the goodnesses of the first [being], to that extent it is nearer and more like it, as Dionysius says. And so it is in humans, because understanding and sense and the other things that are in us retain their own nature.

[iii] To the third we have to say that many things are needed as disposing and assisting factors for wise contemplation but very few as making up its essence. Because of this it is not easily impeded.

[iv] To the fourth we have to say that the objects of wisdom are made proportionate to humans by habit or by a theophany elevating and strengthening nature.

[5. Is Such Contemplation Most Pleasant?]

[5a. It Seems Not]

Fifth, it seems that such contemplation is not most pleasant.

[i] For where that which pleases is not perfectly conjoined, there cannot be perfect pleasure. But divine things are not perfectly joined with us, because we do not fully comprehend them. Therefore, etc.

[ii] Moreover, pleasure arises from being joined with what is agreeable. But divine [things] do not entirely agree with us, because they are above us. Therefore, etc.

[iii] {752B} Moreover, that which is more desired in nature is pleasanter. But science (*scientia*) is more desired than wisdom (*sapientia*), because all humans by nature desire to know (*scire*), as is said at the beginning of the *Metaphysics* (I 1, 980a21). Therefore, wise contemplation is less pleasant than scientific contemplation.

[5b. A Further Question]

I ask further, whether there is perfect pleasure in only one of the things that can be contemplated in wisdom or in all?

[iv] It seems that it is in all of them, because something is perfect when it has whatever it is by nature capable of having. Perfection therefore consists in [having] all. But all are not possessed in one. Therefore, etc.

[v] Moreover, from the habit of principles we can behold all principles. But wisdom is the habit of first principles. Therefore, its pleasure will be in the beholding of all principles.

[5c] For the Opposite

[vi] As knowables (*scibilia*) stand to one another, so do the things that can be contemplated in wisdom stand to one another. But all knowables come back to one which is first, and in it is the perfection of knowing them. Therefore, the perfect pleasure of all wisdom will also be found in one first object of wisdom (*in uno primo sapientiali*).

[vii] Moreover, this is seen from the Commentator [Averroes], who says in [commenting on] *Metaphysics* XI (comm. 51) that the question about which all naturally desire to know is the question about the divine understanding. So it seems that the greatest pleasure is in contemplating God.

[5d. A Further Question]

Further, it seems that philosophical pleasures do not excel in purity.

[viii] For that seems purer which purifies more. But the moral virtues purify more than the intellectual, because they calm the passions. Therefore, their pleasures are purer.

[ix] Moreover, in [Macrobius'] *Commentary on the Dream of Scipio* distinctions are made between the virtues of a cleansed spirit, cleansing virtues, and civic virtues, all of which concern matters of action. Therefore, it seems that contemplative pleasures do not exceed in purity.

[5e. Two Further Questions]

[x] Further, it seems that they do not exceed in stability, because certain intellectual virtues, such as art and prudence, are about contingencies. But contingencies have little or no stability. Therefore, etc.

[xi] Moreover, I ask how these three things he says about the pleasures of philosophy are to be taken – that they are wonderful, pure, and stable.

[5f] Solution

{753A} We have to say that the pleasures of wisdom are the greatest, insofar as they are more remote from mixture with a contrary because they do not have anything contrary to them; nor is any regret mixed with them, for no one has ever regretted contemplating. But because of negligence, difficult circumstances, and reversals in the affairs in which we are active civic activities are mixed with many regrets. Because of this, contemplative pleasures are outstandingly higher, and especially those found in contemplating God himself, because in him is the source of light, and impurity is entirely vanquished.

[5g. Replies to the Opening Arguments]

[i] To the first we therefore have to say that although divine things are not perfectly joined with us in their own mode, nevertheless they are perfectly conjoined according to the measure of our [cognitive] habit, whether acquired or infused, and in this respect they are also agreeable to us.

[ii] From this the solution to the second is clear.

[iii] To the third we have to say that everyone universally does indeed naturally desire to know, but in particular cognition of divine things is especially desired, as is clear from the text cited from the Commentator.

[iv] Because of this we have to say to the fourth that there is perfect pleasure in one thing – or in one thing that is first in such a way that it is the reason and light of all that can be cognized and is the end of the whole of human inquiry (*finis totius inquisitionis humanae*).

[v] To the fifth we have to say that in principles themselves there is an order, so that some are brought back to others, and so on to one that is first.

[vi, vii] We concede the sixth and seventh.

[viii] To the eighth we have to say that the pleasures of philosophy are called pure insofar as they follow on the pure reception of simple quiddities, although the moral [virtues] purify from the passions.

[ix] From this the solution to the ninth is clear.

[x] To the tenth we have to say that they are called stable as to the middle [term in the pertinent syllogisms], because wisdom proceeds by means of a necessary cause.

[xi] To the last we have to say that they are called wonderful according to the order of 'that' to 'because,' for when we see only that something is the case we wonder at the cause, as is said at the beginning of the *Metaphysics* (I 2, 982b12–17). They are called stable because of the order of 'because' to 'that,' but [they are called] pure because of the disposition of the 'because' in itself, because it is grasped in a simple quiddity.

[6. Is the Contemplation Pertaining to Wisdom Most Sufficient?]

[6a. It Seems Not]

{753B} Sixth, it seems that wise contemplation is not most sufficient.

[i] For that is called sufficient which supplies what is lacking. But wise contemplation supplies nothing lacking in life. Therefore, etc.

[ii] Moreover, what is more necessary for life supplies more of what is lacking. But as is said at the beginning of the *Metaphysics* (I 1, 981b13–25), everything else is more necessary than this. Therefore, etc.

[iii] Moreover, it [only] *happens* with regard to justice that many things are required for its activity, and so also for the other virtues, because of the matters on which they bear. Therefore, if it is proved from this that wisdom is most sufficient, it seems that the fallacy of accident is committed.

[iv] Moreover, what the Commentator [Michael of Ephesus] says seems false: that cabbage and water suffice for the contemplative and that he does not ask for partridges, because from more delicate foods more delicate and refined humors are generated, which are more fit for refined contemplation. Therefore, it seems that the contemplative ought to ask for refined foods.

[6b] Solution

We have to say that wisdom is called most self-sufficient because it needs nothing or very little beyond the necessities of life. For one who has it can contemplate in the desert, although for contemplating well the company of fellow philosophers is of value. But the activities of the civic virtues need many external goods.

[6c. Replies to the Opening Arguments]

[i] To the first we therefore have to say that in contemplation wisdom does supply what is lacking. Nevertheless, supplying what is lacking is a useful sufficiency and not what is owed to an end. Accordingly, the more necessary things are also called sufficient, because they are all more useful for life.

[ii] Hence the solution to the second is clear.

[iii] To the third we have to say that the very activity of justice occurs

in dealings with others, for which one person alone does not suffice. Thus justice needs many things essentially [not accidentally], and so do the other moral virtues, but for contemplating one is sufficient by oneself.

[iv] To the fourth we have to say that by cabbage and water the Commentator here refers to those things by which nature can be sustained in good health in relation to its proper work. By pheasants and such he understands foods that are sought after only for pleasure (*voluptatem*), and the contemplative does not ask for these, because no voluptuary can be a philosopher, as Rabbi Moses [Maimonides] says (*Guide to the Perplexed* I 5). That is why Solomon too says (Ecclesiastes 2:3) {754A} that he thought to withdraw his flesh from wine that he might transfer his soul to wisdom.

[7. Is the Contemplation Pertaining to Wisdom Lovable Per Se]

[7a. It Seems Not]

Seventh, it seems that wise contemplation is not lovable (*diligibile*) *per se*.

[i] For the objects of understanding and will are not the same. But to behold is the object or act of the understanding. Therefore, it is not an object of love ((*dilectionis/delectionis* [var.])), which is in the will.

[ii] Moreover, what achieves nothing is pointless. If, therefore, contemplation is not sought after for the sake of anything else, as he says, it seems that it is pointless.

[iii] Moreover, enjoyment (*fruitio*) is fulfilled in love (*amore*), for it is the seeing of what is possessed and loved. But there is enjoyment in the contemplation involved in happiness because there is pleasure in it. Therefore, the contemplation itself is ordered further to love.

[iv] Moreover, Bernard says (*Sermon 36 on The Song of Songs* 3) that to know in order to know (*scire, ut scias*) is pointless. But the contemplation involved in happiness is not pointless. Therefore, it is for the sake of something else.

[7b] For the Opposite

An end is loved (*diligitur*) for itself. But the contemplation involved in happiness is the end of human life. Therefore, it is not sought after for the sake of anything else.

Moreover, what is best is not sought after for the sake of something else. But the activity of understanding is what is best in humans. Therefore, etc.

[7c] Solution

We have to say that the contemplation involved in happiness is loved for itself, because it is the chief thing, namely, the contemplation of God, which according to the theologian (cf. Augustine, *On the Trinity* I 8.17) is the end of human life. We concede the arguments for this.

[7d. Replies to the Opening Arguments]

[i] To the first on the other side we have to say that, insofar as they are virtues, habits of this sort exist in the affective understanding (*in intellectu affectivo*), in which there is an act of will inclining to the work of the understanding. Thus the understanding's object is loved as its good.

[ii] To the second we have to say that when something that exists for an end is so disposed that it does not take in the end, it is pointless, but this does not apply to the end itself.

[iii] To the third we have to say that to love (*amare*) and to possess what is seen follow on seeing and exist in the same [act?]. For this reason it does not follow that the seeing is ordered to something else. {754B}

[iv] To the fourth we have to say that Bernard is speaking of science related to works that is not put to work. Or he is speaking as about someone who wished exclusively to know and not to communicate with anyone else. But philosophers do not do this but rather communicate their science to everyone as much as they can.

[8. Does the Contemplation Pertaining to Wisdom Exist with Leisure?]

[8a. It Seems Not]

Eighth, it seems that wise contemplation does not exist with leisure.

For leisure is a sort of idleness. But Tully says (*On Duties* III 1.1), quoting Socrates [rather, quoting Scipio Africanus], that the wise person is never idle, least of all when alone. Therefore, etc.

Moreover, that which is most continuous does not seem to coexist with leisure. But wise contemplation is like this. Therefore, etc.

Moreover, leisure implies cessation from act. But the wise do not at all cease from their own act. Therefore, they are not at leisure.

[8b] Solution

We have to say that 'with leisure' is not said [here] as implying interruption of a proper act but as excluding a further act to which the first act is ordered. Such leisure agrees with an activity that is the ultimate end.

From this the solution to the objections is clear. . . .

Lesson 12

{756A} '[Now the activity] of the practical [virtues]' (1177b6).

After he has shown that there is perfect happiness in the activity of the virtue of speculative understanding, proving that all the conditions making for the perfection of happiness exist in it, here he intends to show that it alone is perfect, by arguing that the indicated conditions do not agree with the civic happiness found in the activity of the virtue of practical understanding.

About this part three points are doubtful.

[1. Is Aristotle's Division of the Moral Virtues into Civic and Military Adequate?]

[1a. It Seems Not]

The first concerns the division of the moral virtues into civic and military (1177b6), which seems inadequate.

[i] For the virtues are divided into civic, domestic, and moral. But the military fall under none of these. Therefore, the virtues ought not to be so divided.

[ii] If you say that courage is military, to the contrary: It does not seem to be military except for a soldier's courage. This, however, is not a virtue, as was said in Book III (8, 1116b4–23). Therefore, etc.

[iii] Moreover, even should this be granted, the same cannot be said about any other virtue. Therefore, he is wrong to put 'military' in the plural.

[iv] Moreover, wars are ruled more by art than by virtue. But the arts

are not moral virtues. Therefore, he ought not to have given military virtue as a part of moral virtue.

[1b] Solution

We have to say that 'civic' (or 'political') has two senses. One pertains to the disposition of citizens in a city. In this sense the civic is divided against the military, because wars are never organized among citizens. This is the civic strictly so called. In another sense 'civic' refers to whatever pertains to the disposition of citizens, either their disposition to one another or their disposition as regards enemies. This is the civic commonly so called, which is divided into the military and the civic taken strictly. Taking 'civic' strictly, therefore, we have to say that all the moral virtues are both civic and military but with respect to different modes or uses. For according as the citizens themselves are disposed by them with regard to innate or inculcated passions, with regard to their activities with one another, or with regard to elections, they are called political. According, however, as precautions for resisting enemies are found by prudence, just wars undertaken by justice, the citizens restrained from lasciviousness by temperance (lest their spirits be weakened — as King Cyrus of the Persians subjugated {756B} through lasciviousness some whom he had not been able to subdue in war), and enemies invaded and the dangers of war sustained by courage, they are military. Hence this is not a division of different things [i.e., different virtues] but of different ways [in which the virtues are effective].

[1c. Replies to the Opening Arguments]

[i] And so the solution to the first is clear, because the military [virtues] come under the political as commonly taken.

[ii, iii] The solution to the second is also clear, because even true courage, which is a virtue, is military; and also the solution to the third, because courage is military as to invasion itself and the actual waging and sustaining of war, but the others are military as offering some assistance in wars.

[iv] To the fourth we have to say that there is an art concerned with military matters, insofar as war is managed by art, but other things, such as attacking and other things necessary in wars, need the exercise of the virtues.

[2. Are the Moral Virtues Operative When We Are at Leisure?]

[2a. It Seems that They Are]

Second, it seems that the moral virtues are leisurely.

[i] For leisure is impeded only when external things are sought after, as in servile activities. But a virtuous deed is not done for the sake of anything external, because then that thing would be dearer than virtue, and the act would not be virtuous. Therefore, they are leisurely.

[ii] Moreover, those who work at necessary activities, such as cooks, those who prepare couches, and people of these sorts, do not, according to the theologian, interrupt the leisure of feasts. But are not those acts more servile than the deeds of the moral virtues? Therefore, etc.

[iii] Moreover, that which is 'from' humans shows more goodness than what is 'to' them, because the first occurs as an action and the second as an undergoing. But the practical virtues arise from an activity that is from humans, while the activities of the speculative virtues are to them, insofar as things effect or cause that science. Therefore, the practical virtues are nobler and thus more leisurely.

[iv] Moreover, the divine contemplation that will exist in heaven (*patria*) will be nobler than civic contemplation. But the moral virtues will remain with that contemplation. Much more, therefore, can they remain in contemplative happiness, and so they will be present in leisure, just as contemplative happiness is leisurely.

[2b] Solution

We have to say that 'leisure' is taken differently by the theologian and the philosopher. For theologians mean by leisure cessation from servile {757A} acts, meaning acts of sin and also acts that are not immediately necessary for physical preservation, such as cutting wood, weaving, and suchlike. For acts necessary for the body, such as preparation of food and the like, do not impede leisure, because everyone needs food and drink. In this sense the moral virtues may well be called leisurely. But here the Philosopher means by leisure cessation from extension of appetite to another desired object to be sought after. This is a leisure which agrees only with the ultimate end, and in this sense the moral virtues are not leisurely.

[2c. Replies to the Opening Arguments]

[i, ii] From this the solution to the first two is clear.

[iii] To the third we have to say that even in speculative activities there is activity 'from' a human being – and the noblest – insofar as agent understanding casts its light over the species of things, making them actually understandable and thus perfecting the possible understanding.

[iv] To the fourth we have to say that the moral virtues do also remain in contemplative happiness, yet not as eliciting the ultimate act, which is the end, but as shielding a person from disturbances that could impede the speculative act. In the future life, too, the virtues do not remain in the same way as the [ultimate] act does.

[3. Does Contemplative Happiness Require a Complete Lifetime?]

[3a. It Seems Not]

Third, it seems that contemplative happiness does not require a complete lifetime.

[i] For what can exist in a moment does not require a long span of life. But the contemplative beholding that is itself happiness can exist in a moment. Therefore, etc.

[ii] Moreover, I ask to what point that length of life is to be measured. If it is said, 'to death,' as Solon used to say (cf. I 10, 1100a10–11), then it follows that someone cannot be happy before death but either in dying or after death, and both of these are awkward, because neither {757B} the civic nor the contemplative good or evil of this life exists for the dying or the dead.

[3b] Solution

Enough was asked about these matters above in Book I, because the same reasoning applies to this happiness and to civic happiness.

[3c. Replies to the Opening Arguments]

[i] For this reason we have to say to the first that although in itself the activity of contemplative beholding can exist in an instant, yet in the way

that is relevant to happiness it needs a long time. For we would not be happy except in having such activity as a possession, namely, at will and without labor, and this is only when there is a confirmed habit.

[ii] To the second we have to say that someone can have the happiness he is speaking of here even before death, nor is death the term and measure of length for the generation of happiness. For there will be a confirmed happiness at the point when the passions have been calmed by the moral virtues and contemplative habits have been established. For this much time is needed in some cases, in some cases less. But it is true that for the well-being of happiness, it must continue to death, because as Boethius says (*On the Consolation of Philosophy* I, Prose 4) it is a particular kind of misfortune *to have been* happy. Hence for the perfection and well-being of happiness it is required that there be no change-about from such happiness through forgetfulness or other occupations. . . .

Lesson 13

{758B} 'But such [a life would be] altogether [too high for humans]' (1177b26).

Now that he has shown that the most perfect happiness is to be found only in the activity of speculative understanding, he shows here that a life of such happiness – that is, one in which it is exercised – is above the human. This part is divided in two. First he shows that when contemplative and civic happiness are compared as to their essentials, the former has a stronger claim than the latter, insofar as it is above human life while the civic is human. Second (at 'It will seem, however' [1178a23]) he compares them as to the things that contribute to each instrumentally.

About the first part I ask five questions.

[1. Is the Contemplative Life Better than What Accords with Humans, as Aristotle Says?]

First, whether such a life is better than what accords with humans, as he says.

[1a] It Seems Not

[i] For nothing is beyond itself. But such a life is a human life. Therefore, it does not seem to be beyond humans.

[ii] Moreover, what is proper to anything is not beyond it but accords with what is connatural to it. But human happiness, whatever it is, must accord with a proper human habit, as has been said above. Therefore, the same as before.

[iii] Moreover, the order of natures is never completely changed. But in order of nature human nature is below that which is above the human. Therefore, it seems that it could never attain the latter.

[iv] Moreover, in theological contemplation our souls are purged, illuminated, and perfected by heavenly essences, as Dionysius says (*On the Divine Names* 1.3). It seems that for the same reason this would happen in philosophical contemplation. Therefore, since he does not mention this, [what he says] seems inadequate.

[v] Moreover, his refutation of this [thesis] seems inappropriate, because a mortal must not taste immortal things. This agrees with what is said in the book of Maccabees (2 Maccabees 9:12): 'It is just that a mortal not sense things equal to God.' Antiochus is praised for these words (although he was bad otherwise), because he said them in a condition of humility.

[1b. A Further Question]

[vi] I ask further, whether humans can achieve the life of an intelligence, which is above {759A} the human. It seems not, because an instrument never acquires the virtue of its mover. But our souls are the instrument of an intelligence, as is said in the *Liber de causis* (3). Therefore, etc.

[vii] Moreover, nothing acts on that from which it receives activity, because then the same thing would be mover and moved in the same respect. But an intelligence acts on our souls, as is said in the *Liber de causis* (3). Therefore, it seems that, etc.

[viii] Moreover, as movable is to movable, so is mover to mover. But the human body, which is moved by the soul, never attains to the virtue of the heavens, because it is always bodily and mixed, whereas that which is moved by an intelligence is simple. Therefore, etc.

[1c] Solution [in Replies to the Opening Arguments]

[i] To the first we have to say that the activity of understanding can be considered in two ways. In one way absolutely, according to the nature of the understanding as such. So considered it is above the human, because to have the pure activity of understanding pertains only to the intelli-

gences. Or it can be considered according to a certain connaturalness with other powers, as it is overshadowed and directed to the continuous and time. So considered the activity of understanding accords with humans. According as the human understanding abstracts as much as it can from the continuous and time to consider the simple quiddity of a thing, to this extent it acquires a certain life which is above the human.

[ii] To the second we have to say that the activity of understanding is something proper to humans according to [its] connaturalness [in us] with lower powers, but to have absolute and perfect natural intellectual activity is proper to God and to an intelligence. That is why Dionysius also says in his epistle to Titus that, because of this connaturalness, if our understanding acquires anything intellectual, it tries to invest it with particular shapes and put it together with perceptible appearances (*species sensibiles*).

[iii] To the third we have to say that a lower nature *can* in some way achieve the act of a higher, according as it is moved by a higher power, although it does not achieve the higher [nature's] power of acting so as to engage in that act in the same way as the higher nature. For this reason we say that the soul does in a way achieve the act of understanding – which is to consider the simple quiddities of a thing – according as it is moved by the light of an intelligence. Yet in the conditions of this life (which is all that the {759B} philosophers consider) it cannot attain to understanding them in the way an intelligence does.

[iv] To the fourth we have to say that those three activities due to the action of the intelligences in our souls also occur in this [philosophical] contemplation, but this happens naturally, because [they occur] in proportion to natural aptitude and the perfection that comes from serious application. As a result of these one is made abler than another to take things in from the light of an intelligence. But in divine contemplation [the action of the intelligences] is in proportion to merit and grace. For this reason (and also because they pertain more to metaphysics) he did not discuss those activities here.

[v] To the fifth we have to say that a human ought not to sense things equal to God from a presumption of power, as the same Antiochus had done when he wanted to be feared more than God and to break divine laws. But as to imitating the divine activity in purity of feeling and understanding, everyone ought to strive to taste what is divine, even as the Apostle says (Colossians 3:2): 'Taste ye the things that are above.'

[vi] To the sixth we have to say that an instrument does attain to the act of its mover, because the act of instrument and mover is the same. And

in a way it also attains to the power of its mover, as the power of cutting is in the axe in some way, for otherwise it could never achieve an act of cutting. Nevertheless, it is in it as mixed and moved and in the carpenter as simple and moving. Similarly, the soul achieves the act and power of intellectuality, yet, as has been said, not in the manner of an intelligence, because in it the intellectual light is concrete and overshadowed, as has been said.

[vii] To the seventh we have to say that the soul does not act with regard to the intelligences by making its own light flow into them, as happens the other way round. It understands them by a light that is in some way acquired from them.

[viii] To the last we have to say that those four – intelligence, soul, heavenly body, and human body – are proportional as long as the proportion is taken with respect to those things in which it ought to be taken. For just as the human soul, among all forms, attains to the likeness of an intelligence, so the human body attains likeness to a heavenly body as to absence of contrariety. But what the heaven has by simplicity of substance, because it is not composed from contraries, the human body has by the balance of its makeup and the mixture of contraries {760A} in it. Because of this it is perishable, while the heaven is imperishable.

[2. Are Humans the Best that Is in Them?]

[2a. It Seems Not]

Second, it does not seem that human beings 'are' the best that is in them.

[i] For what is best in humans is the understanding, which is a part of them. But no part is predicated of its own whole. Therefore, they are not what is best in them.

[ii] Moreover, the Commentator's [Michael of Ephesus'] example seems wrong. For he says that humans are the best of themselves, just as a city is its ruler and as Aristotle is Aristotle's understanding and Plato Plato's understanding. For it seems that all of these are false or improper, because in none of them is there a predication by either essence or cause.

[iii] Moreover, if this is said to be the case because everything is defined by what is best in it, to the contrary: The understanding is never put into the definition of a human being, which is 'rational mortal animal' (cf. Boethius, *On the Consolation of Philosophy* V, Prose 4).

[iv] Moreover, that which is best in a thing is what is ultimate in it. But in a definition the ultimate form or differentia is convertible [with the definiendum]. But understanding is not converted with being human, because it also exists in the angels and in God. Therefore, humans are not their understandings as their own best thing.

[v] Moreover, that cannot be said to be any nature which exists in it only secondarily and exists primarily in something else. But understanding exists primarily in God and in the intelligences and secondarily in humans. Therefore, etc.

[2b] Solution

We have to say that the understanding can be considered in two ways: either insofar as it is a power of the soul or insofar as it is its substantial form and the very nature of intellectuality. The latter can be considered in two ways: either insofar as it is the form of a part, in which respect it is the form of a matter, or insofar as it is the form of the whole, in which respect it is essentially the same [as the whole].

[2c. Replies to the Opening Arguments]

[i] To the first we therefore have to say that the understanding is not predicated of humans insofar as it is a potential or essential part of them but insofar as it is essentially the same [as them] and something ultimate, in which the concept (*ratio*) of the human is completed. For that is properly predicated of humans which belongs to them insofar as they are human – as Avicenna says (*Philosophia prima*, tr. 5, c. 5) that the form of the whole is predicated (just as genus and differentia are), not insofar as {760B} they are forms, but insofar as they are essentially the same [as the thing].

[ii] To the second we have to say that a city can be considered in two ways: either materially, and so considered it is a collection of humans and a set of buildings, or formally, insofar as a city is a unity of citizens, and so considered it is completed in its concept by its ruler, insofar as the ruler is animate just[ice] (cf. V 4, 1132a21–22), in whom everything belonging to the city is united.

[iii] To the third we have to say that reason is nothing else than obscured understanding. Hence understanding *is* in the definition of a human being in that we are called rational.

[iv] To the fourth we have to say that [the understanding] is proper to humans if it is taken according to the connaturalness of the human, namely, as it is overshadowed. It is in this sense that a human as human is called an understanding.

[v] To the last we have to say, similarly, that although understanding exists primarily in the first [being] and the intelligences, it nevertheless exists in humans, although it is overshadowed.

[3. Is the Understanding Small in Mass but Great in Power?]

[3a. It Seems Not]

Third, it seems that the understanding is not small in mass [but great in power].

[i] For that which does not have quantity in any dimension is neither large nor small in mass. But the understanding is like this. Therefore, etc.

[ii] If you say that it has quantity incidentally, as whiteness does, [I argue] to the contrary: A form does not have dimensional quantity except insofar as it is the act of a body. But the understanding is not the act of any body, as is said in *De anima* III (4, 429a24–25). Therefore, etc.

[iii] Moreover, something that is overshadowed does not seem to be great in power, but in us the understanding is overshadowed, as has been said. Therefore, etc.

[3b. An Additional Question]

[iv] Moreover, I ask why he says that it is great 'in power and value.'

[3c] Solution

We have to say that things have quantity of mass in many ways: some because they have quantity *per se*, as bodies do; some because they are extended through a quantity, although incidentally, as whiteness is in a surface; some because they are the act of something that has quantity, as substantial forms and the powers of the soul that are affixed to organs are; some because they grasp their objects with the continuous and time, as opinion and {761A} reason do; and some because they are only *related* to a nature that exists with a quantity of mass, and this is to have the least mass. It is in this [last] way that the understanding is said to be small in mass, because it has nothing of the character of mass except as it is something belonging to the soul, which is the act of a body of some size.

[3d. Replies to the Opening Arguments]

[i, ii] From this the solution to the first two is clear.

[iii] To the third we have to say that in us the understanding is said to be great in power, that is, in strength (not passive power), not without qualification (as it is great in God and the intelligences), but in comparison with the other forces of the soul, because other cognitions depend on cognition by the understanding and gain strength from it, as, for example, the cognition of a quiddity in quantity or quality depends on the cognition of a simple quiddity.

[iv] To the fourth we have to say that it is called great in power as to activity but in value as to [its] nature.

[4. Is Civic Happiness More Primary than Contemplative Happiness?]

[4a. It Seems that It Is]

Fourth, it seems that civic happiness is more primary [than contemplative happiness].

[i] Because it is the good of a people, which is more divine than the good of one person, as is said in Book I (1, 1094b9–10).

[ii] Moreover, as Avicenna says, the life of one person alone is worse than it could be. But this is the life that contemplative happiness perfects, and hence it is called a hermit's happiness. Therefore, it seems to be less primary.

[iii] Moreover, that to which the human soul is ordered seems to be most primary in things human. But all the human duties that exist in civic [life] are ordered to civic, not contemplative, happiness. Therefore, etc.

[iv] Moreover, that which agrees with the most excellent men according to the best of themselves is most primary in things human. But kings and princes are most excellent, and for them what is best is civic happiness. Therefore, etc.

[v] Moreover, humans are political by nature. But that happiness is more

primary which is more natural to humans. Therefore, the civic is more primary.

[4b] Solution

We have to say that contemplative and civic happiness can be considered in two ways: [i] either as to worth and moral honorableness, and so considered contemplative happiness is much worthier, because it is in accordance with what is best in humans and has less reference to something other than itself; or [ii] as to usefulness for the necessities {761B} of life, and so considered civic happiness has the stronger claim, and this is to be better in a qualified sense. The solution is similar in theology, when it is asked which life is better, the active or the contemplative.

[4c. Replies to the Opening Arguments]

[i] To the first we therefore have to say that the divine is twofold. For there is an act in God as to himself, such as understanding himself and taking pleasure in himself; and contemplative happiness is more similar to these than is civic happiness and is thus more divine. There is another act with respect to things outside him, in which he pours his goodness and sweetness into all creatures according to their capacity, and as to likeness with this civic happiness is more divine, insofar as it is the good of a people.

[ii] To the second we have to say that the solitary life is said to be the worst incidentally, insofar as it does not suffice for the solitary as to the necessities of life. But Aristotle supposes that a contemplative would have the necessities of life; otherwise, it is better for a needy person to make money than to engage in philosophy (cf. *Topics* III 2, 118a10–11).

[iii] To the third we have to say that things useful for life are more immediately referred to civic happiness, yet there is not a stand there, for these things are ordered further to contemplative happiness, as was said above.

[iv] To the fourth we have to say that as to perfection of nature philosophers are more excellent than those who are in power, but the latter are more excellent as to ruling the multitude.

[v] To the fifth we have to say that humans are naturally political as to the inferior part of themselves, in keeping with which they need the

necessities. But as to understanding – that which pertains to humans as human – they are neither political nor conjugal.

[5. Do the Principles of Prudence Accord with the Moral Virtues?]

[5a. It Seems Not]

Fifth, it seems that the principles of prudence are not in accordance with the moral virtues.

[i] For every virtue has its principles in itself. But prudence is a virtue. Therefore, etc.

[ii] Moreover, what is formal does not take from what is material, but rather the contrary. But prudence is formal with respect to all the moral virtues, as was established in Book VI (13, 1144b26–28). Therefore, it does not take its principles from the moral virtues.

[iii] Moreover, the rightness of a virtue is in accordance with its attaining the mean. But every virtue observes a mean, as was said in Book II (6, 1106b15). Therefore, {762A} the moral virtues have rightness from themselves and not from prudence.

[iv] Moreover, the moral virtues exist in parts of the soul that participate somehow in reason. But all rightness is from reason. Therefore, it seems that they have rightness from the very powers in which they exist and not from prudence.

[5b] Solution

We have to say that every habit directive of action must acquire principles in accordance with the character of the action. For if the principles of an action and its directing habit were different, the direction of the former would never reach the action. Now prudence directs the actions of the moral virtues. For this reason its principles must accord with the moral virtues. The Commentator [Michael of Ephesus] says, however, that it is said to have principles in accordance with the other virtues insofar as it has for its end the ends of the other moral virtues; for the end is a principle in things that are to be done. This is indeed true, because, as was said in Book VI (12, 1144a7–9), prudence sets the end for the moral virtues, and this is its act. Nevertheless, the first [reply] is better.

[5c. Replies to the Opening Arguments]

[i, ii] From this the solution to the first two is clear, because prudence has its principles in itself, but they are acquired in proportion to the action of moral virtue.

[iii] To the third we have to say that without doubt what is right in the other moral virtues comes from prudence, which exists in reason; for every rightness is in reason. And a moral virtue does not observe a mean by itself but insofar as {762B} a particular prudence is present. Now some say that what is right in a moral virtue itself does not come from prudence but from itself and that it does not observe the mean by way of art but in a natural way, just as what is heavy reaches the center [of the earth, its proper place] by its own motion. Those who say this do not take into account that nature too is directed to its end by the intention of a first mover setting an end for each nature and directing it to it. Prudence is similarly related to the other moral virtues, which act in a natural way.

[iv] To the fourth we have to say that just as the lower powers have nothing of reason [in them] except from [what is] reason by [its] essence, so also the habits perfecting those powers have rightness from a habit that perfects reason. . . .

Lesson 14

{763B} 'It will seem, however' (1178a23).

In this part he compares the two happinesses with respect to external goods, showing that civic happiness needs these more than does contemplative happiness.

About this I ask three questions.

[1. Does Moral Virtue Need External Goods?]

First, whether moral virtue needs external goods.

[1a] It Seems Not

[i] For nothing that is sufficiently caused by what is within needs externals. But moral virtue is sufficiently caused by what is within, such as choice, will, and the like. Therefore, etc.

[ii] Moreover, nothing either needs or exists for the sake of what is worth less than itself, as Avicenna says. But externals are less valuable than virtue, as is clear. Therefore, etc.

[iii] Moreover, the poor can have virtues, as he himself will say. But they lack an abundance of externals. Therefore, etc.

[iv] Moreover, the moral virtues dispose us toward the intellectual. Therefore, if external goods are required for the moral virtues, they are also required for the intellectual, which he denies.

[v] Moreover, what needs something else only in order to {764A} manifest itself can exist without the other. But moral virtue, as he seems to say, needs external goods because it cannot be manifested without them. Therefore, etc.

[1b] Solution

We have to say that the perfection of a moral virtue, like that of any other habit, is found in its activity. But its activity is concerned with external goods, from which it takes its species, since they are its object and thus are not only its matter but also its end. On this account the moral virtues need external goods for their own perfect being.

[1c. Replies to the Opening Arguments]

[i] To the first we therefore have to say that what is more inward in the soul does not suffice for causing the moral virtues without the acceptance of externals, at least as objects, because [otherwise], since the more inward [element in moral virtue] is one, all the moral virtues would be one. But in fact they are diversified according to their different objects.

[ii] To the second we have to say that external goods as external are of less worth than the virtues, but insofar as they are the objects of the virtues and the end points of their activities, their activities depend on them.

[iii] To the third we have to say that the poor can have all the virtues as to habit, but there are some that they cannot have in activity, in which is the perfection of such virtue, as is clear with regard to magnificence.

[iv] To the fourth we have to say that the moral virtues dispose toward the intellectual virtues as to habit, by which the passions are calmed in contemplation itself, but not as regards the disposition of externals.

[v] To the fifth we have to say that that manifestation pertains to the completeness of a moral virtue, because it cannot arise without the activity in which it is completed.

[2. Is Moral Virtue More a Matter of Choice than of External Activity?]

[2a. It Seems that It Is]

Second, it seems that moral virtue is more a matter of choice than of external activity.

[i] For each thing consists more in that which is primary in it. But choice is primary in virtue and conduct, as he said in Book VIII (13, 1163a22f). Therefore, etc.

[ii] Moreover, each thing consists more in that in which it can be less impeded. But moral virtue is more impeded in external activity than in choice.

[iii] Moreover, the moral virtues are perfections of the soul. But the soul is perfected by inner activities before outward ones. {764B}

[2b] For the Opposite

That for the sake of which something else exists is more primary. But the inner activities of the moral virtues are for the sake of the outward ones. Therefore, etc.

Moreover, that which is the ultimate perfection of a thing is primary in it. But the ultimate perfection of moral virtue is in outward activity. Therefore, etc.

[2c] Solution

We have to say that inner activities can be considered in two ways. [i] The first is insofar as they are only dispositions, according, namely, as they are not perfect willing or perfect choosing but a sort of vague impulse (*velleitas*) rather than a willing (*voluntas*). Moral virtue does not consist primarily in these inner activities, but acts of this sort are perfected by outward activities, and there will then exist the ultimate perfection of virtue. [ii] Inner activities can also be considered as they are the cause of outward activities. This occurs when they are already completed, so that if they are impeded from taking effect (*ab opere*), this will be incidentally, insofar as the material in which they must work (*operari*) is lacking – yet they show themselves as far as they can. Virtue does consist primarily in inner activities so considered, but for acts of this sort one must assume external goods at least as objects in some way, although not as material, so to speak, in which the act is exercised.

[2d. Replies to the Opening Arguments]

[i] From this the solution to the first is clear, because the Philosopher is speaking there of perfect choice.

[ii] To the second we have to say that that impediment occurs incidentally, as has been said, and not from a defect in the cause, which is sufficient.

[iii] To the third we have to say that moral virtue does not perfect the soul as to its being but with respect to the externals in which its activity occurs. Because of this these things must be in it for the completion of virtue, at least in the mode of object.

[3. Do External Goods Impede Contemplation?]

[3a. It Seems Not]

Third, it seems that external goods do not impede contemplation.

[i] For that which dispels care seems conducive to contemplation. But an abundance of external goods dispels care about procuring necessities. Therefore, etc.

[ii] Moreover, the Philosopher says in the beginning of the *Metaphysics* (I 1, 981b17–25) that philosophizing began when everything useful for the necessities or for pleasure had been discovered. Therefore, it seems that they do not impede it.

[iii] Moreover, he says in the *Topics* (III 2, 118a10–11) that for someone in need of the necessities, making money is more choice-worthy than philosophizing. This would not be so if [external goods] brought with them an impediment to the noblest human act. Therefore, etc.

[iv] Moreover, things that do not concern the same thing {765A} are not of a nature to impede one another. But wise contemplation does not concern external goods. Therefore, etc.

[3b] Against

External goods impede divine and philosophical contemplation for the same reason. But they do impede the divine; that is why Augustine says

(Sermon 261 4.5) that the reason the ancient fathers did not see God more is that they were occupied with riches. Therefore, etc.

[3c] Solution

We have to say that external goods can be possessed in two ways: either for necessary use (and the Philosopher is not talking about this, because everyone, whether wise or civic, needs the necessities) or as things to be managed. In this [second] way they do impede contemplation incidentally because of the anxious care they require, because when the soul is intent on one thing it cannot be intensely intent on others. That is also why it is said of Plato (cf. Jerome, *Adversus Iovinianum* II 9, speaking of Crates, after mentioning Plato) that once when he was carrying gold in his pocket while going to his studies at the Academy, he began to think anxiously about it. Because of this he threw it away, saying that he could more easily bear losing the gold than losing his mind.

[3d. Replies to the Opening Arguments]

[i–iv] From this the solution to the objections is clear, because the first three go through with regard to external goods insofar as they supply needs, while the fourth holds, in that [external goods] do not impede contemplation *per se*. . . .

Lesson 15

{766A} 'Now that perfect [happiness is a speculative activity will also appear' (1178b7)].

In this part he shows what sort of activity happiness is – that it is a divine activity – and in this he shows its perfection in itself. The section is divided in two. First he shows its perfection in its own being; second (at '[There will be] need' [1178b33]), he discusses it insofar as it needs externals to be as good as possible.

I ask five questions about the first part.

[1. Does Aristotle Speak Inappropriately When He Says that There Are Gods?]

First, whether he speaks inappropriately when he says that there are gods.

[1a] It Seems [that There Are] Not [Many 'Gods']

[i] A name that can in no way be shared cannot in any way be said in the plural (this is the case with proper names, for example). But such is this name 'God.' Therefore, etc. Proof of the minor premise: 'The name that cannot be shared (*incommunicabile nomen*)' (Wisdom 14:21). The reason for this is that 'God' is the name of the first principle, which cannot be shared, because there are not several firsts.

[ii] Moreover, the first principle does not fall under any concept (*rationem*) in accordance with which it would itself *have* a principle. But every plurality (*multitudo*) has something one as its principle. Therefore, since God is the first principle, there can be no plurality in him.

[iii] Moreover, what is said superlatively agrees with one thing alone. But this name 'God' names a thing of superlative nobility. Therefore, etc.

[iv] Moreover, Avicenna proves that there is only one necessary being (*Metaphysics*, tr. 1, c. 8). But God is a necessary being, as he says. Therefore, etc.

[1b] Against

The unity of God is asserted by both theologians and philosophers, but in theology 'god' is signified in the plural. Therefore, etc.

Moreover, Plato says (*Timaeus* 41A), 'Gods of gods, of whom [I am] the maker and father.' Therefore, etc.

[1c] Solution

We have to say that this name 'God' {766B} can be considered in two ways. [i] The first way is with respect to that on which it is imposed; and when it is imposed on the divine substance, which is only one, it cannot have a plural. [ii] It can also be considered as to that because of which it is imposed. Now it is imposed among philosophers because of this, that there is [held] to exist a separate substance having influence by its own power (which is neither finite nor infinite) on lower things by the motion of the heavens. And this is first and *per se* in the first intelligence, which is God essentially, and is communicated by it to other, secondary intelligences. Thus the philosophers call the intelligences gods by participation (cf. Pseudo-Dionysius, *On the Divine Names* 2.8), just as theologians too call [them] holy angels.

[1d. Replies to the Opening Arguments]

[i] To the first we therefore have to say that this name 'god' can be shared as to that because of which it is imposed.

[ii] To the second we have to say that every plurality of things univocal in genus or species is caused by something that is outside them all, but when there is a plurality of things agreeing only by analogy, it is not caused by a form that is outside them but by one that exists primarily in one of them, namely, in the first (just as substance, which is first, is the cause of the plurality of beings [in the other Aristotelian categories]). And thus the first intelligence, which is God, is essentially the cause of a plurality of gods and will not itself be caused.

[iii] To the third we have to say that what is referred to superlatively without qualification cannot agree with many things. But many things can be referred to superlatively with respect to some genus or order, and in this way every intelligence is first in its own order.

[iv] To the fourth we have to say that that argument goes through from the side of the nature on which the name is imposed.

[2. Are the Intelligences Always Active?]

[2a. It Seems Not]

Second, it seems that the intelligences are sometimes in [a condition of inactive] habit with respect to their activities and are not always in act.

[i] For anything that can be withdrawn from an act in which it engages can be in [a state of] habit with respect to it. But an intelligence can be withdrawn from some of the acts in which it engages, since it engages in many acts, such as contemplating, moving a heaven[ly sphere], and such-like; and it is not possible to do two things at once. Therefore, etc. {767A}

[ii] Moreover, a rational power is a power for opposites from the fact that it is raised above nature, where a power is bound to act in one way. But the power of an intelligence is raised still further above nature. Therefore, it is more capable of acting or not acting.

[iii] Moreover, what exists of necessity is not praiseworthy. But the activities of the intelligences are most praiseworthy. Therefore, etc.

[iv] Moreover, in Book VII (14, 1154b20–25) he said that always to have one simple activity pertains to a simple nature and not a composite.

But all the intelligences except the first are composite. Therefore, they do not have one continuous activity.

[2b] Against

[v] When the activity of anything that moves by understanding is manifested in one way in a moved body, its activity of understanding exists in only one way. But the activity of an intelligence is manifested in a heavenly body, which is always moved uniformly in one way. Therefore, it acts always in one way in understanding.

[vi] Moreover, the nearer something is to the one first simple [being], which is pure act, the more it has [its own] being in act. But an intelligence comes nearer to God than a human being. Therefore, since a human is sometimes in activity potentially and sometimes actually, it seems that an intelligence should always be actually in activity.

[2c. A Further Question]

[vii] I ask further, whether their activity is only speculative. It seems that it is also productive (*factiva*), because Avicenna says that all lower things exist in the intelligences in the way artifacts exist in an artisan. But the activity of an artisan on artifacts is productive. Therefore, so is the activity of an intelligence.

[viii] Moreover, every understanding that puts itself in a body by motion is practical. But the understanding of an intelligence is like this, because intelligences serve as the primary factor in the motion of the spheres, as the philosophers maintain. Therefore, etc.

[ix] Moreover, the philosophers say that all the actions of lower things come from the first movers. But they only produce actions in lower things by intending. Therefore, since every understanding intending a deed in an external matter is practical, it seems that, etc. {767B}

[x] Moreover, since the first understanding is cognizant and causative of things, it is nobler to resemble it in its being causative. But the understanding of the intelligences resembles it in the noblest way. Therefore, etc.

[2d] Against

[xi] The intelligences have the noblest intellectual activity. But speculation is such, because it alone is sought for itself. Therefore, their understanding, which is [their] activity, is speculative.

[xii] Moreover, they have a more perfect understanding than we do. But we have perfect activity of the speculative understanding. Much more, therefore, do they.

[2e] Solution

We have to say that every plurality is reduced to unity as to its cause in such a way that a greater plurality is reduced to a lesser, and so on, in order, until unity is reached. Therefore, the form of the being of the universe must exist in the greatest simplicity in God (who is the principle of the universe) and flow without interruption into the things that are receptive of it according to the mode of the recipients. The closer those recipients are to it the more they receive it as simple and universal, and the more remote they are the more they receive it as contracted, particular, and manifold. This is why the higher intelligences have more universal forms than the lower and why forms are received in matter in an entirely particular way. Therefore, since the intelligences understand only by reception of the form of the being of the universe and in the light of the first [being], and this form is of itself active, it is clear that they are always in continuous speculation because of continuous reception from a continuously influencing [cause]. And due to the actuality of the form itself, which enacts itself in (*seipsam agit in*) beings capable [of receiving it], they are also in continuous activity toward lower things. This is indeed how it goes according to the opinion of the philosophers, but we have to say otherwise according to the theologian – but that is not to the point.

[2f. Replies to the Opening Arguments]

[i] To the first we therefore have to say that when one activity is the cause and reason for another, it does not weaken the other. This is why the intelligences can simultaneously speculate by reception of light from the first [being] and act on a lower, because the reception is the cause and reason for the second activity.

[ii] To the second we have to say that there {768A} can be determination to one activity in two ways: either by being bound to matter (as is the case in nature), and this is ignoble; or by a determination of habit, and this is noble, because a power perfected by habit is nobler and more determined to one [act]. So it is in the intelligences, who understand with

a natural cognition through a natural light, since they are understandings in their substance and not by an additionally developed habit.

[iii] To the third we have to say that necessity in the sense of constraint or of being bound to matter takes away the character of praiseworthiness from an activity, but necessity from unswervingness in nobility and in what is morally honorable augments it. Such is the necessity of acting in the intelligences.

[iv] To the fourth we have to say that the compositeness of an intelligence does not come from different component natures, but there is in them a mode of composition according to a greater or lesser mixture of the same nature, as has often been said.

[v, vi] We concede the two others.

[2g. Solution to the Further Question]

[vii] To the further question we have to say that as to the reception of light or the form of the being of the universe from the first [being], an intelligence's understanding is speculative in itself, and this is its first and primary activity. Inasmuch, however, as it enacts itself in lower [things] through the form it has received, it has the manner of a practical understanding, but this is secondary in it and it is not practical in the way our understanding is.

[vii–ix] From this the solution to the first three objections on this point is clear.

[x] To the fourth we have to say that if the cognition were separated from the [causal] activity, cognition such as this, which is the cause and reason for the activity and yet does not exist for the sake of the activity as for the sake of an end, is nobler than the activity.

[xi, xii] We concede the two others.

[3. Can an Intelligence Be Called Happy in Its Activity?]

[3a. It Seems Not]

Third, it seems that an intelligence cannot be called happy in its activity.

[i] For contraries by nature come to be in the same thing. But misery cannot exist in the intelligences; therefore, neither can happiness.

[ii] Moreover, to exist in the best way consistent with a thing's natural

being is not to be happy. Otherwise, the beasts could be happy, as the Stoics used to say. But intellectual being is the nature of an intelligence. Therefore, it seems that they cannot be called {768B} happy according to their intellectual nature.

[iii] Moreover, each thing is what it is on some other basis than that on which it is happy. An intelligence is what it is through contemplation. Therefore, it does not seem that it can be called happy through it.

[3b] Against

[iv] That because of which each [thing has a property has the property] more. But humans are called happy by contemplation only through likeness to the intelligences' contemplation. Therefore, an intelligence is happier.

[v] Moreover, what rejoices with one simple activity natural and proper to itself seems to be most happy. But God is like this, as is said in Book VII (14, 1154b26), and similarly the intelligences, through imitating him. Therefore, etc.

[3c. A Further Question]

I ask further, whether contemplative happiness is of the same character in gods and humans. It seems that it is.

[vi] For happiness is a certain intellectual activity. But that activity exists in humans and gods. Therefore, it seems that happiness is of one character in both.

[vii] Moreover, as he says (1178b24f), this happiness does not agree with humans as humans but inasmuch as there is something divine in them. Therefore, etc.

[viii] Moreover, similarity is with respect to a single type. But contemplative happiness agrees with humans through resemblance to the gods. Therefore, it agrees with them according to a single characteristic type.

[3d] Against

[ix] An intelligence has through itself what is divine, because it is something divine in its own nature. But it is not so in a human being, because we are not rational by our own nature. Therefore, since this happiness is present in accordance with the divine in them, it will not be of one character in them [and us].

[x] Moreover, there is not one activity belonging to an essentially understanding [being] and one that understands by participation. But a human being understands by participation, whereas an intelligence does so essentially. Therefore, the activity of understanding does not agree with them [both] according to a single character, and so neither does the happiness related to such an activity.

[3e. A Further Question]

I ask further about the Commentator's [Michael of Ephesus'] statement that an intelligence understands and 'has' itself, while our understanding does not.

[xi] This seems false, for one who has is a subject and what is had is a form. Therefore, if there is a having and a had in an intelligence there will be composition in it. {769A}

Moreover, it seems that our understanding also understands itself and has itself as an object of its own activity. Therefore, it seems that the two cases are entirely alike.

[3f] Solution

We have to say that just as the nature of light exists in different ways in the sun, in the moon, in a live coal, and in opaque bodies, differing in purity and mixture and producing a purer act of lighting the purer it is (so that things that look white in sunlight look pallid in moonlight, and the more mixed and clouded over the light the more it is contracted to a reddish color): so it is with the intellectual nature, because in the first [being] it exists in the highest purity (because it is not a light contracted by something in which it is received, and for this reason it also has the purest activity of understanding and consequently the noblest happiness), and the nearer each intelligent [being] is to the first the greater will be its contemplative happiness. For this reason the intelligences also have this sort of happiness more fully than humans.

[3g. Replies to the Opening Arguments]

[i] To the first we therefore have to say that happiness agrees with the gods by their nature, by which they are intellectual. Because of this, misery cannot exist in them. Or we have to say that an accident can be related to its subject as to what is only a subject or as to what is its cause. In the first

way it does not follow that the accident is inseparable and that its contrary cannot be present. In the second way, because effect follows cause, this sort of accident, which has a cause in the subject, must be inseparable.

[ii] To the second we have to say that being in the best way consistent with any nature whatever does not make something happy, but being in the best way consistent with an intellectual nature does.

[iii] To the third we have to say that in an intellectual power activity and essence do not differ in reality but only in concept. In others, however, they differ both really and in concept. For this reason the basis on which something exists is always other than that on which it is happy – really other or other in concept.

[iv, v] We concede the other two.

[3h. Solution to the Further Question]

To the further question we have to say that happiness is not of one character in God, an intelligence, and a human being univocally but by analogy, because its existence in God is prior to and truer than its existence in an intelligence and it is in an intelligence more truly than in a human. Nor does it follow from this that {769B} because it differs only with respect to more and less it is of one type in all, for more and less according to approach to and recession from the same nature (as a limit) do not make for difference in type, but with a more and less that is based on difference of nature there must be a difference of type. And so it is in the case at hand.

[vi] Therefore, when he shows that the activity is of one character, we have to say that this is true by analogy and not univocally.

[vii] To another we have to say that what is divine in humans (in accordance with which they are happy) is also in them in a posterior way.

[viii] To another we have to say that the resemblance is not in relation to something the same in type but in the way previously indicated, according to which each [thing] brings itself into likeness with the first [being] as much as it can.

[ix, x] We concede the other two.

[xi] To what was asked afterwards about the Commentator's statement, we have to say that the first intelligence understands itself and has itself and the very act of understanding, not only as its form, but as an effect of its nature, because it does not understand other things by receiving from them but rather by its influence on them. For this reason there is no

composition. A second intelligence, on the other hand, understands itself by receiving from the first, and there is some composition in it, although not of different essences but in the manner indicated. But our understanding – and the agent understanding, whose activity is to bring its own likeness (*species*) to bear upon intelligibles – falls short of the simplicity of the first intelligence, because it is not its own activity. Hence also the possible understanding, whose activity is in receiving, falls short of the activity of a second intelligence, because it receives more contracted forms, and for this reason it is not of the same character.

[4. Do the Gods Have the Moral Virtues?]

[4a. It Seems that They Do]

Fourth, it seems that the gods have the moral virtues.

For Plotinus posited certain exemplary virtues in the genus of morals. But those can only exist in the gods. Therefore, it seems that the gods have the moral virtues.

Moreover, according to the theologian it is said that the moral virtues will remain in heaven. But human happiness in heaven will be in the same mode as that of the angels. Therefore, etc.

Moreover, in the *Liber de causis* it is said that the first [being] {770A} is rich through itself and also in others; and thus it seems to have certain riches of its own and all the riches of others. But the greatest human riches are the moral virtues. Therefore, etc.

Moreover, Boethius says (*On the Consolation of Philosophy* V, Prose 4) that whatever a lower [being] can do a higher one can also. But a human can have moral ((*morales/humanas*)) virtues. Therefore, etc.

[4b] Solution

We have to say that higher [beings] have in an eminent way whatever belongs to lower ones, and the lower ones fall short of what belongs to the higher. As a result, we say that the moral virtues do not exist in the gods or remain in heaven with respect to the same acts that they have among humans in civic life but with respect to others. For example, courage does not exist in the former as a standing fast in the dangers of war but as an impossibility of being shaken by any violence; and similarly with regard to the other virtues. They are called exemplary by Plotinus with respect to these acts.

From this the solution to the whole question is clear.

[5. Can Beasts Be Happy?]

[5a. It Seems that They Can]

Fifth, it seems that the beasts can be happy.

[i] For happiness consists in the best undergoing, because in the highest pleasure. But beasts can experience in a way that is best in relation to their own natures, as, for example, an ass when it eats wild thistle. Therefore, etc.

[ii] Moreover, happiness is the best action consistent with the nature of the agent, agreeing with it according to its best state. But in beasts there is a best state, between growth and decline, their youth. Therefore, etc.

[iii] Moreover, as humans are to the intelligences, so are beasts to humans. But humans participate in the happiness of an intelligence in some way. Therefore, it seems that a brute may also achieve human happiness in some degree. {770B}

[iv] Moreover, there is happiness in an activity that has been learned. But some animals are teachable. Therefore, etc.

[5b] Solution

We have to say that happiness is a certain activity (*operatio*). For this reason there cannot be happiness or misfortune for things that do not have it in them to act (*operari*) — except by likeness, as someone once said that the stones from which altars were made were fortunate. Now the Epicureans and Stoics maintained that there could be happiness in them [the beasts], because they were taking happiness according to their own conception of it, Epicurus as the best undergoing (*pati*), meaning pleasure, which is a certain passion, the Stoics, on the other hand, as action (*actionem*) according to a thing's own nature, not taking into consideration what nature it was that the acting pertained to.

[5c. Replies to the Opening Arguments]

[i, ii] From this the solution to the first two, which proceed according to their two opinions, is clear.

[iii] To the third we have to say that in comparing human to intelligence and brute to human the likeness does not hold in every respect, because humans participate in that [property] of an intelligence according to which it is happy, namely, understanding, but the brute does not participate in reason, according to which a human is happy.

[iv] To the fourth we have to say that certain brutes are teachable through memory but not through reason. Because of this they cannot have the happiness of reason. . . .

Lesson 16

{771B} 'There will be need, however' (1178b33).

In this last section on contemplative happiness he intends to show in what way a happy person needs external goods and how his own views about contemplative happiness are consonant with the views of others – and also with their deeds.

I ask seven questions about this.

[1. For Contemplative Happiness Does a Human Being Need External Happiness?]

First, whether for contemplative happiness a human being needs external happiness.

[1a] It Seems Not

[i] We read in the letter the Brahmins sent to Alexander [the Great] that they did not build houses but were accustomed to dwell in caves (which served them for houses while they were alive and tombs when they died) and many things of this sort. Since they were great philosophers, as can clearly be seen from the same letter, it seems that those who are happy in this way do not need external goods.

[ii] Moreover, the same thing is seen from the example of Diogenes [the Cynic, in Diogenes Laertius VI 37], who, when he was carrying a cup and saw some shepherds drinking out of their hands, threw away the gold cup, saying he had not realized that he had been endowed with a cup by nature. Yet a vessel for taking food seems to be a necessity. Therefore, etc.

[iii] Moreover, those who have been most contemplative, such as the holy fathers in the desert, abandoned everything.

[iv] Moreover, he says that private individuals and common people who serve others can be happy (1179a27f). But {772A} servants do not necessarily have other servants under them, for otherwise it would go on to infinity. Therefore, someone who is happy in this way does not need an establishment of servants.

[v] Moreover, nature does not fall short in necessities, especially those needed for its own end. But the ultimate end of human nature is contemplative happiness. Therefore, one does not need anything for this except what nature has provided. Now external goods are not of this kind. Therefore, etc.

[1b] Against

The rule of a household and of an individual within a household resemble nature's rule. But as is said in chapter 16 of *On [the Generation of] Animals* (II 3, 737a18–24), nature does not give us all our members and full size all at once, but we must acquire the growth that is due us by something like commerce. Therefore, it seems that it is left to a human being to acquire those external goods by which (in addition to what nature has given) both the contemplative and anyone else may be sustained.

Moreover, moral matters are ordered to household management. But wealth is the end of household management. Therefore a moral individual must aim at wealth in some way. But contemplatives must also be moral, if they ought to live with others. Therefore, etc.

Moreover, someone who is always anxious about procuring externals is miserable and is impeded from contemplation. But someone who is entirely deprived of external goods has to be continually anxious about the means of sustenance. Therefore, etc.

Moreover, in *Metaphysics* I (1, 981b17–25) it is said that philosophizing began in Egypt when everything required for pleasure and necessity had been provided for. Therefore, it seems that philosophy presupposes abundance in externals.

[1c] Solution

We have to say that with respect to external goods 'necessary' has two senses: necessary for a dignitary (*personae*) or necessary for an individual. Those are called dignitaries in civic affairs who are established in a rank of office, as a king, prince, or someone of this sort. Such people do indeed have need of many externals, because their labors are not only for themselves but for the whole multitude. But the necessary for an individual is what any private person at all needs for being and for well-being – not only for subsistence but also for good physical health and for carrying out his proper activity without impediment. Now the activity of contemplatives is carried on by themselves alone and not in a multitude. Because of this they need only what is necessary for an individual, whether this is provided by their property {772B} or by nature (as in certain lands where the fruits [of the earth] are more widespread and sufficient for human nourishment, which does not happen elsewhere). But they do not need superfluous things but are in fact impeded by them.

[1d. Replies to the Opening Arguments]

[i–iii] On this basis, the first three arguments are valid. There is yet another argument concerning the desert saints, because they were looking not only for perfection of the understanding but also for mortification of the body. For this reason they were accustomed to deny themselves even what was necessary for well-being and were content with only what could sustain them in being.

[iv] To the fourth we have to say that an establishment of servants does not mean here an establishment in which one human being serves another but the aid rendered by external goods to human nature, which is in many ways a servant (cf. *Metaphysics* I 2, 982b29f).

[v] To the fifth we have to say that nature does not fall short in the tools necessary for transforming external things into nature, but she does not give everything needed for our sustenance in the form in which it is actually needed; otherwise we would not need to eat.

[2. Does Morally Virtuous Action Require a Great Abundance of External Goods?]

[2a. It Seems So]

Second, it seems that morally virtuous action requires a great abundance of external goods.

For he said in Book I (8, 1099a31–b2) that someone who is happy engaged in politics has many needs: friends, riches, necessities, and the like. Now these bespeak a great abundance of externals. Therefore, etc.

Moreover, it is impossible to reach an end without things that are instrumental. But an abundance of externals is instrumental to happiness. Therefore, etc.

[2b. An Additional Question]

Moreover, what are we to call a 'great abundance' of externals? What is superfluous for an individual? This is necessary for a dignitary. Or what is superfluous for a dignitary? But this too is necessary for a superior dignitary. What is superfluous for a duke is little for a king.

[2c] Solution

We have to say that civic happiness can be considered in two ways. In its own being it is an activity of moral virtue and can belong to moderate individuals who live for themselves alone and do not need external goods except to sustain their nature in being and well-being – and if they should have more things than this they will be impeded by them, because they will not be able to manage them adequately by themselves. Civic happiness can also be considered according to its maximum potentiality, as {773A} it belongs to someone who is over a whole multitude and acts for the good of a people. So considered, it is not an act of virtue alone but of virtue along with all the requisite instruments. For this reason those who are in such positions need a great abundance of external goods befitting their rank. If they have less ((*pauciora/plura*)), they will not be able to govern adequately.

From this the solution to the objections is clear.

[3. Should Discourse Be Believed When It Is Out of Harmony with Deeds?]

[3a. It Seems that It Should Be]

Third, it seems that discourse should be believed even if it is out of harmony with [the speaker's] deeds.

[i] For what is true should always be believed. But as he said in Book II (4, 1105b2ff), there are many who have knowledge but act contrary to it. Now those who have knowledge speak the truth, in accord with their knowledge. Therefore, etc.

[ii] Moreover, Matthew 23:3: 'Do what they say, [not what they do].'

[iii] Moreover, intellectual virtue is perfected by experience, discovery, and teaching. But teaching is done through discourse. Therefore, since he is concerned here with happiness in relation to the intellectual virtues, it seems wrong to say that discourses should not be believed but deeds.

[iv] Moreover, the understanding's virtue is truth. But truth is related equally to good and bad deeds, because fornicating is just as true as acting temperately. Therefore, it seems that in the intellectual virtues deeds should not be attended to.

[3b] Solution

We have to say that because matters of action concern particulars argumentation about them is incomplete. For this reason, discourses are not completely convincing by themselves but certify [what they say about] these matters by the examples of deeds, as Anselm says (*On Truth* 9) about the wholesome herbs being eaten by someone who says they are poisonous. For this reason, in matters of action the deeds of good people are taken as particular universals, so to speak, applicable to each case as a last is applied to all shoes. But it is different according to the theologian, because even if discourses have not been adequately proved and do not deserve credence from the authority of the speaker, who is nothing, they nevertheless deserve credence from [divine] inspiration, because someone who lives badly puts forward the teaching of God. And for this reason he must be believed.

[3c. Replies to the Opening Arguments]

[i, ii] The solution to the first two is clear from this.

[iii] To the third we have to say that intellectual habits are called virtues according as an act of will ordering {773B} the whole of life to the best contemplation precedes the act of understanding, and this also applies to contemplative happiness. Accordingly, we ask about the deeds of those who have contemplated best – about how they conducted themselves in life.

[iv] The solution to the fourth is clear from this.

[4. Does God Care for Lower Things?]

[4a. It Seems Not]

Fourth, it seems that God has no care for lower things.

For the principle of the universe's being is related equally to everything there is, as the saints and philosophers commonly say. But something of this sort does not seem to care more about one thing than another. Therefore, etc.

Moreover, God's care is either efficacious or it is not. If it is not, it is imperfect, which is not suitable to God. If it is efficacious, it draws all things to that which it intends, and so it would make everyone contemplative and virtuous, which we do not see.

Moreover, care involves concern. With concern, however, comes anxiousness of mind, which is not suitable to God.

[4b] Against

In the book of Wisdom (6:7) it is said that, 'God cares for all,' and Peter (1 Peter 5:7) also says, 'He cares for you,' and the Psalm (40:17): 'The Lord is concerned for me.'

[4c] Solution

We have to say that the manner in which God's care is extended and allocated to outer things is a higher question than is to the point here. For this reason we have to say, as pertains to the point, that he cares for everything he has created and that he is said to care more for one thing than for another, not because of any variation in his affection, but because of the different effects according to which one thing shares more in his goodness and another less. This is not due to his being related in a different way to different things but to their being related in different ways to participating in his goodness. Hence it is clear that if some things do not achieve the highest mode of participation, this is not due to a difference in divine providence but from their falling short. And although 'care' (*cura*) is attributed to God, nevertheless 'concern' (*sollicitudo*) does not exist in him except loosely speaking.

From this the solution to the objections is clear.

[5. Is Contemplating the Same as Philosophizing?]

[5a. It Seems that It Is]

Fifth, it seems that to contemplate is the same as to philosophize. {774A}

[i] For contemplating as referred to here is the act of [the virtue of] wisdom. But philosophy is wisdom and its act is philosophizing. Therefore, etc.

[ii] Moreover, contemplating, as is said in the text, is an activity of the understanding. But there is an activity of understanding in relation to all the intellectual virtues. Therefore, it seems that there is contemplating in relation to the acts of prudence, art, and all the others.

[iii] Moreover, he said above (cf. c. 4, 1175a13–15) that a musical mind takes pleasure in theorems. Now a theorem is a contemplating or what is contemplated. Therefore, it seems that there is also contemplation relating to music and, by the same reasoning, to the other sciences.

[5b] For the Opposite

All the acts referred to fit both the good and the bad. But to contemplate pertains only to a good human being, as is said in the text. Therefore, it differs from all of the preceding.

Moreover, a morally virtuous disposition is required for contemplating, as is said in the text. But this is not required for philosophizing or for musical contemplation. Therefore, they are not the same.

[5c] Solution

We have to say that contemplating as it is taken here implies unimpeded activity of the understanding relating to the end of happiness. Now an impediment can be due to the subject or to habit. An impediment due to the subject must be removed by the moral virtues, which free us from the disturbances of the passions. One is freed from the impediment of habit, however, by having an effective means for drawing conclusions about a problem and by being able, from practice, to do this without difficulty. Now contemplation is referred to the end of happiness when everything that can be contemplated is taken in order to what is ultimate – that in the contemplation of which there is the highest happiness, namely, the first [being]. For when the activity of understanding is such, then nature flourishes above itself, inasmuch as it thereby attains its best, and thus there is the happiest activity.

[5d. Replies to the Opening Arguments]

[i] To the first we therefore have to say that philosophizing is more general than contemplating, because philosophizing also pertains to someone who wonders – one who does not have a habit that extends from considering that something is so to cognizing why it is so. But contemplating pertains only to one who has a perfect habit. {774B}

[ii] The solution to the second is clear, because not every activity of understanding is contemplating but [only] the one that has been referred to.

[iii] To the third we have to say that the contemplation of musical [things] is a material [element] in the act of contemplation, but what is formal in it is its reference to the divine that can be contemplated.

[6. Are Theological and Philosophical Contemplation the Same?]

[6a. It Seems that They Are]

Sixth, it seems that theological and philosophical contemplation are the same.

For activities of the same [thing], to the same [end], and in accordance with the same habit seem to differ in nothing. But theological and philosophical contemplation are alike in being the consideration of intellectual [things] in [their] order to God and in accordance with the habit of wisdom. Therefore, etc.

Moreover, just as philosophical contemplation is an unimpeded activity, so must theological contemplation be unimpeded, or it would not be pleasant. Therefore, etc.

Moreover, just as the activity of the moral virtues is prerequisite to philosophical contemplation, so also to theological. For we do not call those who live badly contemplatives. Therefore, etc.

[6b] Against

Philosophical contemplation is by an acquired habit, theological by an infused light. Therefore, they are not the same.

Moreover, philosophical contemplation is without wonder. That is why it is said in the beginning of the *Metaphysics* (I 2, 983a19–20) that the non-geometer wonders at things that the geometer does not wonder at. But with theological [contemplation] there is the greatest wonder. That is why Augustine says (*Confessions* IX 6.14) that he was not *satiated* in contemplating the height of the divine purpose. Therefore, etc.

[6c] Solution

We have to say that theological contemplation agrees with philosophical in some respects and differs from it in others. Hence they are not entirely the same. They agree in this, that in the theological there is also an inspection of some spiritual [things] by the understanding without impediment from the passions on the side of the subject or from doubtfulness on the side of belief, an inspection ordered to resting in God, which is the highest happiness. It differs, however, in habit, end, and object: in habit because the theological contemplates by a light infused by God but the philosopher by an acquired habit of wisdom; in end because the theological places {775A} its ultimate end in the contemplation of God in heaven but the philosopher in a vision by which he is seen to some extent in this life; in object, too, not as to substance but as to mode, because the philosopher contemplates God according as he has him as a demonstrative conclusion, but the theologian contemplates him as existing above reason and understanding. Because of this the mode of contemplating is different, because the philosopher has the certainty of demonstration and depends upon it, but the theologian depends on the first truth because of itself and not because of reasoning (even if he should have it). On this account the theologian wonders but not the philosopher.

From this the solution to the objections is clear, because in theological contemplation there is similarly presupposed a moral virtue that is infused, not, as is the case in philosophical contemplation, acquired.

[7. Is the Contemplative Loved Most by God?]

[7a. It Seems Not]

Seventh, it seems that the contemplative is not most loved by God.

[i] For Richard of St. Victor [rather, Gregory the Great, *Homilies on Ezekiel* I 12.30] says that no work is more acceptable to God than that which bears fruit in souls. But this is a work of action. Therefore, etc.

[ii] Moreover, what is most useful is most loved by God. But what is most useful is to lead human beings back to likeness with the divine and to become a co-worker with God, as Dionysius says (*On the Celestial Hierarchy* 3.2). Therefore, etc.

[iii] Moreover, when someone is said to be most loved by God, this either posits something in God or nothing. If nothing, it seems inappropriate to say that love posits nothing in the lover. If it does posit [something], it therefore seems that that in God from which it follows that someone is most loved by him is not related in the same way to everyone [which also seems inappropriate].

[iv] Moreover, 'most loved' implies something more [in relation to one person] than to others. That 'more' is posited either only in the human being or else in God. But not only in the human, because whatever more there is in a human being comes from God. Therefore, it is necessary that there be in God at least an inclination toward one individual more than another. And again, I ask about that inclination. If you say that it posits something only in the human, it will go on to infinity. Nor again does it posit anything in God, because God is related in one way to everything. Therefore, it seems that the contemplative is not most loved by God.

[7b. An Additional Question]

[v] {775B} Moreover, I ask about the words of the Commentator [Michael of Ephesus] when he says that [the contemplative] is called 'most

akin (*cognatissimus*),' namely, to God, 'not as to substance but as being able to live within himself and see himself and being able through the conversion and conjunction that is in himself to be stretched to the divine, loving it and being deified and as far as possible assimilated. The understanding of each one among us is therefore akin to God as to similarity of activities, for he understands himself, and we [understand] ourselves when we have been raised above fantasy.' And below (ibid.): 'For all opinion works with irrational sense and fantasy, having recourse [from these] to science and understanding; after this, however, to the intellectual life and simple activities ((*operationes/appositionibus* [var.])).' The Commentator again (ibid.): 'Those cherish an understanding akin to God's who embrace all virtue, fleeing the multiform appetites and their fellow servants the senses as things that deceive the mind, fleeing fantasies as things that can shape and divide [their understanding] and produce all manner and degree of impossibilities, and turning away from [mere] opinions as things that are variable and bear [their minds] off to outer things mixed with sense and fantasy. When this has been done, they receive those resplendences from thence and are filled with the purest light.' I ask about the meaning of those words, for it does not seem that from being turned to oneself one immediately reaches the contemplation of God.

[vi] Moreover, it seems that a contemplative ought not to dismiss outer things and recur to those that are within, because much good contemplation can be found in outer things.

[7c. A Further Question]

[vii] Moreover, I ask what are the resplendences he says are received by those in whom there are simple activities ((*operationibus/appositionibus*)).

[7d] Solution

We have to say that someone can be called most loved by God in two ways: either because of purity, in which one is more like God (*deo similior*), and the contemplative is said to be most loved by God in this way; or because of usefulness, and one who converts souls to God is more accepted by God in this way and has greater merit and reward. There is a similar question in theology about the active and contemplative lives and the married and virgin states, because in each of these one is of greater purity and worth but the other can be of greater utility and merit. As a result, it happens that {776A} at death someone flies up to heaven at once because of purity of life but will get a lesser reward than one who spends a long time in purgatory.

[7e. Replies to the Opening Arguments]

[i, ii] And from this the solution to the first two is clear.

[iii] To the third we have to say that 'most loved by God' implies something in God and something in the creature, but the difference does not arise from God's being related in different ways to things but from the different ways in which creatures are related to God. Because of this, one creature will take less of his goodness than another, and according to the greater effect of goodness he is said to love something more or less.

[iv] From this the solution to the fourth is clear.

[v] To what is asked about the Commentator we have to say that the form of a thing can be grasped in three ways: either as a simple quiddity, as grasped in its essential principles, and it is grasped thus by a simple intelligence; or as it is joined to quantity, and thus there are forms of imagination joined with the continuous; or as it is further joined with active and passive qualities, and thus there are sensible forms joined with time because of motion – but we grasp forms of this sort from outer things through the senses. As a result, when we resolve sensory forms into forms of imagination and these into simple quiddities, the soul is withdrawn from outer to inner things and from these to the most inward, and in those it is enfolded in the simplicity of intellectual light and joined with the intelligences. Dionysius (*On the Divine Names* 4.8) calls this activity the circular motion of an angel. Now the rays proceeding from the first source of intellectual light are called resplendences. They come into our soul only as cognition but into the intelligences in the manner of active forms {776B} which can unfold (*explicibilium*) into matter through the motion of a heavenly orb.

[vi, vii] From this the solution to the whole is clear. . . .

Lesson 17

{777A} 'If, therefore, about both these things' [1179a33].

This is the last part of this teaching if we divide the whole book. Now that he has imparted moral teaching, he wants in this part to show the necessity for political science or legislation, so that the connection of science to science may be apparent. Hence this {777B} part is divided into two. First he shows the necessity for legislation, second (at 'Therefore, after these,' chapter 17 [c. 9, 1180b28]), he connects this science with that one. The first is divided into two. In the first he shows that the science that teaches the virtues and the other things discussed above is inadequate for achieving its own ultimate end. Second (at 'If, therefore, in whatever way' [1180a14]), he shows how it is attained through legislation.

About the first part I ask eight questions.

[1. Is the End of Moral Science Knowing or Acting?]

First, whether the end of moral science is knowing or acting.

[1a] It Seems that It Is Knowing

[i] For in any teaching whatever, features are proved of a subject. But the effect of this is to know. Therefore, the end of any teaching whatever is to know.

[ii] Moreover, every teaching is ordered to the understanding. But the good of the understanding is truth, which we do not arrive at through acting but through knowing. Therefore, etc. {778A}

[iii] Moreover, one does not reach an end without the means to it. But there can be good activity without the teaching of conduct. Therefore, etc.

[iv] Moreover, just as this teaching about the virtues produces only knowledge, so also does his teaching about laws. Therefore, just as this one is inadequate for achieving its end, so is that one.

[1b] Solution

We have to say that there are certain problems where we wish to know for the sake of knowing, because the subject or cause or feature is great and wonderful, as in all the sciences that are essential parts of philosophy, which are concerned with things that do not exist as a result of our deeds. There are some, however, where what we wish to know is instrumental, as in teaching about reasoning, the method of philosophy. But the problems of morals do not have anything great about them, raised above what we can do, nor are they investigated for their own sake, nor is there anything here that is instrumental for knowing other things. On this account, it remains that in such [problems] we do not in any way investigate to know but only to act.

[1c. Replies to the Opening Arguments]

[i] To the first we therefore have to say that [in moral science] a feature is not investigated for its own sake but as referred to action.

[ii] To the second we likewise have to say that this teaching is only referred to the understanding as ordered to action. Hence it is not strictly speaking a teaching.

[iii] To the third we have to say that acting well is impossible without moral virtue. Now moral virtue is impossible without prudence, which is built by teaching about conduct. For this reason acting well is impossible without moral teaching, although there can be good activity [without it].

[iv] To the fourth we have to say that laws are not taken [here] only as they direct action by way of instruction but as their binding to action is like a chain, insofar as they have been sanctioned by the rulers of the commonwealth.

[2. Can Anyone Be Made Morally Serious through Discourse?]

[2a. It Seems Not]

Second, it seems that no one can be made more morally serious (*studiosius*) through discourse (*sermones*).

[i] For to be serious about the moral virtues depends on action. But discourse is not action. Therefore, etc.

[ii] Moreover, the [anonymous] Commentator says, [commenting on] Book II, that knowing does nothing toward generating a habit, although it does a little toward acting according to a habit. But becoming morally serious relates to the generation of a habit. Therefore, it seems that no one can become morally serious through discourses producing knowledge of what should be done.

[iii] Moreover, discourse does not make for being morally serious unless it is hortatory. The discourse about the virtues in this book is not put

forward in the manner of exhortation, however, but as a kind of teaching. Therefore, etc.

[iv] Moreover, the same virtue has the same kind of effectiveness in all cases that are of the same kind. Therefore, if discourse can make the good virtuous it seems that it can also transform the bad. He says the opposite (1179b10f).

[v] If you say that evil is resistant, to the contrary: Augustine says (*Enchiridion* 13) that the smallest good is stronger than the greatest evil, because evil can do nothing except through something good in which it subsists. But discourse instructing in conduct is something good. Therefore, etc.

[2b] Solution

We have to say that the young are called generous-minded (*liberales*) here, not from the virtue of generosity (*liberalitas*), but from the generosity of a spirit that is not tied down to serving the passions but of itself loves (*diligit*) the good. As a result, when what is good is shown to it it is kindled to love (*amorem*) of it and acts according to that discourse. But the good of virtue is not to the taste of those who are slaves of the passions and whose taste has been corrupted by unnatural pleasures. Because of this {778B} they are not drawn to acting by discourse.

[2c. Replies to the Opening Arguments]

[i] To the first we therefore have to say that virtue depends on action to effect it but on discourse as something inclining to action.

[ii] To the second we have to say that knowing does nothing *per se* toward generating a habit, but it does something incidentally, insofar as it inclines to action.

[iii] To the third we have to say that although his discourse in this teaching has not been hortatory in form, it has nevertheless had the virtue of exhortation inasmuch as it has praised and taught the virtues, because by this means a ready spirit is kindled to action and exhorts itself.

[iv] To the fourth we have to say that there is an impediment in bad people to [the effectiveness of] discourse, namely, the lordship of the passions, and discourse cannot have effect in them.

[v] To the fifth we have to say that although good is more powerful

than evil *per se*, evil can nevertheless be more powerful incidentally, insofar as free judgment consents to evil and does not consent to good.

[3. Is Aristotle's Division of Ways of Being Made Good Adequate?]

[3a. It Seems Not]

Third, it seems that the division [between being made good by nature, by habituation, or by teaching (1179b20–21)] is inadequate.

[i] For law and punishment make some people good, as he also says. But none of these includes them. Therefore, this division of ways of being made good is inadequate.

[ii] Moreover, he said in Book I ([4] 1095b7–13) that there are some who take in teaching by themselves, while some get it from others. The reasoning is similar here with regard to acquiring virtue. Therefore, it seems that he ought to have posited only two [ways of being made good].

[iii] Moreover, from what he said in Book II (1, 1103a23–26), it seems that no one becomes good by nature, for he said that only the aptitude is from nature, perfecting comes from repeated practice, and only after this perfecting is someone called morally serious. Therefore, etc.

[iv] Moreover, what exists by nature is not voluntary. But being morally serious is voluntary. Therefore, etc.

[v] Moreover, what nature is it by which some become good? It is either common, and in that case all human beings, who are of one nature, would need to be good by the moral virtues; or it is a proper nature, by which the common is individuated, and this is a nature that is also in a certain way common, and, to be brief, a proper nature always arises from the common. Therefore, it seems that no one can become morally good by nature. {779A}

[vi] Moreover, nature follows its own principles. But the principles forming our makeup are the same in everyone. Therefore, it seems that there is the same reason for goodness and badness in all.

[vii] Moreover, if this is true, it seems that he is remiss in not discussing what this sort of nature is, either here or in his works in natural science.

[viii] Moreover, he seems to be wrong in saying that in happening to have such a nature one is lucky. For lucky events occur as a result of two subjects acting beyond the intention of either of them. But this does not

happen in the orderly sequence of nature. Therefore, it seems that one cannot be called lucky in having such a nature.

[ix] Moreover, habituation alone suffices for the attainment of moral virtue. Now by this one becomes morally serious. Therefore, the other two are superfluous.

[x] Moreover, habituation completes nature. But a perfection and what it perfects do not cause anything as being different but as being one and perfect. Therefore, it seems that habituation ought not to have been divided in contrast to nature.

[xi] Moreover, teaching consists of discourses. But discourses do not transform anyone, as he says. Therefore, etc.

[3b. Two Further Questions]

[xii] Moreover, he says that between teaching and virtue there must be some intermediary which perfects virtue, namely, preparation, which is by habituation. I ask whether nature likewise needs such an intermediary to make someone morally serious. It seems that it does, because what exists in potentiality in natural principles must be brought into act by the act of some agent. Now virtue exists in natural principles only by way of aptitude. Therefore, it seems that there must be some intermediary completing nature.

[xiii] Moreover, I ask on what basis these three are taken.

[3c] Solution

[xiii] First we have to say to this last question that these three can be taken to make someone morally serious either all together or each by itself. If all are joined together, there will be something directing, and this is teaching, and something effecting, and the latter in two ways: either as aptitude, and this is nature, or as perfection, and this is habituation. If, however, each is taken as making someone morally serious by itself, then it should be understood that as a body approaches more closely to a balanced makeup it is allotted a soul {779B} that is nobler and more like the intelligences. Therefore it sometimes happens that a soul is entirely pure and entirely vanquishes the body, and so there will exist the understanding that Avicenna calls holy, because it gets by itself the speculative sciences and also the principles for matters of action and the rules of living, and it is in no way (or hardly at all) impeded from living well by bodily passions. In that

case nature alone brings it about that the individual is morally serious. Sometimes, however, there is a pure understanding which is able to get the rules of living by itself but is impeded in carrying them out by bodily passions which it does not entirely vanquish. In that case, for the individual to become good habituation must be added to temper the subject [i.e., the body] with regard to the passions. Sometimes, however, the understanding is more mixed, and then it cannot get even the rules of living by itself. In that case teaching must be added.

[3d. Replies to the Opening Arguments]

[i] To the first we therefore have to say that the Philosopher is speaking here about the things that make the generous-spirited good. Law, however, makes the servile good.

[ii] To the second we have to say that 'by themselves' has two senses: when nature alone suffices for living well or when nature must add to itself habituation but with no need for direction from someone else.

[iii] To the third we have to say that the Philosopher is speaking generally there with regard to everyone and not with regard to those who are privileged – who have been allotted a good soul and pure body.

[iv] To the fourth we have to say that the voluntary nevertheless remains, because although nature inclines toward acting, action nevertheless proceeds from the will.

[v] To the fifth we have to say that the nature that makes one morally serious is not nature in general but one's proper nature, insofar as the body has been brought to a balanced makeup and the best soul has been allotted.

[vi] To the sixth we have to say that although the first principles forming our makeup are the same in everyone, they nevertheless do not produce a makeup of the same rank in everyone.

[vii] To the seventh we have to say that that nature cannot be determined absolutely from natural principles but from natural and astronomical principles together, because it depends on the principles of our makeup – the factors that actually enter into our makeup – which the natural [scientist] considers, and also on first principles, according as the different conjunctions of the stars {780A} in various ways advance or impede matter from achieving a noble form. For this reason it pertains to that part of the science of astronomy which is concerned with judgments, because it is mixed from the principles of both sciences, as Ptolemy says (*Almagest, dictio* 1, c. 1). But perhaps Aristotle discussed [this] in his book *On the Properties of the Elements*, not all of which has come down to us.

[viii] To the eighth we have to say that without doubt 'luck' is taken improperly here, because in the operations of nature there is no luck or chance properly so called. But there is something like luck. For that is said to come about by luck which happens from the concurrence of two things, [each] acting with a purpose, but apart from the intention of either. Similarly, there are two intending [factors] here, namely, the proximate principles, such as hot and cold, in which there is the intention of the first mover, in accordance with which they act to a determinate end; and there are the first movers, which intend in their own right to move lower movers, and the intention of the latter is to follow and obey the higher movers. As a result, that a nature is brought to such a form happens apart from the intention of either, from the fact that the first movers find the second movers so disposed. For although they were moved to some effect in accordance with determinate [astronomical] conjunctions, that effect would nevertheless not follow in matter unless the matter were found prepared for it. Because of this Ptolemy says that the wise master the stars, inasmuch as they alter the arrangement of things and thus impede (or also aid) the stars' effect. Such a connection of causes is called by some '*ymarmenes*' or fate.

[ix] The solution to the ninth is clear, because in certain cases nature itself, without habituation, suffices for someone to be good, even morally [good].

[x] From this the solution to the tenth is clear.

[xi] To the eleventh we have to say that discourses transform the generous-spirited, and the Philosopher is speaking of them in setting forth these causes.

[xii] To the twelfth we have to say that as the soul is nobler and conquers the body and the body is purer, the virtues are accordingly more actual in the soul itself, and the more actual they are the less they need habituation to perfect them.

[xiii] The last has been solved.

[4. Do the Bad Understand Moral Discourse?]

[4a. It Seems that They Do]

Fourth, it seems that the bad understand moral discourse. {780B}

Because he said above in Book II (4, 1105b12–18) that there are many who philosophize about morals, yet do not act [accordingly]. But those who do not act [accordingly] are bad. Those who know, however, do understand what should be done. Therefore, etc.

Moreover, to understand pertains to a human being as being rational. But every human is rational. Therefore, it seems that both the good and the bad can understand discourses about conduct.

[4b] Against

Those who do not hear or understand themselves also do not understand when someone else speaks. But he said above in Book VII (3, 1147a13–14, 19–21) that although those who are impassioned speak the words of Empedocles about conduct, they do not know what they are saying, like those who speak when drunk.

[4c. A Further Question]

Moreover, I ask why both the good and the bad understand other discourses, but only the good understand moral discourse.

[4d] Solution

Here we have to say briefly, on the basis of what was treated more extensively in Book VII, that the cognition of the incontinent and of those who live according to the passions is corrupt regarding the minor premise [of a practical syllogism], and in that respect they do not understand those who speak about conduct. But they remain sound regarding the major, and they understand moral discourses to that extent. Now in the other sciences the minor premise is not about action concerning the passions (by which the continent are assailed). Because of this there is no impediment to understanding either the minor or the major premise.

From this the solution to the whole question is clear.

[5. Can Someone Be Made Morally Serious by Punishment?]

[5a. It Seems So]

Fifth, it seems that someone can be made morally serious by punishment.

[i] First from what he says in the text.

[ii] Moreover, it is said in the laws (*Digest* 47.10.7) that the class of slaves is improved only by punishment.

[5b] Against

[iii] Punishment does not control the soul. But no one can be made morally serious except by being transformed in soul. Therefore, etc.

[5c. An Additional Question]

[iv] Moreover, I ask why in the civic sphere there is punishment only for the purpose of correction, while in the divine it is for many other causes.

[5d] Solution

We have to say that punishment makes someone morally serious, not by immediately and *per se* transforming the soul through inducing a habit, but because it draws him back from an evil deed, and thus, according as {781A} habituation to an evil deed is eliminated and he becomes accustomed to doing good ones, what he has become accustomed to will please him. From such acts, when they begin to be pleasing, a habit will be generated.

[5e. Replies to the Opening Arguments]

[i–iii] From this the solution to the first three is clear.

[iv] To the last we have to say that God sees into the heart. Because of this he ordains punishment for some things that are hidden, to which the civil judge (who judges only by appearances, that is, by deeds) cannot attend.

[6. Does Everyone Need Law?]

[6a. It Seems Not]

Sixth, it seems that not everyone needs law.

[i] For ordering pertains to law. But it does not pertain to the wise to be ordered. Therefore, etc.

[ii] Moreover, the 'animate just' [i.e., a judge; V 4, 1132a21–22] is just *per se*. But what is right *per se* does not need something else to make it right. Therefore, etc.

[iii] Moreover, Romans [rather, 1 Timothy 1:9]: 'A law is not imposed on the just.'

[6b. A Further Question]

[iv] Moreover, I ask, if everyone needs law, what are the different ways in which it is needed by a bad person, a child being raised, a just person, and a judge?

[6c] Solution

We have to say that law can be considered in two ways: either as it is a chain binding, as it were coercively, to acting well – and so considered it is not needed by the just but by those who are to be corrected or forced to virtuous deeds; or it can be considered inasmuch as it is something that regulates – and so considered it is needed by all. For this reason, the Apostle says of the just that 'they are a law unto themselves.' For although judges are put in the place of justice itself, so that we may measure our acts by their judgment, as we would do if there were a self-subsistent (*separata*) justice, yet they themselves are just by participating in justice. Because of this both their own acts and those of others must be measured by the rule of justice that they have. Similar reasoning applies to the wise.

[6d. Replies to the Opening Arguments]

[i–iii] From this the solution to the first three is clear.

[6e. Reply to the Further Question]

[iv] We have to say to the last that a bad person needs law so that he may be punished or moved away from evil; children, however, to restrain them from the passions to which their age is subject; the just so that they may regulate their acts by it; and the judge and the wise so that they may regulate themselves and others.

[7. Should Virtuous Activity Be Rewarded?]

[7a. It Seems Not]

Seventh, it seems that a reward ought not to be given for virtuous activity. {781B}

[i] For when a reward is [already] attached to something, it ought not to be rewarded further. But the greatest reward is attached to virtuous activity, because it acts for the sake of its own good, as has often been said. Therefore, it ought not to be rewarded again.

[ii] Moreover, Augustine says (*Confessions* I 12) that every inordinate spirit is itself a punishment to itself. Therefore, no one who is bad ought to be punished further.

[iii] Moreover, no one ought to pay more in punishment than what he is guilty of committing. But no one is so guilty in sinning as to be forced to pay with the loss of his life. Therefore, it seems that this punishment is unjust.

[iv] Moreover, punishment exists only for the correction of conduct, as medicine exists for the sake of health. But medicine does not prescribe being killed for any sickness. Neither, therefore, ought anyone to be punished by being killed.

[7b] Solution

We have to say that although the virtuous do not act for the sake of another, more external good, yet because the kind of reward they have in the act of virtue itself is not felt by those who are not virtuous the virtuous should for this reason also be given external goods as a reward, so that others may be incited to acting well ([a course] from which they are held back because of its difficulty). Likewise, not everyone feels the punishment of a disordered soul. For this reason an external punishment needs to be applied.

[7c. Replies to the Opening Arguments]

[i, ii] From this the solution to the first two is clear.

[iii] To the third we have to say that although considered in itself no one's guilt is equivalent to the punishment of being killed, yet according as one person's fault affects the whole community by tending to the

dissolution of civility and good conduct, the penalty due could not be paid by a thousand deaths.

[iv] To the fourth we have to say that one human being in a city is analogous to a limb. As a result, just as the physician amputates an incurable limb lest the body be corrupted, so too the judge cuts off one pestiferous [individual] lest the whole city be corrupted.

[8. Should Punishment Always Be by Contraries?]

[8a. It Seems Not]

Eighth, it seems that punishment ought not always to be administered by contraries.

For many sins are punished by one punishment. But one thing cannot be contrary to many. Therefore, etc.

Moreover, punishments are quite frequently commuted, {782A} especially in the judgment of souls in theology. But contraries are not commuted. Therefore, etc.

[8b] For the Opposite

Bede (rather, Pseudo-Jerome, commenting on Mark 9:28) says that what cures the eye does not cure the heel. He means that every sin whatever has its proper medicine. Therefore, since medicine works by contraries, etc.

Moreover, a punishment is inflicted for correction. But the bad can only be improved by a contrary habit. Therefore, etc.

[8c] Solution

We have to say that vice is cured in two ways. The first is when that which directly causes it is removed, as when the opportunity for sex is taken from a lecher. Sometimes, however, vice is cured when something that provides an occasion for it is taken away, as when someone emboldened by wealth gives himself to lasciviousness and other evils and is cured when his wealth is curtailed. Because of this, since punishment exists to cure vices, it will be by contraries when that which is *per se* the cause [of vice] is withdrawn, but it admits of commutation when that which was occasionally the cause is removed.

From this the solution to the whole question is clear. . . .

Lesson 18

{783B} 'If, therefore, in whatever way' [1180a14].

Now that he has shown the need to live according to a law having coercive force, he shows what something of this sort is.

About this, I raise doubts on six points.

[1. What Does Aristotle Mean by 'Devices'?]

First, what does he mean by 'devices' (*adinventiones*)?

[1a] It Seems that It Is Not Necessary to Live by Devices

[i] For that which is infinite cannot provide rules in life. But devices are potentially infinite. Therefore, etc.

[ii] Moreover, as Justinian says (*Digest* I, *lex* 1, n. 7), there are five things that direct us in morals, namely, law, {784A} plebiscites, resolutions of the senate, decisions of rulers, and edicts of magistrates. But none of these is a device. Therefore, a device does not provide rules.

[iii] Moreover, natural law chiefly provides rules for life in relation to blessedness. But such a law is not devised (*adinventum*). Therefore, etc.

[iv] Moreover, no device can eliminate all violence and ignorance. But these two are the causes of involuntariness. Therefore, it seems false to say that someone living by devices does not act wickedly either willingly or unwillingly.

[1b] Solution

We have to say that 'device' is sometimes taken in a good sense, sometimes in a bad. For certain devices are bad, namely, when from their own conceiving people discover some new way of sinning, either against themselves or against others. The Psalm (81:12) says about those who do this that 'They will go on in their own devices.' The expression 'morally serious devices' (*adinventionibus studiosis* [1180a14; 'worthy occupations,' Barnes]) refers, however, to a particular determination of reason for living well, according as we think out some rule for right living for ourselves or others.

[1c. Replies to the Opening Arguments]

[i] To the first we therefore have to say that although devices are infinite with respect to all particular cases, yet their rationales are finite and determinate.

[ii] To the second we have to say that all five of these are particular devices, and they only differ with respect to differences in those devising them.

[iii] To the third we have to say that although natural law is not something devised by opinion (which is about particular cases or conclusions in matters of conduct), yet it is a discovery (*inventio*) of the understanding, just as universal principles in speculative matters are certain conceptions of the understanding.

[iv] To the fourth we have to say that what is done involuntarily due to violence is excused completely, and as to this no one sins. Now what is involuntary due to ignorance is also excused, if it is ignorance of fact or even ignorance of a particular law before its enactment has been published. But ignorance of natural law or of a universal law that is close to natural is not excused. Thus it is clear {784B} that the legislator eliminates both voluntary and involuntary sinning.

[2. Is It Only a King's Word that Has Coercive Power?]

[2a. It Seems Not]

Second, it seems that it is not only a king's word (*sermo*) that has coercive power.

[i] For he says in the text that as laws are in cities, so is the father's word in the home. But laws in cities have coercive power. Therefore, also the father's word.

[ii] Moreover, he said in Book VIII (10, 1160b24–25) that in domestic matters the father is like a king in cities. Therefore, etc.

[iii] Moreover, men of the common people are not kings, nor, likewise, are the prudent. But plebiscites and the *responsa* of the prudent have coercive power. Therefore, etc.

[iv] Moreover, in a timocracy many rule who are not kings and yet they have coercive power.

[v] Moreover, anyone at all can establish with another a law of living. But law has coercive power. Therefore, the same.

[vi] Moreover, it seems that correction by something other than the law does not arouse hatred, because reason itself proves to those who act badly that what they do is shameful. Therefore, someone who argues with them about what is shameful does not move them to hatred.

[vii] Moreover, the Commentator's [Michael of Ephesus'] reasoning seems invalid when he says that legal correction does not arouse hatred because the law was enacted many years ago and hence cannot seem to those who are sinning to have been enacted on their account. By that reasoning, it seems that if a new law is passed it cannot correct anyone without arousing hatred.

[2b] Solution

We have to say that no one's word has sufficient coercive power except that of a king or someone who holds a king's place in a multitude, such as a senator or praetor.

[2c. Replies to the Opening Arguments]

[i] To the first we therefore have to say that the Commentator resolves that contradiction in two ways. The first is by proposing that when it is said that paternal command does not have compulsory force this is meant with respect to {785A} a defiant son, whereas what he says later (that it has the force of law) is meant with respect to a good son, who reverently obeys his father as a king. Alternatively, he proposes that the father does indeed have some coercive power in the home but that it is insufficient, since out of natural love he may conceal his son's offenses even when he should be put to the sword. That is why in legal proceedings (cf. Justinian, *Digest* V, t. 1, *lex* 77) a father is not allowed to be judge in a criminal case involving his son, although he can be judge in a civil case involving him.

[ii] To the second we have to say that although a father has some likeness to a king in the singularity of his rule, he nevertheless does not have

perfectly compulsory force as does a king, in whom there resides full power (*tota potestas*).

[iii] To the third we have to say that the common people and the wise can indeed make laws materially, but these do not have the form of law and compulsory force except from being confirmed by the ruler.

[iv] To the fourth we have to say that in a timocracy, many have the place of one king. As a result they can make laws just as a king can.

[v] To the fifth we have to say the same as to the third.

[vi] To the sixth we have to say that reason is darkened in those whose affection is caught up in their own wickedness, so that they do not recognize the evil they are doing. Because of this, they manage to think that those who correct them do so from hatred.

[vii] To the seventh we have to say that it is not only from the antiquity of its date that legal correction does not arouse hatred but also from its universality, because it is not imposed on one [individual] but on all equally.

[3. Is Aristotle's Definition of Law Adequate?]

[3a. It Seems Not]

Third, it seems that the definition of law he lays down ('law is a discourse existing on the basis of a certain prudence or understanding and having coercive force') is inadequate.

[i] For Justinian says (*Institutes* I, t. 1, sect. 3) that only that is law which the Roman people enact, with a senator proposing as one governing and the people consenting. But this definition does not mention coercion. Therefore, it seems that it ought not to have been mentioned here either.

[ii] Moreover, nothing can proceed from two habits. But understanding and prudence are two different habits, as was said in Book VI (8, 1142a23–30). Therefore, it does not seem that law exists on the basis of understanding and prudence.

[iii] Moreover, understanding is of things that are necessary, as {785B} was said in Book VI (6, 1141a7–8). But law is laid down about contingent cases. Therefore, it is not based on understanding.

[iv] Moreover, Tully (rather, Stephen of Tornai, *Summa decretorum*, ad d. 1, c. 3) defines law as 'what is right, written down, approving the morally

honorable and prohibiting the contrary.' There is no mention of coercion in this either. Therefore, etc.

[v] Moreover, every right [i.e., every body of norms determining what is right or just] has certain laws. But there exists a right that is natural; therefore, it must have laws. But natural law does not compel. Therefore, neither ought it to be defined by coercive power.

[3b] Solution

We have to say that the definition of law Aristotle lays down here is quite adequate. For in it he posits the substance of law (what is material in it and, as it were, its genus) in saying that it is 'a discourse.' He also posits its form (in accordance with which it has the character of law), for law is a rule of living directing toward the end of life, and he touches on this when he says 'based on prudence,' because it belongs to prudence to set forth an end in conduct and to direct to it, as was said in Book VI (13, 1145a4–6). He also posits its way of bringing [us] to the end (in which there is also an explanation of its name, for law [*lex*] is so called from binding [*ligando*]) when he says that 'it has coercive force.'

[3c. Replies to the Opening Arguments]

[i] To the first we therefore have to say that Justinian's definition is not given as a statement of law's essence but only indicates the way of establishing a law – and that [only] for a particular time and place, for since the Roman people used to have a monarchy, it belonged to it to make the law by which all might be ruled.

[ii] To the second we have to say that in matters of action there is understanding with regard to principles and prudence with regard to what are, as it were, conclusions. Now it is not inappropriate for something that is one to be produced from a habit pertaining to principles and [another habit] pertaining to conclusions.

[iii] To the third we have to say either that he takes understanding here otherwise than he did in Book VI (as is clear from what has already been said) or that although universals are necessary even in matters of action, the particular cases handled under them are contingent, and law is laid down about these.

[iv] To the fourth we have to say that Tully does not touch on the

essence of law but only its end. Again, when he says that law is written right, he defines it as taken more narrowly than Aristotle, who says that it does not matter to the being of law whether it is written or unwritten but that its being written is of advantage for the government of later generations. {786A}

[v] To the fifth we have to say that natural right only has law materially, for it gets the form of law from being established by the rulers of the commonwealth.

[4. Are Laws Needed for the Raising of Children?]

[4a. It Seems Not]

Fourth, it does not seem that laws are needed for the raising of children.

[i] For a law ought not to be made about anything except those things for which people are taken to court. But no one is taken to court for raising a child in this way or that. Therefore, etc.

[ii] Moreover, laws direct only according to the virtue of justice. But child rearing must aim at inculcating every virtue whatever. Therefore, it does not seem to fall under the direction of law.

[iii] Moreover, direction by laws only occurs in distributions and in contracts about exchange. There is nothing of this sort in raising children. Therefore, etc.

[4b] Solution

We have to say that in the raising of children, certain things must be attended to for the children's physical health (for example, that the child be suckled by a nurse who is of similar makeup to its mother), and as to this the raising of children is not subject to civil laws but to the laws of medicine. Certain things must be attended to, however, for good habituation in the virtues, and there is no doubt that these should be ordered by laws. But the laws considered by philosophers are different from forensic laws, which provide direction in cases coming to judgment in court. The raising of children is not directed by these. But philosophers consider laws in their order to happiness in accordance with all the acts of the virtues. For this reason even the raising of children is directed by such laws (as, for example, Plato teaches [*Timaeus* 19A] that children's behavior should be observed and they should be assigned those studies to which they apply themselves on their own, because they will be more proficient in these).

[4c. Replies to the Opening Arguments]

[i, ii] The solution to the first and second is clear from this, because legal justice is common to every virtue.

[iii] Similarly also to the third, which is concerned with forensic laws.

[5. Are There Bad Laws?]

[5a. It Seems Not]

Fifth, it seems that no law can be bad.

For in the definition of law it is laid down that it approves {786B} what is morally honorable and prohibits the contrary. Now all such things are good. Therefore, etc.

Moreover, everything that conduces to a good end is good. But every law is like this, because the legislator's intention is to make the citizens good. Therefore, etc.

Moreover, nothing is commanded, as the theologians say, except acts of virtue. But law is a kind of command. Therefore, it only concerns acts of virtue. Thus every law seems to be good.

Moreover, a rule (*regula*, a rod for drawing a straight line) of life cannot be crooked, or nothing in life would remain right (*rectum*, straight). But law is a kind of rule of living. Therefore, etc.

Moreover, everything done in accordance with prudence is good. But law is a discourse based on a certain prudence, as he says. Therefore, etc.

[5b] Against

Isaiah 10:1: 'Woe to those who make wicked laws.'

Moreover, it happens that there are laws in accordance with every polity. But some polities are corrupt. Therefore, etc.

[5c] Solution

We have to say that a law can be considered in two ways: either materially, as it is a particular edict, and thus there can be good laws and bad ones; or formally, according as it is an edict informed by prudence and directing life to its due end, and thus it is always good.

From this the solution to the whole question is clear.

[6. Should Laws Be Promulgated about Particular Cases?]

[6a. It Seems Not]

Sixth, it seems that laws should not be promulgated about particulars but about common matters.

For particulars are infinite, and hence there cannot be an orderly study of them. Therefore, etc.

Moreover, he said in Book V (10, 1137b24–27) that the equitable are better than the just, inasmuch as they know how to make determinations with regard to particulars. But there would be no difference in this respect if laws, which direct the just, were promulgated about particulars. Therefore, etc.

Moreover, everything that gives general direction is universal and universally propounded. Therefore, etc.

Moreover, whatever is valid for one and for another seems to be universal. But law is like this. Therefore, etc.

[6b] Against

Proper care should be adapted to each [thing], as he says in the text. But proper care is taken by means of the laws, as he also says. Therefore, it seems that laws ought to be promulgated about particulars. {787A}

Moreover, someone who has experience cares for things better than someone who has art without experience, as he says in the beginning of the *Metaphysics* (I 1, 981a21–23). But experience is about particulars. Therefore, since particular care is taken by the laws of the soul itself, it seems that they ought to be promulgated about particulars.

[6c] Solution

We have to say that to proceed perfectly in sciences of action one must know both the universal and the particular. For if one knew only the particular, then one would not know the reasons for one's action but would act in the same way as fire burns. Again, if one knew only the universal, one could not apply it in an action, since activity is about particulars. Because of this, laws need to be promulgated about common matters that are nevertheless applicable to particulars, even if not in one and the same way. Because of this there must be equity, which operates in the manner of [the flexible, leaden ruler used in] building on Lesbos, as he said in Book V (10, 1137b29–31); and if a law is promulgated in some particular case, it is understood as having universal force, in the sense that it applies in all similar cases.

From this the solution to the whole question is clear. . . .

Lesson 19

{788B} 'Therefore, after this' [1180b28].

After Aristotle has shown the necessity for legislation, here he shows how one can become a legislator, so as to make a connection in this way with the teaching that follows [i.e., the *Politics*].

I ask seven questions about this part.

[1. Is Politics a Single Science?]

[1a. It Seems Not]

First, it seems that politics is not a single science.

[i] For no one science includes both making and doing (*factualia et actualia*), since for each of these there is a different habit. But politics includes both, because it directs both the virtues, whose activities are doings (*actuales*), and the arts, whose activities are makings (*factuales*), as was said at the beginning of Book I (1, 1094a1–b12). Therefore, etc.

[ii] Moreover, there is no science in which {789A} use is separated from teaching, because no one makes use of a thing who does not have it. But this happens in political [science], because many use it without [prior] teaching, as he says in the text. Therefore, it is not a science.

[iii] Moreover, the characteristics of cities (*urbanitates*) are many – such as kingship, aristocracy, timocracy, and their corruptions – and these are not reducible to one another. Therefore, since politics considers all of them, it does not seem that it can be one science.

[1b] Against

A single scientific habit directs us to a single end, as, for example, medicine [directs us] to health. But the end of politics is one, namely, the human good. Therefore, etc.

Moreover, about the good of a single nature there is a single science. But there is a single human nature, whose good political [science] is about. Therefore, etc.

Moreover, he always speaks as if about one particular science.

[1c] Solution

We have to say that the character of a science fits some habits more primarily than others. Those are most truly called sciences in which we seek to know for the sake of knowing, such as natural science, metaphysics, and mathematics. Next there are those in which knowledge is sought to assist [in further knowing], such as dialectic. The character of a science fits least those in which we do not seek to know as an end, that is, for the sake of knowing, but for the sake of acting. As a result, these are not called sciences without qualification but practical sciences. Politics is among such sciences. We willingly concede that it is a single science – according as it is science.

[1d. Replies to the Opening Arguments]

[i] To the first we therefore have to say that politics only considers making in an order to doing, insofar, namely, as the things made by the arts come into the context of justice.

[ii] To the second we have to say that in sciences that are only sciences there cannot be use unless one has something of the science. But in those that are active there can be use – that is, acting – without teaching, although not perfect use. But the use that pertains to the science [as such] – namely, to consider the reasons for actions – cannot be engaged in without teaching, as is clear in medicine when an old woman heals without knowing the reasons involved in the art.

[iii] To the third we have to say that although polities are not reduced to one univocally, they are nevertheless reduced to one by analogy, because

the character of a polity is found in kingship primarily and in the others secondarily.

[2. Is Politics Subordinate to Ethics?]

[2a. It Seems that It Is]

{789B} Second, it seems that politics is subordinate to ethics (*morali*).

For any science that gets its 'because of which' (*propter quid*) from another science (as optics does from geometry) is subordinate to it. But politics gets its 'because of which' from ethics, which considers virtuous acts, the ends of which are the principles [of politics]. Therefore, etc.

Moreover, the whole of politics is ordered to happiness. But happiness is essentially the activity of some virtue and thus pertains to the consideration of ethics. Therefore, politics is under ethics as that which sets forth its end.

Moreover, if subject is under subject, science is also under science. But the human act of human beings in their civic existence, which someone concerned with politics considers, falls under the human act of humans insofar as they are human absolutely, which the ethicist considers. Therefore, etc.

Moreover, the human being is the principle of the household, and the household is the elementary unit of the city, as the Commentator [Eustratius] says. But the ethicist directs human beings in themselves, while someone concerned with politics directs them in the city. Therefore, ethics gives politics its principles. Therefore, etc.

[2b] Against

[i] A lower science never considers more things than a higher one, because more cannot be contained under the less common than under the more common. But politics considers many things that ethics does not consider, such as polities and many things of this sort. Therefore, etc.

[ii] Moreover, the most primary science does not seem to be under any other. But he said at the beginning (I 1, 1094a26–28) that politics was most primary (*principalissimam*). Therefore, etc.

[iii] Moreover, the good of a people is more divine than the good of a

single human being. But politics has as its end the good of a people, ethics the good of a human being. Therefore, it is more primary than ethics.

[2c] Solution

We have to say that politics is subordinate to ethics, and someone concerned with politics must get its 'because of which' from ethics. And we concede the arguments for this.

[2d. Replies to Objections to the Contrary]

[i] To the first objection to the contrary, on the other hand, we have to say that if we consider those things which pertain to the very nature under consideration, more things are considered in the subordinating science. Thus, geometry considers more features of lines insofar as they are lines than does optics. Nevertheless, certain things can be considered in the subordinate science that are not considered in the subordinating one. Thus, optics but {790A} not geometry is limited to considering a line insofar as it is visual, [but] as a result optics but not geometry considers what follows from being a line insofar as it is visual. Similarly, the human good or the human act, which ethics considers absolutely, is limited, when it is considered in politics, to what relates to a people or a city – but on that side politics considers certain things that ethics does not.

[ii] To the second we have to say that politics is said to be most primary with respect to the mechanical arts, which it directs in relation to the tasks of the city, but not with respect to ethics.

[iii] To the third we have to say that ethics considers human good absolutely. But it is true that some divinity comes to it insofar as it specifically regards a people.

[3. Is Legislation the Whole of Politics?]

[3a. It Seems that It Is]

Third, it seems that legislation *is* politics, not a part of it.

[i] For laws are laid down about everything political. But all laws pertain to legislation. Therefore, they seem to be of equal scope.

[ii] Moreover, in Book I (2, 1094a28–b6) he said about politics ((*poli-*

tica/politico)) that it determines who ought to be assigned which tasks. Likewise he also said above that legislation directs the rearing of children. Therefore, it seems that they are the same.

[iii] Moreover, laws are a kind of principle in civic matters. But principles have a universal influence on everything that follows. Therefore, it seems that legislation is universal in relation to the whole of political affairs.

[3b] Against

Someone concerned with politics must consider what a polity is and what its parts and their differentiae are. But laws are not made about these. Legislation is therefore [only] a part of politics.

Moreover, politics is a concern for all who are part of civic life, but legislation is not. It is therefore a part, which concerns only those who are in charge of others (*rectoribus*). Therefore, etc.

Moreover, Tully (in the *Paradoxes* and in the book *On Duties*) and many others have imparted certain things concerning politics in which, nevertheless, laws are not included. Therefore, it seems that politics consists of more than legislation.

Moreover, a thing and a right relating to it are not the same. But legislation treats the right relating to politics. Therefore, they do not seem to be the same.

[3c] Solution

We have to say that legislation is a part of politics. For it belongs to politics to consider not only {790B} civic acts but also the species and differentiae of polities, but legislation only gives universal directives, albeit directives bearing on all civic acts.

[3d. Replies to the Opening Arguments]

[i] To the first we therefore have to say that laws are laid down about all political acts but not for knowing about polities and things of that sort.

[ii] To the second we have to say that although they have the rearing of the young in common, yet in certain other matters politics has a broader scope.

[iii] To the third we have to say, as was said in Book VII (3, 1147a25–28), that in matters of action the conclusions are deeds. As a result, it

cannot be concluded from the fact that laws are principles that they have a universal influence on all civic matters.

[4. Should Aristotle Have Connected Politics with Household Management?]

[4a. It Seems that He Should Have]

Fourth, it seems that he ought to have connected this science with [the science of] household management (*oeconomicam*).

For just as human beings need to be ordered in themselves and in civic affairs, so too as they live in a household, since there are some acts which pertain to them in this respect. But human acts are not ordered in this respect by either ethics or politics. Therefore, it seems that these two are not sufficient and that there must be [a science of] household management.

Moreover, household management is closer to ethics than politics is, because a human being is an elementary part of the household. Therefore, he ought to have put household management before [politics].

Moreover, the consideration of human beings as conjugal is prior to the consideration of them as civic, because it is more common. But household management considers the acts of human beings insofar as they are conjugal. Therefore, etc.

[4b] Against

That which is derived by likeness from something else must be discussed after it. But the government of the household is gathered by likeness from that of the city, as he said in Book VIII (10, 1160b22–1161a9). Therefore, etc.

Moreover, what is more sufficient for attaining an end is prior and worthier. But the law's command is more effective in making human beings morally serious than that of a father. Therefore, etc.

[4c] Solution

We have to say that without doubt the philosophy of things human in these two sciences – namely, politics and ethics – is not sufficient, but there must [also] be a [science of] household management. It is indeed [logically] posterior in order to politics, inasmuch as the government of the household is gathered by likeness from that of the city, in which the perfect character of government is found. Nevertheless, in the natural order the household is prior {791A} to the city. Aristotle does not observe nature's order but an order for teaching.

From this the solution to the whole question is clear.

[5. Is Politics the Same as Rhetoric?]

[5a. It Seems that It Is]

Fifth, it seems that politics is the same as rhetoric.

[i] For as the Philosopher says in *De anima* III (rather, Averroes, comment 38 on *De anima* III), those things are the same whose differentiae are the same. But Tully divides rhetoric using the same three kinds of cases by which he divides politics or legislation (*De inventione* I 5–7). Therefore, etc.

[ii] Moreover, where there is one instrument there is one art, because every art uses its own instrument, as is said in *De anima* I (3, 407b25–26). But rhetoricians and those concerned with politics use the same syllogism, namely, one drawn from the circumstances of the matter or of the person concerned or according to other differentiae. Therefore, etc.

[iii] Moreover, those habits are the same the activity of which is the same. But to accuse or defend pertains to the rhetorician and likewise to legislation. Therefore, it seems that they are the same.

[5b] Against

Boethius says (*De differentiis topicis* IV) that the whole of what can be spoken of is matter for the rhetorician. But not everything that can be spoken of is matter for politics. Therefore, etc.

Moreover, rhetoric is one of the seven liberal [arts] and is an art of language. Politics, however, is not. Therefore, etc.

[5c] Solution

We have to say that politics and rhetoric are not the same science, nor is one a part of the other, because politics is a science of action but rhetoric is an art of language.

[5d. Replies to the Opening Arguments]

[i] To the first we therefore have to say that in the division of rhetoric by kinds of cases, these are not essential parts but are rather where rhetorical language is more frequently used. In the same way, if demonstration were divided into geometry and arithmetic, into which mathematics is divided, it would not follow that it was the same as mathematics, because it is part of logic.

[ii] To the second we have to say that the rhetorician uses the syllogism in instruction, but those concerned with politics apply it to a specific subject-matter, just as geometry uses the demonstrative syllogism.

[iii] To the third we have to say that to accuse and {791B} defend is not the proper act of rhetoric except insofar as rhetoric is more frequently used in such matters.

[6. Is It Appropriate for Those Not Engaged in Politics to Teach the Subject?]

[6a. It Seems that It Is]

Sixth, it seems that the mode of teaching used by those who imparted political [knowledge] without being active is appropriate.

[i] For to teach theoretically is a proper mode of teaching, because it pertains to one who knows (*scientis*) to be able to teach. But [those whom Aristotle is criticizing] were teaching theoretically. Therefore, they were teaching appropriately.

[ii] Moreover, Avicenna says that a science is not called practical because it acts but because it considers how things should be done in terms of the reasons for actions. But although they were not engaged in action they used to teach how things should be done. Therefore, etc.

[iii] Moreover, practical science is a kind of science. But politics is a practical science; therefore it is also a science. Therefore, it is adequately taught if someone makes another person know (*scire*), even without acting.

[6b] Against

To know a habit perfectly one must be able to apply it to that which it is about. But political science exists for the end of being good. Now this end cannot be attained except by becoming active through experience.

Therefore, it seems that those who taught without experience teach imperfectly.

Moreover, as the Philosopher says (cf. III 3, 1113a2) deliberative discourse (*verba*) requires [consideration of?] the unlimited, and that discourse is called deliberative which pertains to choice. But political knowing is a kind of deliberative discourse. Therefore it requires [consideration of?] the unlimited that is characteristic of making. But those who lacked experience did not know how to make anyone political. Therefore, it seems that they did not know politics and thus did not teach it suitably.

[6c] Solution

We have to say that in sciences of action, where knowledge is sought only for the sake of action, one does not have perfect command of the science when one knows the universal reasons for actions unless one also knows how to apply them to particular acts. It is impossible to know this, however, except from experience. As a result, it is clear that those who are not experienced in civic matters cannot be concerned with politics or have a perfect command of political science, because to be concerned with politics is {792A} to be in a certain way active, and because one can teach only what one knows. On this account, such inexperienced individuals were unable to teach politics perfectly. That is why they made no effort to teach how law might be applied to action but only used to teach certain collections of laws and how to choose those more useful to the case at hand, which pertained rather to a rhetorician than to someone concerned with civic matters.

[6d. Replies to the Opening Arguments]

[i] To the first we therefore have to say that teaching theoretically is the mode appropriate to a science in which one seeks to know for the sake of knowing.

[ii] To the second we have to say that in order to become practical in the manner of someone concerned with politics, it is not enough to know the reasons for actions unless they can be applied to action. But it is true that the reasons for actions are sought in certain sciences of action more than in others insofar as there is something beautiful to know in them, as in medicine. In politics, however, there is nothing great to know apart from its being put into action.

[iii] To the third we have to say that insofar as it is a practical science it

requires a mode of teaching that it does not require insofar as it is [simply] a science.

[7. Should Such Imperfect Teachers Be Called Sophists?]

[7a. It Seems Not]

Seventh, it seems that such imperfect teachers should not be called sophists. {792B}

For those are called sophists who deceive by using some sophistical commonplace. But they were not using anything sophistically to deceive, because they were teaching what was true. Therefore, etc.

Moreover, a sophist is so called on another basis: one who falls short in proof – as a dialectician using syllogisms in matters of demonstration. But this is not relevant here, because politics does not use the demonstrative syllogism. Therefore, such [teachers] can in no way be called sophists.

[7b] Solution

We have to say that they are called sophists from likeness to the act of a sophist. For the sophist promises wisdom without having it, since he overflows with an apparent but unreal wisdom (cf. *De sophisticis elenchis* 1, 165a21). Likewise, they claim to have the political habit and to convey it to others, although they cannot do it.

BONAVENTURE
CONSCIENCE AND SYNDERESIS

Introduction

Bonaventure was born John of Fidanza in Bagnoregio in Tuscany around 1217. He took the name Bonaventure on entering the Franciscan order in 1243, after completing studies at Paris for the Master of Arts degree. He studied theology with the major Franciscan masters at Paris 1243–48, lectured there on the *Sentences* of Peter Lombard from 1250 to 1252, and taught as the Franciscan regent master at Paris until he was elected Minister General of the order in 1257, a position he held until his death in 1274. He was made Cardinal Bishop of Albano in 1273 and participated in the Second Council of Lyons the following year. Bonaventure's disposition prompted some to declare that in him it seemed as if Adam had not sinned. He nevertheless earned the enmity of many of his confreres, who contended that it was imperative for Franciscans to follow a rigorously poor style of life and one innocent of academic culture. Bonaventure defended the importance of university studies against these members of his order and justified a rule of life sufficiently relaxed to allow pursuit of such studies. He was considered a reactionary by some of his university colleagues, however, because of his antagonism to the growing dominance of the teachings of Aristotle. His most celebrated work is a compact synthesis of intellect and devotion, *The Journey of the Mind to God*. A similar fusion is evident in his discourses *On the Ten Commandments*, *On the Seven Gifts of the Holy Spirit*, and *On the Six Days of Creation*. Bonaventure's most purely academic work is his *Sentences* commentary, from which the present selection is taken.

The medieval treatment of conscience and synderesis as distinct moral capacities originated in a misunderstanding of Jerome's fifth-century commentary on the book of Ezekiel. '*Synderesis*' is the transliteration of a Greek term exactly parallel with Latin '*conscientia*,' and in referring to 'what the Greeks called "*synteresis*"' as the spark of conscience Jerome intended no distinction between the two. The misunderstanding was a fruitful one, however, for it stimulated finely discriminating discussions of moral knowledge and motivation. Bonaventure's own contribution is marked by an unusually clear distinction between the cognitive and affective dimensions of morality, a distinction which allowed him to maintain both that there is moral knowledge – partly innate, partly acquired – and that making sense of our moral life also requires positing an inextinguishable although far from invincible impulse toward the good. Bonaventure is typical of contemporary scholastic teaching in holding that it is always a sin to act against one's conscience. He is somewhat less lenient than Aquinas in dealing with the case of a mistaken conscience. His conclusion that one ought (in conscience) to comply more with the command of a superior than with one's own conscience, especially when superiors command what they can and ought to command, is implicitly contested by Ockham in Translation 15.

We omit the consideration of additional problems posed by Lombard's text which Bonaventure adds to his discussion of the main issues.

For further reading on this subject, see CHLMP IX.36, 'Conscience,' and Douglas Langston, 'The Spark of Conscience: Bonaventure's View of Conscience and Synderesis,' *Franciscan Studies*, 53 (1993):79–95. On Bonaventure, see Bonnie Kent, 'Bonaventure,' in Edward Craig, ed., *The Routledge Encyclopedia of Philosophy*, vol. I (London and New York: Routledge, 1998), pp. 828–35.

Conscience and Synderesis

Article 1. Conscience

{898A} For an understanding of this part [of the *Sentences* of Peter Lombard], I raise questions on two topics. I ask first about conscience, which is a certain directive rule of the will. Second, I ask about synderesis, which is called the spark of conscience. About the first, there are three questions. First, about conscience with reference to its subject: Is it in the cognitive or the affective part [of the soul]? Second, with reference to its origin: Does it exist by nature or is it acquired? Third, with reference to its effect: Does every conscience obligate?

Question 1. Does Conscience Reside in Understanding or in Affect?

We proceed to the first question: Does conscience reside in understanding or in affect?

[1. Preliminary Arguments]

[1a. Arguments that Conscience Resides in Understanding]

It seems that it resides in understanding.

[i] First from the text of Ecclesiastes 7:22: 'Your conscience knows that you yourself have often cursed others.' But knowing is an act proper to a cognitive power. Therefore, if knowing belongs to conscience, conscience is on the the cognitive side.

[ii] Again, Damascene says (*De fide orthodoxa* IV 22) that conscience is the law of our understanding. But only Scripture, which directly respects the understanding, is called a law of the understanding. Therefore, conscience resides in understanding.

[iii] Again, every knowing (*scientia*) is on the side of understanding. Every [act of] conscience (*conscientia*) is a knowing. Therefore, every [act of] conscience is on the side of understanding. The major proposition is obvious *per se*. The minor is proved: Everyone aware (*conscius*) of something is a knower (*sciens*) of it. Therefore, on the basis of the elements combined in the term, every [act of] conscience is a knowing.

[iv] Again, conscience is divided into right and erroneous. But being erroneous relates to a habit or act of understanding. Therefore, if what is divided and what divides it pertain to the same power of the soul, it seems that conscience resides in a cognitive power.

[v] Again, the same thing is shown by its acts. For to read, judge, direct, witness, and argue are all acts pertaining to cognition. {898B} But all these acts are attributed to conscience, for conscience is a book in which we read, conscience also judges inwardly, conscience witnesses, conscience argues, and conscience rules and directs. Therefore, it seems that conscience is wholly on the cognitive side, since acts and their habits belong to the same power.

[1b] *Against*

[i] If conscience is on the cognitive side, it is as either a power, a passion, or a habit. Not as a passion, because passions relate especially to the affective; nor as a habit, because conscience is sometimes pure and at other times impure, but no habit is transformed from purity to impurity or conversely. It remains, then, that if conscience is on the cognitive side, it will be nothing other than the cognitive power. Therefore, if the cognitive power is concerned with everything – not only with what can be done but also with what can be contemplated – it seems that conscience will extend not only to moral matters but also to things taught in the various disciplines, which is obviously false.

[ii] Again, as understanding is to the true, so is affect to the good. Therefore, if there is anything whose perfection consists in goodness, it will pertain more to good affect than to understanding. But conscience is like this, for the Apostle says in 1 Timothy 1:5, 'Love (*caritas*) issues from the heart {899A} and from a good conscience'; and again in the same epistle (1:18–19): 'that you may fight the good fight, having faith and a good conscience.' Therefore, etc.

[iii] Again, the law of the flesh fights against the law of the mind, as Damascene says (*De fide orthodoxa* VI 2). But the law of the flesh resides in a motive [power]. Therefore, so does the law of the mind. But conscience is the law of the mind, as Damascene said above. Therefore, conscience is on the side of the affective.

[iv] Again, remorse is the act of an affective power, for wherever there is remorse, there is a certain grief and passion. But being remorseful belongs to conscience, as is said concerning the verse in 1 Corinthians 4: 4, 'I am aware of nothing [against myself].' The Gloss: 'My conscience afflicts me with remorse in nothing.' Therefore, it seems that conscience is on the side of the affective.

[v] Again, the pleasant and the painful reside in an affective power. But we have pain and joy from the side of conscience; hence the damned will be in great pain from the gnawing worm of conscience. It therefore seems that conscience resides in an affective power, not a cognitive one.

[2. Conclusion: Conscience Is a Habit of a Cognitive Power insofar as the Latter Is Practical, Not insofar as It Is Speculative]

I answer. To understand the preceding, it is important to note that, just as the term 'understanding' is sometimes taken for the power to understand, sometimes for a habit, and sometimes for a principle that is understood, so the term 'conscience' has customarily been taken in three senses by teachers of sacred Scripture. Sometimes it is taken for the thing of which one is aware, and it is in this sense that Damascene says it is the law of our understanding; for what we know by conscience is a law. Sometimes 'conscience' is taken for that by which we are aware, namely for a habit, just as {899B} 'knowledge' (*scientia*) is taken for a habit, namely, a habit of the knower (*cognoscentis*). Sometimes, however, 'conscience' is taken for the power to be aware, so to speak, as when it is said that the natural law is written in our consciences. Yet although the term 'conscience' is often taken in all three ways, it is more commonly taken for the habit, as is the term 'knowledge' from which it is constructed.

Therefore, if we ask of what power conscience is a habit, we have to say that it is a habit of a cognitive power, yet in a way different from speculative knowledge. Speculative knowledge is the perfection of our understanding insofar as it is speculative, whereas conscience is a habit perfecting our understanding insofar as it is practical or directs us in action. In a certain way, the understanding thus has the character of a mover, not because it effects movement, but because it dictates and inclines to movement. For this reason such a habit is not named 'knowledge' (*scientia*) without qualification but 'con-science' (*conscientia*), to signify that this habit does not perfect the speculative power in itself but as it is joined in a certain way to affection and activity. On this account we do not say that a dictate of conscience is a principle of the same kind as 'Every whole is greater than its part' or the like, but we do well to say that conscience dictates that God should be honored and similar principles, which are rules of things that should be done. Therefore we have to concede, as the arguments show, that conscience resides in a cognitive power, although not as the power is speculative but as it is practical. For as the Philosopher says, 'speculative' and 'practical' understanding refer to the same power and differ only in that to which it is extended. Nor should this at all be taken to mean that practical understanding is appetite or will, for the Philosopher himself denies this.

[3. Replies to the Preliminary Arguments 1b(i–v)]

[i] To the objection that conscience cannot be a cognitive power, passion, or habit we therefore have to say that {900A} the term can indeed name both a power and a habit. When it names a power, it does not name the cognitive power universally but as it is applied to knowing about conduct or morals. When it names a habit, it names not only a natural habit, but it can also name an acquired habit. And because an acquired habit can purify or defile the soul, conscience is called pure and impure, right and not right. Nevertheless, those differentiae relate to 'conscience' more as it stands for the name of a power than as it stands for the name of a habit.

[ii] To the objection that conscience is said to be good and bad, we have to say that goodness and badness relate not only to affect but also to practical understanding and its habit – in this respect, that practical understanding relates not only to the true but also extends to the good. Because conscience is the kind of judicatory that it is, it is good when it dictates and inclines to good and draws back and flees from evil. It does not follow because of this that conscience resides in an affective power. For something to be called good, it need not be affective in its essence; it is enough if it has a certain concomitance with will and affection.

[iii] To the objection that the law of the flesh is opposed to the law of the mind, we have to say with master Hugh of St. Victor (*De sacramentis* VII 34) that there is corruption in sensuality or in the outer man not only with respect {900B} to the moving and inclining power but also with respect to the sensory. Because of this, although the law of the flesh consists primarily in a wanting (*concupiscentia*) that inclines us to evil, it nevertheless presupposes a disordered representation of carnal things in fantasy and cognition. These two also occur in the law of the mind. Of itself, however, conscience is more directly opposed to the law of the flesh by reason of preceding cognition than by reason of the wanting.

[iv] To the objection from remorse, we have to say that conscience is said to be remorseful because when it shows something evil to an affect that is itself upright, it induces remorse, inasmuch as that affect kicks against the evil. As a result, remorse does not come from conscience as the primary mover but as dictating [what is good or evil]. With respect to its mover, remorse comes from the spark of conscience, synderesis. This will be made clearer later.

[v] To the objection that the painful and the pleasurable are on the side

of conscience, we have to say that they are not from conscience or in conscience except as in something disposing and dictating. For rejoicing and being sorrowful properly belong to affection. When a conscience that is a good witness testifies about a good deed that it is good and about an evil deed that it is evil, it generates sorrow or joy in affect. That is why the Apostle also says (2 Corinthians 1:12), 'This is our boast, the testimony of our conscience,' principally attributing to conscience itself not the passion of rejoicing but the act of testifying.

Question 2. Is Conscience an Innate or an Acquired Habit?

{901A} Second, is conscience an innate or an acquired habit?

[1. Preliminary Arguments]

[1a. *Arguments that Conscience Is Innate*]

It seems that it is an innate habit.

[i] Romans 2:14–15: 'When the gentiles who do not have the law do by nature what the law requires they are a law to themselves, because they show that the work of the law is written in their hearts, their conscience bearing witness to them.' And the Gloss there says that 'Even if the gentiles do not have the written law, yet they have the natural law, by which they are aware [of good and evil].' It is clear from the text and the Gloss, then, that conscience bespeaks a habit naturally inscribed in the human heart.

[ii] Again, Augustine in *On Free Choice* III (c. 20): 'It is no small thing to have received, before any merit from good deeds, a natural judicatory (*iudicatorium*; *iudicium* in Augustine) by which anyone may prefer wisdom to error and rest to difficulty.' Therefore, if conscience is a judicatory of this sort, then it is a habit innate in a human being.

[iii] Again, Isidore: 'Natural right is that which nature has taught animals.' Therefore, if nature has taught animals what belongs to natural right, much more has it taught human beings, who excel all animals. But the cognition of natural right is nothing other than conscience. Therefore, etc.

[iv] Again, we have a natural instinct to seek blessedness and honor

parents. {901B} But this cannot be without some prior cognition. Therefore it seems that some cognition is naturally impressed in us for doing such
things. But the cognition inclining to this is conscience. Therefore, etc.

[v] Again, human beings have some cognition of natural law; therefore [they have it] either by acquisition or by nature. If by acquisition,
then it ought not to be called natural but acquired, as is the case with the
political virtues. On the other hand, if it is by nature, and the cognition of
natural law is nothing other than conscience, therefore, etc.

[vi] Again, natural right binds the will naturally. But an act of cognition
necessarily precedes a binding of the will, for understanding precedes
affect. Therefore, if the will is bound to that law naturally, it seems that
the soul cognizes that law naturally. Therefore, if conscience is the cognition of that law, it is plain, etc.

[1b] Against

[i] The Philosopher says in *De anima* III (429b31–430a2) that the soul at
birth is like a blank tablet, on which nothing has been inscribed. It
therefore seems that in its first condition the soul has no innate cognition.
Therefore, if the habit of conscience implies cognition, it seems that it is
not innate but acquired.

[ii] Again, in the *Retractations* I (c. 8), {902A} Augustine retracts the
following, which he had said previously: 'The soul is created with knowledge, but burdened by the weight of the body it forgets the things it used
to know.' But he would not retract this unless he held it to be false.
Therefore according to Augustine it is false that the soul naturally has
cognition of what should be done. Therefore, it seems that if conscience
is this sort of cognitive habit, it is not innate but acquired.

[iii] Again, we have no cognition of the complex unless we have
cognition of the incomplex. That is why we do not have cognition of a
principle unless we have cognition of its terms. For this reason the Philosopher says (*Posterior Analytics* I 3, 72b23–25) that we cognize principles
insofar as we cognize their terms. But we do not have cognition of
incomplexes except by means of the senses – no one knows color except
by sight. Because of this, those who lose a sense necessarily lose knowledge. If all knowledge of incomplexes is by means of the senses, then, all
cognition of complexes is necessarily acquired and taken from sense. But
conscience is cognition of a complex, inasmuch as it is cognition of some

rule of natural right. Therefore, it seems that conscience is not an innate habit but an acquired one.

[iv] Again, things pertaining to conduct are as difficult or more difficult to know than those pertaining to simple contemplation. But the knowledge that is a cognitive habit relating to what can be contemplated is not innate in us but acquired. Therefore, there is equal reason to conclude that conscience, which is a habit directing us in what should be done, is also not innate but acquired.

[v] Again, every natural habit is always right. But conscience is sometimes right, sometimes erroneous. Therefore, conscience is not a natural habit but an acquired one.

[vi] Again, natural habits are present in everyone and at all times, because those things are natural which are the same for all and which go with a nature inseparably. But consciences are not the same in all. Instead, they are often opposed. Conscience is also not present in us at all times, because a human being often begins to have a conscience that was not there before. For example, as a result of entering a religious order one has a conscience that forbids acting against the counsels [of perfection], a conscience one did not have before. Therefore, etc. {902B}

[2. Conclusion: Conscience Is an Innate Habit by Reason of
Both an Inwardly Given Light in the Soul and Moral First
Principles. It Is, However, an Acquired Habit Both by
Reason of Its Cognizing Species and with Respect to
Particular Activities]

To understand the preceding, it is important to note that, besides the Platonic position, which asserts that all cognitive habits are without qualification innate in the soul but are forgotten at birth because of the weight of the body, a position which both the Philosopher and Augustine refute and reprove, there have been three opinions among the learned about the origin of cognitive habits. All three of these positions agree that just as habitual virtues are neither entirely natural nor entirely acquired but are in a certain way innate and in a certain way acquired, so too, cognitive habits are neither entirely innate nor entirely acquired but are in a certain way innate and in a certain way acquired. They differ, however, in assigning the ways in which these habits are innate and acquired.

Some have wanted to say that they are innate in the active understanding (*intellectui agenti*) but acquired as regards the possible understanding (*intellectum possibilem*) and that it is with reference to the latter that the Philosopher says that the soul is created like a bare tablet and has to be perfected by means of the sensory powers.

But this does not seem consonant either with the Philosopher's words or with truth. For if the active understanding had cognitive habits, why could it not communicate them to the possible understanding without help from the senses below? Again, if the active understanding had cognitive habits, the soul would not from its own initial condition be ignorant. Rather, it would be a knower. Along with this, it is also difficult to understand how species may be said to exist in the active understanding when the possible understanding is called that by which [the mind] becomes all things, the active that by which it makes all things.

For this reason, there is a second way of saying that cognitive habits are in a certain way innate, in a certain way acquired. [On this view] they are innate with regard to cognition {903A} of the universal, acquired with regard to cognition of the particular; or innate with regard to cognition of principles, acquired with regard to cognition of conclusions. As a result, worth (*dignitas*) is that which everyone approves once it has been presented (cf. Boethius, *De hebdomadibus*).

But that way of speaking is not consonant with what the Philosopher and Augustine say either. For the Philosopher proves in the *Posterior Analytics* (II 19, 99b25–27) that cognition of principles is not innate in us, deducing many awkward consequences [from the opposite view]. He shows there that cognition of principles is acquired by way of sense, memory, and experience. Augustine, too, in *On the Trinity* XII (c. 15), speaking of the boy who gave answers about all the principles of geometry, says that this was not because the boy's soul had known those things before, but rather, that he was seeing those things in a certain unique incorporeal light, as the fleshly eye sees things in front of it in physical light, having been created with a capacity for this light and congruent with it.

Accordingly, there is a third way of saying that cognitive habits are in a certain way innate in us and in a certain way acquired, speaking not only about the cognition of particulars and conclusions but also about the cognition of principles. For two things must necessarily concur for cognition to take place, namely, the presence of something cognizable and a light by which we make judgments about it (as we see in sight and as

Augustine indicates in the preceding text). Therefore, the cognitive habits are in a certain way innate in us by reason of an inwardly given light of the soul, and they are also in a certain way acquired, by reason of the species [i.e., the likenesses of things by which they are present to the knower]. Now this indeed agrees with what the Philosopher and Augustine say. For all agree in this, that there is an inwardly given light of the cognitive power, which is called a natural judicatory. We acquire the species and likenesses of things by means of sense, however, as the Philosopher says expressly in many places. Experience also teaches this, for no one would ever know whole or part or father or mother unless their species were acquired by some outer sense; and this is why those who lose a sense necessarily lose some knowledge. On the other hand, that light or natural judicatory directs the soul itself in making judgments both about things that can be cognized and things that can be done. {903B}

But we have to pay special attention to this. Just as some things that are cognizable are very clearly evident, such as axioms and first principles, while some are less evident, such as particular conclusions; so also in things that can be done, some are evident in the highest degree, for example, 'Do not do to another what you do not want done to you' and that one should submit to God and suchlike. In the same way, then, as the cognition of first principles is said to be innate in us by reason of that light, because (due to their self-evidence) that light suffices for cognizing them (after the reception of species) without any additional persuasion, so also the cognition of moral first principles is innate in us, in that that judicatory suffices for cognizing them. Again, in the same way as cognition of the particular conclusions of the sciences is acquired, because the light innate in us does not fully suffice for knowing them, but some persuasion and fuller acquaintance are needed, so on the side of things that can be done we must understand, similarly, that we are bound to do some things which we know only through additional instruction. Therefore, since 'conscience' names a habit that directs our judgment with respect to things that can be done, on this account it names a habit that is in a certain way innate and in a certain way acquired. I say that it names an innate habit with respect to things pertaining to the first dictate of nature; an acquired habit, on the other hand, with respect to those that come through additional instruction. It also refers to a habit that is innate with respect to the directive light but one that is nevertheless acquired with respect to the species of what can be cognized. For I have the natural light, which suffices for knowing that parents should be honored and neighbors should not be harmed, yet I do not have the species of a father or the species of a neighbor naturally impressed on me.

[3. Replies to the Preliminary Arguments]

Now that these points have been considered, the answer to the proposed question and the objections is plain. I concede that conscience refers to a habit that is in a certain way innate (namely, by reason of that 'light shining above us' which indeed 'shows us good things' [Psalm 4:6]) and that it is the seedbed for acquiring other habits. This is what the arguments introduced on the first side show. {904A} Nevertheless, I [also] concede that conscience is a habit that is in a certain way acquired (namely, by reason of the species of cognizables), as the first three arguments on the second side show. I also concede that it is in a certain way an acquired habit with respect to specific things that can be done, as the other three arguments show. If, however, there are cognizables that can be cognized through their own essence, not through species, then with respect to these it will be possible to call conscience a habit that is innate without qualification, as, for example, with respect to what it is to love God and to fear God. For God is not cognized through a likeness taken from sense. Instead, an awareness (*notitia*) of God is naturally implanted in us, as Augustine says (rather, Damascene, *De fide orthodoxa* 1 and 3; cf. Augustine *In Ioann. Evang.* tr. 106, n. 4). We do not know what love and fear are by representations taken from without but by essence, for affects of this sort exist in the soul in their essence.

From these points the answer to the question {904B} of whether every cognition comes from sense is clear. We have to say, no. For we must necessarily posit that the soul knows God and itself and the things that are within itself without the aid of the outer senses. As a result, if the Philosopher sometimes says that there is nothing in the understanding that was not previously in sense and that all cognition has its source in sense, we must understand such remarks in relation to those things which have their being in the soul through an abstracted likeness. These are said to be in the soul like writing. For this reason it is especially notable that the Philosopher says that nothing has been *written* in the soul, not because there is no awareness in the soul, but because there is no picture or abstracted likeness in it. This is also what Augustine says in *On the City of God* (XI 27): God has implanted a natural judicatory in us, where what belongs to light or to shadows is cognized in the book of light, which is truth, because truth is naturally impressed in the human heart.

Question 3. Must We Do Everything that Conscience Dictates as Necessary for Salvation?

{905A} Third, I ask about the effect of being bound by conscience. The question here is whether we must do everything that conscience dicates as necessary for salvation.

[1. Preliminary Arguments]

[1a. Arguments that We Must]

It seems that we must.

[i] Romans 14:23: 'Whatever is not of faith is sin.' The Gloss: ' "What is not of faith," that is, is against conscience, so that we believe {905B} it to be evil, "is sin." ' But this would not be so unless conscience bound to everything it dictated. Therefore, we must do everything that comes from a dictate of conscience.

[ii] Again, a law obligates (*obligat*) one to do what it dictates, for law (*lex*) is so called from binding (*ligando*). But conscience is the law of our understanding. Therefore, we must {906A} do everything that conscience dictates as necessary for salvation.

[iii] Again, we must do what a judge commands. But conscience is our judge, according to the Gloss on Ecclesiastes 7:23. [Gloss: 'Your conscience knows, by which judge no one doing evil is absolved.'] Therefore, we must do everything that conscience dictates.

[iv] Again, it is a rule that whenever anyone does something believing it to be a mortal sin, it is a mortal sin, since it shows contempt for God. Therefore, if we cannot *not* believe what conscience dictates, it seems that, whatever the dictate may be, we sin mortally if we act against it. Therefore, it seems that we must do everything that conscience dictates as necessary for salvation.

[1b] Against

[i] If we are obligated to do everything conscience dictates, but conscience sometimes dictates doing something that is against God, we must therefore

act against God. But no one sins in doing what must be done. Therefore, we do not sin in doing something against God [which is absurd].

[ii] Again, there are some things that cannot be done to a good end, which are evil in themselves in such a way that God cannot do them or command them. But conscience cannot obligate to anything to which God cannot obligate, since conscience is below God. It therefore seems that if conscience should dictate such things, it could not obligate us to do them. Therefore, we are not obligated to do them.

[iii] Again, it seems that it can bind to nothing *per se*, because, as Augustine says (*Against Faustus* XXII 27), every sin is a saying or doing or wanting against God's law. Therefore, if conscience dictates something that does not come from a mandate of divine law, acting against it is not sin, since it is not acting against God's law. Therefore, it is not the case that one must do it. So, conscience does not in virtue of itself bind to anything.

[iv] Again, no one can be absolved from an obligation by a dictate of conscience. Neither, therefore, can one become bound as a result of such a dictate. Therefore, it seems that conscience of itself and *per se* cannot bind to anything.

[2. Additional Questions]

The question is, to what does conscience bind? Does it bind to everything it dictates? Does every conscience bind? Is a human being caught in perplexity when conscience dictates one thing and divine law dictates the contrary? To which is more submission due {906B} when they conflict with one another, the dictate of conscience or the command of a superior?

[3. Conclusion: Every Conscience Either Binds to Doing What It Dictates or Binds to Setting It Itself Aside If It Is Erroneous]

We have to say that conscience sometimes dictates what is according to God's law, sometimes what is aside from God's law, sometimes what is against God's law – and here we are speaking of a dictate as a command (*praeceptum*) or prohibition, not as a counsel or persuasion. In cases of the first kind, conscience does indeed bind without qualification and universally, in that divine law binds us to do such things, and conscience, agreeing with it, shows that we are bound. In cases of the second kind, however, conscience is binding as long as it remains. Hence one must either set conscience aside or carry out what it dictates – as, for example, if conscience dictates that picking up a straw from the ground is necessary for salvation. In cases of the third kind, finally, conscience does not bind to doing or not doing but to setting it itself aside. For since such a conscience is erroneous in a way that conflicts with divine law, it necessarily puts a human being outside the state of salvation while it remains. For this reason it is necessary to set that conscience aside, because whether we do what it says or the opposite, we sin mortally. For if we do what conscience dictates, and that is against God's law, and acting against God's law is mortal sin, without doubt we mortally sin. On the other hand, if we do the opposite of what conscience dictates while that conscience remains, we still sin mortally, not by reason of the deed we do, but because we are acting in a bad way. For we act with contempt for God as long as we believe, with conscience so dictating to us, that what we are doing is displeasing to God, although it may [actually] be pleasing to God. This is what the Gloss says on the verse in Romans 14: 'Whatever does not proceed from faith is sin.' The Gloss says there: 'Everything pertaining to conscience, if it is done otherwise, the Apostle says it is sin. For even though what is done is actually good, if it is not believed that it should be done, it is sin.' The reason for this is that God attends not only to what we do but to the spirit in which we do it. Whoever {907A} does what God commands while *believing* that the act is against God's will does not act in a good but in a bad spirit and because of this sins mortally. So, then, it is clear that every conscience either binds to doing what it dictates or binds to setting it itself aside. Yet not every conscience binds to doing what it dictates, as, for example, a conscience dictating that something to which one is otherwise obligated should not be done. Such a conscience is called erroneous.

[4. Replies to the Opening Arguments]

Now that these points have been considered, the answer to the proposed question and the objections on both sides is clear.

[4a. Replies to 1a(i–iv)]

[i] To the first objection (everything that 'is not of faith' means 'is against conscience') the answer is already clear. For I say that it is always a sin to act *against* conscience, because it always shows contempt for God, yet to act *according to* conscience is not always good, as when conscience dictates something that is against God. As a result, the proposition 'To act against conscience is sin' has two ways of being true: either because conscience binds us to do an act, or because the act cannot be done well while such a conscience remains. For this reason there is a sophism *secundum consequens* [in the objection], because the argument goes from many causes of truth to one.

[ii, iii] To the objection that conscience is the law of our understanding we have to say that it truly is a law but not the supreme law, for there is another law over it, namely, divine law. When it is said, however, that a law binds to doing everything it dictates, we have to say that this is true when a lower law does not dictate something contrary to a higher law; but conscience often does this. The next objection (about the judge) must be answered similarly.

[iv] On the other hand, we have to say that the last objection (that whenever we believe we are sinning mortally, we are sinning mortally) is true. For the saying is universally true, that whoever acts against conscience works toward Gehenna. Yet it does not follow from this that we must do all that conscience dictates, because, as has been said, there are two causes of truth here.

[4b. Replies to 1b(i–iv)]

[i, ii] There is no need to reply to the first arguments to the contrary, however, since their conclusions are true, for they show that conscience is not binding in every case.

[iii] On the other hand, to the objection that conscience binds us to nothing *per se* (because what is done {907B} against conscience is not called sin but rather what is against God's law) we have to say that acting against God's law can occur in two ways: truly or interpretatively, in truth or according to what is reputed to be the case (*secundum reputationem*). There is mortal sin in both ways, for there is contempt for God in both ways. Although when we act against conscience we do not always act against God's law in truth, yet we do act against it either in truth or

according to what is reputed to be the case. This is because conscience is like a herald or messenger of God, and it does not command what it says from itself, but it commands, as it were, from God, like a herald proclaiming the edict of a king. It is in virtue of this that conscience binds in things that can – in some way – be done well.

[iv] To the objection that conscience cannot absolve us from anything [and therefore cannot bind us], we have to say that the cases are not alike. Conscience cannot break another law; that is why it cannot absolve us either from God's command or from the command of a superior to whom we have obligated ourselves by the law of a vow. Yet it does not follow from this that conscience cannot finally bind. Rather, the argument is *a minori destruendo*. As a result, just as it is invalid to argue that since conscience has no power over a superior it has no power over an inferior, so it is invalid to argue that since conscience cannot absolve us from the command of a superior, it therefore cannot obligate us. Yet it does indeed follow that it cannot obligate us against the command of a superior. Nevertheless, it can obligate us to something, for in a certain way it is above us and between us and God, as a herald is between king and people.

[5. Replies to the Additional Questions]

From the preceding, the answer to the questions asked at the end (namely, when conscience is binding and when it is not) is clear. It is also clear that no one is caught in perplexity except temporarily, namely, for as long as the [erroneous] conscience remains. Yet one is not perplexed without qualification, in that one ought to set aside that conscience. If we ourselves do not know how to judge matters, in that we do not know God's law, we ought to consult those who are wiser, or, if human counsel is lacking, turn to God in prayer. Otherwise, if we are negligent, what the Apostle says applies to us: 'Whoever does not recognize [a command of the Lord] will not be recognized' (1 Corinthians 14:38).

It is also clear that one ought to comply more with the command of a superior than with conscience, especially when superiors command what they can and ought to command.

Article 2. On Synderesis

{908A} Next I ask about the second main [topic], synderesis, the spark of conscience. There are three questions concerning it. First, about synderesis itself, with respect to its essence: Is it in the genus of the cognitive or the affective? Second, with respect to its use: Can it be extinguished by sin? Third, with respect to its misuse: Can it become depraved through sin?

Question 1. Is Synderesis in the Genus of the Cognitive or the Affective?

We proceed to the first question and ask whether synderesis is in the genus of cognition or affection.

[1. Preliminary Arguments]

[1a. Arguments that Synderesis Is in the Genus of the Affective]

It seems that it is in the genus of affection.

[i] By the Gloss on Ezekiel 1:10, where it is said about synderesis (after much else): 'This is the spirit that intercedes for us with sighs too deep for words' (Romans 8:26). But to sigh is an affective act. Therefore, if it belongs to synderesis to sigh, synderesis pertains to an affective power.

[ii] Again, Ambrose says (as quoted in the text [of the *Sentences*]) that, though subject to sin, we naturally will the good. But that which naturally inclines us to good is either synderesis or conscience. Therefore, that will inclining us to good is either synderesis or conscience. But it is not conscience. Therefore, it is synderesis.

[iii] Again, 'Against evil there is an opposing good' (Ecclesiasticus 33: 15). But in our sensory motive part we have something impelling us to evil. Therefore, in our rational motive part there ought to be something impelling us to good. Now this is nothing except synderesis. Therefore, synderesis is in the affective part. {908B}

[iv] Again, just as the understanding needs light for judging, so affect needs a certain heat and spiritual weight for loving rightly. Therefore, just as there is a certain natural judicatory in the cognitive part of the soul, which is conscience, so there will be a weight in the affective part of the

soul directing and inclining to good. Now this is nothing except synderesis. Therefore, etc.

[1b] Against

[i] On the text of Malachi 2:15, 'Guard your spirit, and do not put away the wife of your youth,' Jerome comments as follows: 'Understand by "the wife of your youth" the natural law written in the heart; by "spirit" is not meant the animal part, which does not grasp the things that are of God, but the rational.' Now this he calls synderesis. Therefore, it seems that synderesis resides in reason or the cognitive. If you say that 'spirit' is taken there for understanding and affect in common, what follows in the same gloss is an objection: 'This is the spirit that intercedes for us with sighs too deep for words.' But to intercede is an act of reason. Therefore, etc.

[ii] Again, on the text of Luke 10:30, 'They departed, leaving him half dead,' the Gloss says, 'They stripped off immortality, {909A} but they cannot abolish the sense of reason and keep him from tasting and knowing God.' If the sense of reason resides in reason, and a sense of this sort remaining in us is nothing other than synderesis, it therefore seems, etc.

[iii] Again, the spark of conscience and conscience are in the same part [of the soul]. But as has been proved above, conscience pertains to the cognitive, and according to what is said [in the gloss] on Ezekiel 1 synderesis is the spark of conscience. It therefore seems that synderesis resides in the cognitive.

[iv] Again, if synderesis is on the motive side, it is either a power or a passion or a habit. It is certainly not a passion. It seems that it is not a habit, because it would be either a good or a bad one; not a good one, because then it would be a virtue; and not a bad one, because then it would be a vice, neither of which is conceded about synderesis. It does not seem to be a power, because the power of will is related equally to any object of appetite whatever. Now synderesis is not spoken of with respect to food and drink and appetibles of this sort. Therefore, it does not seem that synderesis is in any way on the side of the affective.

[2. Additional Questions]

There is a question, then, as to what synderesis is and how it is related to natural law and conscience – whether they are the same or different.

Again, how is it related to the three powers of the soul, namely, the capacity for wanting (*concupiscibilem*), the irascible, and the rational. For it seems from the gloss on Ezekiel 1:10 ('A human face,' etc.) that there is something besides these three. The Gloss says, 'Many follow Plato in referring the soul's rationality, irascibility, and capacity for wanting to a human being, a lion, and a calf, while they posit a fourth outside and over these, which the Greeks call synderesis, a spark of conscience which was not extinguished even in Cain, by which we sense that we sin when we are conquered by pleasures or anger or are sometimes deceived by a semblance of reason. They represent this as an eagle, which does not mingle with the others but corrects them when they err.' From this gloss it seems that synderesis differs from the other three. But against this is what is said in the book *On Spirit and Soul* (c. 13), that these three {909B} (namely, the wanting, the irascible, and the rational) sufficiently divide the soul's powers. Therefore, if synderesis is something in the soul it seems that it necessarily resides in one or more of these three.

[3. Conclusion. Synderesis, Since It Urges Us to Good, Resides in Affect]

We have to say that opinion varies about the distinction of synderesis from the other powers of the soul and also about the distinction of the other powers from one another.

On the basis of the preceding gloss on Ezekiel 1, some have wanted to say that the supreme [part] of the soul is called synderesis. But the supreme [part] of the soul is the higher portion of reason, by which the soul is turned toward God. That higher portion rules the lower portion of reason and the irascible and wanting [parts of the soul]. Now when it is turned toward God this higher portion is always right, but it deviates as it descends to things here below. And they say that the difference between synderesis and conscience and natural law is as follows. 'Synderesis' names the power itself (that is, the higher portion of reason); 'conscience,' however, names its habit, in accordance with which it rules the lower portion; 'natural law,' finally, names that to which conscience directs us. Now this way of speaking seems probable enough, except that it would conflict with the gloss quoted above, which says that synderesis does not mingle with the others when they are sinning. For since there cannot be mortal sin without an act of the higher portion (because the completion of sin consists in a man's consuming it), if synderesis were the higher portion of reason, it would certainly mingle with the others in sinning. Moreover, the higher portion of reason bespeaks an orientation toward God. The act of synderesis regards not only God, however, but also one's neighbor, as natural law regards both.

Because of this, there is another way of speaking, which holds that, since motivation in the rational powers (understanding and affect) is twofold, namely, by way of nature and by way of deliberation, so, just as free judgment {910A} consists of reason and will as they move deliberatively, conscience and synderesis relate to reason and will insofar as they move naturally. Both synderesis and conscience, and also the natural law, always incline to good; but free judgment sometimes inclines to good, sometimes to evil. Hence, just as free judgment embraces both reason and will together, so does synderesis embrace both reason and will together, and so do natural law and conscience – and they can be taken for the same thing. When each term is given a distinct meaning, however, 'synderesis' refers specifically to a power, 'conscience' to a habit, and 'natural law' to an object. Or, in another way of assigning meanings, 'synderesis' refers to a habit with respect to good or evil in general; 'conscience' to a habit with respect to good or evil in particular; 'natural law,' finally, is related to both indifferently. But because, as was established above, 'conscience' refers to a habit residing in understanding, it will be necessary either to posit something directive in us besides conscience and synderesis, or to posit that synderesis resides in affect.

Because of this, there is a third way of speaking, which is as follows. In the same way as, from the very creation of the soul, the understanding has a light which is a natural judicatory for it, directing the understanding itself in what is to be known, so affect similarly has a certain natural weight directing it in what is to be sought. Now things that are to be sought are of two kinds. Some are in the category of the morally honorable (*honesti*) and some in the category of the advantageous (*commodi*). Things that can be cognized are also of two kinds. Some are in the genus of objects of contemplation, and some relate to morals. And just as 'conscience' names that judicatory only insofar as it directs us to moral actions, so 'synderesis' names that weight of the will (or the will with that weight) only insofar as it inclines it to the morally honorable good. And just as the term 'conscience' can be taken for the power with such a habit or for the habit of such a power, so also can 'synderesis' be taken. Nevertheless, in the more usual way of speaking, 'synderesis' names a power susceptible to habitua-

tion rather than a habit, as is plain in the texts cited above. And because
the power is never separated from the habit, habit and power are included
under one name, and the power as thus habituated is allotted the name of
its habit. {910B}

From this the answer is clear to the first question proposed (whether
'synderesis' refers to something affective or to something cognitive). For I
say that 'synderesis' refers to that which urges toward good and hence that
it resides in the affective, as the arguments alleged for the first side show.

[3. Replies to the Arguments on the Other Side]

[i] To the first objection to the contrary (that synderesis is the rational
spirit that intercedes and appeals for us) we have to say, as Gregory does,
commenting on Job 1, that we speak to God not only by thoughts and
spoken words but also in affect and desire. Moreover, when by its constant
urging synderesis makes a human being desire the good, it is said 'to appeal
to God with sighs too deep for words.'

[ii] To the objection about the sense of reason, we have to say that by
'rational sense' the natural judicatory is meant there, rather than synderesis.
Now lest anyone should contend that synderesis is meant by that [rational]
sense, we must make a distinction. 'Reason' is sometimes taken properly
for the cognitive part [of the soul], sometimes generally, so that it includes
the whole rational spirit. In this [general] way 'sense of reason' is taken
not only for the cognitive but also for the affective, as is clear with regard
to spiritual taste and touch. Hence it does not follow from this that
synderesis is on the side of cognition.

[iii] To the objection that synderesis is the spark of conscience [and
hence is cognitive, as conscience is], we have to say that it is called a spark
because conscience by itself alone can neither move nor sting nor urge
except by means of synderesis, which, as it were, urges and ignites. As a
result, just as reason cannot move except by means of will, so neither can
conscience move except by means of synderesis. Hence it does not follow
from this [the fact that synderesis is the spark of conscience] that it is on
the cognitive side but rather, on the contrary, that it is on the affective
side.

[iv] To the question whether it is a power, a passion, or a habit, we
have to say that properly speaking it is a power, yet nevertheless 'synderesis' does not name the power of will in general but only will insofar as it
moves naturally. Further, it does not name the will universally but only

with respect to the morally honorable good or its opposite. Nonetheless, the term can also refer to a habit, but that habit ought not to be called either a virtue or a vice, for virtue and vice properly relate to free judgment and to will as deliberative, not as natural. {911A}

[4. Replies to the Additional Questions]

From the preceding, the answer to the questions asked at the end is clear. To the question of how synderesis is related to conscience and natural law, we have to say that synderesis (as a habit) is to conscience as charity is to faith, or as the habit of affect is to the habit of practical understanding. Now natural law relates to both in common, namely, to synderesis and to conscience. For 'natural law' can be taken in two senses. In one sense it refers to a habit in the soul, and in this sense, because we are instructed by natural law and are rightly ordered by it, it indicates a habit that includes both understanding and affect, and so it includes synderesis and conscience. In another sense natural law is called a collection of the precepts of natural right, and in this sense it names the object of synderesis and conscience, of one as dictating and of the other as inclining. For conscience dictates and synderesis seeks or refuses. {911B} Natural law is spoken of in both these ways in various places. Nevertheless, it is more properly taken in the second sense. So, to speak properly, synderesis is an affective power insofar as it is by nature easily turned (*naturaliter habilis*) to good and tends to good. Conscience, however, is a habit of practical understanding. Natural law, finally, is the object of both.

From this the answer to the last question (how synderesis is related to the 'wanting,' 'rational,' and 'irascible' powers) is clear. These three name powers of the soul as they move either naturally or with deliberation. 'Synderesis,' however, names the affective power as its motion is natural and right. For this reason it is not distinguished from those powers according to the essence of the power but by its manner of moving, and because it always moves rightly it is said, in accordance with that manner of moving, to fly over the others, not mingling with them when they err but correcting them.

Question 2. Can Synderesis Be Extinguished by Sin?

Second: Can synderesis be extinguished by sin?

[1. Preliminary Arguments]

[1a. Arguments that It Can Be]

It seems so.

[i] On the text of Psalm 14:1 ('They are corrupt, they do abominable deeds') the Gloss says 'Deprived of every rational power.' But synderesis is a rational power. One can therefore be deprived of synderesis, at least as to its act, by the magnitude of sin.

[ii] Again, on the text of Psalm 56:2–3 ('All the day long {912A} I shall fear') the Gloss says 'It is a numbness which does not feel' and adds later that 'Foolish arrogance is like a numbness, when someone trusting himself neither fears nor is cautious.' Therefore, just as the body can become insensible to bodily sickness through numbness, so it can also happen that the soul becomes insensible to spiritual sickness. It seems, then, that if synderesis [normally] protests against spiritual sickness, it sometimes happens that it is extinguished.

[iii] Again, heretics endure death for the sake of their errors without any remorse of conscience. Therefore, if it pertains to synderesis to react against evil, while in them it does not react in any way, it seems to be entirely extinct in them.

[iv] Again, the tinder [of sin] stands in opposition to synderesis. But the tinder can be totally extinguished, as is clear with regard to the Blessed Virgin. Likewise, then, it seems that synderesis can be extinguished by a multitude of sins.

[1b] Against

[i] In the gloss on Ezekiel 1 cited above ('The eagle's face . . . '), it says that 'The spark of conscience is not extinguished in Cain.' Therefore, if Cain was a great sinner it seems that it is not extinguished through sin.

[ii] Again, Augustine says in Book II of *On the City of God* (c. 26) that 'The force of probity and chastity is so great that everyone or nearly everyone is moved by human nature to praise them, nor is there any shamefulness so vicious that it makes one lose all sense of what is morally honorable.' Therefore, if that sense of what is morally honorable is synderesis, it seems that it cannot be extinguished through sin.

[iii] Again, things that are naturally inherent are inseparable [from that in which they inhere]. But synderesis is naturally inherent in us. Therefore,

it seems that we cannot entirely lose its act through sin, since vice, as Augustine says (*On the City of God* XIX 12), does not destroy the last traces of nature.

[iv] Again, if it ought to be extinguished in anyone, it would especially be extinguished in the damned. But synderesis is not extinguished in the damned, because remorse of conscience comes from the action of synderesis, and this remorse is especially intense in them, because neither 'shall their fire be extinguished nor their worm die' (Isaiah 66:24). Therefore, etc.

[2. Conclusion. Synderesis Can Be Impeded Temporarily in Its Act, but It Cannot Be Extinguished Permanently and in Relation to Every Act]

We have to say that synderesis can be impeded in its act, but it cannot be extinguished. {912B} The reason it cannot be extinguished is that it is something natural and because of this cannot be entirely taken away from us. That is why the gloss on Luke 10 ('They departed, leaving him half dead') also says that 'They stripped off immortality, but they cannot entirely abolish the sense of reason and keep him from tasting and knowing God or ever efface the last traces of nature.'

Now although the act of synderesis cannot be entirely taken away or extinguished, it can nevertheless be impeded temporarily, by the darkness of blindness, the wantonness of pleasure, or the hardness of obstinacy. The darkness of blindness impedes synderesis from reacting against evil when evil is believed to be good – as in heretics, who believe that they are dying for the piety of faith when they are dying for the impiety of error. Because of this, they do not feel remorse but rather a certain vain and fictive joy. Synderesis is likewise impeded by the wantonness of pleasure, for in sins of the flesh a human being is sometimes so absorbed by a carnal act that there is no place for remorse – because those who are carnal are carried along by such an onrush of pleasure that at the time there is no place for reason. Synderesis is also impeded by the hardness of obstinacy, so that it does not urge toward good – as in the damned, who are so far confirmed in evil that they can never be inclined to good. [In them] because of this, synderesis is endlessly impeded from inciting to good, and with respect to that act it can thus be called extinct. Yet it is not extinct without qualification, because it has another function, namely, reaction [against evil]. In this function, in which it pertains to synderesis to stab and react against evil, it will be especially vigorous in the damned. I say this inasmuch as the reaction against evil has the character of punishment, not inasmuch as it has the character of justice [in the damned], because that [painful] reaction will exist to commend divine justice, not to elicit fruitful repentance. As a result, in the damned synderesis will react against guilt, yet this will be as punishment.

Thus it is clear that synderesis can be impeded in its act yet never universally extinguished, permanently and with respect to every act, as the arguments for the second side of the question show. Hence they should be conceded.

[3. Replies to the Arguments on the Other Side]

[i] On the other hand, to the objection from the Gloss (that one can be deprived by evil of every rational power) we have to say that 'reason' is used there for a deliberative power {913A} and for something moving by deliberation, a power that in some people is entirely turned to evil. Now, as was shown before, 'synderesis' does not refer to a power of the rational soul moving by deliberation but to one moving by nature. Hence that gloss does not support the point at hand. Nor should we understand it to mean that through sin there is privation with respect to the power but with respect to the rightness of the power.

[ii] To the objection that one is rendered numb by sin, we have to say that the likeness [to being physically numb] holds with respect to deliberative power. It is in relation to this that foolish arrogance exists in us. Yet it could be said that numbness does not take sensation away without qualification but only temporarily. It can well be that for a time the soul is bent so far toward sin that it feels no remorse at all, either due to the intensity of pleasure or because of blindness, when it believes evil to be good.

[iii] The answer to the objection about heretics is already clear. For I concede that synderesis does not function to react against the evil of the error into which they have fallen. Nevertheless, as it reacts against other evils and against things that the heretics believe to be evil, it is not extinct.

[iv] To the objection about the tinder, we have to say that the cases are not alike, because the tinder is a viciousness outside of nature, and thus it can be totally abolished while nature is preserved. This is not the

case, however, with synderesis, which is inherent in us from the first establishment of our nature. Because of this, while nature is preserved, synderesis cannot be entirely taken away. Another reason is that there is a grace, or a freely given gift of grace, that directly opposes the tinder and removes the corruption of the flesh. Now vice and sin do not exist with regard to the act of synderesis, and because of this, however much [the first?] human being may have sinned, both conscience and synderesis have remained.

Question 3. Can Synderesis Become Depraved through Sin?

Third, we ask about synderesis with respect to misuse. The question is whether synderesis can become depraved through sin.

[1. Preliminary Arguments]

[1a. Arguments that It Can Be]

It seems so.

[i] On the text of Ezekiel 1:10 ('an eagle's face on their four right sides'), the Gloss, speaking of conscience and synderesis, says that 'We often see in shameless sinners that it is overthrown and loses its place. To these it is deservedly said "You have the face of a whore" [Jeremiah 3:3].' Therefore, if overthrowing does not occur without fault, it is plain, etc.

[ii] Again, on Jeremiah 2:16 ('The children of Memphis,' etc.), the Gloss says that 'A malignant spirit reaches all the way from the lower members to the top of the head when the sickness of defiance corrupts the mind's chaste height.' But the mind's chaste height is synderesis itself. Therefore, it can be corrupted by sin.

[iii] Again, this is seen by reason. Punishment and fault occur in relation to the same thing. But {913B} the soul is punished by the act of synderesis reacting against sin. Therefore, there can be a commission of sin by the same act.

[iv] Again, synderesis follows conscience as its natural judicatory. But conscience can be right or erroneous. Therefore, it seems that the motion of synderesis is necessarily sometimes right, sometimes deviant.

[v] Again, opposites occur by nature in the same thing. But the gift of

wisdom and the blessing of mourning exist in connection with synderesis, since the gift of wisdom is given to the supreme part of the soul, and synderesis intercedes for us with sighs too deep for words. Therefore, if fault is opposed to the gift of wisdom and to the beatitude of mourning, it seems that fault exists in connection with that power.

[vi] Again, synderesis is either among the greatest goods or among the intermediate goods or among the least goods. If among the greatest, it is therefore a grace or a virtue, both of which {914A} are false, since synderesis remains at the same time as sin. If it is among intermediate goods, then, since these can be used badly, synderesis can be used badly. But bad use is a fault. Therefore, there can be fault in an act of synderesis. Synderesis is undoubtedly not among the least goods, since these are goods of the body.

[1b. Arguments that Synderesis Cannot Become Depraved through Sin]

Against:

[i] The Gloss on Ezekiel 1: 'Synderesis they represent as an eagle, which does not mingle with the others but corrects them when they err.' Therefore, if it does not mingle with the three but rather corrects them, it seems that sin does not exist in connection with its act.

[ii] Again, on Romans 7:16, 20 ('I do what I do not want to do'), Ambrose says (and the Master quotes him in the text) that by nature we always will the good. Therefore, since that will is nothing other than synderesis, synderesis always wills the good. And if it always wills the good, then it never sins.

[iii] Again, that force which by its own movement directly opposes sin is not depraved by sin. But the act of synderesis always reacts against fault, even in the worst sinners. Therefore, it seems that it cannot become depraved and disordered through fault.

[iv] Again, when a whole nature is destroyed by sickness, there is no further possibility of health. Therefore, if the whole rightness of the soul were taken away by fault, there would be no further hope of returning to grace. But it is certain that there is hope of returning, because we should not despair of anyone who is still in this life. It therefore seems that some rightness remains. But the rightness that adheres most tightly is rightness of will by way of nature, and this is synderesis. Therefore, it does not seem that it can become depraved through fault.

[2. Conclusion: Synderesis Cannot Become Depraved in Itself through Sin but Only Overthrown with Respect to Its Ruling Lordship]

We have to say that according to those who say that synderesis is nothing other than the higher portion of reason, there can be sin in its act. For they say that the higher portion of reason has two ways of moving: either as it is turned toward God and is ruled and directed by eternal laws, and in this way sin does not exist in it; or insofar as it is turned toward lower powers, and in this way it takes from them occasion for deviation and can {914B} become depraved through sin. They propose an example in the sin of Arius, who erred about the [divine] Trinity and Unity and so erred according to the higher portion of reason or synderesis. They say that the gloss on Ezekiel cited earlier means to say this, for it says first that 'It does not mingle with the others when they are sinning,' but later it says that 'It is overthrown and loses its place.' They say both are true in different respects of the higher portion or of synderesis itself

But since, as the saints and glosses obviously say, synderesis of itself always urges to good and reacts against sin as long as we are in our present state, others have maintained a different position, namely, that 'synderesis' names the will itself as it moves naturally. Since sin does not occur in the act of will as it exists by nature or moves naturally but only as it moves deliberately, synderesis does not become depraved through sin. Nevertheless, because it belongs to it to rule and direct others and can lose its ruling lordship, it can hence be overthrown through fault. For a lord's presiding depends on two things, namely, the rectitude of the one presiding and the submissiveness of the one serving. Now although synderesis of itself is always right, yet because reason and will frequently hinder it (reason through the blindness of error and will by the obstinacy of impiety) synderesis is said to be overthrown, in that its effect and its presiding over the other deliberative powers is repelled and broken through their resistance. The example is used of a soldier who always sits well on his horse as far as this depends on him, yet when the horse runs wild he is said to be overthrown. We must understand the case at hand in this way.

Many uphold this way of speaking as the more reasonable. Hence the arguments presented for this side should be conceded.

[3. Replies to the Arguments on the Other Side]

[i] On the other hand, the answer to the first objection from the Gloss (that we see synderesis overthrown) is already plain. For it does not follow that if it is overthrown it would on that account be depraved through sin, because its overthrow concerns not only its own act but also that of other powers over which synderesis ought to preside.

[ii] To the objection that the sickness of defiance corrupts the mind's height and that the soul is defiled all the way to its top, we have to say that what is there called the top and height of the mind is not synderesis {915A} but the higher portion of reason. Now 'the higher portion of reason' does not name a power of the soul insofar as it moves naturally but insofar as it moves deliberately. Sin is in it in this way, especially that which is observed in the highest acts of reason, as in the sins of unbelief and despair and other sins directly opposed to the theological virtues.

[iii] To the objection that punishment and fault occur in the same thing we have to say that this is not true, speaking precisely, in that the whole body is punished for the will's sin. Nevertheless, it is true that just as the will is primary in sin, so also it is primarily punished. Hence also the worm of conscience afflicts the will more as it is deliberative than as it exists by nature, because of the mutual opposition. Whether the will alone is subject to punishment, however, or something else is also, will be made clear below in the proper place.

[iv] To the objection that since conscience (a judicatory that precedes synderesis) can be right or not right, therefore synderesis can be also, we have to say that this does not follow. For conscience does not remain only at the level of the universal but also descends to the particular; it moves not only with a simple motion but also with a combining one. Nor is this surprising, because it consists of reason, and it pertains to reason to discriminate and compare things with one another. As a result, although conscience is always right when it stays at the level of the universal and moves in a single direction, when it descends to particulars and makes comparisons it can become erroneous, because here it mingles with the acts ((*actibus*/*actus* [var.])) of deliberative reason.

This is clear from the following. The conscience of the Jews was accustomed to dictating, from the first natural dictate itself, that God should be obeyed. They later accept that God now commands circumcision and discrimination among foods. From this their conscience is formed in particular, so that they practice circumcision and abstain from certain foods. Now that error does not come from the first principle, which was true. Instead it comes from the minor premise, {915B} which was not from conscience as a natural judicatory but rather resulted from erroneous reasoning, which pertains to free judgment. Synderesis, however, taken in itself, moves with a simple motion in reacting against evil and inciting to good. Moreover, it is not moved against this or that evil but universally. Or if synderesis is in some way inclined to detest this or that evil, it is not this evil as *this* but as *evil*. Thus it is that synderesis is not turned aside, although conscience errs.

Another argument could also be given. 'Synderesis' names a natural power as it is naturally habituated. 'Conscience,' however, names not only a natural but also an acquired habit. Nature, taken by itself, always moves rightly. What is acquired, however, can be either right or deviant in character. Hence it is that, while synderesis is always right, conscience can be both right and erroneous.

[v] To the objection that the gift of wisdom concerns synderesis, we have to say that this is false. For all gifts, virtues, and blessings relate to the will as it is deliberative. When synderesis is said 'to intercede for us with sighs too deep for words,' however, this is meant causally, because it incites us to sigh for the evils in which we are immersed.

[vi] To the objection that intermediate goods can be used badly, we have to say that this is true about those that move at the behest of free judgment, in relation to whose act the concepts of use and misuse properly apply. Synderesis, however, since it is a natural power and moves naturally, is not under the command of free judgment. Thus it does not follow [from its being an intermediate good] that free judgment can misuse it. Moreover, let it be the case that it could be misused, it still does not follow that because of this there would be sin in it. For although free judgment misuses the eye in a lustful gaze, sin is not said to be in the eye, for sin is not in that which is misused but in the one misusing it. . . .

GILES OF ROME
ON THE RULE OF PRINCES (SELECTIONS)

Introduction

Giles of Rome (Aegidius Romanus, Egidius Colonna) was born in Rome around 1243–47. He joined the Hermits of St. Augustine at the age of fourteen. Sent to Paris in 1260, he completed his liberal arts studies in 1266 and entered the faculty of theology. He was studying there when Thomas Aquinas returned for his second period as regent master (1269–72). As a young theologian, Giles was soon caught up in disputes within the university over the teaching of Aristotle in the Faculty of Arts. In 1277 Stephen Tempier, the bishop of Paris, condemned as erroneous 219 propositions in theology and natural philosophy, fifty-one of which were drawn from Giles's commentary on the *Sentences* of Peter Lombard. Withdrawing to Bayeux and thence to Italy, Giles nevertheless continued to work on a series of commentaries on Aristotle's philosophical texts. These included the *Physics, Metaphysics, De anima,* and *On Rhetoric.* In 1285 Giles was rehabilitated, returning to Paris as the Augustinians' first regent master in theology, and in 1287 his writings were made the official teaching of the Augustinian order. Giles was elected General of the order in 1292 and was made Archbishop of Bourges in 1295. Besides *On the Rule of Princes,* Giles's other major political work was a sweeping defense of papal plenitude of power, *On Ecclesiastical Power* (trans. R. W. Dyson, Woodbridge, 1986), which he composed in 1302 for Pope Boniface VIII. Giles died in 1316.

On the Rule of Princes (or, to give the work its full title, *On the Instruction of Rulers and the Governance of Kings*) was one of the most influential texts of scholastic political thought. Traditionally thought to have been written in the late 1270s during Giles's enforced absence from Paris, it appears to have been composed at the request of Philip III of France for the instruction of his son, the future Philip IV. Giles's text was immediately and widely disseminated in its Latin original and was rapidly translated into French and Italian and thereafter into German and English. It thus became an important vehicle for the mediation of scholastic political ideas to a much wider audience than that of the Paris schools. It also provided much more in the way of analytical thought than the digests of Aristotle's *Politics* and *Ethics* already available in such collections of excerpts as the *Auctoritates Aristotelis* (ed. J. Hamesse, *Philosophes Médiévaux* XVII, Louvain-Paris, 1974). Nor was its content limited to Aristotle. Giles also drew heavily on a wide range of other classical authors, most notably Cicero and Vegetius, a range which bears comparison with another text that mediated the new learning, Brunetto Latini's vernacular encyclopedia, *Li Livres dou Tresor* (ed. F. J. Carmody, Berkeley, 1948).

On the Rule of Princes was written firmly in the tradition of the 'Mirror for Princes' (*speculum principis*), a genre of political writing that had flourished in the Carolingian period and which had recently been given a new lease of life at the court of Louis IX in the hands of Franciscan and Dominican friars. Giles of Rome himself signaled this affiliation by dividing his work into three books dealing with, respectively, rule of self, rule of the household, and rule of the kingdom. His intention was thereby to present predominantly Aristotelian content in a traditional form. Giles's discussion of the relative merits of rule by a good man and rule by good laws provides a revealing illustration of the fusion he was able to achieve. Carefully steering his reading of Book III of the *Politics* away from any interpretation that might compromise the power of a king of France, Giles directs his discussion toward the relationship between justice and mercy, a topic already familiar in this context from Cicero's *On Duties* and Seneca's *On Clemency*.

Giles's accommodation of Aristotle to the Mirror for Princes genre extends further than content, however. The prologue to *On the Rule of Princes* makes it clear that Giles had also thought long and hard about the precise nature of 'political thought,' that is, about the nature of what he was writing and the relationship between dialectic and rhetoric on which the effectiveness of his treatise would depend. These reflections had been prompted by Giles's study of Aristotle's *On Rhetoric*, a text which contains a considerable amount of material that duplicates and extends the content of both the *Ethics* and the *Politics*. The result of Giles's close reading was a threefold justification of an approach to his subject that was 'general and typical.' First, ethical and political writing deals with moral conduct, subject-matter that is necessarily indeterminate and therefore not susceptible to the sort of demonstrative proof which can be provided in geometry. Second, ethical and political writing is designed to be put into practice and, as a result, must persuade the will rather than simply convince the intellect; it must therefore appeal to human emotions and not just to human reason. Third, ethical and political writing must be tailored to its intended audience – in this instance, not only a future king of France but his prospective subjects as well. In using a comparison between *On Rhetoric* and the *Ethics* as the basis for analyzing the relationship between dialectic and rhetoric, the prologue to *On the Rule of Princes* provides a still pertinent reminder that scholastic political thought should not be viewed through the prism of its subsequent humanist critique. The method Giles puts forward here also reveals the fundamental consistency which underpinned his own political writings. Examination of Giles's understanding of the relationship between rhetoric and political thought makes clear how an Aristotelian *speculum principis* written for the future Philip IV could be followed by an Augustinian defense of papal plenitude of power written against the attacks of that same ruler some thirty years later.

For further reading on Giles of Rome, see CHLMP, p. 861 and *Dizionario Biografico degli Italiani*, vol. XLII. For the condemnation of 1277, see R. Hissette, *Enquête sur les 219 articles condamnés à Paris le 7 mars 1277* (Philosophes Médiévaux XXII, Louvain-Paris, 1977). For the Mirror for Princes genre, see W. Berges, *Die Fürstenspiegel des hohen und späten Mittelalters* (Leipzig, 1938). For *On the Rule of Princes* itself, see the series of articles by R. Lambertini in *Documenti e Studi sulla Tradizione Filosofica Medievale* I–III, 1990–92, and M. S. Kempshall, *The Common Good in Late Medieval Political Thought* (Oxford: Oxford University Press, 1999), chapter 5; for its dissemination and influence, see C. F. Briggs, *Giles of Rome's De Regimine Principum – Reading and Writing Politics at Court and University ca. 1275–ca. 1525* (Cambridge: Cambridge University Press, 1999). For Capetian royal ideology, see J. R. Strayer, 'France – the Holy Land and the Most Christian People' in his *Medieval Statecraft and the Perspectives of History* (Princeton: Princeton University Press, 1971). For the accommodation of Aristotle's arguments to Capetian kingship, see J. H. Dunbabin, 'Aristotle in the Schools' in B. Smalley, ed., *Trends in Medieval Political Thought* (Oxford: Blackwell, 1965), and, for the specific issue of rule by a good man or by good laws, T. J. Renna, 'Aristotle and the French Monarchy, 1260–1303,' *Viator* 9 (1978), pp. 309–24.

On the Rule of Princes (selections)

Book I

Prologue

{aira} To the Lord Philip, descended from royal and most holy stock, first born and heir of the most distinguished Lord Philip, by the grace of God most illustrious King of the Franks. Brother Giles of Rome, Order of the Hermit Brothers of Saint Augustine, devotedly commends himself to his special lord and to all parts of his household.

The judgment of those involved in politics proclaims that not all governments are of equal duration and that individual regimes are not measured by equal periods of time, but some last a year, some a lifetime, while some, through inheritance and filial succession, are indeed judged to be, in a certain sense, perpetual. Since it is generally agreed that nothing violent is perpetual, everything in nature testifies that whoever desires his rule to be perpetual (in his own person and in the sons who come after him) ought to devote the greatest attention to ensuring that his regime is natural. Now no ruler ever succeeds in being natural if he wants to govern by passion or will. He is natural only if, as the guardian of what is just, he decrees that nothing be commanded without reason and ((*et/ex*)) law. For as the Philosopher testifies (*Politics* I 2, 1252a31–32), just as an individual who is physically powerful but weak in intellect is a natural slave, so the individual who flourishes in the application of his mind and in ruling prudence is a natural master. Wherefore if, Glorious and Nobly Born, you have amicably requested me to compose a book on the instruction of rulers and the governance of kings so that you may wield power in a natural regime where greater diligence is exercised toward governing the kingdom according to reason and law, such a request, so it seems, is clearly prompted not by human but by divine instinct. For Almighty God, in whose praise it is written 'Lord of Lords and King of Kings' (1 Timothy 6: 15), seems to take special care of your most holy house, since he has inclined your modest and honorable childhood to want to maintain the kingdom's most just regulations, not by passion and will, but by law and intellect, following in the footsteps of your fathers and ancestors, in whom the zeal of faith and the Christian religion has flourished and continues to flourish ever more fully and more perfectly. I am therefore unhesitatingly inclined toward this praiseworthy and noble request, which for myself I

regard as a command and as supported by the good of the people, something that is more divine and more general than any individual good. With
the aid of the Most High, without reluctance and with pleasure, I will set
about the work as your Reverend Nobility has requested.

Chapter 1. The Method of Proceeding in *On the Rule of Princes*

As the Philosopher maintains in *Metaphysics* VII, any discussion should be as
extensive – no more and no less – as the nature of the thing being discussed
requires. If, then, we intend to impart the art and knowledge of the governance of rulers or kings {airb} so that no more is said than the present work
requires, we must first address the method of proceeding in this art. It is important to know, then, that according to the Philosopher the [proper]
method of proceeding in all moral matters is in terms of what is typical and
general (*Ethics* I [3], 1094b19–22). For it is necessary to go through such subjects by type and in terms of what is typical, because moral actions are not
susceptible to narration in their entirety. Now there are three paths by which
we can hunt down why the method of proceeding in this science should be
general and typical. The first approach is from the point of view of the material with which an art of this kind is concerned, the second from the point
of view of the end aimed at in this art, and the third from the point of view
of the audience to be instructed by it.

[1a. *Moral Matters Require General and Typical Treatment*]

The first approach reveals [the need for such treatment] in the following
way. Teaching about the rule of princes concerns human acts and falls
within [the category of] moral matters. Moral subject-matter (as has been
said) is not open to detailed and thorough investigation but is about
individual situations which, as is set out in *Ethics* II (2, 1103b34–1104a5),
have a great indeterminacy about them because of their variability. The
individual acts which form the subject-matter of this work show, accordingly, that the approach should therefore be general and typical. Now the
Philosopher seems to touch on this reasoning in *Ethics* I ([3] 1094b11–14;
7, 1098a26–29) when he says that enough will be said about moral matters
if what is revealed is in accordance with the subject-matter, whereupon he
adds that in each branch of knowledge one should only look for as much

determinacy as the nature of the thing [studied] allows. For it appears that the nature of the subject-matter in morals is completely opposite to what it is in mathematics, since mathematical demonstrations have a determinacy of the first degree (as the Commentator says in *Metaphysics* II), whereas moral reasonings are superficial and general. It is therefore for the geometer not to persuade but to demonstrate, whereas it is for the orator or the person involved in politics not to demonstrate but to persuade. On this account it is written in *Ethics* I ([3] 1094b25–27) that to accept persuasion from a mathematician is as much, or almost as much, a sin as to demand demonstration from an orator.

[1b. Such a Method Is Required by the Aim of This Art]

The second approach is from the point of view of the end aimed at in this art. As is written in *Ethics* II (2, 1103b27–29), we undertake a work on moral matters, not for the sake of contemplation or in order to know, but to become good. The end aimed at in this science, therefore, is not cognition of the matters [studied] but action, not the true but the good. Although detailed arguments illuminate the intellect more, superficial and general arguments have a greater capacity to move and kindle the emotions. It is especially [the case] in the speculative sciences, where the primary objective is illumination of the intellect, that the approach should be demonstrative and detailed. In moral matters, however, where the objective is rightness of will and to become good, the approach should be persuasive and typical. That is why it is written in *Ethics* I ([3] 1094b19–22) that the treatment of moral matters is worthy of *love* if, in speaking about such things, and about things that are true for the most part, it shows the truth generally and typically.

[1c. Such a Method Is Required by the Audience to Be Instructed]

The third approach is from the point of view of the audience to be instructed in this art. Although this book is entitled *On the Instruction of Rulers*, it is nevertheless also a means by which the whole populace is to be instructed. For while not everyone can be king or ruler, everyone still ought to devote the greatest attention toward being the sort of person who is worthy to rule and govern, which they cannot be unless they know and observe the contents of this work. Therefore, in a sense, the whole populace is the audience for this art. Only a few people, however, {aiva} excel in keenness of intellect, which is why it is said in *On Rhetoric* III (12, 1414a9–10) that the larger the number of people, the further they are from understanding. Thus, the audience for a treatment of moral matters is simple and general, as is shown in *On Rhetoric* I (2, 1357a3–4, 11–12). Therefore, since the whole populace cannot comprehend refined argumentation, the approach in treating moral matters should be typical and general. In fact, according to the Philosopher in the *Politics* (cf. I 7, 1255b34–35), the subject needs to know how to do those things which the lord needs to know how to command. As a result, if this book instructs rulers how they ought to conduct themselves and how they should command their subjects, then this teaching must be extended to the populace so that they may know how they ought to obey their rulers. And because (as has been touched on) this cannot be done except through arguments that are superficial and appeal to the senses, the method of proceeding in this work must be general and typical.

Chapter 2. The Order of What Is to Be Said

[2a. Principal Topics of the Following Four Books]

Since all teaching and all disciplined learning derive from already existing knowledge, as is said in *Posterior Analytics* I (1, 71a1–2), it is beneficial to relate here the order of what is to be said so that some foreknowledge of it may be acquired. An understanding of what is to be said will be secured more easily with this foreknowledge, once it is acquired. It should be known, then, that we intend to divide the whole book into three partial books. The first of these will show how his Royal Majesty (and as a consequence how anyone at all) ought to rule himself. The second will make clear how he ought to govern his household. The third will indicate how he ought to preside over community and kingdom. The first book will therefore be devoted to ethics or individual conduct (*monastica*), the second to household management (*yconomica*), and the third to politics (*politica*).

This order is rational and natural. It is rational inasmuch as those things which relate to another individual originate from those things which relate to ourselves. That is why it is written in *Ethics* IX (4, 1166a1–2, b1–2; 8, 1168b4–5) that friendliness toward one's friends seems to derive from friendliness toward oneself. For a friend seems to be an individual who conducts himself toward the person to whom he is a friend in the way that he behaves toward himself. What is said about the nature of friendship, then, holds true for diligence in ruling, for whoever wishes to rule others diligently ought to be diligent in governing himself. This is why it is reasonable to determine the [truth about] rule of the self before the rule of household or kingdom.

This order is not only rational but also natural, for nature always proceeds from the imperfect to the perfect, as for example it is natural for someone to be imperfect as a boy before he is perfect as a man. In speculative matters as well, we always proceed in a natural order from the imperfect to the perfect, as for example an individual first has imperfect and afterwards more perfect knowledge and cognition, and thus, by devoting himself continuously to speculation, he is perfected in knowledge until he has the measure of perfect knowledge of which he is capable. What has been said of the natural order in speculative matters also holds true for actions, for just as imperfect cognition naturally precedes perfect cognition in speculative matters, so imperfect discernment precedes perfect diligence in actions. Therefore, since the diligence required for ruling oneself is not as much as that required for governing a household, and the prudence required for ruling a household is not as much as that required for governing community {aivb} and kingdom, it is in keeping with a natural order for his Royal Majesty to know first, how to rule himself; second, how to govern his household; and third, how to rule kingdom and community.

[2b. Principal Topics of Book I]

Now in the first book, which treats rule of the self, four things are to be set out: First it will be shown what his Royal Majesty ought to have as his end and where he should locate his happiness; second, what virtues he ought to have; third, what passions he ought to follow; and fourth, what ways of behaving (*mores*) he ought to imitate. For since no one can live well and rule himself well unless he gives himself over to good acts and good deeds that are regulated by the order of reason, anyone who wishes to treat rule of the self ought to impart knowledge of all those things which make some actions and ways of behaving different from others. This is therefore what the Philosopher intends to do when he says in *Ethics* II (2, 1103b29–30) that it is profitable in moral matters to examine thoroughly what concerns activities and how they should be done.

Now as regards the present discussion, it would seem that our activities arise from, and are differentiated from one another by, four factors, namely, ends, habits, passions, and ways of behaving. For since the end is the principle [or beginning] of our activities – so that as anyone sets himself one end or another so he performs one deed or another – then, in order to know what we ought to do, it seems highly profitable [to know] what end we ought to set ourselves. Moreover, because (as is said in *Ethics* II [3, 1104b3–5]) pleasure ((*delectationem/ declarationem*)) or distress in what is done is the sign of an acquired habit – in the sense that we take pleasure in one act or another according as we have one habit or another – [we ought therefore to discuss habits]. Third, actions and deeds are differentiated not only by their ends or habits but also by the passions, since those who are impassioned in one way or another perform one action or another. We see, for example, that, because fear and despair are not the same passion as hope, those who are fearful and who despair of victory act shamefully, leaving the ranks and fleeing the battle, whereas those who hope to be victorious attack in battle and make inroads into the enemy. What is said about hope and fear should therefore be understood of the other passions: Specific emotions and passions bring about an inclination in us to perform one deed or another. Fourth, moral behavior itself seems to differentiate deeds, since those people whose ways of behaving are characteristic of the old act differently from those whose ways of behaving are characteristic of the young. For old people, as will be shown in due course, are naturally skeptical and avaricious, whereas young people are naturally trusting and generous.

These four factors seem to have some analogical relation to each other, since different passions emerge from different ways of behaving, different habits arise from different passions, and different ends are set by different habits. For just as there are different ways of behaving in the young and the old, so there are different emotions and passions, and just as there are different emotions in good and bad people, so there are different habits. Moreover, from different habits we set ourselves different ends, for as is said in *Ethics* III (5, 1114b21–23), what seems to each individual to be an end is in accordance with the sort of person he is. It seems to the intemperate person that the entire end and great happiness [of life] is sexual indulgence. Likewise, those who have other habits are inclined to set themselves ends that conform to their habits.

In the first book, then, {aiira} we will deal with all four of these factors, namely, the end or happiness of rulers, their virtues, their passions, and their ways of behaving. Now we will first speak of the end, happiness itself, because the end of what is to be done is a principle that is more primary ((*principalius/principalis*)) than any of the others.

Chapter 3. The Utility of What Is to Be Said

We are undertaking this work, as has been said, in order to instruct rulers. Now no one is ever fully instructed unless he is favorably disposed, teachable, and attentive. Having rendered his Royal Majesty favorably disposed (by showing in the first chapter that we will handle the topics to be discussed in an easy manner) and teachable (by relating in the second chapter the order of what is to be said), it remains to make him attentive by setting out in this third chapter how much utility there is in what is written here. Because people generally hate a discussion that goes into great detail, most audiences are favorably disposed toward those who offer them one that is easy and superficial. Although this is a corruption of the appetite in other sciences, nevertheless, in moral matters, where the nature of the thing requires handling that is typical and general, it is not a corruption of appetite but rather the correct and due order. In an art of this kind, then, ease of handling renders an audience favorably disposed; the order of what is said renders it teachable, for anyone is made particularly teachable (i.e., capable of grasping what is taught) if what is said to him is put forward with some order and arrangement; while the utility of what is to be said renders it attentive, for everyone listens attentively if they hope to hear something useful.

Now if what is to be said here is correctly understood and duly observed, then, as regards the present work, his Royal Majesty will attain four things for which anyone ought to have the greatest love and desire. First, he will gain (*lucrabitur*) the greatest goods; second, he will gain himself; third, others; and the fourth consequence is that he will have the Lord Himself and eternal happiness.

[3a. The Greatest Goods Are to Be Gained from This Work]

One way in which goods themselves are differentiated is in terms of some being least, some being middling, and some being the greatest. The least goods are those which are external. Middling goods are those internal goods which can be common to good and bad people alike (such as mental diligence, natural intelligence, and the powers of the soul, for even evil people participate in these). The greatest goods, on the other hand, are those interior goods in which evil people cannot participate (such as the virtues, which, according to saints and philosophers, no one uses badly; for it is said in *On Rhetoric* I (1, 1355b2–6) that only the virtues cannot be used badly).

Goods are distinguished in another way (as is clear from the Philosopher in both the *Magna Moralia* [cf. II 11, 1209a20–21] and the *Ethics* [cf. Aquinas, *Sententia libri Ethicorum*, commenting on VIII 2, 1155b16–21]) in terms of some being pleasurable (*delectabilia*), some being useful (*utilia*), and some being morally honorable (*honesta*). Now morally honorable goods are goods *par excellence*, because according to [the Philosopher] these goods include pleasurable and useful goods. For if a good is morally honorable, it possesses in itself great pleasure and includes the utility of useful goods. Therefore, since the aim of this book is [to show] how his Royal Majesty may become virtuous and how he may bring those whom he has as his subjects to be morally honorable and virtuous, there is the greatest utility in its contents, because when they are observed the greatest {aiirb} and morally honorable goods will be possessed.

[3b. The Ruler Will Gain Himself]

There is a second great utility in what is to be said, because from it one will gain not only the greatest goods but also oneself. For as has frequently been touched on, [the purpose of treating] moral matters is that we should become good. Now it appears that a good person possesses himself, whereas an evil person loses himself. We ought to imagine accordingly that, just as in a community and in a kingdom the many are ordered toward one leader and one king, so in one and the same human being the powers that are rational by participation are ordered toward the intellect, which is rational in essence. Therefore, just as a king is not said to have a kingdom or a leader a community if there are some people in the kingdom or community who do not obey their king or leader, so an individual human being is not said to possess himself if his appetite dissents from his reason and if what is rational by participation does not obey what is rational in essence. For according to the Philosopher in *Ethics* IX (4, 1166a16–17; 8, 1168b35), a human being *is*, above all, intellect and reason. Therefore, when reason is not lord over those things which are within a human being, the human being is not lord over himself. He neither rules himself nor does he properly possess himself. Rather, he wills one thing with his reason and does another under the guidance and inclination of passion. That is why, if an evil human being does not possess himself, whereas a good human being does, then, through this treatment [of moral matters], which exists so that we may become good, a person gains himself.

[3c. The Ruler Will Gain Others]

Third, [the ruler] gains others, since the fact that someone rules himself rightly makes him worthy of being made ruler and lord over others. For if he flourishes in prudence and in the other moral virtues which will be dealt with in this book, then he is worthy to govern, whereas if he is lacking in these, then, even though he may rule through civil power, he is nevertheless more worthy to be a subject than to rule. He is, by nature, more a slave than a master.

[3d. The Ruler Will Attain the Lord Himself and Eternal Happiness]

The fourth consequence of observing those things of which we will impart knowledge in this book is that we will attain the Lord Himself and eternal happiness. For God Himself is the essence of unity because He is supremely one, and He is the essence of goodness because He is supremely good. The more someone approaches unity and goodness, therefore, the more he conforms to the first principle and the more perfectly he attains God Himself. Now evil people have the least degree of unity, for their whole kingdom is scattered. The 'kingdom' of any human being derives from the fact that the powers of the soul are 'ruled' by reason and intellect. Therefore, when reason dictates one thing and appetite pursues another, which happens in those who have a perverse soul, then the human being is not united but has ((om. *non*)) within him a fissiparousness which deforms him from [likeness to] the first principle. But those in whom the virtues flourish and in whom morally honorable goods abound (because these goods, which are good without qualification and not according to the senses, follow on from the rule of reason) possess unity and goodness in themselves, on account of which they conform to the first principle and are said to possess within themselves God Himself.

[3e. Conclusion]

So great, therefore, is the utility of what will be said here that, if we observe it, we will gain the greatest goods, ourselves, and also others; we will possess God Himself and, as a consequence, eternal happiness. Indeed, because those things of which we will impart knowledge cannot be observed without divine grace, it is fitting that every human being whatever {aiiva} should pray for divine grace – and his Royal Majesty above all others, for the higher the place occupied by his Royal Majesty, the more he requires divine grace to be able to perform virtuous deeds himself and lead his subjects toward virtue. . . .

Book III

Chapter 29. Which Is the Better Way of Ruling a Political Community or Kingdom? Is Rule by the Best King Better than Rule by the Best Law?

{oira} In *Politics* III (15, 1286a8–9) the Philosopher asks whether a kingdom or political community is ruled better by the best king or by the best law. He puts forward two arguments [to support the proposition] that it is better for the polity of a kingdom (*politia regni*) to be ruled by the best law than by the best king. The first is taken from the fact that the king ought to be the mouthpiece, as it were, and the instrument of the law, the second from the fact that a king is corrupted more easily than a law.

The first line of argument opens out as follows. As is said in *Ethics* V (6, 1134a35–62), a ruler ought to be the guardian of what is just – that is, of the just law. If a ruler {oirb} rules as he ought, therefore, he is a mouthpiece, as it were, of the just law, such that a king ensures that those things which the just law commands to happen will be observed by means of [his] civil power. This is why, if greater primacy is preferable in governance to a mouthpiece and instrument, to be ruled by the best law is preferable to being ruled by the best king. This is therefore what the Philosopher says in *Politics* III (16, 1287a18–22), [namely] that it is preferable for the law to rule, because kings or rulers should be set up to be guardians of the law and ministers of the laws.

The second line of argument in investigating the same [question] is taken from the fact that a king is led astray more easily than a law. Since a king is a human being, he is said to be not only a good intellect but an intellect with desire. Given that a king is not led astray by the fact that he has an intellect, he can nevertheless be led astray by the fact that he has desire connected to it. As a result, it is said in *Ethics* III that anger and desire sometimes lead the best men astray and ultimately destroy them. (If the best man is destroyed by desire, this is not with respect to the existence of his nature but with respect to his best existence because, although he is the best man, he begins to rage and to desire perverse things. Even if he is not destroyed with respect to the existence of his nature, he is ((om. *non*)) destroyed with respect to his best existence, because he is no longer the best [man].) And so the king is termed intellect with desire. But the law, because it is something that pertains to reason, seems to be termed pure intellect. As a result, it is said in *Politics* III (16, 1287a28–30) that whoever bids the intellect to rule bids God and the law to rule, whereas whoever bids a human being to rule also sets up a beast to rule, on account of the desire that is connected to him.

These arguments seem to show, therefore, that it is better for a kingdom and a political community to be ruled by law than by a king.

However, this conclusion should not be put forward without qualification. This is shown by the Philosopher in Book III (15, 1286a9–11) of the same [work]. As he says there, the law makes a universal pronouncement which is not universally [observed]. This is because human laws, however detailed they may be, will necessarily be deficient in particular cases. It is therefore better for a kingdom to be ruled by a king than by a law, since deficiencies in the law can be corrected by a king.

Thus, to reveal what should be said about this subject, it is important to know that a king (or any ruler whatever) is an intermediary between natural and positive law, in that no one rules rightly unless he acts as right reason dictates, because reason ought to be the rule of human deeds. This is why, if the name 'king' (*rex*) is taken from 'ruling' (*regere*) and if it is fitting for a king to rule others and to be a rule (*regula*) for others, a king ought to follow right reason in ruling others and, as a consequence, ought to follow natural law. This is because he only rules correctly to the extent that he does not deviate from natural law, even though he is above positive law because he instituted it on his own authority. And so, just as a king never rules correctly unless he relies upon natural law and acts as right reason dictates, so positive law never binds correctly unless it rests on the authority of the king ((*regis/legis*)) or of another ruler. For as was said above, in terms of their basic principle there is no difference between positive and legal justice in this way or in another. However, when it is established that they differ due to the authority of the person who institutes them, there is a difference, because positive law is beneath the ruler, just as natural law is above him. If it is said that some positive law is above the ruler, {oiva} then this is not insofar as it is positive law but insofar as it contains within it the virtue of natural law.

Therefore, since the question concerns whether it is better for a kingdom or political community to be ruled by the best king or by the best law, then if we are speaking about natural law, it is clear that this should have greater primacy in ruling than the king himself on the grounds that no one is a correct king except to the extent that he relies on that law. On this account, it is a good suggestion of the Philosopher in *Politics* III (16, 1287a28–32), [namely] that in correct governance it is not a beast that ought to rule but God and the intellect. For a beast rules whenever anyone strives to rule others, not by reason, but by the passion and desire which we share with beasts. On the other hand, God rules whenever someone, in ruling others, does not deviate from right reason and the natural law which God discloses to the intellect of every [human being].

If we are speaking about positive law, however, then it is better to be ruled by the best king than by the best law, above all in those cases in which this sort of law is deficient and makes a universal pronouncement which is not to be universally observed. In accordance with this [argument] therefore, the opposite conclusion is reached, [namely] that it is better to be ruled by a king than by law, in that the law is unable to determine particulars. As a result, it is advantageous for a king (and for anyone else who is ruling by means of right reason or the natural law which God imprints in the mind of every human being) to control positive law, to be above legal justice, and not to observe the law where it should not be observed.

From this it can be made clear how severity and clemency are able to stand side by side with justice. For as the Philosopher suggests in *Ethics* V (10, 1137b10–32), because of particular circumstances and because of their changeability, human acts cannot be measured by an inflexible rule, such as iron. Instead, it ought to be the case that they are measured by a [flexible] leaden rule, which is capable of being applied to human acts. Therefore, the law ought sometimes to be pliable in one direction and the wrongdoer dealt with more leniently than the law dictates. Sometimes it ought to be pliable in the opposite direction and the wrongdoer punished more strictly than the law determines. For circumstances, which are particular to a case and cannot be determined by law, sometimes mitigate the crime, whereupon it is in accordance with justice and right reason to act with clemency toward the offender. On the other hand, sometimes such circumstances make the crime worse, whereupon the approach should be more strict. Therefore, although strictness and clemency might seem to lie beyond legal and positive justice, in fact they do not. They lie beyond justice without qualification but, under the demands of particular circumstances, they may not do so with respect to reason. It is on this basis, therefore, that in delivering a judgment some things are said from equitability, some things from strictness, and some things from clemency. As long as the rule of a king remains correct and equitable and shows unbending impartiality, judgments measured according to this sort of rule are said to proceed from equity. On the other hand, if the rule bends slightly to one side when the legal circumstances of the offender demand it, the judgment that is then made is said to proceed from grace or from clemency. However, if the aforesaid rule is bent toward the opposite side, the judgment will be made from strictness or severity. Because all these things can occur in accordance with justice and reason, clemency and severity can {oivb} exist side by side with justice.

PETER OF AUVERGNE
COMMENTARY AND QUESTIONS ON BOOK
III OF ARISTOTLE'S POLITICS (SELECTIONS)

Introduction

Peter of Auvergne was regent master in the Faculty of Arts at Paris between 1272 and 1295. The connection between his appointment as Rector in 1275 and his role in the controversy with more radical Aristotelians in the faculty is unclear. Traditionally considered to be a follower of Thomas Aquinas, at least initially, he also came under the influence of Henry of Ghent and Godfrey of Fontaines, finally becoming a master of theology by 1296. He was made Bishop of Claremont in 1302 and died in 1303.

Peter of Auvergne produced two commentaries on Aristotle's *Politics*. The first of these was a continuation of Thomas Aquinas's unfinished commentary on the work, which had broken off in the middle of Book III (at 1280a6). Peter's completion of this text stands alongside his work on modist logic as his most significant contribution to the teaching of the Faculty of Arts at Paris. Although it cannot be dated with any greater precision than to the period in which Peter was regent master, his part of the commentary was probably composed some time in the 1270s. Far more certain is the influence it soon exerted as it became the standard exposition of William of Moerbeke's translation of Aristotle's text. The primary aim of this 'literal' (that is, phrase by phrase) commentary was to impose order and discipline on a difficult and often opaque original. Peter therefore held back his own interpretation for a second analysis (only datable, once again, to the period between 1272 and 1296), this one in the form of a commentary *cum quaestionibus* (that is, a recasting of the text as a series of questions). This format allowed Peter much greater freedom both in the choice of topic to be scrutinized and in his own endorsement of the conclusions which Aristotle proffered. This second commentary, Peter's *Questions on the Politics*, also came to exercise considerable influence well into the fourteenth century. In particular, it appears to have guided the interpretation put forward in the anonymous Milan commentary and in this way provided an important source for Marsilius of Padua's *Defender of Peace*. Marsilius's understanding of the 'weightier part' (*valentior pars*) of a multitude and of the collective wisdom of the whole political community was not drawn simply and directly from Book III of the *Politics*. It was mediated by the teaching of Aristotle's text with which he was familiar from the Faculty of Arts at Paris and in particular by what Peter of Auvergne had taught about the composition and participation of 'the multitude.'

By presenting an unvarnished English version of Moerbeke's Latin translation of Aristotle alongside Peter of Auvergne's literal commentary, we hope to give some indication not only of the task which Peter faced in trying to make sense of what Aristotle was presented by Moerbeke as having said but also of how Peter could use even the most restrictive of commentary genres to emphasize some points at the expense of others and thereby put forward a particular interpretation of his own. In the case of Book III what is so striking is how Peter softens the impact of Aristotle's apparent preference for the wisdom of the collective judgment of the whole community and, by the same token, highlights those points at which kingship could still be regarded as the best polity. In chapter 9, sections 9 and 12, for example, Peter picks up on a single word, 'perhaps' (*forte*), and uses it to explain why Aristotle may have hesitated in concluding that the collective judgment of the whole multitude should be better than that of a few good men. According to Peter, Aristotle hesitated because he wanted to limit the universal application of such a principle so that he could make an exception for kingship. Likewise, Peter is always careful to define just what 'the multitude' means in this context. Thus, in expounding the analogy of pure and impure food he underlines the point that those people in the multitude who lack wisdom will be persuaded and corrected by other members of the multitude who are wise and prudent. In chapter 14, section 6, he accordingly attributes superior judgment to 'a large crowd or several individuals' but makes it clear that this is the achievement of the latter (*plures*) – of good and prudent members of the multitude – rather than of the multitude as such. Finally, when Peter comes to summarize Aristotle's account of the historical development and transformation of successive constitutions, 'polity' (that is, the constitution where many people are alike in virtue) is omitted altogether.

By juxtaposing the text of Peter of Auvergne's literal commentary with that of his commentary *cum quaestionibus* we hope to give some indication of how Peter used a different genre of exposition to strengthen his interpretation of Aristotle's work with additional arguments of his own and thereby show how he sought to *apply* the content of the *Politics*. Peter's first strategy is to select topics that facilitate the statement of his own views. From the passage in Book III translated here he accordingly selects three topics for detailed analysis: the election and correction of rulers, the relative merits of being ruled by a good man or by good laws, and the comparative advantages of election and hereditary succession. Peter does *not* choose to discuss whether there is greater collective virtue in the whole community acting as a single entity than in any one part of the community acting on its own. His second strategy is to extend the interpretation which was only implicit in his literal commentary. Thus, when he does discuss 'the multitude,' he is careful to define it as a multitude which is not only distinct from a vile or 'beastlike' multitude but is also characterized by the guidance of its wise and prudent members. This 'mixed and ordered' multitude may derive power (that is, *potentia*, in the sense of capacity or strength, rather than *potestas*, in the sense of authority) from its inclusion of the populace, but it derives its prudence and virtue from the inclusion of wise individuals. Moreover, Peter is careful to put practical limitations on the election and correction of a ruler even by this 'proper' sort of multitude. Election and correction by the community are appropriate only for those communities which have no superior authority over them.

Peter of Auvergne's apparent concern to safeguard the position of kingship continues to be in evidence in his second and third questions, where the solutions he offers rest on a distinction between something which is true absolutely or without qualification (*per se, simpliciter*) and something which is true incidentally and within certain terms of reference (*per accidens, secundum quid*). For Aristotle, the good man would always be susceptible to passion inasmuch as he is a human being, whereas the law could be defined as intellect without passion. Conversely, the law is limited to putting forward universal propositions, whereas a human being can judge their particular application.

What is noticeable about Peter's response to these points is that, although he accepts that it is better to be ruled by laws rather than by a good man, he insists that this is true only *per accidens*. Rather than emphasize Aristotle's definition of law as pure reason, therefore, he picks out Aristotle's observation that laws are relative to the constitution and are therefore only as rational as the legislator who made them. Likewise, in answer to his third question, although Peter accepts that election is better *per se* because it bestows rule on the most prudent and virtuous individual, he insists that hereditary succession is nevertheless better *per accidens* because of a number of practical considerations. He accordingly repeats the reservations made in his literal commentary (electors can be of suspect probity; subjects will be more accustomed to obey a ruler when they know the son will succeed the father) but also adds new qualifications from his own experience (the dangers of pride; the perils of a vacancy). Knowing that his son is to succeed him makes a ruler better and also ensures that the son will be trained in good conduct. On balance, therefore, Peter concludes that hereditary succession presents less danger to the political community than election. Whereas he had been content in his literal commentary to use the distinction between *per se* and *per accidens* as a means of leaving this question open, in his commentary in question form he comes down firmly on the side of hereditary kingship. As in his discussions of the participation of the multitude in government and the rational character of law, here too, Peter's own sympathies are clear. Correction by the wise and prudent few, legislation by the good man, and the practical advantages of hereditary succession all point in the direction of kingship rather than a state of affairs in which the populace exercises lordship (*status popularis*).

For further reading on Peter of Auvergne and his commentaries on Aristotle, see CHLMP IX.34, 'The Reception and Interpretation of Aristotle's *Ethics*' and X.38, 'The Reception and Interpretation of Aristotle's *Politics*,' and J. M. Blythe, *Ideal Government and the Mixed Constitution in the Middle Ages* (Princeton: Princeton University Press, 1992), chapter 5. For Peter's significance, including his influence on Marsilius of Padua, see C. Flüeler, *Rezeption und Interpretation der Aristotelischen Politica im späten Mittelalter*, 2 vols. (Amsterdam/Philadelphia: B. R. Grüner, 1992), 1:86–131.

Commentary

Chapter 8

[Aristotle, *Politics* III 10, 1281a11–39]

{189}   Now there is a problem about who ought to exercise lordship in a city. Is it the multitude or the rich or the fair-minded or the single best individual or a tyrant?

[A]   But all of these alternatives seem to present difficulties. Why?

[A1a(i)]   If the poor, because they are many, plunder what belongs to the rich, is this not unjust? It would certainly seem just to those exercising lordship, by heaven! Then what would we have to call supreme injustice?

[A1a(ii)]   Moreover, once everything has been taken, if the many {190} then plunder what belongs to the few, it is clear that they destroy the city. Surely, however, virtue does not destroy what possesses it, nor is what is just destructive of a city? It is clearly impossible for this law to be just.

[A1a(iii)]   Further, whatever actions a tyrant performs would necessarily all be just as well, for he exercises force, in that he is more powerful (*potentior*), just as the multitude does toward the rich.

[A1b(i)]   Is it just, then, for the few and the rich to rule? If they too do these things and plunder and remove the possessions of the multitude, is this just? Then the other is too. It is indeed clear that all these actions are wicked and not morally serious.

[A1b(ii)]   But should the fair-minded rule and be lords over all? Then everyone else who is not honored with political offices is necessarily dishonored, for we term offices 'honors.' Now if the same people are always in office, then others are necessarily dishonored.

[A2a]   But {191} is it better for a single most morally serious individual to rule? But this is still more oligarchical, for more are dishonored.

[A2b(i)]   But perhaps someone will say that it is bad for a human being (whose soul is affected by passion) to exercise complete lordship, but not for the law.

[A2b(ii)]   If, then, the law were to be oligarchic or democratic, what difference will it make to this problem? For the same things will happen as were said before.

1. {413C} After the Philosopher has distinguished between polities in terms of their ruling offices (*principatus*) and has set out [the end] for the sake of which the city is established, in this section he investigates who ought to rule in the city. And because office ought to be distributed according to the excess of some good [in some individual, or individuals, in relation to others], he investigates the good in accordance with whose excess such a distribution should be made. This section is accordingly divided into two parts. In the first (III 10–11, 1281a11–1282b13) he investigates who ought to rule in the city; second (III 12, 1282b14–1283a23), he investigates the good in accordance with whose excess office should be distributed (at 'Since therefore . . .'). The first part is in two sections. In the first he raises a problem and touches on a sort of solution. Second, he argues against this solution (at 'But all of these . . .'). In the first section he says that, after it has been determined on what basis the polities should be

distinguished, [namely] according to their distinction from one another in offices, a problem follows from this, namely, who ought to exercise lordship in the city. Now since someone ought to exercise lordship, this will either be the multitude (as in a polity, which is a popular state [*status popularis*]), or the wealthy (as in the state of the few [*status paucorum*]), or the virtuous (as in a state of the best [*status optimatum*]), or the one best person (as in a kingdom), or the one worst person (as in a tyranny).

2. Then, when he says 'But all of these alternatives . . .' he argues against each one of these, or at least against several of them. This section is divided into two parts. In the first [A] he does what has been said; second [B], he makes a particular inquiry into whether it is more advantageous for the multitude to exercise lordship than for a few virtuous individuals to do so (at 'Concerning other'). The first part is divided into two further sections. In the first [A1] he argues that it is not advantageous for the multitude to exercise lordship, nor for the rich to do so; second [A2], that neither [is it advantageous] for a single morally serious individual (at 'But is it better . . .'). The first of these sections is divided into two. First [A1a] he shows that it is not advantageous for the multitude to exercise lordship; second [A1b], that neither is it advantageous for the rich few to do so (at 'Is it just, then . . .'). The first is divided into three, corresponding to the three reasons with which he proves that it is not advantageous for the multitude to exercise lordship. The second of these begins 'Moreover . . .' and the third 'Further, whatever actions . . .'

[A1a(i)] In the first of these he maintains that all of these alternatives appear to pose problems. For if it is said that it is advantageous for a multitude of the poor to exercise lordship, then, since a multitude of this sort would have power (*potentia*) but lack virtue, it would follow that, because of their poverty and their power, they would plunder the goods of the rich. But is this not unjust? In other words, yes [it is unjust], for a city ought to have just lordship in accordance with virtue. As a result, it is clear that this is 'extreme' injustice (i.e., the worst).

3. [A1a(ii)] Then, when he says 'Moreover, once everything . . .' he puts forward a second argument. If it is maintained that it is advantageous for the multitude to exercise lordship, then, he says, it would follow, as before, that the multitude would plunder the goods of the rich and of the few – as if this were virtuous ((*virtuose/virtuosorum*)). But this is to destroy the city. Yet virtue does not destroy that to which it properly belongs, nor does what is just corrupt a city. As a result, it is clear that a law which

enjoins the multitude to exercise lordship is not just. Therefore, it is not advantageous for the multitude to exercise lordship.

4. [A1a(iii)] Then, when he says 'Further . . .' he puts forward a third argument. He says that all the actions performed by a tyrant as a tyrant are unjust, because a tyrant does violence by means of his power and takes the goods of his subjects. Now such activity is unjust. But where the multitude exercises lordship, it does violence to the rich in the manner of a tyrant by plundering their goods. For this reason, it is clear that the multitude is like a tyrant and that, as a result, the actions of the multitude are unjust. Therefore, it is not advantageous for the multitude to exercise lordship.

5. [A1b] Then, when he says 'Is it just, then . . .' he shows that it is unjust for the rich few to exercise lordship. This section is divided into two parts. In the first [A1b(i)] he shows that it is not advantageous for the rich few to exercise lordship; second [A1b(ii)], that it is also not advantageous for the virtuous to exercise lordship, whether they are few in number or many (at 'But should the fair-minded . . .').

[A1b(i)] In the first he says, as if asking a question, 'Is it just for the rich few to exercise lordship in the city?' It is as if he were saying that it is unjust for a smaller number to exercise lordship, because through their power they will plunder the goods and possessions of the poor, just as the multitude would do in reverse if it were exercising lordship. It would thus be just for the rich to plunder the goods of the multitude, and, conversely, it would be just for the multitude to plunder the goods of the rich. But the latter is unjust, as has been seen. As a result, it is clear that it is wicked, unjust, and not virtuous for the rich few to exercise lordship.

6. [A1b(ii)] Then, when he says 'But should the fair-minded . . .' he shows that it is not just for the virtuous to exercise lordship, whether they are many or few. For someone might say that it is true that it is not advantageous for either the rich few or the multitude to exercise lordship but it is surely beneficial and just for the virtuous to exercise lordship and to be lords among all. But this seems false, because if only the virtuous rule, then everyone else will be dishonored, because they do not attain the {414A} honor of office. Offices are honors, because they are the reward of virtue, and this is honor, as is maintained in *Ethics* I and IV. Therefore, whoever does not attain office does not attain honor. When the virtuous are ruling, then, everyone else remains without honors. But this is inappropriate, for it is a cause of dissension, since everyone naturally seeks

honor. On this account, everyone seeks to be honored by the good and the wise, who can judge better and more correctly. If honor is removed from them, therefore, the consequence is dissension and many evils in the city. Hence it is unjust for the virtuous to exercise lordship.

7. [A2] Then, when he says 'But is it better . . .' he shows that it is unjust for one virtuous person to exercise lordship. This section is divided into two parts. In the first [A2a] he does what has been said. In the second [A2b], because someone could say that it is not advantageous for a human being to rule but for a human being to rule by law, he shows the opposite (at 'But perhaps someone will say . . .'). In the first part [A2a] he maintains that it is not advantageous for one very virtuous person to rule, because if one very virtuous person were to exercise lordship many more people would be dishonored with regard to the honor of office. But this is inappropriate, for from this follow dissension and disturbances in the city, as has been said. Again, this polity would appear to be worse than the state of the few, because in the rule of a few [the subjects' goods] are paid out to many, whereas in this polity [they are paid out] to one individual. Now this seems worse, because the more an evil is divided the less it is and the more tolerable it is. As a result, it is clear that it is not beneficial for one virtuous person to exercise lordship.

8. [A2b] Then, when he says 'But perhaps,' because someone might say that law ought to exercise lordship and not a human being, he argues against this position. First [A2b(i)] he puts forward the reason why it would seem that the law ought to exercise lordship; second [A2b(ii)], he argues the contrary (at 'If, then . . .'). In the first [A2b(i)] he says [that it seems] that it is wicked and unjust for a human being to rule and not the law, because a human being has passions connected to him. Now passions distract the will and make it deviate from its correct end. As a consequence, they pervert the judgment of reason. Law, however, has no passions and, as a result, does not deviate from the correct judgment of reason. Therefore, since rule is better and more justly exercised by something that cannot deviate from a correct end than by something that can do so, and since a human being can deviate from a correct end whereas law cannot, it is clear that it is just for the law to exercise lordship and not a human being.

9. [A2b(ii)] Then, when he says 'If, then . . .' he argues the contrary and maintains that it does not seem to be true that it is just for the law to

exercise lordship in all cases, because there can be laws that tend to the power of the few or the many, and such laws are made and instituted with reference to their end. Now (as has been said before) it is not supposed that in these laws there is an end that is correct without qualification. Therefore, neither are these laws just without qualification. As a result, it is clear that it makes no difference to what may be said whether the law or any of the other alternatives [i.e., one or another group or individual] is to rule, because the same inappropriate result always occurs, as has been shown before for each of them.

[*Politics* III 11, 1281a39–b21]

{191}

[B1] Concerning the others, there may indeed be a different line of reasoning. Now, that the multitude ought to exercise lordship rather than those who are indeed the best but few, will certainly seem questionable and to raise problems but perhaps certainly to have some truth as well.

[B1a(i)] For when many people come together, each of whom is not a morally serious individual, they are nevertheless better, not as individuals but {192} as all together, just as feasts brought together are [better] than those bestowed at one person's expense.

[B1a(ii)] For when there are many, each has a part of virtue and prudence, and gathered together they become, as it were, a single human being with a multitude of many feet and many hands and many senses. So too in understanding and in ways of behaving. On this account, the many are also better ((om. *kries* [var.])) at works of music and of poets, some [at] one particular, others [at] another, but all [at] all.

[B1a(iii)] But morally serious men differ from each one of the multitude just as the good are said to differ from the not good and things depicted in art from true things. This is because separate elements are collected into one, although one particular eye or some other detail may be, on its own, more beautiful than what is painted. {193}

[B1b] Whether this distinction between the many and the morally serious few applies to the whole populace and the whole multitude is not clear. Or rather, by heaven, it is clearly impossible to apply to some [multitudes], for the same line of argument would also fit beasts, and what, indeed (it will then be asked) is the difference between some individuals and beasts? However, nothing prevents what has been said from being true of some multitudes.

10. [B] Then, when he says 'Concerning the others,' he puts the other alternatives on one side and concentrates in particular on inquiring whether it is more advantageous for lordship to be exercised by the

multitude or by a few virtuous individuals. This is divided into two sections. In the first [B1] he establishes that there is no need to discuss all the other alternatives, because a different line of reasoning applies to them, for it is clear that it is not advantageous for the worst individual to exercise lordship – this is clear *per se*. A different line of reasoning applies to this case, because although there is some doubt about the others, there is no doubt about this one, and so the Philosopher does not produce arguments for it. But inquiry should nevertheless be made as to whether it is more advantageous for lordship to be exercised by the multitude than by those who are virtuous but few in number. For there seems to be a problem here, and there is a solution [B1] which resolves the argument previously put forward to prove the opposite [A1a], for it seems to be truer and more advantageous that the multitude ought to rule than the virtuous few.

11. [B1a(i)] Then, when he says 'For when many,' he proceeds [with this inquiry]. First [B1] he shows that it is more advantageous for lordship to be exercised by the multitude than by the virtuous few. Second [B2], he solves the problem and another one connected to it (at 'As a result . . .'). The first section is in two parts. First [B1a] he puts forward a single proposition; second [B1b], he argues from it (at 'Whether this distinction'). The first part is further divided into two. First [B1a(i)] he makes the proposition clear; second [B1a(ii)], he establishes the difference between some of the things mentioned (at 'For when many').

[B1a(i)] In the first of these he maintains that even if the many are not virtuous without qualification, when they come together into a unity they will make up a virtuous individual – not in such a way that any one of these individuals is something virtuous by himself or something better [than one of the virtuous few] but in such a way that all of them together make up something virtuous and are thereby something better than any of them taken separately. He explains this with a simile. He says that it is like people celebrating a feast at common expense with each individual bringing a moderate amount of food – the result of gathering together everything that has been brought is a large quantity of food. Likewise in the case at hand – if there are many individuals and each one of them has a certain amount of virtue and prudence – then when they come together into a unity they make up a unity that is great and virtuous. For in whatever respect one individual happens to be deficient another will abound. For example, if one individual is not inclined to bravery, another will be, and if someone else is not inclined to temperance, another will be, and if one individual is not able to exercise good foresight, another will be. And thus, when they come together, they constitute, as it were, a single, perfect, and virtuous human being. I say 'human being,' in that it possesses a multitude of senses by means of which it can discern and a multitude of hands and feet by means of which it can be moved to act and can act. It is also the same with regard to {414B} understanding and ways of behaving. For when all come together, they are turned into a single human being, as it were, perfect in understanding (in terms of the intellectual virtues) and perfect in appetite (in terms of the moral virtues). He adduces another simile, saying that because many things joined together are something better than any one of them on its own, it happens that musical works and works of poets are done better and brought to perfection through many rather than by one. This is how the arts and the sciences were discovered, in that initially, one person discovered something and passed it on, perhaps without order; someone else then took it on, added to it, and passed on the sum of their efforts in greater order; and so on, until the arts and the sciences were completely discovered. It is also clear that, while particular individuals have made particular discoveries, all individuals together have discovered everything. It is also clear that what everyone has discovered is greater and more complete than what any single individual has discovered by himself.

12. [B1a(iii)] Then, when he says 'But virtuous men differ,' he makes a distinction between a single man who is virtuous without qualification and any one of those individuals from whose convergence into a unity something virtuous is produced. He maintains that in the same way that a good person is distinct from someone who is not good, so virtuous men (i.e., those who are particularly virtuous) are distinct from any one of those many individuals from whose convergence into something singular something virtuous is produced. This is because virtuous men are good without qualification, whereas any one of the latter individuals, taken in himself, is not good, since he is not completely virtuous. Again, virtuous men differ from these individuals taken separately in the same way as things depicted in art differ from true things. By this I understand that a painter who wishes to depict something in art, such as a human form, concentrates on the good state of the eyes in one person and ignores the poor state of his other parts; likewise, he concentrates on the good state of the hand in another person and ignores the poor state of his other parts; and so he concentrates on the better qualities of different parts in different people

and ignores those which are bad. Then, from all these different parts gathered together, he makes an image that is more beautiful than any one of those individuals from whom he has taken something. It is also clear that any one of those from whom he has taken something possesses something of beauty but not beauty without qualification, whereas what he has taken from [all of] them is beautiful without qualification. Likewise in the case at hand. Any one of these many individuals possesses something of virtue but is not virtuous without qualification, whereas that which has been collected from [all of] them without qualification is virtuous without qualification. This is what he means by 'artificially,' because those things which are true without qualification are taken, collected together into a unity, and the image which is composed from the simultaneous [arrangement of] parts that exist in a good state in different individuals is more beautiful than any one of them. In one of these a beautiful eye is found, in another a beautiful hand, for it may well turn out that one person has a more beautiful eye than the one that is painted, although he is deficient in other respects, and, similarly, that another person has a more beautiful hand than the one that is painted, although he is deficient in other respects, and similarly with the other particulars. Likewise in the case at hand. The particularly virtuous individual differs from each one of the individuals who have been described, because, [although] these individuals when taken together may possess all the good qualities that pertain to the soul, and [although] each individual may possess one of them in his own person (in which respect he may, perhaps, be superior to the virtuous person), nevertheless, the individual in the multitude is without qualification inferior to the virtuous individual.

13. [B1b] Then, when he says 'Whether this distinction,' he argues from the proposition which he has just put forward, declaring that it is not clear whether a difference of this sort turns out to exist with regard to the multitude and with regard to a whole populace in relation to the virtuous few, namely, that the whole multitude is better than the virtuous few. However, this is impossible in terms of the virtue that exists in some people, as is the case in a beastlike multitude, in which human beings are inclined to perform beastlike acts and possess very little reason. In this sort of multitude, it is *not* true that something virtuous can arise from these human beings if they come together into a unity. A multitude in which each individual has a degree of virtue and prudence and in which they are all inclined toward virtuous acts is different. In this sort of multitude it *is*

true that what arises from them when they come together into a unity is something virtuous. And this is what the Philosopher maintains, namely, that in some multitudes it is not true that the multitude constitutes something virtuous but that in other multitudes this can be true. From this the following argument can be formed: It is better for what is better and more virtuous to rule. But it can happen that a multitude is better and more virtuous than a few virtuous individuals, as has been proved. Therefore, etc.

Chapter 9

[*Politics* III 11, 1281b21–1282b13]

{193}

[B2a(i)] As a result, a solution is thereby clearly provided both for the problem set out earlier and

[B2a(ii)] for the problem connected to it, namely, what lordship should be exercised by free people and by the multitude of citizens, by such individuals as have no standing (*dignitas*) and no virtue.

[B2b(i)] For it is not safe for them to have a share in the highest offices (because of their injustice and imprudence, the former making them act unjustly, the latter making them do wrong).

[B2b(ii)] There is cause to fear, however, in not allowing them to participate, for when {194} there are many poor people barred from honors, such a city will necessarily be full of factional dissent (*seditiones*).

[B2b(iii)] And so it remains for them to participate in deliberating and judging.

[B2c(i)] It is for this reason that Solon and some other legislators drew up statutes to elect to office and to correct rulers but did not allow them to rule as individuals. For when they are all gathered together they have sufficient sense, and when they are mixed with their betters they are of benefit to their cities (just as impure food mixed with pure food makes a whole that is more advantageous than a small amount [of pure food]), whereas, as individuals, each one of them is imperfect in judgment.

[B2c(ii)] =

[C1a(i)] This arrangement of the polity has an initial problem, however, because it would seem that the individual who judges whether someone is correctly medicated is the same person who provides the cure and restores the sick {195} to health. Now this is the physician. And it is also like this in other skills and arts. Just as a physician ought to administer correction in medical matters, so too should others in like cases. Both the practitioner (*operator*) and the superintendent (*architectonicus*) are physicians, however, and, thirdly, the individual who is instructed (*eruditus*) in the art. There are some such in all arts, so to speak. Now we attribute judgment no less to the instructed than to the knowledgeable (*scientes*). It would seem to be exactly the same, then, with election. For to choose correctly is the function of the knowledgeable, as a geometer is of geometers, a helmsman of helmsmen. For even if there are certain functions and arts in which ordinary people (*idiotae*) too sometimes participate, this is not to a greater extent than the knowledgeable.

[C1a(ii)]   As a result, according to this reasoning, the multitude should certainly not be given lordship, either in electing to office or in correcting.

[C1b(i)]   However, perhaps not all of this is well said, on account of {196} the earlier argument (if the multitude is not too vile, for each individual may indeed be a worse judge than the knowledgeable, but when they are all gathered together they are better or not worse) and because

[C1b(ii)]   there are certain things about which the maker is neither the sole nor the best judge, where those who do not possess the art [nevertheless] also know (*cognoscunt*) the works. For example, knowing a house is not only for the person who made it; in fact, the person who uses it (the user being the householder) judges it better. Likewise, the helmsman is a better judge of a rudder than the carpenter, the guest but not the cook of a feast. Perhaps this problem would seem to have been solved sufficiently, then, in this way.

[C2a]   However, there is another [problem] here. For it seems wrong for the bad rather than the fair-minded to be lords in greater matters. Corrections, however, and elections to office are the greatest matters. In certain polities (as has been said) they are handed over to the people, {197} for the assembly (*ecclesia*) is lord over all such things. Yet those who have few honors and are of any age whatever participate in the assembly, offer counsel, and give judgment, even though control of finances, leadership of the army, and ruling in the greatest offices pertain to individuals of greater status (*maiores*).

[C2b]   And so this problem may also be solved in a similar way. For perhaps they have these things right. For it is not the judge or the counselor or the speaker in the assembly who is ruler but the lawcourt, the council, and the populace, of which each of the aforementioned individuals is a part (now I term 'a part' the counselor, the speaker in the assembly, and the judge). For this reason, the multitude justly exercises lordship over those of greater status, for the people and the council and the lawcourt consist of many individuals, and the possession of honor by all of these is fuller than that [possessed] by those individuals (single or few in number) who rule in the great offices. Therefore, these [problems] {198} have been determined in this way.

[C3a]   The first problem set out shows nothing so clearly as that correctly established laws ought to be lords; the ruler, however, whether a single individual or many, must be lord over those matters on which the laws cannot speak with certainty (because it is not easy to determine universally about everything).

[C3b]   However, it is not yet clear what 'correctly established laws' must be like, and the original problem still remains. If laws are necessarily like polities (in being either bad or good, just or unjust), and yet it is clear that laws are bound to be established with reference to the polity, then, if this is the case, it is plain that those which are in accordance with correct polities are necessarily just but those which are in accordance with deviant ones are unjust.

{414B} 1. [B2] After the Philosopher has raised the problem of whether it is more beneficial for the multitude to exercise lordship than for the virtuous to do so [B1], in this section he solves it, together with an additional problem connected to it. This section has two parts. First [B2a(i)] he infers the solution to the question from what has just been determined and poses a connected question [B2a(ii)]; second [B2b], he solves the latter (at 'For it is not safe . . .').

[B2a(i)] In the first part he maintains that on the basis of what has just been said a solution can be given to the problem raised in asking whether it is more beneficial for lordship to be exercised by the multitude than by the virtuous few. For it appears from what has been said that there are two types of multitude. One is beastlike, in which no one possesses reason (or at least very much reason) but each individual is inclined to beastlike acts. It is clearly not advantageous for this sort of multitude to exercise any kind of lordship, because it is without reason both collectively and separately. The other type of multitude is one in which all individuals have some degree of reason, are inclined toward prudence, and are readily open to persuasion by reason. It is more advantageous for lordship to be exercised by this sort of multitude {414C} than by the virtuous few, for although not everyone may be virtuous, nevertheless, what arises from all of them when they come together is virtuous. In this way a solution to the question becomes apparent, because where there is a multitude of this sort it is more advantageous for lordship to be exercised by it than by the virtuous, but where there is not this sort of multitude but the beastlike type, it is in no way advantageous.

[B2a(ii)] From this it will also be possible to solve another question which arises as a consequence of it, namely, whether the multitude and the free ought to elect their lords and correct them and, if this is advantageous, from whom it is advantageous for these lords to be drawn. And he explains who it is about whom this question is asked: They are the sort who do not have any standing or the good of virtue.

2. [B2b] Then, when he says 'For it is not safe,' he solves the question. First [B2b] he solves it; second [B2c(i)], he corroborates the solution from

the laws of the ancients (at 'It is for this reason . . .'). The first part is in three sections. In the first [B2b(i)] he shows that it is inappropriate and precarious for the multitude to rule; second [B2b(ii)], that for the multitude to have no share at all in ruling is a source of fear (at 'There is cause to fear, however . . .'); third [B2b(iii)], that it is advantageous for the multitude to have some sort of rule (at 'And so it remains . . .').

[B2b(i)] In the first section he maintains that for free people and the multitude to attain ruling power is a danger of the first and greatest degree, since these people are unjust and imprudent. Because of their imprudence they will fail to judge correctly, and because of their injustice they will be inclined to unjust acts. From this it will follow that they will do much that is evil with regard to themselves and much that is unjust with regard to others by injuring and harassing them. This is dangerous. It is supremely inappropriate, therefore, for such people to participate in ruling.

3. [B2b(ii)] Then, when he says 'There is cause to fear, however . . .' he shows that for these people to have no share at all in honors seems to be a source of fear. It seems inappropriate and a source of fear if there is no way in which ruling power is conceded to them and if they cannot attain it, because they will consider themselves dishonored. When they are numerous and poor, sedition and disturbance in the city will follow – something which is to be feared.

4. [B2b(iii)] Then, when he says 'And so it remains,' he concludes the third [argument]. He maintains that from the fact that many evils in the city will result if there is no way at all in which they can attain ruling power, the alternative that remains is that they ought to participate in rule in some way, at least in terms of deliberating and judging.

5. [B2c(i)] Then, when he says 'It is for this reason,' he corroborates this solution by the laws and arrangements of the ancients. This is divided into two parts. In the first [B2c(i)] he does what has just been said; in the second [B2c(ii) = C1a(i)] he argues against the arrangements of the ancients (at 'This arrangement . . .'). In the first [B2c(i)] he declares that, because it was maintained that many evils (such as sedition and disturbance in the city) will result if the multitude is given no share at all in ruling, Solon (lawgiver to the Athenians) and certain other legislators established [a role for] the multitude in the election and correction of rulers. However, they refused to allow any individuals to have the power to elect and correct on their own. This was rational, because none of them has virtue

on his own, and hence each would be found wanting in electing and correcting. We maintain that these legislators refused to allow any one individual to have the power to elect and correct rulers but only [granted this to them] all together for the reason maintained above [B1a(ii)]. This reason is that, although each individual may not have the perfect virtue needed to conduct himself rightly in ruling, nevertheless, the whole multitude has sufficient virtue and discernment for election and correction. For in this multitude there are some who are wise and virtuous and some who are not, and if all these people are taken together they will have more effect than if only the virtuous and the wise are taken. This is the case here as it is in nutrition, in that impure food taken with pure food is more beneficial than impure food taken by itself, for the badness and corruption of impure food is rectified by means of the pure food mixed with it, and from their mixture good food results and the impure is rendered neutral. Thus, within a commonwealth those who lack wisdom in deliberating and discerning are in some way rectified by those who are wise so that they can be of some benefit to the commonwealth.

6. [B2c(ii) = C1a(i)] Then, when he says 'This arrangement,' [he puts forward] an objection against this arrangement of the ancients. It is divided into two according to the dual nature of the objection. The second [C2] begins 'There is another . . .' The first [C1] is divided into two. In the first [C1a] he touches on the objection. Second [C1b(i)], he solves it (at 'However, perhaps not all of this . . .'). The first of these [C1a] is in turn divided into two. First [C1a(i)] he establishes two propositions; second [C1a(ii)], he argues from them (at 'As a result, according to . . .'). The first of these [C1a(i)] is divided into two, corresponding to the two propositions which are put forward. The second begins 'Then, it would seem to be . . .' In the first he says that it has been maintained that Solon and certain other legislators decreed that the multitude should have the power to elect and correct the government [but that] this arrangement seems open to doubt. To explain why, he sets out the following proposition: The person who is to treat someone and cure an attendant illness is also the one to judge who has been cured correctly. Now this is done by a physician. The reasoning behind this proposition is that it pertains to the same person to do something by deduction from causes and principles and to resolve it to its first causes by considering from what causes and what kinds of causes it exists and has being. This, however, is to judge. Therefore, it pertains to the same person to establish something and to

make a judgment about it. It is the same in other arts, for just as the physician judges and corrects in medical matters, so do others in their [own] arts.

He subsequently declares that physicians are of three types: those who do not know the art but know to some extent how to put into practice what has been decreed by others; those who are the principal possessors of the art, who know without qualification {415A} all the causes and principles of medicine; and third, those with experience, who know some things but not without qualification. Therefore, when we say that a physician makes a judgment about the person he is curing, we understand 'physician' in the second and third senses. And just as in medicine there are three types of physicians to consider, namely, the practicing (*practicus*), the knowledgeable (*sciens*), and the experienced (*expertus*), so it is in almost all the other arts. In all of them, we attribute correct judgment about the things with which they are concerned no less (or only a little less) to the experienced than to the knowledgeable. Now he says 'no less' because those who know without qualification make better judgments in all matters.

7. Then, when he says 'Then, it would seem to be . . .' he puts forward a second proposition and maintains that it is the same with election as it is with judgment. It pertains to the knowledgeable to choose correctly. This is his function, just as the geometer judges correctly about things involved in geometry, the helmsman judges correctly about things involved in steering a ship, and likewise in other cases. There is a reason for this. [Election or] choice is appetite that has first been informed by deliberation, and deliberation is reasoning about those things which are the means to an end. Now to reason correctly about the means to an end pertains to the knowledgeable. This is why it is clear that judging and choosing correctly are for the knowledgeable. And if ordinary people sometimes choose correctly, they do so not as being knowledgeable or as being better than the knowledgeable, because if they choose or judge correctly, they do so by chance. Not so, however, the wise.

8. [C1a(ii)] Then, when he says 'As a result,' he argues from these two propositions that it is not advantageous for the populace to have the power to elect to office and to correct. He maintains that it is clear from what has been said that it is not advantageous for the multitude to exercise lordship in the election and correction of rulers because, as has been

maintained, it is for the knowledgeable to choose and for the prudent to correct. But the multitude is ignorant and imprudent. Therefore, it is not advantageous for the multitude to exercise lordship in election and correction.

9. [C1b] Then, when he says 'However, perhaps . . .' he solves this problem. It is divided into two, corresponding to the two ways in which he solves it. The second [C1b(ii)] begins 'there are certain things.' In the first [C2b(i)] he declares that perhaps all these points are neither true nor well argued. He says this on account of the argument put forward above, for if the multitude is not vile or beastlike but has a degree of reason and virtue, then it is quite capable of being persuaded, since it has wise people by whom it can be persuaded correctly. It is then certainly advantageous for such a multitude, taken as a whole, to have the power to choose and correct a ruler. Even if each individual in the multitude does not possess sufficient reason and virtue by means of which he can make a correct choice or judgment, nevertheless, when all of them are taken together, they do. What is constituted from all of them when they come together is something virtuous without qualification. It would appear from this that the Philosopher is replying by denying the minor premise, where it was maintained that the multitude is imprudent and ignorant. [That it is not advantageous for the multitude to exercise lordship] is true if the multitude is of this sort, as has been said. He says 'perhaps,' because in some polities, such as kingship, it is not advantageous for the multitude to have the power to elect and correct. For in kingship, if one individual is prudent without qualification and everyone else is ruled, as it were, by a lordly government such that, as subordinates, they obey a superior, then it is not advantageous for the multitude to have the power to elect and correct. But it is advantageous in a polity in which the multitude is on an equal footing (*aequalis*).

10. [C2b(ii)] Then, when he says 'there are certain . . .' he removes the objection a second time by, as it were, destroying the major premise. He maintains that what was previously accepted (namely, that in any art it pertains only to the knowledgeable to judge their own work) is not true. For example, if those who have made certain things do not use them, it is not true that they will judge well about them. Instead, it is those who use them who judge correctly. It is thus not only the builder who judges a house. Indeed, it is the person who makes use of the house once it has

been built, such as the head of the household, who makes the better judgment. Likewise, the sailor takes possession of a rudder from a carpenter and judges it better than the carpenter. Likewise, the guest at a feast judges better than the cook. This problem [C1a(i)], therefore, seems to have been resolved sufficiently in this way, since the same is also true in the proposition. Those who make the better judgment are those who make use of government; now this is the multitude.

It should also be understood that there are three arts related to one another. One is concerned with the material, such as the art which prepares the material – for example, by hewing and preparing pieces of wood. Another is that which introduces form into the prepared material – for example, shipbuilding. The third is the using art, which makes use of the ship when it has been built. These arts have the following relation to one another. The first takes the rationale for its work from the second and exists on its account, for it prepares pieces of wood in a certain way because of such and such a form which it considers ought to be introduced into such and such a material. Yet it does not, in itself, know the form. Likewise, the second takes the rationale for its work from the third and exists on its account, for it introduces into the pieces of wood the sort of form that is appropriate to the sort of end which is considered by the third, the using art. On this account, the using art also considers the first cause of all the others. Now a more certain judgment is made about a thing by resolving it to its first cause. Because of this, the using art judges more correctly than the art which introduces form into the material. If, however, there is a science which both brings something into being and uses it, that science judges better and with greater certainty than all the others.

11. [C2] Then, when he says 'However, there is another . . .' he puts forward a second objection against the arrangement [of the ancients]. It is divided into two. In the first [C2a] he puts forward the objection; in the second [C2b] he solves it (at 'And so this problem . . .'). In the first he declares that there is another problem with the arrangement and one which is related to the first: It is inappropriate to entrust the greatest matters to those who are wicked and imprudent. But the election and correction of rulers are the greatest things in a city. Therefore, it is inappropriate to entrust them to the wicked. But the multitude {415B} is wicked and imprudent. Therefore, it is inappropriate for the multitude to have the power of correction and election over rulers and over the virtu-

ous. But, as has been said, in certain polities, these things *are* entrusted to the populace, for the multitude has lordship in these polities in both election and correction. This is because there are cities in which members of the populace (*populares*) and lesser individuals (*inferiores*) attain ruling power and judicial and deliberative functions. They even make judgments about lesser honors, have superiority over the rich, lead armies, and rule in the greatest offices more than the magnates (*maiores*). As a result, it is clear that the ordinances of these [ancient legislators] are inappropriate.

12. [C2b] Then, when he says 'And so this problem,' he solves the problem. First he does this, and then [C3] he sets out what can be regarded as clear from what has been said and what cannot (at 'The first problem . . .'). In the first part [C2b] he states that this difficulty can be resolved in the same way as the first. Perhaps it is true that it is advantageous for some multitudes to have the power to elect and correct rulers, for in some multitudes it is not one judge (*iudex*), counselor (*consiliarius*), official (*praetor*), or public speaker (*concionator*) who, by himself, judges the government or is lord in an election, but it is the whole aggregate of officialdom, council, and populace, of which each of these individuals (counselor, public speaker, and judge) is an aggregate part. And it is clear that it is more advantageous for lordship to be exercised by the whole multitude than by certain individuals, because the whole multitude is more virtuous than some few individuals. For the multitude is made up of the wise, the mediocre, and the inferior, and the populace, the council, and the law-court (*praetorium*) are there. Clearly, the whole multitude is more deserving of honors than any one individual or any few taken by themselves. It is clear from this that the aforementioned objection carries no weight, since it should be maintained that it is not true (as was said) that the multitude is wicked and imprudent, for although some are like this, not all are. But if there were a vile multitude of this sort, one in which no one was wise or prudent, then it would not be advantageous for such a multitude to have the power to elect and correct its rulers. From these arguments the Philosopher appears to mean that it is more advantageous for the power of election and correction to be possessed by the whole multitude than by a few individuals. And here he terms 'a multitude' the aggregate of the wise, the magnates, the prudent, the mediocre, and the populace. It is more advantageous for lordship to be exercised by a whole multitude of this sort than by a few individuals. However, it is not advantageous for lordship to be exercised by a vile multitude. (He says 'perhaps' because in the polity

[i.e., kingship] in which there is one individual preeminent in virtue whom others are born to obey, it is not advantageous for the multitude to attain these powers.) There are two requirements for the government of a polity: one is right reason (a multitude possesses this through those who are wise), the other is power (*potentia*) so that it can coerce and punish the wicked (it possesses this through the populace).

13. [C3] Then, when he says 'The first problem,' he shows what is clear and what is not clear about the problem mentioned above. First [C3a] he shows what is clear; second [C3b], what is unclear (at 'However, it is not yet clear').

This text can be expounded in two ways. The first is if we refer this passage to the problem which was raised earlier [B1] as to whether it would be more advantageous for lordship to be exercised by the multitude than by the virtuous few and if we resolve this problem by saying 'yes.' The first problem, namely, the one just expressed, clarifies nothing except for the way in which lordship should be exercised in the city by the law and by the ruler (whether the ruler is one individual or several). For the law ought to be lord and ruler over all those things which can be determined by laws, but the ruler ought to be lord over all those things which the laws cannot determine with any certainty. For law is directed toward the universal and, for this reason, an exception [to the law] is sometimes made in a particular case, since the legislator cannot foresee all the particular cases in which the law can be found wanting (and hence *is* sometimes found wanting). Now these are the cases in which the ruler exercises lordship. This is indeed clear from the problem mentioned above and its solution. For the ruler in a city ought to have a rule by which he may be directed in his own actions, by which he may direct others, and by which he may deliver judgment. This can be done by means of law. This is why the law ought to rule. And because sometimes a ruler cannot judge by means of the law (because the law is found wanting in some cases) and because it is not clear what the ruler ought to correct in such a case, for this reason it is advantageous that the ruler ought to exercise lordship in this case.

The other way in which this passage can be expounded is if we relate it to what was said earlier when it was maintained [A2b] that it is not necessary for a human being to rule according to law just because a human being has passions connected to him which pervert rational judgment. The opposite was argued on the grounds that sometimes the law is wicked and that it is not advantageous for such law to rule. From this a problem arises as to which it is more advantageous to have as the ruling authority – the law or a human being. In that case, this passage may be read as follows. The initial problem, namely, the one mentioned earlier, is not asking anything other than 'When should the law rule and when should the ruler?' (whether the ruler is a single individual or several). And, as was said earlier, in those cases which the law can determine with certainty it is advantageous for the law to rule, and in others, which it cannot determine, it is beneficial for the ruler to exercise lordship.

14. [C3b] Then, when he says 'Nevertheless, it is not yet clear . . .' he shows what is not ((add *non*)) clear from what has been said, because it was maintained above that certain laws are correct, yet it is still not clear which laws are correct and which are not, and there is still a problem with the question that raised similar problems earlier. But what should be maintained for polities should also be maintained for laws, for just as some polities are wicked and unjust and some forms are virtuous and just, so certain laws are just and virtuous and certain {415C} laws are wicked and unjust. This is because laws are laid down with regard to what furthers the end of the polity. Therefore, if the end of the polity is correct without qualification, then the polity is correct and so too is the law which has been laid down with regard to the means toward such an end. If the end of the polity is not correct, then neither is the polity correct, nor is the law which has been laid down with regard to what furthers the end of such a polity. If this is so, then it is clear that laws are laid down relative to the polity and its end, and it is clear that laws laid down according to correct polities are correct and that those laid down according to deviant forms are not.

Chapter 14

[*Politics* III 15, 1285b37–1286b40]

[A]   {219} Consequently, the investigation is about just two issues. One is whether or not it is advantageous to cities for there to be a perpetual commander of the army (and, if so, whether from one family or in turns);

[A1]   one is whether or not it is advantageous for a single individual to exercise lordship over everything. An examination of this sort of {220} leadership of the army is more about law than polity (for this can occur in all polities), and so it can be dismissed for the present.

The remaining mode of kingship *is* a polity, and so it is necessary to examine it and to run through the problems inherent in it. The starting point for the inquiry is this: Is it more advantageous to be ruled by the best man or by the best laws?

[A2a]   And so it seems to those who think it advantageous to be ruled by a king that laws make only universal pronouncements and do not provide for eventualities. This is why, in any art whatever, it is miserable to be ruled by the letter. Indeed, in Egypt physicians are permitted to set things in motion after the third day. If they do so earlier, however, it is at their own risk. It is clear, therefore, that for the same reason a polity according to the letter of the law is not best. {221}

[A2b]   On the other hand, it is necessary for rulers to have this universal statement (*sermo*), because that which is entirely without passion has more weight (*valentius*) than that to which passion is congenial. Passion is not present in law, whereas it necessarily belongs to every human soul.

[A3]   But perhaps someone will still say, in response, that an individual will deliberate better about particulars.

[A4a]   Therefore, it is indeed clearly necessary for him to be a legislator and to establish laws but not lords (whereby they transgress, since lordship should be from others). In all those cases which {222} it is impossible for the law to judge (either at all or not well), must rule be exercised by one best man or by everyone?

[A4b(i)]   For now, when they meet together, they debate, deliberate, and judge, but these are all judgments about individual cases. Taken individually, therefore, any one of these people may be worse. But a city is made up of many individuals, and just as a communal feast that is brought together is more beautiful than one that is solitary and simple, for this reason a large crowd (*turba*) judges better than any one person.

[A4b(ii)]   Moreover, the many are more indifferent in the way that a larger amount of water is. A multitude is likewise also more indifferent than a few. When an individual has been overcome by anger or by some other passion, his judgment is necessarily corrupted. There, however, it is difficult for everyone to be carried away at the same time and to do wrong. {223}

[A4b(iii)]   Assume that the multitude consists of free people and does nothing beyond the law except in those cases in which the law is necessarily deficient. Now if this is not easy in many, but if several are good men and citizens, is a single ruler more incorruptible or is a greater number (good men, however)?

[A4c]   Is it not clearly the greater number? But these will, indeed, create factional divisions (*seditiones*), whereas one individual is without such division. But as a counter to this, the virtuous are, in terms of the soul, just like this single individual.

[A5a]   And so, if rule by a greater number, all of whom are good men, should be put forward as aristocracy, and that of a single individual kingship, then aristocracy will certainly be preferable to kingship for cities (whether the government does or does not have the power), provided that the greater number is taken to be alike.

[A5b(i)]   This is the reason, perhaps, why they were initially ruled by a king – because it was rare to find men who differed much {224} in virtue. And in any case, at that time they were living in small cities. Yet kings were instituted, moreover, from the good they did (*beneficium*), which is indeed the work of good men.

[A5b(ii)] Now when it happened that there were many alike in virtue, they no longer submitted but looked for something shared (*commune aliquid*) and instituted a polity.

[A5b(iii)] When they became worse, enriching themselves from what was in common, it was rational, at this point, for oligarchies to be created (for they made wealth a form of honor).

[A5b(iv)] These, however, were first transformed into tyrannies and then

[A5b(v)]   from tyrannies into democracy, for always heading toward fewer for the sake of wicked gain, they made the multitude stronger so that it rose up and democracies were created. However, since it has turned out that cities have become bigger, it may now be the case that no other polity besides democracy can readily be established.

[B1]   If someone maintains that it is best for cities {225} to be ruled by a king, what will they do about his children? Must his family also reign? But depending on the quality of his progeny, some of them may turn out harmful. But the ruling lord will not pass on [government] to his children. But this is not readily believable, for it is difficult and something of greater virtue than accords with human nature.

[B2a]   Now there is also a problem over power (*potentia*), whether it is necessary for someone who is going to rule to have a strong force around him with which he can compel those who are unwilling to obey, or else how will he come to administer his rule? For if he exercises lordship in accordance with the law, doing nothing beyond the law by his own will, it is nevertheless still necessary that he have the power to protect the laws.

[B2b]   Perhaps {226} it is not difficult to determine this for this type of king, for he must indeed possess a power such that it is greater than that of one individual on his own or of one or more together, but less than that of the multitude. This is the way the ancients provided guards when they set up over a city someone whom they called an Aesymnete or tyrant. When Dionysius requested guards, someone counseled the Syracusans to give him this many.

1. {419B} After the Philosopher has distinguished the different types of royal monarchy and established the five forms it can take, he investigates the first form (the primary sense of the term), namely, kingship. First he pursues certain problems, from which the nature of kingship becomes

apparent. Then, at the end of this third book he shows that the virtue of the best king is the same as the virtue of the best man (at 'About the king . . .' [16, 1287a1]). The first part is divided into two. First he investigates whether it would be more advantageous for a city to be ruled by the best laws or by the best human beings; second, whether it would be more beneficial for it to be ruled by a single best man or by several (at 'Since, however, there are three . . .' [18, 1288a34]). This first section is further divided into two. First [A] he investigates whether it is better for a city to be ruled by the best laws or by the best men; second [B], he puts forward further problems (at 'If someone . . .'). The first part is divided into two more. First [A1] he sets out a problem; second [A2], he pursues it (at 'And so it seems to those who think . . .').

[A1] In the first part, therefore, he declares that the first thing to be investigated about kingship is whether it is more advantageous for a city to be ruled by the best man or by the best laws.

2. [A2] Then, when he says 'And so it seems to those who think,' he proceeds. First [A2a] he argues that it is better for a kingdom to be ruled by the best man; second [A2b], he argues the contrary (at 'On the other hand').

[A2a] That it is better for a kingdom to be ruled by the best man than by the best laws he shows by reason and by example. He declares that some people are of the opinion that it is more advantageous for a city to be ruled by the best man because it is better for a city to be ruled by that which is able to determine every case which arises. This the law cannot do, because the law makes only universal pronouncements and says nothing about the particular (particulars are infinite and cannot all be comprehended). Moreover, the law does not refer what it says to new cases which emerge, whereas the best man can do this through his prudence, for he has correct judgment about what can be done and correct appetite through moral virtue. Then, before he closes with his conclusion, he interjects an example. He maintains that we may witness the same in other arts, [namely] that it is not always good to act according to the letter of an art, because some things are written down which, if they were acted upon, would sometimes be harmful. This is apparent in medicine, for the physician does not always pay attention to medical writings, because many things have been left up to the physician's prudence. Among the Egyptians, for example, it was written that a physician is permitted to 'set things in motion' (that is, employ medicine to expel a disease) after the third day, because before the third day he would be unable to see clearly the nature of the disease. If he set things in motion before the third day, then it was at his own peril. To observe this prescription in all cases was not good practice, however, for in some instances it was advantageous to act more swiftly and in others [to act] more slowly, according to differences in the medicine and the disease. It is the same in a polity: It is not always advantageous to be ruled by what is written down or by law, because law is sometimes found wanting in a particular case, and then there is need for someone to direct matters. As a result, it is clearly better for a kingdom to be ruled by the best man than by the best laws.

3. [A2b] Then, when he says 'On the other hand,' he argues that it is better for a city to be ruled by the best laws. First [A2b] he does this, and then [A3] he objects to the contrary (at 'But perhaps'). In the first [A2b] he maintains that universal reason ought to be present in rulers and that, for this reason, it is better for a city to be ruled by something that does not have passions connected to it than by something that has them by nature, because the passions pervert the judgment of reason. For passion is the movement of the appetite under the influence of what appears to be good or evil. But law does not have passions connected to it, whereas a human being does. As a result, it is better for a city to be ruled by the best laws than by the best man.

4. [A3] Then, when he says 'But perhaps,' he objects to the contrary. First [A3] he puts forward the objection, and then [A4] he removes it {419C} (at 'Therefore it is . . .'). In the first [A3] he declares that someone may claim to the contrary, as it were, that although human beings have passions connected to them by nature, a good human being will nevertheless deliberate about individual cases and will judge correctly in accordance with this deliberation. As a result, it is still better for a city to be ruled by the best man than by the best law.

5. [A4] Then, when he says 'Therefore it is,' he removes this objection by citing another problem, from whose resolution the solution to the original objection becomes apparent. This section is divided into two. In the first [A4] he does what has been said; second [A5], he infers certain corollaries (at 'And so, if . . .'). The first part is divided further into two sections. In the first [A4a] he puts forward the problem. Second [A4b], he solves it by proving the other side (at 'For now'). In the first section [A4a] he main-

tains that it is clear that the ruler of a city ought to know the laws and to lay them down. Yet he need not be lord over everything. For from the fact that he exercises lordship in accordance with the law it is not necessary that he be lord in all matters, but it is necessary that he be lord in those things which cannot be determined (either at all or not well) by the law. Then there is the problem as to whether, in this case, a single individual or several should rule in judging the particulars which the law cannot satisfactorily determine.

6. [A4b] Then, when he says 'For now . . .' he solves this by proving the other side. It is divided into three, corresponding to the three arguments with which he proves that in this case it would be better for several individuals to judge. The second [A4b(ii)] begins 'Moreover, the many are . . .' and the third [A4b(iii)] begins 'Assume that . . .' In the first [A4b(i)] he says that when a particular case arises that cannot be determined by the law, several individuals come together and debate with one another about it, and they investigate it by deliberating about it, and after deliberation they deliver a judgment. All judgments about particular cases that cannot be determined by law are of this kind. Now several individuals can do this but a single person cannot, because several people deliberating about something can see more than a single individual can. It is therefore clear that one individual, when compared to several, is worse in judging and that one individual's judgment, when compared to the judgment of several, is worse. For just as a city made up of many people is finer than one made up of a few, the judgment of many is better than the judgment of a single individual (just as a meal made up of many dishes – i.e., a meal in which there are several dishes – is finer than a simple meal where there is only one single dish). On this account, it is clear that a large crowd, or several individuals, will judge better and with greater certainty than any individual within the crowd. The Philosopher's reasoning, in brief, consists of this: Judgment in a case that is not determined by law ought to be made by whoever is capable of making a more certain judgment. But in such a case several individuals can make a better and more certain judgment. Therefore, in such a case judgment ought to be made by several individuals. [In the present section] he sets out the minor premise of this argument.

7. [A4b(ii)] Then, when he says 'Moreover, the many are more . . .' he puts forward a second argument for the same conclusion. He maintains

that it is clear that with respect to the passions which disturb and pervert correct judgment, several individuals are more impartial than one or a few. The same is true of water, where a greater and deeper amount flows more evenly than a small amount, in that a larger amount flows to many places whereas a small amount of water flows quickly to one part. For this reason, a single individual is more liable to be possessed by passion than several individuals. Now when a single individual is possessed by some passion or another, judgment is corrupted. Where there are several individuals, however, it is difficult for judgment to be corrupted by the driving force of passion, because if some are impassioned their passions will be restrained by the reason of others. Because of this, it will be difficult for them to sin. This is particularly the case if the multitude is not a vile one but consists of those who are free with respect to virtue, for such people will do nothing beyond the law except where the law is found wanting. Now the Philosopher's reasoning consists of this: In such cases as are not determined by the law, judgment ought to be made by whoever is more indifferent with respect to the passions. But several individuals are more indifferent with respect to the passions than a single individual. As a result, judgment ought to be made better by several than by one.

8. [A4b(iii)] Then, when he says 'Assume that,' he puts forward a third argument. First [A4b(iii)] he puts it forward; second [A4c], he objects to the contrary (at 'Is it not clearly'). In the first [A4b(iii)] he maintains that if it is said that it is not easy for several individuals to judge well in such a case, however impartial they may be, even if they were good men and citizens, it would still have to be asked (if this is said) whether it is more difficult for one ruler to be perverted and corrupted than a larger number of good men. It is clear that it is more difficult for several good men to be perverted and corrupted than one good individual; and better judgment is made by whomever it is more difficult to corrupt and pervert. But it is more difficult for several individuals to be corrupted and perverted than a single individual. As a result, it is better that judgment be made by several individuals than by one.

9. [A4c] Then, when he says 'Is it not clearly,' he objects to the contrary and declares that someone will say that it is better for judgment to be made by a single individual than by several because several individuals will disagree with each other according to their factional interests (*seditiones*),

whereas a single individual cannot disagree with himself. Hence it is better for judgment to be made by a single individual than by several. He solves this when he says that it should be maintained against this argument that these several virtuous individuals are like a single individual. It is clearly impossible for virtuous individuals to disagree with each other insofar as they are of this sort [i.e., virtuous].

10. [A5] Then, when he says 'And so, if . . .' he infers two corollaries. This section has two parts, corresponding to the two corollaries he infers. The second [A5b] begins 'This is the reason, perhaps, why.' In the first [A5a] he concludes that the state of the best (*status optimatum*) is superior {420A} to kingship. He maintains that if it is the case, as has been asserted, that it is better for several good people to judge than one, then, since the polity in which several wise individuals rule is the state of the best and that in which a single wise person rules alone is a kingship, it is clear that the state of the best is better than kingship.

11. [A5b] Then, when he says 'This is the reason, perhaps . . .' he puts forward a second corollary. This concerns the order in which the different polities came into being. It is divided into five parts. First [A5b(i)] he establishes how royal monarchy was first introduced; second [A5b(ii)], how the state of the best was introduced (at 'Now when it happened'); third [A5b(iii)], how the power of the few was introduced (at 'when they became worse'); fourth [A5b(iv)], how tyranny was introduced (at 'These, however, . . .'); and fifth [A5b(v)], how the popular state (*status popularis*) was introduced (at 'from tyrannies,' etc.). In the first part he declares that because it is better for a city to be ruled (and for judgment to be passed) by several individuals rather than by a single person, cities were initially ruled by a single king because it was easier to find a single wise person in a government than to find several. It was for this reason that royal rule was initially granted to a single individual. Moreover, at first cities were small, and because of this a single individual was sufficient to rule them. Moreover, they made someone king over them because of a benefit this individual had conferred upon them, either because he fought on their behalf against their enemies or because he discovered some art that was a necessity for them. Now this is the work of a good man, and for this reason they made this sort of person king over them (as a good and virtuous individual).

12. [A5b(ii)] Then, when he says 'Now when it happened,' he explains how, afterwards, the state of the best was introduced. He says that it happened afterwards that as more people became virtuous they devoted themselves to virtuous deeds. Likewise, they then sought a government of several individuals who were alike in virtue, and they no longer tolerated royal rule but instituted the rule of those who were equal in virtue. Now this is the state of the best. After kingship, therefore, came the state of the best.

13. [A5b(iii)] Then, when he says 'When they became worse,' he explains how the state of the few came afterwards. He says it happened afterwards that those rulers became rich from communal goods and began to incline toward pleasures (as they became deficient in reason) and to rule for the sake of wealth. In this way the state of the best was converted into the state of the few (*status paucorum*), for they made wealth honorable and that for the sake of which rule ought to be exercised.

14. [A5b(iv)] Then, when he says 'These, however,' he explains tyranny. He maintains that it happened afterwards that a single individual became wealthier than the others, and more powerful in his associates, and that he subjugated the others. This is the way in which the state of the few was converted into a tyranny, where the ruler rules for the sake of his own advantage.

15. [A5b(v)] Then, when he says 'from tyrannies,' he explains how the state of the many (*status multorum*) was introduced. He says that the state of the many arose after tyranny. For since the tyrant was oppressing the rich for the sake of his wicked gain, the citizens brought about a less extortionate polity and got away from the tyrant's [thirst for] wicked gain by bringing in the multitude, which was stronger (*fortior*), and getting it to rise up against the tyrant. In the event, the populace rose up against the tyrant and drove him out. Power (*potestas*) remained with the populace, and there was then a popular polity. This is the reason why the populace exercises lordship in many cities. Because the populace is large in number, it therefore has power. Nevertheless, where the populace exercises lordship, something is taken from the other polities, for they make some people captains (*capitani*) and put one individual over them. He maintains further that because cities tend to become larger, it may not be easy for another polity besides the popular [state] to come into being.

Now from what has been said a solution is apparent to the objection made earlier (to prove that a single individual ought to exercise judgment), namely, that although he has passions connected to him by nature, he will deliberate about particular cases and will therefore judge correctly. It should be said in response that several individuals were better able to deliberate, and thus make better judgments, than a single individual. As a result, it is still better for a city to be ruled by several individuals than by one.

16. [B1] Then, when he says 'If someone,' he introduces other problems. This section is divided into two, corresponding to the two problems he puts forward. The second [B2a] begins 'Now there is also a problem.' In the first [B1] he declares that if someone should say it is best for a city to be ruled by a single individual, then there will be a problem as to how he should accede. Is it by election or by hereditary succession? He shows that he ought not to accede by hereditary succession, because there is doubt as to what sort of people the sons succeeding will be − it can turn out that a son is evil. If this individual accedes by means of hereditary succession, therefore, it may turn out that an evil person will accede to government. Now this is inappropriate. Therefore, accession should not be by hereditary succession.

But because someone might say, perhaps, that when a father who is a good man sees that his son is evil he will not pass on the kingdom to him but to someone else, he removes this objection. He maintains that this is hard to credit, namely, that a father will reject his son and pass the government on to someone else. For this would be beyond the general capability of human beings. He must leave ((*mittat/dimittat*)) the government to whomever he loves more, and what is closer by nature is by nature loved more. Now the son is like another father, and for this reason, just as a father loves himself more than he loves anyone else whatever, so, after himself, he has a greater natural love for his natural son than for anyone else whatever. As a result, he will sooner leave the kingship to him than to anyone else.

It should also be understood that it is always better *per se* for a king to accede by election than by succession but that to accede by succession is better *per accidens*. The first is clear in the following way. It is better for a ruler to accede in the manner in which it turns out *per se* that the better individual is taken up. But {420B} it happens that the better individual accedes by election than by hereditary succession, because it is generally found that in a whole multitude there is a better person than the single individual [who would accede by hereditary succession]. And election [or choice] is, *per se*, appetite determined by reason. Nevertheless, it is better *per accidens* for the ruler to accede by means of hereditary succession, because in an election dissension can arise among the electors. Moreover, sometimes the electors are wicked, and because of this it may turn out that they elect a wicked ruler. Now both of these are evils in a city. Moreover, the customary exercise of lordship contributes much to someone's being [willingly] subject to another person. Hence, while the father is reigning [his subjects] become accustomed to being subject to the son because they are subject to the father, and because of this they are inclined to be subject to the son. Moreover, it is alien and very hard to accept that the person who is an equal with someone today will be exercising lordship and ruling over him tomorrow. For this reason, it is better *per accidens* for the ruler to accede by means of hereditary succession than by election.

17. [B2a] Then, when he says 'Now, there is also,' he raises the second problem, and it is divided into two parts. In the first [B2a] he raises the problem; in the second [B2b] he solves it (at 'Perhaps it is not'). In the first [B2a] he declares that there is a problem about the ruler's power in a royal monarchy, [namely] whether he ought to have the power by means of which he can coerce and punish rebels who refuse to obey him, and how he ought to conduct and administer his government. It appears that he should have the power needed to punish rebels, because we see that a ruler who rules according to the law and who does nothing beyond the law according to his own will ought to have the power with which he may punish those who refuse to obey the law or who act against it. This is why a ruler who rules according to his will (the kind who exists in a royal monarchy) ought likewise to have the power needed to punish those who refuse to obey him.

18. [B2b] Then, when he says 'Perhaps it is not,' he solves this problem. He maintains that perhaps it is not difficult to solve this problem about a king. For it is clear that he ought to have a power (*potentiam*), and a greater power than that of a single individual, because if he did not have a greater power he would not be able to punish this individual, or these individuals, if they refused to obey him. Moreover, he also ought to have a greater power than several individuals together; otherwise, he would not be able to punish them. Yet he ought to have less power than that of the whole city when considered as a multitude, because if he had a greater power

than the city, he would oppress it and convert the government into a tyranny. This is what some of the ancients did when they made someone king over them and called him an Aesymnete. They gave him guards with a power greater than that of a single individual or of several put together but less than that of the whole city. Likewise, when another [ancient], Dionysius by name, was seeking guards from the Syracusans, someone advised them to give him as many guards as would not exceed the power of the city or multitude (lest he oppress them) yet be greater than that of a single individual or of several individuals together. It is clear, therefore, that a ruler who rules by law should have the power to punish rebels.

Questions

Question 17. Is It Advantageous to a City for the Multitude to Elect and Correct Its Ruler, and Is This Just?

[1. Preliminary Arguments]

[1a. Arguments Against the Proposition]

[i] {214} Argument against ((*quod non/sic*)) the proposition: It is for the wise to elect and to correct. In most cases, however, the multitude lacks prudence. Therefore, these [functions] will not pertain to it. The major premise is clear, because correction belongs to those who can judge. Judgment, however, belongs to the prudent, as is said in *Ethics* VI (7, 1141b10; 5, 1140a25; 9, 1142b30; 11, 1143a20).

[ii] Again, election is for those who can deliberate and confer. But these things pertain to the wise (cf. *Ethics* III 3, 1112a20). Therefore, etc. The minor premise is clear from the Philosopher in this third book (*Politics* III 11, 1282a8–10).

[iii] Again, the Philosopher said earlier (III 11, 1282a25–27) that it is dangerous to make the multitude lord over the greatest goods in a city. But the election and correction of a ruler seem to be just this. Therefore etc.

[1b. Argument in Favor of the Proposition]

Against this there is the Philosopher and what has been said earlier.

[2. Answer to the Question]

{215} It should be maintained here that it is not advantageous for a vile and beastlike multitude to attain these [functions]. Nevertheless, it is just for a mixed and ordered multitude to attain them.

First, election. The election of a ruler requires two things: counsel in finding a good ruler and (especially in those offices of government where the burden is greater than the honor, such as in sentencing murderers) power to compel the individual elected to take on the burden. It is therefore most advantageous for election to belong to something which has, in itself, both counsel and power. This is the multitude, because through its wise parts it has prudence and by itself it has power.

Again, according to *Ethics* V (cf. 7, 1134b10), humans love their own deeds as their children. A multitude will [therefore] show greater obedience to a ruler whom it elects.

Second, correction. When a ruler has sinned, discernment is required to establish a penalty and power is required to inflict it. Now this is what happens in a multitude, because the wise discern the penalty while the populace can inflict it, and neither of them could by itself do both. The wise would discern the magnitude of the punishment but would lack power to inflict it. Conversely, the populace, while having power, would not discern the [appropriate] size of the punishment. For this reason, if it is advantageous for the city that its ruler be corrected (as it is if the order of the community would not otherwise be preserved, for the ruler would destroy the citizens one by one), then it is advantageous that this be done by such a mixed and ordered community. (I understand such a city not to be subordinate to another, for when it is, correction of their ruler lies with the superior.)

Again, it is more beneficial that a ruler be corrected in such a way that, after correction, the corrected ruler is less able to hate those who have corrected him. But this happens if the multitude corrects, since [the ruler] will then be unable to fashion a hatred against specific individuals.

[3. Reply to the Preliminary Arguments]

[1a(i)] To the [first] argument it should be said that the wise are lacking in power, and for that reason (as well as because of the lesser [opportunity for] hatred, as has just been made clear), it is better that the multitude should correct [the ruler].

[1a(ii)] To the second argument it should be said that this must be understood of a beastlike multitude which is not open to persuasion, concerning which Aristotle said earlier that it is born to serve a despotic government.

Question 22. Is It Better for a City to Be Ruled by the Best Man or by Laws?

[1. Preliminary Arguments]

[1a. Arguments for the Rule of Law]

[i] {216} The argument [in favor of] laws is that it is better for a city to be ruled by something that has no connection with the passions than by something that is connected to them, for {217} passion perverts judgment and, as a consequence, both political prudence and prudence (*Ethics* VI 5, 1140b10–15; 8, 1141b24–25). Now law does not have passion connected to it. The best man, however, will still have passion connected to him, because, as is said here, it is difficult (or completely impossible) to separate the human soul from the passions. Law, however, does not have passion, both because it does not have appetite and because it is universal (the passions, on the other hand, are concerned with singulars). Therefore, it is better for a city to be ruled by laws than by a good man.

[ii] Again, it is better for a city to be ruled by what is incorruptible than by what is corruptible. Now law is not corruptible either by power or by money. A good man, however, is still capable of being corrupted. Therefore, etc.

[1b. Arguments for Rule by the Best Man]

[i] [The argument] against: It is better for a city to be ruled by something that attains right reason to a greater degree and *per se* than by something that attains it less and only *per accidens*. Now the best man attains right reason *per se* and to a greater degree than the law, for the law attains it only *per accidens*, inasmuch as it participates in the reason of whoever instituted it.

[ii] Again, it is better for a city to be ruled by something that judges universally about all matters. Such is the best man, but not the law, for law does not determine particulars. Therefore, etc.

[2. Answer to the Question]

It should be maintained here that a man is called good on the basis of virtue, which perfects those who have it and renders their deeds good. A man will be called 'best,' therefore, on the basis of the best virtue. Now this is political prudence, to which all the moral virtues are necessarily attached. The best man will also be said to be one who, having political prudence, also has all the other virtues. Having these virtues, he still remains susceptible to passion, however, because he must necessarily have sensation (otherwise he would not be human, nor would he understand). And if sensation is present, there will also necessarily be appetite. Appetite is susceptible to passion, because passion is the movement of appetite from the imagining of good and evil (*sub fantasia boni et mali*). Because of this, no matter how perfect the best man may be, he is nevertheless susceptible to the passions. Law, however, is a universal proposition about things ordered toward an end that is in accordance with the character of that end. Now this order of possible actions is necessarily in accordance with political right reason {218} or with prudence pure and simple. Because of this, there is a sense in which the best man and the law are determined by the same thing, namely, by the best right reason and by political prudence. However, there is a difference. A good human being attains this political prudence to a greater degree, more perfectly, and essentially, whereas law attains it to a lesser degree, *per accidens*, and by means of whoever instituted it. Moreover, through right reason and prudence the good man can make a good judgment about all things, universals as well as particulars, since he can apply reason to particular instances. Since law is a universal proposition, it cannot do this. In fact, it only judges universals in accordance with the character of a universal end. It leaves particulars to be determined by the prudence of a judge.

When it is asked, therefore, whether a city would be ruled better by law or by the best man, I maintain that, if we are speaking about those things which the law determines, then it is better *per se* for the city to be ruled by the best man than by laws. I maintain that this is the case *per se*. The reason is that it is better *per se* for a city to be ruled by what attains right reason and prudence *per se* than by what does not, since [in the former case] ruling and judgment derive from reason *per se*. The best man attains prudence *per se* and essentially. Law, on the other hand, does so only *per accidens*. Therefore, etc.

However, it is better *per accidens* for it to be ruled by laws. The reason is that it is better *per accidens* for it to be ruled by what is completely lacking in passion than by what has passion connected to it, at least *per accidens*. Now a good man is susceptible to passion, but the law is not, both because it has no appetite and because it is only concerned with universals (while passion is concerned with singulars, as is said in *Ethics* VII).

On the other hand, if we are speaking about those matters which law does not determine, namely, singulars, then it is completely necessary for a city to be ruled by a good man and not by law. The reason is that a city must be ruled in particular cases by whoever {219} is capable of making judgments about them. Now the good man can do this but not the law. In these matters, therefore, [the city] must be ruled by the good man.

This is not to say that it would then ((*tunc/cum* [var.])) be *better* to be ruled by a good man than by the law, because saying this would allow [the possibility] that it would in some way be *good* for a city to be ruled by law in such cases [i.e., singulars], because comparable things must agree, at least in kind, in the respect in which they are being compared. This is not at all the case here with law, and so there is no sense in which it is good for a city to be ruled by law – because there is no point of comparison at all between law and a good man in such cases. And for this reason there is also no way in which law determines them.

[3. Reply to the Preliminary Arguments]

The solution to the [preliminary] arguments is now clear.

[1a] The initial arguments do indeed show that in those matters which the law does determine [i.e., universals] it is better *per accidens* for a city to be ruled by laws than by a good man.

[1b] The second set of arguments [show] that it is better *per se* for the city to be ruled in these matters by the good man. There is no argument as to whether it would be better to be ruled by law or by the good man in matters not determined by law [i.e., singulars], because here there is absolutely no comparison.

Question 25. Is It Better for a King or Ruler to Accede by Birth or by Election?

[1. Preliminary Arguments]

[1a. Arguments for Election]

[i] The argument [in favor of accession] by election is that the ruler needs to be the best person, since he ought to possess perfect moral virtue, as is said in *Ethics* V (1, 1130a1–10). It is therefore better for a ruler to accede by the route which always turns out to find the better person. This route is election, for election is the result of long deliberation and for that reason searches out the best person. Therefore, it is better for the ruler to accede by election than through hereditary succession. {220}

[ii] Again, it is said to be dangerous to entrust the greatest things to fortune. But government is one of these. It is therefore dangerous to entrust it to fortune. This is done, however, if the ruler always accedes by hereditary succession. Therefore, etc. The minor premise is clear, because [heredity] involves chance, nor is it necessary that the good will always succeed the good.

[1b. Argument for Hereditary Succession]

[The argument] against: It is better for a ruler to accede by the route which leads to greater uniformity with the first government. But this is what occurs, clearly, if the ruler always accedes by hereditary succession, for in the first government there is always one and the same [best individual] ((om. *finis* [var.])). Now although a son is not numerically the same as his father, he is nevertheless more like him in character and conduct than many [others]. Therefore, it is better for the ruler to accede by the route of hereditary succession than by election.

[2. Answer to the Question]

It should be maintained here that the ruler needs to be the best person in prudence and virtue. It is therefore better that a ruler accede by the route by which the better person can always accede, for in this way there will be a greater approximation to the first government, where the best person always rules. But election is such a route. Because of this, it is always better, of itself and in terms of the nature of the route, for the ruler to accede by election. The reason is that election [or choice] is appetite informed by counsel (*appetitus preconsiliatus*), and it is therefore inherent in the nature of election to be in accordance with deliberating reason. Thus, insofar as it has this [nature], *per se* it always finds the better person. Therefore, it is better *per se* for the ruler to accede by election than by succession.

However, it is better *per accidens* for the ruler to accede by succession. This is clear from a consideration of the dangers of each [alternative].

First, on the side of succession and [its effect on] the father. As was said in Book III of this work, what is one's own is loved more and given greater care. Now when a father believes that his son will succeed him in ruling, he will consequently value the kingdom as if it were his own, because it is going to belong to someone who is a part of him. As a result, he will have greater love and care for the kingdom and will work more for its good. {221}

Again, custom contributes much to being [willingly] subject to another person, because the customary is pleasant, while the unaccustomed makes people obdurate, as is said in *Metaphysics* II (3, 994b32–995a6) and *On Rhetoric* I (10, 1369b16–20). Therefore, [if], when the father was reigning, the citizens knew that the son ought to reign after his father, they would already be accustomed to being subject to him. With election, however, the opposite occurs. If someone who is an equal citizen today is elected ruler, the remainder, being less accustomed [to him as a superior], will be less obedient to him.

Moreover, it is possible that someone who is abruptly elevated by election from the lowest rank will be prouder than someone who is raised from a superior rank to a more superior rank (who accedes, as it were, by moving the shortest distance from potency to act, which occurs with succession). A ruler's pride is a great danger to a kingdom.

Again, with election the kingdom is vacant [of government] for some time, because it is necessary to call together the electors, which is not done in an instant. This does not happen, however, with succession.

Again, when dissension arises among the electors, either there will be no ruler or, if there is, a bad one may be chosen due to the corruption of the electors. Because of this, the dangers that occur in the course of election are greater and more numerous than those which occur in the course of hereditary succession.

[2a. One Respect in Which Hereditary Succession Might Be Said to Be
More Dangerous]

[It might be objected that] there is a greater danger in hereditary succession that sometimes a bad person will become ruler.

[2b. Reply to 2a]

To this, however, it should be said that it is contrary to nature for good to give birth to evil. For this reason, since this occurs more rarely (for nature is the cause of things that happen always or for the most part, as is said in *Physics* II [5, 196b10–11]), it is accordingly more natural for the good always to succeed the good. It is less natural, however, that a good ruler always be elected. For a good ruler has already trained his successor for some time in good conduct (even beyond any natural disposition he has from birth). Electors, on the other hand, do neither of these things for an elected ruler.

Therefore, from an examination of the dangers of each route, [it is clear that] it is better *per accidens* for the ruler to accede by hereditary succession than by election. {222}

[3. Reply to the Preliminary Arguments]

[1a(i)] To the [first] argument it should be said that *per se* and as far as the nature of election is concerned, it is better of itself [that the ruler] accede by election. However, this can turn out to be worse *per accidens*, for it sometimes happens that this route is never even started on, and moreover, if it is, the election sometimes proceeds more on the basis of passion than reason.

[1a(ii)] To the second argument it should be said that although mischance can occur with succession, nevertheless, because succession is the more natural route, it is susceptible to lesser dangers and it also encounters mischance more rarely. Therefore, etc.

HENRY OF GHENT
IS IT RATIONAL FOR SOMEONE WITHOUT HOPE OF A FUTURE LIFE TO CHOOSE TO DIE FOR THE COMMONWEALTH?

Introduction

Henry of Ghent was born around 1217. He taught at Paris as a secular master in the Faculty of Theology from 1276 until his death in 1293. As a member of Stephen Tempier's commission of inquiry, he helped determine the 219 articles in theology and natural philosophy which were censured by the bishop in 1277. Henry's own particular fusion of Augustinian metaphysics and Aristotelian epistemology has left modern commentators both intrigued and perturbed by the tensions which such a combination produced. The core of Henry's teaching has been preserved in two major works, the *Summa quaestionum ordinarium* and a collection of fifteen *Quaestiones quodlibetales*. The quodlibet is the genre of academic inquiry which offers perhaps the most direct insight both into issues of contemporary intellectual concern and into a regent master's own opinions. Originally a penitential exercise at Easter and Christmas each year, it required a master to respond to a question on 'any' subject (*de quolibet*) and was often used to put him on the spot. Quodlibets can thus provide an index of those contentious issues which were dividing theologians at any given moment. In Henry's case, for example, this form of disputation provided the forum for his exchanges with Giles of Rome and Godfrey of Fontaines over the nature of the distinction between essence and existence. Henry's quodlibets also provide a commentary on issues of directly political and ethical import, such as the debate over the privileges of the mendicant orders, opposition to royal taxation, the connection between the moral and theological virtues, and the relationship between the individual good and the common good. Thus, Henry's quodlibets can be used as a case study for testing the coherence of the connection between his metaphysics and his political thought, between his neo-Augustinianism and his use of Aristotle, and between his exchanges with other theologians on metaphysics and epistemology and his exchanges with the same theologians on politics and ethics.

Henry's twelfth quodlibet was delivered in December 1288. The subject of its thirteenth question – the motivation for laying down one's life for the sake of the community – had been triggered by Aristotle's discussion of self-love in Books VIII and IX of the *Ethics*. These books, which have been seen by some modern commentators as the *locus classicus* for a 'philosophical egotism' among radical Aristotelians in the Arts Faculty, certainly invited discussion of the relative priority which should be given to the good of a virtuous individual and the good of the community of which that individual is a member. When the individual lays down his life, should he be intending primarily to secure his own good (that is, the performance of a supreme act of virtue) or should he be intending primarily to secure the common good? Thomas Aquinas had answered this question by insisting that the individual good is the same as the common good, in that it is included in the common good as the good on which it depends for its own existence. A virtuous individual is therefore like a hand which will expose itself to danger for the sake of the whole body of which it forms a part. For Henry of Ghent the solution was not quite so straightforward.

First, there is the question of approach. Henry clearly thinks that it is necessary to make the point that there is no such thing as a 'double truth' and that philosophical and Christian reasoning must be consistent with one another in such a way that any conclusion is applicable to Christian and non-Christian alike. As a result, he spends much of his analysis correlating Aristotle's *Ethics* not just with Cicero's *On Duties* but also with Augustine's *On Free Choice* and *On the Trinity*. It is Augustine who accordingly provides Henry with the distinction between the evil of punishment or suffering (*malum poenae*) and the evil of guilt (*malum culpae*) which is central to his overall solution. Then there is the question of content. Henry is prepared at least to query Aquinas's presupposition that the individual's good must be the same as the common good, that the individual's good must be included in the common good, and that the organic or corporeal analogy is strictly applicable to an individual's participation in the political community. Instead, Henry differentiates between positive good and negative good (that is, between acquiring good and avoiding evil), a distinction which he justifies, once again, with a combination of Aristotle and Augustine. Henry also considers the apparent detachment of an individual who is engaged in a life of contemplation rather than a life of political and social action. This time, however, in order to prove that even a contemplative individual is, in some limited way, still included in the community, he appeals, not to Aristotle, but to Augustine alone. The reason human society is inclusive of all individuals is that the political community is, at root, a providential remedy for sin. In appealing to Augustine, Henry is clearly prepared to move well beyond Aristotle's own terms of reference. Not only does he discuss the question of whether an individual should sacrifice his own spiritual well-being (that is, incur damnation) if this will result in salvation for the rest of the community, but he is also prepared to assert that Aristotle's understanding of happiness is fundamentally flawed. For all his attempts at harmonization, therefore, Henry does not conceal the limitations of a philosophy that locates happiness within the confines of this earthly life.

For further reading on Henry of Ghent, see CHLMP, p. 863 and, for his discussion of self-sacrifice, Georges de Lagarde, 'La Philosophie sociale d'Henri de Gand et Godefroid de Fontaines,' *Archives d'histoire doctrinale et littéraire du moyen âge*, 14 (1943–45):73–142, and *La Naissance de l'esprit laïque au déclin du moyen âge*, 3rd ed; 5 vols. (Louvain: E. Nauwelaerts 1956–70), 2:180–83; E. H. Kantorowicz, *The King's Two Bodies: A Study in Medieval Political Theology* (Princeton: Princeton University Press, 1957), pp. 479–80; and M. S. Kempshall, *The Common Good in Late Medieval Political Thought* (Oxford: Oxford University Press, 1999), chapter 6. On quodlibets, see J. F. Wippel, 'The Quodlibetic Question as a Distinctive Literary Genre' in *Les genres littéraires dans les sources théologiques et philosophiques médiévales* (Louvain-la-Neuve: Institut d'Études Médiévales de l'Université Catholique de Louvain 1982). On 'philosophical egotism' in the Faculty of Arts at Paris, see de Lagarde, *La Naissance de l'esprit laïque au déclin du moyen âge*, 2:46–47; and B. C. Bazán, ed., *Siger de Brabant, écrits de logique, de morale et de physique*, Philosophes Médiévaux, XIV (Louvain: Publications universitaire, 1974), pp. 103–5.

Is It Rational for Someone without Hope of a Future Life to Choose to Die for the Commonwealth?

{67} Ought someone who has no hope of a future life to choose, according to right reason, to die for the sake of the commonwealth?

[1. Preliminary Arguments]

[1a. Arguments against Making This Choice]

[i] No one acting according to right reason ought to choose something through which he is miserable, because according to Augustine (*On the Trinity* XIII 3–4), just as we all will naturally to be blessed, so we all will not to be miserable. But in dying for the commonwealth such an individual, insofar as he has no hope of a future life, is miserable. For according to Augustine in *On the Trinity* XIII 7, discussing hope of a future life, 'Whoever is blessed with hope awaits with patience a blessedness not now possessed, but whoever is without such hope and suffers without any such recompense will not be truly blessed (however much patience he exhibits) but intensely miserable.' Therefore, etc.

[ii] Whoever is without such hope ought to love his own natural life no less than someone who has such hope ought to love his own spiritual life (that is, the life he lives through grace and charity), because just as the latter possesses true good for himself in his spiritual life so does the former in his natural life. But it does not accord with right reason for the person who has such hope {68} to choose a death contrary to it (namely, the death that comes through sin) for the sake of the commonwealth. For as Anselm says in his book of *Meditations* (3), 'If to sin is to dishonor God, then human beings ought not to sin, even if it were then necessary for everything that is not God to perish.' Therefore, etc.

[1b. Arguments for Making This Choice]

[i] According to right reason, the common good ought to be preferred to the private good. Since the life of such a person is a private good and the well-being of the commonwealth is a common good, therefore, etc.

[ii] Just as limbs are related to each other in the body, so are different people related to each other in the commonwealth, according to the Apostle in 1 Corinthians 12:12–20. But a limb ought to risk its life for the sake of the body. Therefore, so too should any person for the sake of the commonwealth.

[2. Answer to the Question]

I maintain that what ought to be done according to right reason ought to be done equally by all, and everyone who possesses right reason ought to judge equally that it ought to be done. The judgments of philosophers and catholics ought not to diverge on this, nor should someone with hope of a future life judge otherwise than someone without such hope (or vice versa). For just as what is true for some is true for all, and just as there is nothing true according to true philosophy which is not true according to theology (or vice versa), so it is with what is right or what should be done according to right reason.

Thus, in this question the good theologian ought not to be of a different opinion from the true philosopher or vice versa. The same goes with regard to what is false and contrary to right reason. In the present instance, someone with hope of another life ought to judge, according to right reason, that it is preferable to die for the well-being of the commonwealth not so much because he hopes that the penalty of death will be restored, and compensated for, by the reward of a future life {69} but rather because whoever did not make this choice and risk his temporal life for the commonwealth would sin and offend against God. Therefore, someone without hope of a future life ought to make the same judgment, namely, that according to right reason one should choose death for the sake of the commonwealth and should do so because one would sin in not making this choice. This is the case even if he is not afraid of giving offense to God for fear of a future punishment in which he does not believe.

According to right reason, virtuous actions should always be chosen and vicious ones avoided even if one has no hope of another life. With regard to avoiding sin, one philosopher has said: 'If I knew the gods to be unconcerned and human beings to be unaware, I would still think it unworthy to sin.' With regard to exercising virtue, Bernard of Clairvaux maintains in a letter to Abbot Guarinus (Epistle 254): 'True virtue knows no end. The just individual never says "It is enough." If he were to live forever, he would always strive as much as was within him to be more just.' This is because the virtues are in accordance with right reason, by which human beings ought to live insofar as they are human, since this is to live according to their nature. The vices, on the other hand, are contrary to right reason.

I maintain, therefore, that according to right reason even someone without hope of another life ought to choose to die for the sake of the commonwealth. Now I do not add 'when it is necessary' or 'for the sake of the well-being of the commonwealth,' because someone who chooses to die when it is *not* necessary for the well-being of the commonwealth (when, for instance, its well-being could readily be provided for in another way), does not choose to die, strictly speaking, for the sake of the commonwealth but for the sake of his own rashness. Similarly, someone who chooses to die, not for the well-being of the commonwealth (that is, not to defend its justice and protect it from harm), but for the sake of honor and glory and to preserve such things as are opposed to the justice of the commonwealth, would not be said to be choosing to die for {70} the commonwealth but rather for the sake of vainglory and greed. (Such a person does not exhibit true bravery, only an approximation. It would seem that the Philosopher calls such people brave only in the sense of political bravery. He says of them [*Ethics* III 8, 1116a18–22]: 'They seem to submit to danger because of the legal penalties and [to avoid] opprobrium and for the sake of honors. Homer makes such people brave – Diomedes, for example, and Hector.')

As a result, death and other evils that are suffered ought to be avoided when they are considered in themselves. Thus, discussing the just man in *On the Trinity* XIII 7, Augustine maintains that 'Although he may be prepared through bravery to accept and bear with equanimity whatever adversity brings, nevertheless he prefers this not to happen and, if he can do so, makes sure it does not.' I take him to mean 'unless the act of avoiding such things ought to be a cause of shame for us.' Vice is called shameful and is always to be avoided. Therefore, in order to avoid vice, one should not avoid death. One ought to submit to every kind of evil suffered (*malum poenae*) rather than consent to the evil of guilt (*malum culpae*). That is why the Philosopher says in *Ethics* IV (III 6, 1115a27) that 'Nothing is thought to be either good or bad for the dead' (because, as the Commentator states, 'The dead avoid nothing as evil and desire nothing as good') and adds (1115a28–31): 'He does not seem brave who is fearless of death in any form whatever but of death in the greatest and supreme danger' ('or,' as the Commentator states, 'for the well-being of his country, for the laws, for friends, and for freedom'). It is in these circumstances, then, and in such dangers, that the brave are properly fearless. That is why the Philosopher also adds (1115a32–35): {71} 'He will be called brave in the first instance who is undaunted in the face of a good death and whatever brings it about. Such criteria are present above all in war.' Further on (III 7, 1115b10–13) he states: 'The brave man, being as undaunted as a human can be, will therefore fear such things as he should and endure them as reason dictates for the sake of the good, since this is the end of virtue.' So too in Book IX (8, 1169a18–20): 'What is said is true of the morally serious individual (*studioso*): He does many things for the sake of his friends and his country and will, if necessary, die for them.' In expounding this text the Commentator says: 'He does not do *everything* for the sake of a friend – for example, the sorts of things that bring shame or embarrassment and do not result in a genuinely honorable benefit.'

According to right reason, therefore, one should die for the sake of the commonwealth even if there is no hope of a future life.

[2a. Is the Answer the Same for Contemplative Happiness as It Is for Political Happiness?]

There is no doubt that this is the Philosopher's own opinion concerning the individual who is happy in the sense of political happiness. Discussing this in *Ethics* I (7, 1097b8–11), he says: 'We apply the term perfect and self-sufficient good, not to a solitary life of living on one's own, but to a life lived with parents, children, wife, friends, and citizens.' This good consists of performing deeds of moral virtue (of bravery, temperance, and justice) without hindrance and in accordance with perfect virtue (namely, prudence). Here it is better and more blessed to do one great virtuous deed in a brief moment than to live for a long time doing lesser deeds. On this account, dying for the sake of the commonwealth is not only better in itself (because it is for the sake of more people) but also better for the individual. This accords with what he says in *Ethics* IX (8, 1169a17–26): 'Every intellect chooses what is best for itself, {72} and the fair-minded man obeys his intellect. For an individual will cast aside money, honors, and all the goods that people fight for if he can secure good for himself, since he would rather choose a short period of living well than many years of nondescript existence, and one great and good action than many lesser ones. This presumably (*forte*) applies to those who die [for others]. They choose a particularly great good for themselves.'

If the Philosopher holds this opinion of an individual who is happy in terms of political happiness (namely, that according to right reason he ought to choose to die for the commonwealth because in doing so he chooses a greater good – this seems to be the gist of his argument), what, I ask, is his opinion of the individual who is happy in terms of contemplative happiness? He says of this happiness in Book X (7, 1177b26–28):

'Such a life is better than the human level of life, for someone who lives this life does so, not as a human being, but insofar as he has something divine within him.'

[2b. The Problem of Justifying Self-Sacrifice for a Contemplative]

If the Philosopher is of the opinion that an individual who is happy in terms of contemplative happiness should choose, according to right reason, to die for the sake of the commonwealth, is this, I ask, because he thinks it is good for the contemplative himself or because it is good in itself but not good for the contemplative? Not [it seems] because it is good for the contemplative himself, for since he would do this in accordance with political bravery and in a political manner, he would derive no good for himself from this action except in the manner of the political good already described (namely, that it is better and more blessed to do one great deed in a brief moment, etc). This is not true, because it is impossible for the contemplative to experience as much pleasure in any activity relating to political virtue, however great it might be, as he would experience in activity relating to contemplative virtue, since the latter brings its own 'wonderful pleasures,' as [the Philosopher] maintains in *Ethics* X (7, 1177a25). Therefore, it would not be good for the contemplative himself, because he would be descending from {73} a greater and more permanent pleasure to a lesser and more transitory one. Therefore [it seems that] either [i] the Philosopher is of the opinion that according to right reason a contemplatively happy individual ought not to choose to die for the sake of the commonwealth because it is better for himself, or [ii] if, according to right reason, he ought to choose death, then this is because it is better in itself, even though it would not be better for him in the way the Philosopher asserts it is better for a political individual. What is the Philosopher's opinion on this?

[2c. Self-Sacrifice to Avoid the Evil of Guilt]

I believe that either the Philosopher's opinion of contemplative happiness was wrong, or else he thought that according to right reason a contemplative individual ought to make that choice [to die for the commonwealth] because it is better in itself and also for him, since even if it is not better for him in terms of acquiring any good (either overall or for one brief moment), it is nevertheless better for him in terms of avoiding the evil of guilt. In this way, the political individual ought also to choose to die even if it were in no way better for him in terms of acquiring a good. It is better in itself and also better for him in terms of avoiding the evil of guilt.

I maintain, then, that both of them – the politically happy individual just as much as the contemplatively happy individual – are obliged by the law of nature to choose to die and would sin and live shamefully if they did not make this choice. Now it is better to die than to live a shameful life. In this regard it is also better for them. Admittedly, by dying in this way they do not acquire good for themselves but lose every good they have, for according to what is said of the political individual in *Ethics* IV (III 9, 1117b9–13), 'The happier a man is, the more distressed he is at death, for life is most worth living for such an individual, and yet he is knowingly deprived of the greatest goods, which is distressing.' Thus, although good would not come to them (which the Philosopher hints at in the passage which follows [1117b13–15]: 'But he is no less brave and perhaps is more so, since he chooses good in war in its stead'), nevertheless, {74} they ought still to make that choice, according to right reason, because by doing so they will avoid the shamefulness of vice. For as is said in *Ethics* IV (III 8, 1117a16–17), 'The brave person endures the things that are terrifying for human beings' for the sake of 'good *or evil.*' [In this case, it is] not for the sake of a good (that is, acquiring a good) but for the sake of not incurring something shameful (that is, incurring the shamefulness of guilt).

And so the individual who has no hope of another life ought to choose, according to right reason, to die for the sake of the commonwealth, just as the individual who *does* have hope of another life ought to do so [acting] from charity, and just as the latter, according to right reason, would be obliged to do so in the manner described even if he did not merit being received into another life through such a death. It is for this reason that Tully declares in Book I of *On Duties* (22): 'It has been splendidly written by Plato that we are not born for ourselves alone. Our country claims for itself one part of our birth and our friends another. Moreover, as the Stoics believe, everything the earth produces has been created for the use of humans. Humans are produced for the sake of humans in order that one may be of benefit to another among themselves. We ought to follow nature as our guide in this and make a public contribution of things that are beneficial to the community by acting reciprocally in our duties to one another.' He also says in his *Popular Oration to the Senate* [*Pridie quam in exilium iret*] (8–9): 'Thus, I was inspired from the beginning to think of myself less as born for my own sake than as produced for the sake of the commonwealth. I find nothing hard and nothing bitter that protects the commonwealth. For neither is death miserable when it is incurred for the sake of the commonwealth nor is effort shameful when it is undertaken in the course of virtue, particularly since these penalties have some consolation in them.' He also states in the first of his *Invectives* [*In Catilinam*] (I 27): 'My country is dearer to me than my life,' and in Book IV (3) of the same work: 'My position is such that I would submit to every bitterness, every grief, and every suffering, not only bravely but even freely, as long as the dignity and the well-being of both city {75} and commonwealth would result from my labors. I would die prepared and with equanimity. For a shameful death cannot happen to the brave nor a miserable one to the wise.'

The wise, therefore, never accept death unwillingly, while often the brave even seek it out. That is why the Philosopher – because he was of the opinion that the brave political individual and the wise contemplative should choose, according to right reason, to die for the commonwealth even if no good comes to them as a consequence but only the loss of good in the manner already described – when he said in Book IX (8, 1169a24–26) that one great action should be chosen in preference to many lesser ones, added that '*presumably* those who lay down their lives choose a particularly great good for themselves,' because even if this great good did not come about it would still be in accordance with right reason for them to choose to die in this manner. Following this [reasoning], the two arguments put forward in favor of the proposition (1b[i–ii]) must be conceded.

[2d. Arguments Exempting the Contemplative from the Obligation to Die for the Commonwealth]

What, then, if someone maintains that the Philosopher would deny that the happy contemplative ought to choose to die in the manner described, on the grounds that the contemplative lives as though he is completely cut off from human society, existing not as a mortal human being but as though he were divine and immortal (as the Philosopher states in *Ethics* X [7, 1177b27–28]) and is for that reason *not* obliged to descend from his contemplative happiness to engage in political activity for the sake of the commonwealth?

[i] Someone maintaining this position would say in reply to the first

argument in favor of the proposition (1b[i]) that it is true that the public good should be preferred to the private good but only while the private good is included in the public good; otherwise not. Although the common good should be preferred in itself {76} when it is considered in its own terms, this is not the case when it is considered in terms of the individual whose private good is not included in the public good.

[ii] Similarly, it would be said in reply to the second argument (1b[ii]) (that an individual limb exposes itself to the danger of death for the sake of preserving the whole) that this is true when the limb does not have its own intellect and cannot have its own individual good separately from the good of the whole. Yet if a part or a limb were to have its own intellect, or even a good that it could obtain separately (such as the good that the contemplative has), then there is no way in which it would make that choice [to sacrifice itself].

[2e. Replies to the Preceding Arguments]

These arguments cannot stand. Even if the Philosopher held according to right reason many opinions on the means to the end of human life that the catholic faith also holds, nevertheless, in ordering these things toward their end and with regard to the end itself, he was wrong on many points. In this he was like other philosophers, because, as Augustine maintains (Epistle 155), they have constructed for themselves a certain happiness to be found in this life, which is [for them] the end of virtuous deeds, and have accordingly ordered the deeds of virtue toward an end other than the one toward which the catholic faith orders them, namely, the blessedness to be found in the life to come. This is where [the Philosopher] erred.

[i] If, on the other hand, it is argued that he held the happy contemplative to be so removed from human society that the contemplative would not be obligated to the commonwealth in any way, I do not believe that this was his position, for as has been pointed out, this is against the law of nature, from which the contemplative could not be released (unless, that is, he held that in contemplative happiness an individual is outside the sinful condition, as the blessed are in glory – which is completely wrong). Therefore, because the individual always remains under a natural obligation to the commonwealth and is in a state in which he can act meritoriously or demeritoriously, he is always obliged to choose to die for the commonwealth in the manner described. This is because his own private good, although it is not included in the public good as something positive

{77}, is still included in it as something negative, namely (as has been said), as the avoidance of shamefulness and the evil of guilt. This suffices for the original proposition, because if the contemplative's private good were not included in the public good in this way, then I think that there would be no sense in which he ought to choose to die in the manner described, just as the saints in heaven (*patria*) are not obliged to make this choice. The contemplative would then not be under any obligation to the commonwealth in this matter, just as the saints in heaven are not, since just as the latter are not a part of the community of the church militant or within its jurisdiction, so the contemplative would not be a part of human society. This accords with what seems to be the Philosopher's opinion in *Metaphysics* IX (X 4, 1055b23–24), where he maintains that a hermit is neither good nor bad and where the Commentator says 'Because he is not a part of the community.' The hermit, according to the Philosopher, is happy in terms of contemplative happiness.

[ii] Likewise, the response to the second argument (that a limb that has its own intellect and its own separate good ought not to choose to die in the manner described unless its good is included in the common good) is that this is not valid. Even if the individual limbs had individual intellects, their several intellects ought still to be as one in judging according to right reason whether to choose that act. For even if (as has been said) the limb's private, positive good is not included in the public good [of the body], its own good is nevertheless included in the latter as a negative good. What is more, although its private positive good may not be included in that public good, it nevertheless depends on it to this extent, that unless it chooses to die in the manner described it would lose its private good through the vice and shame it would incur, because the good of virtue or happiness of any kind cannot coexist with vice.

[2f. A Final Argument for Exempting the Contemplative]

On the other hand, it might be maintained, following what has already been argued, that the contemplative is not a part of the community and is thus not a limb and for this reason is in no way obliged to risk death for the sake of the commonwealth and would therefore not sin in failing to choose that course of action. {78}

[2g. Reply to 2f]

I reply that in my opinion if it were indeed the case that the contemplative was in no way part of the community, then there would be no way in which he ought to choose that course of action, because by dying he would lose all his goods and would acquire no good and avoid no evil – just as there is no one alive, just person or sinner, who ought to choose to commit a sin or damn himself for eternity so that everyone else may be eternally saved (a position touched on by the second argument against the proposition [1a(ii)]). But this is not the case. For the hermit, however removed he may be from human society, is nevertheless always in need of some assistance from it and for that reason remains under a permanent natural obligation to it. As a result, even if he is not part of it in terms of performing many of the acts that pertain to political life (those concerning the government of the household and the family, for instance, and those which concern friends), he nevertheless always remains part of it in terms of performing acts that are necessary to preserve the well-being of the commonwealth. As a result, if the commonwealth should need the hermit – philosophical, contemplative, and removed from the life of the community – to become ruler (*rector*) of a kingdom, province, or city, then he would be obliged to abandon his contemplation, descend to a life of action, and become ruler of the city and commonwealth, just as philosophers have been accustomed to do until now, as will be set out more fully below in the penultimate question (*Quodlibet* XII 29).

[3. Replies to the Preliminary Arguments (1a)]

[i] In response to what was put forward in the first argument [against the proposition] (that no one should choose, according to right reason, to die for the commonwealth, because, as Augustine says, he would be miserable in making this choice), I maintain that, according to what has just been argued, it is indeed true that the individual would be miserable without qualification, because he would lose every good he has, of whatever sort, both natural and acquired, and, according to the intention behind Augustine's statement, would descend to eternal punishment (*poena aeterna*). However, he would be *more* miserable were he not to make that choice, because he would incur guilt, and the misery of guilt is greater than that of any suffering whatever, be it suffering the loss [of God] (*poena damni*) or physical suffering (*poena sensus*). According to right reason, however, an individual should choose that course of action by which he is less miserable in preference to that by which he is more (on condition, that is, that he has to incur one or the other, as is the case here), although neither would be worthy of choice in itself. {79}

[ii] In response to the second argument (that no one who lives without such hope ought to choose his own natural death, just as no one who lives in grace ought to choose his own spiritual death), I maintain that, according to what has been argued, these cases are not similar. By spiritual death the latter would lose every good he has and incur every evil (namely, the evil of guilt and the evil of suffering, both of which he would have brought upon himself). This is not true of the former, however, because by his natural death he would avoid at least the evil of guilt, which he would have incurred had he not chosen to die. For this reason he ought to choose to die a natural death. There is no way, however, in which one ought to choose to die a spiritual death, as is clear from what has been said.

6

GODFREY OF FONTAINES
DOES A HUMAN BEING FOLLOWING THE
DICTATES OF NATURAL REASON HAVE TO
JUDGE THAT HE OUGHT TO LOVE GOD
MORE THAN HIMSELF?

Introduction

Godfrey of Fontaines was born around 1250. He studied the liberal arts at Paris during the second regency of Thomas Aquinas (1269–72) and then studied theology under Henry of Ghent and Gervase of Mt. St. Elias at the Sorbonne from around 1274. He taught as a regent master in the Faculty of Theology from 1285 to 1298–99 and again around 1303–4, before his death *ca.* 1306–9. Like Henry of Ghent, Godfrey of Fontaines produced his most important work in metaphysics, epistemology, and moral theology in the form of quodlibetic questions. Unlike Henry, however, Godfrey was a close adherent of Thomas Aquinas and, perhaps as a result of an education in the Faculty of Arts under Siger of Brabant, a more sympathetic reader of Aristotle. Thus, not only was Godfrey a firm opponent of Bishop Tempier's 1277 condemnation, but some of his most distinctive positions were established in dialogue with, and in opposition to, arguments set out in Henry's quodlibets.

Godfrey's approach to the issues raised by Book IX of the *Ethics* exemplifies much that is characteristic of his thought: direct engagement with Henry of Ghent, a close reading of Aristotle, and an attachment to Aquinas. In his tenth quodlibet, delivered in 1294–95, he sets out the problems presented by the passage in *Ethics* IX in which Aristotle appears to suggest that a virtuous individual's act of self-sacrifice is motivated primarily by desire to secure the greatest good for himself. Godfrey then proceeds, however, largely on the basis of Aquinas's view that the individual's good is included in the common good, on which it depends for its existence, to provide a critique of Henry's distinction between positive and negative goods. Moreover, for Godfrey the problem of the relationship between self-love and love for the common good involves more than questions about self-sacrifice for the sake of one's fellow humans and the applicability of the corporeal analogy to human society. For Godfrey, self-sacrifice and the organic relationship of individual to community serve, as they had for

Aquinas, as the standard models for understanding the relationship between an individual's love of self and an individual's love for God. Any exposition of Aristotle that gave priority to the individual's love of self (or to the individual's love of good for himself) would therefore invite the corollary that this same priority should operate when an individual lays down his life for God. Set in this context, Aristotle's account of self-sacrifice in Book IX of the *Ethics* precipitated a much wider discussion of the relationship between natural love and gracious love. Godfrey's conclusion here is un-equivocal. The same principle of action must underpin both the natural love of human friendship described by Aristotle (*amicitia*) and the divinely infused love discussed in theology (*caritas*). It cannot be the case that natural love prompts an individual to love himself more than God while divinely infused gracious love prompts an individual to love God more than him-self, since this would leave nature and grace in contradiction. Whether an individual is acting solely according to the dictates of right reason or solely according to the revealed truth of Scripture, the result must be the same, since, according to Aquinas, grace does not abolish nature but perfects it (*gratia non tollit naturam sed perficit*).

For further reading on Godfrey of Fontaines, see CHLMP, pp. 861–62. For his discussion of self-sacrifice, see G. de Lagarde, 'La Philosophie sociale d'Henri de Gand et Godefroid de Fontaines,' *Archives d'histoire doctrinale et littéraire du moyen âge*, 14 (1943–45):73–142, pp. 101–3, and *La Naissance de l'esprit laïque au déclin du moyen âge*, 3rd ed., 5 vols. (Louvain: E. Nauwelaerts 1956–70), 2:172–73; and M. S. Kempshall, *The Common Good in Late Medieval Political Thought*, chapter 8.

Does a Human Being Following the Dictates of Natural Reason Have to Judge that He Ought to Love God More than Himself?

[1. Preliminary Arguments]

[1a. Argument in Favor of the Proposition]

{318} Since good should be loved, natural reason dictates that the greatest or best good should be loved more. But God is the best good not only absolutely but also for a human being, because God is more intimate to each particular thing than that thing is to itself. Natural reason dictates, therefore, that a human being ought to love God more than himself.

[1b. Argument against the Proposition]

This is one of the differences asserted between theologians and Peripatetics, between those who follow the dictates of reason according to the illumination of supernatural light and of faith and those who used to follow the dictates of reason according to the illumination of natural reason alone. According to the leader of that sect, namely, Aristotle, in *Ethics* IX (4, 1166a1–2, b1–2; 8, 1168b4–5), friendliness toward another derives from friendliness toward oneself. But a cause is more potent than its effect. According to them, therefore, an individual loves himself primarily and more than anyone else. According to theologians, however, the friendship with which an individual loves himself ought to derive from the friendship with which he loves God. Thus, according to theologians, a human being ought to love God primarily and more than himself.

[2. First Answer to the Question]

I answer. It should be maintained that we ought not to 'love' God if we are speaking about what is properly called amicable love (*amor amicitiae*), which is a love between individuals who are more or less equals, who participate in goodness and perfection of the same character (namely, the virtuous and morally honorable good), and who share with one another accordingly because they are, as it were, one in this good. [In this case] each individual, in loving the other, loves, as it were, another self. However, by extending the term 'friendship' (*amicitia*) to higher and more eminent things, then, in the way that someone loves those from whom his nature and character derive their being and to whom he has the relation and condition of a dependent caused by them or of a partial good with respect to them, so we 'love' our parents, country, and God himself. In terms of this [extended] definition it should be maintained that since the object of the will is the good [both absolutely and] as it is suitable to the individual who loves, and since God is the supreme good absolutely and is, as it were, the common good on which every particular good of every existing thing depends, then according to the order of natural inclination every existing thing is inclined toward God with a natural love as toward its final end and best good. Likewise in the natural order, every part has a greater natural love for the common good of the whole than it does for its own individual good, as {319} we see in natural [beings] that the part risks itself by a natural inclination to preserve the good of the whole. For example, a less important limb is risked without deliberation to preserve the whole body, and in a political context the virtuous individual risks death to preserve the common good.

Therefore, because God is the greatest universal and common good (common, that is, in terms of virtue and perfection), and because God is said to be all good, in which the human being (or rather, every creature) is included, it follows that a human being loves God with a natural love more – and more primarily – than himself. The result is that, if he were not weighed down by the gravity of sin and deflected toward carnal love, a human being would love God above himself and above all other things not only with a deliberate love informed by charity but also with a deliberate natural love (i.e., even without charity). And so, according to the dictates of natural reason, even a human being who is without grace has to judge that God should be loved above all things. If this were not the case, then grace and charity would destroy, not perfect, nature and natural inclination. If a human being did *not* have the capacity to love God above all according to natural rectitude and natural reason (albeit not graciously, meritoriously, and worthily, so as to merit eternal life) but were inclined in the natural order to love something other than God equally or more, then such a love would be vicious and contrary to the love that is charity. There is an inconsistency here, because natural love (where nature is upright and not vicious) and the love that is charity are in harmony and tend toward the same [end], albeit in different ways and with greater and lesser perfection. This is evident from the words of Christ in John 15:13: 'Greater love has no one than this . . .' etc. This [natural] love is even deserving of eternal life if the will eliciting it is formed by charity. A human being who follows the dictates of natural reason has to judge that he ought to endure every evil of suffering (*mala poenae*) and risk death to preserve the divine honor. If it were possible for God to suffer harm to himself, then a human being ought all the more to choose to endure harm to preserve him. There is no other way that we can emphasize more that a human being should love God more than himself. Therefore, etc.

[3. The Question Reformulated]

These arguments do not seem to remove the difficulty of the question, however, because the mode of loving [just discussed] seems to coincide with the mode in which someone loves the common good in a political context. The Philosopher says of this in *Ethics* IX (8, 1169a18–20) that in loving the good of his country a morally serious (*studiosus*) individual will even be prepared to die to preserve it, should this be necessary. [Yet] according to what seems to be Aristotle's intention here, the morally serious individual loves himself in this more than anything else, because anything he casts away in this action and seems, as it were, to despise is almost insignificant compared to the greatest good of virtue which he intends [to secure] for himself through the action and which he actually exercises in performing it. Hence, as is said in the same passage (1169a16–18, 22–25), such an individual acquires for himself the best and greatest good according to what is best and most primary within him, namely, his intellect. For he would certainly choose a short period of intense pleasure rather than a long period of peace and quiet, one year of living well rather than many years of nondescript existence, {320} and to perform one good and very great action ((*actionem/acceptionem*)) rather than many lesser ones. And so, in all matters worthy of praise the morally serious individual appears to be acquiring more good for himself and thus seems to love himself more.

According to this [argument], therefore, it seems that the individual in the proposition who risks death to preserve the divine good also loves himself more than anything else, because he does this with the intention of performing a good deed, namely, to exercise the virtues to the greatest extent. And so, even someone who loves God through charity would not seem to be loving him above all, because in doing this he too seems to aim chiefly at his own greatest good (since the good of charity is not less than the good of the political virtues).

It has to be understood that such an individual loves God and *also* loves himself and his own good. For since, according to Augustine, each individual naturally and invariably seeks his own blessedness in general (i.e., the character of blessedness, that is, his own well-being or best state), no one can love or seek any good whatever except insofar as his own good or his own well-being is also included within it. For this reason, it must be that an individual who loves God and (as has been said) risks himself on God's behalf also has, in this act, the greatest love for himself, such that

there is no other ((*quod non/quod*)) case in which he could love himself
more and, in doing so, aim at and acquire good for himself to the greatest
extent.

The question may then be raised [however]: Which of these goods does
he love more, the divine good and its preservation or his own good,
which is present in him as a result of the sort of love with which he so
loves God that he is prepared to risk himself to preserve God's good?

[4. Answer to the Reformulated Question]

It should be maintained that since [i] an act has its form and perfection
from its object, and [ii] the object [of the act] in which God is loved is *per
se* and primarily the divine good, and [iii] the divine good is without
qualification the greatest good, while [iv] the object of the love with
which anyone loves himself loving God and achieving perfection in virtue
is a lesser good, it is clear that [v] the former love is absolutely and without
qualification greater and more perfect. Thus, it seems that I love God in
his perfection more than I love myself being perfected by this sort of love
and the other virtues.

[4a. An Objection]

It might be argued that this is not the case on the grounds that, although
the divine good is without qualification and in itself greater than the
individual good just described, the individual good is nevertheless a greater
good for the one who is loving and that for this reason it seems that he
should also love it more.

[4b. Reply to the Objection]

This is not a valid argument. It is true that a good is worthy of love
inasmuch as it is good in itself and suitable to the individual who loves it.
Of such goods, some are extrinsic to the lover, such as wealth and honors,
and some are intrinsic, such as the good of virtue (which perfects the
individual by forming him and intrinsically inhering in him). The latter
good should be loved more than any other good whatever (which, as the
Philosopher says, the morally serious individual casts away and, as it were,
despises in comparison with this good). However, this [intrinsic] good

takes its [own] form and perfection from another, extrinsic good which is *per se* the primary object of love, which is said to be loved more, and for whose preservation the individual who loves it risks himself. For this reason, although this [extrinsic good] is not a good for the individual who loves it in the sense of something forming and intrinsically inhering in him, nevertheless, it *is* a good for him in the sense of an object perfecting him inasmuch as through it {321} he has the perfection of a perfect ((*perfecti/perfectus*)) act (and this is [in turn] a good in the sense of a perfection forming [and inhering in] the individual who is loving). It is loved more as a good of the individual who loves it in this sense, namely, as an extrinsic end, than any other good whatever. For according to the Philosopher, the good of the community is not itself reckoned among the goods that the morally serious individual despises and, as it were, casts away to preserve the common good. Instead, he virtuously chooses to suffer loss in anything *else* whatever to preserve the good of the community. Thus, he loves the good of the community more than he loves any of the other goods of this kind. In short, therefore, it could be said that the love with which I love the divine good as an end and as an extrinsic good is different in character from the love with which I love the good of virtue as an end and as an intrinsic good. For this reason, they are, strictly speaking, not comparable with one another.

[5. A Second Reformulation of the Question]

However, the intellect may still be uneasy. Although these loves are different in character and are not properly comparable with one another (as they would be if they were of one genus or species), nevertheless, because they are entities that are neither completely similar to one another nor entirely different, they do have some relation to one another and are in some way comparable. And so the original question still remains, namely, whether a human being loves God more than he loves himself loving virtuously, and so on.

[6. Answer to the Question in Its Second Reformulation]

It should again be maintained that an individual has a greater love for God for the sake of God and above the love that he has for himself loving God.

For when the individual who is loving does not look for any good of his own in what is loved other than the good of love itself (in which the good of what is loved is included as the *per se* object of this love), and when his loving this [good] is ordered toward nothing else but is fixed on what is loved (or on the good of what is loved) as its primary end, then what is loved is loved for its own sake. (For when something is loved for the sake of some good coming from it other than the loving itself or the good of what is loved, it is not loved for its own sake.) This is therefore the case in every true friendship, and most potently in that which relates to the supreme good.

Justice, which is concerned with activities relating to another individual, does not seek *per se* the good of its agent but the good of whomever its activity is directed toward. For this reason, justice is called the most distinguished of the virtues, because an individual uses it primarily for the good of another person, whereas in the other virtues, which are primarily concerned with those things which intrinsically pertain to the agent, an individual primarily aims at his own good. Now of all friendships, that which exists toward one's parents, toward the common good, and above all toward God has more of the character of justice, inasmuch as it has more of the character of rendering what is due [to another person].

It is clear from this that when an individual loves God *per se* and for the sake of God (i.e., because God is in himself supremely good and supremely worthy of love, and *not* so that some other good might result from this), then even though this includes other goods for the individual who is loving, which follow from it (namely, the vision and full enjoyment of God), nevertheless, if the individual loves God because God is good in this sense and would want to love him without these goods resulting from it, then [God] is loved for his own sake and the human being also loves God above himself. The reason is that when someone chooses to lose every good that is intrinsic to him in order to preserve some extrinsic good, {322} he loves that extrinsic good more than his own intrinsic good. Such is the case in the proposition, because however much an individual may love himself when he is made perfect (or his intrinsic perfection, which includes loving God), he nevertheless chooses to lose every good of this kind and even not to exist at all (if that were possible), rather than for the divine good not to exist. This is also the Philosopher's position in *Ethics* IX. However much the morally serious individual may love himself and his own individual and intrinsic good, he still chooses to die well and virtuously, and not to exist, rather than for the common good to perish.

Indeed, since it is the case that anyone, even an individual who follows the dictates of natural reason without illumination from the light of faith, ought to choose to die and not to exist rather than do anything morally dishonorable (*inhonestum*) against the good of virtue, [it would seem that an individual can love an extrinsic good other than God more than himself]. Imagine that someone has been put in a position where it is necessary for him to die or else what constitutes the good of the community would perish or he would be deserting the good of virtue. Suppose, for example, a situation in which someone else will destroy the good of the community if an individual who is capable of resistance does not oppose him. It seems that in all such instances it has to be said that an individual can love some other good which is extrinsic to him and is not formally God more than he loves himself.

But because, as has been said, I cannot will and love anything unless this includes my own well-being as well as an intrinsic good for me, then when I am good and formally perfect in willing – for the sake of preserving another, extrinsic good – that my good and I myself not exist, I acquire a greater intrinsic good for myself and a better existence (because it is a virtuous existence). But because this intrinsic good derives its goodness from the goodness of the object that is primarily loved, for that reason I accordingly will the greatest good possible for myself. Yet this is not what I will first, primarily, or most, because this is not the first and *per se* object of will. Instead, [the first and *per se* object] is that from which this sort of act (which is [indeed] good for me) derives its own goodness. For if I were to will that my good be preserved in existence rather than the divine good, I would not thereby be willing the greatest good for myself, because this would be to will something inordinate and vicious, like the soldier who flees and throws away his shield to preserve himself, spurning the preservation of the community.

As a result, although in willing that God exist (or in loving the divine good) there is a certain intrinsic and virtuous good for me, and although in willing myself to will that God exist (and in loving myself loving God) reflexive acts are included whose perfection derives from the perfection of the primary object and the primary act, it is clear that simply willing that God exist or loving [God] is more perfect than the reflexive act itself and that I am under a greater obligation to love ((*diligere/eligere*)) [God] and to will that God exist than I am to will myself to will that God exist. Thus, it is clear that I love the divine good, or love God to exist, more than I love my own good.

Likewise, in a political context, when a morally serious individual loves the good of the community and is willing to risk himself for the sake of its preservation and also loves himself loving the common good and risking himself on its behalf, it should be maintained that he loves the common good more. Otherwise, there will be inconsistencies in what is being asserted. For if he loves himself more, he therefore wills that the {323} common good not exist while he remains thus perfected more than he wills that he himself not exist in this perfection while the common good remains. But his perfection in loving the common good in this way includes willing that the common good be preserved even through his own death. The preservation of the common good does not, however, include his own preservation in existence, because the common good can exist without him existing. It is therefore possible for someone to will that the common good be preserved without him, but it is impossible for someone to will that he himself be preserved in such a virtuous deed (namely, the deed in which he wills that the common good be preserved and is willing to risk himself on its behalf) without willing that the common good be preserved rather than himself. In this act, therefore, the individual wills and loves the common good more [than himself].

What has just been said does not seem to contradict the Philosopher, because it is true that in this act the morally serious individual chooses what is best for himself, since the good of virtue which he chooses is the best good for a morally serious individual. For none of those things which an individual puts at risk (and would be able to keep if he refused to risk himself) is [in these circumstances] good. And so, according to the Philosopher, in this act the morally serious individual imparts to himself the best and greatest goods, namely, the goods that are suitable to him in terms of his reason or intellect, because even in dying he chooses to live well for a short period rather than a long period of nondescript existence, etc.

Thus, according to the right order of nature, through which charity perfects [us], a human being loves God more than himself. Nevertheless, in so doing he loves himself more (because he also loves his own greater good) than if he did not love God in this way. The intrinsic good of the individual who is loving is not the final reason, as it were, for loving God or the common good, because the good of a part cannot be the final good for the sake of which the common good is loved and preserved. Instead, the perfect goodness of the common good itself, toward which the good of the part has an order and a disposition, is the reason for which it is loved for itself as an end, as has been said. Otherwise, loving God would be using God [as a means to an end].

[6a. A Possible Difficulty]

But it seems from this that loving God is the most perfect of human acts, since (as has been said) in loving God an individual also wills the greatest good for himself consequentially and, as it were, implicitly.

[6b. Response to the Possible Difficulty]

It should be maintained that although God is that which is best and is to be loved supremely, nevertheless, the act by which he is loved need not be loftier than every other act by which he is attained. It can indeed be maintained that I ought to love God more than any of my acts whatever, whether it is this act [of loving God] or another act in which he is more fully attained. But I love the act of vision in which God is more perfectly attained by the intellect more than I love the act of love in which he is attained by the will, just as, in a political context, a morally serious individual ought to love the common good more than any of his own acts and yet loves the act of contemplation (if he is a contemplative) more than this act [of loving the common good].

[7. Formal Answer to the Original Question]

Therefore, it should be maintained that since the love of God is not greater in kind than that regulated and ordered love by which an individual risks even death for the sake of his country (although it can be greater or lesser in terms of intention), a human being also has to judge from the order of natural reason that he ought to be prepared to suffer death for the love of God, {324} since right reason declares that this should be done even for the sake of preserving the good of the community, as is clear from the Philosopher in *Ethics* IX (8, 1169a18–20). Now [since] someone who loves in this way seems to love that on behalf of which he suffers so much harm more than he loves himself, it is clear that the dictates of natural reason prove conclusively that a human being ought to love God more than

himself. For according to the right order of nature any one individual part
has a greater natural love for the common good of the whole than for its
own particular good, since the individual good is ordered toward the
common good and also depends on it. Now God is the common good of
all things, etc. [Therefore, the individual who follows the dictates of
natural reason has to judge that he ought to love God more than himself.]

By loving the common good more than himself, the individual also
loves himself more, better, and more perfectly, than if he refused to suffer
these losses for the sake of the good which he loves. So too, by ordinately
loving God more than himself (i.e., [loving him] according to the order of
natural inclination and from a dictate of natural reason) the individual
cannot love him without also loving himself more – and more perfectly –
than if he did not love God in this way. Now reason and the natural order
demand that each individual should so love himself that he wills the best
goods for himself and does what is suitable for himself by loving God
more than himself, because this is his most perfect act.

It cannot be maintained, however, that an individual ought to will to
love the divine good more than his own good in such a way that his own
good is included in this act but to a lesser extent than if he simply loved
his own private good primarily or he did not love God in this way. For it
should not be understood that one ought to perform any act (either an
interior act of loving or an exterior deed) unless in doing it one can be
unqualifiedly better. As a result, there is nothing for the preservation of
whose good an individual ought to do or to choose a vicious act, that is,
an act by which he would become worse.

[7a. Corollary: The Good in Self-Sacrifice Is Not a Negative Good]

On these grounds, it seems wrong to maintain, as some do, that when a
political individual risks death for the common good, it is because in doing
so he acquires a greater good for himself, namely, a perfect act of bravery,
but that when a contemplative individual risks himself in this manner, he
does not do so for the sake of a greater good which he thereby acquires
but to avoid becoming worse by incurring the evil of guilt. This is because
an act of bravery or an act of any political virtue whatever is more
imperfect than the act of contemplation which the contemplative individual forfeits by risking himself in this way (because by risking death in this
way he is unable to exercise this act). As a result [it is claimed], to risk

oneself in this way is not better for the contemplative individual in terms of acquiring a good but only in terms of avoiding an evil.

On the contrary. In this act the contemplative, too, acquires for himself a greater good. It seems impossible to maintain that someone can perform a perfect act to avoid the evil of guilt without at the same time acquiring the great good of virtue. For just as the individual would incur evil by not acting (namely, by not risking himself when he ought), so he acquires the good of virtue if he does risk himself when and as he ought (for he would not incur the evil of guilt by not risking himself unless he were bound to do so). It is generally agreed, however, that just as voluntarily omitting {325} to do something good that one is bound to do incurs evil or makes one worse, so by doing from choice something good that one is bound to do one acquires good and becomes better.

Also, although an act of bravery, or of any political virtue, is not in itself and absolutely without qualification more perfect or better than the act of contemplation (on account of which the activity of contemplation should not without qualification and absolutely be neglected in favor of political activity), nevertheless, this can [be better] in certain circumstances. For example, when the common good cannot suitably be preserved unless some contemplative individual deserts the activity of contemplation and risks himself in political acts, it is better to neglect the former. In such a case it is also a greater good for the contemplative to act in this way and he acquires a greater good for himself, just as it is better for a needy person to make money than to engage in philosophy (cf. *Topics* III 2, 118a10–11).

[8. Reply to the Preliminary Argument against the Proposition (1b)]

To the argument that friendliness toward another derives from friendliness toward oneself, it should be said that the Philosopher is speaking about the strictly defined friendship which exists between equals (or virtual equals), in which friends share equally, as it were, in the good on which the friendship is based (or which is the object of such friendship), and which exists in them in a mode of, as it were, participation. He is not speaking about the [unequal] friendship toward another in whom the good that is the object of the friendship is found as a principle of superiority and as a sort of whole including, as it were, every good. In terms of this [distinction], it is clear that a difference of opinion is wrongly ascribed to Aristotle (and the Peripatetics) and any doctor of theology [if this means] imputing to Aristotle [the position] that according to his teaching every individual ought to love himself and his own individual good more than anything else whatever. In fact, in those matters which pertain to true friendship, the teaching of Aristotle and the Peripatetics is in harmony with that of the intelligent theologian. (It should be understood, nevertheless, that sacred Scripture treats friendship in a more perfect way and of a more perfect kind than philosophical science.) Therefore, according to this way of expounding the statement of the Philosopher referred to above, it is clear that he is not out of harmony with the most perfect Christian theologian. Indeed, what Aristotle says about friendliness toward another [deriving from friendliness toward oneself] seems to be no different from what Christ says: 'Love your neighbor as yourself,' etc. The Commentator also expounds this dictum of Aristotle's to mean, not that the reason for loving another person is the individual who is doing the loving or his good, but that through the acts of friendship in which we engage we manifest toward others ((*alios/amicos*)), if we are friends, what a loving individual does toward himself. That is why he maintains that friendliness toward friends and the way it is determined seems to derive from what one determines for oneself – that is, it will be clearly recognizable that an individual is a friend to someone when we know that whatever and however much he wants to have or to happen to himself, he wants (and strives to bring about) for this other person.

7

JAMES OF VITERBO
DOES A HUMAN BEING HAVE A GREATER
NATURAL LOVE FOR GOD THAN FOR
HIMSELF, OR VICE VERSA?

Introduction

James of Viterbo was born around 1255. Having joined the Augustinian
Order about 1270, he went to Paris to study theology *ca.* 1278–83. He
became a regent master around 1293, succeeding Giles of Rome to the
Augustinian chair and teaching there until 1297, when he left Paris to
direct the Augustinian school at Naples. James was made Bishop of Benevento in September 1302 and Archbishop of Naples three months later.
He died in 1308. He is better known, perhaps, for his pro-papal treatise
De regimine Christiano (trans. R. W. Dyson, Woodbridge, 1995), written
after, or just before, he became Bishop of Benevento. His teaching at Paris
survives in the form of four quodlibets. The approach taken in these
disputations is notable for its reserve and prudence. It is thus characteristic
of James to clarify various alternative views before setting down his own
answer to a question. In the debate over the relationship between essence
and existence, for example, he referees between the positions already
established by Giles of Rome, Henry of Ghent, and Godfrey of Fontaines
(CHLMP, pp. 404–5). When he confronts the problem of self-love in
Book IX of the *Ethics*, it therefore comes as no surprise to find him
clarifying a range of different expositions before tentatively ('as I think')
putting forward his own. At the same time, and as is also the case in *De
regimine Christiano*, such studied moderation should not necessarily be taken
at face value.

In the quodlibetic question translated here, James criticizes arguments
recently set out by Godfrey of Fontaines (see Translation 6). Using the
same distinction between natural love and gracious love, James sets out to
demonstrate how Aristotle's account of the basis of friendship in self-love
can be accepted as giving natural priority to the individual's love of good
for himself without threatening the theological principle that human beings should love God more than anything else, including themselves.
James's account of self-sacrifice in the political community accordingly

locates the primary motivation of such an act in the natural love which an individual directs toward himself. The organic analogy of a hand exposing itself to danger for the sake of the body is therefore not, strictly speaking, applicable. If the individual is to have a greater love for the common good than for his own good, then this is the product, not of the natural love found in friendship, but of gracious, divinely infused Christian charity.

The fact that James of Viterbo was careful to confirm this argument with the authority of Bernard of Clairvaux did not spare him a swift response from Godfrey of Fontaines (Translation 8). In his thirteenth quodlibet, delivered in 1297–98, Godfrey takes the nature of love as a case study for the apparent disparity between theology and moral philosophy, the former dealing with grace and charity, the latter with nature and friendship. In fact, he argues, faith and right reason do not produce contrary conclusions and, to prove it, he appeals once again (as in Translation 6) to the Thomist principle that grace does not abolish nature but perfects it. James of Viterbo's argument is then submitted to a point by point refutation concerning the union of an individual with himself and the union of a part with its whole. Godfrey concludes that although the individual may secure his own best or greatest good as a result of willing the common good of the community or by loving God, this does not entail that this *maximum bonum* be his primary goal in such acts. It is possible and rational, in nature as well as in grace, to love another more than oneself.

For further reading on James of Viterbo, see CHLMP, p. 865. For James's debate with Godfrey of Fontaines, see B. Neumann, *Der Mensch und die himmlische Seligkeit nach der Lehre Gottfrieds von Fontaines* (Limburg: Lahn-Verlag, 1958), pp. 32–39, and M. S. Kempshall, *The Common Good in Late Medieval Political Thought*, pp. 214–18.

Does a Human Being Have a Greater Natural Love for God than for Himself, or Vice Versa?

[1. Preliminary Arguments]

[1a. Argument against the Proposition]

{202} It seems that a human being loves himself more than God, because the greater the unity the greater the love. But the unity of a human being with himself is greater than [the unity of a human being] with God. Therefore, there is a greater love as well.

[1b. Argument for the Proposition]

The counter-argument is that the greater the good, the greater the love. But God is the supreme good and is thus a greater good than the human being himself. Therefore, God should be loved more.

[2. Review of Approaches Adopted by Others]

In response, it should [first] be declared that there are several ways in which this question can be discussed.

[2a. Human Beings Have a Greater Natural Love for Themselves than for God without Qualification but Have a Greater Natural Love for God in a Certain Respect]

Some have said that if one is talking about amicable love (*amor amicitiae*), then a human being has a greater natural love for himself than for God without qualification and absolutely but that the reverse is true in a certain respect (*secundum quid*). This is clear [according to those who hold this view] from the following.

To love is the same as to will a good. The amount (*magnitudo*) of a love can therefore be marked either according to the act of loving itself (and in this manner a human being loves himself more than God, because he wills good for himself before, and more intensely than, he wills good for God) or according to the good that an individual wills for someone (and in this manner a human being loves God more than himself, because he wills a greater good for God than for himself, for he wills God to be God yet does not will the same for himself but wills for himself the good that is suitable and proper to him). When the amount of love is considered in terms of the act of loving, it is an amount without qualification, whereas when it is considered in terms of its object, it is [an amount] in a certain respect. This is clear from the amount of charity involved in giving. For those who give from a greater affection – from [greater] charity – give more without qualification, even if they give little. Those who give from less affection, however, give less, even if they give more. Thus, it is said in the proposition (2a) that without qualification an individual has more love for the person for whom he wills good with a greater affection, whereas in a certain respect he has more love for the person for whom he wills a greater good but with less affection {203}.

[2b. Human Beings Have a Greater Natural Love for God than for Themselves without Qualification and Absolutely]

But others are not satisfied with this way of speaking, and as a result they argue differently, namely, that a human being has a greater natural love for God than for himself without qualification and absolutely. They explain this in a number of ways.

[i] [They argue] first from gracious love, i.e., charity. Charity is a love that perfects natural love. Therefore, since a human being loves God more than himself with charitable love, it follows that he also loves God more than himself with natural love, because if he loved himself more than God with natural love, then natural love would not be perfected by charity but would be contrary to it and would thus be perverse – which is not true.

[ii] Second, they explain this as a dictate of reason. For natural reason dictates that a human being ought to love God more than himself. But nature is not inclined to the opposite of what reason naturally dictates. As a result, a human is naturally inclined to love God more than himself.

[iii] Third, they explain the same [conclusion] from characteristics of the good that is God. For the divine good is a causal good, a total good, and a final good. From these three characteristics they derive three arguments in favor of the proposition.

[iii.a] The first argument is taken from the fact that God is a causal good. God brings all things into being and preserves them in existence. Now he preserves them in this way: because he is more intimate to each individual thing than that thing is to itself. And so the good of what is created is preserved in God more than it is preserved even in the created thing itself, because God contributes more to its existence than it does itself. For this reason, a creature will have a greater natural love for God than for itself.

[iii.b] The second argument is taken from the fact that God is a total good. The character of the goodness of every good is contained in God, and every other good compares to him as a part to its whole. Now a part has a greater natural love for its whole than for itself. This is apparent from the fact that a part naturally risks itself for the preservation of the whole, as for example the hand risks itself by natural inclination in resisting, or receiving, a blow for the preservation of the whole body. Because reason imitates nature, the same is also found in political acts. For a good citizen exposes himself to the danger of death for the preservation of the commonwealth, and if a human being were a natural part of a political community, an inclination of this kind would be natural to him.

[iii.c] The third argument is taken from the fact that God is a final good. For God is the end of all things, that on account of which they all exist, and for this reason all things are to be loved on his account. But that on account of which each thing is [such] is also that and more so. Therefore, God should be loved naturally most and above all things. {204}

This, then, is the second way of speaking about the question.

[2c. Human Beings Have a Greater Natural Love for God in the State of Innocence but Not in Their Fallen State]

A third approach, which has been put forward many times, is that in the state of unfallen nature (*in statu naturae integrae*) human beings have a greater natural love for God than for themselves but that in a corrupted or fallen state they do not have a greater natural love for God than for themselves. But for God to be loved above all, grace is needed to heal a nature wounded and made powerless by sin.

[3. Answer to the Question]

Now that the various ways of speaking about the question at issue have been summarily set out, what needs to be put forward next is the conclusion on the subject that seems to me to be tenable as the more capable of proof.

[3a. Amicable Love and Wanting Love]

For the sake of clarity it must be understood here that it is the common custom to distinguish between two kinds of love, namely, a 'wanting' kind of love (*amor concupiscentiae*) and amicable love (*amor amicitiae*). It is called amicable love when we love something in such a way that we will good for it. Now such a love is shown only to those things, such as rational beings, which can love with a similar love in return. Hence this sort of love does not exist toward irrational beings. Wanting love, on the other hand, is the love with which we love something as a good (which we will for ourselves or others). And this good is either an end or a means to an end.

Now rational creatures love God with both kinds of love. We love God with amicable love inasmuch as we will for him his own good, namely, himself, because we will him to be God and to be supremely perfect. We love him with wanting love inasmuch as we will the good that is God for ourselves or for others by seeking to resemble him and to participate or be joined with him. Irrational creatures, on the other hand, do not love God with amicable love but with wanting love – not that there is wanting in all of them, strictly speaking, but that the natural love with which they seek God has a likeness to wanting love, because they love God by seeking some resemblance to him. {205}

Human beings likewise also love themselves with both kinds of love – with amicable love inasmuch as we will some good for ourselves, with wanting love inasmuch as we love for ourselves some good that is either substantially or accidentally in us (for example, to be, to live, to understand, and such like).

Consideration should [also] be given to the fact that (as some have rightly said) when someone is said to love God and himself with amicable love, the term 'amicable' should be taken broadly and according to its common usage. For strictly speaking there is no friendship toward God but something greater than friendship, since the equality required for friendship in the strict sense does not exist between God and a creature. Nor is anyone said to have friendship in the strict sense toward himself but something greater than friendship. For the cause of friendship toward someone is a union of resemblance to him with respect either to nature or to virtue or to something else. Strictly speaking, however, there is neither resemblance nor union with oneself but something greater than union and resemblance, namely, unity. For every individual whatever is one with himself. Nevertheless, friendship as it is commonly understood does exist toward both God and oneself in the manner described above.

[3b. Three Ways of Understanding the Question]

Once this distinction has been premised, therefore, it should now be said that when it is asked whether a human being has a greater natural love for God than for himself, the question can be understood in three ways.

[i] One way is in terms of the human being loving God with wanting love while loving himself with amicable love. Understood in this way, the question is not a reasonable one, since wanting love and amicable love differ in character and because of this are not properly comparable with one another as greater or lesser (just as it is not reasonable to ask whether a human being loves himself more than blessedness or vice versa, because the mode and character of the love with which someone loves himself and that with which he loves blessedness are not the same).

[ii] The present question can be understood in another way, such that each of the loves (the love with which someone loves himself and that with which he loves God) is wanting love. On this understanding, there are some who say that {206} a human being loves God more than himself because he wills the divine good for himself more than his own good, since the divine good is a greater good. But this does not seem right, for in one sense the divine good is said to be the good that is God himself in himself, and in this sense it is not loved with wanting love, since nothing naturally seeks for itself the good of another thing in itself, because the perfection of one thing in itself cannot become that of another. In another sense, the divine good is said to be resemblance to God. Now such a divine good is indeed loved with wanting love, but in this sense the creature's good *is* the divine good, because it is a resemblance to God. There is thus no real distinction between the divine good understood in this sense and the creature's good. As a result, they are not properly comparable with one another as greater or lesser.

(Yet there can be a comparison in goodness and love between different goods, any of which is said to be [both] a creature's good and a divine good [in the second sense], inasmuch as there is a greater resemblance to the good that is God in one [creature] than in another. The more a good resembles God the more divine it is, the greater a good it is, and as a result the more lovable it is, since something is loved or sought to the extent that it is like God. That is why, in this sense, all things are said to seek God, namely, to resemble him.)

[iii] The present question can be understood in a third way, such that each of the two loves (i.e., the love with which someone loves himself and the love with which he loves God) is amicable love.

*[3c. Reply to 3b(iii): Human Beings Love Themselves More than God
with Amicable Love]*

On this understanding, it seems that a human should be said to have a
greater natural love for himself than for God, as the first of the arguments
set out above asserts (1a). This can be shown by two [further] arguments.

*[3c(i). An Argument from the Unity of Lover and Loved as Based
on Natural Being]*

The first argument is taken from the perspective of natural love, which
follows the mode of natural being. For since a thing has being and oneness
on the same basis, [then] just as, on the basis of its natural being, something
is said to be one with itself and one with another (as, for example, Socrates
is one with himself and one with Plato on the basis of his humanity), so,
on the basis of its natural existence, something is said to *be* what it is and
to be something else. Similarly, since love makes the individual who is
loving in some way one with what is loved, the lover ((*amans/amor*)) *is* in
a certain way what is loved. As a result, when someone loves both himself
and another, he is said to be one with himself and with the other on the
basis of love. Now it is obvious that in terms of its natural being a thing
cannot be more something else than what it is itself. For it is what it is
through {207} numerical identity, while it is something else through
conformity or resemblance. Now to be something through numerical
identity is more than to be [something] through conformity. Likewise, this
is why someone cannot love something else more than himself, because
he loves himself on the basis of being numerically the same as himself,
while he loves the other on the basis of being in some way in conformity
with the other. Now to be the same in number as something is more than
to be in conformity with it by natural love, which follows the mode of
natural being. [Therefore] an individual loves himself more than anyone
else at all, whether another human being or God.

[3c(ii). An Argument from Charity]

The second argument for the same conclusion (3c) is taken from charitable
love (*dilectio caritatis*), which elevates nature. On this subject it should be
understood that, although love is twofold (i.e., wanting love and amicable

love, as was said above), each type is suitable to charity, and charity elevates nature with respect to both. For as charity makes us love God with wanting love, so it elevates nature with respect to the character of what is loved ((*dilecti/ diligendi*)), because God is loved with natural love as the universal good on which every good in nature depends, whereas God is loved with charitable love as a good that beatifies with supernatural blessedness. Now as charity makes us love God with amicable love, it must be maintained that it elevates nature in this way too. But it does not seem to do this otherwise than with respect to the order and mode of loving, for besides the elevation present with respect to the character of the object [as, respectively, universal good and beatifying good], there is no other mode of elevation except in terms of the order and mode of loving. The order and mode of loving suitable to charity is for God to be loved for his own sake and above all things. Therefore, if charity elevates nature with respect to this mode of loving, it follows that nature by itself cannot love God in this manner (i.e., above all), because, if it could do this [by itself] it would not need to be elevated to it by charity.

The reason why charity elevates nature so that it loves God above all things can be derived from the following. Charity is a gracious love (*dilectio gratuita*). Now just as natural love follows the mode of natural being, so gracious love follows the mode of gracious being. The gracious being of a human, however, is to be, in a certain sense, divine. This is because a human being is made by grace a participant and {208} partner in the divine nature by a certain resemblance. For this reason, just as grace in a certain sense turns a human being into God, so gracious love (i.e., charity) makes a human being love God more than himself and more than anything else, because just as God loves himself more than other things, so a human, having been made God through grace, loves God more than anything else whatever.

It should be maintained, therefore, that there is a converse order in natural love and gracious love. Natural love tends toward itself more than, and before, it tends toward God. That is why what the Philosopher says is true with respect to this love, namely, that friendliness toward another derives from friendliness toward oneself (*Ethics* IX 4, 1166a1–2, b1–2; 8, 1168b4–5). On the other hand, gracious love, charity, is the reverse, because it tends toward God more than, and before, it tends toward neighbor and self, and so, in this love, friendliness toward self or neighbor stems from friendliness toward God. This is clear from the parallel with

natural and supernatural cognition. For natural cognition starts from creatures and moves from them toward God, whereas, conversely, supernatural
cognition starts from God and moves from him and toward the creature.

From these arguments, then, it seems that when we are speaking about
amicable love, humans love themselves more than God with a natural
love.

[3c(iii). Confirmation from Bernard of Clairvaux]

This can also be confirmed from the authority of St Bernard in his book
On Loving God (8–10, 15) where he assigns four grades to love. The first
is when a human loves only himself and for his own sake. This is natural
love. The second grade is when someone loves not only himself but also
God; however, he loves God in such a way that he loves him, not on
God's account, but on his own human account, that is, for his own benefit.
Now it is generally agreed that in each of these two grades a human loves
himself more than God, because in the first he loves nothing except
himself, while in the second he loves God on his own account. The third
grade is when someone loves God on account of God himself. The fourth
grade is when someone not only loves God on account of God himself
but also loves himself on account of God and does not love himself except
on account of God. {209} Each of these two grades of love, that is, the
third and the fourth, pertains to gracious love, as Bernard says. In fact, he
says that the fourth grade (when humans do not love themselves except
on account of God) is scarcely attainable by anyone in this life except
briefly and suddenly (*raptim*). And because to love oneself on God's account is to love God more than oneself, something which even gracious
love is scarcely able to attain in this life, it should not be attributed to
natural love.

[4. Replies to the Arguments Put Forward by Others]

Now that these points pertaining to the truth of the question have been
considered, therefore, in order to provide more clarity and confirmation
of what has been said, solutions must now be given to the arguments set
out above which some have brought forward to show that humans love
God more than themselves with natural love. There are five arguments,
the first of which is taken from charitable love, the second from the

dictates of reason, and the other three from three characteristics of the good that is God. These will be replied to in order.

[4a. Reply to 2b(i)]

In response to the first argument, therefore, which was taken from the fact that charity perfects natural love, three points need to be made, from which the solution will become clear. First we have to see how any love is said to be natural. Concerning this, it must be understood that love is termed natural in three senses.

[4a(i). Three Senses in which Love is Natural]

In one sense, every love of which a nature is capable by its own principles, without anything being added to it, is natural. This is the sense in which natural love is distinguished from gracious love: Nature is incapable of the latter without the gift of grace infused by God. In another sense, love is called natural more specifically, namely, as the love of which nature is capable by its own principles and which tends toward its object in a natural way, i.e., determinately. In this sense, natural love is distinguished from elective love. An ultimate end is loved with natural love [in this sense], together with those things without which the end cannot be attained, whereas those things are loved with elective love which are means to an end, especially those things without which the end can [still] be attained. The third sense in which love can be called natural is as a certain receptive potentiality existing in rational creatures through which they are by nature capable of being elevated to gracious love. For the capacity of a rational creature through which it is capable of grace and charity is something natural, even though grace and charity [themselves] are above nature. That is why Augustine maintains in his book *On True Innocence* [Prosper of Aquitaine, *Sentences*; PL 51, 476] that 'The ability to have {210} faith, like the ability to have charity, belongs to human nature. [Actually] having faith, however, like [actually] having charity, belongs to the grace of the faithful.'

Now in the present question natural love is taken, not in the third sense, but in the first and second senses, and more strictly in the second sense. For an individual loves God and himself with a natural love in this [second] sense, because he loves in a natural way, i.e., determinately, and cannot *not* love himself and God with natural love when both are actually considered.

With elective love, however, an individual sometimes does not love God and himself, since some people order their choices against ((add *contra* [var.])) themselves and against God.

[4a(ii). How Charity Perfects Natural Love]

Second, we have to see how charitable love is said to perfect natural love. Concerning this, it must be understood that if natural love is taken in the third of the senses outlined above, then charity is said to perfect natural love because it perfects the very nature which is capable of that gracious love (i.e., charity). On the other hand, if natural love is taken in the second sense (i.e., in the sense that strictly pertains to the question), then charity perfects natural love, not because both loves are present in the will in actuality, where one is the perfection of the other, but because with the advent into act of charitable love, which is perfect, natural love, which is imperfect, ceases to be in act. (It nevertheless remains as a capability, such that, if nature is left to itself, it will be imperfect in its love, just as it was before the infusion of charity.)

[4a(iii). Natural Self-Love Is Weak and Imperfect but Not Perverse; Reply to 2b(i)]

Third, we have to consider that natural love is not perverse from the fact that through it human beings tend toward themselves more than, and before, they tend toward God. For this does not come from the perversity of nature but from its defective and powerless state, which cannot be raised to loving God more than itself without the additional gift of grace. Likewise, charitable love does not pervert the order of nature from the fact that through it human beings love God more than themselves, because it destroys nothing of natural love. For a human being loves himself no less through charity than through natural love, but through charity he loves God more than he does through natural love. For this reason, charity perfects natural love and elevates it to what it was powerless [to achieve by itself]. This is also clear from the parallel with natural and supernatural cognition. {211} For although natural cognition moves from creature to God and supernatural cognition the other way around, natural cognition is nevertheless not termed perverse but powerless and deficient. Supernatural cognition does not pervert nature but perfects it by elevating it.

Moreover, there would indeed be perversity in natural love if it loved something else as an end more than it loved God. However, this is not the case. In fact, human beings love God with a natural love as an end above all. When they love something else as an end more than God, this love is perverse and contrary to natural love. As a result, the sin arising from such love is said to be against nature. Yet the love with which someone loves God as an end above all is a wanting love. A human being does not love God more than himself with the natural love that is amicable love. This happens, not through perversity of nature, but through weakness, as was said above.

It is clear, therefore, what should be said in response to the first argument (2b[i]).

[4b. Reply to 2b(ii)]

To the second argument, which is taken from the dictates of reason, it should be said that nature cannot do through its own principles everything that natural reason dictates. For reason dictates and convinces us that God is the greatest thing that can be known, and yet we do not naturally have the greatest knowledge of God. So too all the precepts of the law are dictated by natural law, yet humans cannot fulfill them without the grace of God. In the same way, although natural reason dictates that God is worthy of being loved above all other things, it does not follow on this account that natural love can love him above all things with amicable love.

[4c. Reply to 2b(iii.a)]

To the third argument, which is taken from the fact that God is a causal good, it should be said that with respect to what causes it to remain in existence God is [indeed] more intimate to a thing than the thing is to itself, because anything whatever depends on God more than on itself with respect to the character of causality, since a thing is not its own cause but God is its cause. With respect to the character of union or unity, however, anything whatever is more intimate to itself than to God. But union is the most important consideration in friendship or love. {212}

[4d. Reply to 2b(iii.b)]

To the fourth argument, which is taken from the fact that God is a total good, it should be said that a part can be considered in two ways. In one way, [it can be considered] as included in the whole, and in this sense it is one with the whole. As a result, [considered] in this way it loves itself and its whole with the same and equal love. There is no comparison between them, because considered in this way they are not different things. A part can be considered in another way as different from the whole, for although in some sense it is the same as the whole, it still has a certain difference from it. [Considered] in this way a part loves itself more than the whole.

Now the example which is brought forward as proof, namely, the arm or hand in relation to the body, is problematic. For it would seem that a part does not risk itself for the preservation of the whole but that it is the whole which risks the part for the sake of its own well-being, and risks a baser part, such as the hand, for the well-being of a nobler part, such as the eye. So too in the universe, where God permits evil [to befall] a part for the sake of the good of the whole. That a part is risked to deliver the whole does not stem, then, from what the part naturally seeks but from what the whole naturally seeks, using the parts in this way.

There is also a problem with the additional observation concerning the good citizen who risks himself for the sake of the community, because it would seem that such a citizen loves himself more than the community. For he loves the good of virtue for himself, a good which results from aiming at the common good. And so he loves the common good, yet ((*tamen/cum* [var.])) he loves the good of virtue for himself more than he loves the good of well-being for the community. For just as those who expose themselves to dangers for the well-being of the community so that they may be praised for doing so do not love the community more than themselves (in fact, they love themselves more than the community when they aim at their own praise and glory), so those people who risk themselves for the well-being of the community so that they may act virtuously in doing this love themselves more than the community. Indeed, this is to be said all the more of these people than it is of those who act for praise, in proportion to the ((om. *quamvis* [var.])) degree to which the good of virtue is a greater good, and more pertinent to human perfection, than the external good of praise. Therefore, although the virtuous citizen wills that the community be saved in preference to being saved physically himself while the community perishes, he nevertheless does not on this account love the community more than himself. In fact the reverse is true, because he loves a virtuous deed for himself more than well-being for the community, even though this good of virtue would not exist without love for the common good. This is clear from the fact that a citizen such as this refuses to lose the good of virtue {213} for the sake of saving the community. As a result, he loves the community more than himself only within certain terms of reference, namely, with respect to the good of physical well-being. He loves himself more without qualification, namely, with respect to the good of virtue, which is a greater good. In fact, even with respect to physical well-being, he would not love himself less [than the community] unless it resulted in the good of virtue for him, which he loves for himself more than a physical good. This is why the Philosopher too, in *Ethics* IX (8, 1168a28–29) and *Magna Moralia* II (13, 1212a28–29), asking whether someone ought to love himself most, determines the question in the affirmative with respect to the best goods (i.e., virtuous deeds) and in the negative with respect to other goods, because by loving himself most with respect to goods of this sort the individual falls short of the good of virtue, which should be loved most of all.

[4e. Reply to 2b(iii.c)]

To the fifth argument, which is taken from the fact that God is a final good, it should be said that we do not always have a greater love for those things which are better but for those which are joined more closely to us. Therefore, although God is the greatest good, any individual is nevertheless naturally one most of all with himself, and for this reason a human being has a greater natural love for himself than for God. The argument shows, then, that God is supremely worthy of love because he is supremely good but not that he is supremely loved by us with natural love, just as from God's being supremely true it is shown that he is supremely knowable but not that he is supremely known by us.

Now when it is subsequently declared that other things should be loved on account of God and thus that a human being ought to love himself on God's account and therefore love God more, it should be maintained that God is loved naturally by human beings with both wanting love and amicable love, as was said above, [but that this does not show that we love God *more* than ourselves with amicable love].

Moreover, when something is said to be loved on account of something else, this preposition 'on account of' (*propter*) can signify either the relationship of a [final] cause, as when something is said to be loved on account of an end (and for something to be loved on account of something else in this way locates it in wanting love, for an end is loved with this sort of love), or it can signify the relationship of a motive cause, as when someone is said to love one human being on account of another (such as when a slave is loved on account of the master, because loving the master is the motive cause of loving the slave). In this second sense, an individual is also said to love a friend on account of himself, because love of a friend originates in love of self. In this way, something's being loved on account of something else locates it in the amicable love with which a friend is said to be loved.

[5. Summary Conclusion]

From these considerations, then, it should be maintained, in response to the proposition, that a human being has a natural love {214} for himself on account of God as on account of an end. For this reason, he has the greatest love for God as an end with a wanting love. But a human being does not have a natural love for himself on account of God as on account of a motive cause. In fact, it is the other way around. He loves God on account of himself, because according to natural amicable love friendliness toward another stems from friendliness toward oneself. With the love of charity, on the other hand, a human being loves himself on account of God as on account of a motive cause, because according to love of this kind his friendliness toward himself and his neighbor stems from his friendliness toward God, as was said above.

It is clear, therefore, how a convincing response can be made to the arguments set out above. From this, the solution to the arguments advanced at the beginning is also apparent.

GODFREY OF FONTAINES
REPLY TO JAMES OF VITERBO ON LOVE OF
GOD AND SELF

Introduction

For information on Godfrey's life and writings, see the introduction to Translation 6. For the place of the present selection in late thirteenth-century discussions of the rationality of self-sacrifice, see the introduction to Translation 7.

Reply to James of Viterbo on Love of God and Self

[1. An Argument that Theology Is a Practical Science in a Different Sense from Moral Philosophy]

{180} It might be argued further that it must at least be held that theology is practical in a different way from moral science, because love of the end, or of God, which ought to be a principle with respect to all possible actions pertaining to practical science, has a different character when it is considered by the theologian and by the moral philosopher. This is because the love with which human beings love God as considered by the moral philosopher (namely, as a love of the sort that arises from natural principles) is such that, with it, human beings love themselves more than God, in accordance with *Ethics* IX (4, 1166a1–2, b1–2; IX.8 1168b4–5): Friendliness toward another [derives] from friendliness toward oneself. The love with which God is loved as considered by the theologian, however (namely, as a love caused by a supernatural principle, i.e., by charity), is such that, with it, human beings love God more than themselves. Therefore, etc.

[2. The Differences between Theology and Moral Philosophy as Practical Sciences]

It should be maintained that this much is true, namely, that the actions pertaining to practical science are in some way considered differently by the theologian and the moral philosopher, because even the actions pertaining to the purely moral virtues are in some way considered differently in theology and in moral science. This is because they are considered in theology in terms of their order toward the final good {181} of human beings in the blessed life by reason of merit. In theology the friendship toward God that human beings can have from their natural capacities is likewise considered in terms of its order toward that final good. And just as [in moral science] a certain form of justice is posited – legal justice – through which the good of every particular virtue is referred to the common good insofar as this is possible from our natural capacities, so too [in theology] charity is posited, which (as has been said) is a certain general virtue through which all human acts are ordered and referred to God such that everything a human being does may be done to the glory of God and ordered to God as to an ultimate, supernatural end.

When it is said, then, that with respect to the love with which God is loved [theology] ought in fact to be called practical in a very different way from moral science because of the difference between loving God in terms of what is possible through one's natural capacities (which the moral philosopher considers) and loving God in terms of what is caused by the mediation of charity (which the theologian considers), it should be maintained that it is true that there is a greater difference between the friendship that pertains to the reflections of moral science (which is possible through one's natural capacities) and the friendship that pertains to the theologian (which is possessed through the infusion of a supernatural habit) than there is concerning the other moral virtues considered by the moral philosopher and the theologian. (This is especially the case for those who do not hold that the moral virtues, other than the virtue of friendship at least, are infused.) This is because, according to the theologian's consideration of the acts of any of the moral virtues (whether they fall under legal justice or the virtue of friendship) that can be exercised toward God from one's natural capacities, the virtue of legal justice or friendship does not sufficiently refer the things a human being does to the end that, as was said above, theology considers.

But beyond this, there is an additional [difference between theology and moral philosophy as practical sciences, a difference] of another sort, not indeed as the matter is taken in the [opening] argument but in another way. Charity implies a certain friendship. Now friendship is based on sharing (*communicatio*) by those who love [one another]. The friendship that pertains to charity, however, namely, human friendship toward God, does not consist of sharing in natural goods or in things that are naturally attainable but in the goods of grace, which are found primarily in the things that constitute the blessed life, a life which exceeds the capacity of nature. As a result, God is the object of such friendship inasmuch as he is the object of blessedness. And just as God is not knowable in this respect through natural capacities or by sensory means but through the infused habit of faith, so also he cannot be loved in this respect through our affective inclination toward him as he is apprehended on the basis of our natural capacities through things that are sensible and visible. For this an infused supernatural habit is required. Just as the intellect is raised up by the infused habit of faith, so affection or will is raised up by a habit corresponding to faith, namely, charity.

[3. Reply to 1]

It cannot be shown from this, however, that theology is not a practical science. Rather, it is indeed a practical science but a nobler one than the human science {182} called moral [philosophy], because it directs us toward performing activities in a nobler way and for a nobler end. In this respect, just as charity directs or orders toward its own end the acts of all the acquired virtues (particular justice, general justice, and the others), it also directs to this end the acts of the virtue of love in which God can be loved on the basis of our natural capacities.

From this it is immediately apparent that it is inconsistent to maintain that human beings love themselves more than God through their upright natural capacities and without the assistance of grace, because the presupposition is that grace perfects nature in such a way that it orders the things that are suitable to human beings according to their nature toward its own supernatural end and raises human nature to a level at which it can achieve acts, and an end, that it could not achieve by its purely natural capacities.

Therefore, since the love with which a human being is loved more than God cannot be ordered toward God by the love with which God is loved more than the human being, it cannot be maintained that the first sort of

love is suitable to human beings in accordance with their upright and
ordered natural capacities. When grace perfects and raises nature, therefore,
this should be understood to mean, not that we love God more than
ourselves [only] through it, but that, although we can in some way do this
without grace, we cannot do so as perfectly or do so insofar as God has
the character of a beatifying object and so that we may be capable of
communion (*communicatio*) with him in perfect blessedness. For if human
beings had a greater natural love for themselves than for God, then the
grace which made them love God more would not perfect nature (i.e.,
natural inclination) but would instead destroy it, because such acts are not
related to each other as less perfect and more perfect but as unqualified
contraries. (It is also clear from this that if loving God without qualification
above all other things is intrinsically praiseworthy and virtuous, then loving something else above God is a blameworthy and vicious act, because
these acts are unqualifed contraries.)

Nor is this [argument] invalidated by saying that contrariety and opposition between these acts is prevented by the fact that they emanate from
different principles, the one from natural principles, the other from supernatural (because one of these loves is natural and the other supernatural).
This does not prevent [contrariety], because such acts are contrary and
opposed in terms of what they are by their own nature, as is also the case
in [corresponding] acts of cognition. For just as we are able to love God
both supernaturally (through charity) and naturally, so we are able to know
God through both supernatural faith and natural reason, yet it cannot
simultaneously be the case that, supernaturally and by faith, I know God
to be triune while, by natural reason, I know him not to be triune.
[Genuine] natural and supernatural knowledge are not opposed. For although the ways or means of arriving at these two [putative acts of]
cognition differ in character, this still does not preclude {183} them being
opposed without qualification so that they cannot stand together [as both
being right]. So it is in the proposition.

As a result, although what is known by natural right reason and through
the illumination of faith cannot be contrary, something can be known
through the illumination of faith for which natural reason is insufficient,
or it can be known more perfectly than it could without such a light. So
too, although it is impossible for the will's inclination to love God from a
natural capacity to be opposed to its inclination to love God with the
assistance of charity, it can happen that with the assistance of charity the

will is inclined toward an object in a respect and in a way in which it could not be so inclined without it.

It is wrong, therefore, to say that the love with which human beings love themselves more than God naturally and the love with which they love God more than themselves supernaturally do not contradict each other but stand together. It cannot be maintained that it is the judgment of natural reason that we ought naturally to love ourselves more than God. For this seems erroneous. Moreover, for natural reason to dictate that human beings ought to love God more than themselves and for natural inclination not to respond to this is inconsistent, since the will is by nature innately inclined toward that which is judged [appropriate] by reason, even if (because of its freedom) it does not necessarily follow [such judgment] in everything. Therefore, the Philosopher's text (*auctoritas*) should be expounded as it was elsewhere (Translation 6).

[4. Another Argument for the Primacy of Self-Love]

What if it is said that friendship is based on union (or implies a certain union) and that there is a greater union or unity with oneself [than with anything else] and that therefore every single being has a greater natural love for itself than for anything else?

[Reply to 4]

It should be maintained that if this argument were conclusive then no agent could bring it about that something could keep its nature and, according to a right judgment of reason, love something else more [than itself], because the sort of greater union that [supposedly] causes such a love always remains. For this reason, it should be understood here that nothing is loved by another except inasmuch as it is in some way one with it, because whatever is loved is loved on the basis of being suitable to the lover and thus of being in some way one with it. Therefore, because each particular being is by nature a part of some whole, and because God is, so to speak, a whole in terms of virtue and perfection, containing and preserving all things within himself, each particular being has, for this reason, a truer union or unity appropriate to it in its order toward that whole of which it is a part (or a sort of part) than that [union or unity] which it has as something existing on its own. And so, when someone is [defined] in terms of a part loving the common good of a whole, he loves it naturally in accord with it being suitable and one with him. Therefore, because the union that is a *per se* requirement of friendship does not consist solely of conjunction with the principles constituting the nature of an entity as something singular existing on its own but [also consists of conjunction with the principles of the thing] as a part of some whole, on this account its natural inclination also includes this, [namely] that the good of the part should be ordered toward the good of the whole and that each individual should love itself both as it is by nature one singular being and also in such a way as is useful in [its] order to the good of the community. This [common good] is the primary good and the primary object of an ordered will in such a way that, included in this, is [the principle] that the part loves the common good more than its private good, inasmuch as it even orders its private good toward the common good and not the other way around (although its own greatest good is also included in this).

As a result, although it is a good for the part that it order itself in this way toward the common good – this, in fact, constitutes its greatest good – it nevertheless ought not to be maintained that in doing this it loves its own good more than the common good. For an individual does not risk death for the community for the sake of his own good as his first and primary objective but for the good of the community for its own sake, which is the *per se* and first object of such an act. But it is true that in doing this the individual is also the best [he can be], because by ordering himself and what is his toward the common good and by not referring the good of the whole *per se* and primarily to himself, he acts as he ought to act – although even in this, as has been said, his own best good results.

HENRY OF GHENT
IS A SUBJECT BOUND TO OBEY A STATUTE WHEN IT IS NOT EVIDENT THAT IT PROMOTES THE COMMON UTILITY?

Introduction

(For information on Henry of Ghent's life and writings, see the introduction to Translation 5.)

Thirteenth-century scholastic political and ethical thought stands in a direct and continuous line of tradition with the moral and pastoral theology of the twelfth-century schools. The academic milieu which had inspired the decrees of the Fourth Lateran Council in 1215 also provided the training and the personnel which subsequently put its reforms into practice. From Robert Grosseteste onwards, there was thus an intimate connection between the teaching of Aristotle's *Ethics* in Paris and the provision of effective pastoral care through sermons and confession. The effects of such a direct engagement with pressing social, ecclesiological, and political concerns can be traced throughout the quodlibetic questions determined by Parisian masters. Two issues stand out as having a particular relevance to political thought: first, the longstanding tension between secular clergy (that is, clergy who did not belong to a religious order) and the mendicant orders (that is, Dominicans and Franciscans); second, the imposition of taxes by the Capetian kings of France and by successive popes in Rome.

Hostility between secular and mendicant masters within the University at Paris was the source of acrimonious controversies in the 1250s and 1270s. In 1281, Martin IV issued *Ad fructus uberes*, a bull which granted privileges to mendicant friars and, in the process, appeared to dispense them from the statutes passed by the Fourth Lateran Council. Disquiet had also been aroused by repeated papal grants of tenths (that is, a tenth of annual clerical revenues) to temporal powers to enable them to prosecute essentially political crusades against other Christian rulers. In the 1280s this concern concentrated on taxation of the clergy to support a French 'crusade' against Aragon. By the 1290s the dominant issue was the increasingly high levels of taxation which were being demanded from both clergy and laity by Philip IV of France. By the late thirteenth century, in other words, the nature and scope of papal dispensation from statutory law and the nature and scope of papal and royal authority over their subjects' goods had become issues of intense material and political interest. Both issues were addressed in the quodlibets of Parisian masters.

In December 1290, Henry of Ghent was asked to examine the general principles which should govern obedience to the statutes of a superior authority. That the statutes to be obeyed might include demands for tax is indicated in the formulation of the question by the reference to the possibility that a statute might lack 'evident utility,' since the presence of *evidens utilitas* was a statutory requirement for taxation of the church from the Fourth Lateran Council onwards. That Henry understood the question to apply to the authority of French kings in particular is made clear in the main body of his response, where he countenances resistance to oppressive rulers 'irrespective of the length of their lineage' – an unmistakable reference to the much lauded pedigree of the Capetian line. Henry of Ghent was aware, however, that a general discussion of the basis and limits of obedience had implications for ecclesiastical authority, too. Indeed, he deliberately invites such an application by framing his reply with reference to 'superiors, whether rulers (*principes*) or prelates (*praelati*)' and by leaving the precise meaning of *salus* ambiguous ('salvation' as well as 'well-being'). Henry's own opposition to *Ad fructus uberes* as a secular master was already a matter of record. Two years previously he had delivered a quodlibet (subsequently expanded into a treatise and maybe even circulated in Rome) which disputed the friars' interpretation of Martin IV's grant. Henry made it clear, and in no uncertain terms, that disobedience would be an entirely legitimate response to any pope who sought to ratify the mendicants' reading of the bull. In November 1290, one month prior to the quodlibet translated here, Nicholas IV sent two cardinal legates to Paris (one of them Benedict Gaetani, the future Boniface VIII) to prohibit all further discussion on the subject. In this context, Henry of Ghent's articulation of a general theory of authority that clearly left room for disobedience, ostensibly disobedience to a temporal power and ostensibly over the issue of taxation but with implicit application to the spiritual power as well, was a deft act of defiance.

There was, of course, a long Christian tradition of justified resistance, based ultimately on Augustine's insistence that an unjust law is not a law (*lex iniusta non est lex*), which cut across the more straightforward reading of Romans 13 as a demand for obedience to all authority as power ordained by God. As Thomas Aquinas had shown, however, a theoretical justification for disobeying a command that was not in conformity with divine or natural law, or which did not promote the common good, could still be hedged about with substantial practical qualifications. Whether disobedience was legitimate in act as well as conscience might depend on whether there was any possibility of appealing to an authority higher than the errant ruler and, above all, on whether an even worse evil might result from resistance. There are strong notes of caution in Henry of Ghent's analysis too. Henry pays more than token respect to the principle that proper devotion to the well-being of the community may demand the sacrifice of more than this or that proportion of a subject's material goods. If it is genuinely necessary for this end, subjects may be obliged to give 'not just a tenth but a half, the whole, and even their very selves.' He also rejects an explicit contractualism in terms of which each particular obligation to obey must be based on a specific oath to a superior to do so. Even if there is no verbal promise of obedience, everyone in the community can still be 'interpreted' as having made an oath or a promise in that they have accepted someone as their superior. Thus, even when a superior issues a bad statute, he should first be petitioned to revoke it and must be tolerated in office for as long as these requests are being made. It is only when there is no hope of the superior submitting to correction that the process of removal should be set in train. Nevertheless, when these conditions are met, Henry is in no doubt as to the legitimacy of resistance. For all his emphasis on dutiful obedience, Henry firmly endorses the act of resistance to those superiors who have signally failed to promote the peace and well-being of their communities, and he assembles a cogent case for the deposition of such rulers, spiritual as well as temporal.

For further reading on *Ad fructus uberes*, see P. Glorieux, 'Prélats français contre religieux mendiants. Autour de la bulle *Ad fructus uberes* 1281–90,' *Revue d'Histoire de l'église de France* 11 (1925), pp. 309–31, 471–95; K. Schleyer, *Anfänge des Gallicanismus im 13. Jahrhundert: Der Widerstand des französischen Klerus gegen die Privilegierung der Bettelorden* (Berlin: Verlag dr. Emil Ebering, 1937); Y. M. J. Congar, 'Aspects ecclésiologiques de la querelle entre mendiants et séculiers dans la seconde moitié du XIIIe siècle et le début du XIVe,' *Archives d'histoire doctrinale et littéraire du moyen âge* 28 (1961), pp. 35–151. For political crusades, see N. Housley, *The Italian Crusades: The Papal-Angevin Alliance and the Crusades against Christian Lay Powers, 1254–1343* (Oxford: Clarendon Press, 1982). For taxation, see G. Post, *Studies in Medieval Legal Thought* (Princeton: Princeton University Press, 1964), chapter 10; E. A. R. Brown, 'Taxation and Morality in the

Thirteenth and Fourteenth Centuries: Conscience and Political Power and the Kings of France,' *French Historical Studies* 8 (1973):1–28, pp. 1–8.

Is a Subject Bound to Obey a Statute When It Is Not Evident that It Promotes the Common Utility?

[1. Preliminary Arguments]

[1a. Arguments for Obedience]

{352ra} Concerning the first of these [questions about statutes made by superiors], the following argument is put forward [to prove] that subjects are obliged to observe the statute of a superior in those matters which further the common utility even when it is not evident that this is the case.

[i] Whatever principle binds them to observe one statute of this sort, the same principle also binds them to observe any other. Either they are bound to observe none of the statutes of this sort, then, or all of them. [It is] not [the case that they are bound to observe] none of them; therefore, [they are bound to observe] all of them.

[ii] Again, such statutes constitute deeds of virtue. Now in virtuous deeds, subjects are bound to obey a superior. Therefore, etc.

[1b. Arguments against Obedience]

[i] Against: Subjects are not bound to obey a superior in those things which do not pertain to a particular oath of theirs unless these matters concern what is necessary for their well-being (*de necessitate salutis*). Otherwise there would be no difference between an obligation to those things which fall under an oath and an obligation to anything else whatever that does not fall under an oath. Now such statutes do not pertain to any particular oath taken by the subjects, nor do they concern what is necessary for their well-being. Therefore, etc.

[ii] Again, if subjects were bound to observe such statutes, then, since the payment of a tenth of all one's goods falls within the category of such statutes, rulers could therefore decree that the laity should pay them a

tenth of all their goods, and the laity would be bound to obey, just as the Lord Pope has imposed this decree on the clergy in their payment of tithes. Now this seems improper and oppressive. Therefore, etc.

[iii] Again, if rulers could issue statutes of this sort, then the power to dispose of {352rb} their goods at will would be taken away from the laity by their superiors' statutes. This likewise seems improper. Therefore, etc.

[2. Solution]

I maintain that superiors, whether rulers or prelates, ought to have as their end the peace and well-being of the commonwealth. This also ought to be the end of individual subjects insofar as they are parts of the community. They too are bound to aim at this end, in unison with the ruler, as that which constitutes the good of both the ruler and of any individual within the community, such that both the ruler and any individual within the community are bound to refer their own good and (when need be) their every action to it. For as the Philosopher says in *Ethics* I (2, 1094b7–10), '[To attain] the good for one person alone is worthy of love; [to attain it] for a people and for cities is better and more divine.' And as Tully declares in his *Popular Oration to the Senate* (*Pridie quam in exilium iret* 8–9), 'From the beginning, I was inspired to think of myself less as born for my own sake than as produced for the sake of the commonwealth. I find nothing hard, nothing bitter, that will protect the commonwealth. For death is not to be grieved at when it is incurred for the sake of the commonwealth, nor is effort shameful when it is undertaken in virtue.'

Now because an end imposes necessity on those things which are [the means] toward it, if [rulers and subjects] are bound to aim at this end, then they are also bound to aim at things which are [means] toward it and to perform such deeds as are ordered toward this end. It is for the ruler, however, and for superiors in general, to ordain such things (namely, what, what sort, when, and how things are necessary for this end) in accordance with the architectonic science about which the Philosopher says at the beginning of the *Ethics* (I 2, 1094a27–b2): '[Politics] ordains which disciplines should exist in cities, which should be learned by each individual and up to what point.' For this reason, then, I maintain that every subject is bound to obey statutes issued by superiors on matters necessary for this end or for something without which the end itself cannot be achieved (or at least not readily), even if it is not evi-

dent to any of them that this statute is necessary for the end or for
something ordered toward it.

[I maintain] this because the ruler, by dint of being outstanding in
every virtue, ought to be clearly superior to everyone else in the community, with the result that there is a sense in which the good of the
whole community exists in him, his good is the good of each individual in
the city, and his good ought to be the source of good for each individual in the community, as Tully maintains in his *Popular Oration to Julius
Caesar* (*Oratio pro Marcello* 25): 'I listened unwillingly to those words of
yours: "I have lived long enough . . ." I believe [you have lived] long
enough, perhaps, for nature but all too short a time for your country
which is the great thing. But I would listen if you lived only for yourself
or if you had been born for yourself alone. It is the well-being of all the
citizens, it is the entire commonwealth, which your achievements have
embraced.'

Thus, {352va} in the generally accepted sense of utility, the ruler is
'useful' to everyone in the community, and according to Avicenna in
Metaphysics I, he is termed source, profit, lord, and steward. On the other
hand, subjects are 'useful' to the ruler with a usefulness that is almost
servile. No ruler is in any way ordered thus toward another [ruler], nor, as
was maintained above in the question on the freedom of the will and of
the intellect, is a free human being [ordered thus toward another free
human being], although in common parlance a free person may be useful
to others.

On this account, subjects ought to adhere to the statutes of superiors in
these matters even if, because of doubt over the issue, they do not know
whether, or how, they redound to the common utility. This is because,
from trust in the prudence and goodness of their ruler and his counselors,
they ought to have faith in him on this matter and assume that these orders
are indeed of the kind which redound to the public utility. *Unless*, that is,
it is generally agreed that the opposite is the case and, above all, unless
several other similar statutes which have hitherto been observed by the
subjects have not redounded to this end. In this instance, before anything
else [is done], the subjects ought to petition their superior for the revoca-
tion of such a statute. If he refuses to revoke it, obedience should still be
shown to the statutes of superiors for as long as these [superiors] are
tolerated in their superior status. If there is no hope whatever of correcting
him, his subjects ought to take action to depose their superior rather than
tolerate him and disobey.

[3. Replies to the Preliminary Arguments]

[3a. Replies to the Arguments for Obedience (1a)]

[i, ii] The first two arguments proceed from a sound assumption about the prudence and diligence of the ruler. These [virtues] should indeed be presumed by reason of his status. For ((*autem/artem*)) according to the Philosopher in *Politics* I (2–3), a village derives from a household, a city from a village, and a kingdom from cities, and thus the governments of village, city, and kingdom derive from the government of a household. Now, as he says (1252b20–22), every household is ruled by the most senior individual, and as a result so is the village. This is understood to mean seniority of mind, by which an individual is by nature free and noble (*ingenuus*). And because it should be presumed that there was a ruler of this kind at the beginning, it should for this reason also be presumed that all his descendants who succeed him are of this kind. For as the Philosopher says [quoting Theodectes] in the same book (6, 1255a37–38, b1–3), 'Who would presume to call me a slave when I am on both sides sprung from the divine' (that is, from roots of free and noble stock). 'For they presume that, just as a human being comes from a human being [. . .], so a good person comes from good people. Now on many occasions nature wills this to happen but is unable to bring it about.'

However, when there is no presumption of the ruler's diligence but rather the reverse, then for as long as he is nevertheless still tolerated he can issue statutes and should be obeyed. It is preferable, though, to act to depose him, however long the line of ancestors through whom he has inherited his kingdom. When a ruler has been deposed, he cannot issue statutes, nor is there a duty (*debitum*) to obey him, because it should not be presumed {352vb} that his statutes contain virtuous deeds. Nevertheless, if his statutes are not evidently opposed to virtue, then for as long as the superior is tolerated they should be completely obeyed.

[3b. Replies to the Arguments against Obedience (1b)]

[i] To the first argument to the contrary (that such statutes neither pertain to any particular oath nor concern what is necessary for well-being and as a result should not be obeyed) I reply that they *do* pertain to a particular oath or promise of the community and of the individuals within it insofar as they are parts of it (albeit not insofar as they are individual persons who

are able, as free people, to transfer themselves freely from one community to another as they please). Even if the individuals in a community make no verbal promise of obedience (although leaders [*maiores*] within a community sometimes do so to a newly instituted superior on behalf of the community and the individuals within it), everyone in the community can still be *interpreted* as making an oath or a promise (*votum sive promissum interpretative . . . facit*), namely, by accepting someone as their superior (which can occur either through their own choice, or through the choice of certain individuals acting on behalf of everyone, or through provision by a higher superior, or through right of hereditary succession). As a result, those who live together in communities that are ruled by some form of public council, whether in beguinages or any other sort of congregation, are greatly in error if they believe that they are not obliged to conform to the public edicts decreed by their superiors for the utility of the community.

[ii] To the second argument (that lay subjects would then be bound to pay tithes to a ruler just as the clergy do to the pope) I reply that this is true *if* it is necessary for the end I have mentioned – and not just a tenth but a half, the whole, and even their very selves. However, subjects certainly ought to be wary lest their superiors make such decrees or exactions without it at least being evident to them that this is for the common or public utility and not simply the private [utility of the ruler]. And they should take care that these statutes and edicts are sufficiently reasonable to be issued by their superiors, not through the actual power they have to issue them, but through the power of law (*non de potentia facti sed iuris*), not from absolute power but from power that has been weighed and directed by unerring reason. On this matter, I do not see any difference between clergy and laity with respect to their superiors, although clerical prelates can be deposed more easily than [lay] rulers (because they have no hereditary right to their offices as [lay] rulers do) and the laity have freer disposition of their own goods than the clergy (since they are not constrained by any statute made by a superior, whereas the goods of the clergy, above and beyond what they use for themselves, are to be shared with the poor, according to *Aliqui de numero pauperum*, a text which I have expounded sufficiently elsewhere).

[iii] To the third argument (that then subjects could not dispose of their own goods) I reply that this is true when it would be contrary to the statutes of their superiors but that otherwise they certainly could.

GODFREY OF FONTAINES
ARE SUBJECTS BOUND TO PAY A TAX
WHEN THE NEED FOR IT IS NOT EVIDENT?

Introduction

(For information on Godfrey of Fontaines' life and writings, see the introduction to Translation 6.)

Godfrey's discussion of obedience and resistance in 1295–96 deepens the analysis of two of the topics which had been broached by Henry of Ghent five years earlier (Translation 9). Henry's suspicion of rulers who simply appealed to 'common benefit' or 'common utility' as a justification for taxation was rooted in the connections which canonists and Roman law jurists had already established between taxation, utility, and consent. Just how utility should be judged and just what constituted consent, however, were open to very different constructions. Henry's own conception of tacit consent (that an individual's agreement can be assumed from his remaining physically present in a community) indicates that consent could be construed very widely indeed. When Godfrey of Fontaines came to discuss obedience and resistance, therefore, he made the assessment of utility and the exact nature of consent central to his argument.

Like Henry, Godfrey proceeds to outline the grounds on which disobedience can be morally legitimate. In the aftermath of Philip IV's levies for war in Aquitaine and Flanders this was hardly surprising, as Henry's earlier warning lest rulers abuse the appeal to evident utility appeared to have been all too prophetic. For Godfrey, customary appeals to 'defense of the realm' provided no guarantee that a particular tax was actually justified. Godfrey therefore insisted that *proof* of the utility of such a demand should be provided by the consent of the community. However, Godfrey also saw that appealing to the principle of consent was, in itself, insufficient, since there remained the question of how such consent should be measured. Like Henry, Godfrey identifies the importance of consent but, unlike Henry, he gives a detailed account of how such a principle was to be implemented in practice.

Godfrey was familiar with canon law. His opposition as a secular master to the privileges granted to the mendicant orders in *Ad fructus uberes* was based on a detailed discussion of the relevant texts from Gratian and the *Decretals*. That he was also familiar with Roman law is clear from his appeal to the principles governing individual property rights as well as to the maxim 'what touches all ought to be approved by all' (*quod omnes tangit ab omnibus comprobetur*). Nevertheless, in the quodlibet translated here, the key text for consent is provided, not by law, but by Book III of Aristotle's *Politics*. In particular, Godfrey explores the consequences of Aristotle's discussion of whether it is better to be ruled by a good man or by good laws and whether rulers should accede by hereditary succession or by election. The result is an argument that gives a central role not simply to consent but to counselors, and to counselors who are not only wise and prudent members of the political community but who are also independent from undue influence by the ruler. The absence of such independent counsel, the absence of any satisfactory means of proving utility to the community, was a recipe for tyranny on the part of rulers and slavery on the part of subjects. Such was the condition, in fact, to which, in Godfrey's somber conclusion, almost all of contemporary society had sunk.

For further reading on consent, see J. R. Strayer, 'Consent to Taxation under Philip the Fair' in J. R. Strayer and C. H. Taylor, eds., *Studies in Early French Taxation* (Cambridge, MA: Harvard University Press, 1939), pp. 3–105. For defense of the realm, see J. R. Strayer, 'Defense of the Realm and Royal Power in France' in his *Medieval Statecraft and the Perspectives of History* (Princeton: Princeton University Press, 1971); G. Spiegel, 'Defence of the Realm – the Evolution of a Capetian Propaganda Slogan,' *Journal of Medieval History* 3 (1977), pp. 115–33.

Are Subjects Bound to Pay a Tax When the Need for It Is Not Evident?

{76} Can a ruler impose a levy, and are his subjects bound to pay it, when he says that his cause is the utility of the commonwealth but when the need is not in itself obvious?

[1. Preliminary Arguments]

[1a. Argument in Favor of Such Power]

Next it was argued, [in response] to the second [question in this group], that a ruler can impose a levy on his subjects without making the cause clear, because those with responsibility for waging war by their own authority and providing soldiers with what is pertinent to this can impose such a levy as shall seem advantageous to them. But so it is in what has been put forward. Therefore, etc. The major premise is clear from Augustine in Book XXII (c. 75) of *Against Faustus*, where he says: 'The authority and decision to undertake war belongs to rulers, while that of carrying out the commands of war belongs to ministers.' And he prefaces this with (c. 74): 'contributions are made for this [purpose], so that wages may be provided for the soldier for the sake of wars.'

[1b. Argument against Such Power]

The opposite is argued, when it is shown that this is not permissible in a correct government, where someone rules over others as over free persons and not as slaves, because it pertains to a free person to be the cause of his own actions and not to be completely acted upon by someone else. Therefore, if some such levy is going to be made for the benefit of a community, it ought to be ordered by the agreement and knowledge of the more eminent and discerning members of that community.

[2. Solution to the Question]

Answer: It should be maintained here that according to the Philosopher (cf. *Politics* III 13, 1284a3–11), the ruler of a multitude in a good and correct form of government ought to be the best and most prudent individual, a man who is almost divine in comparison with others. And because the best does not necessarily give birth to the best in the course of natural generation, it would for this reason be more suitable for rulers to be instituted by the people through election, so that the better person would always be placed in charge. For although, because of general wickedness, electors too are sometimes deficient in choosing, election nevertheless provides, in itself, a clearer route toward having a good ruler than natural generation.

Therefore, since kings are *not* generally instituted by election in this way, it should not be presumed from the fact that they are kings that they are the better and more prudent individuals. [Moreover,] however good a particular ruler may be, he is still not entirely immune from passions, which can affect him in different ways, for better or for worse, and thus make his judgment better or worse. For this reason, and because his kingdom ought primarily to be ordered toward the good of the whole community and not toward his own private good, such an individual ought to rule in accordance with correctly instituted laws and not in accordance with his own prudence, as the Philosopher says in *Politics* III (15, 1286a16–20). He maintains there that whatever can be instituted or judged by law should not be entrusted to the ruler but should be determined by the law, because, since there are no passions in it, the law is something weightier {77} and more constant than a human being, in whom the passions are necessarily present. This is why he [also] says there (16, 1287a28–32) that whoever bids intellect to rule (that is, laws instituted in accordance with right reason) would seem to bid God to rule as well as the just laws themselves, whereas whoever bids a human being to rule also appoints a beast. For when desire and anger have been in government – that is, when a human being is free to rule in accordance with the different ways in which he is affected by different passions – he will likewise end up by killing the best men. On these grounds, [the Philosopher] concludes that whatever law can determine should be judged by the law and not by a good man. Now if this is the case when the ruler is generally agreed to be the best sort of person, the point ought to be conceded all the more when it is not generally agreed that he is such a person.

Therefore, when someone rules over others as over free persons and not as slaves, he does not have the right to rule except by virtue of the whole community either electing him or instituting or accepting and agreeing on him, and his government ought not to exist except for the sake of the common good and the common benefit. For this reason, he should not impose anything on the community that weighs heavily on it or harms it, *unless* this proceeds from the consent of his subjects. Inasmuch as they are free, they ought to obey willingly, not by compulsion, knowing the reason for which a burden is imposed upon them and knowing that it is the sort of reason which merits approval. This may be either because it is deduced from statute law instituted in harmony with reason and the prudence of discerning people or because it has been deduced beyond the bounds of the law (when the law does not directly or immediately extend to the matter) by the counsel of the ruler (provided it is generally agreed that the ruler and his counselors show rectitude of intellect in prudence and of will in choosing and that they are so just and faithful that they are able and willing to consider more soundly than others what is better and more advantageous in the situation at hand). Consideration ought to be given in such a case to whether there is an obvious error and to whether it is agreed that in other instances the ruler and his counselors have been accustomed to conduct themselves faithfully and with discernment. However, if [i] what is instituted, or what is announced to the ruler's subjects, is something momentous and burdensome, and if [ii] there is no apparent benefit for which so great a burden ought reasonably to be imposed, and if [iii] compared with others the ruler is not markedly superior in prudence, faithfulness, and love for the common good, and if [iv] those whose counsel is primarily used are not the sort of people who are markedly more trustworthy than others, then, because such an imposition is not reasonable, subjects are not by right (*de iure*) bound to obey. For although a ruler may have been accustomed in such situations to allege that this sort of burden is imposed for the necessity of the commonwealth and for the benefit of all his subjects, if this is not the case, he cannot by right impose it.

Since a free subject, if he is a good person, ought to pay what is for the benefit of the commonwealth willingly and through choice, not from compulsion and violence, it ought to be clear to him in some way that this is very likely the case. To maintain that it is enough for the ruler to say that this is so and that he is acting {78} with good and great counsel carries no weight, because tyrants too have been accustomed to argue in such a manner. And so, if it is not otherwise clear how one differs from the other, then, just as the tyrant strives to rule according to his own will, so too does a good ruler — which is false. In such a situation, therefore, although not [all] individuals from the populace ought to be involved in discussing, ordering, and instituting such things, nevertheless a large enough number of discerning and faithful individuals in the government ought to be involved and to approve these things to make it generally apparent to everyone that the cause for which such a burden is being imposed upon them is reasonable and, on that account, to be undertaken willingly. Now for this [to happen], those with whose counsel such things are discussed and instituted must not be particularly close to the ruler or members of his household, because they would be suspect (on the grounds that they could not easily speak against the ruler's will). Instead, they should be such that the burden to be imposed can affect them and their own subordinates as it affects others — if not, then they would not be concerned and attentive about it.

However, in the case of a ruler who is content solely with his own private counsel and who imposes this sort of burden without being willing to make known to others the cause and necessity for which it is being imposed, his subjects ought to resist, if they can, until such time as the matter has been discussed sufficiently by the aforementioned prudent persons. Otherwise, the realm will gradually be converted into a tyranny, and free subjects will be reduced to the condition of servile subjects. It is to be feared that because of the pusillanimity of many and the faithlessness of others, this may be happening generally today. On this account, there is scarcely ((*vix/vis*)) a correct and just government to be found, but almost all rulers are attempting to rule as tyrants, referring everything to their own honor or advantage, even if this is to the detriment of their subjects, etc.

[3. Reply to the Opening Argument (1a)]

To the opposing argument it should be said that although the authority to declare war and to provide what is necessary for soldiers pertains primarily to the ruler, nevertheless, in very difficult and unclear cases these things ought not to be done without the counsel of their free subjects in the manner set out above.

JAMES OF VITERBO
IS IT BETTER TO BE RULED BY THE BEST
MAN THAN BY THE BEST LAWS?

Introduction

(For information on James of Viterbo's life and writings, see the introduction to Translation 7.)

Giles of Rome, Peter of Auvergne, Henry of Ghent, and Godfrey of Fontaines all used Book III of the *Politics* to highlight the importance of Aristotle's discussion of the relative merits of rule by a good man and rule by good laws. For Giles and Peter, the goal seems to have been to accommodate the Philosopher's views on the collective wisdom of the multitude, on the merits of election and consent, and on the nature of law as pure reason unaffected by passion, but without allowing these views to impugn the status of kingship as the best form of government. In the case of Giles of Rome, writing a treatise for the future king of France, the motivation is clear enough; in the case of Peter of Auvergne, it is more problematic, especially given his own contribution to the debate over taxation in 1298. For Henry of Ghent, however, and for Godfrey of Fontaines, the agenda was more radical. Spurred on by their discontent with the papal bull *Ad fructus uberes* as well as by repeated papal and royal demands for taxation, Henry and, above all, Godfrey used Book III of the *Politics* to emphasize the critical importance of the consent and counsel of wise and prudent members of the community. *This* was the means of securing the common good of the political community in a world where rulers could not always be given the benefit of the doubt.

For James of Viterbo, the position is different again. In 1295–96, when he was asked whether it was better to be ruled by a good man or by good laws, he began his reply, characteristically, with a survey of the alternative views on offer. On the one hand, it is better to be ruled by law, because law is by definition free from passion and because the ruler merely serves as its mouthpiece and instrument. On the other hand, it is better to be ruled by a good man, because law by definition consists of universal propositions and can accordingly be found wanting in particular instances.

One solution, therefore, is to distinguish between rule by natural law and rule by positive law. Another is to hold that rule by a good man is better *per se* but that rule by law is better *per accidens*. James's own position is that it is better to be ruled both by the good man *and* by good laws, or, if it has to be one *or* the other, that it depends on the type of goodness under discussion and on the distinction between nature and grace. Viewed in terms of humankind's limited natural capacity for goodness, it is better to be ruled by law. Viewed in terms of the goodness infused by grace, it is better to be ruled by the good man. Like Godfrey of Fontaines, James reveals a willingness to accompany his analysis with an appeal to Roman law (*quod principi placuit habet vigorem legis*) and to the distinction between nature and grace. Otherwise James's frame of reference remains firmly Aristotelian. Indeed, read alongside the contributions of Giles of Rome, Peter of Auvergne, Henry of Ghent, and Godfrey of Fontaines, the interpretation offered by James of Viterbo gives a clear demonstration of the flexibility and variety which could underpin the scholastic appropriation of Aristotle's *Politics*.

For further reading on the question of rule by a good man or good laws, see Translations 3 and 4. For Peter of Auvergne's views on taxation, see E. A. R. Brown, '*Cessante causa* and the Taxes of the Last Capetians: The Political Applications of a Philosophical Maxim,' *Studia Gratiana* 15 (1972):567–87, pp.585–87.

Is It Better to Be Ruled by the Best Man than by the Best Laws?

[1. Preliminary Arguments]

[1a. Argument for Rule by the Best Man]

{107} It seems better to be ruled by the best man, for the better government seems to be the one which extends over a greater number of things and has a greater likeness to divine government. But government by the best man extends over a greater number of things than government by laws, because, however good laws may be, they cannot determine everything. By the same token, it will also be more like divine government, which is the most general and has no deficiency at all. Therefore, government by the best man is better than government by the best laws.

[1b. Argument for Rule by the Best Laws]

The counter-argument is that the better government is the one which is more permanent and stable. But it is clear enough that government by the best laws is of this sort. Therefore, it is better.

[2. A Possible Solution Given by Others]

I answer. It should [first] be declared that it can be shown on the basis of two arguments that it is better to be ruled by the best law than by the best man.

One argument is that the best man or ruler is the instrument and mouthpiece {108} of the law in executing it and causing it to be observed. That is why he is also called the minister of the law. And so the law is more primary than the ruler. Now that which is more primary is better than, and preferable to, that which is like an instrument.

The second is that the law cannot be led astray. But by dint of the fact that he has the capacity to want and to become angry, a human being, however good he may be, can be led astray.

But, on the basis of a further principle, the opposite can be shown, namely, that it is better to be ruled by the best man than by the best laws, on the grounds that the deficiencies that sometimes occur with laws can in some cases be corrected by the best man.

Therefore, certain people maintain both positions by introducing a distinction. If we are speaking about natural law, then it is better to be ruled by the best law than by the best man. The first two arguments support this. If we are speaking about positive law, then it is better to be ruled by the best man than by the best law, on account of those cases in which such law can be found wanting. The third argument holds in this way.

It is also customary to make another distinction concerning this [subject], namely, that speaking *per se* it is better to be ruled by the best man, but speaking *per accidens* it is better to be ruled by the best law (that is, on account of the deficiencies that can occur in rulers).

[3. Solution]

However, there is also another way of proceeding toward a solution to this question. First it should be established in advance who is the best man and what is the best law.

The best man is the one whose reason is right through prudence – and not only private prudence but also political [prudence] – and whose appetite is right through the moral virtues. Now those laws are called best which harmonize with (or at least do not conflict with) natural right and which are appropriate to the political (*politica*) [community] or commonwealth. For just as nature brings about what is best, not {109} in an unqualified sense, but in terms of what is suitable to the substance of each thing, so the good lawgiver institutes laws that are best, not in an unqualified sense, but in accordance with what is required by the state and condition of the community he is aiming to direct.

Once this is [established as] a premise, therefore, it should be maintained that a government is not complete unless both of these are present, namely, the best law and the best man. For law without a human being is not sufficient for perfect government, both on account of the [need for] observance of the law (because a human being causes the law to be observed) and on account of the [need to] supplement the law (because not everything can be determined by law, but every day new cases occur which are not determined by law). For this reason, it is necessary for a human being to determine them, both for the sake of direction by the law [and] because there are some cases in which the law is deficient. That is why there is a need for human direction in cases of this sort.

Likewise, neither is a human being without law sufficient for perfect government, [i] because time is required for right judgment and, whereas laws have been laid down over a long period of time and from much deliberation, a human being must judge swiftly due to the large number of cases which arise, [ii] because no one is so good that he may not sometimes be deceived and be disordered in his feelings, whereas law is not found wanting in this way, and [iii] because there are also very few 'best men' to be found.

Therefore, neither law without a human being nor a human being without law is sufficient for good government.

But what if it is necessary to take only one of these [alternatives]? In that case it should be stated that, if we are speaking about the goodness a human being can possess by acquiring it through natural principles, then it is better to be ruled by the best law than by the best man. For although the human being and a law can both be found wanting, nevertheless, assuming that the law is observed, there would be fewer unsuitable results from government by law than from government by this sort of best man. This is because law considers what is [right] in the majority of cases, whereas without the grace of God a human being can be led astray in any number of ways. {110}

On the other hand, if we are speaking about the infused goodness of a human being, which exists through the grace of God (the sort of goodness that we read has existed in many rulers), then it would be better to be ruled by this sort of best man than by human law (with which this question is concerned), although not better than being ruled by law that has been handed down at God's instigation. For such a man would be guided by his infused gift in judging swiftly about particulars and would be preserved from being deflected or led astray.

If it is objected that a human being is the minister of the law, it should be stated that a human being is also the founder of the law and is himself animate law (*lex animata*). For what pleases a ruler with right reason has the force of law.

[4. Reply to the Preliminary Arguments]

From what has been argued, it is clear what should be said to the objections.

12

JOHN OF NAPLES
SHOULD A CHRISTIAN KING USE UNBELIEVERS TO DEFEND HIS KINGDOM?

Introduction

After teaching at the Dominican school in Naples from around 1300, John of Naples was sent to Paris in 1310 for further theological study. He was a strict adherent of Thomas Aquinas and was commissioned in 1313 (together with Pierre de la Palu) to examine the teachings of their fellow Dominican, Durand of St. Pourçain. In 1315 John became a regent master at Paris, where he taught until returning to Naples in 1317 as Dominican lector. His work survives in the form of forty-two *Disputed Questions*, thirteen *Quodlibets*, and a series of sermons. He died around 1350.

John's discussion of just war provides further illustration of the close connection between teaching within the Faculty of Theology at Paris and issues of pressing political and ecclesiological concern in western Europe. In discussing whether evil can be used for a good end, in exploring the parallel drawn by Augustine between military and legal contexts, and in expounding Aquinas's reflections on the justification of war and the legitimacy of non-Christian lordship, John makes detailed use of Scripture and of the law — canon, Roman, and customary. His conclusion is nothing if not bold: It is indeed permissible for a Christian ruler to use non-Christian mercenaries to defend a Christian commonwealth. Basing his argument on the distinction between what is true without qualification (*simpliciter, per se*) and what is true in certain circumstances (*secundum quid*), John is careful to add important practical reservations. It would be impermissible to employ non-Christian mercenaries if the need was not pressing (that is, if a ruler already had sufficient Christian soldiers), if such an act had been specifically prohibited by the church, if there was risk of contamination from the mercenaries' unbelief, and if the number of non-Christians employed was so large that they might seize lordship over Christians. Nevertheless, with these provisos, John grasped the nettle of how unjust wars could be waged by Christians and just wars fought by non-Christians. In the political context of 1315–17, these were important and delicate conclusions to advance.

Throughout the thirteenth century the papacy had countenanced crusades against rulers within Christendom who were guilty of heresy or rebellion or of acting as an obstacle to the ultimate objective of an expedition to the Holy Land. In the case of Frederick II, Manfred, and Conradin, the papacy also drew particular attention to the 'blasphemous alliance' (*impium foedus*) into which these Staufen rulers of southern Italy and Sicily had entered with their Muslim subjects in the mainland colony of Lucera. After the conquest of southern Italy by Charles of Anjou, however, the terms of such condemnations had to be adjusted. From the 1280s onward, successive popes gave support to Angevin kings of Naples to drive Frederick of Aragon out of Sicily, efforts which depended in part on the military utility of employing the same Muslim soldiers who had caused such offense under the Staufen. Even though the papacy was reluctant to continue giving these campaigns the status of a crusade after 1302 (when Frederick of Aragon was confirmed in his possession of Sicily on condition that it would not be passed on to his heirs), Robert of Naples (1309–43) continued to emphasize that his struggle for Sicily had begun under the aegis of a crusading indulgence. Moreover, from the early fourteenth century, the papacy (resident at Avignon after 1305) also faced the resurgence of Ghibelline opposition in Lombardy following the invasion of Henry VII (1310–13). In 1312 Clement V accordingly appointed Robert of Naples Vicar-General in northern Italy, an appointment which was confirmed in July 1317 by Clement's successor, John XXII. Once again, the prospect of an expedition to the Holy Land, a crusade which had already been preached in 1316 and which had the full support of Philip V of France, became dependent on the precarious politics of the Italian peninsula. In December 1317 the leader of the Ghibelline alliance, Matteo Visconti, was excommunicated; in April 1318 he was cited to appear before the pope as a 'tyrant,' a summons to which he responded by besieging the strategically vital port of Genoa. In July 1318 Robert of Naples came to Genoa's aid with an army and a fleet. By 1321 John XXII had placed his campaigns in northern Italy under the direction of cardinal legates and given them the status of a crusade.

In 1317, therefore, raising the issue of what constituted a just war was a significant contribution to a wider political debate. Opponents of the papacy were openly criticizing the legitimation of attacks on Christian rulers as crusades (Dante, *Inferno* 27; Marsilius of Padua, *Defender of Peace*

II 26). Supporters of the papacy, meanwhile, responded by vigorously defending the pope's right to direct crusaders against 'tyrannical and rebellious' Christian rulers (Augustine of Ancona, *Summa de ecclesiastica potestate* XXVI 5). It was even more pertinent for a *Neapolitan* theologian to raise this issue as a question about the legitimacy of employing Muslim mercenaries. John's references to Robert of Naples are clear: A ruler who does see fit to employ Muslim mercenaries should be particularly wary if he, or his predecessors, have attacked Muslim cities in the past (Lucera had been destroyed in 1302), and he should employ them only if his own soldiers were not sufficient to defend his kingdom (an argument used by Robert himself in seeking military assistance from the French king).

For the attitude of scholastic theologians to the just war and to mercenaries, see CHLMP X.41, 'The Just War,' and F. H. Russell, *The Just War in the Middle Ages* (Cambridge: Cambridge University Press, 1975). For the political and ideological context of papal involvement in Italy, see N. Housely, *The Italian Crusades: the Papal-Angevin Alliance and the Crusades against Christian Lay Powers, 1254–1343* (Oxford: Clarendon Press, 1982). For the legal background to the conflict between Henry VII and Robert of Naples, see K. Pennington, 'Henry VII and Robert of Naples' in J. Miethke, ed., *Das Publikum politischer Theorie im 14. Jahrhundert* (Munich: Oldenbourg, 1992).

Should a Christian King Use Unbelievers to Defend His Kingdom?

{323} Disputed Question XXXVIII. If He Lacks the Necessary Number of Believers Bearing Arms, Can a Christian King, Who Is a Believer, Use Unbelievers for the Just Defense of the Commonwealth (for Example, Saracen Mercenaries Who Come to Him for the Aforementioned Just Defense) and, in Accordance with the Christian Religion, Ought He to Do So?

[1. Preliminary Arguments]

[1a. *Arguments against the Proposition*]

It seems first that [he cannot and ought] not [to make use of unbelievers] because:

[i] It does not seem possible to make use of such assistance without some sort of association between believers and unbelievers. But believers are prohibited from all association with unbelievers according to 2 Corinthians 6:14–15: 'Do not be yoked together' (that is, have any association whatever) 'with unbelievers.' The text adds: 'For what do righteousness and wickedness have in common? What association can light have with darkness? What agreement is there between Christ and Belial? What does a believer share with an unbeliever?' Therefore, etc.

[ii] Moreover, in Deuteronomy 7:2 the believing children of Israel are commanded to 'make no treaty with them,' that is, with unbelievers. But the assistance of such people [in the proposition] cannot be used without a treaty being made between the king and them. Therefore, etc.

[iii] Moreover, a ruler – or any human being whatever, even the pope – cannot give someone else a license to sin; indeed, in doing so he would sin more than the other person. But by fighting against a believer an unbeliever sins. Therefore, etc. Proof of the minor premise: It is generally agreed that an unbeliever acquires no merit in such an act, because without faith it is impossible to please God (Hebrews 11:6). Therefore, he acts demeritoriously and sins, because, as is commonly said, no individual act is indifferent when it is the product of deliberation – all are therefore either meritorious or demeritorious.

This argument is confirmed by the fact that although it is said that God can make a dispensation from the precepts of the second table [of the Ten Commandments] but not from the first, nevertheless, a human being cannot make a dispensation from God's commandments, just as an inferior power cannot dispense from the commands of a superior power. Therefore, no human being can give someone else a license to sin.

[iv] Moreover, what is not permissible for believers is not permissible for unbelievers either. But it was not permissible for believers who were subject to the Emperor Julian [the Apostate] to wage war against believers, as is said in *Decretum* 11, q. 3, c. 'Julianus' (II.11.3.94). Therefore, this is even less permissible for unbelievers. Therefore, etc.

[v] Moreover, the excommunicate and the unbeliever can be equated,

because each is cut off from the church. But by law no one is permitted to authorize an excommunicate to act for him in a lawsuit, because an excommunicate is not permitted to appear in his own person in a lawsuit. Therefore, neither is it permissible for a ruler who is a believer to authorize an unbeliever to defend the commonwealth of which he is in charge.

[vi] Moreover, by law wars and legal cases can be equated. But in trials or cases no one is permitted to make use of false and illegitimate witnesses. Therefore, neither is it permissible in wars to use people who are unbelievers.

[vii] Moreover, by law wars require wealth and people to fight them. But it would not be permissible in war to make use of wealth which had been acquired illegitimately. Therefore, neither is it permissible to use people who are unbelievers.

[viii] Moreover, by law a body of soldiers cannot be subject to an unbeliever. But soldiers are especially used in wars. Therefore, etc.

[ix] Moreover, unbelievers are members of the Devil, just as believers are members of Christ the Lord. But it is not permissible to use the assistance of the Devil, because this could not be done without some mediating agreement or some honor or service being performed by a human being to the Devil – something which is absolutely impermissible for a Christian according to the Apostle in 1 Corinthians 10:20: 'I do not want you to become associates of demons.' Therefore, neither is it permissible to use the assistance of unbelievers, who are members of the Devil.

[x] Moreover, a human being ought not to be the cause of evil so that he can avoid some evil of which he is not the cause. For example, an individual ought not to procure an abortion for a woman even if it means that the woman will then die, because that person would be the cause of the child's death. [By not procuring the abortion] however, the individual is not the cause of the woman's death, but her own physical weakness. But if a ruler does not defend the commonwealth against aggressors, he is not himself the cause of evil to the commonwealth – instead, the aggressor is. By admitting unbelievers, however, the ruler is the cause of the evil that follows from this. Therefore, etc. Proof of the minor premise: In such a conflict either the unbelievers will be defeated, in which case he has admitted them in vain, {324} or they are victorious, in which case the believers they have vanquished are their slaves, because a conquered person is his conqueror's slave, as is said in 2 Peter 2:19 and as the Philosopher also maintains in *Politics* I (6, 1255a6–7). This is evil, irrational, and dangerous, because through such servitude some might readily be led astray from the faith, for a slave readily follows the will of his lord. The ruler

would be the cause of this evil. Therefore, etc.

[xi] Moreover, anyone who knowingly makes use of a false instrument sins. Likewise, then, whoever uses the assistance of a human being who is an unbeliever and 'false' sins. Therefore, etc.

[xii] Moreover, to cause a believer to sin is itself a sin, according to Matthew 18:6: 'Whoever causes one of these little ones who believe in me to sin, it would be better for him to have a millstone hung around his neck,' etc. Mark 9:42 makes a similar point. But it does not seem possible to introduce such unbelievers without causing believers to sin. Therefore, by doing this the ruler sins.

[xiii] Moreover, it is impermissible for a believer to fight against an unbeliever in an unjust war. Therefore, it is also impermissible for an unbeliever to fight against a believer in any war whatever, because every war of unbeliever against believer seems unjust on the part of the unbeliever.

[xiv] Moreover, if a ruler who governs part of a multitude introduces enemies of the whole multitude in common in order to defend his own part of the multitude against another part which is opposed to him, he is considered by law to have deserted and betrayed the ruler who governs the whole multitude. This is clear from the tribune who summons enemies of the emperor to fight against enemies of the part of the multitude that he himself is defending and governing. But the Saracens are enemies of the whole multitude of the church, because common enemies are defined in law as those against whom the Roman people has declared war or, conversely, those who have declared war against the Roman people. According to the law of Mohammed, however, Saracens ought to fight continuously against believers. Christians are also actively at war with them on account of the Christian lands which they unjustly occupy. Every Christian realm is part of the multitude of the church. Therefore, it is not permissible for any Christian king to admit Sacracens [to fight] against other Christians.

[xv] Moreover, by law (*Codex Theodosianus* 7.1.1; *Codex Iustinianus* XII.35.9), anyone who provides an opportunity for Roman goods to be captured commits the crime of lese-majesty. But unbelievers are barbarians (that is, aliens) with respect to believers. All who are subject to the Roman pontiff, however, can be termed Romans. But by admitting unbelievers [to fight] against believers [the ruler] provides an opportunity for the goods of believers to be captured by unbelievers. Therefore, etc.

[xvi] Moreover, by law, an emperor who brings in a doctor who is an unbeliever, even in a case of necessity, sins. But the good of the emperor

is the common good. Likewise, then, it is also not permissible to bring in an unbeliever to defend a commonwealth of believers, even in a case of necessity.

[xvii] Moreover, by law (*Digest* 8.3, 43.20), someone who channels into his land water to which he is not entitled is deprived of the water to which he is entitled, namely, the water that someone else is obliged by a service to channel through his field. Likewise, then, someone who admits an unbeliever to fight against a believer deserves to lose the legitimate lordship that he has over the believer.

[xviii] Moreover, it is impermissible to provide Saracens with weapons that they can use to attack believers. But according to *Posterior Analytics* I (2, 72a29–30), that because of which anything is such is also such, and more so. Therefore, it is a much greater sin to give unbelievers *authority* to fight against believers.

[1b. Arguments for the Proposition]

But against [what has just been argued]:

[i] Necessity, as is commonly said, is not subject to law and renders permissible ((*licitum/illicitum*)) what would otherwise be impermissible. This is clear regarding theft, pillage, murder, and the like. But the ruler who is a believer seems to be subject to necessity if it is supposed that he lacks the necessary people from among believers. Therefore, in such a case it is permissible for him to take on mercenaries who are unbelievers to defend a commonwealth of believers.

[ii] Moreover, it seems that this would be permissible for him even if he were not suffering from such a deficiency, because something imperfect in character is done better and more appropriately by imperfect means than by perfect. But waging war is something imperfect in character. That is why it is prohibited to men who are perfect, such as bishops, clergy, and the like, according to the whole of *Decretum* 23, q. 8 (II.23.8.1–7). Now unbelievers are imperfect in relation to believers. Therefore, etc.

[iii] Moreover, the perfection of a created will consists in its conformity to the divine will, just as everything that is capable of being measured is perfect [by its conformity] to its measure, because in each genus there is a first [being] which is the measure of the other [members of the genus], as is clear from *Metaphysics* X (1, 1052b18). But God punishes evil human beings in hell by means of demons, when he could, should he so will, punish them by angels. Therefore, even if the ruler has good believers

subject to him, he ought to combat those evil people who have unjustly attacked the commonwealth by means of evil unbelievers.

[iv] Moreover, a ruler ought to prefer to defend the commonwealth against aggressors by means of those whom he presumes should fight against them with greater ardor. But it may be presumed to be highly likely that an unbeliever will fight against a believer with greater ardor than a believer will, because there is greater enmity between unbelievers and believers than there is between believer and believer. Therefore, in the face of a believer who is unjustly attacking the commonwealth, the commonwealth is better defended by an unbeliever than by a believer. Consequently, a ruler who is a believer ought to protect the commonwealth by means of unbelievers rather than believers.

[2. Reply to the Question]

I answer. In this question it seems that the following approach should be taken. First {325} certain points must be set out to explain the title of the question; second, the conclusions which pertain to the question have to be proved.

[2a. Preliminary Points]

With regard to the first, I set out four points.

[i] The first is that the people 'necessary' to the ruler can be understood in two ways pertinent to the present question. Either this can be understood as people who in some way 'belong' to the ruler – that is, who are subject to him. This seems to be the sense of 'necessary' in Job 6:13: 'My intimates (*necessarii*) have also gone away from me,' that is, 'my neighbors and whoever belongs to me.' Hence [the text] continues: 'My brothers pass me by.' Alternatively, ['necessary'] can be understood in the sense of being useful for an intended end, such as the defense of the commonwealth in the proposition. This is how 'necessary' is understood (i.e., as something useful) in the chapter on 'Necessary' in the *Metaphysics* (V 5, 1015a20–26) and in *Physics* II (c. 9), where it is said that food is necessary for life and a horse is [necessary] (i.e., useful) for a journey.

[ii] Second, it should be understood that a deficiency of necessary people can be interpreted either in the sense that the [number of] people is insufficient to defend the commonwealth or in the sense that the [num-

ber of] people who are believers is sufficient to protect the commonwealth but they are not as warlike as people who are unbelievers and consequently are deficient in comparison to the latter with respect to military skill (this being true whether the people who are believers are subject to the ruler or not).

[iii] Third, it should be understood that this question is taken to be about lawful power and not *de facto* power, as is clear from what follows [in the title of the question]: 'and in accordance with the Christian religion ought he to do so,' as when the jurists say, 'We can do what we can do by law (*de iure*).'

[iv] Fourth, it should be understood that something which is absolutely good in its general character may be impermissible on account of some circumstance: for example, [a] because it is prohibited, such as eating meat during Lent; or [b] because it causes someone to sin or a great evil results from it, as with the punishment of sinners when there is a fear of schism (on which account the punishment of sinners should then cease, as Augustine teaches in Book III of his *Contra epistolam Parmeniani*) and as with fraternal correction (a virtuous action and a form of spiritual almsgiving), which is sometimes omitted out of charity so as to avoid serving as a cause of sin for others (as Augustine teaches in *On the City of God* I 9); or [c] due to some circumstance on the part of the agent, as, for example, storing up food for the morrow is permissible in itself but would be a sin for someone who did it because he had no faith in divine providence and relied entirely on his own prudence to rule his life; or [d] because it would be done better and more appropriately by someone else, as for example, baptism by a woman or by a lay person when a priest is present (as Isidore states in Book II, chapter 25 of *De [ecclesiasticis] officiis*, and as is stated in *On Consecration*, Distinction 4, c. '*Constat*' and the following two chapters [*Decretum* III, *De Consecratione* IV, 19–21]), or blessing by a bishop or a priest when an archbishop or some other superior is present, because 'Without any doubt the lesser person is blessed by the greater,' as the Apostle teaches in Hebrews 7:7.

[2b. Conclusions]

Now that these points have been set out, there are five conclusions to be proved for this question:

[2b(i). First Conclusion]

The first is that

> [Conclusion 1] *For a king who is a believer to admit unbelievers for the just defense of the commonwealth, or even to summon them (which is more), is not impermissible in its general character.*

This can be proved in a number of ways.

[2b(ia). First Proof]

First, because using permitted means for a permitted end is a virtuous and permitted act, because it is an act of synderesis, as is clear from *Ethics* VI (10, 1143a6–8; *synesis* [understanding] in Moerbeke's translation of Aristotle). Synderesis, it is said there, is a virtue connected with prudence, which, as is clear from the same book, is connected with all the virtues. But to make use of such assistance for the aforementioned end is to make use of permissible means for a permissible end. Therefore, etc. The major premise has been explained. One part of the minor premise is also clear, namely, that the defense of the commonwealth is a permissible and obligatory end. For the other part, namely, that such a means is permissible (i.e., that it is permissible for unbelievers to fight on the authority of the ruler against anyone whatever for the sake of the aforementioned defense), the proof is threefold.

First, on the basis of Isidore's definition of a just war, *Etymologies* 18.2, as found in *Causa* 23, question 2 (*Decretum* II.23.2.1): 'A just war is one that is waged by decree (that is, by the decree of a ruler) for the sake of retrieving goods or repelling enemies.' From this it can be concluded that for a war to be just these two conditions alone are required, namely, the authority of a ruler and a due end for the combatant. Brother Thomas expressly maintains this in *Summa theologiae* IIaIIae, question 40, article 1. But here [in the proposition] the authority of the ruler is posited and a due end (namely, defense of the commonwealth) is intended. Therefore, as regards the general character of the act, it is not a sin for unbelievers of this sort to fight in such a war.

Moreover, an act that is virtuous and permissible in terms of its general character (such as, for example, almsgiving and the like) is not impermissible for an unbeliever because of his unbelief. Otherwise an unbeliever could never dispose himself toward grace before [receiving] it (because no one has a disposition toward grace through sin; rather, sin disposes one against it), nor would Daniel have advised Nebuchadnezzar (who was an unbeliever {326} and an idolater): 'Therefore, O King, be pleased to accept my advice to you: Renounce your sins by giving alms' (Daniel 4: 27). But to fight for the commonwealth is an act that is virtuous and permissible in its general character, namely, as an act of bravery, as is clear from *Ethics* III (cf. 6, 1115a29–30; 8, 1116a15–29). Therefore, it is not impermissible for an unbeliever because of his unbelief. Rather, it is a good act (in terms of moral goodness) if what he intends is the just defense of a commonwealth of believers, something which he can indeed intend, since love of what is just and morally honorable seems to be natural, and guilt [i.e., the guilt of unbelief] does not destroy nature, particularly for someone in the present life. So too, in giving alms an unbeliever can aim at a laudable and morally honorable end, namely, coming to the aid of the needy, even though no act of his can merit eternal life.

Moreover, the common good of believers is better and more divine than a private good (especially that of an unbeliever), as is clear from the prologue to the *Ethics* (I 2, 1094b9–10). But it is permitted on the authority of the law for anyone, even an unbeliever, to fight against an unjust attacker and kill him. And because by law it is permissible to repel force with force under the rubric of blameless defense, then everyone, even an unbeliever, ought to will and take care of his own life in preference to that of another and ought consequently to protect it by killing an unjust attacker. Therefore, it is much more permissible for an unbeliever acting on the authority of a ruler, who is 'animate law' (as is clear from *Ethics* V [4, 1132a21–22]), to protect a commonwealth of believers, even against unjust attackers who are believers.

Thus the aforementioned minor premise has been proved in three ways, and the conclusion follows accordingly, namely, that it is permissible for a ruler to make use of such mercenaries for the defense of the commonwealth.

[2b(ib). Second Proof]

Moreover, second, in support of the principal conclusion: It is permissible for someone to use for his own good someone else's evil, even when it is evil in its general character. Therefore, it is much more permissible to use something that is good in its general character (and is consequently a good for the unbeliever, as has been proved) for the common good, namely, the preservation of the commonwealth. The inference is clear, because the common good is to be preferred to the private good, and it is more permissible to use someone else's good for a correct end than to use his evil. The antecedent is proved in three ways.

[First,] according to Augustine in his letter to Publicola (Epistle 47) and in distinction 39 of *Sentences* III (39.8), if anyone has sworn by false gods and has not kept faith with his oath, he has committed two sins, because he has both sworn by those he should not have sworn by and he has acted against his promise of good faith; but whoever makes use of the good faith of this person (who is generally agreed to have sworn by false gods) and uses it for good and not for evil does not associate himself with the sin of someone who has sworn by demons but with the good word of someone who has kept faith. From this it seems that it is the person who swears by false gods who sins and not the person who uses the oath for his own good.

Moreover, in support of the same point: Accepting something that has been lent at usury by someone who is prepared to lend to anyone in this manner is not a sin, provided that one does not induce him to lend in such fashion. Nevertheless, the person who lends in this fashion sins – not, however, the person who uses the sin for his own good. Therefore, it is permissible to use someone else's culpable evil for one's own good.

That is why God, too, makes use of all sins for some good, since according to Augustine in the *Enchiridion*, chapter 11, God elicits some good from every evil whatever. Now every perfection of the created will consists in its conformity to the divine will, just as [the perfection of] everything capable of being measured [consists] in conformity to its measure.

Thus the antecedent has been proved in three ways.

[2b(ic). Third Proof]

Moreover, third, in support of the main conclusion: It seems more permissible, or at least no less permissible, for an unbeliever to fight for the utility of a commonwealth of believers than for a believer to fight for the utility of a commonwealth of unbelievers. This is because the common good of believers is a better end (and consequently a more permissible object to aim at) than the common good of unbelievers and also because it is more permissible and rational for a mercenary who is an unbeliever to be subordinate to a believer than the other way around. But we read in 1 Samuel 27:8–12 that David fought against various peoples for the utility of the commonwealth of the Philistines, who were unbelievers, aiding the unbelieving King Achish. Conversely, therefore, it is permissible for a king who is a believer to make use of the assistance of unbelievers for the defense of a commonwealth of believers.

Moreover, in Genesis 14:13–16 we read that Abraham was with Mamre,

Aner, and Eschol and fought with their assistance against four kings who had captured his nephew Lot. Now it is probable that Mamre, Aner, and Eschol were unbelievers, because at that time (as is commonly maintained) the worship of the one God took place in only one family, namely, that of Abraham (although I would maintain that it is more true to say of some who are mentioned in Scripture, such as Job and others like him, that they were worshippers of the one God). Therefore, it is much more permissible to use the assistance of unbelievers for the sake of the common good of believers. Hence Brother Thomas too, in IIaIIae, question 10, article 9, expressly maintains that in time of necessity it is permissible for believers to associate with unbelievers (who are not excommunicates), such as Jews, Saracens, and the like. From this it is clear that if the act is good in its general character and if it is a case of necessity, then a ruler into whose charge the care of the commonwealth has been committed can and, according to the Christian religion, ought to make use of the assistance of unbelievers for the aforementioned end, the example being Abraham himself. Thus it is also the case that the person responsible for the care of the commonwealth is bound in the manner of a commandment to do whatever is advantageous for the commonwealth.

[2b(ii). Second Conclusion]

The second conclusion is that

> [Conclusion 2] *If the ruler can call upon sufficient people who are believers for the defense of the commonwealth (whether subject to him or foreigners), then it is not permissible to call upon unbelievers, even if they are more warlike.*

This can be proved in several ways.

[2b(iia). First Proof]

The person responsible for the care of the commonwealth {327} ought not to employ in its defense those who cannot plausibly be presumed to will, or to care for, the good of the commonwealth in preference to others who *can* be presumed to will and to care for its good, because by doing this the ruler would be exposing the commonwealth to danger. But believers, whether they are subjects or foreigners, are presumed to will and to care for the good of a commonwealth of believers; not so unbelievers, who are enemies of the faith and of the community of believers. Therefore, etc. This argument is confirmed in two ways.

First, because the distance between believer and unbeliever is greater than that between foreigner and subject. But if a ruler can sufficiently defend the commonwealth with those who are subject to him, it would be wrong to bring in foreigners, because subjects are presumed to will and care for the good of their own commonwealth more than foreigners. Therefore, if the ruler can employ believers, it would be wrong to employ unbelievers.

Second, because it is generally maintained that a believer ought not to enter into a contract [of marriage] with an unbeliever, because this is an obstacle to the good of bringing children up to worship God. For it is not presumed that an unbeliever will introduce his children to the true worship of God; in fact, he will hold them back. Therefore, since the common good is more divine and better than the private good, as is clear in the prologue to the *Ethics* (I 2, 1094b9–10), a ruler is under a much greater obligation not to admit unbelievers to defend the commonwealth if he can employ believers (whether they are subject to him or are foreigners).

[2b(iib). Second Proof]

Moreover, provided that the defense of the commonwealth is secure, a ruler who is a believer is under a particular obligation to be wary of anything that can redound to the shame and infamy of believers and consequently of the faith. But to make use of the assistance of unbelievers seems to redound to the infamy, confusion, and shame of believers in the eyes of unbelievers, because from such an act unbelievers could plausibly conclude that believers were not sufficient to defend their commonwealth (either from weakness or from faithlessness to their lord). Therefore, if a ruler who is a believer can employ any believers whatever and is not in dire necessity as a result, then he should not admit unbelievers, since he ought to will and care for the good of believers, particularly their good reputation, in accordance with what the Apostle writes in Romans 12:17: 'Be careful to do what is good not only in God's eyes but also in human eyes.'

[2b(iic). Third Proof]

Moreover, third, in support of the main conclusion: It pertains to a ruler who is a believer, as an example to others, to avoid all familiar contact and friendship with unbelievers unless necessity demands it. That is why, in 2 Chronicles 19:2, Jehu the prophet says to Jehoshaphat, a king who is a believer: 'Should you be joined in friendship with those who hate the Lord? Because of this you will merit the anger of the Lord.' But the assistance of particular people cannot be used to defend the common-wealth without some sort of familiar contact or friendship with them, at least financial contact. Therefore, if a ruler is not suffering from a lack of sufficient believers, he ought not to make use of unbelievers.

This argument is confirmed by the Apostle's prohibition of every asso-ciation with unbelievers, when he says in 2 Corinthians 6:14–15: 'Do not be yoked together with unbelievers,' that is, have any sort of association with them whatever. He adds: 'For what do righteousness and iniquity have in common? What fellowship can light have with darkness? What agreement is there between Christ and Belial? What does a believer have in common with an unbeliever?' Hence the common teaching is that, unless necessity demands it, a believer ought not to associate with unbe-lievers, [even those] who are not excommunicates, such as Saracens, pa-gans, and the like. See Thomas, IIaIIae question 10, article 9.

[2b(iid). Fourth Proof]

Moreover, it seems irrational and inappropriate for an unbeliever to have any superiority over a believer, and consequently this should be avoided altogether unless there is a great and pressing necessity. That is why in 1 Corinthians 6:1 the Apostle prohibits believers from engaging in lawsuits before a judge who is an unbeliever, saying: 'If any of you has a dispute with another, dare he take it to the wicked to be judged instead of to the saints?' i.e., to unbelievers and not to believers, as the text is generally expounded. The church also forbids all lordship and new authority (*prae-latio*) of unbelievers over believers (Book V of the *Decretals*, *Extra* 'On Jews and Saracens' [*Decr. Greg.* IX V.6]). For those who are powerful in intellect ought to have superiority over others (as is clear from *Politics* I [cf. 2, 1252a31–32]). Now unbelievers are deficient in right reason. The de-fenders of a commonwealth, however, have a certain superiority over the others to whom the commonwealth belongs, for everything that is de-pendent is subjected in this respect to that on which it depends. A com-monwealth, however, and consequently the people whose commonwealth it is, are in a certain way dependent on those who defend the common-wealth against aggressors. The same is also true in nature, where the irascible power [of the soul], which in a certain way both defends and fights for the desiring power, is more perfect than it and in a sense superior to it. So too in moral matters, where bravery is superior to temperance. That is why the Philosopher maintains in *On Rhetoric* I (9, 1366b3–6) that the greatest virtues are necessarily those which are the most honored by others – indeed, it is because virtue is a capacity to do good that people give the greatest honor to the brave and the just. Therefore, unless necessity demands it, for a ruler who is a believer to make use of the assistance of unbelievers to defend the commonwealth is inappropriate, irrational, and consequently impermissible. So then, unless it is demonstrable that a king who is a believer is unable to call upon sufficient mercenaries who are believers for the aforementioned defense (whether they are subject to him or are foreigners), it seems that he should altogether avoid employing unbelieving mercenaries as something impermissible and sinful, even if they are more warlike.

[2b(iii). Third Conclusion]

The third conclusion is that

> [Conclusion 3] *It would not be permissible to bring in such a group of unbelievers to protect* {328} *the commonwealth when this has been prohibited by God or by the church, as it was prohibited to the children of Israel in Deuteronomy 7:2 ('Make no treaty with them,' that is, with unbelievers) or when it stems from a lack of faith in divine assistance.*

For to do something against the command of whoever is able to command is a mortal sin, and consequently it is impermissible. Likewise, it is also a mortal sin to have faith in human assistance on its own while lacking faith in divine assistance. That is why such people are cursed by God in Jeremiah 17:5: 'Cursed is the man who trusts in man, who depends on flesh for his strength,' etc. Moreover, we read that God has punished such people and those who have given them assistance. Therefore, etc. This is what we read in *Decretum* (II) 23, question 3. It is what we read in Isaiah 18 and the following two chapters, when Egypt was devastated by Nebuchadnezzar because it promised assistance to the children of Israel in their defense against the Assyrians. The people of Judah were themselves led away as captives, as the final chapter of 2 Kings relates, because they had placed their hope of liberation, not in God, but in humans. It could also plausibly be maintained that this is prohibited in Book V of the *Decretals* (*Extra* 'On Jews and Saracens and their slaves,' chapter *Ita quorumdam*, etc. [*Decr. Greg.* IX V.6.6]), where all believers are prohibited under penalty of excommunication from providing unbelievers with weapons which they could use to attack Christians. Therefore, there is a much greater prohibition against any ruler giving them *authority* to fight against Christians, since that because of which anything is such is also such, and more so, as has frequently been said in the course of this argument.

[2b(iv). Fourth Conclusion]

The fourth conclusion is that

> [Conclusion 4] *If there is a fear that some believers could be infected by any sort of unbelief as a result of the conduct of such people in their kingdom, it would again be impermissible to [bring in unbelievers].*

[a] This is apparent, first, from the fact that, according to the right order of charity, the spiritual good of one's neighbor should be preferred to one's own temporal good or to the temporal good of someone else. But the good of faith is a spiritual good; or rather, it is the foundation of the entire spiritual edifice, whereas peace, or the peaceful lordship of any kingdom, is a temporal good. Therefore, etc.

[b] Second, [it is apparent] because this was prohibited to the children of Israel – because, that is (as is generally maintained), they were prone to idolatry. That is why in Deuteronomy 7:2–4 the words already cited ('Do not enter into treaties with them') are followed by: 'For they will turn your children away from following me to serve other gods.' Therefore, by the same reasoning this would be impermissible for anyone else.

[c] Third, because, as was stated above, even fraternal correction can be put to one side if it would create an opportunity for sin, and fraternal correction is not a lesser good than the protection of a temporal commonwealth. Therefore, etc. This is expressly maintained by Brother Thomas in IIaIIae, question 2, in the article already cited.

[2b(v). Fifth Conclusion]

The fifth conclusion is that

> [Conclusion 5] *It would not be permissible to make use of the assistance of such people where there are demonstrable grounds for fearing the lordship of unbelievers over believers [would follow].*

It is highly likely that this would be the consequence if a ruler employed such a large number of unbelievers that they could usurp his lordship. For the appetite for lordship seems to be particularly natural except to the extent that it is reined in by right reason – something which is not presumed to be present in unbelievers. As a result, it is highly likely that unbelievers would wish to usurp lordship over believers and consequently would do so if they could. Clearly, it is not only stupid but also impermissible to bring in this many unbelievers, because an act that is permissible in its general character should be set aside on account of a greater evil that it is presumed could follow from it, as is clear from what has been said. But the lordship of unbelievers over believers (which is readily followed by believers turning away from the faith, because a slave readily follows the will of his lord) is a greater evil than any conquest of a commonwealth of believers by a ruler who is a believer. It is a greater evil, even, than the tyranny of a ruler who is a believer over believers whom he has attacked and vanquished. Therefore, etc.

What was maintained in the second conclusion can also be concluded from this, because if it is impermissible to employ these unbelievers on their own to defend a commonwealth of believers (on account of the danger that they could usurp lordship), then neither is it expedient to employ them together with believers (if, that is, a sufficient number of believers can be had, whether subject to the ruler or foreigners). This is because a virtue is stronger when it is united than when it is divided. Now the greatest division seems to be between unbelievers and believers, greater than that between subjects and foreigners when both are believers. It is in no way permissible, then, to employ unbelievers for the aforementioned end if sufficient believers (of whatever provenance) can be had. This is because the ruler responsible for the care of the commonwealth ought to look after its good by the best and safest means possible and avoid the evil ranged against it.

Now it seems that in trusting to the assistance of Saracens particular caution should be shown by a ruler whose ancestors have inflicted some loss on the Saracens, either by destroying a city in the Saracens' own land or by attacking cities in lands that belong to them, because although they are dispersed everywhere they still consider themselves to be one people. Thus, there are good grounds for supposing that they would freely avenge themselves on a son in return for what their people have suffered anywhere at the hands of his predecessors. And it is very likely that in doing so they would consider themselves to be performing an obedient service to God and to Mohammed. Nor should it be presumed that they would care for the good of such a ruler. Consequently such a ruler should be extremely suspicious of association with them and should avoid it altogether.

[3. Replies to the Preliminary Arguments]

[3a. Replies to the Arguments against the Proposition (1a)]

[i] To the first argument against the proposition, therefore, it should be said that with these words the Apostle forbids those Corinthians who had recently been converted to the faith from being Gentiles to associate {329} with unbelievers because of the danger that they will be led astray from the faith. That is why he had already told them in 1 Corinthians 5:6: 'Do you not know that a small amount of yeast works through the whole batch?' In such circumstances (namely, where there is a fear of this happening), a ruler who is a believer ought not to admit unbelievers to assist him, as has been said above. Alternatively, it should be said that the Apostle is forbidding believers to associate with unbelievers when there is no pressing necessity to do so. The opposite is assumed in the proposition.

[ii] To the second it should be said that the children of Israel were prohibited from making treaties with idolatrous unbelievers because, as is generally maintained, they themselves were prone to idolatry. When a ruler fears that some such danger is hanging over the people subject to him, there is no imminent necessity which would permit him to bring unbelievers into association with believers, as is clear from the fourth conclusion proved above [2b(iv)].

[iii] To the third it should be said that although no individual deliberate act is indifferent (i.e., neither morally good nor morally evil), nevertheless, some actions can be neither meritorious with respect to eternal life nor demeritious or sinful. One such instance is an act that is good in its general character (for example, giving alms or fighting in a just war) when it is performed by an unbeliever from a good intention (such as coming to the assistance of the needy or defending the commonwealth in a just war or supporting oneself by payments received in a just war), as was proved above in the first conclusion [2b(i)]. From this [the response] to the confirmation [for this argument] is clear.

[iv] To the fourth it should be said that it was not permissible for

believers who were subject to Julian the Apostate to wage war against believers whom Julian was fighting unjustly because of their faith. However, in a war that was just on Julian's part and unjust on the part of believers (for example, if believers had unjustly attacked the commonwealth), it would have been permissible for believers and unbelievers to fight against believers. This is presupposed in the proposition, as is clear from the title of the question.

[v] To the fifth it should be said that an excommunicate is prohibited from acting on another's behalf in a lawsuit and consequently no one else is permitted to have an excommunicate act for him in a lawsuit because in doing so he would cause him to transgress a prohibition. But we do not read that in the time of the New Law unbelievers are prohibited from defending a commonwealth of believers, even against believers (if they are unjustly attacking it) or that a ruler who is a believer is prohibited from employing them for this purpose. Nevertheless, if this were prohibited by the church, then it would not be permissible, and therefore the present case is not like [the one outlined in the objection].

[vi, vii] To the sixth it should be said that although unbelievers are wicked in themselves they can nevertheless be permitted to wage war on the authority of a ruler in justly protecting a commonwealth, and they will accordingly be legitimate combatants, as was proved in the first conclusion above [2b(i)]. And from this the response to the seventh argument is also clear.

[viii] To the eighth it should be said that although it is inappropriate for unbelievers to have [authority over] a body of soldiers in terms of the privileges that are granted to soldiers by law, it is nevertheless not inappropriate for them to hold enough authority to protect a commonwealth legitimately, as was said above.

[ix] To the ninth it should be said that, as is generally maintained and as was also touched on in the course of this argument, it is not permissible to make use of the assistance of demons because [a] a demon will only provide assistance to someone who has a tacit or explicit pact with him and shows him some undue honor or reverence, something which cannot take place without the sin of idolatry, and because [b] in giving such assistance the demon is supposed to aim as far as possible at the damnation of the person to whom the assistance is given. A human being can, however, make use of the assistance of an unbeliever without any sin of idolatry, nor is it necessary for an unbeliever in this life to set himself an evil end in every act, as was explained in the first conclusion [2b(i)]. For

this reason, the Devil and unbelievers are not alike here, even though the latter are members of the Devil. Otherwise, the same would have to be said of all wicked people, all of whom have the Devil as their head, as Gregory states in his *Forty Homilies* (16).

[x] To the tenth it should be said that those who have been vanquished by mercenaries are not slaves of the mercenaries but of the person on whose authority the mercenaries are fighting. The mercenaries themselves should be content with their pay, in accordance with the teaching given to them by John the Baptist in Luke 3:14: 'Be content with your pay.' For victory should be ascribed to the ruler at whose command the mercenaries are put into action, rather than to the mercenaries themselves, since the person who does something by means of others seems to do it by himself (for mercenaries pillage on the ruler's authority). Nevertheless, if it is feared that as a result of such a victory unbelievers would usurp lordship over believers, then it would not be permissible for a ruler who is a believer to employ mercenaries who are unbelievers, as was explained in the fifth conclusion [2b(v)].

[xi] To the eleventh it should be said that although unbelievers are wicked with respect to their faith, they can still be morally good with respect to an act that is good in its general character, such as fighting in a just war. As far as such an act is concerned, therefore, it is not a sin to make use of their assistance when there is a pressing necessity, as was explained in the first conclusion [2b(i)].

[xii] To the twelfth it should be said that if there is a fear that any sort of scandal could follow from the admission of such unbelievers (that is, causing some [believers] to fall spiritually into sin), then it is not permissible to use their assistance, as was explained above in the fourth and fifth conclusions [2b(iv), (v)].

[xiii] To the thirteenth it should be said that a war between believer and unbeliever can be just and permissible on the part of the unbeliever, namely, when it is unjust on the part of the believer. {330} This is presupposed in the proposition, as is clear from the title of the question.

[xiv] To the fourteenth it should be said that if there is a pressing necessity, then by law it is permissible in a just war to bring in enemies of the whole multitude against a part of the multitude, as long as they are brought in as warlike mercenaries, not as enemies of the whole multitude. Nor is this to the prejudice of the person who is [in authority] over the whole multitude, but it is for the just defense of a part of the multitude.

[xv] To the fifteenth it should be said that giving unbelievers authority

to fight against believers does not give them the opportunity to take plunder from the believers whom they conquer, because it seems that such plunder ought to belong to the ruler on whose authority they are fighting. They themselves should be content with their pay, as was said above. Nevertheless, if the ruler were to give them authority to take plunder from their enemies, the response to the argument would be that it is a sin to give them the opportunity to take plunder from believers except when the combat is for the sake of the Christian faith or is in some way just on the part of the unbelievers ((*infidelium/fidelium*)).

[xvi] To the sixteenth it should be said that according to a truer opinion, a ruler who brings in an unbelieving doctor to care for his body in a case of necessity does *not* sin, because necessity is not subject to law and renders what is not permissible permissible.

[xvii] To the seventeenth it should be said that the person who brings in water to which he is not entitled sins and, for that reason, deserves to be deprived of the water to which he is entitled as a service from someone else. But bringing in unbelievers in a case of necessity for the just defense of the commonwealth is not a sin, as has been explained above, and for this reason the situations are not alike.

[xviii] To the eighteenth it should be said that if the prohibition forbidding a believer to sell or give weapons to Saracens includes a prohibition on giving them authority to fight against believers who have justly or unjustly attacked a commonwealth of believers (as could very likely happen), then employing mercenaries who are unbelievers ((*infideles/fideles*)) for the just defense of a commonwealth of believers is impermissible – not because it is wicked in itself but because it is prohibited. Alternatively, it should be said that believers are forbidden to provide unbelievers with weapons when it can be presumed that they will attack believers as believers with them. It would not be prohibited, however, if it were assumed that with these weapons they would be able to protect a commonwealth of believers against anyone who unjustly attacked it.

[3b. Replies to the Arguments for the Proposition (1b)]

[i] To the first counter-argument it should be said that there is no necessity on account of which it would be permissible for a ruler to admit mercenaries who are unbelievers if [i] there is a fear that some believers would be turned from the faith by their association with unbelievers, or if [ii] there is a fear that a greater evil than the temporal danger to the common-

wealth could result from such an admission of unbelievers, as was explained above in the fourth and fifth conclusions [2b(iv), (v)].

[ii] To the second it should be said that it is impermissible for clergy to wage war on account of the incongruity of their ministry with the shedding of blood, as is generally maintained, and not on account of their perfection, because we read that particularly perfect men such as Abraham (Genesis 14) and David (1 and 2 Samuel passim) have fought in wars. Moreover, although believers are more perfect than unbelievers, not all believers can be said to be perfect without qualification.

[iii] To the third it should be said that it is more suitable for wicked human beings to be punished in hell by demons than by good angels, [since] in the present life they have conformed themselves to the will of these demons and because in the present life they have even been overcome by them, in accordance with the rule that is written in 2 Peter 2:19: 'A man is a slave to whatever has overcome him.' But [even] unbelievers who are unjustly attacking a commonwealth of believers are more suitably fought off by believers than by unbelievers for the reasons stated above in the second conclusion [2b(ii)].

[iv] To the final [argument] it should be said that as is maintained in Ecclesiasticus 33:14, 'Good is opposed to evil and life opposed to death; so the sinner is opposed to the just man.' Consequently the reverse is also true, namely, that the just man is opposed to the sinner. As a result, a believer sins no less than an unbeliever when he is an unjust aggressor. In fact, according to the Apostle in Hebrews 10:29, a believer sins more: 'How much more severely do you think someone deserves to be punished who has trampled the Son of God underfoot, who has treated as an unholy thing the blood of the testament by which he has been sanctified?' The just ((*iustus/iniustus*)) believer ought to fight against an unjust believer with no less ardor than against an unbeliever, or conversely, than an unbeliever against a believer, for he does not fight against him as against a believer but as against someone who is unjust. Moreover, the ardor of combat should be weighed above all by the end that is aimed at in the fighting. A believer should be presumed to will and care for the good of a commonwealth of believers more than an unbeliever does, as was explained above in the second conclusion [2b(ii)].

13

WILLIAM OF OCKHAM
USING AND ENJOYING

Introduction

William of Ockham was born around 1287, probably in the village of Ockham near London. After entering the Franciscan order he studied at Oxford and completed the requirements for the master's degree in theology. He never became a regent master, however, probably because of the need to defend his teachings on grace, free will, and other topics from charges of heresy brought against them at the papal court in Avignon in the mid-1320s. While Ockham was in Avignon, he concluded that Pope John XXII was himself a heretic on points of doctrine held by most Franciscans at the time to be essential to Christian belief. Ockham fled the curia in 1328 with the Minister General of his order and a few confreres, taking refuge with Ludwig of Bavaria, who was at odds with the papacy over his title as Roman emperor. Ockham then wrote against the teachings of John XXII and John's successor Benedict XII, composed a massive treatise in dialogue form on heresy (with special reference to papal heresy), and discussed at some length the basis and functions of secular and religious governmental institutions. He is usually thought to have died in Munich in 1347 during an outbreak of plague.

Ockham was formally excommunicated for leaving Avignon without permission and was implicitly condemned as a heretic for his opposition to John XXII's bulls against the dominant Franciscan conception of the poverty of Christ, the apostles, and the Franciscans themselves. The doctrines on which he had been examined at Avignon were never officially condemned, however, and his early theological works, commentaries on Aristotle, and logical treatises exercised considerable influence at Oxford and Paris during his own lifetime and for at least the following two centuries.

In the five questions translated here from Ockham's major theological work, his commentary on the *Sentences* of Peter Lombard, the point of departure is Augustine's contention that only God is to be *enjoyed* (where to enjoy is to inhere in something with love for its own sake), while other things are to be *used*. Ockham's account of using and enjoying in Question 1 is distinctive in allowing for a third act, intermediate between loving someone or something as the highest possible good and merely using a person or object for the sake of something else. In this middle act, what is loved (virtue or pleasure, for example) is loved for its own sake (that is, without reference to a higher good) but not as itself either being or not being the highest possible good.

Ockham's celebrated but often misunderstood voluntarism comes to the fore in the thesis of Question 2, that enjoyment is solely a volitional act, not a cognitive one; in the central claim of Question 3, that the will rather than the enjoyed object is the immediate cause of the pleasure involved in enjoyment; in his contention in Question 4 that love of God rather than love of the vision of God is the essence of enjoyment; and in his arguments in Question 6 (against Thomas Aquinas, among others) that the will enjoys God, the ultimate end, contingently and freely, not from a necessity of its own nature.

Although he does not cite it, Ockham clearly had in mind Augustine's address to God at the beginning of the *Confessions*: 'Our hearts are restless until they rest in Thee.' The heart of Ockham's own position as a Christian theologian is indeed that God and only God satisfies or gives rest to the human will. Ockham's fine-grained analyses of the causation of pleasure and God's immediacy as object of love echo this Augustinian text vividly. At the same time, his rigorous critique in Question 4 of Duns Scotus's attempt to derive knowledge of this ultimate end from our purely philosophical or scientific knowledge of human nature leaves both the possibility and the need for such an end uncertain apart from faith. Ockham holds that it cannot be demonstrated 'naturally' that a vision of the divine essence (or anything analogous proposed by various philosophers) is possible to us or, if possible, will be completely satisfying. It is also impossible to demonstrate naturally that nothing 'this side' of God *would* give the will rest.

Then are we free, apart from faith, to set up anything we please as our ultimate end? Yes, according to Ockham, in the sense that nothing prevents us from loving supremely anyone or anything whatever and ordering the rest of our lives accordingly. What our freedom cannot accomplish, however, is to make all such projections of an ultimate end equally rational, equally 'ordinate,' or equally satisfying. These limitations on Ockhamist will (if we should call them limitations) apply apart from faith as well as within it, for the comparative nobility of the objects to which we can devote ourselves and the right ordering of one thing to another are matters to be determined by reason, not by will. The present selection thus illustrates two themes whose interplay characterizes much of Ockham's thought: on one hand the supreme value of loving God and on the other a rational ethics and politics not grounded in religion or speculative metaphysics.

For further reading on this subject, see CHLMP VIII.32, 'Free will and free choice'; VIII.33, 'Thomas Aquinas on human action'; and IX.35, 'Happiness: the perfection of man.' See also Paul Spade, ed., *The Cambridge Companion to Ockham* (Cambridge: Cambridge University Press, 1999), and A. S. McGrade, 'Enjoyment at Oxford after Ockham' in Anne Hudson and Michael Wilks, eds., *From Ockham to Wyclif* (Oxford: Blackwell, 1987), pp. 63–88.

Using and Enjoying

Question 1. Are All Things Other than God and Only Things Other than God to Be Used?

{371} Concerning the first distinction, in which the Master [Peter Lombard] treats enjoying and using, I ask first whether all and only things other than God are to be used.

[1. Preliminary Arguments]

I argue that this is not the case in two ways.

[1a. Arguments that Not Everything Other than God Is to Be Used]

First, that not everything other than God is to be used.

[i] First, as follows. The act of using is not itself to be used. Therefore, not everything other than God is to be used. The inference is clear. I prove the antecedent: If the act of using is itself to be used, it will be either by the same act or by another. Not by the same act, because [one and] the same act is not [both] direct and reflex; nor by another, because then there would be two acts in the will at once.

[ii] Second, as follows. Whatever can be used can be misused. But there are some things that cannot be misused. Therefore, there are some things that cannot be used. The major [premise] is clear, because opposites belong to the same thing [cf. Aristotle, *Categories* 11, 14a15–16]. But using and misusing are contraries. Therefore, what can be used can also be misused. The minor is clear, because the virtues cannot be {372} misused, since according to the Master, no one uses the virtues badly [cf. Augustine, *On Free Choice* II 18–19]. Therefore, no one misuses them.

[iii] Third, as follows. That is to be used which can be referred to God. But there are many things that cannot be referred to God. Therefore, etc. The major is clear, because to use is to love something for the sake of another [cf. Augustine, *On the Trinity* X 11.17]. Consequently, anything that is to be used can be loved for the sake of another. But everything whatever is especially to be loved for God's sake. Therefore, everything that is to be used can be referred to God. The minor is clear, both (i) because second intentions, which cannot ground a real relation to God, cannot be referred to God (similarly, they are not to be loved, since they are not things), and (ii) because evils, which are not to be loved either for themselves or for another, cannot be referred to God.

[1b. Arguments that God Is to Be Used]

Second, I show that God is to be used. This is because everything that can licitly be an object of a 'wanting' kind of love (*amoris concupiscentiae*) is to be used. But God can licitly be loved with wanting love. Therefore, God is to be used. The major is clear, because anything loved with wanting love is loved for the sake of someone or something else loved with amicable love (*amore amicitiae*). For to be loved with wanting love *is* to be loved for the sake of someone or something else loved with amicable love, because to be loved with wanting love is to be wanted (*concupitum*) or desired (*desideratum*) for another. But whoever loves something for the sake of another uses it. Therefore, whoever loves something with wanting love {373} uses it. The minor is clear, because whatever is useful to someone or something that is loved with amicable love can be wanted for him, her, or it and consequently loved with wanting love. But God is useful to a rational creature loved with amicable love. Therefore, God can licitly be wanted for the creature. Therefore, the creature can use God.

[1c] For the Opposite

All and only that which can be ordered to another is to be used. But everything whatever other than God can be ordered to God, who is the end of all, and God cannot be ordered to another. Therefore, etc.

[2. On the Meaning of the Question]

Concerning this question, we first have to explain the meaning of the question; second, [we will speak] to the question.

Concerning the first, it is important to know that the question is not about the using which is the activity of any power whatever (as 'use' is taken when we say 'the use of which,' etc.); neither is it about the using meant when we are said to use powers to elicit the acts of powers, or the using meant when we are said to use habits when we will, or the using meant when we are said to use the act [of will] itself when we will. Rather, the question is about the using meant when we are said to use something as an object. Understanding the question in this way, I say that 'to use' has two senses, broad and strict. Broadly speaking, every act of will is a using, according to blessed Augustine (*On the Trinity* X 11.17). In the strict sense, however, using is an act of will distinct from an enjoying, and the question is meant more particularly in this sense. {374}

Concerning this we have to see first how an act of using is distinguished from an act of enjoying and, second, what the object of an act of using is.

[2a. How Is an Act of Using Distinguished from an Act of Enjoying?]

Concerning the first, it is important to know that someone can take something into the faculty of will in two ways: for its own sake or for the sake of something else. Something [A] presented to the faculty of will by the understanding is taken into the will in the first way when it *would* be taken into the faculty of will even if it were presented without anything else. Something [B] is taken into the faculty of will in the second way when it is taken after something else [A] has been presented, so that if [A] were not presented to the will or were not taken into the faculty of will, [B] would not be taken into the faculty of will. [I] The first act – when, namely, the will elicits an act concerning something in such a way that it would elicit the same act even on the assumption that nothing else was shown to it — is *nonreferring*. An example would be if God were shown to someone, nothing else had been shown, and the individual sought God. [II] The second act — when an act would not be elicited about one thing if nothing else were shown to the faculty of will or if nothing else were taken up into it — is *referring*. For example, someone seeks a bitter potion that he would not seek if he were not seeking health. But an act can be nonreferring in two ways. The object {375} may be accepted [by the will] [Ia] as the highest that could possibly be presented to it (that is, as to be loved supremely by it); or else [Ib] absolutely — that is, it may be accepted and taken into the will neither as highest nor as not highest. The first act [Ia] — when something is accepted as highest without qualification — is an act of enjoying. The second act [Ib], properly speaking, is neither an enjoying nor a using. The third act [II] is a using in the most proper sense.

[2b. On the Object of Use]

Concerning the second, I maintain that the object of use in general (considering both ordinate and inordinate use) is anything whatever, created or uncreated. This is clear, because whatever the will can refer to something else is an object of use. But the will from its freedom can refer anything whatever to something else. Therefore, it can use anything whatever. The major is obvious. The minor is clear, because when anything whatever has been shown to it, it can love something else more, and consequently can love the first thing for the sake of the other.

A second thesis is that God is not an object of ordinate use, because if he were, he would be an object of either ordinate [referring] willing or willing against (*volitionis aut nolitionis*). Not of willing against, because no one can ordinately hate God. Nor of [referring] willing, because then something could ordinately be loved more than God. Similarly, an ultimate end is not referrable to anything else. But God is without qualification an ultimate end.

A third thesis is that everything other than God can be an object of ordinate use. This is proved, because everything other than {376} what is supremely accepted can be taken into the faculty of will for the sake of what is supremely accepted. But God is ordinately supremely accepted. Therefore, everything other than God can ordinately be taken into the faculty of will for God's sake, and consequently everything else can ordinately be used. The major is clear, because everything other than what is supremely accepted is either good or bad. If good, it can be loved for the sake of what is supremely accepted. If bad, it can ordinately be willed against by the will for the sake of what is supremely accepted. Therefore, everything other than what is supremely accepted can ordinately be taken into the faculty of will for its sake. Therefore, etc.

[2c. Three Difficulties about the Preceding]

There are three difficulties about the preceding. The first is about the middle act [Ib]. Is such an act possible, and is it necessarily good or bad?

The second is about the act of using in its most proper sense. Is it numerically one act without qualification, or does it include several numerically distinct acts, one with respect exclusively to the end and another with respect exclusively to what is for the sake of the end?

The third difficulty has been touched on in the first argument at the beginning (1a[i]). Is the act of using in which one uses one's own proper act of using numerically the same act [as the proper act of using, i.e., the act of using an object] or another one?

[2d. Solution of the First Difficulty]

Concerning the first I maintain that there is such a middle act, in which something is neither loved as an unqualifiedly ultimate end nor actually referred to something else. {377}

It may be said [against this thesis]: 'If it is not loved for the sake of something else, therefore for itself. But every such thing is loved as an ultimate end.' I answer that such a thing is loved for its own sake, because if nothing else were shown to the will it would still be loved. Yet [it is] not [loved] as an ultimate end, at least positively, because something is loved as an ultimate end when it is accepted as being loved more, or as *to be* loved more, than anything else, whatever might be shown to [the will] as something to be loved. But not everything loved for its own sake is loved in that way, as an ultimate end. For someone apprehending virtue and not thinking of happiness seeks virtue and yet does not do so for the sake of happiness. Nevertheless, such an individual does not seek virtue as something to be sought more or to be sought less than anything else that might be shown to him. So it is concerning what is loved, and so there is a middle act, as I have said.

The Philosopher testifies to this in *Ethics* I, where he wants to maintain that some things are choice-worthy for the sake of other things, something exclusively for its own sake and in no way for the sake of anything else, and something both for its own sake and for the sake of something else. Hence in *Ethics* I 8 (I 5, 1097a30–b6) he says the following. 'Now we call what is worthy of pursuit for itself more perfect than what is for the sake of something else, and what is never choice-worthy for the sake of something else we call [more perfect] than those things that are choice-worthy both for the sake of this and for themselves. And [we call] perfect without qualification what is always choice-worthy for itself and never {378} for the sake of something else. Now happiness especially seems to be like this, for we always choose it for its own sake and never for the sake of something else. On the other hand, we do indeed choose honor, pleasure, understanding, and all the virtues for their own sake, for if nothing came of them we would still choose each of them, but we also choose them for the sake of happiness, looking to be happy in so doing. No one chooses happiness for the sake of these, however, or for the sake of anything else at all.' From this it is clear that something can be willed when nothing else is presented to the will, so that it is not then chosen positively for the sake of something else, while nevertheless not being an ultimate end but being choice-worthy for the sake of another end.

It may be said [as a further objection] that when something which is a means to an end is loved but not *as* a means to the end, the act is bad. I answer that an act relating to something that is a means to an end can be non-evil even if the object is not positively referred to, or loved in relation to, the end. This is especially so if the end is not apprehended.

It may be said [as a third objection] that every lack of a circumstance required for a good act makes an act evil. But the end is a circumstance required for a morally good act. Therefore, whenever it is lacking the act will be evil. But it is lacking in the case proposed. Therefore, etc.

I answer that not every lack of a circumstance required for a morally good act makes an act evil or a sin. For then ignorance would never excuse, yet according to learned teachers and saints ignorance sometimes excuses totally. But when some circumstance is lacking that the individual eliciting the act is at that time obligated to observe, then the act is evil. If, however, the individual is not at the time obligated to observe that circumstance the act is not evil. So it is here. The individual in this case is not obligated to {379} will what he wills for the sake of [something else as] an end. Yet if someone in this situation elicited an act that set the object up as an end in relation to everything else, it would be a sin.

[2e. Possible Solution of the Second Difficulty]

Concerning the second difficulty, it could seem to some that there is another act [involved in the act of using as described above] – other both numerically and in kind – so that there cannot be such an act of using without there being distinct really different acts.

[i] This can be argued first as follows. When something that is a means to an end is loved for the sake of the end, both the end and the means to it are loved. But the end and the means to the end cannot be loved in one act. Therefore, there are several acts here. The major is clear, because it is certain that what is a means to an end is loved, for otherwise there would not be an act of using, since there is not a willing of it. It is clear that the end would also be loved, because what causes [something in another has] it more [in itself] [cf. Aristotle, *Posterior Analytics* I 2, 72a29–30]. Therefore, if what is a means to an end is loved for the sake of the end, it is necessary that the end be loved more. The minor is proved, because the end is loved by an act of enjoying, because it is loved for itself. That which is a means to an end is loved by an act of using. Therefore, if they were numerically one act, the numerically identical act would be both an act of using and an act of enjoying. The consequent is false, because they are opposite kinds [of acts].

[ii] Second, it can be argued as follows. If there were only numerically one act, the act of using would be more perfect than the act of enjoying. The consequent is false, therefore [also] the antecedent. The falsity of the consequent is clear, because [if it were true] there would be an act of will more perfect than enjoyment of the divine essence and {380} consequently [more perfect] than blessedness. The inference is clear, because when the act of a power relates equally perfectly to several objects that act is more perfect than an act that relates to fewer [objects]. But, on the assumption being considered, enjoyment or an act of enjoying would relate only to the end, [whereas] an act of using would relate to both the end and the means (and it would relate to the end equally perfectly as the act of enjoying does, because one does not love God less as a result of loving a creature for God's sake). Therefore, the act of using the creature would be more perfect than the act of enjoying God.

[iii] Third, as follows. There cannot be two perfect acts in the will at one and the same time with respect to the same object. But if we posit a meritorious act in the will, an act of loving God for God's sake, the understanding can then offer the will something that can be ordered to

and loved for the sake of God, which the will can [then] love for God's sake. And it is not necessary for the will to let go of the first meritorious act. Then, therefore, that second elicited act will terminate exclusively in the creature [as its object]. Otherwise there would be two acts in the will with respect to God at once.

[iv] Fourth, as follows. Just as one can love something for the sake of something [else] one loves, so one can detest something for the sake of something one loves. Therefore, if the act of loving something for the sake of something else is numerically one act having both as objects, for the same reason the act of detesting something for the sake of something else (or for the sake of one's love of the other), is one act having both for an object. But this is impossible, because then an act of loving and an act of hating would be numerically one act. The last inference is clear, because if the act terminates in the end [as an object], the end is either loved in that act or it is hated. It is not hated, {381} therefore it is loved. Therefore, the act is an act of loving. But because something is hated in that act it is also an act of hating. Therefore, etc.

[v] Fifth, as follows. The numerically identical act cannot be both intense and weak, perfect and imperfect. But anyone who loves something for the sake of something else — that is, for the sake of an end — loves the end more intensely and more perfectly while loving the means to the end more weakly and more imperfectly. Therefore, both are not loved in the same act.

Confirmation [of the last argument]: If both were loved in the same act, one would therefore meritoriously love a creature by as perfect an act (and consequently as much) as one loved God, and so it would not be the case that God is to be loved supremely and above all, which is absurd.

[vi] Sixth, as follows. 'Choice is not will, because choice regards means to an end, will regards the end,' *Ethics* III (2, 1111b26–27). But if they were the same act, choice, from the very fact that it relates to something for the sake of an end, would relate to the end.

[vii] Moreover, just as the understanding cannot understand several things [at once], so the will cannot will several things [at once]. Therefore, there is neither one act [regarding means and end] nor are both willed at once.

[2f. Tenable Solution to the Second Difficulty]

Notwithstanding these arguments, it seems tenable that there can be two acts [involved in using] and that there can be one act.

This can be explained [as follows]. The will has the same relation to ends and means as the understanding has to principles and conclusions. But the understanding can know a conclusion in an act distinct from the act in which a principle is cognized, and it can [also] {382} cognize both in a single act. In the same way, therefore, the will can have distinct acts with respect to end and means, and it can have one act with respect to both. The major is clear in itself, because the will can do no less with its objects than the understanding can with its objects. The first part of the minor is clear, because the awareness of a principle causes awareness of the conclusion. But a cause is really distinct from its effect. Therefore, there can be an act in which the principle is cognized that is other than the act in which the conclusion is cognized. The second part of the minor is clear, because it no more conflicts with the understanding to understand one discourse or one inference in a single act than one proposition. But it can understand one proposition in a single act. This is clear from what the Philosopher says in *De anima* III (6, 430a26–b21), where he divides the activity of the understanding into activity with respect to simple and composite [objects]. If the division is correct, there will therefore be one [act of] understanding with respect to a complex [i.e., a proposition], just as there is with respect to an incomplex [i.e., a term].

Moreover, in *De anima* III (c. 2) [Aristotle says that] the common sense cognizes differences among the various sense objects of the same sense. Therefore, [it does this] either in a single {383} act or in distinct ones. If in one act, therefore much more can both understanding and will have a single act relating to several objects. If in distinct acts, a particular sense can do this. Therefore, it is not necessary to posit a common sense for that activity.

It may be said [as an objection to the preceding] that if there are distinct acts [involved in using], then neither of them will be an act of using. Not the first, obviously, nor the second. Proof: If an act is not an act of using apart from another act from which it can be separated, it will not be an act of using even when joined with the other act. This is because the numerically identical act is not made into an act of using by another act if it was not an act of using beforehand (or conversely). But an act that terminates exclusively in a means to an end could exist apart from any act relating to the end, because the will can freely bear on any object whatever that is shown to it, even when no other absolute thing is present ((*absoluto posito/ablato* [var.])). But if this is the case, it will not be an act of using, because [the object] is not loved for the sake of something else. Neither, therefore, will it be an act of using when it exists together with an act relating to the end. This [reasoning] is confirmed: An act that terminates exclusively in one [object] and can exist apart from anything else does not tend toward one thing for the sake of something else. Therefore, neither is it an act of using, tending toward one thing for the sake of something else, if it does not tend toward the something else.

To this it can be answered that, speaking strictly about the act of using, an act terminating exclusively in something that is not supremely accepted (not accepted, that is, as the highest [possible good]) is not an act of using. Hence a threefold distinction can be made about 'act of using.' In one sense [an act of using is] any act that is not an enjoying; in another sense, an act terminating in some object, when the act is caused by an act of enjoying relating to something; in a third sense, it is taken to be an act that, {384} existing as one [act], tends toward one thing for the sake of something else. In the first sense the act in question [i.e., an act terminating exclusively in something that is not accepted as the highest possible good] is an act of using whether it is joined with another act or not. In the second sense that act is not an act of using except when it is caused by another act joined with it. When 'act of using' is taken in that sense the numerically identical act can at first be an act of using and can later, even while it remains [the same act], not be an act of using. This is because it can at first be caused by an act relating to an end or by an act of enjoying, and later, if the act of enjoying has ceased, the will can continue that numerically [same] act. For example, if someone first loves a potion simply because of loving health, then that love of the potion will be an act of using, because it is caused by another act; but if it is continued from the will's freedom even when health is not actually loved, then it will not be an act of using, because then it is not caused or conserved by the act relating to health. 'Act of using' is taken most strictly in the third sense, and here the same [act] always relates to different [objects]. And so I maintain that it is not inappropriate for there to be a numerically single act relating both to the ultimate end and to things that are means to the end.

[2g. Replies to the Arguments for the Possible Solution to the Second Difficulty (2e)]

[i] To the first argument to the contrary I reply that when [terms] signify one thing and connote different things, then, although verbally they may seem different or opposite and imply opposition with respect to the same thing, they can nevertheless apply to the same [directly signified thing]

with respect to different [connoted things]. This is the case, for example, with the natural and free and with the contingent and necessary, which cannot apply to the same thing with respect to the same thing, yet it is not inappropriate for them to apply {385} to the same thing with respect to different things. For example, everyone agrees that the [divine] will is a principle producing the Holy Spirit necessarily and is nevertheless a principle producing a creature contingently. So it is in the case at hand. The same act can be an act of enjoying with respect to the ultimate end and yet be an act of using regarding means to the end. This is clear, because the act of loving God is an enjoying with respect to the divine essence, and yet the creature is not enjoyed but used. We shall be able to say the same in the case at hand. Similarly, in one act the understanding 'knows' (*scit*) a conclusion and consequently in that act it not only understands the conclusion but also the terms of the conclusion, and yet in that act it knows the conclusion and it does not by that act know any incomplex [i.e., any term] of the conclusion. So the same act is called knowing (*scientia*) with respect to the conclusion [cf. Aristotle, *Posterior Analytics* I 2 and *Nicomachean Ethics* VI 3] while it is not called knowing with respect to the term but [in that respect] it can be described in some other way. Therefore, it is not inappropriate for the numerically identical act of will to be given different descriptions from having different objects, so that in that act the will may be said to enjoy one object and use another object. Similarly, there is sometimes an act of using without any act of enjoying.

[ii] I concede to the second that it is not inappropriate for an act of using to be more perfect than an act of enjoying, when the act of using is also an act of enjoying another ((*alio/illo* [var.])) object. Hence it seems that an act in which a creature is loved exclusively for God's sake is more perfect than an act in which God exclusively is loved. This is so if the act is equally intense [in the two cases as regards loving God], which does not always happen. Perhaps, however, beatific enjoyment in heaven (*patria*) will arise exclusively from God alone and relate to God alone {386} but will nevertheless be more perfect than any possible act relating to both God and creature, for an act relating to God and creature can be elicited by the created will, whereas the other [i.e., the beatific act as here imagined] cannot.

[iii] I concede to the third that the will can have two perfect acts relating to the same object at the same time, especially when the object is the total object of one act and a partial object of the other. So it is in the present case. When an end is loved exclusively for its own sake then it is the total

object of the act, because the act terminates in nothing except the end. When, however, the means to an end is loved for the sake of the end, the end is then only a partial object. In this way (as I said earlier) when one understands first an incomplex and later a complex, it will be possible for the first awareness to remain along with the second. Otherwise, when terms have been apprehended the understanding could not at once, in the same instant, form a proposition from them, and consequently the apprehension of terms would not be *per se* presupposed for composition and division [i.e., for forming affirmative and negative propositions], because nothing is presupposed *per se* for any effect unless it can remain with that effect. Because of this the Philosopher holds that privation is a principle only *per accidens*. (I will show elsewhere how this is to be understood.)

[iv] It can be conceded to the fourth that the numerically identical act can be described as detestation or an act of detesting with respect to one [object] and {387} an act of loving with respect to another when in a single act I detest something for the sake of something else that is loved in the same act.

It may be said [in objection to the preceding] that willing and willing against are opposite acts. But detesting is a willing against and loving is a willing. Therefore, etc.

It can be answered that just as an act of loving and an act of hating are not opposed except when the same thing is loved and hated (because when one thing is loved and another hated, they are not opposed), so we have to say about willing and willing against and using and enjoying. According to the particular connotations involved, these cannot apply to the same [act] with respect to the same [object], although they can apply to the same [act] with respect to different [objects].

[v] I concede to the fifth that the same act cannot be both intense and weak, yet in the same act one thing can be loved intensely and something [else] weakly. For example, God loves himself with the greatest intensity and yet loves every creature whatever with less than the greatest intensity.

In reply to the confirmation, I deny the inference: 'He loves the means to the end in an equally intense act, therefore equally intensely.' The reason in all of these cases is that 'to love equally intensely' connotes more than an equally intense act. How this ought {388} to be understood will be made clear elsewhere. This answer is confirmed: God may be more accepted than all other things in a single weak act, and yet, when this has been assumed, it is possible that an act relating to a creature may be more intense. So 'It is loved in as intense an act, therefore it is loved as much' does not follow.

[vi] I reply to the sixth that what the Philosopher means is that choice is not will because there is will with respect to something with respect to which — as a total object — there is not choice. Similarly, one can will impossibles, but choice does not exist with respect to them. Hence what is called will relates to one thing only and not to one thing for another; choice, however, relates to something already willed [i.e., to an end, for which means are chosen].

[vii] To the seventh it is commonly said that the understanding cannot understand many things at once *as* many but [that it can understand] many things as one. In the same way [on this view], the will cannot bear on many things as many but on many as one. Hence it is said specifically with regard to the present question that the will can bear on things that are means to an end either as they are ordered to the end, in which case the same act of will relates to the end and to the means, or it can bear on them as they are particular things desirable in themselves, in which case the will bears on them in distinct acts. Hence it is said that in the first way of bearing on those things, the end is a formal object and, as it were, the reason for bearing on them, while that which is a means to the end is a material object, and that [together] they are one object, just as light and color are one object. {389}

But that reply is not valid, because something is as distinctly understood when it is understood along with another as when it is understood without the other. And it is understood thus under a concept proper to it, because it can be understood under its proper defining concept, in which case it is not understood inasmuch as it is one but rather (frequently) inasmuch as it is diverse [when the defining concept involves an analysis into essential parts].

Moreover, if the end were the formal object and the means to the end the material object, then the act would not be varied as a result of varying the means, because an act is not varied by varying its material object. But this is false, because then it would be numerically the same act to love God for God's sake and to love a creature for God's sake.

On this account I say to the argument that (as will be made clear elsewhere) the understanding can understand many things both in one act and in distinct acts. If it is asked whether it understands them inasmuch as they are many or as one, I say that it understands them neither 'as' many nor 'as' one. Hence neither of these is true with [such] a qualifying note.

[2h. On the Third Difficulty]

About the third difficulty, [the solution] will be made clear in another question. Therefore, let it be deferred until then.

[3. Replies to the Preliminary Arguments]

[1a(i)] To the first argument at the beginning I reply that (as will be made clear later) the act of using is itself used in an act other than that in which an object is used. And I concede the conclusion that there can be two acts of willing in the will at once.

[1a(ii)] To the second I reply that something can be used or misused in two ways: either as the object of an act of will or as {390} a habit inclining one to an act proper to itself. (There are still other ways of using or misusing, but they are not relevant.) In the first way I say that whatever can be used can be misused but not conversely. This is because using in this sense (where use is contrasted with misuse) is using ordinately. Now it is possible to misuse God but there is no way in which it is possible to use God, because no one can use God ordinately. Yet whatever *can* be used ordinately can be misused, because anything that can be an object of ordinate use can be an object of misuse. And when it is said that the virtues cannot be misused, I say that it is possible to misuse the virtues as objects. For someone who desired charity for itself as an ultimate, supremely loved end would be misusing charity, and similarly for the other virtues. According to some [e.g., Duns Scotus], the first angel was misusing blessedness in that way, by seeking to have it inordinately and for its own sake as an ultimate end.

In the second way charity itself cannot be misused, because it does not incline to an evil act. This is what the Master and Augustine mean. Nevertheless, any absolute reality in any virtue distinct from charity can be misused, as will be made clear in the third book. And when it is said that contraries belong to the same thing, I say that contraries belong to the same *subject*, and hence in whatever {391} subject there can be use, there can also be a contrary misuse and conversely. But [contraries] do not occur with regard to the same effect or, always, with regard to the same object. Hence, however much misuse there can be with regard to God, it is not necessary that there be a possible contrary use regarding the same [object]. Similarly, although it is possible to use a habit with regard to some effect, it is not necessary that we be able to misuse the same habit with respect to some effect, because [in some cases] the habit does not have any bad effect.

It may be said [in objection to the preceding] that it follows from this that it is possible to use God ordinately. This is because ordinate use and misuse are contraries, but there can be misuse in the will with respect to God. Therefore, there can be ordinate use in the will with respect to God, for in whatever subject it is possible for one of [a pair of] contraries to exist, the other can exist.

I answer that misuse of God does not have any ordinate use contrary to it, because every using of God is inordinate and is thus a misuse. Hence it is not necessary that they be able to exist in the same subject, because they are not possible in the nature of things. Still, we have to concede that some usings with respect to God are contraries, but each will be a misusing.

[1a(iii)] I reply to the third that all things can be referred to God, because all are to be taken into the faculty of will for God's sake. To the first proof I say that second intentions can be referred to God, because someone can, for God's honor, will them to be and to be understood in the way they are. When it is said that they cannot ground a real relation, I concede it, but it does not follow from this that they cannot be referred to God. Hence, when {392} someone desires a future potion for the sake of health or health for the sake of God, those things are referred, because they are desired for the sake of another, and yet they do not ground a real relation, because they do not exist. The same can be said here. And when it is said further that they [second intentions] are not things [*res*], therefore they are not referred to God, I deny the inference (following the opinion asserting that they have only objective being), because beings of reason can be referred to God on this basis alone, that they can be accepted for God's sake as being in the way that they are. To the second proof [which denied that evils can be used] I say that for something to be ordered or referred to God can be understood in two ways, either as being willed for God's sake or as being willed against for God's sake. In the first way there is no use of the evil of guilt, because it is not to be willed for God's sake. In the second way there is a use of the evil of guilt, because it is to be detested for God's sake. Hence with respect to anything whatever the will can have some act – of willing or willing against or accepting or bearing – that it would not have unless God had been shown to it by the understanding.

It may be said [in objection to the preceding]: 'The object of an act of using is useful. But not everything other than God is useful, as for example evils, second intentions, and things of this sort. Therefore, not everything [other than God] is the object of an act of using.'

I answer that not every object of an act of using is useful, because properly speaking the useful is that which is to be sought so that something may result or so that something may be conserved. But the object of an act of using is anything that can be taken into the faculty {393} of will, by any act whatever, for the sake of another. [What is required is] that, unless the other were presented to it ((omit *vel . . . voluntatis* [var.])) (concerning which it also has some act), the will would not elicit such an act concerning [the object], whether an act of willing or an act of willing against or detesting or suffering or any other [volitional act] whatever.

[1b] To the fourth I reply that the will does not always use what it loves with wanting love. When it loves exclusively with wanting love and not [also] with amicable love, *then* it uses [what it loves]. The will does not love God exclusively with wanting love, however, but also with amicable love. And when it is said that to use something is to love it for the sake of another, I answer that this is true when the thing is loved exclusively for the sake of the other. This is what was said before: Properly speaking, something is used when the will elicits an act concerning it that it would not elicit unless something else were presented to it concerning which it [also] has an act.

Question 2. Is Enjoying Solely an Act of Will?

{394} Second, I ask about enjoying; and first, whether enjoying is solely an act of will.

[1. Preliminary Arguments]

That [it is] not [is argued as follows].

[1a. Arguments that Enjoying Is an Intellectual Act]

[i] The best and pleasantest act exists in the noblest power. But that act [enjoying] is best and pleasantest, and according to the Philosopher in

Ethics X (c. 7) the intellect is the noblest power, because he places happiness in it. Therefore, enjoying is in the intellective power.

[ii] Second, as follows. Enjoyment (*fruitio*) is formally [the same as] blessedness, because it is so called from 'fruit,' which is something ultimate, and blessedness is like this. But according to the Philosopher in *Ethics* X (c. 7) and I (7, 1098a15–17), blessedness is an activity of intellect. Therefore, enjoying will be an activity of intellect.

Confirmation: Natural and supernatural blessedness ought to be placed in the same power. But natural blessedness is placed in the intellect, according to the Philosopher. Therefore, supernatural blessedness is also. {395}

[1b] For the Opposite

According to blessed Augustine, to enjoy is to inhere in something with love for its own sake (*frui est amore inhaerere alicui propter se*) (*On Christian Doctrine* I 4). But loving pertains solely to the will. Therefore, etc.

[2. Reply to the Question]

Concerning this question, we first have to show that enjoying is solely an act of will. Second, we have to see how the will is related to that act.

[2a. Enjoying Is Solely an Act of Will]

The first cannot be proved decisively, since words are conventional, and hence they are to be used as their authors use them, but [the relevant] authors hold that enjoying is solely an act of will.

[i] This is clear, because according to them [e.g., Duns Scotus and William of Ware], 'enjoying' (*frui*) is so called from fruit. But fruit is something ultimate. Therefore, enjoying will be an ultimate act. But an act of will is ultimate.

[ii] Again, only in an act of will is there the greatest rest (*actus solius voluntatis est maxime quietativus*). But enjoying is the act in which there is the greatest rest. Therefore, etc. The major is clear, because the greatest rest is in that act which is either pleasure or the direct cause of pleasure. But only an act of will is of this sort, because if pleasure is in another

power or exists without an act of will, then, given an equal act of the other power there would be equal pleasure, or at least some pleasure. The consequent is false. It is clear from experience that someone who understands something intensely but does not love it will not take pleasure in it, and will rather be distressed if he hates it. {396}

This is confirmed, because distress belongs solely to the will, because according to blessed Augustine (*On the City of God* XIV 6) it arises when things happen to us that we do not want to happen. Therefore, the contrary pleasure will belong solely to the will, since contraries are in the same subject. Therefore, etc.

[iii] This is also clear from blessed Augustine in *On Christian Doctrine* I (4): 'To enjoy is to inhere in something with love for its own sake.' But it pertains to the will alone to inhere in something through love. Therefore, etc. Again, [Augustine] *On the Trinity* X 10: 'We enjoy things cognized in which the pleased will finds rest.'

Nevertheless, it is important to understand that when I say that enjoying is solely an act of will, I do not mean to deny that properly speaking and in virtue of [the strict meaning] of the terms (*de virtute sermonis*) enjoying is an act of the intellect, for as I will show elsewhere intellect and will are entirely the same [thing]. Hence whatever is in the intellect is in the will and conversely. So enjoying is in the intellect and is an act of intellect from the fact that it is an act of the will. But I mean to say that enjoying is not understanding or knowing, and so on about other acts that are in any way called cognitive acts. And that is what I mean when I say (conforming to the way others speak) that enjoying is not an act of intellect but of will (and the same goes for similar statements).

[2b. How Is the Will Related to the Act of Enjoying?]

Concerning the second, I say that 'enjoying' has many senses. In a broad sense it means any act in which something is taken into the faculty of will {397} for its own sake as supreme, whether it be present or absent or possessed or not possessed. In this sense we are said to enjoy now, in this life, when we love God for himself as supreme and above all things. In another sense, it is taken strictly for the ultimate beatific act, in which the blessed are said to enjoy in heaven. We are not said to enjoy God now in that sense.

On the basis of this distinction, I maintain, first, that when an enjoyable object has been shown to the will by the intellect, whether clearly or obscurely, whether in particular or in general, the will can actively elicit an act of enjoyment with respect to the object by its own natural powers. Second, [I maintain] that with respect to the beatific act the will is in no way active but only passive.

[2b(i) First Thesis]

The first thesis is clear as to its first part (that if an object is shown obscurely and in general the will can elicit an act of enjoyment – that is, love the object supremely and beyond all else). This is clear because the will can conform itself to a right dictate of reason. But the intellect can rightly dictate that such an object should be loved in that way. Therefore, the will can conformably elicit such an act.

The other part [of the first thesis] (that the will is capable of an act of enjoyment in this way when the object is seen clearly) is clear, because the will can do no less with regard to a more perfectly known object than with regard to one that is known less perfectly. But the will can elicit such an act with regard to an obscurely known object. Therefore, much more [can it do so] with regard to one that is known clearly. {398}

This is confirmed by the preceding reasoning, because the will can conform itself to a dictate of reason. But when an object is seen clearly, it may be dictated or can be dictated [by reason] that that object should be loved supremely. Therefore, etc.

Moreover, every free power is capable of some act regarding an object shown to it. Therefore, the will is capable of some act regarding God when God is seen clearly. And it does not necessarily have an inordinate act. Therefore, by its own natural powers it can have an ordinate act, though not a meritorious one. But it would not be an ordinate act unless it tended toward God for himself. Therefore, etc.

[2b(ii). Second Thesis]

The second thesis (that the beatific act of enjoyment does not arise from the will actively) can be persuasively argued as follows. First, when some things are essentially ordered and are in the same genus, if the first and less perfect does not arise actively from any creature, either totally or partially, but from God alone, the supreme and ultimate [thing in the genus] will come actively from God alone. But the vision of the divine essence and enjoyment (which is the beatific act) have such an order and are in the same genus, because both are supernatural. Therefore, since the bare vision comes actively from God alone, the enjoyment will come actively from God alone.

Nevertheless, because this could be denied about both, I argue as follows. First, when any two things are supernatural, if the less perfect, {399} because of its perfection, can be created only by God, the more perfect will also be creatable only by God. But the habit of charity and the light of glory (if it is posited) are supernatural and are less perfect than the supernatural acts corresponding to them, and according to the common way of speaking they come actively from God alone. Therefore, much more [will] the acts also [come actively from God alone]. Therefore, etc.

Moreover, I argue specifically about the act of will as follows. Every power that acts freely and contingently can cease from its own act by its own absolute power (and this mediately or immediately, which I say because of an objection to be brought up against a certain opinion in another question). But the will acts freely and contingently with respect to any object whatever. Therefore, simply by its own power it can cease from its own act. Therefore, the will could simply make itself not blessed, and so the will of the blessed would not be confirmed in good (as the will of the wayfarer is not) [which is an unacceptable conclusion]. The major is obvious. The minor is clear, because the will cannot be necessitated with respect to anything.

Moreover, it is no more ((*magis/minus*)) repugnant to the will of the blessed to receive the beatific act from God alone than for the will of the damned to receive an act of will from God alone. But the damned are not active with respect to any act of will, because, if they were, they could bring it about that they were without that act and consequently without distress and consequently without punishment. (This reasoning will be made clear in the second [book].)

I do not offer these arguments as irrefutable, because a way of replying to them will be given in various questions afterwards. {400} Nevertheless, I hold this side as more probable, that with respect to blessedness, whether of intellect or will, God alone is the effective cause, and this because of the nobility of blessedness itself.

[2b(iia). Objections to the Second Thesis]

Against the preceding it can be argued as follows.

[i] First, every act of will with respect to God clearly seen is beatific,

because every such act brings rest supremely. But it has been conceded that when the object has been seen clearly the will can enjoy God actively. Therefore, it will be able to be active with respect to beatific enjoyment.

[ii] Moreover, it is more noble to act than to undergo. Therefore, this can belong to the will with respect to what maximally perfects it. But it is maximally perfected through the beatific act. Therefore, it ought to be active with respect to that act.

[iii] Moreover, reward corresponds with merit. Therefore, reward and merit belong to the same thing and in the same way. But the will merits, and actively merits. Therefore, it will be rewarded, and actively rewarded.

[2b(iib). Replies to the Preceding]

[i] To the first of those I reply that such a person seeing the divine essence can elicit an act of loving God, but it will not be beatific nor will the greatest rest be in it, because there will be more rest in another [act] that is more perfect.

It may be said [in objection to this reply] that then the blessed would always have two acts of enjoying God, one from God alone and another actively from themselves. The consequent seems unacceptable. The inference is clear, because the will {401} of the blessed is bound to love God as much as it can and in every way that it can. Therefore, if it can be active in any enjoyment, it elicits it unless it is impeded. But it is not impeded by the beatific act, because those acts are distinct in species and are not contrary, hence one will not impede the other.

To this it can be said, conceding [the inference], that it is not unacceptable to conclude that the blessed have two acts with respect to God, one from God alone and another from God and from themselves. Whoever wishes to deny this can say, however, that the [second] act will not [in fact] be elicited by the will, because God does not wish to cooperate with it in producing that act.

[ii] To the second I reply that although acting is nobler in general than undergoing, because the most noble agent is nobler than the most noble patient, yet some undergoing is nobler than some acting, both with respect to the same thing and with respect to different things. This is clear with respect to the same thing, because if intellect and sense were exclusively passive, undergoing these cognitions would still be nobler than bringing them about. Hence the receiving power would be nobler than the effecting object, because intellection itself would be nobler. It is also clear with

respect to different things, because it is nobler to receive an intellection than to produce heat. On this account I say that it in no way conflicts with the nobility of the will to be exclusively passive with respect to the beatific act.

If it is said that it at least follows that the will is imperfect, I answer that the will is not perfect without qualification, but it has some imperfections.

[iii] To the third I reply that the argument is more to the opposite effect, because merit and reward ought to be opposites {402} as regard the activity of the one who merits and the one who rewards. It is in the nature of merit that it come actively from the one who merits, but it is more in the nature of reward that it exist passively in the one rewarded, because reward ought to come actively from the one who rewards. Now something may indeed occur actively in the one rewarded, but it does not have the nature of reward, since if [activity] were *totally* from the one rewarded, it would not have the nature of reward. Hence I answer that to merit and to be rewarded do belong to the same thing, but it will merit actively and be rewarded passively, and the reward will come actively from the one from whom it is merited, namely, from the one who rewards.

[3. Replies to the Preliminary Arguments]

[1a(i)] To the first argument at the beginning, I concede that enjoying exists in the noblest power. When it is said that intellect is the noblest power, I concede it. Similarly, the will is the noblest power, because that power which is intellect and that which is will are in no way distinct either in reality or in concept, as will be explained elsewhere, because those are names *signifying* the same thing, precisely *connoting* distinct *acts*, namely, the acts of understanding and willing.

Yet if they were distinguished, I would maintain that the volitional power would be nobler. Thomas says this, although elsewhere he may have said the opposite. Thus in the first book [of his commentary on the *Sentences*], first distinction, first question, he says the following. 'The supreme part [of the soul] has intellect and will, of which intellect is higher in order and will in perfection. {403} There is a similar order in habits and also in acts, namely, vision and love. Now as to perfection "enjoyment" names the highest activity.' So, as if forced by the truth, he says here that enjoyment, which is an act of will, is nobler than the act of intellect, although in many places elsewhere, following the errors of his own head, he says the opposite [cf. *Summa theologiae*, I, q. 82, art. 3; *Summa contra gentiles*, III, q. 26].

[1a(ii)] To the second I reply that one part of blessedness is in intellect, another in will. About this elsewhere. To the confirmation I reply that natural blessedness, if there were such a thing, would be in the will just as it would be in the intellect. Nor, when he places it in the intellect, does the Philosopher deny that happiness is in the will, because it does not consist exclusively in one act but in two.

Question 3. Is Enjoyment a Quality Really Distinct from Pleasure?

Second [with regard to enjoying], I ask whether enjoyment is a quality really distinct from pleasure.

[1. Preliminary Arguments]

That it is not [is argued as follows].

[1a. Arguments that Enjoyment Is Not Distinct from Pleasure]

[i] Because the will is ultimately at rest through enjoyment. But the will cannot be ultimately at rest except through pleasure. Therefore, enjoyment is pleasure. The major is clear, because enjoyment is an ultimate; it therefore brings rest ultimately. The minor is clear, because bringing rest to the will implies a certain {404} pleasure. Therefore, pleasure is what ultimately brings rest. Similarly, whatever [else] the will might have, if it lacked pleasure it would still look for it. Therefore, the will is never ultimately at rest except through pleasure.

[ii] Second, as follows. If they are really distinct, either pleasure is more perfect than enjoyment or conversely. If the first, then happiness would be located chiefly in pleasure. The consequent is false, therefore the antecedent [is also]. The inference is clear, because happiness is the most perfect attribute that can pertain to a rational creature. The falsity of the consequent is clear, because according to the Philosopher (and according to everyone) happiness consists in activity. Now pleasure is not activity but supervenes on activity, *Ethics* X (4, 1174b31–33).

If it is said that enjoyment is the more perfect, to the contrary: Things prior in generation are posterior in perfection, *Metaphysics* IX (8, 1050a4–6). If enjoyment is really distinct from pleasure, then, it will be prior to it in generation, so it will be posterior in perfection.

[iii] Third, as follows. If enjoyment were another thing prior to pleasure, then, since every prior thing can occur without a posterior, there could be enjoyment without pleasure. The consequent is false, because everything compatible with one of a pair of contraries is compatible with the other. Therefore, if enjoyment is compatible with pleasure and can exist without it, then it is compatible with distress. Consequently, someone could enjoy God and be miserable and so be blessed and miserable at once [which is absurd]. {405}

[1b] For the Opposite

Enjoyment is an elicited act. But pleasure is not an elicited act but supervenes on activity, *Ethics* X (4, 1174b31–33). Therefore, enjoyment is not pleasure.

[2. The Opinion of Peter Aureoli]

To this question some say that 'Every affirmative act of will is a desire or a pleasure, such that every love is a desiring love (*amor desiderii*) or a pleasurable love (*amor delectationis*). On the other hand, all hatred is divided into flight and distress, so that every hating is either an abhorring and fleeing or a being distressed and displeased. Accordingly, all acts of will, insofar as they involve wanting (as do willing against and willing), are of four kinds, namely, desiring willing and pleasant willing and fleeing willing against and displeased willing against.'

[i] This is proved first as follows. 'Animal appetite in beings with sensation and will in intellectual beings are like natural appetite in beings lacking sensation. But natural appetite has only two positive acts and two privative ones. The positives are moving to an end and resting in it, the privatives are fleeing from the opposite and being disquieted while near it.' Similarly, then, sensitive appetite and will have two positive acts, namely desire and pursuit [on one hand] and [on the other hand] rest in the object, namely, being pleased, and two negative [acts], the first of which corresponds to flight and recoiling, {406} namely, abhorring or

detesting and fleeing from evil, whereas the second corresponds to disquiet, namely, displeasure and being distressed.

[ii] Second as follows. 'If there were some love other than desire and pleasure, it would surely be the love that arouses desire and makes one take pleasure [in something]. But that is nothing else than taking pleasure in (*delectari*) and being pleased with (*complacere*) an object and the things associated with it, as is clear from the terms. For it is the same thing to say "I love such a thing" and "Such a thing is pleasing to me and pleasurable." ' Therefore, there is a pleasure that comes before desire and a pleasure in a present object following desire.

[iii] Third, because every love is a wanting love (*amor concupiscentiae*) or an amicable love (*amor amicitiae*). But every wanting love is a desire and every amicable love is a pleasure, either in something absent or in something present.

[iv] Fourth, every love is a desire or a being pleased (*complacentia*). But every being pleased is a pleasure. This is clear from the terms: 'You please me, you are pleasant to me.'

[v] Fifth, if it were the case [that there was some other love], this would be so that one might be united with the object and be transformed into it and rest in what is loved and give oneself to it. But these all pertain to pleasure.

[vi] 'Moreover, Augustine in *On the City of God* XIV 7 says that "Love that is avid" (that is, desiring) "to have what is loved is yearning; love having what is loved and enjoying it is joy" (or pleasure); "whereas love fleeing what is adverse to it is fear." He continues: "And if it should happen, feeling it {407} is distress." Therefore, since he here divides love into avid love, which is desire, and love enjoying what is loved, which is pleasure ((omit *sive tristitia* [var.])), and divides hatred into flight from what is adverse, which is fear, and abhorrence of an evil that is present, which is distress ((add *qui est timor, et in abominationem mali quod praesens est, quae est tristitia* [var.])), it manifestly appears that he intended to divide all hatred into flight and distress, and love, on the other hand, into pleasure and desire.'

So, then, this opinion asserts that some love is really pleasure and some is not. Hence the arguments of others [e.g., Scotus] proving that love and pleasure are really distinct do not succeed against this opinion or even against the opinion against which they argue, as will be clear.

Hence I argue against this opinion as follows.

[3. Refutation of Aureoli's Opinion]

[3a. Arguments against the Position]

[i] When two things are related in such a way that one of them remains when the other does not, they are really distinct. But love can remain when desire has been destroyed and also when pleasure has been destroyed. Therefore, it is really distinct from both. It is important to know that this form of argument is not valid as it sounds: 'When two things are related in such a way that one remains when the other does not remain, they are really distinct; but it is possible that love remains and that neither pleasure nor distress nor desire ((add *nec desiderium* [var.])) remains; therefore love is really distinct from pleasure and distress and desire ((add *desiderio* [var.])).' But there is a fallacy of accident [here], as has been explained elsewhere. But this conclusion follows: 'Therefore, {408} this is possible: love is really distinct from distress and pleasure and desire ((add *desiderio* [var.])).' And this suffices against the preceding opinion. The major is obvious. The minor is clear, because when the Devil tempts a human being and leads him to sin he wants him to be in that sin, and he then has an act of will regarding that sin, because he keeps him in that sin as much as he can, which he would not do without any act of will regarding that sin. Nevertheless, [on Aureoli's view] he does not have desire, because according to him [Aureoli] desire relates to something not possessed; nor does he have pleasure, because the damned have no pleasure. (This can be proved: Just as the blessed stand with regard to distress, so the damned stand with regard to pleasure. But the blessed have no distress at all. So neither do the damned have any pleasure.) This is confirmed: All agree that after the [Last] Judgment the damned will have no pleasure, but after judgment the damned will have many acts of will regarding things before them, as for example the Devil will want others to be punished with him. Therefore, they will have some act of will other than desire and pleasure.

[ii] Moreover, not every hate is a flight or a distress. Therefore, for the same reason not every love is a desire or a pleasure. The inference is clear, because there is some love opposite to every hate, therefore there is a distinct love opposite to a distinct hate; and so, opposite to that hate which is neither flight nor distress there is a love that is neither desire (which is opposed to flight) nor pleasure (which is opposed to distress). I prove the antecedent: Just as every desire, according to him, presupposes a love by which it is caused, so every flight presupposes a hate by which {409} it is

caused. But flight does not necessarily presuppose distress. Therefore, the hate that is presupposed is neither flight nor distress. The point assumed (that flight does not necessarily presuppose distress) is clear, because the blessed flee something, wanting something not to be which still exists or desiring something to exist that does not yet exist. Therefore, the blessed have an act opposite to desire and consequently have [an act of] flight and consequently a hate by which the flight is caused but do not have any distress, as all agree. Therefore, that presupposed hate is neither flight nor distress.

[iii] Moreover, according to the Philosopher in *Ethics* X (5, 1175b16–24; cf. VII 14, 1154b13–14), supreme distress excludes not only the pleasure opposite to it but also pleasure that is not opposed to it. For example, someone supremely distressed about the loss of a temporal thing does not take pleasure in investigating anything theoretical. But that distress does not exclude all love of that investigation. This is clear, because assuming this [distress] one could still labor to carry the investigation on.

[3b. Replies to Aureoli's Arguments]

Moreover, his own arguments do not support his conclusion but rather the opposite.

[i] The first does not prove its conclusion, because animal appetite in beings with sense perception and will in beings with intellect are *not* like natural appetite in those that lack sensation. This is because in actually seeking [something] natural appetite acquires nothing absolute formally inhering in it, [whereas] {410} animal and intellectual appetite do, in their seeking, acquire something absolute formally inherent [in them], because [they acquire] an appetitive act, which is an absolute quality, and a cognitive act, which is an absolute quality. And so, if it were a good analogy it would follow that just as natural appetite does not have two absolute acts formally inhering in it, so neither does animal or rational appetite, which is obviously false. Similarly, when it is claimed that natural appetite has only two positive and two privative acts, that is obviously false, because it does not have two positive acts. This is because [for example] a heavy thing has no positive act when it is in the center [of the earth]. For if it does, I ask about that act whether it is really the same as heaviness or really distinct. Not the first, because then it would have that act when it was away from the center, just as it has heaviness when away from the center. Nor is it really distinct, because it is obviously not an absolute, nor is it a

respect (because there are no respects here except with regard to the category of place); but that act is not natural appetite [i.e., no such act is involved in natural appetite]. It is clear in the same way that [natural appetite] does not have two privative acts, for when a heavy thing is away from the center it has no act except with regard to something keeping it [from reaching the center], because it breaks the beam if it can, and so it acts on the beam. Hence if it could not get past the obstacle, the heavy thing would have no act.

Therefore, I say to this reasoning that the cases are not alike, because natural appetite does not have elicited acts like those of rational appetite and animal appetite. Similarly, natural appetite is always active with respect to the act it elicits. Hence a heavy thing has no appetency unless it acts actively (by moving in place or by destroying something opposing it). Animal appetite, however, and, similarly, rational appetite can have an act, no matter how purely passive their condition may be. Hence they are not alike. {411}

[ii] The second argument does not succeed, because what it ought to prove is that it is the same to say 'I love something' and 'It is pleasant (*delectabile*) to me.' Here he tells us something false, which he does not prove. For it has been proved that this is false ([3a(i) above]). This is also clear because the Devil and all who are damned love themselves intensely and yet they have no pleasure with respect to themselves. Similarly, they desire blessedness and many things, and nevertheless do not take pleasure in them, for if they did, they would take intense pleasure in things when they desired them intensely, which is obviously false. Similarly, someone who is angry does not take pleasure in the revenge that he intensely desires, although he would be pleased if it actually occurred. Therefore, not every desire is caused by pleasure.

This is confirmed: An angry person who believes that vengeance is impossible but nevertheless supremely desires it is distressed and not pleased. Therefore, that desire is not caused by pleasure, and yet it is caused by a love of self or love of a friend whom he desires to avenge. Therefore, not every love is a desire or a pleasure. So the argument is to the opposite effect, going this way: 'Every desire is caused by some love that is not a desire. But not every desire is caused by pleasure. Therefore, there is a love that is neither desire nor pleasure.' We have the major premise from him. The minor is proved by the desire of the angry person, the Devil's desire for blessedness, and many other instances.

Hence I reply to this argument that not every love which arouses desire is a pleasure. Yet 'being pleased' (*complacere*) can be taken in two senses, either for any willing with respect to something possessed, in which sense not {412} everyone who is pleased (*complacens*) takes pleasure (*delectat*), or as the same thing as taking pleasure, in which sense not everything loved pleases. This is clear from the case of the Devil, who wants the sinner to sin and nevertheless does not take pleasure in the sin.

[iii] The third argument does not succeed either, for it ought to prove that every amicable love is a pleasure. The opposite has been proved, because [it is possible for] someone to love himself with an amicable love and yet not take pleasure.

[iv] To the fourth, it was made clear earlier (3b[ii]) [in what sense] being pleased is a pleasure and [in what sense] not.

[v] [The reply] to the fifth is clear from the same [distinctions], because, strictly speaking, some of the four things named are effects of love rather than love itself, and sometimes they are separable effects, as has been explained above.

[vi] It would be easy to reply to [the text from] Augustine that there is a causal predication there, because enjoying love is a cause of pleasure and joy unless it is impeded. How it could be impeded will be explained in the second [article below]. {413}

[4. Division of the Question]

Hence we have to reply otherwise to the question. We must proceed with it as follows. First we have to see how love and pleasure are related to one another as to identity and difference; second, how they are related as to their efficient causes and effects; third, how they are related as to the subject receiving them; fourth, how according to nobility: which of them is nobler.

[5. Article I. The Distinction between Love and Pleasure]

As to the first, I say that love and pleasure are really distinct, because if any love were really pleasure, it would be especially that which is present in obtaining something previously desired. But that is not really pleasure.

Therefore, no love is really pleasure. What is assumed here has been proved in arguing against the preceding opinion.

[6. Article II. The Efficient Causes of Love and Pleasure]

[6a. Duns Scotus's Opinion]

Concerning the second [article] it is said [by Duns Scotus] that love and pleasure have different efficient causes, because love is effectively from the will {414} but pleasure is effectively from the object.

[i] This is because, just as a sensible object is a cause of pleasure in sensitive appetite, so an intelligible object is a cause of pleasure in intellective appetite.

[ii] This is also proved [as follows]. It is clear that the act of loving is effectively from the will, because the act of hating is effectively from the will; therefore the acts of willing and loving are also. The inference is clear, because they are opposite acts, therefore they are acts of the same power. Similarly, both acts are equally free. The antecedent is clear, because just as an act of loving relates to a good inasmuch as it is good, so an act of hating relates to an evil inasmuch as it is evil. I ask, then: Does the act of willing come from the will or from the object? If from the will, the point is made. Not the second [i.e., not from the object], because a privative is not as such the cause of anything positive. Evil is, as such, a privative, however, and an act is something positive. Therefore, it [the act of willing] is not caused by the object, so [it is caused] by the will. But the act of pleasure is not caused by the will but by the object. For the Philosopher says in *Ethics* X 4 (1174b14–31) that when a sensible object has been sensed there is always an act of pleasure. And he says in *On Rhetoric* I (11, 1369b33–1370a3) that the pleasant is a cause of pleasure.

[iii] Similarly, distress, which is the opposite of pleasure, comes from the object, not from the will, because no one distresses himself. Therefore, pleasure does not come from the will either.

[6b. Arguments against Scotus's Opinion]

But this opinion is not true.

[i] Because when something [A] can exist equally without another thing [B] as with it and cannot exist when that thing [B] is given unless yet

another thing [C] is given, it [B] is not its [A's] effective cause. But given an act {415} of will [C], pleasure [A] can exist equally without the object [B] as with it, and if the object is given and the act of will destroyed, there can in no way be pleasure. Therefore, the object is not the cause of the pleasure, at least not the immediate cause.

[ii] Moreover, plurality should not be posited without necessity or certain experience. But given only an act of will it seems there is a sufficient cause of pleasure. Therefore, the object seems superfluous.

[iii] Moreover, what does not exist is not a positive cause of anything. But the object can be a nonentity. As a result, there is pleasure with respect to many things that do not exist. (It may be said that they exist in the cognition of the intellect and that this suffices for them to be a cause of pleasure. To the contrary: If this is the case, then the cognition itself will be the cause of pleasure, because nothing really exists here except the cognition itself or the volition; so one of those is the cause. But neither of those is the object. Therefore, the object is not the cause.)

[6c. Ockham's Opinion]

Hence I maintain concerning this article that the object is not the immediate cause of pleasure, but the immediate cause of pleasure is the act of will itself. The reason is that, given an equal act of will there follows equal pleasure whether the object exists or not, and without the act of will pleasure can in no way follow. Therefore, the act of will alone will be the immediate cause.

[6d. Objections]

[i] It may be said that this argument does not suffice, because with respect to the same effect there can be many causes, any one of which is sufficient, and therefore that however much a volition may be a sufficient cause of pleasure, from this it does not follow that the object is not a cause.

[ii] Similarly, from the fact that there cannot be pleasure without volition it does not follow that the volition is the cause, because things neither of which is a cause of the other are sometimes ordered so that there is an order of effects {416} with respect to the same cause, while they are nevertheless not ordered among themselves in an order of causality. For example, if the sun illuminated some region near it, and if a more distant region, because of its opacity, could be illuminated *only* by the sun, then

the sun – not, however, the first region illuminated – would illuminate the distant region. In this case there would be an order between the near and the distant region as effects of the same cause, yet not an order of cause to effect [between themselves]. Similarly, in the case at hand volition could be necessarily presupposed for pleasure and not be its cause.

[iii] Moreover, by the same reasoning it would follow that it [pleasure] would not arise effectively from the will.

[6e. Replies to the Preceding Objections]

[i] To the first of these I reply that although there can be several causes with respect to the same effect, yet this should not be posited without necessity – say, because it can be shown from experience either that with one thing given and the other destroyed the effect follows or that with the one not given and anything whatever given the effect does not follow. An example of the first: It is proved that fire is a cause of heat because, given fire with everything else removed, heat follows in something capable of being heated that is close to it. An example of the second: It is proved that an object is a cause of intuitive [i.e., direct] intellection because, with everything else given and the object alone removed intuitive awareness does not follow. Therefore, the object is the cause of intuitive awareness. Such argument holds on the basis of some such proposition {417} as 'Whatever absolute thing is required in real existence for the existence of a thing is a cause of that thing by some kind of causation.' The first argument holds on the basis of the proposition 'Everything on which something else follows when it is given is a cause of the other.' That one thing is the cause of another can be proved otherwise, without such experience, by reason. In that way it is proved that the will is an effective cause of its own act, because every free power which cannot be necessitated is an effective cause of its own act. Perhaps this is the only convincing argument that the will is an effective cause of any of its acts. Other arguments, however, based on mediating [propositions] such as 'What pertains to an inferior nature ought not to be denied of a superior,' 'A universal second cause partially concurs immediately in producing the effect of a particular cause; therefore, the first cause [concurs] without qualification,' likewise, 'A body is not the total cause of anything spiritual,' and suchlike are [only] plausible rather than being demonstrative or necessarily convincing arguments.

Since, therefore, it is not clear that there is any such way to prove that pleasure is caused by the object, we ought not to assert that it is caused by it. For this clearly cannot be proved from experience. Not in the first way [mentioned above], because when the object is given in any way whatever, pleasure does not follow if cognition or also willing of it is absent. Nor, clearly, [can it be proved] in the second way, because with the object destroyed there can be pleasure. If it could be proved that, given some act of will, pleasure would not follow when the object was destroyed, then it could be proved that the object was the cause of that pleasure. Therefore, too, if it could be proved that, given, by divine power, an intuitive awareness without the object, there would not follow as great pleasure as with the object really existing, then it could be proved that the object was a cause {418} of the pleasure, or at least of the volition preceding the pleasure. It is likewise clear that it cannot be proved by reason. Not by the first [example of proof by reason in the previous paragraph], because an object does nothing toward the free production of an effect; it therefore cannot be proved by freedom that it is the cause of anything at all. Likewise it cannot be proved by other reasons, especially because when pleasure is given it is possible that the object not exist. (It follows from this that it cannot be proved sufficiently that the intellect is an effective cause of cognition, but it suffices for saving all [the facts] that it is the subject of cognition. About this elsewhere.)

[ii] To the second I reply that from such an order it is always possible to infer causality in the prior with respect to the posterior, especially if the prior can exist (even naturally) without the posterior and not conversely. This can be done on the basis of a proposition granted by that doctor [Scotus]: 'No absolute is necessarily required for the existence of anything unless it is its cause by some kind of causality.' Therefore, if the prior is required for the existence of the second (because the second cannot exist without the prior), it will be its cause by some kind of causality.

If it is said that although it is prior it is nevertheless not necessarily required for the existence of the second, I ask to the contrary: If it is prior, by what kind of priority? Either by priority in perfection (and this is beside the point, because a posterior can exist without qualification without such a prior) or by priority of time, nature, or causality. Whichever of these is given, if it is prior essentially and not accidentally, the prior will be a cause of the posterior. This is clear regarding the first priority, because if it is prior in time, {419} and not merely accidentally but *per se*, then the posterior cannot exist without the prior. Therefore (by the preceding and by the principles of that doctor mentioned just now and in the first question of the prologue), it is caused by it. If it is a priority of nature, the point is made by the same principles. If it is a priority of causality, the point is made. Nor does it seem that any other priority is relevant. This is clear by induction.

When it is said that 'There is an order of effects with respect to the same cause, while they are nevertheless not ordered among themselves in an order of causality,' I maintain that this is not possible, unless perhaps it is an order of perfection. And it is compatible with such an order not only that the prior is not a cause of the posterior but equally that the posterior is a real effective cause of the prior. Universally, there cannot ((*non/nullus* [var.])) be an order of effects with respect to the same cause without an order of causality of the prior to the posterior except when, as far as its own nature is concerned, it is possible for the posterior in such an order to be without qualification a real cause of the prior in such an order. And so, if a volition is prior in nature or time or in any such order (and this *per se* and not merely accidentally), it can be inferred that the volition is a cause of the pleasure.

It may still be objected that it has not been proved sufficiently that volition is a cause of pleasure, because when two things are inseparable from one another it cannot be proved that either of them is a cause of the other. But the act of willing and pleasure are naturally inseparable. Therefore, it cannot be proved that the act of willing is a cause of the pleasure any more than the converse, but it suffices {420} that they are [both] caused by one and the same cause, because it is not inappropriate for the same cause to have at the same time effects distinct in kind without such an order, except perhaps with an order of perfection.

I answer that if it could be proved that by divine power one would be separable from the other and not conversely, causality could perhaps be proved in one with respect to the other and not conversely. So if there could not be pleasure without an act of willing – since it has been proved above that there can be an act of willing without pleasure – it would follow that the act is a cause. Yet I say that they are naturally separable [i.e., even without an appeal to God's power], so that there can be an act of willing without pleasure and not conversely. This is clear, because someone who is supremely distressed can will something and yet not take pleasure in it when what is willed follows. Therefore, there can naturally be an act of willing without pleasure and not conversely. Therefore, it is its cause.

[iii] To the third I concede that it cannot be proved sufficiently that pleasure arises effectively from the will.

[6f. Replies to the Arguments for Scotus's Opinion]

[i] To the first argument for the first opinion I reply that the sensible object is not the immediate cause of pleasure in sensitive appetite, but rather the cognition itself is the immediate cause, according to the Philosopher, *Ethics* X (4, 1174b31–33), where he seems to attribute causality with respect to pleasure to the activity itself. {421}

If it is said that by the same reasoning that shows sensitive cognition to be the immediate cause of pleasure in sensitive appetite, intellective cognition will be the immediate cause of pleasure in intellective appetite, I answer by denying the inference. This is because besides intellective awareness and pleasure there is an act of will between them; hence that will be the cause. But besides sensitive cognition and pleasure in sensitive appetite there is not such an act between them; hence sensitive cognition will be the immediate cause. [More] about this elsewhere perhaps.

[ii] To the second argument I concede that love and pleasure arise from different agents, but those different agents are not the will and the object but the will and an act of will.

To the proof I concede that an act of willing is from the will, although the reasoning [in the proof] is not valid, because even love does not come from the will as from a total cause, since it also comes effectively from the cognition itself, as will be explained elsewhere. But I maintain that the pleasure is not from the object, because the same thing is object of the act and of the following pleasure. Therefore, there cannot be an act of will from any object whatever, because the object itself is not [always] a positive entity. For the same reason there will not be pleasure from it, since pleasure is a positive entity. So if evil as evil is purely privative, it will be no more possible for pleasure to come effectively from evil as evil than for an act to do so. And so one part of that argument obviously destroys the other. When it is proved from the Philosopher that when the object has been sensed pleasure follows, I concede. So the sensation itself {422} is cause of that pleasure; and in the same way, because pleasure follows when the object has been willed, the volition will on that account be the cause. To the other text I answer that the pleasant is a mediate cause of pleasure – when the pleasant is necessarily present, naturally speaking, as with the pleasures of the special senses – yet it is never the immediate cause.

[iii] To the third proof I reply that distress does not arise from the object, except perhaps sometimes mediately, but it arises immediately from the act of will itself.

It may be said against all of these [arguments] that then pleasure or distress would always follow when an act of will was posited, because the act of will is not a free cause but a natural one. I answer that unless there is an impediment pleasure or distress always does follow. But sometimes there is an impediment, as when extreme distress impedes an act of will (on account of that distress) from [causing] the pleasure that ought to follow.

[7. Article III. The Subject of Pleasure]

Concerning the third article, the problem is whether pleasure exists in the will itself as subject or in the act of will. I maintain that it exists subjectively in the will itself. The reason for this is that every subject receptive of some contrary is receptive of the other contrary. Therefore, if the act of willing were receptive of pleasure, the same act would be receptive of the distress contrary to it. But it is awkward and perhaps impossible that someone should love something supremely and yet be distressed with it, unless perhaps because of some other act. {423}

[7a. Objections and Replies]

[i] It may be said that this reasoning is not valid, because fire is receptive of heat, yet not of cold. To this it can be said that by God's absolute power fire can receive cold.

[ii] It may be said that, in the same way, it seems that by God's absolute power an act of love can exist along with distress, because just as every subject receptive of one contrary is receptive of the other, so whatever absolute is compatible with one of [a range of] contraries is by God's absolute power compatible with the rest. This is clear by induction, because whatever exists along with whiteness can exist along with blackness.

[iia] This [objection] is confirmed: An intense act of love can exist with distress regarding the same object, namely, when someone is afraid of losing what he loves.

[Reply to (ii)] It can be said to this that such an act of love does not exist along with the opposite distress contrary to the pleasure of which it is naturally the cause.

It may be said [in objection to this reply] that a single thing has a single contrary [cf. Aristotle, *De caelo* I 2, 269a14–15; *Metaphysics* X 4, 1055a19–20] and that therefore if that pleasure is opposed as a contrary to that distress, the act of will will not be opposed to it as a contrary and therefore will be able to exist along with it.

It can be said [in reply to this further objection] that although that act of will is not properly opposed as a contrary to that distress, it nevertheless conflicts with it. As a result, just as in substantial forms there is an incompatibility of some forms [with one another] even though they are not properly opposed as contraries, so it can be said that there is some incompatibility in accidental forms even though they are not properly opposed as contraries. And so we must deny the proposition that 'With whatever contrary {424} an absolute is compatible, it is compatible with the other contrary.' Therefore, although the act of will that is love is compatible with pleasure, it nevertheless need not be compatible with the distress opposed to it.

It may be said [in further objection] that in the case of substantial forms whenever something is incompatible with one of those conflicting forms it is also incompatible with the rest and that therefore in conflicting accidental forms, too, whatever absolute is compatible with one is also compatible with the rest.

It can be said [in reply to this objection] that a substantial form is incompatible with one specific form and not with the rest, just as the sensitive form in a human being, which is really distinct from the intellective, is compatible with the intellective form and not with the form of an ass. Similarly, in accidental forms whiteness and intellection are conflicting forms (because it is impossible for them to exist in the same immediate subject), and yet something is compatible with a whiteness that is not compatible with an intellection. The same can be said here.

[Reply to (iia)] To the confirming argument I reply that distress from fear of losing a good that one loves (or any other [distress] whatever) is not opposed to pleasure in the object; therefore love can exist with such distress. (If one concedes that at least by God's absolute power an absolute compatible with one contrary stands with the rest and that contraries are one to one, one must then say that by God's absolute power love can stand with distress.)

On this article, therefore, I maintain that it is more plausible to say that pleasure exists subjectively in the will, not in an act of will, although perhaps this {425} cannot be proved adequately enough to escape [counter-]arguments. Nevertheless, I say that this can be proved adequately on Aristotle's principles. For as is clear in the book of *Categories* (5, 4a10–11), the special property of substance is to be susceptible to contraries, so that this can pertain to no other [category]. Since pleasure and distress are contraries, then, they will exist immediately in some substance, and consequently neither of them will exist immediately in any accident. And so neither of them will exist subjectively in an act of will but in the will itself (which is the rational soul itself).

(If it is said that quantity is receptive of contraries, I answer that Aristotle held that quantity is not another thing (*res*) from substance, and so according to Aristotle it is true both that 'Only substance is susceptible to contraries' and that 'Quantity is susceptible to contraries.')

[8. Article IV. On the Nobility of the Act of Love]

Concerning the fourth article I say for the time being that the act of love is without qualification nobler than pleasure. This can be made plausible as follows.

[i] First, that of which the contrary is worse and less perfect is nobler. But hatred of God is worse than distress. Therefore, love is nobler than pleasure. The major seems obvious. The minor is clear, because since both are accidents, that which is more to be avoided is worse; but hatred of God is more to be avoided than any distress whatever. {426}

[ii] Second, as follows. A rational creature is more perfect than any irrational creature. Therefore, an accident by which it is especially distinguished from the irrational creature will be more perfect. But it seems that the rational creature is more distinguished by volition than by any pleasure whatever. What is assumed is clear, because it is especially distinguished by freedom, which is a principle of volition.

[iii] Moreover, it seems that amicable love is the most perfect accident that can belong to anyone. Therefore, it is more perfect than pleasure. The antecedent is clear, because it [amicable love] is especially accepted by God.

[iv] Moreover, love in this life is more perfect than pleasure in this life; therefore, love in heaven is more perfect than pleasure in heaven, and consequently love as a whole is more perfect than pleasure.

[v] Moreover, just as sensitive activity is related to the sensitive pleasure following it, so is intellectual activity related to the pleasure following it. But sensitive activity is more perfect than pleasure. Therefore, etc. What is assumed is clear from the Commentator [Michael of Ephesus], who says in comment 12 on *Ethics* X that 'Since we rather pursue

pleasure for the sake of activities and in order to live, from these [facts] someone would certainly believe more [in the greater perfection of activities?], and first from [considering] virtuous activities, for however pleasant these are, it is not for the sake of pleasure that they are eagerly engaged in. {427} For we choose many virtuous activities even though engaging in them is a cause of distress, labor, and grief.' From this text it is clear that activities are not worthy of choice for pleasure but conversely, as the Commentator explains there. Therefore, pleasure is not more perfect than activity.

It may be said that that text is not to the point, because it only indicates that *some* activities are not worthy of choice for the sake of pleasure (but conversely). This is clear with respect to virtuous activities, which are not more perfect on account of sensitive activities (because the latter do not properly elicit virtuous activities) but on account of the activities of will commanding those activities, which [activities of will] are properly and in the first instance virtuous. It is true that *they* are more perfect than sensitive pleasure, although sensitive activities would be less perfect than pleasure.

This is not valid, because according to the Commentator in that place pleasure exists for the sake of activity not only in humans but also in brutes. Thus he says, 'Let us say that it is known for a certainty that nature has given pleasure to animals for the sake of activities.' But in brute animals there is only sensitive activity. Pleasure is for the sake of sensitive activity, then, and not conversely. Therefore, it is less perfect.

There are many doubts about the preceding, which I now pass over, because they will be resolved in the fourth book and the third. {428}

[9. Replies to the Preliminary Arguments]

[i] To the first argument at the beginning I reply that for something to give rest to the will 'ultimately' can be understood in two senses: either because it is ultimately worthy of choice for its own sake and not for something else or because it is something after which nothing else gives rest. In the first sense I say that enjoyment gives rest to the will, because it is worthy of choice for itself, not for the sake of acquiring something else. In the second sense pleasure gives rest ultimately, because after pleasure nothing comes to the will to give it rest. So it is clear that there is a fallacy of equivocation in the argument.

[ii] To the second I reply that enjoyment is more perfect than pleasure, as has been explained. And when it is said that things posterior in generation are prior in perfection, I answer that this is true when they are of the same genus and one is essentially ordered to the other and exists for the sake of the other. Thus sperm exists for the sake of [generating] a human being (the Philosopher gives this as an example [*Metaphysics* IX 8, 1050a4–6]), and the boy is ordered from the intention of nature to become a man. But enjoyment does not exist in this way for the sake of pleasure. Therefore, etc.

[iii] To the third some [Scotus] concede that God by his absolute power can bring about an enjoyment without the following pleasure. And when it is inferred further, 'Therefore it can exist along with distress,' it is clear above what can be said to this. {429}

Question 4. Is God the Only Due Object of Enjoyment?

Third [about enjoyment], I ask whether God is the only due object of enjoyment.

[1. Preliminary Arguments]

[1a. Arguments that God Is Not the Only Due Object of Enjoyment]

[i] [The object] of an act that can satisfy the appetite can be a due object of enjoyment. But an act having an object other [than God] can satisfy the will. Therefore, an object other than God can be a due object of enjoyment. The major is clear. The minor is proved: When some acts of a power are so related that one is without qualification less perfect and the other without qualification more perfect, if the less perfect act can satisfy the power much more will the more perfect act satisfy it. But it is possible for some act of will with respect to a creature to be more perfect and more intense than an act of will with respect to God. This is because the act with respect to God is finite and consequently has a certain proportion in perfection to other acts. Hence it does not seem to involve a contradiction for an act more perfect than that finite act to arise. Therefore, if the less perfect finite act satisfies, much more will the other, more perfect one satisfy.

This argument is confirmed: If a single act of will with respect to God can satisfy the will, then acts [with respect to other things] multiplied so {430} much that they exceed in perfection the act of will with respect to God can satisfy the will. Therefore, etc.

[ii] Second, as follows. That is to be enjoyed which is to be loved supremely. But something other than God is like this. Therefore, etc. Proof of the minor: According to the Philosopher, *Ethics* IX (c. 8), each individual ought to love himself more than anything else.

This argument is confirmed: If God is to be loved supremely, this would only be because the supreme good is to be loved supremely. But according to the Philosopher, *Topics* III (8, 137b20–27), just as supreme is to supreme and more to more, so too is unqualified to unqualified. Therefore, if the supreme good is to be loved supremely, what is better is to be loved more, and consequently it would be the case that a human being should love an angel more than himself, which is against the philosophers and against the saints.

[iii] Third, as follows. That is to be enjoyed which is to be loved for itself. But something other than God is to be loved for itself. Therefore, etc. The minor is clear, because every morally honorable good is to be loved for itself, because it is to be loved even if everything else is left out of consideration. But there are many morally honorable goods, such as the virtues and similar things. Therefore, etc.

[1b. An Argument that God Is Not to Be Enjoyed]

Second, chiefly [it is argued] that God is *not* to be enjoyed, because that is not to be enjoyed which cannot satisfy the capacity of the will or give it rest. But God cannot satisfy or give rest to the capacity of the will. Therefore, God is not to be enjoyed. The major seems {431} obvious, because enjoyment involves the will's being at rest. The minor is proved: When the capacity of some power is satisfied, that power cannot seek anything further. But a will having an act with respect to the divine essence can seek something further, because it can seek an act with respect to a creature. Therefore, it is not then satisfied.

[1c] For the Opposite

Only that is to be enjoyed to which all other things are ordered and which is itself ordered to nothing else. Only God is like this. Therefore, etc.

[2. Preliminaries to a Response]

Concerning this question I shall proceed as follows. First, some distinctions have to be made about enjoyment; second, the question must be answered.

[2a. Distinctions regarding Enjoyment]

Concerning the first it is important to know that enjoyment is twofold, namely, ordinate and inordinate. There is ordinate enjoyment when something that is *to be* loved supremely *is* loved supremely. There is inordinate enjoyment when what is to be loved less and for the sake of something else is loved supremely and for itself. But ordinate enjoyment is twofold. There is one which gives rest to the will without qualification. Enjoyment in heaven is said to be like this. There is another which does not give rest without qualification but allows of anxiety and distress along with it, even naturally [i.e., without special divine action]. Enjoyment in the present life is like this.

[2b. Division of the Question]

Concerning the second, we first have to see whether it can be proved naturally that any enjoyment giving rest to the will and satisfying it {432} is possible; second, whether such [enjoyment] is in fact to be posited; third, what the object of that enjoyment is; fourth, we have to see about enjoyment that does not give rest or satisfy; fifth, we have to consider inordinate enjoyment.

[3. Article I. Can the Possibility of Enjoyment Be Demonstrated?]

[3a. Scotus's Opinion]

Concerning the first there is one opinion [advanced by Scotus in various places] which posits that it can be proved naturally that such enjoyment is possible for us.

[i] This is proved first as follows. When any power is distinctly and perfectly known, every act to which it is naturally ordered can be known. But human nature can be distinctly and perfectly known. Therefore, etc.

Therefore, since according to the truth of the matter such an act [i.e., enjoyment of God] is possible for us, so that the will has a natural potentiality for such an act, it follows that this can naturally be proved to be possible for us.

[ii] Moreover, when any caused thing is known, the cause on which it naturally depends can be known. But such enjoyment is an end [i.e., final cause] for the will. Therefore, when the nature of the will has been known, that end can be known.

[iii] Moreover, it is naturally knowable that being is the primary object of the intellect. Therefore, it is naturally knowable that anything contained within being is distinctly knowable by the intellect. Therefore, it can be known naturally that the divine essence can {433} be seen nakedly and perfectly by the intellect and consequently, for the same reason, that enjoyment of the divine essence is possible for the will.

[iv] Moreover, the object of the will is being. Therefore, it does not find rest except in the most perfect thing contained within being.

[v] Moreover, when a power has many things in its scope, it does not find rest except in the most perfect among them. Therefore, the will does not find rest except in God.

[vi] Moreover, any good whatever can be sought by the will. Therefore, the supreme good can be sought by the will, and consequently it cannot find rest except in the supreme good.

[3b. Arguments against Scotus's Opinion]

To the contrary, it does not seem that it can be proved naturally that such enjoyment is possible for us.

[i] Because philosophers investigating diligently what is the ultimate end of human deeds have not been able to reach that end. Therefore, it is not likely that this can be proved naturally.

[ii] Moreover, all the arguments brought forward to prove this can be answered. Therefore, the conclusion cannot be proved naturally.

[iii] Moreover, according to all the saints, faith is required for holding that such an end is possible for us. But if it could be proved naturally, faith would not be necessary.

[3c. Ockham's Opinion]

Hence I maintain concerning this article, first, that it cannot be demonstrated naturally that such an enjoyment of the divine essence {434} is possible for us, because it genuinely is something believed, and so it cannot be demonstrated naturally.

Second, I maintain that it cannot be demonstrated naturally that the will cannot be satisfied or be brought to rest in anything this side of God. The reason for this is that if it could be proved naturally that the will cannot be brought to rest in anything finite, the proof would be either [i] through the freedom of the will (namely, because as a result of being free the will can seek anything whatever that can be willed, and so it can never be satisfied except with what is ultimate) or [ii] through the universality of the will's object (namely, because its object is being in general, and consequently whatever is contained [within being], and consequently it cannot be brought to rest except in the supreme [being]) or [iii] through the will's capacity (namely, because it is capable of infinite good). [i] It cannot be proved in the first way, because, as will be shown in the last question of this distinction, it cannot be demonstrated naturally that the will is contingently brought to bear on anything whatever that can be willed. Therefore, it cannot be proved naturally that when the will has an act with respect to anything finite the appetite or will could seek a more perfect good. [ii] Nor can it be proved in the second way, because it cannot be known naturally that whenever anything general is apprehensible by a power whatever is contained within it can be known perfectly by such a power, because there can be an impediment from the disproportion of one of the contained things or from the lack of some other cause. An example of the first: According to the Philosopher, the first being is disproportionate for causing immediately any effect in {435} lower things. Hence if the intellect cannot know anything intuitively and in particular unless it is moved immediately by the object or unless some new effect is immediately caused by the object, it therefore cannot know God intuitively and in particular. An example of the second: If there were some object that could in no way be apprehended by the intellect unless it were first apprehended by sense, [and] if there were an intellectual nature with which that sense was incompatible, such an intellect, although it could apprehend something in general pertaining to all objects, nevertheless could not apprehend in particular each and every thing contained [under the general concept]. This is confirmed: Our intellect in its present state can apprehend something common to substance and accident, yet according to them [the Scotists] it cannot apprehend substance. [iii] Nor can it be proved in the third way, because it cannot be proved that the will is capable of such good, since this is solely supernatural and not natural.

Hence I maintain that it cannot be demonstrated naturally that the will cannot receive a single act from some created being, as from a total immediate cause, that will satisfy the will's whole appetite, just as it cannot be proved that some pleasant sensible object cannot give rest to sensitive appetite as long as the sense retains all the same dispositions it had prior to that pleasure.

Third, I maintain that it cannot be proved naturally that the will can be brought to rest in any act whatever or that with any possible act whatever being posited in the will it could not freely will something else and be distressed if it lacked it. So it can be proved neither that the will can be satisfied and brought to rest by the enjoyment that we in fact posit, {436} nor that it cannot be brought to rest by something else with respect to a creature, nor that it can be brought to rest by anything whatever. Nor do the arguments of others sufficiently prove any of those conclusions.

[3d. Replies to the Arguments for Scotus's Opinion]

[i] To the first: The major is false, as was said earlier in the question about the subject of theology, because it was explained there that a subject can be distinctly and perfectly known [but that] however much [it is known] one cannot as a result have an awareness of anything else whatever.

[ii] To the second I reply that when anything caused is known, any cause you like can be known in general; say, that it has an end and an efficient cause, and many features of those causes can be known from [knowledge of] the thing, but that which is a cause cannot be known in particular or by a proper or equivalent cognition from any caused thing whatever.

[iii] To the third I reply that for something to be the primary object of some power (speaking here about a primary object by primacy of adequation [i.e., in relation to the intellect's capacity, not primacy in order of acquisition]) can be understood in two ways: either because anything falling under it can be apprehended in particular and under its own concept by the power, while nothing is thus apprehensible by the power except [things] of which that [object] is predicated; or because it is the most general among all the things that can be apprehended by the power, and nothing can be apprehended by the power except [things] of which it is predicated. I maintain that it cannot be known naturally that being is the primary object of the intellect in the first way, because it cannot be known naturally that whatever is contained under being is knowable

{437} by the intellect in that way [i.e., in particular and under its own concept]. In the second way it is possible, but then it is not naturally known that everything contained under such a primary object is naturally knowable by such a power distinctly and in particular.

[iv] To the next: It would need to be proved that a power is not brought to rest except in the most perfect thing contained under its common object. This is because, if a sense can have pleasure with respect to several sensibles, then if there were some less perfect sensible always approximated to that sense it would necessarily always bring rest to the sense (because it would exclude all distress contrary to that pleasure), and yet it would not be the most perfect thing contained under that common object. Similarly, when not every content at all is knowable by a power distinctly and in particular, it would not be necessary that it could only be brought to rest in the supreme [content].

[v] By the same [reasoning I reply] to the next: It is not sufficiently proved that such a power cannot be brought to rest except in what is most perfect.

[vi] To the last: It cannot be proved sufficiently that the will can have every good that it seeks in a different way than it does have it. So it does not seem that Avicenna's opinion, which posits that the inferior intelligence is beatified in the superior intelligence, can be disproved sufficiently by natural arguments.

[3e. Objections to the Preceding Replies]

[i] It may be said that when the inferior intelligence sees the superior it either sees it to be finite or sees it [as] infinite, or does not see its finitude or infinitude but believes it to be infinite. If {438} the second ((*secundo/primo* [var.]; omit *vel tertio* [var.])) of these, then it is not made blessed in it, because according to Augustine, *On the City of God* IV (c. 4), nothing stupider can be said than that a blessed soul has a false opinion. If it sees neither its finitude nor its infinitude it does not see it perfectly, nor, consequently, is it blessed. If, however, it sees that it is finite, then it can understand that something could exceed it. Consequently (as we experience even in ourselves that beyond any good whatever we can seek another good that is shown to be greater), it can seek and love that greater good and so not be brought to rest in the intelligence.

[ii] Moreover, Avicenna's argument supports the opposite conclusion, because the second intelligence, if it causes the third, does not do so by its own power but by another. Consequently it is not an end for it in

virtue of its own power but another. Now what is an end [for something] by reason of another end, does not [itself] bring it rest. Therefore, etc.

[3f. Replies to the Preceding]

[i] To the first of these it could easily be said that the [inferior] intelligence sees that the intelligence in which it is made blessed is finite and that there is something more perfect than it. When it is said 'Therefore it can seek that more perfect thing,' it could easily be said that that does not follow, because the inferior intelligence cannot seek anything against right reason. Others would say here, however, that it would be impossible for the lowest intelligence to possess the first intelligence otherwise than as it does have it, and so it cannot be sought otherwise. Or it could be said that the lower intelligence does not know that {439} higher intelligence. From this it is clear that the experience we have would not be cogent against someone with this opinion, because our will can will the impossible, not so that will. So the cases are not alike.

[ii] To the second: They would deny the inference 'The intelligence is an end by reason of another end, therefore it does not bring rest,' just as they would say that something sensed does not give pleasure except in virtue of something else (which yet does not give pleasure), and nevertheless it brings rest to the sensitive appetite.

[4. Article II. An Enjoyment that Brings Rest Is to Be Posited]

Concerning the second [article] I say that in fact such enjoyment is to be posited, but this is only to be believed and is not known by natural reason.

[5. Article III. The Object of Beatific Enjoyment]

[5a. The Opinion of Durandus of St. Pourçain]

Concerning the third [article] there is an opinion which posits that the immediate object of enjoyment is not God himself but the beatific vision of the divine essence. This is proved in many ways.

[i] First as follows. Whenever the will uses *things* (*rebus*) it uses by means

of some other *act*, so that that act is the formal object of the act of using that follows desiring. Therefore, when someone uses some thing with an enjoyment following an act of desiring, he enjoys by means of some act which will be the formal object of that enjoyment. The antecedent is clear by induction: {440} When someone first desires a house and aferwards obtains it and uses it, he uses by means of inhabiting [it] or some such [act].

[ii] Moreover, wanting love does not bear immediately on a thing but on an act in which the thing is possessed. But enjoyment is a wanting love. Therefore, it does not bear immediately on God himself but on the beatific vision in which God is possessed. The major is clear by induction, because when someone loves bread and wants it, the object is not immediately the bread itself but the act in which the bread is had, namely, the act of eating. The minor is proved, because there is enjoyment with respect to God when God is possessed. Therefore, it exists with respect to the act in which he is possessed, and consequently it is a wanting love.

[iii] Moreover, enjoyment succeeds to desire. Therefore, the object of desire and enjoyment is the same. But desire exists with respect to the act in which God is possessed, not with respect to God absolutely, for we only desire God because we desire to see him. Therefore, enjoyment is not of God absolutely but of the beatific vision of him.

[iv] Moreover, enjoyment is with respect to a complex [i.e., a proposition or a state of affairs], because it exists with respect to what is desired. But desire is with respect to a complex. Therefore, enjoyment is also. But God is something incomplex.

[v] Moreover, the object of enjoyment is that which we most greatly desire, but such is the act in which God is seen. {441}

[vi] Moreover, it can be argued as follows. The object of enjoyment is the same as the object of the pleasure consequent on it. But the object of pleasure is the vision itself, because the blessed will supremely rejoice in it. Likewise, pleasure arises from the conjunction of things that agree with one another. Therefore, it arises from that conjunction itself. Therefore it exists with respect to the act in which the conjunction occurs.

[5b. Arguments against Durandus's Opinion]

That opinion seems to be simply false.

[i] Because to enjoy something is to inhere in it with love for its own sake. But nothing is to be loved for its own sake except God alone. Therefore, God alone is to be enjoyed.

[ii] Moreover, that alone is to be enjoyed which cannot be ordered to something else. But everything other than God can be ordered to God as an end. Therefore, nothing other than God is to be enjoyed.

[iii] Moreover, Augustine, *On Christian Doctrine* I (c. 5): 'The things to be enjoyed are the Father and the Son and the Holy Spirit.'

[5c. Ockham's Opinion]

Therefore, I maintain that the object of enjoyment in heaven is God himself:

[i] Because amicable love is the most perfect [love] with respect to any object whatever. But enjoyment is a most perfect love. Therefore, enjoyment is amicable love. But amicable love terminates in God himself in himself. Therefore, so does enjoyment.

This is confirmed: God can be loved immediately by the blessed. For this is possible with respect to a creature: that one love another immediately. But the love that has a more perfect object is {442} more perfect. Therefore, the love in which God is loved immediately is nobler and more perfect than that in which the vision of the divine essence is loved. But enjoyment is the noblest love, so enjoyment terminates immediately in God in himself.

[ii] Moreover, the blessed can have no less an act with respect to the divine essence in itself (besides their act with respect to the vision of the divine essence) than wayfarers have. But besides the act by which wayfarers desire to see and possess God they have an act of loving God in himself, and that is nobler and more meritorious. Therefore, besides the act by which the blessed love the vision of God and the possessing of God they have another, more perfect act terminating first in God himself in himself. What is assumed is clear, because given that God were never to be possessed otherwise than as he is possessed in this life, it would still be the case that he was to be loved supremely, and yet not in this case with an act of desiring; therefore, by another act, one which was not a desire. Consequently, for the same reason he is now to be loved in himself and not only desired. From this it is argued as follows. To the more perfect act of charity there corresponds a more perfect act in heaven. But the act of will that concerns possessing God corresponds to the act of desire in this life. Therefore, a more perfect act will correspond [in heaven] to that act in this life by which God is loved in himself. That can only relate to God in himself, and that is most perfect. Therefore, [it is] enjoyment.

[iii] Moreover, what is to be used is not to be enjoyed. But the act of

seeing God is to be used. Therefore, it is not to be enjoyed. Proof of what is assumed: Objects of the same kind have to terminate acts of the same kind. But the vision of one blessed person and another are of the same kind. Therefore, either both are to be used or both are to be enjoyed. {443} But both are not to be enjoyed, because one blessed person ought not to enjoy the act of another blessed person but use it. Therefore, both are to be used.

[iv] Moreover, what one can according to right reason will not to have is not an object of enjoyment. But one can will not to have that vision, because according to right reason anyone at all ought to ((*debet/potest* [var.])) conform to the divine will. But God can will [a creature] not to have that created vision. Therefore, the created will can will not to have it. Therefore, it is not an object of enjoyment.

[v] Moreover, the object of enjoyment is the same in this life and in heaven, or at least there is not a nobler object of enjoyment in this life than in heaven. But the object of enjoyment in this life is God himself and not the created vision of God. Therefore, etc. What is assumed is clear, because if that vision were the object of enjoyment in this life, then the desire for that vision would be enjoyment in this life. The consequent is false, because then whoever desired that vision would enjoy God. The consequent is false, because someone in mortal sin desires that vision and yet does not enjoy God. Similarly, the damned desire that vision and yet do not enjoy God. Similarly, someone without faith can enjoy God on the basis of purely natural capacities, because he can love [God] supremely and above all, and yet he need not on this account desire that vision, because he can be ignorant of whether such a vision is possible for him.

[5d. Replies to Durandus's Arguments]

To the arguments for the other opinion.

[i] To the first I reply that although the using that follows desire is by means of some act, {444} nevertheless an act of using that neither follows desire nor is a desire relates to a thing in itself. For example, someone can be bound by divine command to love a neighbor even given that he ought not to do anything with regard to him besides the act of love. In this case he would be using the neighbor and yet his act of using would terminate in nothing except the thing itself (and not in any act). So, in the same way, God is to be loved supremely without any such mediating act. It is nevertheless true that just as the use following desire occurs by means of

an act, so the act of the blessed that follows the desire by which God is desired in this life occurs by means of an act, because it occurs by means of the vision itself and by means of enjoyment. And so there can be three acts in heaven, namely, vision, enjoyment, and an act regarding God by means of the two [preceding] acts of intellect and will.

[ii] To the second I reply that enjoyment is not a wanting love, not enjoyment in heaven any more than enjoyment in this life. The reason is that every wanting love that is exclusively wanting presupposes an amicable love, so that when something is loved with wanting love there is something [else] that is loved more with amicable love. So if God were loved exclusively with wanting love, there would be something that was loved more than God, which is unacceptable. For this reason I maintain that enjoyment is an amicable love. When it is said that enjoyment relates to God as possessed, I say that this is true, because God is possessed. Yet it does not relate first to possessing or to the act in which he is possessed but to deity in itself.

[iii] To the third I reply that enjoyment does not succeed to desire except because it comes after it (in the way it succeeds to faith). But it succeeds to the love {445} by which God is loved in himself and for himself in this life, which is something other than an act of desiring, as has been explained. And of those two enjoyments there is the same object, namely, God himself.

[iv] To the fourth it is clear by the same [argument] that even if desire related to a complex, nevertheless enjoyment would not, because the primary object of desire and enjoyment is not the same.

[v] To the fifth I reply that desire properly relates to something future, and because the beatific act (and not God) is future, hence (granting that the beatific act is supremely desired) it ought not to be said that what is supremely desired is the object of enjoyment but that the *object* of what is supremely desired is the object of enjoyment.

[vi] To the sixth it can be said that pleasure does not properly have an object, since it is not an act. Yet granting this, I say that the object of the pleasure following on enjoyment is God himself and not any act. When it is said that the blessed will rejoice supremely in the vision, I say that they will rejoice supremely in God himself, just as they will love him supremely. And when it is said that pleasure arises from the conjunction of things that agree with one another and so from the conjunction itself, I deny the inference. It [the pleasure] will be about the object of that conjunction.

[6. Articles IV–V. The Objects of Other Enjoyments]

Concerning the fourth [article] I maintain that the object of the enjoyment that does not bring rest, such as enjoyment in this life, is God himself, because the object {446} of ordinate enjoyment is that which is to be loved for itself. But only God is such. Therefore, etc.

Concerning the fifth I say that the object of inordinate enjoyment can be something other than God, because, namely, [it can be] anything that appears supremely good to an erring intellect or even what does not [so] appear, because from its freedom the will can love supremely, and so enjoy, anything whatever that is shown to it.

[7. Replies to the Preliminary Arguments]

[i] To the first [argument] at the beginning I reply that no object other than God can satisfy the will, because no act with respect to anything other than God excludes all anxiety and distress. Whatever created object it may possess, however, the will can with anxiety and distress seek something else. To the proof I reply that the act of enjoyment with respect to the divine essence is most perfect and hence it alone will give rest. When it is said that it [enjoyment] is finite, that is true. Nevertheless, it will not be possible to attain to it [i.e., the perfection involved in enjoyment of God] by another act, because it is distinct in kind from the other act. The argument applies when the things of which one is more perfect and another less perfect are of the same kind, but not when they differ in kind. Similarly, that act excludes all anxiety and distress. I say this speaking naturally, although perhaps by God's absolute power {447} distress and anxiety could be compatible with it, as it was in Christ, according to some [e.g., Scotus]. But this will be made clear in the third book.

[I reply] in the same way to the other confirmation: Distress and anxiety are compatible with all other acts.

[ii] To the second I reply that God alone is to be loved supremely, because he is the supreme good.

And when it is said that, 'just as maximum is to maximum, etc.,' I say that that proposition is not universally true. For it is clear that the highest being produces the most perfect effect, and nevertheless the more perfect being does not always produce the more perfect effect, because an angel is a more perfect being than anything whatever here below and yet can produce only accidents [i.e., qualitative changes], when many lower [be-ings] here can produce substances. But I will say elsewhere when that proposition holds true.

[iii] To the third: It was clear earlier that that is to be enjoyed which is to be loved for its own sake and not for the sake of something else. Morally honorable goods such as the virtues are to be loved not only for their own sake, however, but also for the sake of something else. Hence they are not to be enjoyed.

[iv] To the last I reply that the will is brought to rest in beatific en-joyment. When it is said that it can seek something beyond, I say that that is true, but it cannot seek anything beyond with anxiety and distress. . . .

Question 6. Does the Will Enjoy the Ultimate End Contingently and Freely?

{486} Fifth [concerning enjoyment], I ask whether the will enjoys the ultimate end contingently and freely.

[1. Preliminary Arguments]

[1a. An Argument that the Will Does Not Enjoy the Ultimate End Freely and Contingently]

That it does not: The will is naturally inclined to will the ultimate end, just as each thing whatever is naturally inclined toward its perfection. Therefore, it cannot [incline] toward the opposite. This is because some-thing is violated when the opposite of that to which it is naturally inclined occurs. But the will cannot be violated. Therefore, etc.

[1b.] For the Opposite

The will is receptive of willing against and willing with respect to any object whatever. But it is receptive only of that with regard to which it is active. Therefore, it is capable of active willing with respect to any object whatever and also active willing against. Therefore, [it enjoys the ultimate end] freely and contingently.

[1c. Duns Scotus's Opinion]

It is said to this question [by Scotus] that the will does not enjoy the ultimate end necessarily when it is shown to it in general; or second when the ultimate end is shown to it in particular but obscurely; or third when the ultimate end is shown to it clearly in particular. {487}

[i] The first is proved first as follows. 'Natural necessity is incompatible with freedom. This is because nature and will are active principles that have opposite modes of functioning as principles. Therefore, nature's mode of functioning as a principle is incompatible with the will's mode of functioning as a principle. But the will wills an end freely. Therefore, it cannot will an end by natural necessity or, consequently, will it necessarily in any way. What is assumed – that the will wills an end freely – is proved: The same power wills an end and the means to the end. Therefore, it has the same mode of acting [in both cases], because different modes of activity argue different powers. But it operates freely concerning the means. Therefore, also concerning the end.'

[ii] 'Moreover, according to Augustine in *Retractations* I 9, "Nothing is as much in the will's power as the will itself." This is meant only with regard to an elicited act. Therefore, if the will's act is in the power of the will when the act of another power is between [it and an object], it is much more in the will's power [when it is related to the object] directly. But it is in the will's power to will or not will an end when an act of intellect is between [it and the end], because it is in the will's power to turn the intellect away from considering an end.' Therefore, etc.

'The preceding reasoning is confirmed: That which is necessitated to act when it is not impeded necessarily removes [anything] preventing [its] action if it can. Therefore, if the will {488} is of its own nature necessitated to will the ultimate end when not impeded, it necessarily removes everything preventing that volition if it can. Now nonconsideration of an end prevents its being willed, and the will can remove this [obstacle] by making the intellect pause to consider the end. Therefore, the will of necessity will make the intellect stay to consider the end. The major is clear, because what is of itself necessitated to act is never prevented except by something opposing it that overcomes its active power (*virtutem*). This is clear from the example of a heavy object: It is prevented from falling by something opposing it that overcomes its inclination, and by equal necessity it removes the impediment if it can.'

[ii] Second, chiefly, it is argued as follows. 'Everything acting of neces-

sity acts according to the full extent of its power, for just as the action is not in its power, so neither is the measure of acting (i.e., acting intensely or not intensely). Therefore, [if its willing of the end were necessary] the will would always of necessity will the end as much as it could. We experience the opposite of this.'

[iii] Third, as follows. 'A power that is free by participation does not tend toward a perfect object more than toward another object. Therefore, neither does a power that is free in essence. Now there is no difference between an end willed and other [things] willed except with regard to [the end's being] the more perfect object. The antecedent is clear, because to the extent that its act is under the will's command, sight, which is a power free by participation, does not see a beautiful object more necessarily than a less beautiful one. Hence it turns from both and sees both equally contingently.' {489}

Second, it is said that [the will] does not enjoy the end necessarily when it is apprehended in particular [but] obscurely.

The third [point of Scotus's position] (namely, that the will, even elevated by charity, does not enjoy the ultimate end necessarily when it is seen clearly) is proved first as follows.

[iv] 'When an eliciting principle does not elicit necessarily, something having that principle does not act necessarily. But an eliciting principle that is in the same mode as it was in earlier, when it elicited [its acts] contingently, does not in any way elicit an act necessarily. Now when the will at an earlier time had the same charity that it has at present, it elicited the act of enjoying contingently. Therefore, it does not now elicit that act necessarily, since no change has been made from its side. This is clear in Paul's rapture [2 Corinthians 12:2–4]: If he had charity beforehand equal to that which he had in that rapture, there was no change on the side of the will or eliciting principle. Therefore, no more necessity of eliciting then than now and consequently no necessity of acting.'

[v] 'Or an argument is formed as follows. There cannot be a necessity of acting except through something intrinsic to the active principle. From the fact that the intellect now sees an object, however, there is nothing new intrinsic to the active principle in enjoyment. Therefore, neither is there a new necessity of acting. The major is proved: Otherwise the necessity of acting would not be by reason of the active principle, and so [it would come] either from nothing or from an extrinsic principle,' and consequently it would have acted as a result of that. The minor is clear, because seeing is not the cause of enjoyment, or not [the] chief [cause].

But {490} 'there is no necessity of acting except through something intrinsic to the principal active principle. For a secondary [principle] does not give activity to a primary, as neither does it determine it to act; but conversely, the primary, acting of itself in its own mode, uses the secondary, so that if nothing in the primary excludes contingency, the whole action will be contingent.'

[vi] 'Again, either the end moves or the power moves. If the end, it is clear that there is no necessity, because that end does not move necessarily to any created act. If the will, and if there is no difference from the side of the object except for greater or less proximity, then I argue that a different proximity of patient to agent does not cause necessity but only a more intense action. This is clear from [the example of] what is hot in relation to more and less approximated heatables. Now a difference of presence in an object – say, as between seen and not seen – seems to be only a difference of proximity to the will concerning what ought to be the will's act. Therefore, it does not make a difference between necessity and non-necessity but only makes for a more or less intense act.'

[1d. Replies to Scotus's Arguments]

Although, as I believe, these conclusions should be maintained, nevertheless the arguments do not seem to prove them adequately. Hence I argue against them.

[i] Against the first, the strength of which lies in this, that the same power does not have different modes of functioning as a principle, I argue [as follows]. {491} If that proposition means that the same operative thing, indistinct in every way on its side, does not have distinct modes of functioning as a principle with respect to distinct [objects], it is simply false. For according to them [the Scotists] the divine will is a principle necessarily in the emanation of the Holy Spirit, and the same [divine will] is a principle in the creation of creatures contingently. So those holding the other opinion [e.g., Henry of Ghent, against whom Scotus was arguing] would say that the same [human] will is a natural and necessary principle in willing the ultimate end and a contingent and free principle in willing means to the end.

If it is said [in defense against this reply] that functioning as a principle contingently and necessarily can pertain to the same thing with respect to different [objects] but functioning as a principle naturally and freely cannot, this is of no avail, because there is no more conflict between functioning naturally and freely with regard to different [objects] than there is between functioning necessarily and contingently with regard to them. Similarly, if this is granted, the point is made that it is not unacceptable for the will to bear necessarily on an end and yet contingently on the means to the end, so that from such different modes of functioning the opposite cannot be proved, although according to them [the Scotists] it bears freely on both.

Moreover, as will be explained later, intellect and will are in no way distinct in reality (*ex parte rei*), and yet according to them [the Scotists] the intellect causes intellection necessarily and the will causes volition contingently and freely. {492}

Moreover, it seems that not only can the same principle be a cause of things differing in kind in such a way that it is a natural cause of some and a free cause of others, but that with respect to things that are of the same kind it can be a natural and a free cause, because according to that doctor [Scotus] the will contingently and freely causes love of itself in itself, and the same will naturally and necessarily causes love of itself in another will. What is assumed is clear, because according to that doctor the object is a partial cause not only of the act of understanding but also of the act of willing. But an object distinct from a moved will does not cause that will's act contingently and freely, because then the act would be in its power, and consequently it could be not-loved by that will as it itself pleased, which is obviously false. It is therefore caused by it necessarily.

If it is said that the will does not cause volition in another will immediately but only by means of the act of knowing, this does not suffice, because that doctor does not seem to mean that the act of understanding is properly an effective cause of the act of willing. Yet something other than the will is a partial active cause of willing. That partial cause will therefore be the object. Similarly, if this is granted, the point is at least made that the will is a contingent and free cause of the act of loving itself and that the same will is a natural and necessary cause of either the act of willing in another will or the act of understanding (or the intelligible species, if {493} it is required before intellection and an act of will). Whichever of these is granted, the point is made that the same thing can be a natural principle with respect to one [object] and a free principle with respect to another.

If it is said that the object is not properly and *per se* an effective cause but is a cause in a special mode of causing, this answer is against the principles of that doctor, who proves that the object is a partial cause of intellection from the fact that an intellection cannot be posited without an object. He therefore seems to hold that the object is properly a cause. Similarly, it could be asserted equally easily that heat does not cause properly and effectively but in a special mode of causing.

[ii] Moreover, the second argument does not succeed, because it would be easy for them to say to [the text from] blessed Augustine that he means [to speak] about an act of will with respect to means to an end but not about an act of willing with respect to an end.

Moreover, the confirmation does not seem to succeed, because it is not unacceptable for something to be in the power of the will with some act mediating and yet for it not to be in its power immediately, so that if the other [act] is given it will tend to that act necessarily. What is assumed is clear, because when the will tends toward an antecedent it necessarily tends toward a consequent known to be consequent, so that if the first volition and first act of intellect stand, the will is necessitated to the second, nor can it fail to elicit the second unless it destroys {494} the first. So others [cf. Thomas Aquinas, *Summa theologiae* IaIIae, q. 10, arts. 1–2] would say that if the intellection of the end stands, the will is necessitated to willing the end, so that it cannot fail to will the end unless it destroys the intellection of the end.

It may be said [in defense against the preceding reply] that although when one volition stands another volition follows necessarily, this is nevertheless not possible with regard to intellection, because the order of volition to intellection or of intellection to volition is not like that of one volition to another. To the contrary, this does not suffice. For the will can be so disposed that it has some act in its power such that, if nothing is varied prior to the act it can freely elicit or not elicit it, while with only an intellection supervening *de novo* it will elicit the act necessarily, so that it does not [then] have it in its power freely to elicit or not elicit it with everything remaining disposed as before. Therefore, it is not unacceptable for some act to be in the will's power with an act of intellect mediating and yet for it not to be in the will's power without qualification when the act of intellect is posited with the other conditions. What is assumed is clear: Let it be posited that someone efficaciously wills health but does not know whether or not a bitter potion is necessarily required for obtaining it. Given this, he will be able freely to will or not will to have the bitter potion. If, however, he begins to believe that he will in no way be able to be healthy without the bitter potion, if that belief and the prior efficacious willing of health stand, a willing of the bitter potion will follow necessarily – just as necessarily as heat follows in wood at the presence of fire. {495}

From this it is clear that the proposition 'That which is necessitated to acting when it is not impeded removes of necessity what prohibits it from acting when it can,' is not universally true. This is because, as has been explained, if the will has a certain dictate that it can in no way obtain health without the bitter potion and it has an efficacious willing of health, it is necessitated to will the bitter potion, so that, under these conditions, it cannot fail to will the bitter potion. Yet it is not necessitated to remove everything prohibiting it [from *not* willing the potion], because the volition ((*volitio/nolitio* [var.])) for health prohibits that volition [i. e., willing against the potion], and yet it can freely remove or not remove that [volition, i.e., the willing of health]. Hence I say that the proposition is true about a total cause (insofar as a creature can be a total cause), so that if a creature is necessitated to act, every other creature being set aside, it removes everything prohibiting it [from acting] if it can. It is not true, however, about a partial cause, when one creature concurs with another in causing, although sometimes the proposition is true [even then].

From this it is clear [as] to the proof of that proposition. When it is assumed that 'That which is of itself necessitated to acting is never prohibited except by something opposing it that conquers its active power,' that proposition is only true about a total cause, when one creature suffices without another, as is clear from the example of something heavy. Hence, just as one partial cause is impeded solely by the nonassistance of another partial cause, so sometimes one partial cause with another one assisting it causes necessarily – yet by a conditioned necessity: {496} namely, if it does not will to destroy a concurring cause; and if that is removed it sometimes causes contingently.

From this it is clear that not only can the same thing have different modes of causing with respect to different things, but the same thing can have different modes of causing with respect to the same thing at different times and when it is differently disposed. For example, when the will lacks an efficacious willing of health or a firm opinion that it will not be able to obtain it without a bitter potion, it seeks the bitter potion contingently. Yet when an efficacious willing of health and a firm opinion of the intellect that health cannot otherwise be obtained are posited, it does not without qualification will the bitter potion contingently but necessarily – namely, with such a necessity that it cannot not will it unless it wills to destroy either the efficacious willing of health or that opinion of the intellect.

It can be objected against the preceding, as they [the Scotists] object against others: that it is impossible for one extreme [A] to relate to another extreme [C] with any necessity whatever unless it relates with as much necessity to [B] whatever is necessarily required between those extremes. Otherwise, the necessary would necessarily depend on the non-necessary. Therefore, with whatever necessity the will [A] tends toward the bitter potion [C], it tends with the same necessity toward the willing of health [B] without which it does not tend toward the bitter potion.

Moreover, whatever necessarily rests in something when it is present to it necessarily holds it present if it has it and can hold onto it. Therefore, if the will tends necessarily to the bitter potion and, as it were, rests in {497} it, it necessarily holds onto it if it can – but not without the willing of health. Therefore, it necessarily holds onto the willing of health.

To the first of these I reply that the antecedent is true when that extreme is the cause of both (both of the extreme and of what is required for it), and if it relates to the extreme with an absolute necessity, so that it cannot naturally be posited unless the other extreme is posited. When, however, it is not a cause of both, then it is not properly an extreme in such a way as to make what is required something in between. Or if it is a cause of both and can, in the natural order, be posited without qualification without the other extreme, then it would not be necessary. So it is in the case at hand. The will is the cause of both the willing of health and the willing of the bitter potion, and in the natural order it can exist without either of them. When it is said that then 'The necessary would necessarily depend on the non-necessary,' I answer that what is necessary without qualification cannot depend on the non-necessary. But no creature is necessary in this way, nor does any effect depend necessarily in this way on any cause. Yet it is not unacceptable for an effect to be elicited necessarily by a cause in such a way that it is not at that time in its power without qualification except by means of something else that is non-necessary and is in its power.

To the second I reply that when something necessarily tends toward or rests in something, it necessarily keeps itself in it if it can when no other creature that is in its power concurs. But when some creature that is in its power concurs, it is not necessary. {498}

On the basis of the preceding, others [Thomas Aquinas and Henry of Ghent] would reply to the other argument [1c(ii)] by conceding that when there is equal consideration of the end the will would always equally seek the end, just as when there is an equal willing of health the bitter potion is equally sought if the firm opinion [that the potion is required for health] is equal. Hence the proposition 'Everything acting of necessity acts according to the utmost of its power' is true about a cause acting necessarily with everything else circumscribed and also about a cause acting necessarily with nothing that is in its own power concurring, but it is not true about a cause acting necessarily when something concurs that is in its power.

[iii] To the next argument it would easily be said that [these cases] are not alike, because a power that is free by participation relates to all of its objects equally with respect to indfference and contingency, because if it did not, it would not be free by participation but would in some respect be free in essence. But a power that is free in essence does not relate thus to all of its objects equally with respect to indifference and contingency but relates to some contingently and to some necessarily.

From the preceding it is clear that the arguments for the third article [of Scotus's opinion] do not completely succeed, because it could be said that the vision of the divine essence is a partial cause of enjoyment and that when it is posited the will elicits enjoyment necessarily but without it only contingently.

[iv] So it would be said [to the fourth] as to the first argument, that something with the same eliciting principle always elicits in the same way unless {499} some other eliciting principle concurs at one time but not at another. If, however, another eliciting principle concurs, this is not necessary. For example, the will necessarily elicits an act of seeking the bitter potion when an efficacious willing of health and a firm opinion that it cannot obtain health without the bitter potion concur. It does not necessarily elicit [such an act] when these do not concur.

[v] By the same [reasoning I reply] to the next that there can be a necessity of acting due to the concurrence of another active principle.

If it is said [in defense against this reply] that one active principle does not confer a mode of acting on another any more than it confers activity on it and that therefore the same active principle will always have the same mode of acting with respect to the same [object], I answer that just as one partial cause does not confer activity on another in the sense that the other receives something from it, and yet the other cannot act without it, so sometimes one partial cause does not confer a mode of acting on another in the sense that the other receives something from it, and yet with it the other can act in one way and without it in another way. Nor is another cause to be sought except that such is the nature of these partial causes. But on what basis is it certain to us that such is their nature? It is by experience: Because we experience that before an efficacious willing of health we can freely and contingently seek the bitter potion or not seek it, but not when that willing stands with the firm opinion that health cannot otherwise be obtained. Yet even if it were conceded that the same active principle always had the same mode of acting with respect to effects of the same species, the preceding argument would not succeed, because then we would have to say that since it is manifest from experience that sometimes {500} an act of will follows necessarily on an act of intellect and [another] act of will, then that act is sufficiently caused by those preceding acts without [further] activity of the will. And so there would be a new necessity for acting there, not in the active principle that was previously acting contingently, but in a single new active principle that is a sufficient cause for positing the effect without the activity of the contingently acting preceding principle.

[vi] On the basis of the preceding it could be said to the last argument (although not according to the position of those against whom it is directed [Aquinas, Henry of Ghent, and Godfrey of Fontaines]) that such a difference in the presence of a known object, say as between being seen and not being seen, is not only a difference in proximity [of the same cause] but [that the object's being seen] is the presence of a partial cause with which the will is naturally apt to act necessarily and without which [it is apt] to act either contingently or not at all. Alternatively, [it could be said that] it is the presence of a cause that is sufficient without the activity of the will (as I believe is in truth to be posited, with respect to willing the bitter potion, in either of the preceding ways concerning the willing of health and the firm opinion that health cannot be had without the bitter potion).

[2. Ockham's Solution]

To the question: I shall first set out some distinctions; second, I shall assert theses. {501}

[2a. Preliminary Distinctions]

[i] The first distinction is about the contingent, which is taken for present purposes in two senses with regard both to enjoying something contingently and to producing something contingently. In one sense [to enjoy or produce contingently means that] without qualification one can enjoy or not enjoy, produce or not produce. In that sense anything producing any

effect whatever produces contingently, because God can bring it about that it not produce. The contingent is taken in another sense for that which produces some effect and, with nothing being varied on its side or on the side of anything else whatever, has it as much in its power not to produce as to produce, so that by its own nature it is not determined to either. The same is to be said about contingently enjoying. The question is meant in this second sense.

[ii] The second distinction is about enjoying freely. In one sense freedom is distinguished from compulsion, and it is taken thus most improperly, because in that sense freedom can pertain to the intellect. In another sense it is opposed to the servitude of a rational creature, either the servitude of guilt or the servitude of punishment. In this sense the blessed are freer than those in this life, because they are more free from the servitude of guilt and punishment. In another sense freedom is opposed to necessity as necessity is opposed to the contingent in the second sense mentioned in the preceding distinction. In this sense freedom is a certain indifference and contingency, and it is distinguished from a natural active principle. This is how philosophers use the terms 'freedom' and 'will.' Active principles are distinguished in this way in *Physics* II (5, 196b17–22) and *Metaphysics* IX (5, 1048a5–9). This is also clear from Damascene {502} (*De fide orthodoxa* II 27), who proves that brutes do not have free judgment, because they are actuated more than acting (*magis aguntur quam agunt*). He means either that they are actuated according to their substance, and this is nothing to the point, because in that way men and angels would not have free judgment, because they are actuated in that way; or else he means this about their acts, and then that they are actuated either because their acts arise from something extrinsic to them and not from something intrinsic, and this is not [to the point], because then it could be held that sensitive appetite effectively causes its own acts in itself, just as this can be held about the intellect or about the heavy or about anything else whatever moving itself; or, therefore, he means that they do not have free judgment because they are actuated – that is, because they do not have acts in their own power or have lordship over their own acts – and the point is made: that those things which have free judgment have lordship and power over their own acts. But this is not without indifference and contingency; hence, etc.

[iii] The third distinction is that, just as, according to Anselm (*On the Fall of the Devil* 12; *On the Harmony of the Foreknowledge, the Predestination, and the Grace of God with Free Choice* 12–13), there is an affection for the

advantageous and an affection for the just, so there is a willing against the disadvantageous and a willing against the unjust. This is true when willing and rejecting are elicited according to a dictate of reason.

[iv] The fourth distinction is that just as there is a certain willing with respect to an incomplex, which is properly called love, and a willing with respect to a complex (taking complex broadly, as in willing to have bless-edness, willing not to exist, or some such), so there is {503} a willing against with respect to the incomplex, which can be called hatred or detestation, and there is a willing against with respect to a complex, as in being unwilling to have riches or being unwilling to have honors (yet because of this one does not hate riches or honors, except taking 'hating' broadly).

[2b. Theses]

The first thesis will be this:

> [Thesis 1] *The will contingently and freely, in the way explained, enjoys the ultimate end shown in general, because, it can love blessedness or not love it and can seek blessedness for itself or not seek it.*

This thesis can be made plausible as follows.

First, the will can will against what the intellect can dictate should be willed against. But the intellect can believe that no blessedness is possible, because it can believe that only the state we in fact see is possible for it. Therefore, it can will against all that is incompatible with the state we see, and consequently it can will against blessedness. The major is manifest, because, although, as will be explained elsewhere, the will is not necessarily conformed to a judgment of reason, it nevertheless can be conformed to a judgment of reason, both a right one and an erroneous one.

This argument is confirmed: The will can will against that in which it believes it cannot rest. But it can believe that it will not be able to rest in anything possible for it. Therefore, it can will against everything possible for it, and can certainly will against everything impossible for it. Therefore, it can will against anything whatever. {504}

Moreover, whoever can efficaciously will the antecedent can will a consequent known or opined to be consequent. But someone can effica-ciously will not to be, and it can be known evidently that not being blessed is consequent on not being. Therefore he can will not to be blessed and consequently will against blessedness. What is assumed is clear, because many who have the use of reason – both believers, who believe in a future life, and unbelievers, who believe in no future life – have killed themselves and risked death. Therefore, they were willing themselves not to be.

The argument is confirmed: Some believers, believing that they can obtain blessedness if they do not sin, choose to sin, knowing or believing that they will have eternal punishment because of such sin. This would not happen unless they were then willing against blessedness not only in general but even in particular.

A second thesis is that

> [Thesis 2] *Someone can will against blessedness in particular.*

This can be proved by the preceding arguments.

A third thesis is that

> [Thesis 3] *Someone can will against blessedness in particular when it is believed to be possible, so that he can will against having blessedness.*

This conclusion is plausible because whatever can be dictated by right reason can fall under an act of will. But right reason can dictate that an individual will always lack blessedness. Therefore, he can will always to lack blessedness. Therefore, he can will against it for himself.

This is confirmed: Someone who was damned to both sensory punishment and to the punishment of loss [of the vision of God] could, if it were left to him, conform himself in {505} willing to the divine will, both known and believed. But the divine will wills him always to lack blessedness. Therefore, this can be willed by such a will, and consequently, by the same reasoning, by the will of someone in this life.

Moreover, whoever efficaciously wills something wills everything without which he believes that he can in no way obtain what he wills. But some believer believes that he can in no way obtain blessedness without a good life, and yet he does not will to observe a good and holy life. Therefore, he does not efficaciously will blessedness, and consequently, by the same reasoning, he is able not to will it.

A fourth thesis is that

> [Thesis 4] *Someone seeing the divine essence and lacking beatific enjoyment can will against that enjoyment.*

This is proved, because, as has been said before, any will whatever can be conformed in willing to the divine will. But God can will him always to lack beatific enjoyment. Therefore, etc.

Moreover, whatever can be willed or willed against for one time can also be willed or willed against for always. But such a will can will against having blessedness for some determinate time, say, for as long as God wills that it not have beatific enjoyment. Therefore, it can reject it *simpliciter*.

A fifth thesis is that

> [Thesis 5] *Such an individual, seeing the divine essence [but] by absolute divine power lacking love of God (about this it will be clear in the fourth book) can will against God.*

This is proved or made plausible as follows. Everything disadvantageous can be an object of willing against, whether it be truly disadvantageous or esteemed to be such, just as everything {506} advantageous, whether truly or in estimation, can be an object of willing. But God can be disadvantageous to such an individual, or at least esteemed to be such. Therefore, God can be an object of willing against. What is assumed is clear, because such a person could be punished by God, both with the punishment of loss and the punishment of sense.

This is confirmed: Christ, notwithstanding that he was blessed, was punished and sustained bodily pains. But everything punitive or afflictive of an individual can be disadvantageous to him, either truly or in his estimation. Therefore, there is a reason why God can be disadvantageous to such a person, either truly or in his estimation.

Against the preceding there are many doubtful points, which will be clarified in the fourth book in the material on blessedness. Hence I pass over them for now.

[2c. Answer to the Question as Stated]

From the preceding it can be replied to the question as stated that 'ultimate end' can be taken in two senses: either for the created blessedness possible to the will or for the object of that blessedness. In the first sense it is not licit for the will to enjoy the ultimate end, if we are speaking properly about enjoying. It can, nevertheless, contingently and freely enjoy [or not enjoy it]. It can not-enjoy just because this [enjoying] is illicit, and it can enjoy, because if the will can enjoy something created that is less good, much more can it enjoy the highest created good possible to it. If, however, enjoying is taken broadly for the act of seeking, I say that the will can absolutely will or not will or will against the ultimate end, whether it be shown in general or in particular, in this life or in heaven. And {507} the preceding theses have been asserted in this sense. Speaking about the [ultimate] end in the second sense, I say that in this life it can be an object of willing or willing against. If, however, it is shown nakedly and clearly, and God should suspend the will's activity with respect to willing, it can be an object of willing against. If, however, he should not suspend the activity of willing but should leave [the will] to its own nature, then there is more doubt. Something will be said about this in the fourth book.

[3. Reply to the Initial Argument]

I reply to the argument at the beginning that the will is not naturally inclined toward the ultimate end, unless natural inclination is taken as what is done in the common course of things. And about such an inclination it is not true that there is violence in whatever is done against inclination. When it is said that 'Each thing is inclined to its own perfection,' that should be denied, taking inclination strictly, except when the perfectible thing is a natural agent. The will is not like that.

AUGUSTINE OF ANCONA
SUMMA ON ECCLESIASTICAL POWER
(SELECTIONS)

Introduction

Augustine of Ancona (Augustinus Triumphus) was born around 1270\73. He studied at Paris, lectured on the *Sentences* of Peter Lombard there sometime between 1302 and 1306, and returned as a master in theology in 1313–15, after serving as Lector in the school of his monastic community, the Augustinian Order of Hermits, at Padua. He became Chaplain to Charles, son of King Robert of Naples, in 1322. Augustine wrote on logic (including a commentary on Aristotle's *Prior Analytics*), psychology, and metaphysics and composed more than a dozen theological treatises and biblical commentaries. He completed the *Summa de ecclesiastica potestate*, from which the present selection is taken, by the end of 1326, as evidenced by a letter dated December of that year acknowledging receipt of the work at the papal court in Avignon. He died in 1328.

The *Summa on Ecclesiastical Power* is the most extensive medieval articulation of the papalist, curialist, or hierocratic conception of spiritual and temporal power earlier advanced by such authors as Giles of Rome and James of Viterbo and developed (with qualifications regarding secular affairs) by Juan de Torquemada, Cardinal Cajetan, and Albert Pighi. In more than a hundred questions, each consisting of several articles, Augustine considers the pope's power first in itself, then in relation to the acts of lordship or dominion for which it is ordained, and finally in relation to the various personal statuses making up Christian society, which all derive what perfection they have from their papal source.

Not surprisingly, given the general orientation of his work, Augustine contends throughout Question 6 of the *Summa* that no appeal from a papal judgment to any other authority is permissible. In Question 7, however, he insists that it is every Christian's duty to censure an erring pope and that in certain circumstances this duty could involve public declarations of papal wrongdoing or doctrinal error such as might lead to the pope's deposition. A deposed pope would in effect have judged himself (as Augustine puts it elsewhere). In this way the logic of juridical absolutism is preserved, while extra-juridical space is provided for correcting the supreme ruler in exceptional circumstances.

In Questions 22 and 23, on the obedience owed the pope, and in Question 63, on the obligatory character of papal directives in comparison with natural law and conscience, there are similar attempts to reconcile the transcendent status ascribed to papal authority with the claims of natural reason and human institutions. Augustine's *Summa* is of interest, then, both in relation to modern, secular theories of sovereignty and with regard to the political power of religion.

There are more than thirty known manuscripts of the *Summa*, five printed editions in the fifteenth century, and three reprints within three years of the Rome edition of 1582. (The cognomen 'Triumphus' first appears in 1581.)

For further reading, see CHLMP X.39, 'Rights, Natural Rights, and the Philosophy of Law,' and A. S. McGrade, 'William of Ockham and Augustinus de Ancona on the Righteousness of Dissent,' *Franciscan Studies*, 54 (1994–97), pp. 143–65.

Summa on Ecclesiastical Power (selections)

Question 6. Concerning Appeal from a Papal Judgment

Article 1. Can an Appeal Licitly Be Made from the Pope to God?

[1a. Arguments that Such an Appeal Is Licit]

{56A} We proceed to the first article as follows. It seems that an appeal can licitly be made from the pope to God.

[i] Because God does not forsake Christ's faithful. 'For he himself says "I will not leave you or forsake you." So we can say with confidence, "The Lord is my helper, I will not fear what man may do to me"' (Hebrews 13:5–6 [quoting Joshua 1:5 and Psalm 118:6]). But it often happens that the pope acts unjustly, for since he is human he can be affected by emotion and be confused, so that he wanders from the straight

path of justice because of some corruption or fleshly affection. Lest, therefore, the church's faithful seem forsaken by God, it is licit for them to appeal to God in a case of injustice.

[ii] Moreover, we read in Isaiah 64:6 that 'The acts of human justice are like the skirt of an unclean woman,' for they can take on various false colors. But appeal is the remedy for a case invalidated by injustice, {56B} as is written in 2. q. 6., c. *Lice*[a]*t*: 'It is licit for an appellant to carry an invalidated case higher by the remedy of appeal.' Therefore, in such a case it is licit to appeal from the pope to God.

[iii] Moreover, it is written in James 5:4, regarding oppressors and those who commit injustice: 'Listen! The wages of your workers, which you kept back by fraud, cry out, and their cry (*clamor*) has reached the ears of the Lord of hosts.' But there is no appeal from the unjust sentence of a lower judge except complaint (*clamor*) to a higher. Therefore, since the pope has no other superior, it seems that one can appeal from him to God.

[1b] To the Contrary

God would hear a case brought before him on appeal either as God or as a human being. Not in the first way, because 'no one has ever seen God' (John 1:18). Nor in the second, because since the Ascension he has not consorted with human beings in a human way; hence he [Jesus] said to Mary Magdalene, when she wanted to approach him in a human way, 'Do not touch me' (John 20:17). It therefore seems that one cannot appeal to God in the present life.

[1c. Resolution]

I reply that for three reasons relevant to the present question we have to say that appeal from the pope to God in the present life is demonstrably ridiculous and frivolous. These relate to [i] the appeal process itself, [ii] the pope, from whom the appeal is made, and [iii] God, to whom it is made.

[1c(i). Conditions of an Appeal Process Ruling Out Appeal to God]

The first reason is clear from the following.

An appeal is a remedy meant for relief of those oppressed in a judicial case. Accordingly, with respect to the case in which the appeal is made, [the process of appeal] includes relief of the oppressed [from the effects of the judgment being appealed while the appeal is under consideration], because an appeal should not be made except in case of injustice or for those unjustly oppressed.

Second, with respect to the judge from whom appeal is made, [the appeal process] includes a request for Apostles. Thus it is said in 2 q. 6, *Ab eo*, that 'letters of committal, commonly called Apostles, should be sent by the judge from whom an appeal is made to the judge who will consider the appeal,' to make it clearly apparent to the higher judge that the oppressed party has appealed and that the lower judge is aware of this.

Third, with respect to the appeal itself, [the process] includes a public record, so that, if the request for Apostles is denied, it will be apparent to the higher judge {57A} from the written record at hand that the lower judge is not ignorant of the appeal.

Fourth, with respect to time, it includes a set time or due date, so that the appellant cannot cheat both the higher and the lower judge by evading both judgments.

Fifth, it includes the testimony of witnesses, because when the preceding requirements have been completed, witnesses are brought before the higher judge, and the case proceeds according to what is alleged and proved.

Sixth and last, it includes the hearing of the case, because a judgment is pronounced, and the case is concluded.

Now it is ridiculous to say that recourse to God is to be had by such a judicial order in the present life, since God – who knows who deceives and who is deceived and to whose eyes everything is naked and open not only before it is written down but even before it occurs – does not need to observe such an order in judging.

[1c(ii). *Appeal from the Pope to God Is Ruled Out by the Pope's Position as* Vicarius Dei]

The second reason is taken in relation to the pope, for only the pope is said to stand in God's place (*esse vicarius Dei*), because only what he binds or releases is taken as bound and released by God himself. Hence the pope's judgment and God's judgment are one judgment, just as the pope's judgment and that of his delegate judge are one. Since, therefore, an appeal is always made from a lesser judge to a higher, and since no one is greater than himself, no appeal holds from the pope to God. There is one consistory of the pope and of God, and the pope is doorkeeper of this consistory and holds its key. No one, therefore, can appeal from the pope to God, just as no one can enter God's consistory except by means of the pope, who is keyholder and doorkeeper of the consistory of eternal life. Just as no one can appeal to himself, so no one can appeal from the pope to God, because there is one judgment and one court of God and the pope.

[1c(iii). Appeal from the Pope to God Is Ruled Out by Consideration of God's Nature]

The third reason is taken in relation to God, to whom the appeal would be made. For it is said in 2, q. 6, c. *Qui se*, that, 'appeals are to be heard by those to whom the appeal is made,' so that just as the judges from whom the appeal was made are visible and passed judgment against the oppressed party visibly and perceptibly, in the same way the higher judges to whom the appeal has been made ought to give relief to the oppressed visibly and perceptibly. Now it is plain that God is invisible. For it is written in Exodus 33:20, 'A man shall not see me and live,' and in Job 9: 11, 'If he should come to me, I shall not see him.' Therefore, God does not visibly and perceptibly consider a case brought to him by appeal. For it is written in Daniel 2:11, 'What you ask me to speak of is a hard matter, and no one will be found who may judge it except the gods, whose dwelling is not with mortals.'

[1d. Replies to the Opening Arguments]

[i] To the first we therefore have to say that God does not desert his faithful but always comes to their aid in a just cause, either by way of appeal (and so he comes to their aid by human means, in a judicial process conducted among humans) or by way of supplication and prayer, when he changes a judge's heart from injustice to justice, from evil to good – hence an individual ought sometimes to have recourse to God from the pope's judgment by prayer and supplication, as holy Jacob did in Genesis 43:14: 'May God almighty grant you mercy before the man, so that he may send back {57B} with you this your brother and him whom he holds in chains.' Sometimes, however, [God acts] by way of recompense, because by his just judgment he sometimes permits his faithful to be unjustly oppressed, so that he may reward them more for their long-suffering.

[ii] To the second we have to say that human injustice is not always [finally] dealt with in the present life, because even cases dealt with on appeal by judicial means are often subject to great defects, as Augustine says (*On Free Choice* I 5) about the civil law laid down for ruling cities, that it allows many things and leaves many things unpunished which will

nevertheless be judged by divine justice. And the same Augustine, commenting on 1 Peter 4:18 ('If the just will scarcely be saved, what will become of the ungodly and the sinners?'), explains why the just will scarcely be saved. It is because God's justice is agreed to be so great that sometimes what seems in our judgment to be just in human beings will be found unjust in God's judgment. Human injustice therefore remains to be dealt with in a future judgment, but in the present life God does not deal with it by way of appeal except by means of humans and by means of the judicial order he has instituted.

[iii] To the third we have to say what the Gloss says on the text cited there, that it was meant to frighten those who think the poor and oppressed have no protector. The Lord almighty will examine the cases of individuals in a future judgment, in which he will render to all according to their deeds.

Article 2. Is an Appeal from the Pope to God an Appeal against God?

[2a. Arguments that Such an Appeal Is Not an Appeal against God]

We proceed to the second article as follows. It seems that to appeal from the pope to God is not to appeal against God.

[i] Because a living person's appeal carries more weight than that of one who is dead. But Abel appealed to God after the injustice done him by his brother, according to Genesis 4:10: 'The voice of your brother's blood cries out (*clamat*) to me from the earth.' Similarly, therefore, it seems that one can complain (*reclamare*) to God about an injustice done by the pope.

[ii] Moreover, an appeal is a complaint (*clamor*) reaching a higher judge about an injustice done by a lower judge. But such was the cry (*clamor*) of the children of Israel which reached God, according to Exodus 3:7: 'I have seen the affliction of my people in Egypt, and I have heard their cry.' It therefore seems licit to appeal from the pope to God.

[iii] Moreover, to appeal is to petition for a judge over one's cause. But Susannah appealed thus when she said in Daniel 13 [Susannah]:42–43, 'Eternal God, who dost know all secrets and foresee all things, thou knowest they have borne false witness against me.' And it is added there (v. 44) that 'the Lord hearkened to her voice.' Therefore, an appeal to God in a case of injustice is not against God.

[2b] To the Contrary

{58A} The pope is an intermediary (*medius et sequester*) between God and humanity, as Moses was, according to Deuteronomy 5:5: 'I was an intermediary between God and you.' But Dathan and Abiram, who spurned the judgment of Moses, were plunged into the depths of the earth, as if they had spurned the judgment of God, as is written in Numbers 16. It seems therefore that an appeal from the pope to God is an appeal against God.

[2c. Resolution]

I reply that as far as the present question is concerned we have to say that an appeal implies three things. First, a judicial order and, consequently, divine ordination, because, as is said in Romans 13:1, 'The [authorities] that exist are ordained by God.' Second, it implies a set time, because an appeal must be made in a fixed, determinate time. Third, it implies a defense of one's own justice, because those who appeal trust in their own justice and lay down their own justice as a foundation. From these three it can therefore be shown that whoever appeals from the pope to God in the present life appeals against God.

First, with respect to divine ordination: On the text of 1 Corinthians 4: 3 ('But with me it is a very small thing that I should be judged by you or by the day of man.'), the Gloss says that there are two kinds of judgment: one human, by which man judges man in the present life (which the Apostle calls the day of man); another divine, by which God will judge at the end of the age (which the Apostle calls the day of God). Since, therefore, an appeal does not rely on the judgment with which God will judge but on a human ((*humano/proprio*)) judgment by which we are judged in the present life, whoever appeals from the pope to God wants to escape that judgment by which God has ordained that we be judged ((*iudicetur/iudicet*)) in the present age and as much as possible wants to evade what has been divinely ordained. And in resisting the divine ordination, according to the Apostle, one resists the divine will. Therefore, whoever appeals in that way from the pope to God appeals against God.

Second, because such an appeal conflicts with the determination of a time [for judgment already made by God]. For God has set a fixed day on which all who are to be judged by him must be presented at his tribunal, 'so that all may receive according to their deeds in the body,' as the Apostle says in 2 Corinthians 5:10. But since an appeal is a remedy in law, whoever wishes to appeal to God in this life wants to proceed in court by legal means before the day of judgment that is to come after this life. He wants by legal means to anticipate the day ordained by the judge, and thus, by appealing in this way to Christ the judge, he appeals against the judge.

Third, such an appeal conflicts with divine justice. For since every appeal relies upon right and justice, it follows that those who appeal want to establish their own justice (*iustitiam*) as a foundation and that they trust in their own justice. But according to the Apostle in {58B} Romans 10:3, 'Those who seek to establish their own righteousness (*iustitiam*) have not been subject to God's righteousness.' Since an appeal relies on one's own justice, those who appeal to God therefore withdraw from divine justice and call forth divine justice upon themselves, for since no living flesh is justified in [God's] sight, those who want to establish their own justice in the sight of God and to glory in their own justice show, as much as is in them, that they do not have that justice from God, and thus they withdraw themselves from God's justice from the time when they assert their own justice in their appeal. One who appeals to God in that way therefore appeals against God. One can appeal in the sight of humans and establish one's own justice, since one does not receive justice and other inner goods from them and they know only those things that are outwardly apparent, but in the sight of God such an appeal or foundation of justice has no place.

[2d. Replies to the Opening Arguments]

[i] To the first we therefore have to say that the outcry of Abel's blood was not an appeal or an accusation, because, as the Gloss says there, 'The evidence of a completed crime does not require the complaint of an accuser ((*accusatoris/accusationis* [var.])) or an appeal.' Instead, it expressed the vengeance taken by divine justice. Hence the Gloss says there, 'Great is the virtue of justice, which exacts vengeance for the blood of the innocent.'

[ii] Similarly, to the second we have to say that the cry of the children of Israel was an expression of divine vengeance. God did not do this directly by himself, however, but by means of Moses, to whom he said (Exodus 3:10), 'Come, that I may send you to Pharaoh to bring my people the Israelites out of Egypt.' So by means of the pope – through appeal [to him] – God does justice in the present life for all the oppressed. [But] from

the pope's judgment it is extremely dangerous to appeal, just as it was dangerous for Dathan and Abiram not to accept the judgment of Moses.

[iii] To the third we have to say that Susannah's recourse to God was not by way of appeal but in the mode of devout supplication. And these two modes of recourse are licit: By appeal we may have recourse to a human [judge], especially to the vicar of Jesus Christ; by prayer and supplication recourse may be had to God.

Article 3. Should an Appeal to God Be Allowed?

[3a. Arguments that Such an Appeal Should Be Allowed]

We proceed to the third article as follows. It seems that an appeal to God should be allowed.

[i] Because no one should be given cause for despair. But if an unjust judgment by the pope could not be appealed to God, there would sometimes be cause for despair, since recourse could not be had to anyone. It therefore {59A} seems that such an appeal should be allowed.

[ii] Moreover, it is only reasonable that when human aid is lacking divine aid be sought. But in 2 Chronicles 20:12 it is said in the person of that holy king Jehoshaphat, 'We do not know what to do, but our eyes are on you [God].' But human aid is not available for an unjust judgment by the pope. It is only reasonable, therefore, that appeal be made to God.

[iii] Moreover, the casting down of the proud is pleasing to God, according to Judith 9:11: 'From the beginning the proud have not been pleasing to God, but the prayer of the humble and meek has always been pleasing to him.' But in such an appeal – from the pope to God – there follows the freeing of the oppressed and the humiliation of the proud. It therefore seems that such an appeal is only reasonable.

[3b] To the Contrary

To evade a judgment instituted by God is to evade the order of divine justice. But someone making such an appeal seems to want to evade a judgment instituted by God. Therefore, such an appeal should not be allowed.

[3c. Resolution]

We have to say that it is reasonable on two accounts to reject and not allow an appeal from the pope to God. First, because all appellants justify themselves and deny the justice of the judge from whose sentence they appeal, because by the very fact that they appeal they say that they have been unjustly aggrieved and assert that the judge unjustly aggrieves them, and consequently they say that they themselves are just and the judge unjust. Therefore, those who appeal from the pope to God necessarily have to justify themselves before God and deny that the pope is just. But all who justify themselves before God and deny the justice of another deserve to be rejected by God. We have the example of the Pharisee in Luke 18 ((18/13)):11–14, who was rejected by God for justifying himself and denying the publican's justice. Therefore, appeals made from the pope to God should not be allowed but rather rejected with respect to the appellants, because ((*quia/qui*)) from the very fact that they justify themselves and deny the justice of another, their appeals should be rejected.

Second, this is plain with respect to the appeal itself, because an appeal depends on knowledge, since it depends on rules of law, and it is plain that rights and laws are matters of knowledge. Now in knowing and taking cognizance there is a movement of things to the soul. God must therefore be known by us, not directly, but through his likenesses and his effects, as the Apostle says in Romans 1:20: 'The invisible things of God are seen and understood through the things he has made.' Supplication and prayer, however, depend on grace and love, because in loving there is a movement of the soul to the thing [loved]. Hence, although we do not know God directly, we can cherish and love (*diligi et amari*) him directly. Therefore, an appeal, which depends on knowledge, cannot come before God directly, but only by human mediation and by means of judges {59B} instituted by God. But prayer and supplication, which depend on love, can come before God directly, because love enters in where knowledge stays without.

[3d. Replies to the Opening Arguments]

[i] We therefore have to say to the first that our hope in God ought not to be for this life only, because as the Apostle says in 1 Corinthians 15:19, 'If we have hoped in Christ for this life only, we are of all people most to be

pitied.' For it happens in God's just judgment that good persons and saints
are sometimes separated from the church by an unjust sentence of excommunication or deposition. [Yet] if without any insolence they hold and
defend until death what they know is preached in the catholic church, the
holy father, seeing in secret, crowns them, as Augustine says in his book
On True Religion (c. 6).

[ii] To the second we have to say that when human aid is lacking, divine
is to be sought, not by way of appeal, however, but by way of devout
supplication, which the holy father [God] himself always heeds, either
freeing the suppliant, or granting patience, or exchanging what is sought
for something better. For often, according to Augustine, things sought are
not given when they are sought, so better may be given, or (*Tract 102 on
the Gospel of John*) 'they are deferred, so that they may be generously
bestowed at a more suitable time.'

[iii] To the third we have to say that one should not resist the pride of
a superior in this life by one's own strength (*virtute*) but should patiently
bear it, because according to the Apostle, 'We ought not to be overcome
by evil but to overcome evil with good' (Romans 12:21). And most
especially, no one, under any pretext whatever, can without the mark of
pride withdraw from [obedience to] the highest pontiff, who holds God's
place on earth.

Article 4. Can One Appeal from a Present to a Future Pope?

[4a. Arguments that One Can]

We proceed to the fourth article as follows. It seems that one can appeal
from a present to a future pope.

[i] Because a future pope is greater in relation to a present pope than
the Emperor Caesar was in relation to Paul. But Paul appealed to Caesar
against those who were falsely accusing him, as is plain in Acts 25:10–11.
Much more, therefore, can one appeal from a present pope to a future
pope.

[ii] Moreover, we read in 2, q. 6, c. *Qui* [*se*]: 'Those who are placed
above others should not resent having a superior over themselves.'
Therefore, just as the present pope is placed above others in hearing the

cases of all appellants, so he ought not to resent it if appeal is made from him to a future pope.

[iii] Moreover, it is also written in 2, q. 6, c. *Quotiens*, 'Let those who have an untrustworthy judge appeal to the Roman see.' {60A} But the present pope can sometimes be considered an untrustworthy judge. Therefore, one can appeal to a future pope holding the Roman see.

[4b] To the Contrary

Appeals made for the sake of delay should not be accepted, as is written in 2, q. 6, c. *Quicunque*. But an appeal from a present pope to a future pope would be of this kind, because in this way disputes and questions would never have a set end. Therefore, such an appeal should not be accepted.

[4c. Resolution]

We have to say that an appeal made from a present to a future pope is ridiculous. This can be proved by direct argument (*ratione ostensiva*) and by *reductio ad absurdum*. The first argument is as follows. A present pope compared to a future pope as future is not less but greater and more perfect than the future pope, because the present pope is actual, whereas the future pope, as future, is potential. But act is always more powerful and more perfect than potency. Hence, because appeal from a greater to a lesser, or from a more perfect to a less perfect, does not hold, appeal from a present to a future pope in that way [i.e., to a future pope as future] is ridiculous. Now if the appeal is made to a future pope, not as future but as then present (because he would then be actual and have the same authority as the present pope), the appeal does not hold in that way either, because it is plain that an equal cannot command an equal. The one deciding an appeal, however, is always greater than the one from whom the appeal is made.

The *reductio ad absurdum* is as follows. If an appeal could be made from a present pope to a future pope, by the same token an appeal could be made from that future pope to another future pope, and so two impossibilities would follow. First, there would be a process into infinity. Second, questions and disputes among the church's faithful would never be settled, and appeal, which was devised as a legal remedy in the interests of justice, would militate against justice.

[4d. Replies to the Opening Arguments]

[i] To the first we therefore have to say that Paul appealed to Caesar, not as to someone greater than or equal to himself, but as a Roman citizen, as Augustine says (*Answer to the Letter of Petillian* II 58) and as is set down in dist. 10, c. (*Si in adiutorium*): 'If you think fit to adopt the laws of the earthly empire for your aid, we do not blame you, for Paul did this against those who were wronging him, when he testified that he was a Roman citizen.'

[ii] To the second we have to say that a present pope in relation to a future pope is either greater or at least equal to him. Hence such an appeal could not be made without wronging him.

[iii] To the third we have to say that the difficult aspects of all cases are reserved to the determination of the Apostolic See, and its decision (*consultum*) must always be awaited on all of them. {60B} If anyone presumes to attempt to obstruct the proceedings of this see, 'He will learn with peril to his own office to return cases to the same see,' as is written in 2, q. 6, c. *Qui se*.

Article 5. Is It Licit to Appeal from the Pope to the College
of Cardinals?

[5a. Arguments that Such an Appeal Is Licit]

We proceed to the fifth article as follows. It seems that one can licitly appeal from the pope to the college of cardinals.

[i] Because it pertains to those who elect a judge to judge that judge, but it pertains to the college of cardinals to elect the pope as judge. Therefore, it pertains to them to judge that judge.

[ii] Moreover, the pope must judge and give sentence about difficult affairs of the church with the counsel of the cardinals. It therefore seems that at least in such cases, if he does something without their counsel one can appeal to them.

[iii] Moreover, the pope is related to the cardinals as the head is to the members [of the body]. But the head receives some of its power (*virtutem*) from the members, because if the heart were not alive the head could not live. Therefore, just as one could appeal to the heart of a natural body if

the head offended, so if the pope, who is head of the mystical body, offends, one can appeal to the cardinals.

[5b] To the Contrary

Appeal is not made from a greater to a lesser, but the college's authority is less than the pope's. Therefore, such an appeal is null.

[5c. Resolution]

We have to say that the cardinals assist the pope as counselors and as his attendants and servants, for they present alternative ways of proceeding in the difficult matters before him on which he wishes to take counsel. Then it pertains to him to choose and determine what seems more beneficial for the church. That is why cardinals are so called, from *cardo* (hinge), because just as the whole door turns on a hinge, so the difficulties of the whole world that are subject to counsel turn on them. But it would be insane to appeal from a lord to his subordinates and from a king to his counselors. It is similarly insane to believe that one can appeal from pope to cardinals, since the cardinals are related to the pope as his subordinates and counselors. The pope, on the other hand, is related to the cardinals as heaven {61A} to earth. Hence it is said in dist. 10, c. *Suscipitis*, 'Does it seem just to you if the spirit yields to the flesh, if the earthly rises above the heavenly, if things human are preferred to things divine?' Therefore, just as the heavens generate and destroy things below and alter and vary them, yet none of those lower things rise up or appeal against the heavens but patiently endure whatever the heavens work upon them, whether by generation or destruction or alteration, so the papal power, as heavenly, can generate, destroy, and alter all lower powers (*potestates*) of both clergy and laity in such a way that it is not licit for anyone to rise up or appeal against it.

[5d. Replies to the Opening Arguments]

[i] To the first we therefore have to say that the pope chooses the cardinals, and the cardinals choose the pope, yet not in the same way, for the pope chooses the cardinals by his own power (*virtute*), because whatever fruitfulness and whatever authority is in them comes from the pope. Hence in

John 15:16 the Savior said to the disciples, whom the cardinals represent, 'You did not choose me, but I chose you ((*vos/vox*)), and I appointed you to go and bear fruit.' And in John 15:5 he said, 'Abide in me and I in you, because apart from me you can do nothing.' But the cardinals choose the pope by authority of the pope himself, not by their own authority, for it is maintained by the pope's authority that the person chosen by two-thirds of the cardinals should be *ipso facto* accepted by the universal church as highest pontiff. Hence they can choose the pope by their own authority, but in such a way that once he has been elected they cannot judge him or entertain an appeal against him.

[ii] To the second we have to say that it is not essential to the pope as pope that he determine or order the difficult affairs of the church with the counsel of the cardinals, for he can dispatch and determine such matters without their counsel. After all, we do not read that Christ, whose place is held by the pope, was in need of counsel from the apostles or determined anything with their counsel except to test and teach them, as when he said to Philip (John 6:5–6), ' "Where are we to buy bread for these people to eat?" testing him, for he himself knew what he was going to do,' as also when he said to Peter (Matthew 17:25), 'From whom do the kings of the earth take tribute? From their children or from others?' But because the pope is entirely human and can mislead and be misled in such affairs, it is fitting for him to do everything he does with more mature counsel, in proportion as his decisions are set on a lampstand and not under a bushel, and no mortal dares resist them.

[iii] To the third we have to say that it is not essential (*de ratione*) for a head as head to receive anything from the members but always, rather, to influence them. Hence in a natural body the head does not receive anything from the members as a head, but if it receives anything this is by reason of the nourishment it needs from the digestive processes of stomach, liver, and heart – and in this respect it falls short of being simply a head. But the highest pontiff is the head of the whole mystical body of the church in such a way that he receives no power (*nihil virtutis*) and authority from the members but always influences them, for which reason he is fully and essentially a head. {61B}

Article 6. Can One Appeal from the Pope to a General Council?

[6a. Arguments that One Can]

We proceed to the sixth article as follows. It seems that one can appeal from the pope to a general council.

[i] Because one can appeal from a lesser [power] to a greater. But power is greater in a council than in the pope, because the power of the church dies in this or that pope, but in a council and in the whole church it does not die. Therefore, it is licit to appeal from pope to council.

[ii] Moreover, according to Augustine, the common good is preferred to any private good, but a general council represents the common good of the whole church. The pope, on the other hand, since he is a private person, is rightly under the authority and power of a council.

[iii] Moreover, the community cannot err, hence neither is it excommunicated. A pope, on the other hand, can err. But from anything deviant and crooked appeal can be made to what is straight and well ordered (*regulatum*). Therefore, one can appeal from pope to council.

[6b] To the Contrary

A general council receives its authority from the pope, not vice versa, as is plain in dist. 17.

[6c. Resolution]

We have to say, as the Philosopher says in Book III (3, 1113a10–11) of the *Ethics*, that choice is the determining of a council (*determinatio concilii*). For a council is made up of many individuals, so that different ways of proceeding may be proposed by them, from which the person who is over the council can choose one in preference to the others – for according to Damascene (*On the Orthodox Faith* II 22), choice *is* choosing one rather than another from among many things previously given. Therefore, without the pope or his authority in a council, no choice can be made among the things proposed. Hence it is said in dist. 17 ((17/15)) that the authority to assemble universal councils resides with the Apostolic See, because without the authority of the Roman pontiff a council has neither stability nor authority.

Similarly, there is another reason why there cannot be an appeal from pope to council. It is because no one except God can change the order of things natural in the realm of nature (*in regimine naturali*), and in the moral realm (*in regimine morali*) no one can change the judicial order except the pope, who holds God's place on earth. But the judicial order operating among humans presupposes the pope's authority for convoking a council, {62A} assigning authority, and ordering the mode of appeal from one [judiciary] to another. Appeal from pope to council is therefore ridiculous, since a council cannot change the judicial order in the ecclesiastical realm (*in regimine ecclesiae*) without the pope's authority.

[6d. Replies to the Opening Arguments]

[i] To the first we therefore have to say that 'being greater,' when it is said of power, is not taken in a univocal sense with reference to the power residing in the church and in the pope, because it exists in the church or in a council as in a root and habitually (because in the absence of a pope and college of cardinals a Roman pontiff could be provided for), but such a capacity exists in the pope actually; and because what is in act can act, whereas what is in habit and in potency does not act. Therefore, in terms of potential or habitual greatness, the power of the church is greater in a council and in the whole congregation of the faithful than in the pope, because in a council of the faithful such power never dies. In this or that pope, on the other hand, it does die. But in terms of actual greatness the power of the church is greater in the pope than in a council, because a council cannot act by that power, but the pope can act when he will. Therefore, since an appeal bespeaks an act (from pope to council), such an appeal will not hold, just as an appeal from greater to lesser does not hold.

[ii] To the second we have to say that according to Augustine, commenting on Genesis 1:31 ('God saw everything that he had made, and it was very good'), all the things produced by God were indeed good in themselves but *very* good because of the order they keep in relation to one another. Accordingly, therefore, since the leader and head of the whole ecclesiastical order is the pope, just as that order would be destroyed by an appeal, so the corresponding good would be destroyed, because (since the good of an army exists only on account of the good of its leader and the good of the church only on account of the good of the pope) the good of the leader is greater than that of the whole army, and the good of the pope is greater than that of the whole church.

[iii] To the third we have to say that at such time as a pope may err, in

such a case recourse can be had to a council, as was said above. This is because a pope ceases to be pope on account of heresy, but while he remains in authority, no one can withdraw from [obedience to] him in any way whatever.

Article 7. Can the Pope Make a Statute Allowing Appeal from His Judgment?

[7a. Arguments that He Can]

We proceed to the seventh article as follows. It seems that the pope can make a statute allowing appeal from his judgment.

[i] Because a pope can make a {62B} statute allowing himself to renounce the papacy. Therefore, as it seems, all the more can he make {62B} a statute allowing appeal from his judgment.

[ii] Moreover, if it does not involve wronging someone else, one can renounce a right of one's own. Granted, therefore, that there is no appeal from the pope through the [existing] judicial order, because he does not acknowledge a superior on earth, nevertheless, he can, as it seems, change that judicial order himself and renounce such a right.

[iii] Moreover, the pope is exempt from paying tribute, yet if the emperor seeks tribute, the pope does not refuse. Similarly, therefore, granted that he is legally independent of appeal, it seems that he can bind himself by such a law.

[7b] To the Contrary

As is said in dist. 14, c. *sicut*, the pope cannot do anything that is found contrary to, or opposed to, the decrees of the holy fathers. But we find it determined in the chapters of the Council of Ephesus that it is not licit for anyone to appeal from the judgment of the Apostolic See [cf. the reference to Pope Celestine I's authority in Cyril of Alexandria's third letter to Nestorius, which was read with approval at the council; PG 77, 105ff].

[7c. Resolution]

We have to say that with regard to jurisdiction and moral ((*morali/ moralis* [with edn 1473])) action the pope is related to all lower powers in the ecclesiastical order as God is related to all secondary causes with regard to their natural action. Now God is related to secondary causes with regard to natural action in such a way that he can exempt one creature from the 'jurisdiction' of another – as, for example, he can exempt a combustible substance from the jurisdiction of a burning fire, so that someone standing in the fire is not burned, as he did with Daniel and his companions (Daniel 3:23–26) – but he cannot exempt any creature from his own jurisdiction, for according to the Apostle (2 Timothy 2:13), God is faithful and cannot deny himself. If, however, he exempted some creature from his own jurisdiction, he would be denying that he was God. The pope is related in the same way to the powers of the ecclesiastical order, because he can exempt one prelate or group from the jurisdiction of another superior, yet he cannot exempt anyone from his own jurisdiction, because then he would be denying that he was head of the whole church. Therefore, since by such an appeal an individual withdraws from the pope's jurisdiction to the jurisdiction of another, the pope cannot make a statute allowing this, just as he cannot make a statute to the effect that a pope, while remaining pope, is not over the whole church.

[7d. Replies to the Opening Arguments]

[i] To the first we therefore have to say that a pope can renounce the papacy, but that it involves a contradiction for him to deny that he is pope and head of the whole church while remaining pope. Hence the latter cannot be done, whereas the former can.

[ii] To the second we have to say that one can renounce a right of one's own if that right has not been acquired from another, and if such renunciation would not be prejudicial to the other. Now the pope acquires his right from God alone. Hence, while remaining pope he cannot renounce such a right without wronging God himself and the whole church. {63A}

[iii] To the third we have to say that the pope pays tribute from temporal goods, which he can place under the power of others without prejudice to his own jurisdiction. But that anyone should by appeal withdraw universally from his authority would prejudice the pope's jurisdiction, by which he is head of the whole church.

Article 8. Is It an Error to Say that It Is Licit to Appeal from the Pope to God or Man?

[8a. Arguments that It Is Not an Error]

We proceed to the eighth article as follows. It seems that it is not an error to say that appeal can be made from the pope to God or man.

[i] Because error and every vice, according to Augustine (*On the City of God* XI 17), is against nature. But it is natural to appeal in a case of injustice, just as it is natural to repel violence. Therefore, so to appeal is not an error.

[ii] Moreover, according to Augustine in *On True Religion* (I 10), doubtful points of doctrine are to be believed as long as the authority of holy church does not command the contrary. But no authority seems to have defined it as erroneous to say that appeal can be made from the pope to God or to a human being ((add *vel hominem* [with Cod. 71, St. John's College, Oxford])). Therefore, such an appeal ((om. *ad hominem* [with Cod. 71, St. John's College, Oxford])) is not heretical.

[iii] Moreover, all people whatever are held to preserving their natural lives as much as they can. Similarly, therefore, with regard to moral life. But appeal has been devised for this, namely, for preserving justice in moral life. Therefore, it is licit without the sin of heresy, not only to believe in but actually to make [such an appeal].

[8b] To the Contrary

It would be an error to believe that the pope is not the head of the whole church. But whoever believes it possible to appeal in a judicial order from the pope to a human being or to God believes that the pope is not the head of the whole church. Therefore, so to believe is an error. {63}

[8c. Resolution]

We have to say that it is an article of faith to believe in one, holy, catholic, and apostolic church. Now the unity and stability of that church are based on the unity and stability of its head. Anyone, however, who believes that it is possible to appeal from the pope to a human being in the present life believes that there is some other head in the church besides the pope and thus does not believe in the unity of the church. Anyone who believes, however, that it is possible to appeal in a judicial order from the pope to God believes that God has not instituted the existing judicial order to be followed among humans in the present life and thus sins against apostolic authority. Accordingly, I think it is an error to believe that it is possible to appeal from the pope to God or to a human being in the present life, and especially to defend this proposition recklessly and obstinately.

[8d. Replies to the Opening Arguments]

[i] To the first we therefore have to say that what is natural in one thing can be contrary to nature in another. For example, it is natural for fire to heat but contrary to nature for water to do so. So it is natural in a case of injustice that a lower power should have recourse to a higher, but it is against nature for it to withdraw completely from the higher power, because then what is supreme would not be supreme.

[ii] To the second we have to say that whoever obstinately defends things contrary to the decisions of the [first] four general councils falls into heresy, because the church has approved those councils just as it has the four gospels, as is written in dist. 15, c. *Sicut*. But we find in the canons of the Council of Ephesus that it is not licit for anyone to appeal from the judgment of the Apostolic See.

[iii] To the third we have to say that we must generally preserve both our natural and our moral lives as far as possible, but in a matter of the faith, or to avoid a greater danger, or for the benefit of the commonwealth, one must risk death. {64A}

Question 7. On Censuring the Pope

Article 1. Does Fraternal Correction Extend Even to the Pope?

[1a. Arguments that Fraternal Correction Does Not Extend to the Pope]

We proceed to the first article as follows. It seems that fraternal censure does not extend to the pope.

[i] Because it is written in Exodus 19:12–13 that 'A beast that touches the mountain shall be stoned.' By the mountain, we understand the pope; by a beast, anyone below him; and by touching, censure, as the Gloss says.

Again, in 2 Samuel 6:7 it is written that 'Uzzah was struck because he touched the ark of the Lord,' by which the pope is signified. Similarly, in Numbers 12:1–10 it is written that Miriam the sister of Aaron was struck with leprosy because she corrected Moses, the ruler and leader of the people. Therefore, fraternal censure does not extend to the pope.

[ii] Moreover, acts of justice should sometimes be forgone so as not to give occasion for sin. For example, the excommunication of a ruler or community or an action to recover tithes is sometimes forgone for this reason. Therefore, since there could easily be occasion for sin and dishonor to the pope from his being censured, it seems that such censure should be forgone so as not to give occasion for sin.

[iii] Moreover, a censurer is active, while the one censured is passive. But according to Augustine, the active is superior to the passive. Therefore, the pope, who is superior, ought not to be censured by anyone.

[1b] *To the Contrary*

By the Lord's command anyone whatever must correct a brother. This is according to Matthew 18:15 (and it is quoted in 2, q. 1): 'If your brother sins against you, correct him, when the two of you are alone.' But everyone is brother to the pope, because Christ himself, whose place he holds, is not ashamed to call all people brothers, saying in Hebrews 2:12, 'I will proclaim your name to my brothers.' Therefore, such censure extends to the pope.

[1c. *Resolution*]

We have to say that according to some fraternal censure does not extend to the pope unless there is danger to the faith or the crime of heresy, for then, in taking up God's cause, an inferior becomes superior. This happened with the monk Lanfranc ((*Lanfranco/Lanfredo* [var.])), who went with his abbot's permission to confute Berengar, who was attacking an article of the faith. But in {64B} all other cases, since a corrector holds the superior position in relation to the one being corrected, no mortal may in the present life correct the pope's faults, since the pope holds the place of superior in the whole church, as is said in dist. 40, c. *Si papa*. When it is argued from the Lord's commandment ('If your brother sins against you, correct him.') that therefore, if *such* a brother – say, the pope – sins against you [you should correct him], this commits the fallacy of consequence, for such correction is not meant with respect to every brother but only with respect to an inferior or equal.

Nevertheless, without prejudice [to this view], I think that we have to distinguish three ways in which censure or correction can be made.

First, by way of simple admonition, and when it proceeds from charity, that manner of correction extends to the pope and to all superiors, especially when there is hope of their improvement. For although the pope is universally superior to others in office, nevertheless in many things he can be inferior to others. For Augustine says in a letter to Jerome (Letter 82), 'I ask you to correct me faithfully where you see that I need it, for although in the terms of honor now in use in the church a bishop is greater than a priest, nevertheless in many things Augustine is less than Jerome − although correction even by someone less than oneself should not be avoided or disdained.'

Second, [correction] can be made by way of command and the threat of punishment.

Third, by way of denunciation and accusation before a judge. Neither of these [last two] extends to the pope, because in these ways the pope himself judges everyone and is judged by no one.

[1d. Replies to the Opening Arguments]

[i] To the first we therefore have to say that in an inferior's correction of a superior simply by way of charitable admonition, three conditions ought to be observed: first, discretion and due care, so that his amendment may be hoped for or expected. Second, there ought to be obedience and due reverence, so that it is not done rashly and impudently. Third, there ought to be love and good will, so that it is not done for the sake of defamation or detraction. For lack of the first, therefore, it was commanded that no beast touch the mountain − that is, that anyone censuring a prelate bestially and indiscreetly should be stoned. For lack of the second, on the other hand, Uzzah was struck for rashly touching the ark, for since he belonged to the priestly tribe, he ought to have carried it on his own shoulders. And for lack of the third Miriam was struck with leprosy, because she rose up against Moses out of discontent and to defame him.

[ii] To the second we have to say that excommunication of a ruler and of a multitude is forgone, not so much to avoid giving occasion for sin −

the equity of justice should not be forgone for this reason – but because of the danger of schism or to avoid contempt of excommunication. Similarly, an action to recover tithes from knights and rulers should not be forgone to avoid giving occasion for sin, {65A} but because they sometimes say that they have them as a gift of the church.

[iii] To the third we have to say that by such a censure as proceeds from charity and satisfies the preceding conditions, a superior can be censured by an inferior, because if someone is superior in office as a prelate, he can nevertheless be inferior in many other respects.

Article 2. Ought the Pope to Be Censured Publicly or in Private?

[2a. Arguments that the Censure Should Be Public]

We proceed to the second article as follows. It seems that the pope ought to be censured openly, not in private.

[i] Because Paul was inferior to Peter, yet it is written in Galatians 2:11, 14 that, 'When Cephas had come to Antioch Paul withstood him to his face before all the people, because he was blameworthy.' Therefore, the pope ought to be censured openly, not in private.

[ii] Moreover, it is written in 1 Timothy 5:20, 'Rebuke the sinner in the presence of all, that the rest may stand in fear.' Therefore, the pope should be charged before all, so that others may also stand in fear.

[iii] Moreover, it is written in Acts 5:3–9 that Peter publicly denounced Ananias and his wife Saphira, who were secretly practicing fraud about the price of a field, without previously admonishing them in private. Therefore, if the pope sins, either secretly or publicly, he ought to be censured publicly because of his public status.

[2b] To the Contrary

Commenting on the text in Matthew 16:22 ('And Peter took him aside and began to rebuke him.'), Jerome says that Peter took Jesus aside separately, lest he be seen to reproach their master in the presence of the other disciples.

[2c. Resolution]

We have to say that that question is doubtful because of Paul's censure of
Peter, whom he reproached publicly before all, as is plain in Galatians 2.
Following Jerome (PL 26, 338–42), it may be said that this was not a true
censure but was prearranged. Augustine, however, says to the contrary
that it was true and not fictive (Letters 28, 40, and 82). Yet for the present
this doubt can be resolved generally concerning common fraternal correction, as it may be called, {65B} following Augustine in his book about the
words of the Lord. He says that a sin is either public and notorious or
private and secret. If it is public, then (as the Apostle says) you ought to
reprove it before everyone, because then it is not only you that the person
sins against, wrongs, and affronts, but also everyone who sees him, as is
said about the wicked servant in Matthew 18:31: 'When his fellow servants
saw what he did, they were greatly distressed.' If the sin is secret, however,
then following the Savior's word you ought to reproach him for it when
you are alone.

Second, [this doubt] can be resolved particularly about censuring the
pope. Concerning this I think we have to say that such censure would
either concern a matter of the faith and the crime of heresy, and then such
censure should be delivered publicly. Hence the Gloss on the passage in
Galatians 2 says that Paul would by no means have censured Peter in front
of everyone or withstood him to his face unless he had been a peer of his
or an equal, which is true with respect to defending the faith. And Augustine in his letter to Jerome, where he discusses that question, says that Paul
provided an example for posterity, in accordance with which, as long as
fraternal charity is preserved, those who are greater should not scorn
correction from those who are less when they are defending the truth of
the gospel. He adds that when the latter are acting for the truth of faith
they can resist those who are greater when they abandon the path of faith
and truth. Therefore, since to Judaize and to provoke others to Judaize,
once the truth of the gospel was proclaimed, would be against the path of
gospel teaching, Peter was deservedly censured by Paul in such a case, and
the pope in such a case could justly be corrected by any believer whatso-
ever.

If, on the other hand, [censure] is given from charitable zeal and concerns the amendment of other sins, and if amendment is hoped for, it
ought to be done by simple word of admonition in secret, and not rashly
but with observance of the conditions mentioned above.

[2d. Replies to the Opening Arguments]

[i] To the first we therefore have to say that Paul was less than Peter and also greater and equal. He was indeed less in power as a prelate, because only Peter was 'cephas,' that is, head, of the whole church. He was greater, however, by the prerogative of election, because he had been chosen by Christ after his resurrection and glorification. Hence, on the papal seal Paul is placed to the right [of Christ], Peter to the left. But he was equal in the office of preaching and defending the faith, because [preaching] the gospel to the uncircumcised was entrusted to him, as the gospel to the circumcised was to Peter, as he testifies to the Galatians. Hence in such a case he could rightly censure Peter as his equal or inferior.

[ii] To the second we have to say that the Apostle's words are meant to apply to public and notorious sins or they are meant to apply to the correction administered by prelates and by those to whom it pertains to correct not only by fraternal charity, with verbal warnings, but also by punishing wrongdoers and inflicting penalties in conformity with justice, so that others may fear [to transgress].

[iii] To the third we have to say that the sin of Ananias and his wife Saphira had not come to Peter's notice in a human way, by denunciation or {66A} accusation, but by divine revelation. And so he did not proceed regarding that sin in accord with human judicial forms but, as God's executor, according to a form of divine judgment.

Article 3. If the Pope Does Not Listen to Correction, Should the Church Be Told?

[3a. Arguments that the Church Should Not Be Told]

We proceed to the third article as follows. It seems that if the pope does not heed someone censuring him, the church should not be told.

[i] Because according to the Gloss, by 'the church' a higher prelate is meant, but the pope does not have a prelate over him except God. Therefore, if he disregards censure, the church cannot be told.

[ii] Moreover, according to Christ's rule in Matthew 18:15–16, 'If your brother sins against you . . . If he does not listen to you, you ought to take one or two others along with you.' Therefore, it is necessary to call in witnesses before telling the church.

[iii] Moreover, a brother's reputation should be preserved, and the greater the reputation of the pope, the more dangerous it is to detract from it. But from telling the church his reputation would be lost. Therefore, if the pope disregards censure, the church should not on that account be told.

[3b] *To the Contrary*

As was said above, fraternal censure extends to the pope. Therefore, the order of fraternal censure extends to him. But this is the order of fraternal censure: If a private warning is not heeded, the church should be told. Therefore, such an order ought to be observed in censuring the pope.

[3c. Resolution]

We have to say (as said above) that the censure that extends to the pope by way of simple warning should be given with hope of his amendment and with observance of the stated conditions: that it be done with due discretion and care, with love and good will, and with obedience and reverence. We must, however, [now] make a distinction regarding the things censured in the pope. There are certain sins which are private (*occulta*) and harm only the sinner and the one sinned against. Here the order mentioned above should be observed: A private (*secreta*) warning precedes telling the church. On the other hand, there are certain sins which redound to the harm of the whole commonwealth, for example, the sin of heresy and the subversion of the whole Christian faith. For such [sins], {66B} such an order should not be observed, but (unless there are good grounds for believing that after a private warning [the sinner] will want to desist from such subversion), help against the danger should be given at once, because the common good should be preferred to any private (*privato*) good. Augustine and the African bishops took this course when the heresy of the Pelagians arose, denouncing them to Pope Innocent without a private admonition beforehand, saying (Letter 176), 'To the most blessed lord and deservedly revered Pope Innocent, Augustine greets [you] in the Lord [. . .] A new and exceedingly pernicious heresy is trying to break out from the enemies of Christ's grace. By their unholy arguments they are even trying to deprive us of the Lord's Prayer [. . .] I make this known so that your reverence may immediately and quickly provide against it.'

[3d. Replies to the Opening Arguments]

[i] To the first we therefore have to say that 'the church' can mean either a prelate or the congregation of the faithful, which holds the place of prelate in a case where the faith is at issue or in one that involves danger to the people and the whole commonwealth.

[ii] To the second we have to say that that order ought to be observed in sins that harm [only] the sinner or doer, but when the sins are such that the Christian faith can be subverted, that order should not be observed.

[iii] To the third we have to say that the Savior ordered fraternal censure to be administered in this way (by a private warning) so that there would be provision for conscience and so that no one's reputation would be blemished. Nevertheless, because conscience should be preferred to reputation, if a brother's sin cannot be amended without loss of reputation, the Lord ordered that, finally, it should be publicly denounced, inasmuch as such a reprimand by many might be a remedy to save him.

Article 4. By [the Lord's] Command Ought the Pope to Be Censured for Every Sin?

[4a. Arguments that the Pope Ought Not to Be Censured for Every Sin]

We proceed to the fourth article as follows. It seems that the pope ought not to be censured for every sin.

[i] Because on the text of Matthew 18, 'If your brother sins against you,' the Gloss says, 'Note that it says, "If he sins *against you*," because it is not for us to judge sins committed against God.' It is indeed not for a human being to censure the pope (or another person) for blasphemy or other sins committed against God.

[ii] Moreover, in fraternal censure we ought to imitate Christ, according to the Apostle's saying in Ephesians 5:1 [conflated with 1 Corinthians 11: 1], 'Be imitators of me [as I am of Christ], as beloved children.' But Christ punished many sins without first issuing a private warning. Therefore, a private censure is not to be administered for every sin. {67A}

[iii] Moreover, it is written in Genesis 37:12 that Joseph accused his brothers in front of his father for the worst crimes, nor do we read that there was any private warning beforehand. Therefore, such [preliminary] censure is not to be administered for every sin.

[4b] To the Contrary

On the text of Matthew 18, 'If your brother sins against you,' the Gloss says, 'For whatever sin he has committed with your knowledge, you ought to correct your brother.' Therefore, such correction should be administered for every sin.

[4c. Resolution]

There is a difference between public admonition (*denunciatio*), accusation, and complaint (*proclamatio*). *Public admonition* is for the sake of a brother's amendment, and hence fraternal censure precedes it, so that reputation may be preserved as well as the amendment of the wrongdoer. In *accusation*, on the other hand, satisfaction of the church is intended and preservation of the well-being of the commonwealth. Accordingly, accusation should not be made regarding all [sins] but only about those from which it is evident that spiritual or physical danger may arise for the whole multitude and the whole commonwealth. When this is the case, one can proceed to accusation without a private warning beforehand, because the common good should be preferred to private good. Hence it is necessary for an accusation to be written, which is not necessary for a public admonition, as is plain from *Extra, De accusat.*, c. *Super his*. But a *complaint* is made about certain less serious sins and ought to be called a reminder rather than an accusation or public admonition, for it brings to remembrance a fault committed for which the individual must make purgation, but it does not damage his reputation. Now if a complaint were made {67B} publicly for a grave fault, from which someone's reputation could be ruined, and there was no private warning beforehand, it would be illicit and against Christ's command. From this it is plain that fraternal ((*fraterna/fraterno* [with edn 1473])) censure should neither be administered for every sin nor omitted for every sin.

[4d. Replies to the Opening Arguments]

[i] To the first we therefore have to say that 'sins committed against God (*in Deum*)' can be understood in two ways: either with reference to knowledge, in the sense that only God knows and not man, and then censure is not a matter for our judgment; or else with reference to the offense, in that God is offended, because with your knowledge something

is done against his commandments. We are bound to censure such sins more than if they were committed against us.

[ii] To the second we have to say that sins hidden from us are manifest to God. Hence, just as all public sins stand in relation to human judgment, so all sins hidden from us stand manifest in relation to divine judgment. Because of this, he can punish them without a private warning beforehand. Nevertheless, he usually does censure sinners within themselves, by giving them pangs of conscience, which are with a man waking or sleeping, as we read in Job 33:15–16: 'In a dream, in a vision of the night, when deep sleep falls on mortals, while they slumber on their beds, then he opens their ears and terrifies them with warnings, that he may turn them aside from their deeds.'

[iii] We have to say to the third [argument] that we should believe that the ancient fathers did many things pertaining to fraternal charity which have not been recorded. It is possible, therefore, that Joseph warned his brothers before accusing them, although this is not recorded. Or it can be said that that sin was a public crime, at least among the brothers, and hence that it deserved accusation without a private warning before-hand. . . .

Question 22. On Obedience to the Pope

Article 1. Must Christians Obey the Pope in Everything?

[1a. Arguments that They Must]

{129B} We proceed to the first article as follows. It seems that Christians must obey the pope in everything.

[i] For it is written in Colossians 3:20, 'Children, obey your parents in everything.' Much more, therefore, must we obey the pope in everything, because, as is written in Hebrews 12:9, 'If indeed we have had our fathers in the flesh {130A} to discipline us and we respected them, shall we not much more submit to the father of spirits and live?'

[ii] Moreover, an inferior ought not to judge ((*iudicare/iudicari* [with edn 1473])) a superior, because a greater cannot be judged by a lesser, as is written in dist. 21, c. *submittitur*. Therefore, it does not pertain to Christian subjects to judge or discriminate in which [cases] they ought or ought not to obey the pope.

[iii] Moreover, the pope is the prelate of all Christians, but blessed Benedict says in his Rule (c. 68) that if a prelate commands the impossible, the subject ought to attempt to fulfill it.

[1b] To the Contrary

As is written in Acts 5:29, 'We must obey God rather than man.' Therefore, if the pope were to command anything against God, we should not obey him.

[1c. Resolution]

We have to say that the things commanded by the pope fall under either (i) natural law (*iure naturali*), (ii) divine law, or (iii) positive law. (i) If they fall under divine law, and if the pope should command anything contrary to that law, he should not be obeyed. For example, if he commanded that a creature be adored or honored with the worship due only to God, or that God's name be taken in vain, or that time dedicated to the worship of God be withdrawn from it, he should not be obeyed. On the contrary, he should be vigorously resisted. (ii) If what the pope commands falls under natural law, and if he should command that something be done against that law – as, for example, fornication, theft, or the killing of an innocent person, or that one should not eat or contract marriage – he should not be obeyed in such things either. (iii) But if what he commands falls under positive law, since all positive law depends on him, either by direct promulgation (canon law) or by confirmation and approval (civil law), then, just as it pertains to him to establish (*condere*) all the commands of positive law and to confirm or interpret them, so it pertains to him to abolish all of them, either in the whole world or in part of it. Hence in such matters, if he commands anything contrary to positive law or interprets the law otherwise than it is written, he should be obeyed.

[1d. Replies to the Opening Arguments]

[i] To the first we therefore have to say that we should not absolutely and without qualification obey either our fleshly fathers or our spiritual fathers in everything, but only in what relates to subjection to fleshly fathers and reverence and honor to spiritual fathers.

[ii] To the second we have to say that a subject ought not to judge or discriminate as to whether he ought to obey the pope, if the pope commands what accords with God and is customarily observed in the Christian religion consonant with divine and natural law. But if he were to command things visibly (*notabiliter*) contrary to custom and not in harmony with God's commands and the law of nature, since a pope commanding such things would be an unbeliever, he would judge himself, because 'Those who do not believe' rightly 'have already been judged' (John 3: 18). {130B}

[iii] To the third we have to say that blessed Benedict is speaking of perfect obedience to counsels [not commands] and with respect to a lower prelate, in which case the prelate should be obeyed in everything that can be done without sin. For it is plain that if an abbot were to command a monk to sleep on the bare ground, the monk could licitly complain (*reclamare*) about obeying him, because it is not customary in observance of the rule. Yet with respect to a prelate of universal authority (*obedientiae*) – and the pope is such – no complaint is allowed as long as he does not command anything out of harmony with God's commands and the law of nature.

Article 2. Must Clergy and Laity Obey the Pope in the Same Way?

[2a. Arguments that They Must]

We proceed to the second article as follows. It seems that clergy and laity must obey the pope in the same way.

[i] Because [all] children must comply in the same way with their fathers' directives. But according to John 1:12 ('He gave to those who believe in his name power to become children of God'), laity and clergy are in the same way children of God, whose vicar is the pope. Therefore, they must obey the pope in the same way.

[ii] Moreover, no one is exempt from God's lordship. But the pope is God's vicar on earth. Therefore, a layman is no more exempt from the pope's lordship than a cleric.

[iii] Moreover, those who are in a condition of greater servitude must obey the pope more [than those who are freer]. But the laity are in more

servitude than the clergy, because what is written in 1 Peter 2:16 ('Live as free people, yet do not use your freedom as a pretext for evil, but be servants of God') is understood to be addressed to clerics.

[2b] Chrysostom on Matthew Is to the Contrary

[2c. Resolution]

If lay and clerical obedience to the pope are compared, clerical obedience is understood to be (i) more primary, (ii) more universal, and (iii) more direct.

(i) It is more primary because the pope's government and all ecclesiastical government primarily exists for the sake of spiritual good; but it consequently flows over into a concern with material things, because the pope is vicar of him who said in Matthew 6:33, 'Seek first the kingdom of God and all these things will be added unto you.' Lay or secular government, on the other hand, has been introduced primarily for the sake of material goods. Hence the clergy are understood to be more primarily ((*principalius/principaliter*)) {131A} subject to ecclesiastical government than the laity.

(ii) [The clergy are] universally [subject to the pope], because the pope is over clerics by both the [sacramental] power of order and by the power of jurisdiction, because both powers come to clerics from him. But he is over laymen only by the power of jurisdiction, because by the fact that they are laymen they are not suitable recipients of the power of order.

(iii) Similarly, clerical obedience is more direct, because although the pope's power extends to both clergy and laity by direct jurisdiction, nevertheless it does not extend to the laity by direct administration (*executionem*). The pope administers the governance of the laity through secular rulers and judges, except ((add *nisi* [with edn 1473])) in the five cases noted in *Extra, Qui filii sint legitimi, c. Per venerabilem*. The first is when a prince or king grants some temporal possession to the church, either granting only its use and retaining lordship for himself or granting both use and lordship (the church [even] then administers lordship with respect to justice by laymen, not ecclesiastics, as Hugh [of St. Victor] says in his book *On the Sacraments*). The second [case] is when some difficult and doubtful matter arises, and then it should be referred directly to the pope. The third is by reason of a misdeed by a secular ruler, for example, if a secular ruler is found to be a heretic and to deviate from the faith. The fourth is if a defect is found in the judgment given by a secular ruler or judge, because the pope has power to rectify and correct [the act of] a secular [authority] if it is not a good one and to establish and confirm it if it is good, as Hugh says in the book mentioned above.

[2d. Replies to the Opening Arguments]

[i] To the first we therefore have to say what Chrysostom says in discussing the Savior's words in Matthew 21:28–30, 'A certain man had two sons. The first said he would not do his father's will but afterwards did it, while the second said he would do it but afterwards did not.' By those two sons [according to Chrysostom] are meant laity and clergy, because the laity, by the very fact that they choose a secular life and wear secular dress, seem to refuse obedience to Christ and his vicar. Clergy, on the other hand, by the very fact that they [choose] an ecclesiastical life and wear a clerical dress, are understood to promise obedience to Christ and his vicar. If they fail to do so, it is said of them later in the same chapter, 'Amen, I say to you, the tax collectors and prostitutes will enter the kingdom of God ahead of you.'

[ii] To the second we have to say that no one is exempt from both the pope's direct lordship and his indirect lordship. Clergy are under ecclesiastical government directly, the laity are under it [indirectly] through lay government, which has been given to the supreme spiritual authority to serve and assist it, as was said above.

[iii] To the third we have to say that the laity are in a condition of greater servitude and hence must obey in more ways, for they must submit to both lay government and ecclesiastical government. Clergy, on the other hand, are exempt from lay government, because they cannot be summoned before a secular judge. {131B}

Article 3. Must Lay Christians Be More Obedient to the Pope than to the Emperor or a King?

[3a. Arguments that This Is Not the Case]

We proceed to the third article as follows. It seems that the Christian laity are not required to be more obedient to the pope than to emperor or king.

[i] Because granted that an archbishop is greater than a bishop and a

bishop greater than an abbot, nevertheless a subject must obey [his] bishop more than an archbishop, and a monk must obey [his] abbot more than a bishop. Similarly, therefore, given that the pope is greater than an emperor or king, lay subjects must obey emperor or king more than the pope.

[ii] Moreover, each [superior] should be obeyed in accordance with the laws he imposes. But the emperor imposes laws on everyone subject to the Empire. Therefore, they must submit to him in accordance with such laws.

[iii] Moreover, it is due as a matter of justice that we render to all what is their own, in accordance with the Apostle's statement in Romans 13:7, 'Pay to all what is due them – taxes to whom taxes are due, revenue to whom revenue is due.' But the emperor is lord of temporal matters. Therefore, it is due as a matter of justice that in temporal matters the laity obey him more than the pope.

[3b] To the Contrary

A universal lord should be universally obeyed, but the pope is vicar of him who is lord of all, according to Esther 13:9: 'Lord and King who rulest over all, because the whole world is under thy authority.' Therefore, he should be universally obeyed.

[3c. Resolution]

We have to say that the whole world structure (*tota machina mundialis*) is only one principality (*principatus*); hence it ought to have only one ruler, in accordance with the Philosopher's statement in *Metaphysics* XII (10, 1076a4–5): 'Beings are unwilling to be badly organized; hence [let there be] one ruler and one principality.' But the ruler of the principality of the whole world is Christ, whose vicar is the pope, according to Daniel 7:13– 14: 'As I was watching [in the night visions], I saw one like a human being coming with the clouds of heaven. And he came to the Ancient One. To him was given power and honor and kingship, that all peoples, tribes, and languages should serve him.' Now wherever there is a source and origin to which everything can be traced, obedience to a higher [authority] is not abolished by the command of a lower one. Hence in the issues raised above the gloss on Romans 13:1 applies: 'If a procurator orders one thing and a proconsul something else, the proconsul should be obeyed, {132A} not the procurator. And if the proconsul orders one thing and the emperor something else, the emperor should be obeyed, not the proconsul.' In the same way, if the pope orders one thing and the emperor something else, the pope should be obeyed, not the emperor. Yet the faith of Christ does not destroy justice but confirms it, as the Apostle says in Romans 3: 'The righteousness (*iustitia*) of God is through faith in Jesus Christ.' Hence, since every government (*principatus*) proceeds from the ordering of divine justice, according to Romans 13:1 ('All power is from God, and what is from God is ordered (*quae a Deo sunt, ordinata*).'), therefore just as the pope ought to observe all justice and institute and order all governments (without which justice could in no way be preserved), so he ought to maintain and govern – not abolish or undermine – all due subjection and obedience of their subjects to secular rulers and kings. Hence Peter, whose successor the pope is, says in his first canonical epistle, chapter 2:13, 'Be subject for God's sake to every human institution (*creaturae*), whether to the king as supreme or to governors as sent by him to punish evildoers and praise the good.'

[*3d. Replies to the Opening Arguments*]

[i] To the first we therefore have to say that the cases are not similar, because everyone is subject to the pope by divine law, and so with respect to him there is room for no exception. A presbyter, on the other hand, is subject to his bishop by natural law, and so he must [obey] the bishop more than the archbishop, to whom he is subject only in those matters which the church has established and ordained. Similarly, a monk must obey his abbot more than the bishop, especially if he [the abbot] is exempt [from episcopal oversight] and [the commanded act] accords with the [monastic] rule and with constitutions confirmed by the pope.

[ii] To the second we have to say that, as Augustine says to Boniface (as is quoted in dist. 9, c. *Imperatores*), 'Whoever is unwilling to submit to imperial laws passed in favor of God's truth earns a great punishment. Whoever is unwilling to submit to imperial laws passed against God's truth earns a great reward.' If, therefore, an emperor orders anything against the pope's command and against the liberty of the church, one should not submit to him.

[iii] To the third we have to say that obedience to secular rulers should not be withdrawn unless they render themselves unworthy and unless they

administer government unjustly, because then they can be deprived by the pope not only of the subjection of their subjects but also of governmental jurisdiction.

Article 4. Must the Servants of Christians Obey Their Lords More than the Pope?

[4a. Arguments that They Must]

We proceed to the fourth article as follows. It seems that the servants of Christians must obey their own lords more than the pope.

[i] Because no one can serve two lords issuing contrary commands, as is written in Matthew 6:24. {132B} Therefore, if it should happen that the pope and their own lords command contraries, the servants must submit more to their own lords than to the pope, for otherwise they would transgress the Apostle's directive in Ephesians 6:5: 'Servants obey your earthly lords in all fear.'

[ii] Moreover, if anyone takes an oath to two lords, he must obey both, and first the one to whom he swore first. But servants take an oath to their earthly lords before the pope. Therefore, they must obey them first.

[iii] Moreover, the pope is the successor of blessed Peter, but blessed Peter directs in his first canonical [epistle], chapter 2:18, that servants 'be subject to their lords in all fear, not only to those who are good and gentle but even to those who are bad-tempered and overbearing.'

[4b] To the Contrary

A common lord should be obeyed more than one's own lord, just as the common good should be put before one's own good. But the pope is the common lord of all. Therefore, servants must obey him more than their own lords.

[4c. Resolution]

We have to say that with respect to the present question a human being can be considered in four ways. First, with respect to the movement of inner will. Second, with respect to the way of life of the whole Christian religion. Third, with respect to the natural functioning of the body.

Fourth, with respect to external physical behavior. One must obey differently in accordance with these four considerations.

(i) With respect to the movement of inner will, one must obey God alone. For, as the Gloss says, quoting Augustine, on Romans 13:1 ('Let every soul be subject to the higher powers'), obedience is rendered to powers insofar as they are higher (*superior*). It is plain, however, that nothing is higher than a human being in the motions of the will except God. Hence, when roused by God's inspiration (*instinctibus instigatis a Deo*), one ought at once to obey and not resist, as the prophet said: 'Let me hear what the Lord God says to me' (Psalm 85:8).

(ii) With respect to the way of life of the Christian religion, on the other hand, every Christian must obey the pope, because in ordaining how Christians should live no one is superior to him, especially since he is the intermediary between God and humanity or the whole Christian people. Hence, everyone living in the Christian religion – lords and servants, laity and clergy – ought to say to the pope what the children of Israel said to Moses in Exodus 24:7: 'All that the Lord has told us' through you 'we will do, and we will be obedient.'

(iii) With respect to the natural functioning of the body, however, such as bodily sustenance and the generation of children, a human being has no superior. {133A} In such matters all are equal. Hence a servant need not obey any lord forbidding him to eat or to marry.

(iv) But with respect to external physical behavior we must obey different people, because here we can have different superiors. For in managing a ship a sailor must obey the ship's pilot rather than the pope, even if the pope is present, because in such an art he is subject to the pilot and not to the pope. Similarly, in things relating to war a soldier would be held to obey the commander of the army rather than the pope, and so on in other cases.

[4d. Replies to the Opening Arguments]

[i] To the first we therefore have to say that if the pope directs otherwise than a servant's own lord in matters where the servant is subject to him, the servant must obey the pope and not his own lord.

[ii] To the second we have to say that if anyone takes an oath to two bishops, he must obey both if he can. If on the other hand he cannot, he is bound to obey him to whom he swore first, especially if he is beneficed in his diocese. If, however, he has been translated with an explicit dispen-

sation to the diocese of the second to accept a greater benefice, some say that he must obey the second and not the first. Nor is it true that one takes an oath to anyone else before the pope, because one takes an oath to the pope in baptism, when one promises to live according to the faith and rites of the Christian religion.

[iii] To the third we have to say that blessed Peter directs servants to obey their lords in those matters in which they are subject to them. He did not, however, exempt them from the obedience in Christian service owed to him and his successors.

Article 5. Can the Pope Exempt the Slaves of Christians from Servitude and Grant Them Freedom?

[5a. Arguments that He Can]

We proceed to the fifth article as follows. It seems that the pope can exempt the slaves of Christians from servitude and grant them freedom.

[i] Because he who frees from a greater servitude can free ((*liberare/liberari* [with edn 1473])) from a lesser. But blessed Peter, whose successor the pope is, freed all Christians from servitude to the [dietary and ceremonial] Law [of the Old Testament] when he said in Acts 15:10, 'Why are you trying to place on the disciples' necks a yoke that neither you nor our ancestors have been able to bear?' Therefore, the pope can grant freedom from all other servitude.

[ii] Moreover, servitude has arisen through sin, but the pope can absolve from sin by administration of the sacraments. Therefore, he can abolish all servitude. {133B}

[iii] Moreover, it pertains to the pope to bring what is unjust to justice. But many get lordship by tyrannical usurpation and violence. Therefore, it pertains to the pope to exempt Christians from servitude to such lords and restore them to freedom.

[5b] To the Contrary

The apostle Paul baptized Onesimus the slave of Philemon and consequently cleansed him from sin. Nevertheless, he sent him back to his lord Philemon, nor did he exempt him from servitude, but rather he confirmed him in servitude to his lord (Philemon 12–14). Therefore, the pope ought to act in the same way.

[5c. Resolution]

We have to say that by the sin of our first parent the stain of sin was so great in the soul that it could be called the soul's servitude, because whoever commits sin is a slave of sin. The penalty was similarly very great in the body: mortality, infirmity, and external servitude. Now through Christ, whose vicar the pope is, we have been freed from servitude to sin and the servitude of the soul, according to the Apostle in Romans 6:22: 'But now you have been freed from sin and enslaved to God.' But we have not been freed from the servitude of the body or from other penalties, because the baptized die and are ill just like the unbaptized, and one is bound to external servitude after baptism just as before. It may be said here, as Seneca says in Book III of *On Benefits* (c. 19), that 'It is an error to think that servitude penetrates to the whole person, for the better part is excepted. Only the body is liable to punishment and assigned to a lord. The mind has its own law (*mens est sui iuris*).' But this must be understood with respect to compulsory servitude, because it is plain that the soul cannot be forced to serve sin – indeed, if it were forced and sinned involuntarily, it would not be sin. However, this does not mean that servitude to sin does not penetrate into a willing and consenting soul. We could only be freed from this servitude by Christ, because we were able to fall by ourselves, but we could not rise again by ourselves.

Now as to why Christ has not freed us from bodily servitude as he has from servitude of soul, three reasons are commonly given.

One is from the side of natural justice. It is because the natural order requires that, just as in the physical world higher things move lower ones to their actions by the excellence of the physical forces (*naturalis virtutis*) divinely conferred on them, so in human affairs the higher should command the lower by their will, in accordance with the divinely ordained order of justice.

The second reason is from the side of legal justice, without which the stability (*status*) of human affairs could not be maintained. This is because (according to Augustine in Book IV, chapter 4, of *On the City of God*), when such justice is removed, kingdoms are nothing but great bands of robbers. Christ has not abolished the order of this justice among us but has indeed strengthened it, because he who has justified us has not released us from any just debt.

The third reason relates to the present state (*status*) of the world. {134A} This state requires that as long as we live the animal life of the senses we serve God's law with our minds and the law of sin with our bodies, as the Apostle says in Romans 7:25: 'With my mind I serve the law of God, but with my flesh I serve the law of sin.' Only in a future state will the creature be freed from the servitude of corruption and taken up into the freedom of the children of God in glory. Therefore, in the same way the pope ought to try to free believers in Christ from servitude of soul, which is servitude to sin, but not from bodily servitude, by which they are held bound to temporal lords. Rather, holding to the teaching of Christ and the apostles, he ought to confirm them in such servitude.

[5d. Replies to the Opening Arguments]

[i] To the first we therefore have to say that Peter freed from legal servitude because the truth of the gospel was incompatible with the shadow of the Law, since with the advent of truth the shadow becomes void. But the freedom of soul one gains in baptism is compatible with the chain of bodily servitude. On this account the cases are not alike.

[ii] To the second we have to say that by the administration of the sacrament [of absolution] one is freed from servitude of soul, not, however, from bodily servitude and penalties.

[iii] To the third we have to say that the pope ought to rescue Christ's faithful from unjust and tyrannical lordship when it remains unjust and tyrannical. But if it should become just, either by his confirmation or by the adherence of its subjects, he ought rather to confirm [their subjection] than to exempt them.

Article 6. Can the Pope Justly Condemn Free Christians to Servitude?

[6a. Arguments that He Cannot]

We proceed to the sixth article as follows. It seems that the pope cannot justly condemn free Christians to servitude.

[i] Because the truly free cannot be truly slaves, but it is written in John

8:36 that 'If the Son makes you free, you will be truly free ((*eritis*/*erit is* [with edn 1473]))).' Therefore, Christians have been truly freed by the son of God and cannot justly be condemned to servitude.

[ii] Moreover, it is written in Matthew 17:26 that the children of a king are free from tribute. But all Christians are children of an eternal king, according to John 1:12: 'He gave them [all who received him, who believed in his name] power to become children of God.' Therefore, they cannot justly be condemned to servitude.

[iii] Moreover, what is not the cause of a cause cannot be the cause of what it causes. Since, therefore, the cause of servitude is sin, then just as the pope ought not to cause sin in his subjects, so he ought not to be a cause of their servitude. {134B}

[6b] To the Contrary

In a papal judgment passed on rebels against the church there is set down among other penalties that they become slaves of those who capture them.

[6c. Resolution]

We have to say that servitude is of three kinds: natural, conditional, and accidental.

[i] Natural servitude implies a distinction of natural rank, because, according to the Philosopher (*Politics* I 5, 1254b16–1255a2), it is essential to [natural] lordship and servitude that lords naturally excel in understanding, while slaves fall short in understanding and are strong in physical abilities. Now that servitude would have existed in the state of innocence, because before sin some would have excelled more in understanding and some less.

[ii] Conditional servitude, however, implies moral corruption, because just as humans master beasts, lest they follow the appetites of their senses without restraint, so when a human being chooses the life of cattle and submits the whole judgment of reason to sensuality, that individual is deservedly subjected to someone who lives by the rule of reason. Hence Gregory says in the *Pastorals*, Book II, chapter 6, that when prelates correct the vices of their subjects, 'they lord it, as it were, not over humans but over beasts.' Now such servitude was introduced conditionally, because of sin – conditionally indeed, because, just as man was able not to sin, so if he had not sinned he would not have incurred such servitude.

[iii] But accidental servitude implies some sort of violent conquest, for according to Augustine in *On the City of God*, Book XIX, chapter 15, *servi* (slaves) 'are so called from *servando* (preserving),' because long ago 'those who by right of war could have been killed by the victors were preserved by them and made their perpetual *servi*.' Now such servitude is called accidental because, just as the outcome of war is accidental and fortuitous (since 'the sword slays now this one and now that one,' as David said of the death of Uriah [2 Samuel 11:25]), so such servitude has been introduced accidentally.

Therefore the pope ought not to condemn free Christians to natural servitude (because he ought not to diminish anyone's exercise of reason) or to conditional servitude (because he ought not to be a cause of sin to anyone). But he can justly condemn rebels to accidental servitude. For according to Augustine in *Questions on Joshua*, chapter 10, it is just to wage war against persons or against a city that neglects to correct the wicked acts of its citizens or to return what has been taken unjustly. Thus the pope can justly punish rebels with such a penalty.

[6d. Replies to the Opening Arguments]

[i] To the first we therefore have to say that the text from John refers to the freedom of grace and the spiritual freedom we have obtained through Christ. It does not refer to fleshly freedom, which {135A} we do not obtain through him in the present life but only in the future.

[ii] To the second we have to say that in the text from Matthew Christ shows himself to be free from the servitude of tribute because he was the king's natural son. We, however, are the king's children by adoption, which does not free us from the servitude of tribute. Or, as some expound the text, it refers to Christ and his disciples, among whom all things were in common and they had nothing of their own, on which account they were free from tribute.

[iii] To the third we have to say that the pope ought not to be the cause of sin to anyone and consequently not [the cause] of a servitude arising from his sin. But if the servitude to which he condemns someone who is contumacious arises from the person's own sin, it should not be imputed to him [the pope].

Article 7. Ought the Pope to Withdraw Christians Living Under the Lordship of Unbelievers from Their Lordship?

[7a. Arguments that He Ought]

We proceed to the seventh article as follows. It seems that the pope ought to withdraw Christians living under the lordship of unbelievers from that lordship.

[i] Because in 1 Corinthians 6:1 the Apostle directs that believers ought not to be summoned before unbelieving judges, saying, 'When any of you has a grievance against another, do you dare to take it to court before the unrighteous, instead of taking it before the saints?' And later (cf. 5:13) he concludes, 'Drive out the wicked from among you.' Therefore, in the same way believers ought not to live under the lordship of unbelievers.

[ii] Moreover, a sinner does not have just lordship over a just person, but the Gloss on Romans 15 says that the whole life of unbelievers is sin. Therefore, unbelievers cannot justly have lordship over believing Christians.

[iii] Moreover, a believer ought not to contract marriage with an unbeliever, because difference of worship is an impediment to making such a contract and nullifies it if it has been made. Therefore, similarly, a believer should not be placed under the lordship of an unbeliever.

[7b] To the Contrary

In 1 Timothy 6:1 the Apostle says, 'Let all who are under the yoke of slavery regard their lords as worthy of all honor, so that the name and teaching of the Lord may not be blasphemed.'

[7c. Resolution]

We have to say that the Apostle expressly decides this question in the chapter of 1 Timothy cited above, where he says (1 Timothy 6:3–4) that those pseudo-teachers who {135B} were teaching that Christians were to be released from the lordship of unbelievers (because they had been freed from their lordship by Christ) did not 'agree with the sound words of our lord Jesus Christ and the teaching that is in accord with godliness.' And he calls them 'conceited, people who know nothing and have a morbid craving for controversy and for disputes about words,' in that Christ's teaching is blasphemed by them. For Christ's teaching was being called wicked and unjust by unbelievers on the ground that it [supposedly] directed that slaves were to be released from the lordship of their lords, and this was giving rise to scandal.

Nevertheless, it is important to know that there are three grounds on which the pope can justly release Christians from the lordship of unbelievers.

The first is when the lordship has been acquired unjustly. To be sure, Augustine says in *On the City of God*, Book XIX, chapter 20, that the Romans claimed that their power over provinces they had occupied violently was just, because being subject to them was useful, since Roman lordship deprived the wicked of license to harm their subjects. Nevertheless, I think that no matter how useful it may be, this is not a sufficient basis for just lordship over others against their will. Accordingly, if unbelievers have gotten lordship over believers by violence, the pope can justly release the believers from such lordship.

The second ground [on which the pope can release believers from the lordship of unbelievers] is if they use their lordship unjustly, by enjoining illicit [acts, acts] contrary to God's commandments and moral virtue, or by imposing unaccustomed, heavy, and unbearable burdens.

The third ground is an unseemliness in the circumstances (*indecentem statum*). For in the early church, because the whole world was full of unbelieving peoples, the power and lordship of unbelievers was useful for converts to the Christian faith. If they wished to escape their lordship, it would have been necessary for them to leave the whole world, as the Apostle says in 1 Corinthians 5:10. As things stand now, however, because a multitude of peoples has entered the church, it would be very suspicious if Christians able to live under the lordship of believers arranged by their own efforts to remain under the lordship of unbelievers. Hence I think that in present circumstances the pope can and ought to prohibit this.

[7d. Replies to the Opening Arguments]

[i] To the first we therefore have to say that the Apostle prohibited believers from being judged by unbelievers because disagreement and conflicts arise in judicial proceedings, whereas a servant of God ought not to litigate but should be gentle to all. But one does not incur sin by being a slave. For the Apostle says at 1 Corinthians 7:21, 'Were you a slave when you were called? Do not be concerned about it. Even if you can gain your

freedom, make use [of your present condition] now more than ever.' This is because, as the Gloss explains, the more we are despised for God's sake in this world, the more we will be exalted in the next.

[ii] To the second we have to say that a sinner cannot have just lordship over the just in what concerns the soul or the will – and it is through these that sin is incurred or avoided. In these, as the Apostle says {136A} in Galatians 3:28, 'There is no longer slave or free, male or female, Jew or Greek, for all are one in Christ Jesus.' But in what concerns the body a sinner can have just lordship over a just person. Hence the Savior warned us (in Matthew 10:28) not to fear those who kill the body, because they cannot harm the soul.

[iii] To the third we have to say that it is prohibited for a believer to contract [marriage] with an unbeliever because of the danger of the offspring not being dedicated to the worship of God. (Yet a {136B} believer is not commanded ((*iubetur/prohibetur* [margin])) to part from an unbeliever if she married him before her conversion, 'For the unbelieving husband is made holy through his believing wife,' as the Apostle says in 1 Corinthians 7:14.) Now such a danger is avoided in servitude. Nevertheless, in present circumstances (*statu*) individuals who were not under the lordship of unbelievers before conversion to the faith ought not to put themselves under the lordship of unbelievers afterwards, as has been said about marriage. {136A}

Question 23. On the Obedience of Pagans

Article 1. Are Pagans by Right under Obedience to the Pope?

[1a. Arguments that They Are Not]

We proceed to the first article as follows. It seems that pagans are not by right under obedience to the pope.

[i] Because the pope is over everyone by the power of the keys, by binding and loosing, but pagans are neither bound nor loosed, since they have never accepted the faith of Christ. Therefore, the power of the keys does not extend to them.

[ii] Moreover, the pope is over all Christ's sheep, but pagans and other barbarous nations are not among Christ's sheep, because, as he himself says

in John 10:16, 'My sheep listen to my voice.' Now pagans and unbelievers do not listen to Christ's voice. Therefore, they are not among his sheep.

[iii] Moreover, the pope is over the whole church, but pagans and unbelievers do not belong to the church. Therefore, they are not rightfully subject to him.

[1b] *To the Contrary*

The pope is over [his subjects] in Christ's place. But Christ has full juris-diction {136B} over every creature, since 'at his name every knee shall bow, in heaven and on earth and in the places under the earth,' as is said in Philippians 2:10.

[1c. Resolution]

We have to say that by his passion Christ has merited judicial power over every creature, according to the last chapter of Matthew (28:18): 'All power in heaven and on earth has been given to me.' Hence, on the text, 'He will have lordship from sea to sea' (Psalm 72:8), the Gloss says, 'See how broad Christ's kingdom is, because it is "from sea to sea," that is, it will spread from one end of the earth to the other, so widely will the church extend.' Now the pope is Christ's vicar, hence no one can right-fully withdraw from obedience to him, just as no one can rightfully withdraw from obedience to God. But just as Christ has received from the Father authority and the scepter of the church of the nations, going out from Israel over every rulership and power and over everything whatever, so that every knee bends to him, in the same way he has committed the fullest power to Peter himself and to his successors, as the Patriarch Cyril of Alexandria says in his book of *Treasures*.

[1d. Replies to the Opening Arguments]

[i] To the first we therefore have to say that pagans and unbelievers are bound and judged by the power of the keys, because those who do not believe have been judged already, so that if they are willing to wake up and accept the faith of Christ they can be absolved by the power of the keys.

[ii] To the second we have to say that all rational creatures are Christ's sheep by right of creation and, sufficiently, by right of redemption, because he has suffered sufficiently for all. But pagans and unbelievers are not

among Christ's sheep as faithful adherents. Hence the gloss on the cited text says that after Christ had said in John 10:16, 'You are not among my sheep' [rather, 'I have other sheep that are not of this fold'], he went on to persuade them to become his sheep. According to Augustine, we should not despair about anyone, because those who are Jews or pagans today can be Christians tomorrow. Indeed, all can {137A} be Christ's sheep, partly through the charity of the church, because it prays for all to convert, and partly by their own power, because the will and free judgment by which they can convert have been given to all.

[iii] To the third we have to say that 'to belong to the church' can be understood in three ways. The first is in relation to judicial power. In this sense everyone belongs to the church – good and bad, believers and unbelievers – because just as all have one God, so by right all ought to have one shepherd (*pastor*) who acts in his stead. The second sense is in relation to will and way of life (*imitatione*). In this sense only believers and the good belong to the church. The third sense is by being – in various circumstances (*occasionaliter*) – of fruitful use. In this way all pagan unbelievers can be said to belong to the church. For Augustine says in *On True Religion* (c. 6) that, 'The catholic church, spread out through the length and breadth of the whole world, makes use of everyone for its own progress. It uses pagans and gentiles as material to work on, heretics to test its teaching, schismatics for proof of its stability, Jews as a foil for its own beauty. Yet to all it gives the power of sharing in the grace of God, whether they are still to be formed, as pagans are, or reformed, as are heretics, or gathered in again, as schismatics, or admitted, as Jews.'

Article 2. Besides Being Subject to the Pope, Are Pagans Directly Subject to the Emperor?

[2a. Arguments that They Are]

We proceed to the second article as follows. It seems that besides being subject to the pope all pagans are directly subject to the emperor.

[i] Because pagans are directly subject to that lordship which is over all nations, but the emperor is over all nations, as is written in 2, q. 1, c. *Haec siquis*. Therefore, all pagans are directly subject to him.

[ii] Moreover, pagans are directly subject to him under whose power all realms are included, but all are subject to the imperial power, as is written

in 23, q. 8, c. *Convenior.* Therefore, pagans are directly subject to the emperor.

[iii] Moreover, [all] pagans occupy one or another province, but the emperor is over all provinces, as is written in dist. 63, c. *Adrianus.* There-fore, pagans are directly under the lordship of the emperor.

[2b] To the Contrary

The emperor is only over those [who *are*] subject to him, but the church prays that he *make* all barbarous nations subject to him. Pagans and other barbarous nations are therefore not [yet] under the emperor.

[2c. Resolution]

We have to speak first of pagans subject to particular Christian kings by [hereditary] succession, {137B} as appears clearly with regard to the kings of Spain and Aragon, who have many Saracens and Jews subject to them, and as was once true in the kingdom of Sicily with regard to the Saracens of Noceria. It is agreed that such pagans are under the jurisdiction and power of the king to whom they are subject. And if there were some [pagans] in Italy and in areas where the emperor has lordship, they are subject to his jurisdiction (which was obtained by benefit of the church's confirmation). On the other hand, if we are speaking of pagans or barbar-ians who are not under Christian kings or princes but are ruled by their own kings or sultans, it seems that we most likely have to say that they are subject to those under whose power they are living, because all power is given by God, as the Apostle says in Romans 13:1 and as Augustine says in *Against Faustus the Manichaean* (XXII 74–75), as quoted in 23, q. 1, c. *Quid culpatur.* Augustine says there that, 'No power exists unless God either commands or permits it. And the natural order in the government of mortals is accommodated to peace. Hence, if a just man happens to be a soldier under a king who is also personally sacrilegious, he can rightly go to war when the king commands it, if what he is commanded to do preserves the order of peace and is clearly not against a commandment of God or if it is not certain that it is [against God's commandments].'

[2d. Replies to the Opening Arguments]

[i] To the first we therefore have to say that the cited text of the *Decretum* does not say that the emperor is over all nations but rather the contrary.

For it says, 'We will that all who are subject to our ((*nostri/naturae* [with Cambridge University Cod. 1936])) jurisdiction, Romans, Franks,' and [the inhabitants] of various other provinces specifically named, 'should also observe this decision.' Hence that statute extends only to subjects of his own empire.

[ii] To the second we have to say that as to protection all realms are under the power of the emperor and of those who are under his jurisdiction. For sometimes in a general statement certain particulars are tacitly excepted.

[iii] To the third we have to say that the emperor is over all provinces subject to his jurisdiction. Or it can be said that he is over all provinces, because he is especially over Italy, which by preeminence of power and dignity can be called the mistress of provinces. For this reason the emperor is referred to as lord of the world, in that he has the title 'King of the Romans,' and Rome is called the head of the world.

Article 3. Can the Pope Justly Deprive Pagans of Lordship and Jurisdiction?

[3a. Arguments that He Can]

We proceed to the third article as follows. It seems that the pope can justly take lordship and jurisdiction away from pagans.

[i] Because it is unjust that slaves exercise lordship. But pagans, since they are unbelievers, are slaves to the sin of unbelief, for everyone {138A} who sins is a slave to sin. Therefore, they cannot justly exercise lordship.

[ii] Moreover, unbelievers deserve to forfeit power and freedom by reason of their unbelief, according to dist. 74, c. *Ubi ista*: 'Those who abuse a power that has been granted them deserve to forfeit the privilege.' Therefore, the pope can justly deprive them of lordship and jurisdiction.

[iii] Moreover, the church cannot err. But the church pursues and attacks those very unbelievers. Therefore, the pope can justly deprive them of lordship.

[3b] To the Contrary

A benefit of nature is not withdrawn from anyone because of sin. But the lordship and jurisdiction of one person over another is a benefit of nature.

Therefore, such a benefit should not be withdrawn from unbelievers because of their unbelief.

[3c. Resolution]

We have to say that according to the Philosopher in *Politics* I 3 (cf. I 2, 1252a31–34), the lordship of one person over another is reckoned among natural benefits. 'There are,' he says, 'those who are naturally lords, who excel in understanding and can exercise forethought. Those, on the other hand, who have physical strength but are lacking in understanding are naturally slaves.' From this he concludes that the same thing is beneficial for lord and slave. For it is beneficial for the lord to be served, since he is lacking in strength, and it is beneficial for the slave to serve others and be directed by another, since he is lacking in understanding. Moreover, natural benefits are retained not only by unbelievers ((*infidelibus/fidelibus*)) but even by demons, for as the Gloss says on the Apostle's statement in 1 Corinthians 15:24 ('Then comes the end, when he hands over the kingdom to God the Father after he has destroyed every ruler and every authority and power.'), 'While the world lasts, angels are over angels, demons over demons, and men over men.' Therefore, the order of ruling, since it is a natural benefit conceded to every human creature, should not be withdrawn from unbelievers either by the pope or by other Christian rulers, since God, whose judgment the church imitates, bestows such benefits of nature on all, both good and bad, because 'He makes his sun rise on the good and the bad and sends rain on the righteous and the unrighteous,' as is written in Matthew 5:45.

[3d. Replies to the Opening Arguments]

[i] To the first we therefore have to say that unbelievers are slaves by servitude to sin. Hence they lose the power and freedom of grace, the privation of which is sin. And if it is said (with the Gloss on Romans 14, quoting Augustine) that all of the life and conduct of unbelievers is sin, this is true of the things unbelievers do just in virtue of their unbelief. For example, if unbelievers clothe the naked and feed the hungry in honor of an idol they adore, such an intention (because it is unbelieving and proceeds from the root of unbelief) makes these good [acts] bad and sinful. But if unbelievers feed the hungry and clothe the naked from a certain natural compassion (*pietate*), such [acts] {138B} are good in their kind and

are done well because done with a good intention. (They do not merit eternal life, however, because they are done without charity.) Accordingly, unbelievers can possess many things and do many things without sin.

[ii] To the second we have to say that unbelievers deserve to lose the power and freedom of grace but not the power of nature. Hence the natural order of ruling, which is based on natural law, is not withdrawn from them.

[iii] To the third we have to say that the church does pursue unbelievers who attack Christians or assail ecclesiastical rights and our rights with tyrannical fury and repeatedly make savage assaults against Christians. In such cases the pope can justly deprive them of lordship and dominion and declare it licit to make war on them. But if the Saracens and unbelievers themselves do not pursue Christians or attempt any other savage assault against the Christian faith but wish to have peaceful relations with Christians, those things which they can possess without sin ought not to be taken from them, as the Gloss on 23, q. 8, c. *Dispar nimirum est* seems to note.

Article 4. Can the Pope Justly Punish Those Who Act against Natural Law?

[4a. Arguments that He Cannot]

We proceed to the fourth article as follows. It seems that the pope cannot justly punish pagans who act against the natural law.

[i] For it is written in Romans 2:12 that 'All who have sinned apart from the law will perish apart from the law.' Therefore, pagans should not be punished by the pope as transgressors of any law.

[ii] Moreover, the pope can only judge those who are subject to him. But pagans are not subject to him. Therefore, the pope cannot judge them.

[iii] Moreover, natural law is the law of conscience, according to the Apostle in Romans 2:14–15: '[The Gentiles who do not have the Law of Moses have] what the Law requires written in their hearts, their conscience bearing witness and their various thoughts accusing or defending them.' But to judge consciences is not permitted to the pope or to any man whatever in the present life, according to the Apostle in 1 Corinthians 4: 5, 'Therefore, do not judge before the time [when the Lord comes].'

[4b] To the Contrary

The pope is Christ's vicar on earth. But in Genesis 18:20 God judged the Sodomites for acting against natural law. Therefore, it pertains to the pope to punish pagans and other barbarians acting against natural law.

[4c. Resolution]

{139A} Regarding the present question we have to say that law is three-fold: eternal, natural, and positive. The eternal law is neither laid down (*ponitur*) nor set aside (*deponitur*), whereas natural law is laid down but not set aside, and positive law is both laid down and set aside. Therefore, the pope ought to emulate (*esse imitator*) eternal and divine law, because from it all law and all justice are derived. Hence Augustine says in *On Free Choice* I (c. 6) that 'Eternal law is the supreme' divine 'reason itself, by which ((*qua/quia*)) it is just that all things be' right and 'orderly in the highest degree (*ordinatissima*). It must always be obeyed, and it is according to it that every law is rightly passed and rightly changed.' Concerning this law it is written in Proverbs 8:15, 'By me kings reign and lawmakers discern what is just.' And the pope ought indeed to observe the natural law, for he cannot change it. Just as it is not laid down by him, so it is not set aside by him. Such law is directly imprinted on the rational mind by God, nor is it contradicted (but rather approved) by the law and the prophets, according to Matthew 7:12: 'In everything do to others as you would have them do to you, for this is the law and the prophets.' But the pope ought to make and change positive law to suit the times, because just as he lays it down, so he can set it aside.

Therefore, because the pope ought to observe natural law he can justly punish all pagans and transgressors of such law. For anyone can justly be punished for transgressing a law which has been given to him and which he professes to observe. Otherwise, according to Augustine, sentence cannot be passed against anyone unless he is convicted [under positive law?] or freely confesses. On the other hand, pagans and barbarous nations cannot be convicted under the divine law of the Old or New Testament or under [papally enacted] positive law, since they have been given neither of these. Hence, just as they can be convicted solely under the law of nature, which they are forced to profess, so they can justly be punished under it.

[4d. Replies to the Opening Arguments]

[i] To the first we therefore have to say that the Apostle does not mean to say that pagans should not ((add *non* [with Cod. 71, St. John's College, Oxford])) be punished for transgressing the law of nature. He means that just as they have sinned without the written law, which was not given to them, so they will not be judged for transgressing the written law but for transgressing the law of nature.

[ii] To the second we have to say that pagans are not subject to the pope in fact but by right, because no rational creature can withdraw from his lordship by right, just as no one can withdraw from God's lordship. Hence, since it devolves to the pope to judge transgressors of the law of nature he can justly punish them.

[iii] To the third we have to say that the pope does not judge about inner conscience but about the evidence of outer deeds, which are of themselves convicted as deserving punishment, if the natural law cries out against them, because the evidence of a completed crime does not need the complaint of an accuser. Hence on the text of Genesis 18 (cf. 18:20 and 19:13)('The outcry against Sodom came to me.') the Gloss says, quoting Gregory, 'We may not judge our neighbors' bad [deeds] before we see them.' {139B}

Article 5. Can the Pope Force Pagans to Live by Imperial Law?

[5a. Arguments that He Cannot]

We proceed to the fifth article as follows. It seems that the pope cannot force pagans to live by imperial law.

[i] Because one ought to live by the law of [the ruler] whose power one is under. But not all pagans are under the emperor's power, as was said above. Therefore, they should not be forced by the pope to live according to imperial law.

[ii] Moreover, the jurisconsult sets down an imperial decree that in contracting marriage pagans and barbarians need not execute nuptial documents. Therefore, they need not live according to imperial law.

[iii] Moreover, pagans and barbarians cannot be punished by the spiritual

penalties with which Christians are punished, since they are outside the church. Similarly, therefore, they ought not to be punished by the legally assigned temporal penalties with which Christians are punished.

[5b] To the Contrary

Pagans and unbelievers ought not to be more exempt than Christians, for then their unbelief would serve as a protection, not a punishment. Therefore, since law has been made because of transgressors, it is fitting that they be ruled by a law that punishes transgressors with coercive power (*virtute coactiva*).

[5c. Resolution]

We have to say, agreeing with the Apostle in Romans 13:1 ('Let every soul be subject to the higher powers.'), that it is fitting for those who are subject to someone's power to be subject to the law made by that some-one's power. Hence, when pagans or barbarians are subject to Christian kings or princes it is appropriate that they ought to live by the code and laws by which the other subjects of those kings and princes live – except, however, for the customary rites and observances of their superstition, for pagans and barbarians are not bound to do anything detrimental to their superstition. For just as they should not be compelled to believe, so they should not be forced to follow the practices of the catholic faith. Never-theless, so that they cannot, by their damnable superstition, do anything tending to produce doubt or irreverence toward the Christian faith, it is suitable that they be ruled by the same law, which is imposed on all alike.

[5d. Replies to the Opening Arguments]

[i] {140A} To the first we therefore have to say that just as powers vary, so do laws. For those who live in one city or realm are subject to the laws of that city or realm, not those of another (unless one king or prince happens to be under the lordship of another). Hence, if the pagans are under imperial power they ought to live by imperial law, and the subjects of other rulers ought to live by the same laws that those rulers' other vassals live by.

[ii] To the second we have to say that the formality of documents in making a nuptial contract is required only of believers, for they can only

contract marriage with a single person. Pagans and barbarians, on the other hand, can take many [spouses] in keeping with their rite and superstition. Hence they are not held to the formality of dowry instruments, because just as they are not subject to Christian rulers in their rites and superstitions, so they are not subject with regard to nuptial contracts and marriage formalities.

[iii] To the third we have to say that pagans and barbarians cannot be punished with a spiritual penalty in this sense, that if [for example] a pagan should strike a cleric, he would not come under the canon 'of a sentence passed' [in canon law], since he is outside the church. Christian princes with pagans living under their lordship could, however, be punished with a spiritual penalty (because they could be excommunicated), if they did not punish [their pagan subjects for such offenses] with a fine or other appropriate penalty designated by the church. On the other hand, pagans living under a sultan or some other unbelieving ruler ought to live according to the rites, observances, and statutes of that ruler.

Article 6. Ought the Pope to Tolerate the Rites of Pagans?

[6a. Arguments that He Should Not]

We proceed to the sixth article as follows. It seems that the pope ought not to tolerate the rites of pagans.

[i] Because whoever can prohibit sin and does not do so seems to consent to it, as the Gloss says on the passage in Romans 1:32 ('They know God's decree, that those who practice such things deserve to die – yet they not only do them but even applaud [Vulgate *consentiunt*] others who practice them.'), 'Not only those who do [such things] but also those who consent to others doing them deserve to die.' Therefore, pagans should not be tolerated in practicing the rites of their unbelief.

[ii] Moreover, the pope ought especially to be on guard against any appearance of unbelief, since it is only for heresy that he should be deposed. But as is written in dist. 83, c. *Error*, 'Someone who fails to oppose manifest villainy is not free from suspicion of secret alliance with it.' Therefore, the pope ought not to tolerate the rites of pagans when he can oppose them. {140B}

[iii] Moreover, the sin of idolatry and sin committed against God's law is more serious than sin committed against the natural law. But the pope

should punish sins against the natural law as soon as they have been brought into the open, as was said above. Therefore, similarly, the pope ought not to tolerate the sin of idolatry and other superstitions of pagans but should punish them at once.

[6b] To the Contrary

The pope is God's vicar. But God tolerates many evils in the present which will be punished by his justice in future, as Augustine says. Therefore, the pope ought to be tolerant in the same way.

[6c. Resolution]

We have to say that, according to Gregory in the *Book of Pastoral Rule* (II 10), the church ought to conduct itself in five ways in correcting vices: first by deliberate disregard; second, by considered toleration; third, by thorough investigation; fourth, by harsh rebuke; fifth, by wholly getting rid of them (*per omnimodam exterminationem*). For the church imitates the judgment of God, who disregards many evils in the present, tolerates many, brings many to light by thorough investigation, strongly rebukes many with harsh afflictions, and wholly gets rid of many. Hence if the pope sees that the conduct of pagans benefits believers, either by their [possible] conversion ((*conversionem/conversationem* [with Cod. 71, St. John's College, Oxford])) or for avoiding defiance of the Christians and other evils, he can and ought to tolerate their rites and superstition. Otherwise, he ought to shun them completely. Now especially, when believers are so numerous, it is not beneficial for the rites of pagans and other unbelievers to be mixed together with the Christian faith.

[6d. Replies to the Opening Arguments]

[i] To the first we therefore have to say that consent should not be given to the superstition of the pagans, but it should sometimes be disregarded or wisely tolerated, because perhaps some greater evils would arise from getting rid of them [such practices?] and perhaps some greater goods would be impeded. On these two accounts, God permits much evildoing in the universe which he could prohibit.

[ii, iii] From this the solution to the second and third arguments is plain. . . .

Question 63. On Dispensation by Binding

Article 1. Is the Pope's Command More Binding than the Binding of Natural Law?

[1a. Arguments that It Is Not]

{333A} We proceed to the first article as follows. It seems that the pope's command is less binding than a command of the natural law.

[i] Because the changeable and fallible is less binding than the unchangeable and infallible. But the binding of natural law is infallible and immutable, whereas the pope's command is fallible and mutable. Therefore, it is less binding.

[ii] Moreover, an obligation impressed [upon us] by God binds more than one impressed by a human being. But a command of the natural law is an obligation impressed by God (as Augustine says in *On True Religion*), whereas a command of the pope is an obligation impressed by a human being. Therefore, an obligation of natural law is more binding than a command of the pope.

[iii] Moreover, an obligation that is binding by both divine and human command is more binding than one that is binding only by human command. But both divine and human commands bind us with respect to an obligation of natural law, whereas only human laws bind us with respect to a command of the pope. Therefore, an obligation of natural law is more binding than the pope's command.

[1b] To the Contrary

The binding of natural law is corrupted by sin, as the Gloss on Romans 1 says. On the other hand, the pope's command is never abolished, for although Peter's boat is tossed about, it is never sunk.

[1c. Resolution]

We have to say that the natural law can be considered in three ways. First, formally and in relation to what it essentially is. So considered it is formally a certain habit determining and inclining the human understanding so that it cannot easily go astray or err. For everything indeterminate needs something to determine it. Now the power of understanding is indeterminate, hence it needs some habit to incline and determine it to its act. Second, [natural law can be considered] materially and subjectively. So considered the habit [just described] is imprinted in the practical understanding, and it is in the practical understanding as in a subject. For the practical and speculative understanding are one, but they differ by reason of their ends, because truth is the end of the speculative understanding, a deed of the practical, as the Philosopher says. Hence, just as an awareness of speculative principles has been placed in the speculative understanding (for example, 'Every whole is greater than a part of it.'), so {333B} an awareness of principles in matters of action has been placed in the practical understanding (for example, 'One should not do to anyone what one would be unwilling to have done to oneself.'). Properly speaking, the natural law is that awareness. Third, [natural law] can be considered finally, with respect to its object. So considered it relates to universal principles directing our actions, not to particulars.

So: considered formally, natural law is properly a cognitive habit; considered materially, it is naturally impressed on the practical understanding; considered with respect to its object, it relates to universal principles directing our actions, not to particulars. Therefore, because it is formally a habit, it is something potential rather than actual. On the other hand, because it is materially in the practical understanding, it pertains to doing, not to knowing. But because its object is universal, it functions only with respect to universals, not with respect to particulars.

Therefore, the pope's command is more binding than natural law, because the pope's command binds both potentially and actually, while the natural law binds only potentially. Similarly, the pope's command binds with respect to both doing and knowing, while natural law binds only with respect to doing. In the same way, the pope's command binds both universally and in particular, while the natural law binds only universally.

[1d. Replies to the Opening Arguments]

[i] To the first we therefore have to say that the pope's command is personally and instrumentally changeable and fallible, but in terms of authority and rule (*auctoritative et principaliter*) it is unchangeable and infallible, because the divine authority on which it rests is unchangeable and infallible.

[ii] To the second we have to say that the pope's command is also impressed by God, that is, by Christ, who said to Peter (Matthew 16:19),

'Whatever you bind on earth will also be bound in heaven.' And that impression is more infallible than the impression of natural law by as much as the impression of natural law, which is habitual, can be depraved to evil and reformed to good through actual exercise. But that impression can never be universally depraved, just as the faith of the church can never fail universally.

[iii] To the third we have to say that with respect to the obligations of natural law we are bound by both divine and human commands virtually, habitually, and universally. But this sort of obligation has been explicated particularly and actually by various commands in the law of Moses and, later, by additions perfecting it and by particular declarations of the new law [of the Gospel]. Plainly, it pertains to the pope as Christ's vicar to interpret and explain both laws. {334A}

Article 2. Is the Pope's Command More Binding than the Binding of an Erroneous Conscience?

[2a. Arguments that It Is Not]

We proceed to the second article as follows. It seems that the pope's command is not more binding than the binding of an erroneous conscience.

[i] Because an erroneous conscience [sometimes] binds one to do evil, as an individual must follow an erroneous conscience indicating something to be good that is [in truth] evil. For on the text of Romans 14:23 ('Whatever does not proceed from faith is sin.') the Gloss says that, even if what is done is good, yet if it is done against conscience, it is bad. Now everyone must avoid evil and consequently must follow an erroneous conscience. But the pope's command does not bind one to do evil. Therefore, an erroneous conscience is more binding than the pope's command.

[ii] Moreover, it is written in Galatians 5:3, 'I testify to every man who lets himself be circumcised that he is obliged to obey the entire law.' But fulfillment of the [Mosaic] law after Christ's advent was not binding on the basis of divine command. Therefore, it was binding solely on the basis of conscience. And because it was evil (because to observe those legal requirements after Christ's advent was evil), therefore an erroneous conscience binds one to do evil, which the pope's command does not.

[iii] Moreover, in acting against conscience one always sins, whether one does good or evil. Therefore, one must always follow one's conscience. But one need not always follow the pope's command, for if he were to command something against God's law, he should not be obeyed. Therefore, an erroneous conscience is more binding than the pope's command.

[2b] To the Contrary

The false sentence of a judge is not binding. This happens in two ways: first, if the sentence is passed by someone not one's own judge but someone else's; second, if it contains manifest error. In either case the sentence is not binding. But an erroneous conscience is a false judge and contains manifest error, especially if it dictates that something should be done that is contrary to natural or divine law. Therefore, it is less binding than the pope's command.

[2c. Resolution]

{334B} We have to say that an erroneous [dictate of] conscience is an erroneous judgment about what should be done. Now regarding the present question, things that can be done are of three kinds. There are certain things we must do or must avoid on the basis of divine law, as [for example] things coming under affirmative or negative commands. Then there are things that we are led to observe by counsels and admonitions but are not required to observe. There are other things, finally, that we neither must observe, nor are led to observe, as [namely] indifferent actions and natural acts, such as picking up or not picking up a straw, eating or not eating. About the first there is a doubt as to whether we must follow an erroneous conscience. (There does not seem to be any doubt about counsels and indifferent actions, for it is plain that if anyone believes himself bound to enter a religious order, he sins if he does not enter it, and similarly, if anyone believes that he must pick up a straw, he sins unless he picks it up. But there is doubt with regard to [the obligation to follow a dictate of conscience against] the commands of divine law, because here there is a divine obligation to the contrary.)

There are some who say that if anyone conscientiously believes he must commit fornication or theft, it is not true that he must fulfill such an obligation of conscience, because it is not true that one must do (or follow conscience in doing) what is contrary to divine law. Hence they say that an erroneous conscience does not bind us to do evil and to follow it in things prohibited by divine law. Yes, to be sure. But because (as Augustine seems to say) to do anything against conscience is always sin, whether good or evil be done, I think that an erroneous conscience does oblige one to follow it in doing evil – not simply and of itself [however], but with qualifications and accidentally, insofar, namely, as it is believed to be right (while it remains erroneous). For the same act has two contrary chains around it. One, from the natural law, is a chain binding without qualification and of itself – to not stealing, for example, or not committing fornication. The other chain is from the erring conscience, believing that fornicating and stealing are licit. And this chain does indeed bind – with qualification and accidentally – inasmuch as conscience is believed to be right. Hence one sins whatever one does while such an erroneous conscience endures. For if one fornicates, one goes against the binding of a divine command. On the other hand, if one does not fornicate, one goes against the binding of conscience.

But how does one sin in doing either, since one is perplexed and is, as it were, obligated to the impossible? For universally, according to Augustine, what cannot be resisted is not sin. Now in the situation described here it seems that one cannot resist running up against one or the other [obligation].

To this it is said that one is not perplexed without qualification, because one can and ought to set aside an erroneous conscience at the command of the pope or a superior. And thus the question proposed is resolved, because the pope's command binds more than the binding of an erroneous conscience. For it is true that in a qualified way and for the time being an erroneous conscience is more binding than the pope's command extensively, in that while the erroneous conscience remains erroneous it binds both to evil and to good – to good from the obligation of a divine command [to follow conscience?], to evil, on the other hand, from the obligation of an erroneous conscience which is thought to be right – whereas the pope's command {335A} binds only to good. (This is because a papal command to do evil would not be something to be obeyed. On the contrary, it would deserve to be altogether spurned.) Virtually and universally, however, the pope's command is more binding, because one must always and universally in all matters give up an erroneous conscience at the command of one's superior and abide by his determination – and in that determination abandon one's own perplexity.

[2d. Replies to the Opening Arguments]

And from this the answer to the arguments for the opposite view is clear.

Article 3. Is the Pope's Command More Binding than the Binding of a Right Conscience?

[3a. Arguments that It Is]

It seems that the pope's command is more binding than the binding of a right conscience.

[i] Because the mandate of a superior is always more binding than that of an inferior. But the pope is above all human souls, according to Romans 13:1: 'Let every soul be subject to the higher powers.' Therefore, the pope is above the consciences of all, and his command is therefore more binding than the command of one's own conscience.

[ii] Moreover, that from which one cannot release oneself is more binding than that from which one can release oneself. But one cannot release oneself from the pope's command. One can, however, release oneself from the binding of conscience. Therefore, the pope's command is more binding than one's own conscience.

[iii] Moreover, what is certain to be good is more binding than what is not certain. But it is certain that a superior's (*praelati*) command is good, for it is written in Proverbs 16:10 that 'Inspired decisions are on the lips of the king; his mouth will not err in judgment.' Therefore, the obligation imposed by a superior's command is stronger than that imposed by conscience.

[3b] To the Contrary

A bond that releases one from God's command removes the bond of a papal command. But a dictate of conscience releases one from God's command. For if conscience dictates to a woman that a certain man is her husband, even though he really is not, and she is known by him [sexually], she does not sin nor is God's command transgressed, although it would have been transgressed except for the dictate of conscience. Much more, therefore, does the binding of conscience release one from the pope's command.

[3c. Resolution]

We have to say that 'to bind more' can be understood in two ways, either extensively or {335B} intensively. Therefore, if a right conscience is assumed, which is believed to be right, such a right conscience binds a person extensively – in more things – than does the pope's command. The reason for this is that there is a twofold judgment, divine and human. God in his judgment weighs affect more than effect, since he sees into the heart. In human judgment, on the other hand, effect [is weighed] more than affect, since human judgment is based on outward appearances, as is written in 1 Samuel 16:7 ['The Lord does not see as man sees; men judge by appearances but the Lord judges by the heart.']. Hence if one does something good against conscience (doing it [therefore] with an affect that is not good), then, although one does not act against the law according to human judgment, one nevertheless acts against divine judgment and deserves punishment. Conversely, if one does something evil prohibited by human law, [but] believing it to be good according to one's own conscience, then, because one acts with a good affect, one does not act against divine judgment or deserve punishment in such judgment, although in this case one is acting against the law according to human judgment. Therefore, a right conscience which is believed to be right is binding in all matters, whereas the pope's command, because it does not bind one to do evil or to act against God, does not bind in all matters. Nevertheless, intensively, the pope's command binds more strongly than the binding of conscience, because it binds both in the court of outer judgment, where conscience does not bind (since one does not deserve punishment by human judgment solely for one's thoughts) and also in the court of inner conscience, since one ought to conform one's right conscience to the pope's command. (An erroneous conscience one ought indeed to put aside at the pope's command.)

[3d. Replies to the Opening Arguments]

[i] To the first we therefore have to say that the pope is above an individual's conscience in the court of outer judgment. In the court of inner conscience, however, one is subject solely to God, who imputes an end to one's deed according to one's intention. Hence an individual is bound in more things by inner conscience than by papal command, since whatever one does against conscience – believing oneself to be acting against God –

is punished by [God's] judgment. But it is not the case that whatever an individual does against the pope – or [that whoever] transgresses the pope's mandate in any matter – should be punished.

[ii] To the second we have to say that one cannot release oneself either from the bond of conscience or from the pope's command. For if the binding of conscience is right one has to follow it, and so one does not release oneself from it. If it is erroneous one must indeed put it aside – not by one's own judgment but by the judgment of a superior.

[iii] To the third we have to say that that argument shows the pope's command to be a more effective bond than the binding of conscience. And [we have to say] that by the pope's command one has to remain in the bond of conscience, whether it be right or wrong. But as long as it is believed to be right it binds in more things than does the pope's command. {336A}

Article 4. Is the Pope's Command Universally Binding in All Matters?

[4a. Arguments that It Is]

We proceed to the fourth article as follows. It seems that the pope's comand is universally binding in all matters.

[i] Because one who is obligated to the greater is obligated to the lesser. But matters pertaining to the rule of Christian faith, in which one is obliged to obey the pope, are greater than indifferent matters. Therefore, the pope's command is binding in the latter [as well as in the former].

[ii] Moreover, God's command is binding in all matters. But the pope's command is binding by God's power (*virtute Dei*), according to Luke 10: 16: 'Whoever listens to you listens to me, and whoever rejects you rejects me.' Therefore, similarly, the pope's command is binding in all matters.

[iii] Moreover, Bernard says, 'Believe that whatever a prelate has enjoined is wholesome.' Therefore, whatever directive Christ's vicar delivers must be carried out (where he does not command anything contrary to divine law).

[4b] To the Contrary

Bernard says, 'Do not exact more from me than what I have promised.' But in the Christian religion one does not promise to observe [commands concerning] all indifferent matters. Therefore, the pope's command is not binding in all matters.

[4c. Resolution]

{336B} We have to say that in the Christian religion, in which the pope holds sole rulership, some things are commanded as necessary for salvation, some are urged as suitable, and some things are done which are indifferent. With respect to those things in the first category that are explicit, the pope's command is binding in virtue of divine command, whereas with respect to those that are implicit, the pope's command is binding in virtue of the [power of the] keys [cf. Matthew 16:19: 'I will give you the keys of the kingdom of heaven.'], because it pertains to him to determine and declare what those things are that anyone professes to observe in the Christian religion. On the other hand, the pope's command is not binding in the second and third categories (because neither is there a command of God that binds [in these categories]), unless perhaps by reason of contempt [that is, because resisting a papal command in these areas would show contempt for papal authority in general?], or unless the pope commanded that things believed to be indifferent should be understood to be required in professing the Christian religion. For on the text of Matthew 23:2 ('The scribes and the Pharisees sit on Moses' seat; so practice and observe whatever they tell you.') the Gloss says that the commands of prelates hold good in those matters that pertain to [their] authority or in those that are brought to it.

[4d. Replies to the Opening Arguments]

[i] To the first we say that the things contained in the Christian religion as commands are of greater necessity than counsels or indifferent matters, yet they are not greater with respect to suitability. Hence the pope's command binds of necessity in the former, but in the latter only by a certain suitability.

[ii] To the second we have to say that the pope's command binds in virtue of God's command. Hence, concerning those things that are not commanded by God but are only urged or are indifferent, the pope's command ought similarly not to be binding.

[iii] To the third we have to say that that statement of Bernard's should be understood in terms of humility and suitability, not necessity.

WILLIAM OF OCKHAM
IS AN ERRANT INDIVIDUAL BOUND TO
RECANT AT THE REBUKE OF A SUPERIOR?

Introduction

(For information on Ockham's life and writings, see the introduction to Translation 13.)

Ockham's *Dialogue between Master and Student*, from which this selection is taken, grew out of disagreements between Pope John XXII and a small group of dissident Franciscans led by Michael of Cesena, of which Ockham was a member. In his constitution *Cum inter nonnullos* the pope had condemned as heresy a doctrine these friars believed had been endorsed by previous popes and accepted by the whole church. This, in their view, made John himself a heretic, and the majority of Franciscans who had accepted John's constitution were thus in their view either heretics or supporters of heresy. Part I of the *Dialogue* is accordingly a discussion of heresy, heretics, and supporters of heresy. The Master makes no assertions of his own but reports and discusses 'the views of the learned.'

A heresy, in the definition apparently endorsed by the Master, is an assertion that contradicts catholic truth, which is found in the Bible and the teaching of the whole church. A heretic is not simply someone who believes a heresy but a baptized Christian (or one who presents himself as such) who believes some heresy pertinaciously. Pertinacity is unwillingness to accept the rule of faith, namely, the Bible and the teaching of the church. Book 4 discusses how it is proved that someone holds a heresy pertinaciously. The Master describes various sorts of evidence. For example, someone brought up as a Christian who says Christianity is false and converts to another religion is clearly not willing to accept the rule of faith. Altogether, the Master discusses twenty ways of proving pertinacity.

Discussion of the seventh way occupies ten chapters, five of which are translated here. Some say that refusal to retract an opinion at the mere command of a superior with no reason given is not evidence that a person is a heretic. According to this opinion, even those whose beliefs are actually heretical need not cease defending them, even against the pope, until they have been shown clearly that their belief conflicts with the Bible or the teaching of the church.

The Master goes on to discuss a number of other possible ways of proving that someone is a heretic. According to some (and no serious opposition is reported), a pope or other prelate who attempts to impose an heretical opinion on others is pertinacious and a heretic even if it has *not* been shown to him that his opinion conflicts with the Bible or the teaching of the church. The mere fact that he is trying to impose his opinions authoritatively is conclusive evidence that he is not willing to be corrected. This counts heavily against John XXII. It means that if, as the dissident Franciscans offer arguments to prove, the opinions he is trying to impose are indeed heretical, then he is a heretic even if he has not listened to or understood their arguments. On the other hand, as the discussion of the seventh way implied, the dissidents (as long as they are ready to listen and ready to be corrected) are not heretics even if their opinions are in fact heretical, because this has not yet been shown and they are not trying to impose their opinions but merely arguing for them.

Thus, the Master's account of evidences for pertinacity is at the same time a contribution to the campaign against John XXII and a defense of freedom of theological discussion (subject to the rule of faith) within the church.

For further reading, see CHLMP, X.39, 'Rights, natural rights and the philosophy of law.' See also A. S. McGrade, *The Political Thought of William of Ockham* (Cambridge: Cambridge University Press, 1974), chapter 2. A corrected Latin text and English translation of much of Ockham's *Dialogus*, including Part I, Book 4, will be found at http://www.britac.ac.uk/pubs/dialogus/ockdial.html.

Is an Errant Individual Bound to Recant at the Rebuke of a Superior?

Chapter 15

{454} **Master** A person is manifestly convicted of pertinacity if, when lawfully corrected, he does not correct or amend himself by retracting his heresy. This is gathered evidently from Augustine's words quoted above, found in 24, q. 3, *Qui in ecclesia* [If those in the church who think wrongly are corrected but 'resist . . . and will not amend their . . . doctrines and persist in defending them, they are heretics.']. That such a person should be judged pertinacious is also plainly proved: Anyone not ready to be corrected ought to be regarded as pertinacious, but a person who, when lawfully corrected, does not retract his heresy is not ready to be corrected; such a person should therefore be regarded as pertinacious.

Student Since I have often heard about this way of convicting someone of pertinacity and the others are altogether new to me, I want this way to be treated more thoroughly. I ask you, now, to discuss two questions about it, namely: To whom does it belong to reprove someone in error? And what ought the correction to be like if it is to be regarded as lawful and sufficient?

Master We must see first about the correction and second about the corrector.

Student Follow whichever order you prefer.

Master Regarding the correction, it is said that correction should be reckoned lawful and sufficient only if it shows plainly to the person in error that his assertion conflicts with catholic truth in such a way that, in the judgment of people with understanding, he can by no evasion deny that it has been sufficiently and plainly shown to him that his error is inconsistent with catholic truth. For example, if from ignorance of the gospel text someone ignorantly said (as they say someone in Avignon did publicly preach) that the soldiers broke Christ's legs, and the opposite were shown to him from the text of John's Gospel, chapter 19 (where we read: 'The soldiers came, therefore, and broke the legs of the first and of the other who was crucified with him, but when they came to Jesus and found him dead already they did not break his legs'), that correction ought to be regarded as sufficient, because in the judgment of anyone with understanding such a person could by no evasion deny that it had been plainly proved to him that his assertion conflicts with gospel truth.

Also, if someone from ignorance taught as dogma that in Christ there were two persons as two substances and it were shown to him from the text of the Council of Ephesus that this is the heresy of Nestorius condemned by that council, he could by no evasion deny that it had been plainly proved to him that his assertion is a condemned heresy and consequently is opposed to catholic truth. Such correction should therefore be regarded as sufficient and lawful.

Second, we must see about the corrector, concerning whom the following distinction is made. Some persons correct by rebuking and punishing with due penalty, some only by charitable warning and refutation of the error. To correct in the first way those who are in error belongs to superiors and those with jurisdiction, to correct in the second way belongs to any Christian.

Chapter 16

Student From this I understand what, according to many, should be regarded as sufficient and lawful correction. [Now] I am considering the distinction concerning the corrector of someone who errs [i.e., the distinction between a superior who corrects by imposing a penalty and someone who corrects by charitable warning and refutation]. I would like to know whether all the learned believe that anyone in error who is corrected by his superior (*praelatus*) or someone with jurisdiction over him is bound to retract his error even though that person has not shown him clearly that his error conflicts with catholic truth – that is, whether he ought to retract his error at the mere admonition or rebuke of his superior.

Master On this matter different people think differently. Some say that no one corrected by a superior or someone with jurisdiction is bound to retract his error until it has been shown clearly to him, in the way described above, that his error is contrary to the truth. They prove this first as follows. Those who, in explaining divine Scripture and consequently in transmitting things belonging to the orthodox faith, take precedence over superiors and those with jurisdiction are not bound, and ought not, if they err in ignorance, to retract their opinions as heretical (even though in truth they are erroneous), even though they have been corrected by superiors or by others, unless it is shown clearly to them that their opinions conflict with orthodox truth. For someone who has greater authority in some matter is certainly not {455} subject in this matter to a lesser authority. Therefore those who take precedence over superiors in explaining divine Scripture are not subject to them in this. But in explaining divine Scripture, and consequently in transmitting things belonging to the orthodox faith, scholars (*doctores*) and commentators on divine Scripture take precedence over superiors and those with jurisdiction. Therefore, scholars are not bound to retract their opinions, even if they are erroneous, if they are corrected by superiors, unless it is proved evidently to them that their opinions conflict with the truth.

The major [premise] is certain. The minor is proved first by a text of Gratian in *Decreta*, 20 dist., para. 1. He says: 'To settle cases is one thing, to explain the sacred Scriptures diligently is another. . . . It is clear that even if commentators on the divine Scriptures surpass pontiffs in knowledge, nevertheless, because they have not attained their [the pontiffs'] high office, although they are put ahead of them in explaining the sacred Scriptures, they deserve second place after them in deciding cases.' These words clearly establish that in explaining the Scriptures scholars take precedence over pontiffs.

This is also shown by an argument of Gratian's that he puts in these words: 'So far as a person relies on the greater reason, the more authority his words seem to have; but very many commentators – excelling others by greater knowledge, as in fuller grace of the Holy Spirit – are found to have adhered more to reason. Accordingly, it seems that the statements of Augustine, Jerome, and of other commentators should take precedence over the things laid down by some pontiffs.' These words show that in matters belonging to the faith scholars should take precedence over pontiffs, and so, unless they are corrected by them lawfully in the way explained above, they are not bound to retract their opinions if they are erroneous.

Student That argument seems to fail in two ways. First, because Gratian is speaking of scholars approved by the church, such as Augustine, Jerome, and others like them, and not of modern scholars. Hence, although those saints should be put ahead of pontiffs in explaining the Scriptures, modern scholars ought not to take precedence over bishops and inquisitors into heretical wickedness. Second, it seems to fail because [the following argument] does not follow: 'Scholars ought not to retract their opinions at the correction of someone with jurisdiction unless they have been lawfully corrected in the way described before; therefore other, simple, people corrected by superiors ought not to retract their errors unless they are lawfully corrected in the way often mentioned.'

Master It is easy to answer those objections, as is clear from what was said above. To the first, accordingly, they say that Gratian is not speaking only of scholars approved by the church but also of others, just as he also speaks of other pontiffs besides those who lived in the times of the scholars now approved by the church; for he is comparing in general the status of scholars with the status of pontiffs. Hence, just as in the past scholars were to take precedence over pontiffs in transmitting things belonging to the faith, so also now scholars are to take precedence over modern pontiffs – as long as they are scholars (*doctores*) who have been raised to the teaching office because of outstanding knowledge and praiseworthy life, not because of gifts and entreaties or human favors. Accordingly, to explain his meaning clearly, they say that Gratian is not speaking only of 'doctors' as the term is understood these days but of insightful commentators on divine Scripture, whether they be called masters or students. For many who are called students should take precedence over masters in explaining divine Scripture, and hence they should also take precedence over pontiffs in such matters. Accordingly, Gratian's argument applies to modern scholars as well as to past commentators on the Scriptures, for scholars these days 'excel by greater knowledge.' In such matters, therefore, they should take precedence over illiterate and simple bishops and inquisitors.

To your second objection they say that just as experts corrected by superiors or those with jurisdiction are not bound to retract their erroneous opinions unless lawfully corrected by them in the way mentioned, for the same reason neither are simple people who follow the opinions of experts bound in any way to retract the opinions they have accepted from the more expert unless they are corrected lawfully. It follows from this that other simple people are also not bound to retract their erroneous opinions unless they are corrected lawfully, because all simple people seem to be judged by exactly similar law.

Chapter 17

Student If you have more arguments for the above conclusion, please bring them forward.

Master The same conclusion is proved, second, as follows. Anyone who is not bound in matters of faith to show undoubting faith to another is not bound to retract his erroneous opinion at that other's mere assertion, warning, or rebuke. For anyone who retracts an erroneous opinion ought to hold the contrary assertion with firm faith, and adhering firmly to catholic truth and dissenting from the contrary falsehood seem to be conceptually the same. But in matters of faith subjects are not bound to show undoubting faith to their superiors, because then the faith of the subjects would rest upon the wisdom of men [cf. 1 Corinthians 2:5] and because superiors, from simplicity or ignorance or else from pertinacity, can err against faith. Therefore, subjects are not bound to retract their erroneous opinions at the mere assertion, warning, or rebuke of their superiors, but if they are bound to retract, it must be because the superiors show them clearly by the rule of faith that their opinions conflict with the orthodox faith.

Third, as follows. No one is bound to retract his erroneous opinion at the correction of a person who ought to be ready to satisfy someone demanding a reason for the faith unless that person does give a reason why that opinion should be retracted as an error, because if he were bound to retract his opinion as erroneous without any reason being given the other would not be bound to give a reason for retracting it. But superiors correcting subjects of errors against faith ought to be ready to satisfy someone who demands a reason {456} for the faith and consequently ought to be ready to satisfy someone who demands a reason for retracting things they say are opposed to faith. Blessed Peter testifies to this in his first letter, chapter 3 (v. 15), when, writing to superiors, he says to each of them: 'Sanctify the Lord Christ in your hearts, being always ready to satisfy anyone who demands of you a reason for the faith that is in you.' Therefore subjects are not bound to retract their erroneous opinions contrary to catholic faith because of any correction by superiors unless it was a lawful correction in the way described above.

Fourth, as follows. In a case in which they would be permitted to appeal from the judgment of superiors, subjects are not bound to retract opinions they do not know to be erroneous at the correction of superiors. For someone who can licitly appeal from a judgment is not bound to obey that judgment. But appeal is permitted from a superior correcting someone of error and not showing by the rule of faith that the error conflicts with truth. Therefore, no one is bound by such correction to retract an opinion that he does not know to be erroneous. The major [premise] is manifest. The minor is clearly proved by sacred canons. For as we read in 2, q. 6, c. *Si quis*, Victor says: 'If anyone believes himself to be oppressed by his own metropolitan, let him be judged by the patriarch or primate of his diocese, or by the See of the universal apostolic church.' From these words we gather that if anyone believes himself wrongly corrected for error by a superior he is permitted to appeal. This could also be copiously proved by many other sacred canons, but for brevity's sake I pass on.

Student That argument proves that [even] someone *lawfully* corrected for error is not bound to retract his error, because he is permitted to appeal [– which is absurd].

Master The answer to this is that if someone lawfully corrected for error by a superior appeals frivolously or in a way calculated to frustrate judgment, he ought to be punished by the church. He also sins before God, who sees how maliciously he is appealing, since he has been corrected lawfully [i.e., has been shown his error]. . . .

Chapter 23

{459} **Student** According to these people, as I understand their position, bishops and inquisitors reprove the erring in vain unless they clearly prove that they are opposed to apostolic doctrine. But I still do not know what they think about the pope – whether those who err unknowingly are bound to retract their heresies at the pope's simple correction, without the correction they call lawful.

Master They say not, because often the pope is illiterate and simple; also because in matters of faith the pope can err against the faith; also because the pope is bound to give a reason for the faith (because, as the Gloss notes, *Extra, De rescriptis,* c. *Si quando,* 'A reason ought to be given for everything, if possible'); also because in a case concerning the faith it is permitted to appeal from the pope; also because our faith does not rest upon the pope's wisdom, for in matters of faith no one is bound to believe the pope unless he shows the reason for his statement by means of the rule of faith.

Student That seems inconsistent with the custom of the church. For sometimes the pope condemns heresies without giving any reason for his condemnation, and general councils also have framed creeds listing articles which, however, they do not prove by the rule of faith. It does not seem, therefore, that the pope is always bound to give a reason for a condemnation of heretical wickedness.

Master They answer that we never find that the pope has condemned a heresy without giving any reason for his condemnation, but sometimes [he gives the reason] outside the condemnation and sometimes within it. Alexander III acted thus, as is clear, *Extra, De hereticis,* c. *Cum Christus,* and also Innocent III, *Extra, De Summa Trinitate et fide catholica*, c. *Damnamus*. However, if the pope does not give a reason in the condemnation itself, he ought to give a reason for his condemnation in his other assertions.

As for general councils framing creeds, they answer that although in the creeds themselves they may not prove the articles of the creeds by the rule of faith, they are nevertheless manifestly proved outside the creeds, because those who frame the creeds either prove those articles themselves or approve, tacitly or explicitly, proofs given by others.

Student What if in the pope's presence someone were to defend a heresy that he said he believed to be in harmony with catholic faith?

Master They say that if, even in the presence of the pope, he were to defend a heresy a thousand times − unknowingly, with explicit or tacit protestation that he is ready to be corrected when he learns that his opinion conflicts with catholic faith − he should not be judged a heretic unless he were proved a heretic by other lawful evidences. For just as he is permitted the first time to defend an erroneous opinion unknowingly in that way, so he is permitted the second time, and the third, and always, until it has been plainly proved to him that his opinion must be reckoned a heresy.

Student Perhaps the person defending his opinion in this way will say, even after his opinion has been proved heretical, that it has not been shown *to him* that his opinion conflicts with orthodox faith, and thus he could never be convicted.

Master It is not enough for him to deny that his opinion has been proved heretical. He will be compelled to stand by the judgment of experts. If they believe that it has been sufficiently proved to him that his opinion is heretical, he is bound to retract it. Otherwise, he must be reckoned pertinacious and a heretic.

Student What if the experts and all the Masters of Theology together with the pope are wrong?

Master Then they will *de facto* condemn an innocent person. In accordance with the laws, however, he will be able to help his cause by the remedy of appeal. If his lawful appeal is not accepted, however, nothing remains for him but to entrust himself to divine grace and not fear to be deleted from human society by a wicked judgment [of others], since he is not deleted from the book of the living by a wicked conscience [in himself].

Student What if he {460} defends manifest heresy in writing?

Master They say that he should not be regarded as pertinacious or a heretic on that account, because in this regard it does not matter whether he holds or defends his erroneous opinion verbally or in writing. Blessed Cyprian left an heretical opinion in his writings, but because he did not defend it pertinaciously he was not to be judged a heretic. Similarly Abbot Joachim wrote an heretical opinion, as Innocent III testifies, *Extra, De Summa Trinitate et fide catholica,* c. *Damnamus,* and yet he was not to be judged a heretic. The gloss on the chapter *Damnamus* says of Joachim, 'Because he was ready to be corrected and (as the text goes on to say) did correct himself, he ought not to be called a heretic, even though he sometimes erred in faith.' Similarly, although opinions that Peter John [Olivi] left in his writings were condemned as heretical, he himself was not judged to be pertinacious or heretical. Similarly, though blessed Jerome wrote erroneous opinions which also we do not read that he retracted, he is not regarded as a heretic.

Student According to those [examples], it seems that no one could be accused of heresy after his death, but the sacred canons manifestly assert the opposite.

Master It is answered that after death no one should be accused of heresy solely because he maintained a heresy verbally or in writing, but if it can in some way be proved that he *pertinaciously* maintained a heresy verbally or in writing it will be possible to accuse him of heresy after death. If it can be shown that he was pertinacious by other means than simply words or writings expressing heresy, for example by words, writings, or acts declaring pertinacity, he should be condemned.

Student Would you please give an example, so that I can better understand what is being said?

Master If it is proved of someone after death that he maintained verbally or in writing that there were two persons in Christ, he should not for this alone be regarded as a heretic. He could be excused by simplicity or ignorance. If, however, it is proved that he knew that that assertion had been condemned and that afterwards he maintained it verbally or in writing, he must be condemned for pertinacity and heretical wickedness.

Student I suppose that according to these people the procedure must be the same against a person accused of heresy whether living or dead. But for inquisitors it is enough to prove only that someone dead maintained a heresy verbally or in writing.

Master These people say of the inquisitors that they often proceed wickedly and do much harm to God's church, being wholly eager for temporal gain.

Chapter 24

Student Would you speak now about the person corrected by a friend or by another person known to have absolutely no jurisdiction over him?

Master These people say that someone lawfully corrected for heresy by a friend or by his subordinate or by anyone else is bound to lay his heresy aside immediately, without delay, so that if he is convicted of maintaining that heresy verbally or in writing or of regarding it in any way as true after such correction, he should be regarded as pertinacious.

They prove this first as follows. Our faith is not in the wisdom of human beings, according to the Apostle (1 Corinthians 2:5). Therefore, as to being bound to lay aside heresy, it does not matter which human being shows by the rule of faith that an opinion conflicts with orthodox faith. But if it is clearly shown to anyone by his superior that his opinion conflicts with orthodox faith, he is bound to lay it aside immediately, or else he must be reckoned pertinacious. He is therefore obliged to do the same, whoever demonstrates this to him.

Second, as follows. Anyone who is not ready to be corrected if he errs is pertinacious. But if a person has been corrected lawfully by anyone whatever – that is, it has been shown clearly to him that his opinion conflicts with orthodox faith – and he does not lay his opinion aside immediately, he is not ready to be corrected. Therefore such a person is pertinacious and must be judged a heretic.

Third, as follows. A person is no less bound to lay aside an error if he discovers the truth from being instructed by someone else than if he discovers it for himself. But anyone who discovers the truth for himself is bound to lay aside his error immediately, on the example of the Venerable Anselm, *Why God Became Man*, Book I 18, when he says, 'I am certain that if I say something that undoubtedly contradicts sacred Scripture, it is false, and if I become aware of that I do not wish to hold it.' Therefore, if someone finds the truth in harmony with sacred Scripture from being instructed by anyone else at all, whether friend or subordinate, he ought to lay aside the contrary error without delay.

Student According to these arguments, there seems to be no difference between a person corrected by a superior and someone corrected by another who is not a superior, even by a subordinate.

Master It is answered that there is no difference with respect to the fact that the error should be laid aside, but in many other respects there is a great difference. A superior and someone with jurisdiction over another can summon him to give an account, require him to listen to his instruction, compel him to public retraction and, if in these matters (or others pertaining to the superior's office) he is found contumacious and rebellious, can punish him with an appropriate punishment. But someone who has no jurisdiction over the person in error cannot act toward him in these ways.

Student Do they put any difference between the pope's correction of the erring and correction by other superiors?

Master Regarding heresies condemned explicitly, they speak in the same way of the pope {461} and of other superiors, but regarding heresies condemned only implicitly there is a great difference. Over people holding heresies condemned only implicitly, superiors lower than the supreme pontiff are known to have no jurisdiction enabling them to punish them [i.e., the former] or compel them to anything; if they [i.e., the latter] think in their conscience that they are pertinacious, they ought to accuse or denounce them to the Apostolicus [i.e., the pope]. The Apostolicus, however, can examine them and, if he finds them pertinacious, condemn them.

Emendations

[We have emended the text of Goldast's *Monarchia* by drawing on variants from a number of manuscripts. The emendations are listed here by page and line in our translation. Each emendation is preceded by the reading in Goldast.]

485.30 *add* cap 15 485.31 *add* manifeste 485.32 correptus] correctus
485.33 scilicet] *om.* 485.34 28] 24 486.3 iudicari] reputari 486.4 correptus]
correctus 486.8 *add* ut 486.9 corrigere] corripere 486.12 *add*
est 486.15 correctorem] correctionem 486.16 reputanda] *om.* 486.18
posset] possit 486.19 sit] *om.* 486.21 *add* et 486.25 est] erat 486.28
evadendo] *om.* 486.31 *add* et 486.32 hoc] hec 486.33 quod non] quin
486.34 esset] est 486.35 esset] est 487.1 *add* est 487.2 *add* sic 487.2
distinguitur] distinguatur 487.4 primus modus] primo modo 487.4 *add*
errantes corripere 487.5 secundus modus] secundo modo 487.5
pertinet] hoc spectat 487.7 14] 16 487.9 correptio] correctio 487.13
sciant] sentiant 487.14 correptus] correctus 487.17 monitionem]
admonitionem 487.18 Doctores] diversi 487.19 correptus] correctus
487.19 *add* vel 487.27 correpti] correcti 487.32 *add* que 488.2 correpti]
correcti 488.4 Et] *om.* 488.5 quae] qui 488.6 sanctas] sacras 488.6
patet] apparet 488.7 *add* et 488.8 licet] tamen quia 488.10 literarum]
scripturarum 488.10 his] quibus 488.11 expositionibus] expositione 488.11
scripturae] scripturarum 488.14 quia quicunque] quo quisque 488.14
utitur] nititur 488.15 tractatores] tractatorum 488.16 et] ita 488.16 quia
sunt] sicut 488.21 correpti] correcti 488.25 sic] sicut 488.26 non
modernis] *om.* 488.26 *add* non de modernis 488.27 temporis] *om.* 488.31
habentibus] habentis 488.32 correpti] correcti 488.35 ex] *om.* 488.36 *add*
unde 488.37 etiam] et 489.7 violentas] *om.* 489.12 sunt] *om.* 489.17
correpti] correcti 489.18 *add* erroneas 489.19 correpti] correcti 489.22
correpti] correcti 489.24 correpti] correcti 489.25 consilii] consimili
489.26 15] 17 489.29 *add* secundo 489.30 exhibere] adhibere 489.35 et
eadem ratione] eiusdem rationis videtur esse 490.10 correptionem]
correctionem 490.10 quod] qui 490.15 parat] parati 490.18 dicuntur]
dicunt 490.18 *add* in 490.20 sentite] sanctificate 490.23 correptionem]
correctionem 490.24 correptio] correctio 490.27 correptionem]
correctionem 490.28 cui licet] cui valet 490.31 correptionem]
correctionem 490.33 *add* est manifesta minor 490.34 *add* si quis 490.35
add patriarcham vel 490.37 correptum] correctum 491.1 correptus]
correctus 491.4 correptus] correctus 491.6 quin] qui 491.7 videlicet]
videt 491.7 quoquomodo] quam 491.7 correptus] correctus 491.9 20]
23 491.11 corrigunt] corripiunt 491.12 ea] eos 491.12 catholicae]
apostolice 491.14 correptionem] correctionem 491.15 correptione]
correctione 491.17 *add* Tum quia papa sepe est illiteratus et simplex tum
quia papa de fide potest errare contra fidem 491.19 narrat] notat 491.19
add c. 491.22 ergo] enim 491.27 *add* etiam 491.28 *add* fidei 491.31

Respondetur] ad ista respondent 491.33 ex damnatione] extra
damnationem 491.33 cum] in 491.34 *add* extra 492.1 sic enim] sicut
etiam 492.1 *add* et fide 492.2 reddat] reddit 492.7 *add* ipsa 492.11 *add*
esse 492.11 orthodoxae] catholice 492.14 agnoverit] cognoverit 492.14
opiniones suas] opinionem suam 492.20 haereticas] hereses 492.21 talis]
taliter 492.21 diceret] dicet 492.26 cogitur] cogetur 492.27 *add* sibi 492.27
add sua 492.31 errent] errant 492.32 Si] *om.* 492.32 damnaverint]
damnabunt 492.32 scilicet] tamen secundum 492.35 *add* ei 492.36 quia]
quem 493.3 defenderet] defendit 493.4 Quidam] *om.* 493.4 non est]
nec 493.4 iudicandus] est reputandus 493.9 *add* extra 493.15 fuerunt]
fuerint 493.16 iudicandus] iudicatus 493.17 *add* etiam 493.18 reputandus]
reputatus 493.25 facto] scripto 493.27 *add* per 493.28 declaravit per quae
pertinacia] declarantia pertinaciam 493.30 quod] quid 493.33 solum]
solummodo 493.33 simplicem] simplicitatem 493.35 vel] *om.* 494.1
concipio] conicio 494.3 aliquo modo] aliquem mortuum 494.4 ipsum]
om. 494.8 21] 24 494.9 correpto] correcto 494.11 correptus] correctus
494.12 *add* alio 494.15 correptionem] correctionem 494.16 Quod] hoc
494.17 ad] *om.* 494.18 deponere] dimittere 494.23 id] idem 494.23 est hoc
patenter sibi] sibi hoc extiterit 494.25 pertina] pertinax 494.25 correptus]
correctus 494.26 si sibi] cui 494.26 scilicet] *om.* 495.6 illud] ista 495.7
correptum] correctum 495.14 pertinax] contumax 495.14 cum] *om.*
495.16 in eo] in eum 495.18 ne] *om.* 495.18 aliam] *om.* 495.22
solummodo] dumtaxat 495.23 *add* summo pontifice

JEAN BURIDAN
QUESTIONS ON BOOK X OF THE ETHICS

Introduction

Jean Buridan's dates of birth and death are uncertain, but he is known to have been active in the University of Paris between 1328 and 1358. He spent his whole working life as a Master of Arts (unlike many other well-known medieval philosophers, who were theologians). He wrote on logic and produced commentaries in question form on many texts of Aristotle. His questions on Aristotle's *Ethics* break off at the beginning of Question 6 of Book X and may be his last work.

The questions on Book X are concerned with two main topics, freedom and happiness. The connection is that freedom in one sense, namely, 'freedom of final ordering,' is to be attributed to the activity that is the ultimate end of human life, which is also happiness. Freedom of final ordering is not what philosophers these days mean by free will. 'Final ordering' means ordering or directing toward an end (*finis*); freedom of final ordering is characteristic of something that is an end in itself and not a means ordered to some further end. We can understand why this is called freedom by considering Aristotle's understanding of the difference between free persons and slaves: Free persons live for themselves, slaves exist for the benefit of others. Hence Aristotle's description of 'the free' as that which exists 'for its own sake and not for the sake of another.' The act in which happiness consists will be free with freedom of final ordering since it is not for the sake of anything else.

Besides 'freedom of final ordering' there is 'freedom of opposition' (called by some later writers 'freedom of indifference' and by modern philosophers 'freedom of the will'). According to Buridan, freedom of opposition consists in being able to choose at one moment to do something, at another moment not to do it or to do the opposite, even if meanwhile *nothing else in the universe changes* besides the act of will. (Here Buridan seems to follow Ockham; see Ockham's *Opera theologica*, vol. IV, p. 580.) Buridan holds that such freedom is found in acts of will that he calls 'acceptance' and 'rejection' and in no other human act (though other acts can be free with freedom of opposition 'consequently' – that is, they are free in the sense that they result from free acts of acceptance or rejection). According to Buridan, the act in which the highest happiness consists, in which freedom of final ordering is achieved, namely, the direct intellectual apprehension of God, is not free with freedom of opposition. (In holding that the highest act is intellectual and that it is not free in this second sense, Buridan aligns himself against Duns Scotus and with Thomas Aquinas.) Freedom of opposition itself exists for the sake of freedom of final ordering. Acts that are free with freedom of opposition are for the sake of the act that is free with freedom of final ordering, and we have freedom of opposition so that we can withhold acceptance or rejection until we investigate the appearances of good or evil more carefully, so that our acts will be right and bring us to our final goal.

The opening question of Book X is: Which is freer, intellect or will? Buridan's initial answer is that they must be equally free since they are the same entity. However, the question needs refining. Though the terms 'will' and 'intellect' stand for the same entity, the soul itself, they signify by appellation, or connote, different actions. (Again Buridan seems to follow Ockham; see Ockham's *Opera theologica*, vol. I, p. 402 and vol. II, pp. 435 ff.) According to Buridan, intellect is the soul *qua* able to understand, will is the soul *qua* able to will – or more accurately, intellect is the soul *qua* able to *receive* an intellection, will is the soul *qua* able to receive a volition. So the initial question becomes: Are we free more because we can will than because we can understand? His answer is that we are free in the sense of freedom of final ordering because of an act of intellect, and we have freedom of opposition in the will's acts of acceptance and rejection.

Buridan distinguishes between two senses of happiness. In one sense it is the aggregate of all the good things that a human being can possess (cf. Boethius, *On the Consolation of Philosopy*, III, Prose 2), in another sense it is the best of these (just as Aristotle says that the intellect *is* the human being, meaning that the intellect is the best part). Even in the second sense of the term, although it stands for the best, happiness connotes the presence of various other goods: Happiness in the second sense consists in the intellectual apprehension of God, but if by miracle God gave that apprehension without pleasure and with pain, it would not be happiness because of lack of the pleasure connoted by the term. This is Buridan's solution to the question debated in ancient times between Stoics and Peripatetics, whether virtue is sufficient by itself for happiness. According to Buridan, the best act of the best power acting in accordance with virtue is happiness, but the presence of some other goods is required before the term can properly be applied.

He also resolves another ancient debate about the 'continuity of happiness': Is it enough for happiness to achieve the best in an instant, or must one engage in the best activities continuously over a normal lifetime? Buridan answers that 'happiness' in the sense of the aggregate consists in the aggregate of the happinesses of the different parts of the person and of the person's life, and in the sense of the best part it *connotes* the achievement of these partial happinesses to a certain extent. Thus inferior goods are relevant to happiness in both senses of the term. As Buridan admits, these solutions may seem verbal, but they do have the virtue of sorting out a number of confusions. The point of substance is that the best is so very good that it outweighs the lack of other goods – a person who cannot properly be called 'happy' may nevertheless attain all that really matters. (Compare Cicero, *De finibus*, V 30.)

For further reading see CHLMP, VIII.32, 'Free Will and Free Choice,' and IX.35, 'Happiness: the Perfection of Man.' See also Edward J. Monahan, 'Human Liberty and Free will according to John Buridan,' *Medieval Studies*, 16 (1954), pp. 72–86; James J. Walsh, 'Is Buridan a Sceptic about Free Will?' *Vivarium*, 2 (1964), pp. 50–61; J. J. Walsh, 'Buridan and Seneca,' *Journal of the History of Ideas*, 27 (1966), pp. 23–40. The Latin text translated here will be found at: http://www.humanities.mq.edu.au/Ockham/wburlat.html.

Questions on Book X of the Ethics

Question 1. [Is the Will Freer than the Intellect?]

{203r} Next we must ask some questions about Book X. The first part deals with pleasure, about which we asked enough questions in connection with Book VII. We must therefore ask about the second part, in which Aristotle inquires: What act does human happiness consist in? And because Aristotle says that happiness is an activity of the best power in accordance with its best virtue, we must therefore inquire: What is the best power and what is the best virtue? Now everyone asserts that the best power is either the intellect or the will. Therefore, it is necessary to ask how these two powers compare with one another. And because it is immediately obvious that a power is more excellent if it is more free, we therefore ask first, whether the will is freer than the intellect.

[1. Preliminary Arguments]

[1a. Arguments that the Will Is Freer]

It is argued that the will is more free, because a lord is, *qua* lord, always freer than his subject. The intellect, however, compares to the will as subject to lord.

[i] This is clear, first, because one who urges is subject to the one urged, and in *Ethics* I (13, 1102b15–16) Aristotle says that reason 'urges' aright and toward the best objects. And it cannot be said that reason has any superior power that it urges except the will.

[ii] It is clear, second, because the intellect is like an adviser and the will like a lord who has a council or advisers in his affairs. This is clear in our advisings and choices. It is for the lord who seeks advice to appoint the end and to seek advice on the manner and means of achieving it, as is apparent from *Ethics* III. There it is also clear that it is will which relates to the end; in this, therefore, the will is like a lord. Again, once the end has been appointed by the will's decision, the lord seeks advice (*consilium*), which is made and given by intellectual reasoning. Once the advice has been given, again it is for the lord to choose, by will, what first has been judged by advice. As Aristotle says in *Ethics* III (3, 1113a10–12), 'choice will be deliberate desire; for, judging as a result of deliberation, we desire in accordance with our deliberation' (*consilium*). Now judgment belongs to the intellect, desire to the will. Therefore, in these matters every will is like a lord.

[iii] Again, it is clear in the same Book III that it is by will that we are lords of our acts. For this reason voluntary acts, and only voluntary acts, are imputable to us, something which is entirely foreign to intellect.

[iv] Again, it is for the lord to command his subjects. The will, however, commands the intellect to study, to engage in thought; for I study because I will, I cease because I will something else instead, for instance to go to church or to dinner; and I study now metaphysics, now moral philosophy or logic, only because I so will, in accordance with the saying, 'Thus I will, thus I command, let my will be the reason.'

[v] Again, to be compelled or compellable by another is unfree and servile, and not to be compellable is free. But the will cannot be compelled in its act, for to be compelled to something and to will it are incompatible. The intellect, however, is compelled or necessitated to study and engage in thought by the will, for if external obstacles are removed, none of my powers can prevent me from studying if I effectively will it.

[vi] Again, whatever has power for both opposites while everything stays the same is free, and whatever does not have this power but is necessitated and determined by another is unfree. The will, however, and not the intellect, has power in this way for both opposites. For even if the intellect judges that one should go to church, the will can, nevertheless, while this judgment stands, not will to go – indeed it can also will not to go there but to the pub.

[vii] Again, in the preface to the *Metaphysics* (I 2, 982b25–27) Aristotle describes the free, saying that the free is that which exists for its own sake and not for the sake of another. Therefore, the more free is that which has more the manner and nature of an end. Now the will is like this with respect to the intellect, for willing always follows understanding as an act naturally later and more an end, or also later in accordance with Aristotle's frequent maxim that the later in generation is prior in perfection.

[viii] Again, that power seems freest in human beings which can render them free or make them slaves. This is the will. Proof: Virtue and vice, which are a matter of will and appetite, determine slave and free, as is clear in *Politics* I (6, 1255a21). That it is not intellect but will that determines whether we are virtuous or vicious is obvious from experience, for we have seen many who excel in intellect and wisdom but are unjust and very bad – indeed, the demons are very gifted intellectually and yet bad from badness of will. We have seen others, however, who are simple in intellect yet just and holy from goodness of will. Will is therefore lord in making us good or bad and consequently free or slave.

[ix] And every will seems to have lordship over the intellect even in judging of principles that ought to be clearest to the intellect, because in *Ethics* VI (12, 1144a8–36) Aristotle says that 'wickedness' (that is, of will) 'perverts us and makes us go wrong about practical *principles*,' concerning which 'virtue makes our intention right.'

[1b. Arguments that the Intellect Is Freer]

[i] It is argued on the opposite side that according to Aristotle in the preface to the *Metaphysics* (I 2, 982b25–27), the free is that which exists for its own sake and not for the sake of another, and happiness is chiefly such; therefore among human acts happiness is chiefly free. It follows, therefore, that of human powers the power in whose act human happiness consists is the freest. But (as we read in *Ethics* X [c. 7]), it consists in the activity of wisdom, which is a habit of intellect and not of will; therefore, etc.

[ii] Again, as was said in arguing for the other side, a lord is freer than a subject. The *intellect* is like a lord, however, since ordering and determining what should be done and not done pertains to a lord, and the intellect orders and determines what to will (*volendum*) and what to will against (*nolendum*), what to flee and what to pursue, what to love or hate, and the will has no power for those acts without the predetermination of the intellect. Hence in the preface to the *Metaphysics* (I 1, 982a17–19) [Aristotle says that] the *wise* must order – namely, through wisdom.

[iii] Again, in *Politics* III (11, 1282b2–3) we read that rightly enacted laws must rule. On this account, Aristotle also well determines in *Politics* I (rather, *Rhetoric* I 1, 1354a31–34) that it is most fitting that rightly enacted laws determine everything that happens, entrusting as little as possible to judges – that is, because the rule of laws is better than that of judges. In ourselves, then, that power ought chiefly to be called lord to which it pertains to impose laws. That is not will but intellect, which can see and discern what is just, what unjust, what good and what bad. Hence in *Politics* III (16, 1287a28–30) [Aristotle says that] 'whoever bids the intellect to rule, seems to bid God and the laws to rule.' He does not say whoever bids the *will* to rule. Indeed, he means that law rules best from the fact that (as he says) law is intellect without appetite.

[iv] Again, Seneca and Cicero seem to be on this side. In his letter '*Tu me inquis*' (*Ad Lucilium Epistulae Morales*, VIII 7), Seneca says: 'You must serve philosophy, that true freedom may come to you. For to serve philosophy is itself freedom.' Now philosophy pertains to the intellect. And again, in his letter '*Quod maximum*' (XXXVII 3) he says: 'To this,' namely, wisdom, 'betake yourself, if you wish to be safe, secure, blessed, in short if you wish to be – the main thing – free.' And he adds afterwards: 'Wisdom alone is freedom. If you wish,' he says, 'to subject all things to yourself, subject yourself to reason; you will rule many if reason rules you.'

Similarly, Tully in *De Paradoxis* (*Paradoxa* V 33) says that all the wise are free and all the foolish slaves.

[2. Answer to the Question]

In this question we must make distinctions concerning freedom, and also slavery, because slave and free seem to be opposites; {203v} and first in different individuals, where the contrast is more obvious, and second in the same individual, which is more to our purpose.

[2a. Freedom and Slavery in Relations between Different Individuals]

In different individuals freedom and slavery are spoken of in one way with reference to bodies, in another way with reference to wealth and external goods, and in a third way with reference to the soul.

Aristotle speaks of bodily slavery and freedom in *Politics* I (5, 1254b27–31). He says that nature wishes to make different bodies for freemen and for slaves, some strong for necessary use, others upright and useless for such activities but useful for civic life. I set aside this mode of freedom and slavery, because it is not to our purpose concerning happiness or the comparison of intellect and will, because just as slavish bodies can have free souls, so also free bodies can have slavish souls. As Aristotle says in the same place, often the opposite [of what nature wishes] happens: some have the bodies of freemen and others the souls. Seneca brings out the same point nicely in his letter '*Claranum*' (LXVI 4), where he says: 'Claranus seems to me to have been produced as an example, so that we could know that the soul is not disfigured by the ugliness of the body, but the body adorned by the beauty of the soul.'

As a matter of money and external goods, however, slavery and freedom are spoken of with reference to plenty or lack of things necessary to life, just as we say that the poor must 'serve' the rich to get the necessities of life. And neither is this the freedom we are studying at present, because it was said in Book I that human happiness does not consist in such external goods. Indeed, this is not properly called freedom, because, as we read in the letter [of Seneca] just quoted (LXVI 23), 'All those things over which chance exercises lordship are slavish – money, body, honors – fragile, unstable, mortal, of uncertain possession.'

Further, freedom or nobility and slavery or nonnobility are ascribed by extrinsic denomination from one's ancestors. People are commonly called nobles and freemen because they were begotten by the great and well born, and those are called nonnobles and servile who were born of humbler folk, such as citizens, burgesses, merchants, and country people. Certainly, if such nobility and good birth were a matter of intrinsic denomination, it would be very honorable – as they [their descendants] would be also if they had a disposition of soul like the disposition of the ancestors from whom they have derived such denomination, since they derived it from some who excelled in wealth *and virtues.* Hence Aristotle says in *Politics* III (13, 1283a37) that 'good birth is virtue of family,' and again, that 'good birth is ancient virtue and wealth' (IV 8, 1294a20–22). Those, therefore, who are descended from the well born, if they follow their progenitors in the virtues, are formally and properly called noble and well born, and (other things being equal) they should be honored above others. Indeed, if they do not appear obviously wicked, even those who are descended from such a well-born family should (other things being equal) be placed above others in honor. As Aristotle says, those with better ancestors are likely to be better. As he says in *On Rhetoric* II (15, 1390b22–31), however, many such persons lose their family character by not following the virtues of their ancestors and become of little worth, indeed very bad – robbers, murderers, tyrants – because, as he says in *Politics* I (2, 1253a33–34), armed injustice is the most savage. Yet among themselves such people still call themselves nobles, brave, well born, and free, though by a denomination not true but mendacious; and others also call them thus either from flattery or because they dare not say otherwise. It is therefore clear that this freedom derived from ancestors is nothing to our purpose concerning happiness.

Further, Aristotle distinguishes freedom and slavery in another way, touching the soul, in *Politics* I (cc. 5 and 6): namely, that one [kind of freedom or slavery] is natural, another violent. For there is a natural slavery: strength of body with little capacity of soul. Such persons are not worthy to be over others in the governing and ordering of a commonwealth, so it is right that they should serve. This is also more beneficial for them than to exercise lordship and rule, for as we read in *Ethics* VI (13, 1144b10–11), a strong body moving blindly may stumble all the harder. The naturally free, however, those worthy to govern, are gifted and perceptive, as Aristotle says, with bodies upright and useless for such activities as manual work but useful for civic life. Of these, then, Aristotle says in *Politics* I (2, 1252a30–34) that natural ruler and subject are [such] for the sake of [mutual] safety: 'For the one that can foresee with his mind is by nature the ruler and by nature lord, but the one that can do these things with his body is subject by nature and a slave.' As a matter of violence, however, those are called slaves who are compelled against their wills, such as captives and prisoners, or, also, those whom the laws bind bodily to others and who cannot – and whose children cannot – separate from their lord without bodily penalty. The free who correspond to such slaves are those who are not compelled in this way or bound to others.

It is clear, then, that natural freedom and slavery are morally honorable, just, and beneficial in the best and noblest polity, though freedom is much more morally honorable and noble than slavery, just as the soul is nobler than the body. However, freedom and slavery by law and violent compulsion have nothing of beauty about them, nothing of the morally honorable, nothing of love. Hence in *Politics* I (6, 1255b12–15) Aristotle [says that] friendship with one another is beneficial to slave and master if they are deservedly such by nature but that the opposite is the case for those who are not slaves in this manner but by law and by violence done to them. Accordingly, we must also entirely dismiss such nobility or freedom, for it contributes nothing to happiness; for of the slave Aristotle says in *Politics* VII (3, 1325a25–26) that to use slaves insofar as they are slaves is not honorable.

Still other distinctions of kinds of freedom and slavery are taken from *Politics* I. In relation to these, we must note that we call 'free by primary purpose' (*liberum prima intentione*) that which by primary purpose exists and acts for its own sake, and others for its sake, and not for the sake of another (so far as it is called 'free'). We call 'slave' (as such) anything that exists or works for another's sake, as we read in the preface to the *Metaphysics* (I 2, 983b25–27). Therefore, so far as something exists or acts by primary purpose for its own sake and other things for its sake, to that extent it has freedom, and so far as it exists or works by primary purpose for the sake of another, to that extent it participates in a mode of slavery. The same thing is slave and free with respect to different things. For example, counts and dukes would be called slaves with respect to the king and free with respect to their own subjects. We humans are God's slaves, and we are lords and free in relation to brute animals and plants and inanimate things, for we use them for our sakes, as we read in *De anima* II (4, 415b15–20; cf. *Politics* I 8, 1256b15), and because by supernatural order 'the worse' or less worthy 'exists for the sake of the better,' as Aristotle determines in *Politics* VII (14, 1333a21–22). Therefore, he says in Book I (5, 1254b16–

20) that, in the mode of freedom and slavery just spoken of, in every association what is better and more worthy is called free and by comparison with it other things are called slavish and subject. In opposition to this mode of lordship and slavery, however, we find another that is erroneous and unnatural, namely, when the worse and less worthy sometimes take to themselves lordship over the better and more worthy, as happens in the deviations from polities (which from their lack of order {204r} do not deserve to be called polities but deviations from polities). They are enumerated by Aristotle: three opposed to the three right polities, namely, tyranny (opposed to kingship), oligarchy (opposed to aristocracy), and democracy (opposed to timocracy). In these [regimes] those who are naturally slaves become by violence and against nature lords and free, and vice versa. These two modes of freedom and slavery are taken, then, from the division of lordship or rulership into rightly and naturally ordered or distorted and unnaturally disordered.

Further and last, Aristotle notes another division of freedom or lordship or rulership. There is despotic lordship, and there is royal lordship. Lordship is called despotic when it is exercised over things that do not have the power or intelligence (*industria*) to resist or obstruct the will or impulse of the one exercising lordship over them. We exercise lordship in this way over inanimate things and plants, houses and fields, also over brute animals when by art or physical power we are able to subjugate them to us, and even human beings (by the violent lordship we spoke of earlier). Royal lordship, however, and royal freedom is over [subjects] that have the power and intelligence to resist or obstruct the will and impulse of the one exercising lordship over them but do not try to obstruct or wish to do so. Indeed, they are inclined to subjection, because by experience they know, or by good persuasion and custom they understand (*habent industriam*), that it is good for them to be subjected – better than not to be subjected – since (as is said in *Ethics* VIII [11, 1161a11–12]), a king's lordship is of exceedingly abundant benefit to his subjects, for kings benefit their subjects and take care of them so that they act well. Yet despite this, a king acts by chief purpose for his own sake, namely, so that his soul may be inwardly perfected by the virtue of justice and so that outwardly honor and glory may be bestowed on him. Those whom these things do not satisfy become tyrants, as Aristotle well says in *Ethics* V (6, 1134b7–8).

[2a(i). Summary: Modes of Freedom and Slavery in Relations between Different Individuals]

To recapitulate, then, nine modes of freedom and slavery have been put forward, many of which, if they are not distinct in what they refer to, are yet somehow distinguished by different reasons for ascribing them.

The first mode [of freedom] consists in a good and refined bodily makeup disposing to liveliness of perception, and the [corresponding] mode of slavery consists in a makeup of body that is more compact and hard, making bodies strong for necessary use but lacking in aptitude for mental activity, in accordance with the text of *De anima* II (9, 421a25–26): 'Those whose flesh is soft are mentally capable, while those whose flesh is hard are incapable.'

The second mode consists in abundance or lack of money or of goods measurable in money.

The third mode consists in an extrinsic denomination from ancient ancestors.

The fourth mode, so far as it adds something above the first, consists in mental discrimination or lack of discrimination, prudence or imprudence.

The fifth consists in violence, for one who violates is called free and the one violated a slave.

The sixth mode of freedom consists in being better and more worthy and more principal [i.e., ruler-like].

The seventh consists in deviation from the right and natural order.

The eighth mode of freedom and slavery consists in the subject's inability to obstruct the will or impulse of the one exercising lordship and in the lord's necessitating the subject by a necessity either violent or natural.

And the ninth mode of freedom and slavery adds above the sixth that the subject is capable of obstructing the will and commands of the one exercising lordship.

[2b. Freedom and Slavery within a Single Individual]

But since the intellect and will about which the question was formulated are in the same individual, it remains now to speak of freedom and slavery in the same individual. We will compare first, soul to body; second, the superior part of the soul, namely, the rational, to the inferior part of the soul, namely, the sensual; and third, intellect to will.

[2b(i). Soul and Body]

In the first comparison we should follow Aristotle's judgment in *Politics* I (5, 1254b4–5). He says that 'the soul rules the body with a *despotic* lordship.' For the body is unable to resist the soul. I move my feet if I will, or my hands or head or tongue, etc., as each member is capable of being moved, and none of them can resist me if it is not sick or if there is no external obstacle (in which case the soul would not have lordship over that member insofar as it was thus impeded).

[2b(ii). The Rational and the Sensual]

Concerning the second comparison it is said that the superior part exercises lordship over the inferior by a royal lordship, and this is what Aristotle means in *Politics* I (5, 1254b5–6) when he says that intellect rules appetite 'with a political and royal rule.' (For it is said that by 'intellect' Aristotle means the whole superior part, namely, intellect and will, and by 'appetite' the whole inferior part, namely, sense and sensitive appetite. Aristotle therefore immediately adds, concerning the lordship of soul over body and intellect over appetite, that it is clearly according to nature and beneficial for the body to be ruled by the soul and for the passional, i.e., sensual, part to be ruled by the intellect 'and' the part that 'has' reason. Since properly speaking a conjunction should join different things, it seems that when Aristotle said '*and*' the part that '*has*' reason he meant the will, which is said to have reason not because it reasons but 'presuppositively,' because will bears only on what has first been judged by reason.) That the sensual part is able to oppose and obstruct reason was sufficiently explained in Book I of this work. Now it has just been said that the ninth mode of freedom, namely, the royal, presupposes the sixth mode, which is true in the present case, because everyone concedes that the intellectual part is naturally better and more worthy and more excellent in virtue and activity than the sensual, and because it has been said that the sensual part is able to oppose reason. It sometimes happens, from a defect of the intellectual part and the wickedness of the sensual, that the intellectual part succumbs and the sensual part exercises lordship over the intellectual. Therefore, when the intellectual part exercises lordship and the sensual permits itself to be led by reason and is inclined to obey reason, then there exists in a human being a rulership that is royal, ordered, natural, right, and best.

Such is the rulership in all the virtuous and in none but them. When the opposite is the case, however, then the rulership is unnatural, perverse, and very bad, and it is such in all the vicious. Therefore, since it was said in *Ethics* IX (4, 1166a16–17; cf. X.7, 1178a7) that a human being *is* chiefly intellect and ought to be denominated simply from the intellectual part, a human being is therefore said simply to be his own true lord and seems to be free if in him reason exercises lordship over sense. But if, on the contrary, intellect succumbs and is slave to sense, he is said truly to be a slave. And many texts of the philosophers run in accordance with this doctrine, that is, Aristotle's, when he says in *Politics* I (6, 1255a21) that virtue and wickedness determine slave and free and noble and nonnoble; and Tully's, when he says in *De Paradoxis* that all the wise are free and all the stupid slaves (he means that all the wise are good and that none are bad except the stupid, in accordance with the text 'Now all the bad are ignorant,' *Ethics* III [1, 1110b28]). Seneca holds the same in the letter to Lucilius '*Iterum tu mihi*' (XLIV 4), when he says, quoting Plato: 'Plato says that no king has arisen except from among slaves and no slave except from among kings: Long vicissitude has mixed all things and fortune has turned them upside down.' Then he asks, 'Who is well born?,' that is, free and noble, and answers, 'Whoever is by nature well put together for virtue. This is the one thing to consider!' He adds: 'The mind makes {204v} us noble; it can rise above fortune from any condition whatever.' On the other hand, human beings are made slaves by their vices, as he says in his letter '*Libenter*' (XLVII 17): 'One is a slave to lust, another to ambition, another to avarice, all to fear.' The common verse also says this: 'The only nobility is that which adorns the mind with virtues.'

(Some have criticized my habit of bringing forward so many authoritative texts to support my position, since an authority does not demonstrate. I say that I will not give up this way of arguing, especially in morals, for more credence should be given to ancient and famous teachers in morals than to arguments newly discovered and not thoroughly investigated, since, as [Aristotle] says in Book VI of this work [11, 1143b11–14], because they have insight from experience, such teachers 'see the principles.' And again, proof and demonstration of those texts are given where the texts are found. Those who want demonstrations of what I propose can therefore go back to the places from which those quotations come, if they wish. Therefore, I do not think it pointless to adduce them.)

[2b(iii). Intellect and Will]

It now remains to say how intellect and will compare, which was the original question.

[2b(iiia). Intellect and Will Are the Same Entity]

And I suppose, from what was said in Question 3 of Book VI (f. 118r) and in *De anima* III, that intellect and will in a human being are the same entity (*res*), so that the intellect is the will and the will the intellect. From this supposition I infer this first thesis:

> [Thesis 1] *The will is not freer than the intellect or the intellect freer than the will.*

This is because it would [otherwise] follow that the will would be freer than the will or the intellect freer than the intellect, which is not conceded. The inference is clear by means of an expository syllogism, arguing thus: The intellect is freer than the will, and the intellect is the will, therefore the will is freer than the will. Similarly: The will is freer than the intellect, and the will is the intellect; therefore, the intellect is freer than the intellect. And similar arguments hold concerning nobility, being principal, power, causality, priority, and in general all comparisons and relations in which it is not possible for the same thing to be compared with or related to itself. If it is impossible for the same thing to be prior or posterior to itself, or more noble or less noble, or that the same thing should be its own cause or its own effect, it follows that it is impossible for the intellect to be nobler than the will or ignobler, prior or posterior, its cause or its effect, or the reverse. Similarly, from the same root it follows that all such conjunctive propositions as the following are impossible: 'Socrates' intellect understands and his will does not understand,' 'His will wills and his intellect does not will,' 'His will is blind and his intellect is not blind,' 'His intellect has acquired the habit of wisdom or prudence and his will not.' And so of others of the kind.

[2b(iiib). A Doubt]

But then there is a doubt, because it is not only the intellect that is the same as the will. In a human being it is indeed also the same as the sense or sensitive power and the appetite or appetitive power, because we assert that in a human being the same soul is the intellective power and the sensitive and the vegetative. How, then, can we attribute contradictory predicates to intellect or will [on one hand] and to sense or sensitive appetite [on the other] – for example, that the one opposes and obstructs the other, that reason always urges toward the best objects and not sense or appetite (which urge sometimes toward the worst), that the superior part, namely, the intellectual, is nobler than the sensual part and rules it by a royal lordship? All these seem to contradict the foregoing.

[2b(iiic). Resolution of the Doubt]

I answer that all these things are in harmony if we specify the meanings with which they are said and asserted by the wise and if we distinguish the different ways in which we use the terms 'intellect' or 'intellective power,' 'sense' or 'sensitive power,' and similarly with others of this kind. I will say, then, that we call every human intellect an 'intellective power' because it can understand (or we can understand by it) as receptive of intellection; and in the same way we call the will a 'volitive power' because it can will (or we can will by it) as receptive of volition; and similarly we call sense a 'sensitive power' because it can sense (or we can sense by it) as receptive of sensation, and we call appetite the 'appetitive power' because it can desire (or we can desire by it) as receptive of appetition. If, however, something is an active [principle] of human intellection, volition, sensation, or appetition that *does not receive in itself* such intellection, volition, sensation, or appetition, we do not call this a human intellect or human will, we do not call it sense or sensitive appetite. I suppose this, then, from the meaning of the terms. (If anyone wishes to attribute other meanings to these terms, let him speak consistently.) Thus we do not here take 'intellect,' 'will,' 'sense,' and 'appetite' for acts of understanding and sensing, etc., nor do we take 'intellect' for the habit of principles; for these are not primary meanings or usages of those words.

I will say, second, that there is a difference between intellection and volition on the one hand and sensation and sensual appetition on the other, since intellection and volition are not received in the body or in a bodily organ as in a subject from whose power they proceed but are received in that way in the human soul alone. Those acts are therefore not extended by the extension of the body. This is what we mean when we customarily say that in their acts of understanding and willing intellect and will do not use bodily organs. Sensation and sensible appetite, on the other hand, are received in the composite of soul and body, as in the subject from whose power they proceed – from both body and soul. Those acts are therefore extended by the extension of the bodily organ. I have explained this more fully [in the Questions] on the *De anima*.

From these points it seems now to follow that intellect and will are nothing except precisely the soul itself, but sense and sensitive appetite is a composite of soul and bodily organs. Nevertheless, because the soul is much the more principal part in this composition, it is sometimes allowable to take 'sense' or 'sensitive appetite' for the soul, so that the term stands only for the soul while signifying the organ by appellation. To distinguish these two meanings, we can (if we please) call sense in the first meaning 'total sense' and in the second meaning 'partial sense,' and similarly with appetite. Then intellect and will would be identical with 'partial' sense or appetite and would not be identical with 'total' sense or appetite. Insofar as they are not identical, therefore, it is not surprising if contradictory predicates are truly said of them, but [this] never [happens] insofar as they are the same. As such [i.e., as the same], indeed, I may say that sense understands and intellect senses, namely, as partial sense, and intellect does not rule sense (unless sense rules itself), and sense is not opposed to intellect (unless intellect is opposed to itself), and intellect is not nobler than sense or freer, nor sense than intellect.

But you will ask, 'Then is intellect nobler than *total* sense?' I can say that it is not, because the body, which is the subject in which the soul exists, does not diminish the soul's perfection. Rather, the composite of soul and body seems to be better and more perfect than soul itself apart from body – just as Aristotle says in *Ethics* I (7, 1097b17–18) that if happiness were counted together {205r} with the least of goods it would be made more desirable. I will say later how it may be understood that intellect is a much nobler power than sense and will nobler than sensitive appetite.

[2b(iiid). Intellect and Will Are Equally Free]

I return, then, to the comparison of intellect and will, and I assert, in accordance with the supposition laid down above, this second conjunctive thesis:

[Thesis 2] *The intellect is free and the will is free, and both are equally free.*

For if both are free, it is necessary that they be equally free, since it has been said above that neither is freer than the other. That each is free, therefore, I prove as follows. Everyone concedes free choice (*liberum arbitrium*) in human beings. Some, however, say that choice is free because of the freedom of the intellect, others because of the freedom of the will, and others because of the freedom of both; and thus all are in agreement that either the intellect is free or the will is free or both. But if the intellect is free it follows that the will is free, and vice versa, by an expository syllogism (as has been said). It is necessary, then, to concede the freedom of both. Therefore, they are both free, and equally free.

Again, it has been said that the intellect is the soul itself and the will also is the soul itself, and it has also been said that the soul itself is free in respect of the body, for it rules the body with despotic rulership. Therefore, the intellect is free and the will is free.

[3. Doubts Remain – Reformulation of the Question]

But these theses are not the points that were doubted. It should be known, therefore, that although intellect and will are the same [thing], namely, the soul, nevertheless the *terms* ['intellect' and 'will'] differ in concept. For the soul is called 'intellect' (*intellectus*) from the fact that it understands (*intelligit*), or can understand, by receiving an intellection in itself, and the same soul is called 'will' from the fact that it wills, or can will, by receiving a volition in itself. Therefore, whatever is attributed to the soul because it understands or can understand is attributed to it *qua* intellect, and whatever is attributed to it because it wills or can will is attributed to it *qua* will. The chief predicates attributed to the soul *qua* intellect are 'to understand' or 'to be able to understand,' and [the chief predicates] attributed to the soul *qua* will are 'to will' and 'to be able to will' (namely, to be *able* to understand or will [are attributed to it] *qua* intellect or will *in potency*, and [*actually*] to understand and will [are attributed to it] *qua* intellect and will *in act*). When we say, therefore, that the intellect understands but does not will and, conversely, that the will wills but does not understand, or also that the intellect can understand but cannot will and, conversely, that the will can will but cannot understand (indeed, is blind), we ought not to understand such propositions in the sense they would have if taken literally, because they would be false, as has been said. But for brevity we put such propositions in place of other propositions, reduplicative or causal ones. Thus 'The intellect can understand but cannot will' [is put in place of] 'The soul is called "intellect" because it can understand but not because it can will' or 'It is called "intellect" insofar as it can understand' – that is, '[It is called "intellect"] *qua* able to understand and not *qua* able to will.' And the proposition 'The will can will but cannot understand' [is put in place of] 'The soul is called "will" because it can will, not because it can understand' or '[It is called "will"] *qua* able to will, not *qua* able to understand'; and similarly, *mutatis mutandis*, of 'will' and 'understand' as to intellect and will in act.

The question moved at the beginning, namely, whether the will is freer than the intellect, has therefore been answered in the sense it has if taken literally. But if it is formulated in place of another question, namely, a reduplicative or causal one, doubts remain. For example, these questions are doubtful: Do freedom and lordship befit the soul more according to the act of willing than according to the act of understanding? Does the soul have government and rulership over the body and the sensitive appetite more by an act of willing than by an act of understanding? Does the soul produce or receive an act of willing more freely than an act of understanding? And in general, is the act of willing nobler and freer than the act of understanding? We will therefore inquire into these questions in what follows. Let the second question, then, be:

Question 2. Does the Soul Produce in Itself the Act of Willing More Freely than the Act of Understanding?

[1. Preliminary Arguments]

It is argued that it does, for the reasons advanced in the last question to argue that the will is more free and more a lord than the intellect. As we saw, those reasons did not address that question well in the sense it has when taken literally, but they seem relevant and to have their force [if the thesis is taken] in the sense that the soul ought to be called lord and free more because of the reason for which it is called will than because of the reason for which it is called intellect. But it seems that if this is true it must be because the soul itself is freer in producing an act of willing (according to which it is called will) than in producing an act of understanding (according to which it is called intellect). Therefore, it produces the act of willing more freely.

The opposite is argued in a corresponding way, by the reasons advanced in the last question to argue that the intellect is freer than the will.

[2. Answer to the Question]

This question supposes some points and asks something further. It obviously supposes that the soul produces both the act of willing and the act of understanding, and it also supposes that the soul receives both (because of the phrase 'produces *in itself*'). Then it asks: Which of those acts does the soul produce *more* freely or receive more freely? (In this it also seems to suppose that the soul produces or receives both freely, if there is not to be a faulty comparison.) We do not doubt, then, that the human soul is receptive of those acts. I believe that it is also active with regard to them, and I suppose this. (I have discussed it with respect to the act of willing and willing against in Question 2 of Book III of this work (f. 37v) and with respect to the act of understanding in Question 10 on Book II of the *De anima* and in Question 10 of Book III.) To decide this point belongs more to speculative science than to this one. Still, because we have said that, if the comparison is not to be faulty, 'more freely' presupposes 'freely,' we must therefore see about this first as to both producing and receiving.

Let the doubt be, therefore, whether the human soul brings about (*agit*) intellection and volition freely.

[2a. Freedom of Final Ordering and Freedom of Opposition]

It seems that here the learned and the philosophers distinguish two kinds of acting freely. In one way an agent is said to act freely 'by freedom of final ordering' (*libertate finalis ordinationis*), in another way 'by freedom of opposition' (*libertate oppositionis*).

An agent is said to act freely by freedom of final ordering if it acts by chief purpose for its own sake and is said to act like a slave if it acts for the sake of another. Hence God alone acts simply and entirely freely in this way, and in relation to God all other agents act like slaves, because all things that exist and act both exist and act for God's sake; and hence we too ought to be God's slaves – and every external thing God produces and conserves is produced and conserved in its primary and chief purpose for God's own sake, for all existing things are 'finally ordered' to God. Yet despite this, a particular agent is said to act freely if it acts for its own sake *more chiefly* than for the sake of any other particular end which does not 'finally contain' it according to the natural connection and order of ends. (I say this because God finally contains us and all other things, and according to Aristotle we finally contain, according to the natural connection and order of ends, other lower things – for example, brute animals, plants, and inanimate things. {205v} He speaks about this connection at the end of *Metaphysics* XII.) Therefore, although we act like slaves in relation to God (because more chiefly for God's sake than for our own), simply speaking we are said to act freely if we act more chiefly for our own sake than for the sake of anything else except God, who finally contains us. So too, if according to the natural ordering of ends a brute animal acts more chiefly for God's sake and for our sake than for itself, then the brute acts like a slave in relation to God and to us. Nevertheless, according to its own nature it is said, simply speaking, to act freely with this freedom [of final ordering] if it acts for its own sake more chiefly than for the sake of anything else apart from us and God, and apart from any other thing that is (according to the natural connection and order of ends) its end, if anything else is such. Aristotle ascribes this kind of freedom to us in the preface to the *Metaphysics* (I 2, 982b24–27), where he says that just as we call those human beings free who exist for themselves and not for someone else's sake, 'so also this,' i.e., metaphysics, 'of all human sciences is alone free; for it alone exists for its own sake.' (By 'metaphysics' he means theology, from 'meta,' which is 'beyond,' and 'physis,' which is 'nature,' and 'icos,' which is 'science,' as if to say: 'the science of the things that are beyond nature.')

But an agent is said to act freely by freedom of opposition because, when it does something, it is not prenecessitated to do it by anything else or by any concurrence of other things, but *with all other entities (apart from the action itself) being the same* as they are when it begins to act and remaining thus, it is possible for it not to act or perhaps to do the opposite. Whether this manner of acting freely is possible has been determined sufficiently in the affirmative in Questions 1 and 2 of Book III (f. 36r). There it was determined that the will is free with this freedom, that no other power of the soul is more free than the will, and that to will and will against, i.e., volition and nolition, are the first acts of which we are lords in this manner of freedom and lordship. And as is clear there, all these things are explained and determined there in the sense of our present question, namely, that the will (or the soul according as it is called will) freely produces the act of willing or willing against and that it produces no other acts more freely by this freedom of opposition. Let us therefore suppose all these things as true.

[2b. Freedom of Opposition in Acts Attributed to Will]

But much doubt remains whether, by this freedom of opposition, the soul produces freely every act it is said to produce *qua* will, or does not produce every such act freely; and if not every act, then there is a stronger doubt which of them it produces freely and which not. To answer these doubts sufficiently it is necessary to specify distinctly the many different acts we attribute to the soul *qua* will. Although many acts are attributed to sensitive appetite *qua* sensitive appetite, yet there are also corresponding acts attributed to the will *qua* will; the two sets of acts are therefore distinguished correspondingly. You will find their distinction in Question 14 of Book IV (f. 83rb).

In accordance with what was said there let us assert, then, that the first act attributed to the will is favoring (*complacentia*) or disfavoring (*displacentia*) an object, which arises from apprehension of the object as good or bad, suitable or unsuitable. It was determined in Question 3 of Book III (f. 41v) that the will is not free as regards that act and is not its lord by lordship and freedom of opposition; you may look for this there.

Then, upon the act of favoring or disfavoring there sometimes follows another act which we are accustomed to call acceptance (*acceptatio*) or rejection (*refutatio*). This act properly speaking is called volition or nolition, because what I accept I will, and what I reject I will against, and vice versa. And upon this act there immediately follows actual pursuit (*prosecutio*) or avoidance (*fuga*), if it [the thing accepted or rejected] is apprehended as pursuable or avoidable and there is no obstacle. Concerning this act it was determined in Question 1 of Book III (f. 36r) and in the two following questions that the will is free as regards the production of this act and is lord of the act by the lordship and freedom of opposition; this too may be looked for there.

And, third, from the act of acceptance, or, properly speaking, of volition, there necessarily follows love (*amor*) and from the act of rejection hate (*odium*); or perhaps the acceptance *is*, formally, love and the rejection hate. Now if acceptance and love are the same, then just as the will is free regarding acceptance, so it is also free regarding love. If, on the other hand, love is a passion following upon an acceptance or volition that is really distinct from it, I think it follows upon that acceptance or volition necessarily, so that it is not naturally possible for the will to accept something and not love it or to reject it and not hate it. Therefore, because the will is related '*first* freely' to willing and willing against, therefore it is also related '*consequentially* freely' to loving and hating, but not freely in separation so that it can, while accepting, hate or not love, or, while rejecting, love or not hate. With this I pass on for the present from love, about which I will say more later.

But again, from this acceptance or rejection, if together with acceptance there is an apprehension of the thing accepted as something that is to be had but not [yet] possessed, there necessarily follows desire (*desiderium*); and if there is an apprehension of it as something had and possessed, there necessarily follows pleasure (*delectatio*). So also if there is an apprehension of a thing rejected as something had, there necessarily arises distress (*tristitia*); and if [the thing rejected is apprehended] as something to be had but not [yet] had, there arises the opposite of desire, on which we have imposed no special name. From these points we must conclude that the will is not free regarding those acts, namely, of pleasure and distress, except perhaps 'consequentially,' namely, insofar as it is free regarding the preceding act or acts upon which such pleasure or distress necessarily follows. Much was decided about these pleasures and distresses in Book VII, and we saw there, in Question 19 (rather, Question 29, f. 165r), that pleasure and distress are not the same as love and hate and not the same as the acceptance and rejection referred to above, nor yet the same as the favoring and disfavoring that are the first acts attributed to the will *qua* will.

It should also be noted that by the foregoing I do not mean to deny that pleasure and distress follow upon other acts of will as well as acceptance or rejection. Rather, it is also true that upon simple favoring and disfavoring, if accompanied by an apprehension of the object as present and had, pleasure necessarily follows upon favoring and distress upon disfavoring. This can be seen often in the preceding books. For in the 'mixed voluntary' [cf. *Ethics* III 1, 1110a4–13], although an [intrinsically undesirable] object is accepted [from compulsion] and not rejected, nevertheless not only does pleasure follow the acceptance and the presence of the act, but there is also much distress annexed because of the remaining disfavor (though without rejection). And in general, when the object is apprehended as present, pleasure is not entirely absent unless favor ceases, nor distress unless disfavor ceases.

It should be noted further that this thesis – namely, that the will produces the act of acceptance or rejection freely, with freedom of opposition – is to be asserted indefinitely, not universally, because consistent with this is {206r} the thesis that the will as will is not free with respect to *some* act of acceptance – indeed, that in this case acceptance and volition follow necessarily from a preceding intellectual apprehension, and that while this apprehension and judgment stand it is impossible for the will not to will the thing judged. This thesis was explained in Question 8 of Book VII (f. 145rb); look for it there. It appears, then, that the things said in this place have been proved elsewhere and are only recapitulated here.

[2b(i). Summary: Freedom of Opposition in Acts Attributed to Will]

There are seven theses about the will as to freedom of opposition. The first is that

[Thesis 1] *The will is free with freedom of opposition and no power is more free with this freedom than the will is.*

The second is that

[Thesis 2] *The will freely produces the act of willing or willing against and produces no act more freely than the act of willing or willing against.*

The third is that

[Thesis 3] *The will does not produce its first acts freely, which are favoring and disfavoring.*

The fourth is that

[Thesis 4] *The will freely produces the act of acceptance or rejection.*

The fifth is about the act of love [see above, p. 518, 'And, third . . . '].
The sixth thesis is about the act of pleasure or distress [see above, p. 519, 'But again . . . '].
The seventh is that

[Thesis 7] *The will is not free with freedom of opposition regarding some act of acceptance*

(In which act it is free and in which not can be seen in Question 8 of Book VII [f. 144v].)

[2c. Freedom of Opposition in Acts Attributed to Intellect]

Now we must see, similarly, about this freedom of opposition as to the intellect and acts attributed to it *qua* intellect, which are simple concepts not composed of several concepts (which we call 'simple apprehensions') and afterwards complex concepts. The latter are multiple. Some are composed of determination and determinable, others of subject and predicate, either affirmatively or negatively (such as propositions), others [are] assertive judgments, in which we assent to propositions as being true or dissent from them as being false. And further, concerning propositions, there are other acts called 'seemings' (*apparentie*), by which a proposition seems true or false, though we do not yet assent to it or dissent. Thus we often have arguments to the same conclusion that make it seem to us to be true and many others that make it seem to us to be false, but we do not yet judge either side assertively. Judgment, however, is actual belief (*fides*) or knowledge (*scientia*) or opinion, from which are generated habitual belief or knowledge or opinion. There are also other intellectual acts called discourses (from premises to conclusion), discoveries of means of proof, comparisons, abstractions, and the like. These will have to be distinguished and thoroughly examined elsewhere.

As far as our [present] purpose is concerned, however, we have to hold (briefly) for an eighth thesis:

[Thesis 8] *The intellect is not free regarding its first acts.*

This is because, as has been said, the will is not [free] regarding its [first acts], which would nevertheless seem more [likely to be the case].

[2c(i). Doubts]

But about other acts [besides the first] there is more doubt. For example, let us suppose that the intellect is informed by several simple concepts and can form an affirmative proposition from them and can also form a negative – for example, that 'A human being is an animal' and that 'A human being is not an animal.' It can form either without forming the other, and it can form both and, once they are formed, conserve them together in itself. Can the intellect, then, when it is thus informed by simple concepts, freely form an affirmation or not form it, form a negation or not form it, or form one only or both? To determine this question is difficult, since it has been little investigated.

[2c(ii). Arguments that the Intellect Is Free in Affirmation and Negation]

To some it could seem that in this matter the intellect has freedom of opposition *qua* intellect, because although it be conceded that the will may command me to study geometry, it nevertheless does not command me or my intellect to form or lay down such-and-such premises or to arrange them in the first or second figure. For it would seem an obstacle and a drag on the thinking process if in each such particular act one had to go back to an act and determination of the will. We must say, then, that in this the intellect can determine itself freely.

Again, if the thinking process involved such determinations by act of will, then the will would be more the lord of thinking habits than the intellect. It does not seem that this should be conceded.

Again, it also follows that in speculative study a special virtue and habit would be acquired in the will just as in the intellect, because just as a habit is acquired in the intellect from acts of intellect, so a habit ought to be acquired in the will from acts of will. We do not say this.

Again, before I formed the mental proposition 'A human being is an animal' or 'A human being is not an animal,' I was not aware of those propositions. Therefore, since the will cannot be brought to bear on what one is unaware of, it is impossible for the will to determine me by an act of willing to form this or that proposition.

[2c(iii). Arguments that Intellect Is Determined by Will in Such Acts]

But on the opposite side it could seem to someone that in this matter the intellect does not have lordship and freedom but the will does. For if you say to me, 'Form a proposition from the terms "human being" and "animal,"' it is certain that when I obey you it is in the power of my will to form either an affirmative or a negative. If I wish to form a negative, I form it and say that 'A human being is not an animal,' and if you ask why I have formed that false negative and not the affirmative (which is true), I cannot answer except by saying, 'Because I willed to do so.' If I wish to study geometry and also wish to study theology, if I begin with geometry, I can stop, either immediately after the first conclusion or even immediately after forming a major premise, and turn to theology if I wish, as everyone seems to experience in himself. It therefore seems that in these acts and in each of them the will has freedom and lordship.

Again, there are wonderful pleasures in philosophy and philosophical thinking, as we read in *Ethics* X (7, 1177a25), and not only in the end but in every conclusion and in every process [of thought]. Now these pleasures are acts of will. Therefore, the will works and has lordship throughout.

Again, if the intellect had lordship in such matters and not the will, it would follow that the intellect had freedom and lordship over its act before the will had freedom and lordship over its act (i.e., over the act of willing), which is against what we said before. For we said that the soul produces no act more freely than the act of willing or willing against and that these are the first acts of which we are lords with lordship and freedom of opposition. The inference is clear, because the intellect must judge concerning the goodness or badness of an object before the will accepts or rejects it – indeed, before the will has favor or disfavor toward it. Yet that judgment, namely, that something is good or suitable, bears on a formed proposition. If, therefore, the intellect has freedom of opposition in forming the proposition, it has such freedom before the will has it in the act of volition.

[2c(iv). Solution: Acts of Intellect Are Free Only When Freely Commanded by Will]

To make [the truth] concerning this matter evident we must note that according to what was said in Book III the soul is free as regards many intellectual acts – indeed, many sensual and bodily and external acts. For since the will freely produces the act of willing, every act that proceeds from a volition and would not proceed without it is said to proceed freely from our power and freedom (e.g., studying, sitting, {206v} standing, going to class, cutting wood, etc.). For example, my intellect judges that it will benefit me to build a house. From this judgment the will wills that I build it – not necessitated to willing by that judgment but freely forming the act of willing, although it could not form it without the preceding judgment. From that act of willing, sense and sense appetite and my limbs and the axe act to build the house – sense by knowing the wood, etc. and together with the sensitive appetite moving the limbs that move the axe cutting the wood. We, therefore, acting through all these, are said to produce all these actions freely: not because the axe cuts freely, for it is prenecessitated by my limbs; and my limbs do not move the axe freely, because they are prenecessitated to moving it by sense and sensitive appetite; nor again [does] sense [act freely] to move my limbs, nor does sensitive appetite act freely, because they are prenecessitated to it by volition, which is attributed to the will *qua* will. The will, however, produces this volition freely, because it is not necessitated by anything previous. Thus, therefore, we attribute freedom and lordship over all of these to the will and to no inferior power, because none of them is in our power according to freedom of opposition except through the volition over which we first have this freedom. From this volition, if there is no obstacle, everything necessarily follows, in such a way that without this volition they would not follow.

Now that we have noted these points, it is clear that an act is said to be in our free power in two ways: in one way because we produce it without being necessitated by any previous act to produce it when we do produce it. This can be called 'free in itself' – and thus we freely produce an act of willing or willing against. In another way [an act is said to be in our free power] because, if there is no obstacle, it follows necessarily on an act of ours that is free in itself and would not happen without it. Such an act we can call 'free consequentially.' Or some call the first act 'freely elicited,' because the will freely produces it immediately, and they call the second act 'freely commanded,' because the will commands our other powers to carry out those acts. For example, when the will commands the intellect to engage in thought concerning such or such a science, by that command the intellect is necessitated to engage in thought and does so if there is no obstacle. Thus, in a virtuous human being the will commands the sensitive appetite not to accept something pleasant shown to it by sense until reason sees whether it is virtuous. Then it instructs the intellect to consider whether this pleasant thing is virtuous or not virtuous. When that has been considered, it again commands the sensitive appetite to accept it or to reject it. Afterwards it commands sense and sensitive appetite or the motive power to move the limbs to carry out the outward acts willed, for example, to go into a bath or to build a house, and so on. And all these commands are only necessitatings of the powers to work and to work in a certain way, to which, if there is no obstacle, the soul necessitates them through the volition and its other preceding acts.

In accordance with this, then, let us assert a ninth thesis:

> [Thesis 9] *The soul freely produces many intellectual acts but produces them* qua *intellect.*

For we are said to produce freely not only acts freely elicited or free in themselves, but also acts that are freely commanded or free consequentially, as has been said. But the acts that the intellect produces *qua* intellect are often acts freely commanded by the will. For example, study and geometrical thinking are attributed to the intellect *qua* intellect, and yet we sometimes perform those acts through choice and volition. For example, we ask ourselves whether we will go to dinner or first study a little and think a little in geometry. When we have judged that we should study, the will accepts and we will to study. From this volition, since we are not obstructed, it follows necessarily that we will study and think.

We assert a tenth thesis:

> [Thesis 10] *When the soul freely produces those commanded intellectual acts it does not produce them freely only* qua *intellect but also* qua *will, so that freedom in producing them is attributed to the soul not only* qua *intellect but also* qua *will.*

For when the soul produces that thought [in the preceding example] *qua* intellect it is prenecessitated in this by a volition, which is not due to the soul *qua* intellect. So far as it is prenecessitated, however, it is not said to act freely. It is therefore not said to act freely *qua* producing the thought, but *qua* commanding the production. It commands this, however, through a volition, which is attributed to the soul *qua* will. Therefore, freedom in producing that thought must be attributed to the soul as it is called will.

We assert an eleventh thesis:

> [Thesis 11] *We produce an entirely similar act of thinking sometimes freely, sometimes not freely.*

I say freely, as in the case above, because there it is produced by a free command of the will, but I say not freely because [an entirely similar act can be produced] without such a command or act of the will. Suppose the following case. Socrates, waking from sleep, gets up, and a book on geometry meets his gaze. Out of habit he reads from it and studies and does some thinking. It is possible that in this sequence there is no act that is in itself freely elicited but that the power immediately producing each act is predetermined and prenecessitated to produce it if no obstacle intervenes. For he does not wake up freely but by natural (or perhaps violent) necessity. And when he gets up and walks he need not do so freely, for a dog, which we say does nothing freely, or a boy, who does not yet have the use of reason, would get up or walk in the same way. And he does not find the book placed there by free choice, but because it was put there apart from his intention. And if he subsequently sees it and reads and studies it, to do this he need not first consider whether to read, or first judge that he should read, nor, consequently, must he first accept by [an act of] will that he should read, for without this he is sufficiently determined to read by the object's presence and his habit of reading. But you will ask, 'Is this reading or thinking voluntary?' I answer, first, that it is not properly said to be *in*voluntary, because it is not against his will, and it is not in the most proper sense voluntary, because on this occasion a command of the will, i.e., an act of volition, contributes nothing to the action. But it is said to be 'consequentially' voluntary, either because the habit of studying or thinking determines him to this and the habit was acquired by voluntary acts, or because, if his intellect had posed the question whether he should then study and think, then he would have judged that he should and then the will would have commanded it.

Likewise, also, the thesis is clear because sometimes when a [pleasant] object is present an intemperate person rushes to act at once, determined through sense and passion and accustomed habit of intemperance without previous intellectual consideration, like a beast, and acts intemperately. [On the other hand] sometimes he seeks the object from choice and intellectual consideration and, in this case also, acts intemperately on finding it. (Yet despite this, activities that come about from the passions and sense without the cooperation of the will are, properly speaking, culpable and imputable {215r [*recte* 207r]} to us as being in some way voluntary, in the way we determined in Book III.)

Again, if we say that without an act of volition nothing is done freely with the freedom of opposition referred to earlier, it follows that you did not form freely the first proposition you formed, because volition did not concur in that, as we said before; and yet you can now form such a proposition voluntarily and freely; therefore, etc.

I now assert a twelfth thesis:

> [Thesis 12] *The human intellect produces no act of understanding freely as an act in itself freely elicited, although indeed [it may produce such an act] as a 'free commanded' act.*

I do not know how to demonstrate this thesis evidently. I hold it as an opinion, as a result of having a slightly persuasive [argument for it] and not having any reasons against it that are difficult to answer. The persuasive argument for it is as follows. We assert no such freedom in inanimate things, plants, or brutes but only in intellectual natures, and yet we see that a dog can produce opposite effects – for example, now sitting, now walking, walking now to the right, now to the left, now forward, now back again – as if it produced such acts freely. Yet we say that it does no such act freely but in each and every one is prenecessitated by the conjunction of circumstances, namely, either by objects appearing externally or by images kept in the imagination representing themselves in various ways to the common sense, and by the movements of the blood and spirits caused by the vegetative power, and also by the powers of celestial bodies and other things unknown to us, effecting and determining such alternations of different acts. Because we do not know how to assign such causes determining the dog to those different and opposite activities, we think at first glance that it acts as it does freely because it pleases it to do so, just as we would say of ourselves. Let us first suppose all these things. Second, I also suppose that from the above some have taken up the opinion that all things come about in us from predeterminations, just as in brutes, for we could say of ourselves just what we have said of the dog. We have little in the way of argument to disprove this sort of opinion except from our catholic faith, and because if it were true we would be necessarily predetermined in all our acts and consequently they would not be imputable to us for merit or demerit, which seems to conflict not only with our faith but also with the sciences and principles of morals. Therefore, we only attribute this freedom to ourselves more than to brutes to save [the fact] that we act well or ill, meritoriously or demeritoriously, and in ways that are imputable to us.

Since, then, we do not attribute this freedom to every power of our soul, and indeed not to the will in all its acts, it seems that just enough freedom should be attributed to only that power, and only in those acts, as is sufficient to save the above [namely, imputability]. But it is enough if we attribute this freedom to our soul only in acceptances and refusals. Therefore, it is only in those acts that we ought to attribute freedom of opposition to it and not to the intellect, or even the will in its other acts.

Again, some argue that we ought to attribute this freedom of opposition to the intellect rather than the will because the intellect is the noblest power of our soul. But through that means [of proof] I can argue the opposite. We do not attribute this freedom of opposition to the will in its noblest act, therefore we need not attribute it to the noblest power because of the nobility of the power. The antecedent is clear, because the noblest act of will would be that in which it willed and loved God when God was shown to it perfectly and steadily under the concept of the highest goodness, lacking any evil or defect whatever. Yet it would be necessitated to such an act and would not produce it freely with freedom of opposition, as we said in Question 8 of Book VII (f. 145rb).

Again, freedom of opposition is attributed first to God, yet not according to intellect *qua* intellect, because God understands necessarily all things, present, past and future, however they are, will be, or have been. But freedom of opposition is attributed according to his will in relation to things other [than himself], in creating or preserving them, or in willing to create or not create, preserve or not preserve them. It is likely, then, that the same should be said of us, except that God is necessitated by his essence always to understand, while we are not (though from what has been said above we are necessitated to understand when we do understand).

Then the arguments advanced earlier against this thesis can be answered. To the first I concede that when by will I study geometry, a new act of volition need not also concur in forming each proposition and ordering one after another or in a certain figure. Yet neither does the intellect *qua* intellect form and order them freely. It is predetermined either by habit and custom or by the relationship of those propositions to one another or because thus it occurs to me from imagination or dreams or some other such circumstance, just as a lutenist does not deliberate every time he plucks a string or a dog about every step when it walks. Nevertheless, it can often happen that many choices come into it. From these points made now and others made earlier anyone who wishes can easily answer the other arguments.

Now that freely acting has been discussed, I will hasten briefly over freely undergoing, asserting as a thirteenth thesis:

> [Thesis 13] *Whatever act the will produces first freely it also receives freely, because it accepts it into itself and it receives it from itself, and thus, as to that act, acting and undergoing, producing and receiving, are the same.*

Yet here freedom is attributed to the will *qua* agent rather than *qua* patient, because freedom suggests lordship, and the agent *qua* agent is said to dominate what is passive where they differ. Therefore also where they do not differ freedom ought to be attributed to a power *qua* agent rather than *qua* patient. Freely commanded acts need not all be received in the agent, however, but may be received externally in stones and wood, and [so] freedom need not be attributed to [all] passives.

[2d. Freedom of Final Ordering]

After this we have to speak about freedom of final ordering as to both intellect and will. I assert a fourteenth thesis:

> [Thesis 14] *Both intellect and will are free [with freedom of final ordering] and freely produce their acts of understanding and willing.*

This is because the actual thoughts and the habits of thought generated from them are, in their chief purpose, for the sake of perfecting the intellect itself and are not by a chiefer purpose for the sake of anything else except God. And acts of prudence, acts of the moral virtues, and the moral virtues themselves are, in their chief purpose according to the natural ordering of ends, either for the sake of habits of thought (we spoke about this relationship in the last question of Book VI [f. 139rb]), which are again ordered to the soul, as has been said, or else they serve directly for perfecting the will and perfecting the practical intellect (for it was said in Book II that we seek the moral virtues and knowledge of them to become good).

Fifteenth thesis:

> [Thesis 15] *Intellect and will do not produce all their acts of understanding and willing freely with freedom of final ordering.*

Indeed, they produce many of them slavishly and miserably, namely, all vicious acts, because these do not perfect the intellect or the will but corrupt them. It is therefore {215v [*recte* 207v]} obvious that they are not finally ordered to the intellect and the will according to the natural ordering of ends. For it would be absurd to say that something unsuitable to me and wicked and harmful exists by the natural ordering of ends for my sake and is finally ordered to me. It is clear, then, that in such acts intellect and will do not act by chief purpose for their own sake but for the sake of sensual pleasures contrary to their natural perfections.

The previously cited texts of the philosophers are therefore quite valid under this interpretation. For example, Seneca says that 'to serve philosophy is freedom.' I understand this, not as saying that intellect is the slave of philosophy itself, but that a human being is truly free when all other powers and actions of soul and body are ordered to the end that the intellect can think without encumbrance, and that in this way they serve the speculative intellect. And this is true, because in this way the intellect is truly lord and free, and a human being is chiefly his intellect, as was said elsewhere (*Ethics*, IX 4, 1166a16–17; X 7, 1178a7). Seneca also says that 'wisdom alone is freedom' – that is, it is chiefly through wisdom and its work that we are free, that is, more than through any other of our powers or any other act. According to this opinion, Tully's statement that all the wise are free and all the foolish slaves is obvious; also Aristotle's statement that virtue and wickedness determine slavery and freedom (*Politics* I 6, 1255a21) and Seneca's statement about the wicked, that 'One is a slave to lust, another to ambition, etc.' And this was also said in the other question.

[2e. Answer to the Main Question: It Depends on Which of Our Acts Is Best]

Finally, supposing what has been said, we must speak directly to the first question, about freedom of opposition. I assert a sixteenth thesis:

[Thesis 16] *The soul produces the act of willing more freely than the act of understanding.*

For we produce the act of willing first and immediately freely, as in itself freely elicited, but we do not produce an act of understanding freely except consequentially, as free commanded. Therefore, we produce the act of understanding freely because of the free production of the act of willing through which we command it, and that because of which anything is such is also such, and more so [cf. Aristotle, *Posterior Analytics* I 2, 72a28].

Next I assert a seventeenth thesis, about freedom of final ordering:

[Thesis 17] *As to some acts of willing and understanding the will produces an act of willing more freely than the intellect produces an act of understanding, and as to some it is the reverse. And similarly as to acts of understanding among themselves, the intellect also produces one more freely than another, and similarly of the will as to acts of willing.*

This is immediately clear, because we produce an act more freely if we produce other acts for its sake as an end according to the right and natural ordering of ends. But we ought to order all our inferior acts, both of willing and of understanding, to the end of contemplating and loving God, and love and contemplation are themselves acts of understanding or willing, either formally or by connection.

Again, if I will to think, that volition is finally ordered to thinking. Thus prudence and the moral virtues connected with it, which are habits of the intellect and will, exist for the sake of wisdom, which is a habit of the speculative intellect. This was Aristotle's view as explained in the last question of Book VI (f. 139rb). Therefore, acts of will are indeed finally ordered to an act of understanding. By contrast, advising, which is an act of intellect, is finally ordered to choice, choice being an act of the will. The intellect judges that something is better and more choice-worthy, not so that we may stop with that judgment but so that we may accept it and by a volition command performance. The judgment therefore exists for the sake of the volition as its end, though not as a last end.

But a more difficult question remains. Which act does the soul produce most freely with this freedom of final ordering, an act of will or an act of intellect? It ought to be certain that among all the acts our soul produces, it produces most freely with this freedom the act that is best and most perfect of all. For it produces that act most of all for its own sake, because that act perfects it most of all. And that act (whether it is an act of will or an act of intellect) is also most of all the end of the others, because by natural order the worse, that is, the less good, is always for the sake of the better, as Aristotle says in *Politics* VII (14, 1333a21–22). This is because by natural order the things ordered to an end are always good because of the goodness of the end, and that because of which anything is such is such also, and more so.

And again the question remains: Which is worthier and better, the best act of intellect or the best act of will? This question will be discussed afterwards (in Question 5). But so that at last the truth can appear directly concerning the question at the beginning, I will assert two last theses. One is this, namely, the eighteenth:

[Thesis 18] *Freedom of opposition is finally ordered to freedom of final ordering.*

This thesis is deduced as follows. It is certain that often something seems good to us that is not good, and bad that is not bad; and often, too, something seems good to us that is simply good, and bad that is simply bad. It would therefore not be good for us either to accept everything that seems good to us or not to accept everything such. Freedom of opposition, therefore, as was said in Question 3 of Book III (f. [42v] [misnumbered 62], 'alia ratio'), has not been given to us so that we should not accept the seeming good, nor also so that we should accept what seems because it seems, because in that way it would be given to our hurt – sometimes we would not accept what we should accept and sometimes we would accept what we should not accept. Rather, it has been given to us for our good in this way, that if something is not steadily and clearly judged to be simply good or simply bad, we should defer acceptance or rejection until we have investigated as best we can whether the seeming good or bad is simply good or simply bad, so that we may finally accept the simply good and not the bad and reject the simply bad and not the good. Moreover, when the intellect inquires and judges of the simply good that it is simply good and the will accepts it, then these things are done by both intellect and will on their own account and for their own sakes, for these things are, as such, ordered to the perfection of the intellect and will, as we were saying before. Intellect and will therefore act in that way freely with the freedom of final ordering. Thus, therefore, it is clear that the end for which freedom of opposition has been given to us is that in both intellect and will we may act freely with the freedom of final ordering, that is, laudably and well, to our salvation and perfection. And this is what we wished to prove.

Again, the will is not disposed freely by freedom of opposition to the acceptance of the ultimate good perfectly and steadily shown to it under the concept of pure goodness, as was said in Question 8 of Book VII

(f. 145rb), but it is disposed to it freely by freedom of final ordering, as was said above. Yet the end to which all other acceptances, showings, advisings, and choices about which we have freedom of opposition are ordered is the clear showing of that ultimate good and the acceptance or volition of it thus shown. It is therefore clear that all our acts that are free with the freedom of opposition – and freedom of opposition itself – are for the sake of an act that is free with the freedom of final ordering and for the sake of freedom of final ordering itself – that is, so that we may be free in that way.

Again, the highest human freedom of final ordering is in accordance with the highest human good, which is human happiness, and all other human goods are finally ordered to it, as was said in Book I. Freedom of opposition is not that happiness, because freedom of opposition is innate in us and happiness itself is not. Therefore, freedom of opposition is finally ordered to the freedom of final ordering. {208r}

Last I assert a [nineteenth] thesis:

> [Thesis 19] *If the best act of understanding that our intellect produces is nobler and better than the best act of willing that our will produces, then simply speaking our intellect produces the act of understanding more freely than our will produces the act of willing (and vice versa).*

This thesis is clear from the foregoing, because in comparing freedoms in order to decide which is a greater and stronger freedom, we need not attend to any freedom of opposition as if it might be greater but rather always to freedom of final ordering, since we have said that every freedom of opposition is for the sake of freedom of final ordering, and that because of which anything is such is such also, and more so. Therefore, this freedom of final ordering is more of a freedom than freedom of opposition is, and our soul is said to be more free *qua* free by this freedom than *qua* free by freedom of opposition. But it is certain that in producing its free acts the soul would be said to be free most of all by freedom of final ordering in producing its best act, whether that is an act of understanding or an act of willing.

Now it is clear that this last thesis is conditional and must be reduced to a categorical thesis finally determinative of the [main] question by determining this [subsidiary] question: Is the best act that our soul produces an act of understanding or an act of willing? We will speak about this later [in Question 5].

[3. Reply to the Preliminary Arguments of Question 1]

The arguments about freedom brought forward in the preceding question, both on the side of intellect and on that of will, can be answered by the preceding distinctions and theses concerning freedom, or they will be answered in the following questions.

Question 3. Does the Soul Produce the Act of Willing More Freely qua Intellect than qua Will?

Although we have already said plainly in Book III that the will is free as regards the act of willing and freely produces it, even *qua* will, and that it produces the act of willing more freely than the intellect produces some act of understanding (speaking of freedom of opposition), still this does not yet determine whether the *intellect*, even *qua* intellect, also freely produces the act of *willing* by freedom of opposition, nor, also, whether the intellect may be said to produce the act of willing more freely *qua* intellect than the will *qua* will. We must therefore now frame a question about this.

Let the third question, then, be only about the production of the act of willing, namely, whether the soul produces that act more freely *qua* intellect than *qua* will.

[1. Preliminary Arguments]

It is argued first that the question is a nullity, because the soul is not called intellect in relation to the act of willing. Therefore, in the production of an act of will no freedom should be attributed to the soul *qua* intellect but only *qua* will.

The opposite is argued: The soul produces a volition *qua* informed by an intellectual apprehension of an object under the concept of good or bad. But this befits it *qua* intellect, not *qua* will. Therefore, to produce a volition befits the soul *qua* intellect.

But I also argue that the will does not *produce* a volition *qua* will. For it is called will only *qua* willing by *receiving* a volition into itself, as we said should be noted from the verbal definition [of 'will' – see Question 1,

p. 512, Resolution of the Doubt]. But as such it is not said to be disposed toward volition except passively. And yet it is not said to *produce* a volition *qua* receiving it and being disposed passively. Therefore, it does not produce a volition *qua* will. Yet the opposite of this was said and supposed in the previous question.

[2. Answer to the Question]

This question supposes one thing and asks another. It supposes that the soul produces an act of willing both *qua* intellect and *qua* will. Argument was already made about this supposition, and now [in the preliminary arguments] it has been argued from both sides, since it appears that the supposition is doubtful. Afterwards, when we have seen that it is true, we [will] ask whether the soul is disposed more freely toward the act of willing *qua* intellect than *qua* will, or, also, whether it is said to produce that act more freely *qua* intellect than *qua* will or vice versa. And I wish this whole question to be understood of freedom of opposition.

[2a. The Soul Produces the Act of Willing Both qua Intellect and qua Will]

As to what has been supposed, then, we must see how the soul produces an act of willing. We suppose from what was said before that it does produce it. But to see how it does, we must note and suppose that it produces it only when it is informed by knowledge of a willable thing under the concept of good or apparent good, because everyone concedes that animal appetite, insofar as we distinguish it from natural appetite, is not brought to bear on what is unknown. Further, this knowledge must be intellectual, not merely sensitive, because this is how we distinguish conceptually between will and sensitive appetite and between an act of willing and an act of sensual appetite: An appetitive act insofar as it follows intellectual judgment is called an act of willing, and the power desiring in this act is, as such, called will. An appetitive act insofar as it follows sensual judgment is called an act of sensual appetite, and the power desiring in this act is, as such, called sensitive appetite.

Supposing this, we must now see whether intellectual apprehension of the willable thing contributes anything, either actively or passively, to the production of a volition. Concerning this I assert [ten] easy theses. The first is that

> [Thesis 1] *Intellectual apprehension contributes to volition either actively or passively.*

For although we suppose that the *soul* brings about the volition and also receives it, the apprehension is a disposition of soul without which the soul cannot bring about or receive a volition, and thus it is necessarily required. And no one can say how it is thus necessarily required except as a disposition or instrument of the agent for acting or as a disposition or instrument of the patient for being acted on. (It is not a disposition required in the soul for the soul's being, because the soul can exist without it. Therefore, it must be either for the sake of being acted on or for the sake of acting.) But a disposition of the agent necessary for acting is related actively to the production of the effect, although it is active not principally but instrumentally or dispositively. And thus also, if it is a disposition necessary for being acted on, then it is related passively, dispositively, though not principally. Therefore, etc.

Second thesis:

> [Thesis 2] *It is possible for the soul to bring about a volition of some object with the object doing nothing. It follows from this that the willed object is not a principal active [cause] of volition.*

The thesis is clear, for suppose no wine exists (God has annihilated all wine). Nevertheless, if I am now thirsty, I can begin to wish for wine, and so a volition of wine is brought about in me now. And yet wine does nothing now, because it is nothing, and what is nothing does nothing, because an agent acts according as it is actual. (I concede, nevertheless, that the wine has brought about its likeness in the soul, a likeness stored in imagination or memory or wherever you like in the body or in the soul, from which there follows later {208v} intellection and volition of the object. In this sense, which is quite remote from proper speech, we say that understood or willed objects bring about intellections and volitions in intellect and will.)

Third thesis:

> [Thesis 3] *Intellectual apprehension contributes actively to the production of a volition.*

Proof: It is determined in *De anima* III (10, 433a18–b13), that an appetible [object] moves the appetite to appetition, and first of all it moves the intellect to understand. The appetible is, as Aristotle says, the good or apparent good. It is apparent that it first of all moves the intellect to understand, because Aristotle says that it moves appetite *as a result of being thus understood or imagined*, and yet, as is clear from the last thesis, the appetible does not then act in itself but by this intention [of the soul]. For the likeness it brought about, stored in sense, acts toward an intellection of it, and that intellection subsequently [acts] toward a volition of it, which is what we wish to prove. This is confirmed, because Aristotle says that the appetible *moves* the appetite to appetition by its being thus understood or imagined. This would not be so, however, unless an intellection or an imagining contributed actively, for to move is to act.

Fourth thesis:

> [Thesis 4] *Intellectual apprehension does not contribute to volition passively.*

This is explained as follows. Intellection is neither a principal active [cause] of volition nor a principal passive [cause], because the will, as all concede, is the principal passive and receptive [cause] of volition, and the will is not the apprehension but is the soul itself. Similarly, the soul itself is the principal active [cause] of volition more than intellection is. Otherwise, we would have to say that an intellection would be disposed more nobly and more freely in producing a volition than the soul is, which is absurd.

Again, we should imagine that just as the nutritive soul brings about nutrition by means of natural heat, so does the soul bring about volition by means of intellection. Now not the heat but the soul is the principal nutrient [cause], and the heat is a disposition the soul needs to bring about nutrition. So, therefore, we ought to understand that not the intellection but the soul is the principal agent in bringing about volition, and the intellection is a disposition the soul needs to bring about volition. Supposing this, we explain the asserted thesis as follows. If intellectual apprehension contributed passively to volition, that is, so that it was a disposition of the soul for receiving a volition, it would follow that something entirely the same and in the same respect and in relation to the same thing would be both agent and patient, which Aristotle denies in many places. Thus in *Metaphysics* V (12, 1019a15–18) and IX (1, 1046a9–11), he describes an active power as a principle of motion or change in another (or [in the same thing] insofar as it is other), and a passive power as a principle of motion or change by another (or by the same thing insofar as it is other). It belongs to speculative philosophy to specify this truth, but the inference is clear: The soul, remaining the same, would be disposed both actively and passively to the same volition and in accordance with an apprehension remaining the same.

Again, this thesis seems reasonable because it pertains to a being in potency, as such, to be acted on, and it pertains to a being in actuality to act. The human soul is in itself in pure potency toward all the incorporeal dispositions that can exist in a human being and is like a tablet upon which nothing is written. It is in itself (and not through another disposition actuating it) passive and receptive of all these incorporeal dispositions. When [however] it has been actuated by certain dispositions, it is able to bring about other, consequent dispositions. Therefore, it seems to me that the soul *brings about* a volition by means of the intellection by which it is informed and *receives* it through its nature alone.

Then there follows a fifth thesis:

[Thesis 5] *The soul brings about volition* qua *intellect.*

This is because it brings about volition through this [i.e., through the intellect], because it does so *qua* informed by that intellection, as has been said. But *qua* informed by intellection it is called intellect. Therefore, etc.

A sixth thesis:

[Thesis 6] *The soul also brings about volition* qua *will.*

This is because, as was said before, those acts (namely, favoring and disfavoring, acceptance and rejection or volition and nolition; also love, hate, pleasure, distress, desire, etc.) are acts of the soul itself *qua* will, so that the soul *qua* informed by one of these is called will. I suppose this. Next, from points already determined I further suppose that favoring and disfavoring are acts in the will that are by nature prior to acceptance and rejection, which are properly called volitions. (If favor toward an apprehended good and acceptance sometimes come to exist in the will simultaneously, this is no reason why favor should not be naturally and necessarily prior according to the order of nature.) Now among things thus essentially ordered in the soul, the prior is the cause of the posterior. Therefore, just as through apprehension of the good the soul makes in itself favor toward that good, so through apprehension and favor together it makes the resulting act, namely, the volition. The soul therefore brings about volition as informed both by apprehension and by favor. But as informed by apprehension it is called intellect, and as informed by favor it is called appetite and will. Therefore, the soul brings about volition both as it is called intellect and as it is called will.

Seventh thesis:

[Thesis 7] *The soul is passive as regards volition* qua *will, not* qua intellect.

The intellect is not called intellect because it brings about intellection nor sense sense because it brings about sensation, for then the sensible or intelligible object or its likeness would be called intellect or sense. Rather, it is called 'intellect' from having or receiving in itself an intellection by which it formally understands (so too for sense and sensation). Therefore, correspondingly, the will is not called will because it brings about volition or pleasure or favor or the like, but rather because it has or receives such acts in itself, and this is to be passive to them. Hence we must form our picture here with subtlety and care. Although we concede that the will brings about volition under the concept through which it is called will, nevertheless it is not *called* will because it brings about volition but from having in itself favor, which is an act attributed to the soul *qua* will through which it brings about volition. Indeed, the intellect is also not called intellect because it brings about anything (for this is incidental), but from having an intellection in itself. There is a difference, then, between saying that the will brings about volition under the concept through which it is called will, and saying that the will is called will because it brings about volition, for the first is true and the second false. I say the first is true, because the will brings about volition through favor, through having which in itself it is called will. But the second is false, because it is already called will from having favor in itself, even if it brings about nothing; and also because, if the will brought about both favor and volition but did not receive either of them, it would never on this account be called will.

I assert an eighth thesis:

> [Thesis 8] *In receiving a volition the will is free with freedom of opposition, because with everything remaining the same (i.e., with the intellect remaining informed by this apprehension and the will by this favor), it is then possible that the will receive a volition from them and possible that it not receive one.*

[2b. Intellect and Will Together, with Freedom of Opposition]

Ninth thesis:

> [Thesis 9] *In producing a volition, intellect and will together, the former informed by an apprehension and the latter by a favoring, are free by freedom of opposition.*

For being in that state and with everything else remaining the same, they can produce, and they can {209r} not produce, yet neither [can produce] without the other. That is, the soul can freely produce a volition through the apprehension and favoring together, but not through the apprehension without the favoring or through the favoring without the apprehension.

You will ask, 'Where does the soul get this freedom?' I believe it has it essentially and formally from itself, so that it itself is that freedom, and has it, as it has its essence, primarily, actively, and finally from God. Now with that freedom it is able to produce in itself an act of willing through the apprehension and favoring as dispositions, but it is not necessitated by them to produce it.

It therefore appears, at last, that the will, *qua* will, produces volition freely, though not as total producer, and similarly the intellect *qua* intellect. The soul, however, *qua* both intellect (through apprehension) and will (through favoring) at once, freely produces the volition as total producer (yet not excluding the common influence of God).

And so we have spoken about what was being supposed in the question at the beginning. Now we must speak formally of what was asked.

[2c. The Soul Produces the Act of Willing More Freely (with Repect to Freedom of Final Ordering) qua Intellect than qua Will]

About this it seems to me that we have to assert this tenth thesis:

> [Thesis 10] *If there is a comparison in this matter, the soul is freer in producing volition* qua *intellect than* qua *will.*

I say *if* there is a comparison, because there does not seem to be one here as to freedom of opposition, but there is indeed a comparison as to freedom of 'being principal' and of final ordering. For if apprehension is more principal in producing a volition than favoring, then the soul more principally, and consequently more freely, produces volition *qua* intellect than *qua* will. And so it is. Therefore, etc. Proof of the minor: [i] The soul directs through apprehension the whole of what follows, and, since it directs, it is more principal than what is directed. [ii] Apprehension is to favoring as primary to secondary agent (for favoring is brought about through apprehension and volition through both of these, as has been said), but the primary agent, other things being equal, is more principal in producing an effect than a secondary agent, for it influences more, as the author of the *Liber de causis* says (first proposition), and it moves more, as is said in *Physics* VIII (5, 257b16–17). [iii] Favoring is reputed to be of little efficacy and nobility, but the apprehension that shows what is to be done, and how, and what is to be left undone, which is the act of prudence, is reputed by everyone to be of great efficacy and nobility. Freedom of final ordering is more to be attributed to something like that. Therefore, etc.

Now if you say that will *qua* will is freely disposed toward volition both actively and passively but the intellect *qua* intellect is only disposed toward volition actively and that therefore the will is freer *qua* will, I say that if this is conceded it is not against the asserted thesis, because the thesis was only about production. Nevertheless, one need not concede what you now conclude, because freedom is not properly called freedom from passivity but from activity. Freedom properly so called signifies or connotes being principal and lordship, but the agent, *qua* active, dominates the passive and never the passive (*qua* passive) the active.

[3. Reply to the Preliminary Arguments]

The arguments advanced at the beginning of the question are clearly answered by what has been said. So much, then, for these three questions about the freedom or servitude of human beings and their powers.

Question 4. Does Human Happiness Consist in One Act or Several?

Fourth we must ask: Which act or acts does human happiness consist in? The question can be put in this form: Does human happiness consist in one act or several?

[1. Preliminary Arguments]

[1a. Arguments that Human Happiness Consists in One Act]

[i] It is argued that it consists in one. Aristotle says in *Ethics* I (7, 1098a15–17) that human good, that is, happiness, is an *activity* of the soul in accordance with virtue, and if there are many virtues, in accordance with the most perfect and the best. He does not say 'activities' or 'according to the virtues,' but 'activity' and according to one virtue, namely, 'the most perfect and the best.' He also says the same thing again and in detail in Book X.

[ii] Again, in *Ethics* I (8, 1099a24–25) Aristotle says that happiness is both the best and finest thing and the most pleasant. Such a thing is singular, because a superlative applies only to one.

[iii] Again, in *Ethics* I (2, 1094a18–22) Aristotle says that there is some

end of human activities that we will for its own sake and for which we will other things. He says it is good and best, and he is referring to human happiness. Yet this cannot apply to two human acts, because in a perfect human being there ought not to be a lack of order, just as there ought not to be in the greater world. There would be a lack of order among human acts, however, if there were two best and equally final acts neither of which was finally ordered to the other. There must therefore be only one such act, and that is happiness.

[iv] Again, thinking (*speculatio*) is one act, not two, and yet in *Ethics* X (8, 1178b32) Aristotle concludes that 'therefore, indeed, happiness will be some sort of thinking.'

[v] Again, Seneca never ceases to proclaim in his letters that a human being's good is one thing alone and that it is perfect reason. In his letter '*Inimicitias*' he concludes that only perfect reason makes us happy (LXXVI 16). Therefore, happiness seems to consist in one act.

[1b. Arguments that Human Happiness Consists in More than One Act]

Those who think otherwise argue on the opposite side with many texts and arguments.

[i] Everyone who would say that human happiness consists in one act would say that this is either an act of the intellect, for example the vision or thought of God, or an act of the will, for example love of God – whichever of these is most perfect and best. But it is argued that this is impossible, whichever of them you say. For example, if you say that the most noble act that can exist in a human being is the clear vision of God, then I prove that this would not be happiness essentially. For if it were happiness essentially, then with it alone remaining and all other acts being removed (as they could be by God's absolute power, as some theologians say), one would still be happy, as a stone would be white if whiteness remained in it and all other accidents were removed. Yet that conclusion is false, namely, that a human being who saw God clearly without any pleasure and without love of God would be called happy. For happiness must be most pleasant, as Aristotle says (*Ethics* I 8, 1099a24–25). Therefore, etc.

This is quite strongly confirmed. Those theologians say that God could form in Socrates' soul, together with the clear vision of God, an intense distress without pleasure and a hatred of God without love. Would he then be happy? I am sure I would not wish for such happiness!

[ii] Again, any human power is capable of happiness (*felicitabilis*) if its activity is able to attain to the beatifying object, God. Now the vegetative and sensitive powers, the power of locomotion, and the sensitive appetite are not such powers, but intellect and will are, for through intellect we understand God and through will we love him. A human being is thus truly capable of happiness with regard to both of these powers. Therefore, if someone were made happy with regard to only one of them, the happiness would not be perfect or total but diminished and partial. This should not be said, because nothing diminished is attributed to happiness (hence in *Ethics* X [7, 1177b25–26] [Aristotle says] that there is nothing imperfect in the things that constitute happiness). Happiness must therefore essentially consist of acts of [both] those powers and cannot be the single act of only one of them.

[iii] Again, happiness is asserted to consist in the perfect contemplation of God, which is not knowledge of God without love or love without knowledge but is made up of both.

[iv] Again, happiness is asserted to be something most sufficient *per se*, and no single act is most sufficient *per se*.

[v] Again, Aristotle says in *Ethics* I (8, 1099b3–5) that no one who is very ugly in appearance, low born, or lonely and without offspring is at all happy. How would this be true if happiness consisted in one act, whether of intellect or of will? {209v}

[vi] To the same effect one could also quote Aristotle, *Politics* VII (7, 1323b21–23): 'Let us acknowledge that each one has just so much happiness as he has of virtue and prudence and of virtuous and prudent action.' He says, then, not only 'of prudence,' pertaining to the intellect, and not only 'of virtue,' pertaining to the will, but 'of virtue and prudence' together. On this he builds an argument that there is no good work, of a man or of a city, without virtue and prudence.

[vii] This seems indeed to be what other moralists and sacred Scripture also think. Many texts of sacred Scripture seem to say clearly that human happiness consists in the vision of God and many others that it consists in love of God. This is only because it does not consist in the one or the other alone but jointly and integrally in both. And this seems to be true regarding Seneca and Tully. Sometimes they say the one thing, sometimes the other. For example, Tully says in *De Paradoxis* (*Paradoxa* V 33) that all the wise are free and all the foolish slaves, and thus he attributes freedom, and consequently happiness, to wisdom, which is an intellectual habit. But at once in the same book he asks, 'What is freedom?' and answers 'The

power to live as you will' (*Paradoxa* V 34), and thus he attributes happiness to the will. Similarly, Seneca very often attributes happiness to wisdom and right reason and often also to the moral virtues. For example, in his letter '*Agnosco*' (XXXI 8) he says, 'It,' that is, the highest good, and consequently happiness 'cannot be, unless there is knowledge of things and the art by which divine and human matters are known.' In the letter that begins '*Epistola tua*' he says that true goods are those which reason gives, solid and eternal, etc. (LXXIV 16). He says the same afterwards, that nothing is stronger than reason (LXXIV 20). And in the following letter: 'The best thing in a human being? Reason . . . This, if right and perfected, completes human happiness' (LXXVI 9). He therefore concludes afterwards that only perfected reason makes one happy (LXXVI 16). It is clear, then, that in that letter Seneca asserted that happiness consists in reason and wisdom.

[1c. Objection]

But you would say at once: 'All of Seneca's texts and the reasons on which they are based prove the opposite of what you wanted to prove. You were intending to conclude that human happiness consists not in an act of the intellect alone (such as wisdom, science, and reason), but rather in the conjunction of an act of intellect and an act of will. [But] the texts quoted say expressly that it consists in an act of intellect only. Seneca says, "*only*" perfected reason makes one happy, and whoever sees all his books [will see that] he cries up and extols wisdom above all human goods.'

[1d. Answer: Seneca Speaks as Aristotle Does]

The answer is, however, that if Seneca's meaning or opinion is looked into carefully, it will appear that he well knew how to distinguish between the moral virtues (which we have said are virtues of appetite or will) and prudence (which we say is a virtue of the practical intellect). This is clear from that beautiful little book of his called *On the Four Cardinal Virtues*. In that book he has called both of these [i.e., moral virtue and prudence] virtues or kinds of virtue – the former being virtues of our soul *qua* practical appetite, the latter, however, of the same soul *qua* practical intellect. But he did not call either of them separately simply virtues of the human soul *qua* human soul; for a virtue must be a perfect state of that of which it is said to be the virtue, *qua* its virtue, and neither of those separately is a perfect state of the human soul *qua* human soul, nor even of the practical human soul *qua* practical human soul.

And it seems that Aristotle ought to concede this. For it is clear from *Physics* VII (3, 246a13–14) that virtue is a perfect disposition of that which has it: 'A virtue is a perfection; each thing is then most of all perfect when it attains its appropriate virtue.' Similarly in *Ethics* II (6, 1106a15–17) he says that every virtue both perfects that which has it and makes its work good. Afterwards, in Book VI (13, 1144b17–32), it appears that although moral virtue as distinct from prudence makes the practical will perfect *qua* will and its work good so far as it relates to the will *qua* will (and similarly of prudence so far as it relates to practical intellect), nevertheless neither separately makes the whole active soul perfect or its work good – as Aristotle seems to confess when he says that moral virtue in the proper sense cannot exist without prudence. Accordingly, as he says, all who define virtue posit a habit and add 'which is in accordance with right reason.' Finally he concludes that it is clear from what he has said that it is not possible to be good in the proper sense without prudence, nor prudent without moral virtue. And in *Politics* VII (1, 1323b32–33), cited above, he says that there is no good work, of one [individual] or of a city, without virtue and prudence. And so, reasoning according to the preceding inferences, he seems to say that the virtue of the active soul *qua* active is an aggregate of moral virtue and prudence and neither separately. Next we must consider (as Aristotle says in *Ethics* IX [8, 1168b31–35) that since a human being is an aggregate of soul and body and of a sensual and an intellectual part, nevertheless, since the human being is what is most principal in this aggregate, the human being is called chiefly this [most principal part], namely, intellect. And so Aristotle holds of other aggregates, saying that just as a city and every other aggregate seems to be chiefly its most principal part, so also a human being. If, therefore, we say that prudence is the most principal part in the aggregate of moral virtue and prudence that is the virtue of the active soul, it follows (in accordance with this naming of an aggregate from the more principal part) that all human virtue relating to the active life as active 'is' prudence.

This is what Seneca meant by reason and also by wisdom, because he always spoke of practical happiness, in relation to which prudence is called wisdom. For thus Seneca says that all virtues of the soul are reasons and that courage is knowledge. As a result, in the letter '*Si vales*' he asks, 'What is wisdom?' and answers that it is 'always to will the same and will against the same' (XX 5), although willing and willing against are acts of will.

And in the letter '*Claranum*' he says expressly that 'All virtues are reasons' (LXVI 32). In the letter '*Perperceram*' he says that 'Courage is not thought-less rashness or love of dangers or appetite for fearful things but knowing how to distinguish what is evil from what is not' (LXXXV 28). We must suppose that Socrates was following this opinion and manner of speaking when he said that all virtues are reasons and prudences, as Aristotle reports in *Ethics* VI (13, 1144b28–29). Aristotle does not seem very critical of those statements so intended. He criticizes the words, but he criticizes them in the same way as his own words might be criticized [as figurative?] when he says that a city and every aggregate is its most principal part and that the intellect *is* the human being.

[2. Answer to the Question]

In view of all this, it seems we must say that practical happiness, of which the abovementioned philosophers were especially speaking, is not sepa-rately either an act of understanding in accordance with prudence or an act of willing in accordance with moral virtue but an act aggregated from those acts in accordance with a perfect virtue also aggregated from those partial virtues. In this aggregation, however, the part that is more principal, more noble, and better would be prudence and the act of prudence, according to the explanation of what the philosophers quoted above meant. And it seems we must speak correspondingly of contemplative happiness in relation to acts of contemplative intellect and contemplative will, if we are speaking of it as happiness of the human soul and as it is (and is called) contemplative. Hence I think that in heaven (*patria*) there is, corresponding to clear vision (which properly ought not to be called practical), love (which also properly ought not to be called practical love but contemplative).

[2a. A Distinction: Aggregation vs. Division]

{210r} I do not believe it possible to invalidate this way of speaking by arguments of much force, nor do I think that Aristotle would have rejected it in the sense given above. Yet despite this, another way of speaking can be offered, namely, the following. Since that ought to be called happiness which is best and most perfect in kind of the things able to exist in a happy human being (or in a human being capable of happiness), and since the best of things naturally able to exist in us can be considered in two ways, as either best by way of composition or aggregation, or best by way of division or resolution, so human happiness can be spoken of in each of these ways.

In the way of composition, then, the best in a human being is the aggregate of all the virtues, activities, and dispositions we are capable of that make us better, both in soul and each power of the soul and in body and each part pertaining to the wholeness of the body. In this way, therefore, the word 'happiness' would stand for such an aggregation, yet signifying by appellation the possession of external goods sufficient for us to perform without encumbrance every activity suitable to us in accordance with the virtues of both soul and body. This is the happiness described as a 'state made perfect by the aggregation of all goods' (Boethius, *Consolation of Philosophy* III, Prose 2), and thus 'There is nothing imperfect in the things that constitute happiness,' as is said in Book X (7, 1177b25–26) of the present work. And thus Aristotle would say that someone missing a limb, or in the grip of sickness, or in prison, or unlucky, or without friends or outward riches would not be simply a happy human being, as was noted in Book I. [This is the only sense that] philosophers lacking the catholic faith and any special supernatural revelation would recognize in attributing happiness to someone in this life.

In the way of resolution, however, the best in a human being would be said to be the disposition or act (or by whatever word it is called) that would be best of all if this aggregate were resolved into its parts and would be the ultimate end of the others, to which every other would be finally ordered – not that this resolution should be made by really removing parts from one another, but by reason distinctly considering each part. If we say, therefore, that what is best is an act of thought regarding the divine essence, we will say that this act is human happiness, so that the term 'happiness' stands for that act precisely, yet not cut off from connotations; rather, it connotes or signifies by appellation all the things prerequisite to the easy performance of that act of thought and the things naturally following upon or annexed to it. And thus, in the first place, it signifies by appellation the love of God, as naturally following upon that act of thought if it is right and perfect, and the pleasure naturally connected with these acts. And then it also signifies by appellation the virtue of wisdom in accordance with which that thinking is perfect. Next it signifies by appellation prudence and the moral virtues, which prepare a place for wisdom, as was said in Book VI (cf. f. 139rb); then liveliness of the senses, which serves the intellect in thinking; and finally the virtues of the body and exterior goods, as was sufficiently shown in Question 16 of Book I of this work (f. 15r). It is certain that Aristotle used this way of speaking, nor do the arguments advanced before have any force against it, for they are easily answered.

[2b. Reply to the Arguments that Happiness Consists in More than One Act (1b[i–vii])]

[i] To the first let us assert that the clear vision of God is human happiness in heaven. You argue that then someone would be happy seeing God clearly but without pleasure, indeed with distress and hatred of God. I deny this. Indeed such a person would instead be miserable, because that vision would not then be happiness because of the lack of things signified by appellation. Similarly snubness, although it stands only for the nose's curvature, yet signifies the nose by appellation. Therefore, if the magnitude and curvature of the nose (which is snubness) were removed from the nose and placed in a stone, it would no longer be snubness, because of the lack of something connoted. And so, although Aristotle held that happiness is an act of thought, he nevertheless says in Book VII (13, 1153b19–21) of this work (and similarly in Book I [cf. 10, 1100b28–30]) that those who say someone on the rack or in misfortune is happy if he is good are speaking nonsense (even if the unfortunate is actually engaged in thinking). What was said about whiteness is therefore not to the point, because whiteness signifies what it stands for without connoting other things.

[ii] To the next, which says that both will and intellect are capable of happiness, I concede it. But for a clear reply to that argument a certain other distinction about happiness will have to be laid down first. Therefore I now pass on.

[iii] To the following argument, when it says that happiness is the perfect contemplation of God, I can concede it. This contemplation is the thought or vision of God. Yet the word 'contemplation' connotes, just as the word 'happiness' does, the presence of the love and pleasure naturally connected to that thought or vision. And you say, 'Vision is not perfect contemplation.' I say that indeed it is, if love and pleasure are present with it, but if they were not present it would not be perfect contemplation – indeed, it would not be contemplation and it would not be perfect vision. It would indeed be a vision perfect by its essential perfection, but 'therefore, perfect' does not follow until it is also perfect through the perfections able to be

present with it. In the same way someone lacking the moral and intellectual virtues would be perfect in essential perfection but would not be simply a perfect human being.

[iv] To the next, which argues from the *per se* sufficiency of happiness: we said in Question 14 of Book I (f. 14r), where four modes of its *per se* sufficiency were posited (and a fifth can be added), that happiness is *per se* most sufficient if it needs nothing that would be suitable to it or to the happy human being for living perfectly, since I am not in need of what I have. Now the thinking that is human happiness has added to itself everything suitable to us for perfect living in both body and soul. Otherwise it would not be happiness. Hence I concede that thinking could be in need of many things required for a perfect human life, but then it would not be human happiness. Therefore, the statement that happiness is most sufficient, so that it is in need of nothing, is true *per se*, as has been said.

[v–vii] Now all the texts, whether of sacred Scripture or of the philosophers, even if they were to say expressly that happiness consists in love of God or in pleasure or in love and vision together, or that happiness is love or pleasure or a combination of love and vision, would be explained as being meant to indicate that happiness cannot exist without these things, or that they follow necessarily upon happiness or are connected to happiness, or in some such way. For sentences are very often not asserted in the most proper significations and accepted meanings of the words.

[2c. A Second Distinction: Happiness of Whole vs. Happiness of Parts]

Now, then, having introduced this first distinction of happiness (whose members coincide as to the real existence of human goods and their ordering in the happy human being), I will assert yet another distinction concerning happiness. And I will note that if it befits a thing to have its own virtue, then happiness or something corresponding to happiness befits it when it works easily in accordance with that virtue. I say 'happiness befits it' if it is itself able to be happy, 'or something corresponding to happiness' if it is not properly said to be capable of happiness. For everything that attains its own virtue and works easily in accordance with it is, as such, perfect and is in the best state and, consequently, happy or related to happiness correspondingly. Now it is certain that if a whole has different parts naturally ordered to different activities, we must assign {210v} a special virtue to it and also to each of its parts, one to one part and another to another. For the special virtue and best condition of the heart is one thing, that of the brain another, of the hand another, of the eye another. And the special virtue of each part perfects the well disposed part and makes its work good. For example, the virtue of the eye both makes the eye keen and makes the eye's work good, for 'by the virtue of the eye we see well,' as [Aristotle] notes in Book II (6, 1106a18–19) of this work. From these points it follows that a happiness of its own (or a special state [*dispositio*] of the part corresponding to happiness) befits each part of a well ordered whole. If, therefore, we call everything corresponding to happiness 'happiness' in a broad sense, then there will be both happiness of body and happiness of soul in a human being – and happiness of heart, brain, hand, and eye, one happiness of this part and another of that. Therefore, too, since we assert that the soul is potentially divisible into parts, one thing will be the virtue and happiness of the sensitive soul as sensitive, another of the appetitive as appetitive, another of the intellect as intellect, another of the will as will, another of the speculative intellect as speculative, another too of the active intellect as active.

But then we must consider, concerning a whole constituted out of many parts, what is its virtue and happiness, and how it is distinguished from the special virtue and happiness of each part. It can be said that the virtue of the whole results from the ordered and proportioned virtues of the parts and is nothing other than the ordered and proportioned aggregate of the virtues of the parts or powers. The virtue of the whole differs from the virtue of a part in just the way an aggregate of many differs from one of them. So too, if happiness is placed in activity in accordance with virtue, the happiness of the whole differs from the happiness of a part as an aggregate of many actions differs from one of them. This is speaking in the first mode of the earlier distinction. But if we speak in the second mode, namely, according to denomination from the most principal part of the aggregate – for example, if we called the general assembly of the university the rector's assembly and the particular assembly of a nation [within the university] a proctor's assembly – then we would say that the virtue of the whole is the virtue of its most principal part. For example, if we were to say that the virtue of an animal is the state of the heart that is the virtue of the heart itself, then the terms 'virtue of the heart' and 'virtue of the animal' would stand for the same thing – but differently, because the term 'virtue of the heart' would not signify by appellation the virtue or state of the brain or liver, but the term 'virtue of the animal' would signify by appellation the virtuous states of brain and liver and other members. Supposing, then, that the heart was in its best state and not the brain, the state of the heart would then be the virtue of the heart but would no longer be said to be the virtue of the animal, because of a lack of something connoted. And so we ought to imagine correspondingly of the happinesses of whole and parts in relation to the virtuous activities which those happinesses would consist in.

[2d. Application of the Second Distinction]

Now, then, let us come particularly to the happiness of a human being and the happinesses of his parts, and let us speak according to the first mode of the earlier distinction (because it is easier). Let us divide a human being first into [1] an inferior portion, called vegetable and sensual, composed of soul and body (since vegetation and sensation are exercised only in a corporeal organ), and [2] a superior portion, called intellectual, which is the soul alone (since the activities specific to that portion are not exercised in a corporeal organ). Now the inferior portion is divided into vegetable and sensual; the vegetable is divided into particular members each composed of soul and body with its own makeup and its own vegetating, and the sensual is divided into sense and sensitive appetite. It is certain that a natural makeup perfects a sensual power for sensing clearly and distinctly; an appetitive power, however, requires in addition to a good natural makeup a habit of good custom inclining it to obey reason. The superior portion is divided potentially into an active part and a contemplative part (or into practical and speculative), and both parts are divided into intellect and will: that is, the practical part into practical intellect and practical will and the contemplative part into contemplative or speculative intellect and contemplative or speculative will (which I call speculative not because it formally thinks but because its act, as such, follows upon the act of thought). According to Aristotle, then, the virtue of the speculative intellect is wisdom, and the act in accordance with that virtue is thought concerning divine things, which is the happiness of the speculative intellect. The virtue of the speculative will would be habitual love of God and love of the whole ordering of beings as depending on God, and the act in accordance with that virtue would be actual love of God, etc., following upon the abovementioned actual thinking, and this loving would be the happiness of the speculative will. In truth, the happiness of contemplative intellect is the clear vision of God, and the happiness of contemplative will is actually loving God. Thus the happiness of the whole contemplative part would be this love and vision combined. The virtue of the practical intellect, however, is prudence, and its happiness is the act of prudence. The virtue of practical will is the combination of moral virtue with prudence, and its happiness is actual inclination to the judgment of prudence in accordance with those virtues. The virtue, therefore, of the whole superior portion is the aggregate of these virtues, and its happiness is the aggregate of these happinesses.

And so, dealing with blessedness in heaven briefly (because it goes beyond the limits of this investigation), we would not say that someone is in the most proper sense blessed before the resurrection [of the body], because until then he would lack blessedness of body (or its best state), which belongs to the wholeness of human blessedness, or would lack things connoted by human blessedness, since a human being in the most proper sense is a composite of soul and body. (Yet I confess that according to denomination from the more principal part – as Aristotle says that the intellect is itself the human being – blessed Peter, although he has not risen corporeally, is truly blessed and a blessed man from the blessedness of his soul.)

Following Aristotle, we must speak in a corresponding way about this life. For if one is happy according to the superior practical portion it does not follow that one is a happy person, but rather a happy active person – perhaps not happy speculatively, which is required for being simply a happy human being. And if one is happy according to wisdom and prudence – that is, practically and speculatively – still it does not yet follow that one is a happy human being, because perhaps the happiness of some part of the inferior portion is lacking – for example, if eyes, feet, or hands are lacking, or if the vegetative part is impeded by sickness (from which it follows that the sensitive part is impeded and also the intellective part in performing its work), or also if because of lack of nourishment the vegetative part cannot do its work and all the other powers are soon impeded. Nevertheless, the happiness of a human being, insofar as it is a matter of living naturally in this world, is as such (or connotes) an aggregate of the happinesses of all such parts. Therefore, if the superior portion enjoys its own happiness and prosperity, it does not follow from this that one is a happy human being. And this is what Aristotle meant.

*[2e. Resolution of Questions about Bodily and External Goods
from Book I]*

From these points many of the things we were asking about in Book I are clear and obvious. For it is obvious that human happiness does not consist in external goods or in pleasures or in any {211r} corporeal virtues or works – indeed, it does not consist in intellectual virtues or activities except partially; or if, following the second way of speaking according to the first distinction, it is said to consist in the work of intellect, this is nevertheless not without the presence of the other human goods of body and soul. It is also apparent that Seneca's words (some of which were quoted in Question 6 [rather, 16] of Book I [f. 15rb]), in which he often seems to exclaim against Aristotle's opinion (namely, when he says that goods or evils of body, health or sickness, riches or poverty, etc., do nothing to augment or diminish human virtue or happiness or add anything to it or take anything away, etc.) – it is clear that, so far as those words are true, they have no force against Aristotle. For if he is speaking of the happiness of a human being as composed of body and soul and living naturally, he would not be speaking the truth. If, however, he is speaking in a qualified way – that is, about the virtue of a human being with regard to the superior portion – he is speaking the truth concerning virtue once it has been acquired but not about its acquisition (especially as to wisdom, for bodily sickness, captivity, lack of necessities, etc., greatly obstruct study). Nor would he be speaking accurately of happiness if it consists in an act of wisdom. And although he would be right regarding the inner working of practical virtue, he would nevertheless not be right about the outward working, which immediately affects friends, neighbors, the commonwealth, etc. A good state in each of these is required for a human being to be in the best state, which is to be a happy human being.

In these texts Seneca speaks very well and beautifully and piously – comparatively, but not simply and absolutely. I say 'comparatively' because the excellence of the superior portion is so great in relation to the inferior that no comparison of them can be admitted when it is impossible for both to be preserved. We hold this from our faith. Aristotle would hold the same thing, namely, that when it is impossible for both to be preserved it would be preferable to lose riches, friends, a limb, or indeed body and temporal life, rather than stain the superior portion in the slightest. This comparative statement is Seneca's opinion and that of all moralists. For he seems to speak as he says in the letter '*Inimicitias*': 'Nothing will deter [a good man] from what is honorable, nothing will tempt him into baseness' (LXXVI 18). Yet it was not Seneca's opinion that a human being is simply in the best state when afflicted by torments, in the grip of sickness, lacking food, money, and friends; because if he believed himself to be in his best state then, he ought not to seek a state other than this one, which Seneca denies. In his book *On the Blessed Life* he says that 'If we are wise, we will not despise ourselves for being very short, yet we will wish to be tall'; 'We will put up with bad health, but we will wish for good health' (XXII 2–3); 'I will despise fortune's whole kingdom, but if given the choice I will take the better things from it' (XXV 5).

[3. Supplementary Questions]

Although this seems to be a true account of happiness, yet certain small questions arise about it.

One is this. Someone who is in the best state of soul and body must grow old and then, being unable to walk, will not be in the best bodily state; and thus no old person would be a happy human being, which the philosophers did not concede.

A second [question] is whether a sleeping person is a happy human being. It seems not, because no activity then takes place in accordance with the intellectual virtues; yet you say that human happiness consists in this activity, at least as to the part of happiness that is by far the more principal. But against this it seems unsuitable if we must so often lose our happiness.

Third: If a human being under torment or sickness, unfortunate or captive, is not a happy human being, is he therefore miserable or unhappy? It seems not, if he was happy before, since in Book I (10, 1100b34) of this work [Aristotle says that] 'No one who is blessed will become miserable.'

Fourth: If a human being is always in the best state in soul and body until his fortieth year and for the whole of the rest of his life remains in captivity, often tortured, often sick, and the like, was it ever true to say of him that he was a happy human being?

Fifth: Is anyone happier than a happy human being? It seems not, because to be happy is to be in the best state, and there is nothing better than the best.

[4. Replies to the Supplementary Questions]

[4a. *Can an Old Person Be Happy?*]

To the first question I answer that happiness for a human being is being in the best state, but not in the best state simply (for that would amount to being God) but rather to be for the whole time of a complete life in the best state that human nature permits, referring to each part of time the best state that our age at that time permits and requires. Someone must be called simply a happy man, for example, if in boyhood he is in the best state as a boy, in his youth as a youth, in manhood as a man, in old age as an old man. Both in the whole time of his life and in each part of that time it is true to say that he is a happy human being.

Against: You would say that then in the time of his boyhood he would truly be said to be a happy human being; but in that time he has no moral or intellectual virtue, and thus it follows that he would be a happy human being without wisdom, prudence, or moral virtue, which is absurd to say and contrary to what has been determined.

This reasoning is sophistical and more [a problem of] natural [philosophy] than ethics. For I can truly say that 'Socrates runs' at a time when he does not run, for I speak at one time with reference to another time. Otherwise I could not contradict you when you say that Socrates does not run, because I do not know how to contradict you until you have spoken. I will contradict you, therefore, by saying that Socrates runs. And perhaps Socrates was not running when you spoke and was running when I spoke: 'Therefore, both speak the truth and thus both of two contradictories are true.' I say that this is not so, because in contradicting you I was not speaking with reference to the time at which I was speaking but with reference to that in which you were speaking, and thus we were both speaking with reference to the same time but at different times. If, therefore, in the time of Socrates' boyhood, I say, 'Socrates is happy,' I speak the truth, because I do not speak with reference only to the time at which I am speaking but with reference to the whole time of Socrates' life, in which he is truly happy. But you will ask, not of speaking, but of being, 'Is Socrates happy in the time of his boyhood?' I say that he is not – except partly, because he is a happy boy. 'Is he therefore happy in the time of his adulthood, when he is perfectly virtuous, both in soul and in body?' I say that he is, by denomination from the most principal part of human happiness, because he is a happy adult and adulthood is the nobler time of life. But he is not a happy human being, because happiness signifies perfection in every way, in body and in soul and in the span naturally befitting human life. Aristotle notes this in *Ethics* X (7, 1177b24), when he says: 'This will be the complete happiness of a human being, assuming a complete length of life, for there is nothing imperfect in the things that constitute happiness.' 'What!' you say. 'Were not God's martyrs who suffered death in their twentieth or thirtieth year happy human beings?' It would be said that they were not happy human beings simply but happy human beings according to their superior portion, and thus happier than if they had not suffered death for the good and preservation of the superior part, to which the preservation of the inferior part, when it is impossible for both to be preserved, has no comparison, as was said before (above, p. 552). And in the resurrection they will become truly happy human beings totally. Something was said about this before (above, p. 551).

[4b. Can Someone Be Happy while Asleep?]

The second question was answered in Book I, but now I will reply to it in a somewhat different way in accordance with a logical stipulation. I say as before that in the time when he sleeps it is true to say that he is happy. But you ask whether he is happy in the time when he sleeps. I say that he is, because there 'the time' is taken indefinitely, and it is true *with reference to the whole time of his life*, therefore it is simply true. You will infer, 'Therefore, a sleeping person is happy.' I concede this, and no wonder, because the sleeping person is awake, though not at the same time but earlier and later. For I use 'the time' as present not at one moment or one day but with reference to a whole lifetime. But again you will infer: 'Therefore, someone who does not engage in thinking is a happy human being.' I deny the inference. You prove it: 'No one who is asleep engages in thinking.' I deny this, but I concede that one does not sleep and engage in thinking at the same time but earlier and later. 'But suppose he sleeps for a whole hour. Does he engage in thinking in this hour?' I say not. 'So {211v} is he happy in this hour?' I say not, because happiness is [properly attributed to an individual] according to the whole time of his whole life. Indeed, even supposing that during a whole hour or day he contemplates very well and his soul is in an altogether good state as far as it is possible for a human being to be naturally in a good state for one day, I say that in that day he is a happy human being not simply but subject to a qualification: that is, because he is a happy human being so far as relates to the condition of a human being through one day. 'But is someone who *sleeps* for this whole hour happy in precisely that hour, subject to qualification in the above manner – namely, so far as relates to the condition of a human being through one hour?' I say yes, because for him to sleep this hour is for him to be in the best state for this hour, much better than if he were awake and thinking. For I suppose that in an earlier time he was awake so much and thought so much that for this hour his senses needed natural rest, that is, sleep. Then it is certainly better for him to sleep now than to go to excess in wakefulness and thought, for he does not sleep for the sake of sleeping but to be better able to be awake and think more strongly. Hence, as was said before, we do not say that human happiness consists in thought as the aggregate of all the goods requisite to happiness, but as the best part of that aggregate.

Do not imagine that the aggregate of human goods making up happiness, or requisite to happiness, exists simultaneously as a whole. Rather it is spread successively in its parts through the whole life of the happy human being. One part is in one day or one hour and another in another – for example, now speaking with a friend, now going to church, now sleeping, now thinking or eating, etc., and [doing] each of these when and where and how (etc.) one ought. Therefore, if it is asked whether a happy human being is happier in an hour of thinking than in an hour of sleeping, I will say not, because he is not a happy human being in either hour. But I concede that the part of happiness that exists in an hour of thinking is much better and more honorable than the part that exists in an hour of sleeping.

The things said above in this answer to this question complete the study of the continuity of happiness, which was spoken of more superficially in Book I.

[4c. Can a Happy Person Become Miserable?]

On the third question we must say that misery is the contrary of happiness. Contrariety, however, is the greatest distance [between terms], as we read in *Metaphysics* X (4, 1055a4–5), or at least a great and notable distance. Now it was said before that when it is impossible for both to be preserved, the inferior portion [of a human being] is of no nobility in comparison with the superior portion. I say, therefore, that a human being is never called miserable because of a defect of the inferior portion if the superior is in a good state, but only those are called miserable whose superior portion is infected with vices. Concerning unhappiness, however, it must be said that we commonly use the terms 'intemperance,' 'injustice,' 'incontinence,' and 'illiberality' [though in form they are privatives] as contraries of the terms 'temperance,' 'justice,' 'continence,' etc., and thus also we can use the terms 'unhappiness' and 'unhappy' as contraries of the words 'happiness' and 'happy,' and then 'miserable' and 'unhappy' signify the same. Therefore, I will say the same of the unhappy person as was said of the miserable person [that no one who has been happy before can be unhappy]. If, however, unhappiness is opposed to happiness not as a contrary but only privatively, then someone who had been born senseless – that is, without the use of reason for an entire lifetime, for example, natural fools – would be called unhappy. The person about whom the question was asked is therefore not miserable or unhappy but 'not happy,' because he is – but is not *simply* – a happy person [i.e., he is happy insofar as the 'superior portion' is perfect, but is not happy without qualification].

[4d. Does Ill Fortune Later in Life Mean that the Person Was Never Happy?]

To the fourth question, it is clear from what has been said that he never was a happy human being, although he was a happy boy, a happy youth, and perhaps a happy adult, and although he was also happy according to his superior portion.

[4e. Can Anyone Be Happier than Someone Who Is Happy?]

To the fifth question, it seems to me we must say that we ought not to speak of the happy human being according to a mathematical image, namely, of someone always at an extreme good state that could not become better by however small an improvement, for no one was such except Christ alone. Indeed, it is impossible for anyone living naturally in this world not to depart in some degree from the right mean of virtue, unless directed miraculously by a very special supernatural grace. We say, therefore, speaking of natural morality, that when we say a happy human being is the same as a human being in the best state, we understand by being in the best state not being defective in body or in members by any notable defect and being morally virtuous and prudent and wise, rich, and fortunate – that is, so that there is no notable deficiency in any of these. And thus I concede that it is possible to be happier than a happy human being, just as one can be more temperate than someone who is temperate. Grammar teachers therefore say that a superlative does admit of further comparison, for example 'best, more best, most best.'

Now if these are not real solutions to the problems, let them nevertheless be received as dialectical and playful. And it appears that all the arguments advanced so far have no force against the points determined earlier, whichever of the two ways of speaking about happiness reported earlier in the preceding [rather, in this] question we follow. Nevertheless, it is clear that human happiness – that is, [happiness] either [in the sense of] the act which is happiness or [in the sense of] the act which is most principal and the end of the others in the aggregate that is happiness – consists somehow in one act. We must therefore ask, in each way of speaking: 'What act does human happiness consist in?' For as Aristotle says in Book I (2, 1094a22–24) of this work, knowledge of it is a great addition to life, and like archers who have a target we will better attain what we ought: the end and target to which we must finally order all human acts. Thus, as they think the target and end to be one thing or another, different people order their lives differently, some worse, others better. And because none of the great philosophers and moralists asserted that happiness was anything but an act of will or an act of intellect, the fifth question will be formulated in accordance with those views.

Question 5. Does Human Happiness Consist in an Act of Intellect or in an Act of Will?

Fifth, we ask whether human happiness thus [i.e., given that it is somehow a single act] consists in an act of intellect or in an act of will.

[1. Preliminary Arguments]

[1a. Arguments that Happiness Consists in an Act of Will]

It is argued first that happiness consists in an act of will.

[i] For some theologians say that we merit more by an act of will. Therefore, it is also reasonable that we be rewarded more principally in an act of will. Now the final reward is happiness. Therefore, etc.

[ii] Second, some theologians also say that the highest of the virtues existing in a human being is charity, which is a virtue of will. Therefore, its act, actually loving God, is the highest and best act, and consequently human happiness consists in that act. Therefore, the first of the Lord's commandments is about that love: 'Love the Lord your God with your whole heart, etc.'

[iii] Third, because human happiness consists in the act by which a

human being is most united with the beatific object. This is by an act of will, which is love. For one who understands is not intimately united with what is understood by the act of intellection, for we understand what we reject and flee in the same way in which we understand what we accept and pursue. But love unites one who loves with what is loved in such a way that the friend is another self, as Aristotle says, so that friends give themselves to one another.

[iv] Fourth, because an old woman who loves God pleases God because she loves him, although she has little knowledge of God. A great cleric, however, who has much knowledge of God does not please God if he does not love God. But something through which we please God is much better and happier for us than something through which we do not please God. Therefore, to love God is much better and happier in us than to know God.

[v] Again, human happiness consists more in the better act, since happiness is something best in a human being. But it is proved that an act of will is better, because an act determinately directed to the good is better than one that is indifferently related to goods and evils. Now true love, namely, amicable love, does not exist except between those who are good, and we do not love anything except under the concept of good or apparent good. We understand good under the concept of good, however, and bad under the concept of bad. Therefore, etc. Aristotle uses a similar argument in *Metaphysics* IX to prove that an act done by means of a virtuous power is better and more honorable. {212r}

[vi] Again, other things being equal, acts or powers are called better and nobler if they have a better object, as is clear in Book X (4, 1174b26–31; 7, 1177a11–16) of this work and in the prologue to the *De anima*. It follows, then, if there are two acts or two powers relating to the same object, the better and nobler would be the one bearing on the object under the concept of better. Now this is true of the will, for the will bears on God under the concept of good and best, the intellect under the concept of being and true. Therefore, etc.

[vii] Again, of the things that exist in the blessed, blessedness is most lovable to them. But the will is more lovable to the blessed than an act of understanding; therefore, etc. The minor is clear, because each power, like each thing, is naturally inclined to its own act more than to the act of another power. Therefore, in the blessed the will, whose act is loving, loves the act of willing, which is its own act, more than the act of understanding, which is the act of another power.

[viia] Confirmation: Happiness is something most pleasant, according to Book I (8, 1099a24–25) of this work. Now the act of willing is more pleasant to the blessed than the act of understanding; therefore, etc. Proof of the minor: As was said in Book II of this work, in Question 11 (f. 31v), something is called pleasant because it can be apprehended under the concept of what agrees with what seeks it; for when such a thing is obtained it gives pleasure. What seeks is called will, however, and not intellect *qua* intellect, and what agrees most with the will *qua* will is most pleasant; and this is the act of willing, which is the will's own act *qua* will; therefore, etc.

[viii] Again, that is worse of which the opposite is better, as we read concerning kingship and tyranny in *Topics* (VIII 2, 157b18–23) and Book VIII (10, 1160 b8–10) of this work. But hating God, which is the opposite of loving, is worse than being ignorant of God, which is the opposite of knowing; therefore, etc.

[ix] Again, pleasure is an act not of intellect but of will. And yet in Question 28 of Book VII (f. 162v) it was argued that pleasure is something best and most final in us, namely, that on account of which the activities of both intellect and will finally exist. It follows from this that human happiness truly consists in it [and hence in an act of will].

[x] Again, since freedom is a noble condition, the freer power is the nobler and consequently has a nobler and happier act. If, therefore, the will is a freer power than intellect, its act will be nobler and happier. Then, to argue that will is the freer power, take the arguments for this brought forward at the beginning of the first question.

[1b. Arguments that Happiness Consists in an Act of Intellect]

[i] The opposite is argued from the same major, taking [as minor the proposition] that intellect is a freer power than will, which can be argued from the arguments given for this in the first question and also from the tenth thesis of Question 3.

[ii] Again, because thinking is an act of intellect and not an act of will. But according to Aristotle happiness is some sort of thinking. In *Ethics* X (8, 1178 b32) he says expressly, and sets out to prove, that perfect happiness is a certain activity of thought, and at the end of the chapter he concludes: 'Therefore, happiness will indeed be some sort of thinking.' The same appears from Seneca, because reason is an act of intellect and not of will (i.e., *qua* will), and yet Seneca says (as was quoted in the preceding

question) that the best thing in us is reason and that only perfected reason makes us happy.

[1c. A Third View: Happiness Is the Soul Itself]

Then someone could argue that human happiness is neither an act of will nor an act of intellect but is the soul itself. For happiness is asserted to be the best human good, and this is the soul, since it is nobler and better than any accident, as the Commentator says, *De anima* II.

[1d. A Fourth View: Happiness Consists in the Activity of Sense]

It can also be argued that happiness consists in an activity of sense. For it was conceded in Question 1 of this Book X (2b[iiic]) that sense is more perfect than intellect and will, and the more perfect and better activity ought to be that of the nobler and better power, for we attribute to happiness many words in the superlative degree, for example that it is something best, most perfect, most desirable, etc.

[2. Answer to the Question]

[2a. Preliminary Observations]

Concerning some such words [as those involved in this question] it must be noted that, whether they are purely synonymous or differ in concept in some way, we nevertheless regard them as all standing for the same thing. Therefore, when one of them has been proved of some subject, I regard each of the others as having been proved of the same subject, and likewise, when any predicate has been proved of any of them, I regard that predicate as having been proved of each of the others. And I now list some of these words: 'best act,' 'most noble act,' 'most perfect act,' 'most worthy,' 'most excellent,' 'most honorable'; also 'most lovable' (because the greater good should be loved more, other things being equal) and 'most final' (since the end is always better in the essential order of ends than things ordered to it, the ultimate and most final end must be best of all); also, 'most free' (according to what we said earlier, whatever is freest with the freedom of final ordering is simply freest, and the same thing is best and most final, as was also said earlier).

Further, the term 'most pleasant act' must also stand for the same thing [as the terms just listed], since pleasure in some good apprehended under the concept of present and attained is said to be stronger and greater, other things being equal, if the good is apprehended under the concept of better and more fitting and with a more perfect apprehension, as was explained in Book VII. Now it is certain that an intellectual and right apprehension is more perfect than one that is sensual, oblique, and false. We therefore take pleasure most of all in that act which we apprehend by a right and true intellectual apprehension under the concept of best and attained. But it is certain that by a right and true concept we do not apprehend under the concept of best anything except what *is* best, nor under the concept of our best act anything except what is our best act – otherwise the apprehension would be false. Among our acts, therefore, we take pleasure most of all in the best one (or [in the act] that has the best [object]) thus apprehended in the best way. And such a thing, the apprehension of which in the best and most agreeable way is followed by the greatest pleasure, I call most pleasant. Our best act, therefore, is the same as our most pleasant act.

[2b. Theses]

Since, therefore, we supposed at the beginning of this question that human happiness consists either in an act of intellect or an act of will (in the sense there explained), and every such act has some *object* which we aim at or will or will against, love or hate, toward which we have favor or disfavor, etc., I assert this first thesis:

> [Thesis 1] *The act which human happiness consists in (whether it is an act of will or of understanding) has God as its object.*

This is because in comparison with all our other acts of intellect or will that act [i.e., happiness] must be nobler and most noble, as is supposed. But it is certain that the act that has a nobler object is nobler, other things being equal. For to understand God would be far nobler and more excellent than to understand a straw, if both intellections were equally steady and evident and equally specific (indeed even if there were much difference in evidence). All philosophers concede this. But of all goods, whether of intellect or will, God alone is the most noble object. Accordingly, the act which human happiness consists in has God as object. All theologians and moral philosophers agree on this, and it is beyond doubt for all who concede that human beings ought rationally to love God more than themselves, about which we spoke in Question 7 of Book IX (f. 199rb).

For the sake of the next thesis, we must note that every act of will is necessarily preceded by an act of intellect in which what is willable, or an object of will, appears as good or bad. I say good if favor, acceptance, love, desire, or pleasure ought to follow. I say bad if the opposite acts ought to follow. These points were made elsewhere and will be clear [in the Questions] on *De anima* III. For the appetible moves the soul because it is understood or imagined, and it moves because it is good or {212v} seemingly good, as was said there. And when an object has been judged good and good for us, favor toward that object necessarily follows, as was said in Book III. And if it was a certain and steady judgment of the pure goodness of the object without any character of consequent or concomitant badness, then not only favor but love and acceptance necessarily follow, as was said in Question 8 of Book VII (f. 145rb).

Now from these points it seems to follow that: [1] If there is a perfect judgment – that is, one that is steady and certain – of the pure and steady goodness of an object, then perfect love and acceptance or perfect volition follows that judgment, and [2] If the judgment is not perfect, perfect acceptance does not follow. I explain this (although it seems that it ought to be conceded *per se*). [1] First, that perfect acceptance and perfect love follow such a perfect judgment: Perfect acceptance can follow on *some* judgment, and a more perfect acceptance cannot follow on an imperfect judgment than on one that is perfect. Therefore, perfect acceptance can follow on such a perfect judgment. But if it can follow, it does follow, because we have said that it does not follow in the mode of freedom of opposition but rather in the mode of natural necessity. In this mode, however, as much follows as can follow (unless God by his absolute power wills to subtract or add); therefore, etc.

I prove in the same way: [2] If the judgment is not perfect, perfect love or perfect acceptance does not follow. For if the causes necessarily required for the being and production of some effect exist in a diminished state, it does not seem possible for a perfect effect to come about. But a judgment of an object's goodness is a cause necessary for producing a volition, as has been said. Indeed, this judgment is also necessary for the volition to exist or continue, for all volition or favor or pleasure seems to cease when actual cognition ceases, as in perfect sleep without dreaming. (It is true that pleasures and distresses or fears, etc., often come from a dream. This is because a dream is some sort of apprehension.)

Again, just as it is impossible for the will to be brought to bear on an uncognized object, so, with equal reason, it seems that it cannot be brought to bear more on an object than the object is cognized. Therefore, it is not possible to love more than it seems to me I should love. For what is beyond the level cognized is, so to speak, uncognized. It seems, then, that the bearing of the will cannot exceed the level judged.

There is no force against this in the objection that a father or mother often says of a son, 'I know he is bad and that I love him too much, but I cannot stop loving him.' For I say that here sense is obstructing reason. The mother truly concludes that according to reason the son should not be loved thus, but sense judges from natural inclination that he is to be loved very much, and sense conquers and does not permit intellect to stand fast in the judgment of reason. The mother thus loves her son sensually, just as a cock loves his hen, and loves more the more intellect is drawn to sense, and at last judges with sense, from wickedness dismissing reason.

Again, if the will had power beyond judgment, this would come from its freedom of opposition. But it cannot come from that freedom; therefore, etc. The major is conceded. The minor at first glance seems false, since in its freedom the will can will or love less than has been judged good – indeed, it can not-will. If, therefore, it can will less, why not more? This is answered by the earlier argument that less and more are not alike, because the less is included in the greater, and therefore that less is not uncognized. But the greater, as to the degree by which it exceeds, is uncognized, because it is not thus included in the less.

I explain the minor, therefore, because (as was said in Question 3 of Book III [f. 42v, misnumbered 62]) freedom was not given to us finally for evil but for direction. Let us ask, then, what if a judgment concerning the goodness of an object is not perfect? Then freedom not to accept what has been judged, or to accept less, is beneficial to us, either immediately, for not accepting evil, or else as a precaution or safeguard against accepting what is perhaps evil. For if what seems good by that judgment is not good but evil (as when the judgment is erroneous), then not accepting is immediately beneficial, because evil would be accepted. If, however, what seems good by that judgment is good, yet it is not certain that it is good, then, lest we accept evil, it is a precaution and a good safeguard to defer acceptance until the truth (that it is good and not evil) is shown more fully. But freedom in accepting more than has been judged would not be beneficial in any of these ways. For if what seems good in a judgment is not good but evil, accepting it would be harmful, and accepting more would be still more harmful. If, however, what seems good by that judgment is good, but it is not certain that it is good, then accepting it, or accepting it more, is not a precaution or safeguard but a danger and a fault. Therefore, freedom was not given to us for this.

Now that these points have been laid down, I will assert a second thesis toward the question proposed at the beginning:

> [Thesis 2] *Human happiness does not consist in an intellectual apprehension of the divine essence or goodness that is false or unsteady or fictitious, or in any act of will following such an apprehension.*

For every such apprehension is imperfect and defective, and also every following act of will is imperfect, as has been said. But human happiness does not consist in any imperfect or defective act, for there is nothing imperfect in the things that constitute happiness, as we read in this Book X of the *Ethics* (7, 1177b25).

From this a corollary seems to follow: According as we distinguish faith from clear or evident awareness, human happiness does not consist in an act of faith with regard to things of which we can have evidence, whether we are speaking about this life or heaven. For such an act is not perfect. Concerning anything of which we can have evidence, it is always more perfect to know with evidence than to believe without evidence. But you will say, 'Is not our awareness by faith a perfect awareness?' I say not, [in the sense of 'perfect' in which] the corollary is asserted. As a result, although we would say that the faith we have regarding the Trinity remains in heaven with respect to what it is objectively, it does not remain with the connotation of *not* being evident knowledge of the Trinity.

(But is our awareness of the Trinity in this life by faith perfect? I say that it is, so far as regards the status of a wayfarer – indeed, much more perfect than the evident and demonstrative science that a triangle has three [angles that add up to 180 degrees]. But this is not against the corollary, because it says, 'of which we can have evidence.')

Third thesis:

> [Thesis 3] *Human happiness in the way explained at the beginning of the question does not consist in pleasure.*

We have said that the most final good is the best and that consequently human happiness consists in it and not in something else. But pleasure is not the most final good among human acts, because we said in Question 28 of Book VII (f. 162v) that by chief or primary purpose pleasure is for the sake of activity. Therefore, etc.

Some try to demonstrate this thesis as follows. Human happiness ought to be for us the most pleasant of all our acts. But no pleasure is most pleasant to us; therefore, etc. The major is asserted by Aristotle and conceded as being a principle. Proof of the minor: Something is said to be pleasant to us in two ways, in one way objectively, in another way subjectively. Something is said to be pleasant to us objectively [i.e., as an object] because it can be united to us or {213r} attained by us and can be apprehended as united to or attained by us, for pleasure necessarily follows such an apprehension of ours and is connected to it. An apprehension is said to be pleasant subjectively [i.e., as existing in us as subject] if pleasure thus necessarily follows it and is connected to it. (Others, however, assert a third mode [of being pleasant], which they call 'formally pleasant,' and they say that this is pleasure [itself]. But let us dismiss this mode, because it is just like saying that whiteness is white, that the soul [*anima*] is animated, that movement is moved, and such like, and we do not accept such predications except as improper. Let us therefore revert to the two modes above.) It is clear that what is most pleasant *objectively* is nothing but God. For according to what was said earlier we can apprehend only God by a right and true apprehension as best and best for us; and God can be united to us, through grace and glory on God's part and through contemplation of God and love on our part. And thus God can be apprehended by us under the concept of best and best for us and under the concept of united with and attained by us. We cannot thus apprehend anything else by a true apprehension, and only on such an apprehension does the greatest pleasure follow. Therefore, only God is objectively most pleasant. And no pleasure of ours, indeed no act of ours (that is, no act inhering in us), is God. Therefore, no pleasure of ours is most pleasant to us objectively. This deduction well demonstrates the first thesis asserted earlier, namely, that human happiness consists objectively in God (or [in some act] regarding God). But again, it appears that no pleasure of ours is most pleasant to us *subjectively*, because what is pleasantest in this way is the activity or apprehension on which there necessarily follows, and with which there is necessarily connected, the greatest pleasure in us; and that is, as has been said, the apprehension of God, which is not pleasure. Therefore, etc. Since, therefore, pleasure is not most pleasant to us in either way, it follows (as it seems) that it is not our happiness.

Nevertheless, that argument is not, as it appears to me, a demonstration of the above thesis [i.e., the third thesis]. For those who maintain the other opinion would say that our happiness is most pleasant to us objectively, not simply (this is God alone, as was well proved), but *among all our acts*, because in that sense it is best, and the best is the most pleasant. Now it has not been proved that happiness is not objectively the most pleasant of our acts; therefore I stand instead on the first argument [given for the third thesis]. What follows from these statements as a corollary is true, about how human happiness is most pleasant to us: It is not most pleasant objectively (rather, God is), but it is indeed most pleasant objectively among human acts, because the blessed not only love and understand God, but they can understand reflexively, and they understand that they understand and love and take pleasure. Therefore, whichever of those is the best and happiness, they can understand it truly in the manner of something best and present and possessed among our acts, and upon such an apprehension, of which happiness is already the object, there necessarily follows the greatest pleasure that can be had objectively from any of our acts. But also, along with this, happiness is most pleasant to us subjectively, if we assert that it is the most noble apprehension of God, since it is that upon which there necessarily follows, and to which is connected, the simply best and most perfect pleasure, as we have said. When we say, however, that that apprehension is most pleasant subjectively, perhaps this is not a proper way of speaking, because it is not the apprehension but the soul which receives that pleasure, for it was said earlier that apprehension is related actively, not passively, to the consequent act of will. It would be more proper to say that that apprehension is the most pleasant among our acts connexively and causally, by active causality.

Since, then, no one asserts that human happiness consists in simple favor or desire, as distinct from the act of willing, or acceptive love (which we regard as the same), it is clear that it remains only to see whether happiness consists in that perfect apprehension of God or in the consequent act of willing and loving. And I prefer to assert, last, this fourth thesis:

> [Thesis 4] *Human happiness consists in the apprehension or perfect understanding of God.*

I hold this thesis, first, because Aristotle and Seneca and other ancient moral philosophers, in the import of their words, altogether prefer reason and thinking to all other human acts and wisdom to all human virtues.

Second, this thesis can also be made persuasive by the arguments and cited texts in Question 1 of this Book X concerning freedom and lordship of the intellect, and also in Question 3.

And again, the thesis can be confirmed from the fact that many theologians hold that, of any two entities neither of which is God and neither of which is of the essence or wholeness of the other, God can separate either from the other and conserve it without the other. They say, therefore, that by his absolute power God could conserve in Peter's soul a clear vision of God while taking away love and every act of will, and conversely could conserve in it the love of God or the act of will while taking away vision and every act of understanding.

Nevertheless, I do not either approve or reject these statements, because they do not belong to the science Aristotle gave us. They go beyond our faculty of Arts – according to which faculty, however, and not beyond it, it was my purpose to treat of morals in this book (and if I sometimes transgress, I regard this as something incidental). It is true, nevertheless, that it indeed does belong to this faculty of ours to consider what we can further infer from certain assumptions, whether possible or impossible, and this in terms both moral and natural. Let us see, then, what follows if there were clear vision of God under the concept of present to us and intimate and best, as in our true blessedness, if love and accepting volition were set aside – assuming, nevertheless, that God allows the rest to follow and proceed just as they are naturally apt to do. It is clear to me that perfect pleasure would naturally and inseparably follow such an apprehension, for the nature and condition of pleasure consists in this, that it is an inseparable property of such an apprehension, namely, of an object under the concept of good, present, and possessed. But suppose on the contrary that love and volition remain without vision, that is, without intellectual apprehension: pleasure does not follow. Then let us argue thus. That act of ours upon which, posited by itself in the way described, perfect pleasure follows is more perfect than one upon which no pleasure would follow. And so, according to the opinion of those theologians, we will conclude our point.

Again, the act that first and immediately attains God, who is the beatific object, is more noble than an act that does not first and immediately attain God. But it is an act of understanding that first and immediately attains, and love or volition only [attains] with cognition mediating. Therefore, etc.

This is also apparent according to certain theologians, who very plausibly (as it seems to me) assert that in the soul's beatification in heaven God immediately and as total cause brings about in the soul the vision of the divine essence. I say 'immediately' {213v} because it is not by means of another intelligible species or anything else whatever representing God. I say also 'as total cause' because nothing else concurs actively and determinatively in making that vision except God. The volition or love, however, is not thus first and immediately made by God, but [is made] with that vision mediating, and perhaps in the production of love the vision concurs as a secondary and determinative active [cause]. But what is thus from God first and immediately is more noble than what is not, for, other things being equal, what is closer to the most noble ought to be conceded to be more noble – just as Aristotle, when he posits an order of beings in their dependence on God, would assert that the intelligence depending first and immediately is more noble than all the others which follow.

And if these arguments are not demonstrations, they are nevertheless as persuasive as the arguments customarily brought forward for the other side. This will appear more clearly if the replies to the latter are considered.

[3. Reply to the Preliminary Arguments of Question 1 for the Will Being Freer than the Intellect (1a[i–ix])]

To the first argument for the other side brought forward at the beginning of the first question (that intellect compares to will as subject to lord): I deny it, but assert instead the converse. For I say that, if the order is not perverted, intellect rules appetite by a royal government (as is said in *Politics* I), and not only sensitive appetite but also intellectual.

[i] When it is said that intellect 'urges,' I say that sometimes intellect necessitates will, as was said, but does not compel or do violence to it, because such rule would be not royal but tyrannical. Kings and popes do not command their subjects, at least those who are good, by compelling them; rather, they command them to act well, by exhortation and persuasion, showing by their laws and decretals which things must be done and which abstained from. That is the way intellect relates to will. Aristotle calls such royal exhortations and persuasions 'urgings' when he says that the intellect 'urges toward the best objects.' Since Aristotle says that intellect uses this urging upon the sensitive appetite, which he says is sometimes opposed to reason, it is remarkable how masters [in universities] use this text to prove that intellect is subject to will, since no one says that intellect is subject to sensitive appetite except in the depraved and by a perverted order. And Christ, true lord, used such urgings toward his subjects, that is, exhortations and persuasions; and so also do good prelates toward the people subject to them. Nevertheless, I do not deny that there are other

urgings, of inferiors toward superiors, to give them some of their temporal goods – or also their spiritual goods, by teaching, advising, directing. Will would urge intellect in that way, if it knew how to urge.

[ii] To the next (that the intellect is like an adviser): I concede it. But someone who can give good advice is in this respect greater than one who needs it, for those who know better how to give advice are wiser and in this respect worthier. But you say, 'It is for the lord to appoint for himself the end and to seek from advisers subject to him advice on matters ordered to the appointed end.' I concede that it belongs to the lord to be the end or appoint the end for himself and others, but it is intellect which appoints the end for us, when it says that the end is to live in the best way. From that evident judgment the will necessarily accepts and wills the best life. Then also it is the work of intellect to ask and find and judge what the best life is, which is to appoint the end according to a specific concept, and the will cannot accept as end and good anything the intellect has not predetermined to be the end and good. Then when it is said further that the lord seeks advice from his subjects, I say first that it is not so. He seeks it from those wiser than himself, who in this respect are worthier. If, however, the advisers are in some other way subject to the one seeking advice, this is incidental, for we see that the common people, the poor and ignorant, seek advice in the king's palace from advocates much superior to themselves, and the pope, prelates, and good priests advise their subjects for the salvation of their souls, and physicians advise their patients for the safety of the body. Would that God would deign to advise us! Next I say that it is not for the will to seek advice, for seeking and asking are acts of intellect. When it is said further that once advice is given it is for the lord to choose, I say that even in choosing the intellect holds first place. This is because, while the advice and deliberation stand fast that A is simply better and more worthy of choice than B and that they are not simultaneously possible, it is not in the power of our will to choose B and pass over A, although it can choose to do nothing. And this is what the quoted text says: 'Judging from deliberation, we desire in accordance with our deliberation.' Therefore, although advice does not necessitate choosing, nevertheless, *if* we choose, it determines what we choose. For 'we desire,' that is, choose and will, 'in accordance with deliberation,' if we choose and will while the judgment stands.

[iii] To the next (that it is by will that we are lords of our acts): I concede it, because [we are lords] both by will and by intellect, but more

strongly and more principally by intellect, as was said earlier, in Question 3.

[iv] To the next (that the will commands the intellect to think) I say, first, that if the will commands us to think, this injunction is for the sake of thinking, and thus again thinking is more final and better than the injunction. Second, I say that the will's commanding is nothing but willing. Yet it seems that willing is not commanding properly speaking, because I can will that you go to church and yet not command you to do so. Third, I say that if there is a command here, it is the intellect that commands first, and without its command the will can command nothing. For before the will wills that we think, the intellect first judges that thinking should take place, and afterwards the will wills and accepts in accordance with that judgment. The judgment, therefore, is the first command and the will that it be done is the second; and the first command determines [the will] to the second, in such a way that one must will in accordance with that judgment or will nothing. Therefore, intellect still has first lordship in this and therefore seems more to be the lord, since it more principally and more freely gives the command. Nevertheless, if volition is a command, it was said before that the intellect more principally makes that volition than the will, in the senses elsewhere explained.

[v] To the next I say that the intellect is not compelled or violated, just as the will is not, but it is necessitated to think and for the sake of thinking, as was said. Neither is the will sufficient to necessitate the intellect or any other of our powers in this way. Rather, a previous judgment is required. Therefore, those two acts together and neither separately (namely, the judgment that one should think and the resulting volition) necessitate the intellect to think – and according to what was said in Question 3, the judgment does so more principally.

[vi] The other argument is only about freedom of opposition, about which enough has already been said.

[vii] To the next, which asserts that the act of will is posterior in being and generation and is therefore more final and more perfect, I say that this was argued with respect to pleasure in Book VII, Question 28, and the argument was answered there. So look for the answer there (f. 164v).

[viii] To the next I say, first, that although not much intelligence is required for being good absolutely, much is required for being best and for being in the best state, because wisdom and the work of wisdom are needed. These things were discussed sufficiently in the last question of

Book VI (f. 139rb). I also say, second, that the intellect contributes more, and more principally, toward acting well and being good than the will does, as has become apparent.

[ix] To the next, we have said that there is a certain mode of {214r} erroneous and unnatural domination present in a depraved human being, when the sensual part usurps lordship over the intellectual part, and there is nothing good in this as such, but the whole is bad, in intellect and will and sense. Accordingly, there is nothing to the purpose about happiness here, for to dominate in this way is bad, just as it is to be subject. Yet it is only in this case that wickedness perverts us, and makes us go wrong about practical principles. In a good and ordered lordship, however, intellect has lordship and is principally active in appointing the end and in other matters, as was said earlier. About the text that virtue makes intention right, etc., we spoke clearly in Question 19 of Book VI (f. 135r).

It seems to me, therefore, that our last and main thesis is much confirmed by the fact that the arguments others use are not difficult to answer [when brought against us] but are very strong when brought over to our side, as has become apparent.

[4. Reply to the Preliminary Arguments of This Question
(1a[i–x], 1c, and 1d)]

Now we must also reply to the arguments advanced against our side at the beginning of this question.

[i] To the first it can be said that we merit rather, and more principally and freely, through an act of intellect than through an act of will. For right volition is not the only meritorious act, but also the apprehension that brings about and directs that volition. And if we were to say that the first meritorious act is right volition, nevertheless, according to what we said above, the intellect would be related to that volition more nobly and more principally and freely *qua* intellect than the will *qua* will. Therefore, it would be reasonable that the soul also be rewarded more principally, and more, *qua* intellect than *qua* will.

Again, the soul is called different powers, not in such a way that [the powers] are different things, but because there are different activities of the soul itself. Now it is certain that reward and merit are different activities. It is therefore not unsuitable – indeed, it is reasonable – that in relation to meriting and being rewarded the soul should be called different powers.

For the capacity to merit and the capacity to be rewarded are conceptually different, just as being able to will and being able to understand [are different].

[ii] To the next: I think Aristotle would have denied that charity is a more excellent virtue than wisdom, and I think that Solomon may praise wisdom in the way another praises charity. It is true that in comparing these three virtues – faith, hope, and charity – it was said that the greatest is charity – and no wonder, because God is charity and the highest love, even according to Aristotle. But God is not faith or hope (insofar as faith connotes that the articles believed are not evident and hope that the good hoped for is lacking or in the future). And just as there is a great distance between faith in this life and clear vision in heaven, so there is a great distance between charity on the way [i.e., in this life] and charity in heaven, and we must not believe that charity in heaven is nobler than clear vision. Whether charity on the way is better than faith I leave for theologians to determine, however, for I have heard from Christ, 'Your faith has saved you,' as I have also heard, 'Many sins are forgiven her because she has loved much.'

[iii] To the next I say that Aristotle asserts a union of intellect with the thing understood in the same way as a union of will with the thing willed. For he says in *De anima* III (5, 430a14–15) that the soul is in a way all things, which he explains by reference not to appetite but to cognition, saying that knowledge is somehow the knowable, and sensation the sensible (431 b22). This union and presence (*condonatio*) do not occur without apprehension but rather, first and more principally, through apprehension, as we said earlier. And when it is said that the intellect understands things rejected and avoided in the same way as it understands things accepted and pursued, I concede it. But there also follows on both of these an act in the will, namely, volition and nolition. Through the intellection that something is good and the following acceptance I unite myself to it, or it to me, as much as I can. In the same way, through the intellection that something is bad and the following rejection, I separate myself from it, or it from me, as much as I can.

[iv] To the next Aristotle would say that the old woman does not love God more than she judges that God is good and should be loved. The old woman does, however, judge and believe more steadily than the great cleric that God should be loved and worshipped above all things and that God's commandments should be observed, for although he knows demonstratively that God is best and the cause of all things, he nevertheless judges

that God is not better for him than pleasure, money, or honors and does not judge that it is better to observe the divine commandments than to live voluptuously or dominate tyrannically. Indeed, he judges the opposite, which is clear because he chooses and does the opposite, which does not happen without a previous judgment. If he often says that it is better to observe the divine commandments, it is apparent that he says this only with his mouth and is lying. Thus it is clear that the old woman has only true and very steady apprehensions of God, though not evident ones. The cleric, however, has many false estimates of God, although he also has many true ones, some demonstratively. (He holds many of the true ones less steadily [than the old woman], even though he has them demonstratively. This is not impossible, as we read in *Ethics* VII (3, 1146b29–30). For there are some who believe what they opine no less than others believe what they know. In his prologue to *Physics* III the Commentator [says that] the vulgar believe more strongly than the philosophers.) Nevertheless, other things being equal, more intense love follows on a steadier judgment of the goodness and lovableness of the object. Let us say, therefore, that the old woman is more pleasing to God not only because she loves God more but also because she judges more steadily that God should be loved and loved above all else and that his commandments should be observed above all others.

Someone will perhaps tell me, 'You have purposed to speak according to the philosophers, but you only speak theologically. Philosophers arguing purely naturally did not posit divine commandments.' I say that indeed they did. For all the great moral philosophers who were neither Jews nor Christians said that the human intellect is God or something divine. For example, Cato: 'If God is our mind, etc.' (*Disticha*, I 1). And Seneca, in his letter '*Facis rem optimam*' (XLI 1): 'God is close to you, God is intellect and is with you' [following Buridan's text]. And he says who that God is in his letter '*Agnosco*' (XXXI 11), for he says of the mind that is right, good, and great, 'What else would you call this than God staying as a guest in the human body?' And in the letter '*Claranum*' (LXVI 12): 'Now reason is nothing else than a part of the divine spirit immersed in the human body.' And Aristotle in *Ethics* X (7, 1177b26–28): 'Now such a life will be better than a human one; for a human being does not live thus as a human being, but as containing something divine.' They say these things not because they believe that the human intellect is God properly speaking but because it is, beyond all bodily things, similar and close to God and able by its activity to attain the divine essence. Accordingly, every judgment about what should be done made by a human intellect that is perfect and not seduced the philosophers call a divine commandment, and life in accordance with intellect in such a state they call a divine life, as is clear in *Ethics* X.

[v] To the next we must say that will is no more determinately directed toward good than intellect is. For just as the intellect understands good under the concept of good by one act and evil under the concept of evil by another act, so also the will has a single act concerning good under the concept of good, namely, favor or love or volition, and another act concerning evil, namely, disfavor or hatred or nolition. And just as the intellect can judge of evil that it is good, so also the will can consequently accept it as good. Indeed, it is entirely necessary that the intellect be determined to judge that something is good and should be loved before the will *can* determine itself to love it, and there cannot be a right and perfect act of will {214v} unless by natural priority there is a right and perfect act of understanding.

[vi] To the next I say that just as, in our blessedness, the will bears on God under the concept of best, this is also true of the intellect, and earlier. If you say that the intellect also bears on God according to a more universal concept, I say that you are arguing for the intellect's excellence and nobility. For a superior power of the soul has power in more things than an inferior — for example intellect than sense, and common sense than an external sense.

[vii] To the next two we must say that whatever is agreeable to will is agreeable to intellect and is equally agreeable to one as to the other, because the one and the other are the same. Nevertheless, if reduplications helped to prove either side of the question they would help our side, because the will bears only on what has been judged. Therefore, whatever the intellect judges more agreeable, the will wills more, loves more, and takes more pleasure in. But other things being equal, the intellect has to judge its own act more agreeable than the act of another [power]; therefore, etc.

[viii] To the next: This comparison has its place in things that are opposites in the same way. You do not argue thus, for hatred and love are [contrary] opposites, but cognition and ignorance are only privative opposites. Hence I will concede that if judging that God is best and to be loved always is better than loving God, then also judging that God is worst and to be hated always would be worse, if possible, than hating God.

[ix] We send the next argument back to Question 28 of Book VII, so let it be looked at there (f. 164v).

Everything that follows [x–] has been answered (3. Reply to the Preliminary Arguments of Question 1) up to the argument to the effect that the soul itself is happiness because it is the best of human goods (p. 561). I say that we do not call happiness the best human good in that sense, but we call it the best human good among goods that are not part of the human substance. For the human substance is not happiness but is capable of happiness.

[1d] To the next argument (from sense and the activity of sense) we must say that although the aggregate of master and slave is more perfect and better in a good ordering of things than the master taken by himself (at least extensively, though perhaps not intensively), nevertheless an activity in which the master needs to participate with the slave is not nobler than one which is proper to the master. Indeed, the activities common to master and slave are ordered finally to that which is proper to the master, as to something that is nobler and more excellent. Now the aggregate of soul and body is an aggregate of master and slave. Therefore, the activities proper to the master, namely, to the soul, such as acts of understanding and willing, are nobler than the activities of the combination [of body and soul], namely, activities of sense or sensitive appetite.

Question 6. Which Act of Intellect Does Human Happiness Consist In?

We ask, sixth, what act of intellect does human happiness consist in – in a simple or in a complex act, and if in a simple then in which one, and similarly of the complex, and whether in a direct or reflex act . . . [The work breaks off here.]

Emendations

[We have emended the 1513 edition with variants drawn from a number of manuscripts. A few emendations are conjectural, as indicated. Each emendation is preceded by the reading in the 1513 edition.]

500.31 *add* potentiarum et que sit 501.3 *add* quam intellectus 501.6 *add* Arguitur quod voluntas sit magis libera 501.7 *add* sibi 501.10 etenim recte] recte enim et 501.16 per] et 501.17 huius] Ethicorum 501.17 *add* etiam 501.19 illo instituto] iterum statuta 501.22 per consilium] concilio 501.22 et dicit] dicente 501.27 *add* Et iterum in eodem 30 manifestum est

quod secundum voluntatem sumus domini actuum nostrorum; propter
quod actus voluntarii et non nisi voluntarii sunt nobis imputabiles, licet
hec omnino lateat intellectum. 501.33 forum] cenam 501.33 tunc] nunc
502.9 *add* autem 502.15 liberum esse] liberum dicens liberum est 502.17
add autem 502.19 *add* tanquam actus naturaliter posterior et finalior aut
etiam posterior, iuxta illam maximam sepe ab Aristotele, quod posteriora
generatione sunt priora perfectione. 502.25 Politice] Politicorum 502.27
videmus] vidimus 502.29 videmus] vidimus 502.33 manifesta]
manifestissima 502.34 huius] Ethicorum 503.6 *add* humanas 503.8
noluntatis] non voluntatis 503.12 *add* et 503.13 vel] et quid 503.14 vel] et
quid 503.15 determinatione] predeterminatione 503.18 Politice]
Politicorum 503.19 *add* Aristoteles 503.21 ipsas et] et quam 503.23 dici
potest dominus] debet poni domina 503.25 *add* in 503.26 Politice]
Politicorum 503.27 dominum] Deum 503.27 *add* non dicit igitur qui
voluntatem iubet principari 503.34 *add* iterum 503.35 philosophiam]
sapientiam 503.38 *add* te 504.5 etiam] primo 504.12 Politice]
Politicorum 504.14 *add* necessarium; om: vite 504.17 vel] ad 504.22
exemplar] exemplum 505.10 Politice] Politicorum 505.10 *add* generis
505.10 *add* iterum quod ingenuitas est virtus et 505.15 et] immo 505.15
his] eis 505.16 *add* descendunt 505.21 *add* mali 505.21 Rhetorice]
Politicorum 505.24 nominatione] denominatione 505.25 aut] et sic 505.28
om. autem 505.31 robur] robustas 505.32 primi esse] preesse 505.34
dicitur] habetur 506.2 *add* natura 506.2 prestat corpore] potest hec
corpore facere 506.5 captivitati] captivati 506.7 a] se ab illorum 506.11
honesta] valde honestior 506.12 *add* et servitus 506.12 actionem]
coactionem 506.18 *add* omnino 506.19 *add* est 506.22 ad predictorum
modorum oppositorum similitudinem] ex predicto primo Politicorum
506.28 aliquis] aliquid 506.28 *add* vel agit 506.29 *add* et alia propter
ipsum, tantum habet de libertate et quantum est vel operatur gratia
alicuius prima intentione 506.31 virtutis] servitutis 506.33 *add* respectu
506.35 *add* in ordine 506.35 ad] et 506.35 ad] et 506.39 Politice]
Politicorum 507.2 genere] communione 507.2 respecta huiusmodi]
respectu huius 507.3 subdita] subiecta 507.7 potentiarum] pollitiarum
507.8 potentie] politie 507.8 potentiarum] politiarum 507.10
opponitur] opposita 507.10 opponitur] opposita 507.11 opponitur]
opposita 507.12 violenti] violentia 507.16 *add* aliam 507.22 naturali]
corporali 507.22 *add* nobis 507.23 violentiam] violentam 507.25 vel] et
507.27 subiiciendum] subiectionem 507.28 vel ex] et 507.30 huius]
Ethicorum 507.32 et] ut 507.32 operantur] operentur 507.35 sunt] fiunt

508.7 *add* disponente ad sensuum vivacitatem, et modus servitutis
consistit in complexione corporis 508.10 secundo] secundi 508.19 etiam]
om. 508.21 *add* libertatis 508.25 et] vel 508.26 sine] sive 508.27 octavum]
sextum 509.2 Politice] Politicorum 509.4 etiam] aut 509.5 et] aut
509.8 impedimentum] impeditum 509.10 *add* pars 509.11 partem] *om.*
509.12 Politice] Politicorum 509.13 dicit] dicitur 509.16 passibili] *om.*
509.18 parti] passionali parti id est 509.24 semper] *om.* 509.25 *add* et
509.25 *add* nunc 509.32 *add* pars 509.35 huiusmodi] in homine 510.5
intellectus] intellectuali 510.9 phisicorum] philosophorum 510.11 vitium]
malicia 510.15 huius] *Ethicorum* 510.16 *add* tu michi 510.24 *add* in 510.25
avaritie] ambitione 510.25 ambitioni] avaritie 510.29 sed] cum 510.29
auctoritates non demonstrent] auctoritas non demonstret 510.30 dicam]
dico 510.30 *add* specialiter 510.34 experientia] experientiam 511.7
immo] ita 511.8 hac] istam 511.12 *add* vel intellectus liberior intellectu
511.20 et] vel 511.21 et] vel 511.22 et] aut 511.22 impossibiles]
impossibile est 511.22 intellectu] intellectum 511.23 voluntatem]
voluntate 511.34 potentia] anima 512.2 *add* vel voluntati 512.4 rationi]
illi 512.15 ipse] ipsa 512.16 receptivo] receptiva 512.18 *add* vocamus
potentiam appetitivam 512.20 appetitionem] intellectionem 512.21
intellectionem] appetitionem 512.23 ego] igitur 512.25 *add* ipse 512.25 et]
sic 512.30 sensibilem] sensualem 512.33 *add* sic 512.35 puta] *om.* 513.2
secundum extensionem] extensione 513.4 *add* iam 513.6 compositum]
compositus 513.7 principalis] principalior 513.7 illa] in hac 513.8 et]
vel 513.10 una] prima 513.19 est liberior vel nobilior sensu] adversetur
sibi ipsius, nec intellectus est nobilior sensu vel liberior, nec sensus
intellectu 513.26 humana] *om.* 513.28 vel] et 513.34 liber] libera 514.1
probatur] probo 514.2 homines] homine 514.4 *add* sic 514.7 *add* ut
dictum fuit 514.10 sic] *om.* 514.10 *add* ipsa 514.14 solvunt] sunt 514.15
add idem scilicet 514.34 altarum] aliarum 514.35 *add* potest 515.1 *add* i.e.
515.2 sed] et 515.3 ita] ista 515.4 ea ratione qua] quia 515.4 ea
ratione] quia 515.5 et sic] vel ea ratione qua potest velle, non ea ratione
qua potest intelligere, et similiter 515.11 restat dubitatio] restant dubia
515.12 vel] et 515.19 *add* fiat igitur questio secunda 515.32 *add* Igitur
illum actum volendi producit liberius 516.2 aliam] aliqua 516.3 *add*
actum 516.5 que] quem 516.12 secundum . . . tertii] De Anima in
decima questione secundi libri, et in decima questione tertii libri. 516.28
add et agunt et sunt et 517.1 talem] naturalem 517.2 omnia] *om.* 517.4
finaliter] serviliter 517.6 *add* agamus 517.7 *add* aliud 517.8 finem
ordinatum] finium ordinationem 517.12 preter nos et preter deum]

propter aliquid aliud preter deum et preter nos 517.19 intendo] intelligit
517.20 *add* quod est 517.21 *add* quod est 517.22 transcendens] de
transcendentalibus 517.23 *add* agere 517.29 questione] questionibus 517.31
add anime 517.33 omnia illa: hec omnia 517.34 *add* et determinata 517.35
add libere 517.37 supposita sunt] supponamus 518.2 magis] multa 518.2
add anima 518.6 supponere] specificare 518.7 *add* anime 518.8 *add*
etiam 518.10 accipias] accipies 518.17 require] requiris 518.18 aliquis]
aliquando alius 518.21 hoc] quod 518.21 *add* et econtra 518.23 *add* si illud
sit apprehensum per modum prosequibilis vel fugibilis 518.25 tribus]
duabus 518.32 in re] *om.* 518.32 *add* libere 518.33 *add* et 518.35
distinctam] distincta 519.1 vel] ad 519.2 non] *om.* 519.5 et] sed 519.6
acceptati] accepti 519.7 obtinendi] non obtenti 519.17 prius] *om.* 519.19
add odio 519.20 *add* etiam 519.22 *add* est etiam 519.23 consequuntur]
sequuntur 519.35 *add* est 520.4 illa] *om.* 520.5 nunc] *om.* 520.9 *add*
libera 520.15 que] qui 520.20 *add* conclusio est 520.25 septimo] octava
520.26 octava] septimi libri 520.33 ut] *om.* 520.33 assensiva] assertiva
521.1 *add* assentimus 521.7 assensive] assertive 521.7 *add* vel 521.13
tenenda] tenendum est 521.14 videtur] breviter 521.14 *add* pro octava
conclusione 521.15 habet] habeat 521.17 videtur] videretur 521.22 lapis]
homo 521.23 lapis] homo 521.25 pluribus] simplicibus 521.35 utroque]
quolibet 522.6 sequeretur] sequitur 522.10 lapis] homo 522.11 lapis]
homo 522.17 habet] habeat 522.18 dicat] dicas 522.19 et] est 522.21
queratur] queras 522.24 studio] studere 522.30 dicitur] habetur 522.36 *add*
quod est contra prius dicta; dictum est enim quod anima nullum actum
producit liberius quam actum volendi 523.1 non essent] sunt 523.13
primo] immo 523.13 spirituales] sensuales 532.15 dici] dicitur 523.15 *add*
libere 523.16 *add* nostra 523.16 facere] *om.* 523.20 sed] licet 523.22 cum
securi] et securis 523.22 scilicet secando] sensus cognoscendo 523.24 in
scindendo] scindentem 523.29 qua] que 523.31 quam] quia 523.31
premium] previum 523.34 supra] super 524.1 est] dicitur 524.3 tamen]
actum 524.4 *add* libere 524.6 quod] quia 524.7 ita] et 524.8
possemus] possumus 524.8 liberum] libere 524.12 ad speculandum] quod
speculetur 524.12 tales vel tales scientias] talem vel talem scientiam 524.12
ex ea] qua 524.16 precipis] precipit 524.20 exterioris] exteriorum 524.21
intrandum] faciendum 524.22 sunt] non sunt nisi 524.22 necessitates]
necessitationes 524.28 *add* libere elicitos sive 524.31 *add* libere 524.35 *add*
modicum 524.36 sumus] simus 525.8 dicetur] dicitur 525.10 anime
attribuitur] attribuenda est anime 525.16 *add* sed 525.17 posito casu]
ponendo casum 525.18 surgat] surgit 525.19 occurat aspectui] occurit

conspectui 525.21 *add* immediate producens eum 525.23 violente]
violenta 525.27 liberos ibi positos] librum ibi positum 525.28 *add* et
525.30 si est] *om.* 525.30 tunc] esse 525.31 tunc] esse 525.32 istud] *om.*
525.33 ergo] *om.* 525.33 et] *om.* 525.37 communiter] consequenter 526.1
potuisset querere] posuisset questionem 526.2 vel] et 526.3 acceptasset]
imperasset 526.6 intemperate] intemperantie 526.8 *add* et aliquando ex
electione et consideratione intellectuali querit obiectum et inveniens et
agit intemperate 526.10 passionem] passiones 526.18 *add* modo voluntarie
et libere 526.21 *add* actum liberum 526.23 probare] demonstrare 526.24
quia] *om.* 526.28 carnem] canem 528.28 *add* sedere modo 526.29 *add* et
ambulare 526.32 *add* extra 526.33 reputantibus] representantibus 526.34
add ex 526.36 *add* ad 526.38 *add* canem 527.1 scilicet] *om.* 527.1 *add* ei
527.1 sibi] sic 527.2 dicimus] diceremus 527.2 supponimus]
supponamus 527.3 dictis] predictis 527.5 possumus] possemus 527.5
dicimus] diximus 527.7 si] sic 527.8 *add* propter quod 527.9 repugnat]
oppugnare videtur 527.13 *add* nobis 527.17 *add* quod 527.21 alii] aliqui
527.23 possem] possum 527.27 quod] quam 527.27 vel] et 527.38 *add*
quod ita 527.38 *add* sit 527.38 in eo] deo 528.3 ergo] *om.* 528.3 *add*
prius 528.4 concedendo] concedo 528.6 inde] tamen 528.9 contingit]
occurit 528.11 quandocunque] quando 528.13 *add* et 528.17 quecunque]
quemcunque 528.23 quam] qua 528.24 patiens] passum 528.32 species]
speculationes 528.35 quam] nisi 528.36 et] *om.* 529.1 principalem finem
ordinati] naturalem finium ordinationem 529.2 *add* libri 529.3 *add* est
529.3 *add* etiam 529.3 *add* statim 529.4 vel etiam] et 529.4 etiam]
enim 529.5 his] eis 529.9 ac] hac 529.10 miscere] misere 529.10
secundum] scilicet 529.11 suos] *om.* 529.15 *add* turpe 519.15 ordine]
ordinatione 529.16 naturaliter] finaliter 529.16 immo] ideo 529.18
naturalium] *om.* 529.18 *add* naturalibus 529.19 omnes] *om.* 529.20 *add*
verbi gratia 529.21 vera] *om.* 529.22 *add* ipsam 529.22 ad philosophiam]
om. 529.22 *add* omnes alii 529.23 adeo] ad hoc 529.25 speculativo]
speculativi 529.26 *add* et homo maxime intellectus est 529.28 *add* id est
529.29 *add* aliquam 529.32 virtutes] virtus 529.32 malicie] malicia 529.37
dictis] predictis 529.37 proprio] primo 530.3 *add* libere 530.7 *add* quod
530.12 add et 530.23 *add* et voluntatis sunt gratia sapientie que est habitus
intellectus 530.25 *add* libri 530.29 sit status] sistamus 530.30 exsecutionem]
prosecutionem 530.35 liberius] liberrime 531.1 Politice] Politicorum
531.3 unumquoque] quod unumquodque 531.8 pono] ponam 531.9
add est 531.9 *add* decimaoctava 531.16 *add* libri 531.17 ideo] ad hoc
531.18 deacceptemus] acceptemus 531.18 malum] *om.* 531.18 quod] quia

531.26 simpliciter] *om.* 531.29 *add* sui 531.29 hoc] hec 531.30 ordinatur]
ordinantur 531.30 ad] in 531.32 *add* finalis ordinationis 531.32 *add* Igitur
sic manifestum est quod libertas 531.32 que] *om.* 531.38 sexta] octava
531.38 *add* libri 532.5 *add* ostensi 532.8 *add* et propter ipsam libertatem
finalis ordinationis 532.8 sumus] simus 532.9 *add* sic 532.11 hominis]
humana 532.22 nobilior] potentior 532.26 *add* quod 532.30 magis]
maxime 532.32 Ergo etc] *om.* 533.3 *add* pro parte 533.10 *add* aliquem
533.11 *add* adhuc 533.12 *add* etiam 533.15 querere] facere 533.21 Et] *om.*
533.25 *add* volitionem 533.27 *add* non ea ratione qua dicitur voluntas.
Igitur producere volitionem convenit anime ea ratione qua dicitur
intellectus 534.1 scilicet] sed 534.2 *add* tamen 534.4 presuppositum]
suppositum 534.5 alia] precedenti 534.10 *add* quo 534.10 patet] apparet
534.14 quam] qua 534.14 *add* vel econtrario 534.18 suppositionem]
suppositum 534.24 etiam ulterius] et ultra 534.25 *add* sic 534.27 quia]
scilicet quod 535.1 ipsius] *om.* 535.1 faciliter] faciles 535.16 scilicet] tunc
se habet 535.22 pono] pone 535.22 annihilet] annihilavit 535.23 tunc]
tamen 535.23 incipiam nunc] incipio 535.25 in me] *om.* 535.25 *add* et
cum quod nihil est nihil agit 535.29 intentio] intellectio 535.37 movet]
moveat 536.3 patet] apparet 536.5 intentionem] intellectionem 536.6
consequitur] consequenter 536.9 *add* autem 536.14 *add* principale 536.16
add est 536.17 intentio] intellectio 536.18 intentio] intellectio 536.21
illam] *om.* 536.22 intensionem] intellectionem 536.24 intentio] intellectio
536.26 intentio] intellectio 536.28 *add* scilicet 536.33 et] vel 536.33
alterum] altero 536.36 *add* sed 537.2 *add* ut sic 537.6 actualem]
actuantem eam 537.7 ut] per hoc quod 537.14 et] quod 537.14
informatur] informata est 537.17 add etiam 537.18 *add* prius 537.19 *add*
sive 537.21 supposito] suppono 537.22 *add* prius 537.25 fuerint fiant
537.28 omnibus anima 537.28 posterioris] posteriorum 537.32 *add* et
537.34 *add* et 537.37 *add* voluntas, non ea ratione qua dicitur 538.1 *add*
intellectus 538.2 *add* sensus 538.3 dicerentur diceretur 538.4 *add*
dicitur intellectus 538.4 secundum quam qua 538.6 *add* non 538.6 *add*
ex eo quod agit volitionem vel delectationem vel complacentiam vel
huiusmodi, immo 538.8 ex] *om.*, quod] *om.* 538.8 eam sic] *om.* 538.9
sic] hic 538.14 intellectionem] aliquid 538.14 hoc] eo 538.19 habet]
habere 538.20 quod] *om.* 538.21 *add* et 538.26 *add* informato 538.27
tamen] tunc 538.35 animo] alio 538.35 simul *om.* 538.36 *add* simul et
539.4 illas] illam 539.5 necessitatur] necessitata 539.20 *add* bene 539.33
dicit] ostendit 540.2 *add* qua voluntas 540.2 *add* quod 540.4 cum hoc]
tamen 540.5 passibilitate] passivitate 540.19 *add* primus huius 540.21

perfectissimam] *om.* 540.22 et] *om.* 540.23 et] scilicet 540.24 *add* etiam
541.1 ipsum] illum 541.12 homini] hominis 541.13 unum] unicum
541.13 perfectissima] perfecta 541.19 dicunt] dicerent 541.20 dicunt]
dicerent 541.23 quia] ut 541.25 *add* si esset essentialiter felicitas 541.26 *add*
sole 542.4 autem] potentie 542.9 propterea] *om.* 542.20 spem] specie
542.21 *add* in 542.24 confessis] confessum 542.33 *add* ita 542.36 *add* de
542.37 et] esse 542.38 et] est 543.10 consumatur] consummata 543.13 sic]
igitur 543.16 dicis] diceres 543.17 fundatur] fundantur 543.17 *add* tu
543.19 etiam] *om.* 543.28 diximus] dicimus 543.30 vocat] vocavit 543.33
dicit] dixit 544.2 *add* anime 544.2 dicitur] anima 544.7 *add* dicitur
544.12 Sed] sicut 544.17 tuno . . . enim] *om.* 544.19 viri] uni 544.21 *add*
dicere 544.22 aggregatio] congregatio 544.24 aggregatus] congregatus
544.24 *add* et 544.27 id est] scilicet 544.29 principalissima]
principalissimum 544.33 virtutem] vitam 544.36 etiam] enim 545.7 *add*
bene 545.9 impropria] propria 545.11 intellectivum] intellectum 545.17
perfecta] perfectam 545.17 et] etiam 545.18 tum] tamen 545.20
delectationem] declarationem 545.25 et secundum se] *om.* 545.25 debeat]
debet 545.27 et] sed 545.33 virtutem] speciem 545.34 felicitabilis]
felicitabili 546.1 *add* naturaliter innata sunt 546.12 que a Boetio] *om.*
546.13 describitur] descripta 546.16 aliquis] Aristoteles 546.17 detentius]
detentus 546.18 *add* amicis vel 546.20 spirituali ac] speciali 546.21
huiusmodi] homini 546.24 *add* aliorum 546.25 et] *om.* 546.28 sic] *om.*
546.35 *add* et 546.39 *add* libro 547.2 *add* huius 547.13 *add* solum 547.21
add etiam 547.22 Et] *om.* 547.22 *add* igitur 547.32 *add* non 547.33 verum]
immo 547.35 *add* contemplatio nec etiam esset 547.37 *add* donec etiam
est perfecta 547.37 perfectione innata] per perfectiones innatas 548.5 *add*
in 548.5 xiii] xiv 548.6 adhuc] *om.* 548.6 *add* sic 548.7 *add* vel felici
548.11 felicitas] speculatio 548.17 in amore et visione] simul visione et
amore 548.20 annexa] consequentia 548.20 felicitati] ad felicitatem 548.20
consequentia] connexa 548.25 que] quantum 548.26 unam] *om.* 548.28 et]
om. 548.28 habet felicitatem] *om.* 548.28 *add* felicitati 548.29 operatur]
operetur 548.30 natum] innatum 548.33 *add* ut sic 548.33 *add* se habens
548.34 felici] felicitati 548.36 *add* et 548.36 et] *om.* 548.36 est ei propria,
et] etiam propria, et alicuius altera. Alia enim est virtus propria et 549.2
cuiuslicet] cuiuslibet 549.2 alicuius partis] *om.* 549.3 *add* puta, oculi
virtus et oculum studiosum facit et opus eius oculi bene reddit 549.7
proportionabili] proportionabile 549.11 *add* et 549.12 et] etiam 549.12
potentiam partialem] potentialiter partibilem 549.13 inquantum] ut
549.14 inquantum appetitivus] ut appetitiva 549.15 *add* alia

speculativi ut speculativus 549.16 et alia speculativi ut speculativus] *om.*
549.18 *add* partibus 549.19 *add* virtute et 549.27 dicendi] dictum 549.30
add specialem 549.30 specialis] *om.* 549.32 in *om.* 550.1 tamen] tunc
550.9 et melior] *om.* 550.20 et] *om.* 550.20 assuefactionis] consuetudinis
550.21 in] *om.* 550.22 *add* in 550.24 *add* voluntatem practicam et pars
contemplativa in intellectum contemplativum seu speculativum 550.25
pars speculativum] *om.* 550.29 *add* est 550.33 *add* etc. 550.35 speculativi
seu] *om.* 550.35 *add* et 550.36 speculative seu] *om.* 551.2 cuius] eius
551.6 prima] patria 551.8 an] ante 551.9 ei] corporis 551.11 proprie]
proprissime 551.15 tamen] *om.* 551.20 *add* felix 551.24 deficiat oculus aut
pes] deficiant oculi aures pedes 551.32 felici] felicitate et 551.38 earum]
om. 552.2 *add* loquendi 552.6 octava] sexta 552.10 *add* manifestum est
quod 552.13 dicit]diceret 552.18 dicunt] diceret 552.20 diceretur] diceret
552.24 *add* suis 552.28 crederet] teneret 552.30 longe] *om.* 552.31 culpa]
macula 552.33 ita] *om.* 552.33 Vir bonus] *om.* 552.34 spe] *om.* 552.36 et]
in 552.37 deberet optime] optime crederet 552.38 qui] quam 552.39 *add*
suo 553.6 felicitatis] de felicitate 553.6 *add* quedam 553.7 circa] in
553.8 Prima] una 553.8 tamen] eum 553.9 habet] habere 553.14 *add*
tamen 553.15 longe] valde 553.16 contra] econtra 553.16 *add* hominem
553.16 hominem] *om.* 553.18 est] *om.* 553.18 seu] sub 553.21 utrique] *om.*
553.22 est] *om.* 553.23 quartum] *om.* 553.28 optime] optimo 554.2
scilicet secundum] *om.* 554.4 dicendum] dicendus 554.8 dices] diceres
554.8 *add* quia 554.8 punicei] pueritie 554.8. *add* ipse 554.10 queretur]
sequitur 554.14 diligere] dicere 554.20 contradictione] contradictoriae
554.26 hoc] *om.* 554.26 precise] preciso 554.28 qua] quo 554.28 est] *om.*
554.28 queris] quereres 554.29 punicie] pueritie 554.30 ipse *om.* 554.30
quando] quo tempore 554.31 virtutibus] virtuosus 554.32 aperte] a parte
554.34 humane] *om.* 554.39 fuerunt] fuerint 554.39 amore] *om.* 554.39 *add*
qui 555.1 *add* sunt 555.3 *add* homines 555.3 partem] porcionem
555.3 etiam] sic 555.4 *add* mortem 555.4 *add* bono et 555.5 *add* illius
555.6 *add* prius 555.7 *add* vere 555.8 *add* ante. in non . . . libro] *om.*
555.10 quod . . . dicam] Secunda questio soluta fuit in primo libro. Sed
adhuc nunc aliter quodammodo solvo eam secundum logicam
stipulationem et dico 555.12 quod] *om.* 555.17 sed] licet 555.27 *add* hora
vel 555.28 *add* optime 555.28 *add* omnino 555.29 *add* in 555.35 sit] sic
555.37 *add* et speculetur 556.5 nos] non 556.6 non] *om.* 556.11 pro]
una pars 556.11 una] uno 556.11 alia et alia, alia die et alia hora] et alia
alio vel alia 556.17 *add* concedo quod 556.20 materia] consideratio 556.24
add est 556.35 *add* continentia 556.35 *add* sic 556.37 significant]

significunt idem 557.1 sicut . . . infelici] dicam de infelici sicut dictum
est de misero 557.5 sunt] *om.* 557.20 quam habet] quamtumcunque
557.22 deviet] deviaret 557.22 et perfectissimo] *om.* 557.23 valde . . .
haberet] per valde specialem gratiam supernaturalem 557.25 *add* esse idem
557.25 *add* hominem 557.27 bonus] virtuosus 557.30 et] sicut 557.31
magni] magistri [conjecture] 557.35 *add* que 557.35 *add* fuerunt 558.7
scilicet] *om.* 558.13 *add* et moralium 558.23 aliquid] quidam 558.24 *add*
etiam 558.26 Item] *om.*; *add* etiam 558.27 hominibus] homini 558.30 *add*
ex toto corde 559.6 ipsi] amici 559.9 et tamen] *om.* 559.10 *add* autem
559.11 *add* valde melius 559.12 *add* in 559.14 ipsum] deum 559.15 *add*
magis 559.17 *add* actus 559.17 quidem] qui est 559.20 *add* sub 559.22 tali]
simili 559.24 studiose potentie] studiosa potentia 559.25 et] vel 559.25
dicunt] dicuntur 559.26 que] qui 559.26 secundo] decimo 559.29 est]
esset 559.30 *add* autem 559.34 *add* in beato 559.34 intellectus] intellectio
559.35 *add* igitur etc. 559.35 probatio] minor patet 559.36 *add* suum
560.1 beatitudo] felicitas 560.4 secunda] undecima 560.11 peius] melius;
melius] peius 560.13 nono] octava 560.18 et delectabilissimum] *om.*
560.19 *add* et 560.24 *add* potentia 560.24 oportet capere] cape 560.24 *add*
ad hoc 560.25 huius decimi] *om.* 560.27 subsumendo] sumendo 560.28 et]
quod 560.29 *add* ad hoc 560.29 eadem] *om.* 560.30 eiusdem decimi libri]
om. 560.31 *add* actus 560.36 *add* et 560.36 voluntas] voluntatis 560.37 *add*
scilicet 560.37 quarta] precedenti 561.4 intellectus nec voluntatis]
voluntatis nec actus intellectus 561.14 delectabilissimum et
perfectissimum] perfectissimum et delectabilissimum 561.18 *add* sint pure
561.21 *add* similiter 561.23 illorum] aliorum 561.28 liberrimum]
liberrimus 561.29 ut dictum est] secundum dicta 561.30 etiam] *om.* 562.5
determinatum] declaratum 562.7 vel] et 562.9 *add* adepti. Sed constat
quod ratione recta et vera non apprehendimus sub ratione optimi 562.12
id] *om.* 562.22 *add* et 562.22 intelligimus] intendimus 562.23 quod]
nolumus 562.31 etiam] *om.* 562.33 ut] hoc 562.34 *add* solus 562.35 solius]
om. 563.1 *add* concedentibus 563.2 in nono questione septima] in
septima questione noni libri 563.3 secunda] alia 563.3 *add* est 563.4
quod] quo 563.6 *add* amor 563.8 *add* animam 563.9 sic] sit 563.12
verum] *om.* 563.12 iudicium] iudicatum 563.15 hoc] *om.* 563.18 seu] et
563.19 tunc necessario] illud iudicium 563.19 tunc] *om.* 563.22 ad] *om.*
563.22 perfectum] *om.* 563.23 et perfectus amor] *om.* 563.27 licet] sed
563.27 libertatis] necessitatis 563.28 *add* sequi 563.28 dico] *om.* 563.32
diminutus] diminutis 563.37 tamen] *om.* 563.38 *add* etc. 563.38 *add* ideo
564.2 *add* obiectum 564.4 esse] mihi 564.7 que fiunt] *om.* 564.8 *add*

sed 564.8 nec] non 564.12 rationem] *om.* 564.13 illa] *om.* 564.13 illum]
suum 564.16 quia] *om.* 564.17 sua] illa 564.23 quem] quo 564.28 *add* non
564.29 saltem] statim 564.30 *add* tutelam seu ad 564.32 vel sit] sed 564.36
veritati] veritas 564.38 modo] horum modorum 564.39 nocet] noceret
565.1 nocet] noceret 565.2 iam] ideo 565.8 incerta] ficta 565.11 talem
naturaliter est] *om.* 565.11 *add* humana 565.12 *add* seu defectuose 565.12
add actu 565.24 cum beatitudine] obiective 565.24 maneret] manet 565.28
add etc. 565.37 *add* libri 566.1 probare seu declarare sic] sic demonstrare
566.6 *add* nobis 566.11 cui] ei 566.12 quam] quem 566.13 dimittimus]
dimittemus 566.14 si diceremus] dicere 566.16 *add* nisi 566.16 *add*
improprias 566.17 priores] predictos 566.22 boni et] *om.* 566.22 *add* et
nobis optimi 566.26 *add* etiam 566.29 dono] deo 566.35 *add* delectatio
567.1 quia] sed 567.4 omnes] *om.* 567.4 opinione seu] *om.* 567.5 *add*
hiis 567.10 sic] sit 567.11 beatus] *om.* 567.11 *add* hoc 567.12 obiecti]
optimi 567.12 et optimi] *om.* 567.13 *add* iam 567.14 posset] possit 567.21
denominationem] delectationem 567.26 acceptatio] acceptativo 567.26
quos] que 567.32 *add* conclusionem 567.32 *add* primo 567.36 divino]
dominio 567.38 posset] potest 568.4 Nicholai] Petri 568.4 visione]
visionem 568.8 ad presens] *om.* 568.9 nec] non 568.11 ego] *om.* 568.12
factum incidentaliter] esse incidentale 568.19 precedere] procedere 568.19
sunt] se 568.19 precedere] procedere 568.26 consequeretur] consequitur
568.28 concluderemus] concludemus 568.37 aliqua] *om.* 568.37
quecunque] quocunque 569.1 facienda] faciendam 569.4 *add* sic 569.7
sic enim] sicut 569.10 demonstrabiles] demonstrationes 569.15 *add* alterius
partis 569.25 quid] que 569.27 ut] et 569.28 etiam] *om.* 569.30 magni viri]
magistri 570.3 deprecatur] deprecaretur 570.26 *add* ultra 570.29
impossibilia] incompossibilia 571.1 *add* prius 571.4 speculetur]
speculemur 571.5 *add* quam illud praeceptum 571.8 nichil] non 571.10
non] *om.* 571.10 *add* nichil 571.11 presentiat] presententiat 571.15 *add* ad
571.17 omnino] ideo 571.20 sensum] sensus 571.20 declaratum] declaratos
571.25 Sic] *om.* 571.26 necessitatur] necessitant 571.27 sed] et 572.15 *add*
et 572.17 econverso] converse 572.22 *add* huius 573.1 *add* posse 573.6
add extollit 573.7 que sint] simul 573.8 *add* et 573.10 connotat]
connotaret 573.11 differunt] distant 573.22 solum] *om.* 573.22
communem rationem] cognitionem 573.24 omnino] immo 573.30 quod]
om. 573.31 *add* et sic per intellectionem quod est malum et refutationem
sequentem ego divido me ab illo vel illud a me sicut possum 573.35
ipsum] deum 573.38 *add* esse 573.39 principium et] *om.* 574.1
voluptatem] voluptates 574.5 sit] est 574.15 firmior] fortior 574.15

dictum est quod] tamen 574.20 *add* amandum et 574.20 observanda]
super omnia alia esse servanda 574.23 quia] et 574.24 *add* pure 574.24
primo] immo 574.25 *add* posuerunt 574.25 *add* enim 574.26 Unde] ut
574.28 *add* intellectus est 574.28 intus est] *om.* 574.33 immersa] mersa
574.36 aliquod] aliquid 575.2 *add* vitam 575.4 *add* est 575.9 sub
ratione mali] *om.* 575.12 *add* quam voluntas possit determinare ad
amandum 575.13 *add* et rectus 575.14 *add* prius 575.14 precedat] sit
575.14 *add* rectus et perfectus 575.25 tantum] tamen 575.30 *add* proprium
575.38 remittit] remittitur 575.40 *add* solutum 576.7 illam] aliam 576.7
eius] *om.* 576.7 *add* sensus 576.11 *add* cum 576.15 *add* est 576.17
coniunctis] coniuncti 576.20 *add* queritur sexto in quo actu intellectus
consistit humana felicitas an in simplici vel in complexo, et si in simplici
tunc in quo simplici et sic de complexo; et an in actu directo vel reflexo

JOHN WYCLIF
ON CIVIL LORDSHIP (SELECTIONS)

Introduction

John Wyclif (ca. 1330–1384) was an Oxford secular master in Arts and
later in Theology who in the 1370s became involved in political and
theological controversies. As diplomat, preacher, and writer he supported
the government against the pope's claim to levy taxes and the claim of the
clergy to have absolute ownership of property. His chief academic work
in this period of his life was a theological *Summa*. After a massive preliminary treatise *De domino divino* (*On Divine Lordship*), the *Summa* included
Tract I *De mandatis divinis* (*On the Divine Commandments*), Tract II *De statu
innocencie* (*On the State of Innocence*), Tract III *De civili dominio* (*On Civil
Lordship*, from which the chapters translated below come), and other treatises on Scripture, the church, kingship, the papacy, etc. Wyclif's elaborate
treatment of lordship, divine and civil, is largely inspired by the treatise *On
the Poverty of the Savior* by Richard FitzRalph, Bishop of Armagh, a contribution to the controversies over Franciscan poverty in which Marsilius
of Padua and William of Ockham had also taken part. All these writers felt
a need to clarify the various senses of lordship, property, justice, and rights.
As Wyclif's *Summa* progressed it became more and more controversial on
a variety of subjects, such as the nature of the church, the authority of the
pope, and the doctrine of the eucharist. By the end of his life Wyclif had
antagonized most of the higher clergy and the religious orders. Like Marsilius and Ockham, Wyclif has often been seen as a forerunner of Reformation and early modern thought, but also like them he turns out on
closer inspection to be very much a member of the medieval intellectual
community.

On Civil Lordship continues a comprehensive examination of lordship
that Wyclif began in *On Divine Lordship*. In the earlier work he gave a
general definition of the sort of lordship he was concerned with: 'Lordship
is the relational disposition of a rational nature according as it is characterized as being over some person or thing that serves it' ('*Dominium est*

habitudo nature racionalis secundum quam denominatur suo prefici servienti,' De
dominio divino I, p. 4; *servienti* covers both persons and things). Similarly, he
defines servanthood as 'the relational disposition of a creature according to
which it is said formally to be subjected to its lord' (*'Servicium . . . est
habitudo creature secundum quam dicitur formaliter suo subici dominanti'*; ibid.,
p. 7). There is a difference between service (*servitium*) and slavery (*servitus*):
The latter involves coercion and is due to sin, whereas service befits even
Christ and the saints, and every rational creature must serve God at least
(ibid., pp. 7–8). *'Servus'* means ambiguously either a slave, who is compelled to work, or a servant, who works by choice (ibid., p. 7).

These definitions put lordship and servanthood into the category of
relations. According to Wyclif a relation has a subject, a term (or 'object,'
ibid., p. 15), and a foundation. For example, 'Peter's likeness [a relation]
to Paul is subjectively in Peter, terminatively in Paul, and foundationally
in the quality of Peter and Paul according to which they are said to be
similar' (ibid., p. 9). Wyclif often refers to the subject and term together as
the 'extremes.' The foundation of the lord–servant relationship is the
lord's right to service. Thus it is an error to define lordship as *being* a kind
of right or power, but its *foundation* is a right (ibid., p. 8). In *On Civil
Lordship* Wyclif maintains that the foundation of civil lordship is, or presupposes, a right either of uncorrupted nature or of grace. ('Civil right is a
right of nature or grace, or something that necessarily presupposes such a
right'; below, p. 622).

More specifically, 'No foundation [of lordship] is relevant except the
lord's justice (*iusticia*, equally well translated in Wyclif as "righteousness")'
(below, p. 595 [Chapter 1, 3rd argument]). Wyclif's conception of justice
lies at the intersection of several lines of thought that are often pursued in
separation from one another. Justice, he holds, is the most distinguished of
the Aristotelian virtues, it is indeed the whole of virtue. Originally and
most naturally, however, justice is virtually identical with the Christian
theological virtue of charity, and so it animates a life marked by love of
God, love of neighbor, and a lack of possessiveness. In both these respects,
furthermore, justice can be understood in terms of the relation between a
feudal lord and his vassals. God, the generous chief lord of all creation, is
the source of all rights, and disobedience to God's law or abuse of God's
gifts results automatically in forfeiture of all that the lord – that is, God –
has granted. Finally, since charity (hence loving obedience to God and all
genuine virtue) is impossible, according to Wyclif, without divine grace,
all questions of moral, economic, and political legitimacy depend on God's

good pleasure, which Wyclif understands in terms of the doctrine of predestination.

Human lordship, then, is a gift of God; God gives lordship to human beings without in any way reducing his own lordship. Human lordship divides into natural (or original), gospel (*evangelicum*), and civil. Original lordship is the lordship of uncorrupted nature, the lordship Adam had before sin; gospel lordship is a (partial) restoration of original lordship. Civil lordship is established by human beings because of sin; it differs from original and gospel lordship in being coercive (*De civili dominio*, I, chapter 11, pp. 73, 75), and also in involving *property*, i.e., exclusion (ibid., chapter 18, pp. 126–28). Whereas original lordship is based on a right on the part of each person who enjoys it to be served by every one of God's creatures, civil lordship belongs to one person (or body of people) to the exclusion of others. It is 'not [as a whole] communicable on equal terms to each of many lords' (*incommunicable singulis et ex equo multis dominis*, ibid., p. 126; for the sense of *ex equo* see pp. 127–28). As the Roman law puts it, 'Two persons cannot have lordship or possession *in solidum* [i.e., of the whole thing],' *Digest*, 13.6.5.15. Much of Wyclif's doctrine on lordship comes (as he says) from Richard FitzRalph, who in turn was probably influenced (though he does not say so) by Franciscan writers such as Bonagratia of Bergamo and Ockham. (For Ockham, see *Short Discourse*, pp. 87–104, and *Work of Ninety Days*, c. 2, translated in *A Letter to the Friars Minor and other Writings*, pp. 27–48.)

The ten chapters translated below, the first ten chapters of *On Civil Lordship*, argue two main theses. The first is that a person in mortal sin does not have a simple or unqualified right to anything and therefore does not have a simple right to civil lordship. This is because God does not grant any gift except to those who are pleasing to him, i.e., those who are 'in grace.' This thesis again comes from FitzRalph, and behind him are Giles of Rome and Augustine; but whereas Giles of Rome inferred that all civil lordship depends upon the pope, FitzRalph and Wyclif hold that the gift is given by God with grace directly to each person.

The second main thesis of these chapters is that those who are in 'finally gratifying grace' are in reality lords of all God's good things, including God himself and one another. The notion of 'finally gratifying grace' needs explanation. Wyclif believes that humanity is divided between 'the predestined' (i.e., those who will go to heaven) and 'the foreknown' (those who will go to hell). Which division an individual belongs to depends on whether he or she is in gratifying grace, that is, grace that makes a person pleasing to God, at the moment of death. For someone to be predestined means that God wills that that person will be in grace at the moment of death (this will is the grace of 'final perseverance'); the foreknown, on the other hand, will be in mortal sin at the moment of death. A given person may be at some times in grace and at other times in mortal sin; neither that person nor any other human being can know which state he or she will be in at death, i.e., whether the person is predestined or foreknown. The second thesis is, then, that anyone in 'finally gratifying grace,' i.e., anyone who is in grace and will be so at the final moment of life, has lordship over all things. Predestined persons temporarily in mortal sin do not at that time have a right to all things, but they will have again when they return to grace, and meanwhile they have the main thing, the gift of final perseverance. Those of the 'foreknown' who are temporarily in grace have a right to whatever civil lordship they hold, but they are not lords of 'all things' since they do not have the grace of final perseverance and consequently have no right to the kingdom of heaven.

What are the practical or political implications of Wyclif's denial of lordship to sinners? The answer is not clear and interpreters disagree. It seems most likely that Wyclif thought sinners should be deprived of civil lordship. Others had said that sinners are not *worthy* of the civil lordship they hold, of which they are nevertheless not to be deprived (cf. Ockham, *Short Discourse*, p. 96). Wyclif in some places says that those who are perfect will not have civil lordship at all, since it involves sin (see Daly, *The Political Theory of John Wyclif*, pp. 76–77). In the extract translated below, however, Wyclif argues that the civil judge should award civil lordship to Peter against Paul if he knows that Peter is in grace and Paul in mortal sin (below, p. 622). 'The whole body of human law ought to rest upon the gospel law as its essentially directive rule' (*De civili dominio* I, p. 139).

One practical implication that eventually becomes clear is that secular lords can rightly deprive sinful clergy of their property. In chapter 37 (not translated) Wyclif asserts that 'Kings, princes, and temporal lords can lawfully and very meritoriously take riches away from any ecclesiastical person or community habitually abusing them.' Several of the propositions condemned by Pope Gregory XI in 1377 came from chapter 37; Book II of *De civili dominio* is a defense especially of that chapter. Wyclif professes not to be asserting that the clergy are actually abusing riches: 'Whether today the church is in that case is not for me to discuss. It is the business of politicians who supervise the practicalities and state of kingdoms. Indeed, I protest that I am speaking conditional truths concerning what is possible, leaving to them the judgment of fact. I know that it is the business of the temporal lords to examine the question' (*De civili dominio*, I, pp. 269–70). There is not much doubt, however, that he thought not only that the clergy were in fact abusing church endowments but that abuse was inevitable as long as the church remained wealthy. Like Marsilius, Wyclif wanted *all* the clergy to live in apostolic poverty.

For further reading, see the Preface, p. vii–xxxi, Iohannis Wycliffe *Tractatus de Civili dominio liber primus*, ed. Reginald Lane Poole (London: For the Wyclif Society, Truebner and Co., 1885). See also CHLMP, X 39, 'Rights, natural rights and the philosophy of law,' and X 40, 'The state of nature and the origin of the state.' See also Lowrie J. Daly, *The Political Theory of John Wyclif* (Chicago: Loyola University Press, 1962), and M. Wilks, 'Predestination, Property and Power: Wyclif's Theory of Dominion and Grace,' *Studies in Church History*, 2 (1965), pp. 220–36. On Wyclif's life and doctrines see Anthony Kenny, *Wyclif* (Oxford: Oxford University Press, 1985). For translation of another of Wyclif's theological works see John Wyclif, *On Simony*, translated by Terrence A. McVeigh (New York: Fordham University Press, 1992).

A †† at the beginning of a passage indicates that we suspect the passage is corrupt in the Latin we are using. The Latin text translated here will be found at: http://www.humanities.mq.edu.au/Ockham/wwyclat.html.

On Civil Lordship (selections)

Book I

{1} **Chapter 1.** In discussing the civil lordship that human beings have in addition to natural lordship we must first see whether civil lordship presupposes a natural lordship founded in grace, just as civil law presupposes divine law as its essential exemplary cause. For the sake of what is to be said I intend, therefore, to show two truths which I will use as principles for what is to be said later. The first is that no one while in mortal sin has a simple right to any of God's gifts; the second is that anyone who is in finally gratifying grace not only has the right but has in reality all God's good things. But so that the explanation of the doctrine will not be impeded from the outset by equivocation or ignorance of terms, I suppose that a person is said to have simply a right to, or in, some good while he possesses or has the thing purely justly, so that he does not have it {2} at that time unjustly – that is, so that if he holds (*occupat*) something unjustly at a certain time, at that time he does not have (*habet*) it simply justly.

[1. No One in Mortal Sin Has a Simple Right to God's Gifts]

[1a. First Argument]

Then I argue first as follows. Every human law causally presupposes divine law, as is clear from what was said above, Tract I (*De mandatis divinis*), chapter 3. Therefore, every lordship that is just in relation to human beings presupposes a lordship just in relation to God. [a] But those who are in mortal sin lack, as such, just lordship in relation to God. Therefore, they also lack simply just lordship. For as in relateds it is valid to argue from 'in relation to' to 'simply,' so it is valid to argue that if something is just or unjust in relation to God then it is such simply, since the first rule cannot fail in judging. The minor ([a] that those who are, etc.) is clear thus: [b] Every good that such persons possess, they possess unjustly. Therefore, they lack true lordship of anything at all that can be subject to lordship. The premise [b] is proved: Sinners possess only in the mode in which they are. But [c] however sinners are, they are unjustly. Therefore, however they possess, they possess unjustly. The minor premise [c] is clear from the fact that when mortal sin poisons a nature, it much more evidently poisons every mode or accident of the nature; so if people's lives are unjust, so that they live unjustly, then each of their actions is unjust. Since they act no otherwise than as they live and since life is the being of living things (*De anima* II [4, 415b13]), it is clear that if they exist and live unjustly then they are lords unjustly and are unjustly the subjects of any accidental quality that can be mentioned.

Even if this argument should seem sophistical to many, any metaphysician would nevertheless give it full credence, since it is the conclusion of the foremost Philosopher. In Matthew 6:22–23 he says this: 'If your eye is sincere, your whole body will be full of light, and if {3} it is evil, your body also will be shadowy.' Since, therefore, according to the saints, Truth in his usual way means by the organs the actions they elicit, it is clear that the meaning is this: If your intention is right, all the resulting actions will be just, and if your intention deviates from justice, all your actions, even those good in their kind, are unjust: For justice, according to Aristotle

(*Ethics* V [1, 1129b25–31]), is the most splendid of the virtues, shining among the others like the Evening Star among the stars. Christ seems to allude to this meaning when he calls all the actions of the just 'full of light' and all the actions of the unjust 'shadowy.'

And if it is inferred from this that the sinner has body or soul or any other natural good unjustly, clearly the inference is very well drawn. For if such a person lives unjustly, it is clear that he has soul and thus life unjustly. Otherwise Truth, who cannot lie, would not have said so often that 'whoever loves his soul,' meaning loves it pleasurably contrary to justice, 'will lose it' (John 12:25). But no one loses what he possesses or has except when his right is taken away; therefore, etc. Augustine raises this point, among others, in his first homily on John, that sin is nothing and men become nothing when they sin. For no one who sins mortally has (except equivocally), for that time, body or soul or any good of fortune; for since he has being by pure grace and by this being is bound by the law of nature to continue in grace, when he loses the rule of this law he does not remain a creature, or one who possesses anything, except equivocally.

[1b. Second Argument]

Second (principally) it is argued as follows. If it is possible for the unjust to be simply justly a lord of temporal things, then [a] it would likewise be possible for the unjust to use purely justly the temporal things of which he has the simply just lordship. The inference is clear, because no one to whom any usufruct ought justly to be denied has free and pure just lordship. Therefore, any just {4} possessor is lawfully permitted to use his property.

[Objection] But against the given conclusion [a] it is argued as follows. Let Peter be an unjust man who holds temporal possessions from which he gives alms to the needy – in whatever circumstances you wish, provided [only that] he remains all the time unjust. And it is clear that if use of temporal things by an unjust person were ever not unjust this use would most of all be such, since its act would be good in its kind, since nothing would taint it except the injustice by which the almsgiver is unjust. If we suppose [that there is such a taint in this case], it would likewise taint every other good action, because it follows equally well whatever we suppose along with injustice. Let it be supposed, then, that the unjust man, Peter, distributes alms not unjustly but in a purely just way.

Against [this argument]: No external action is simply just except as it proceeds from the virtue of justice. But Peter's almsgiving lacked the virtue of justice in Peter, since he is imbued with an injustice that is inconsistent with it. The almsgiving in question is therefore not simply just. Indeed, since justice is the whole of virtue (from *Ethics* V [1, 1129b25–31]), then if he distributes alms justly he does so virtuously and consequently is a virtuous man acting pleasingly and meritoriously in God's sight. This implication is against every teaching of philosophers and theologians, who say that someone in mortal sin may perform an act good in its kind but cannot act well. Similarly, God requires of Peter, as he requires of every wayfarer, that he do nothing except in grace. But Peter acts without grace, since he is (it is supposed) in mortal sin. Therefore, he acts otherwise than as he ought. The requirement to act differently does not oblige Peter to act differently under just any penalty, but under the penalty {5} of mortal sin. From this it is clear that if he is unjust, then whatever Peter does, whether sleeping or eating or doing any act good in its kind, he continually sins mortally.

This will not be called into question by a theologian who knows how the inner self poisoned with sin poisons all the rest of the person's corporeal nature and each of that person's acts. Now it is unjust for anyone to live as unjust or to be lord over anything. If you seek Scripture's testimony to this teaching, consider the conclusion of the Apostle's antistrophe in 1 Corinthians 13:3: 'If I should distribute all my property to feed the poor and if I should deliver my body to be burned but have not charity, it profits me nothing.' And anyone who understands the terms knows that injustice and charity are two contradictory opposites, so that one or other of them must be in a person, and if one is the other is not, and vice versa.

Again, it is known that, if the unjust cannot use anything without by that very act using it unjustly, or rather abusing it, it is likewise not possible for the unjust to be lord over anything without, as such, being lord unjustly, or rather tyrannizing, since an unjust person unjustly takes by force and holds things that belong to someone else. If you seek the testimony of holy doctors, consider the teaching of the great Augustine. In *Letter* 37 [*Letter* 153 in modern editions], to Macedonius, concerning tyrants he plainly teaches the following doctrine. 'Therefore,' he says, 'if we read with insight the text, "The whole world of riches belongs to the faithful, but to the faithless {6} not a penny," do we not convict of possessing other people's property all those who seem to themselves to enjoy things lawfully acquired but do not know how to use them? For a thing is certainly not another's if it is possessed lawfully, and it is possessed lawfully if it is possessed justly, and it is possessed justly if it is possessed well. Therefore, everything possessed badly is another's, but a person possesses badly who uses badly.' He says that 'No one has justice badly, and whoever has not loved it does not have it. Money, on the other hand, the bad have badly, and the good have it better when they love it less.' Thus Augustine.

[1c. Third Argument]

Third (principally) as follows. There exist (I suppose) many civil lordships of people who exercise civil lordship over temporals. For such lordship, however, it is not enough to posit the [mere] coexistence of someone who can be a lord with something or someone that can be subject to lordship. Some foundation of lordship must therefore be posited in one of the extremes [i.e., in the subject or term of the lord–servant relationship]. But no foundation is relevant except the lord's justice. Therefore, true civil lordship presupposes the disposition of the virtue of justice in such a lord. The minor is clear, because [if mere coexistence is enough] then everyone, simply by existing, has civil lordship of all the temporal things of this world. Also it is clear that lordship is not a relation that follows essentially upon the extremes, as equality and inequality follow essentially upon quantities, as is clear in *Metaphysics* V 2. Since, therefore, no creature is *per se* the lord of anything whatever (because then a creature could not accidentally acquire lordship or lose it), it follows manifestly that in addition to the extremes we must posit in anyone exercising civil lordship some disposition relevant to lordship. {7} All who speak rightly admit this. They say unanimously that all such lords must have a right to the thing over which they have civil lordship (e.g., by hereditary right, purchase, or grant) and that no such right is created unless it has been drawn from the primary right (as is clear from common speech about right). It follows manifestly that no one has right or lordship over anything, unless for this he has his God's goodwill.

This is confirmed: Every created just thing is just because it pleases God, since there cannot be such a just thing that does not proceed from God's goodwill. Similarly, whether a judge has passed sentence or the law has approved anyone's lordship for one of the three reasons stated above [i.e., inheritance, purchase, or gift], this has been done because it is just and reasonable that it be done; and consequently the justice of someone's being lord is naturally prior to its being approved by created law or an earthly judge not in error; and consequently the first title of the justice of any civil lordship is from God.

Catholics cannot rightly doubt this, since that great Lord, by reason of his omnipotence and by the efficacy of his will, has in his kingdom whatever he wills and does not have whatever he is unwilling to have; and it is clear that for any just holding under civil law the Lord must authorize, ratify, and confirm it, since whatever he does not approve is not just. And we need not labor this point, since in John 1:3, Colossians 1:16, and James 1:17, it is said, in harmony with the philosophers, that all things exist through him. Therefore, if a creature's lordship exists, it exists through God's originally approving it. (From that axiom of natural law derives the law of earthly monarchy that an inferior lord cannot rightly alienate immovable property, especially to a 'dead hand,' without permission from the chief lord. This is so because he has a just interest in all things, which it is not just for him to lose without his consent; {8} and it is clear that however people exchange the lord's property by buying, selling, granting, and judging, the exchange is unjust unless he consents.) With this established, then, it is proved that God does not approve the lordship of anyone who is unjust. For let it be so [i.e., that God approves his lordship] concerning Peter, an unjust man. Against this: If God approves that lordship, he likewise approves the use of that lordship and all other things that pertain to it; and since every such person abuses the lord's goods (as is clear from the second argument), it follows that God approves this abuse. Indeed, since every act of such an unjust person is a sin, it follows that God is the helper and approver of sin, not only in relation to its second being but in relation to its first being. For if God wills that Peter be lord and he is lord in this way only by tyrannizing, it follows that God wills him to tyrannize and thus to sin. To say this is blasphemy.

This is confirmed from Scripture. For in Hosea 8:4 God says prophetically of tyrants, 'They have reigned, but not by me'; for pretended 'reignings' ([so called] by equivocation) are called tyrannies (as was said above, chapter 3 [*De mandatis divinis*, p. 18], about right simply and by pretense); and since an unjust person is not lord 'by God,' it is clear that no one who is unjust is simply lord.

Chapter 2. Although the three arguments above may convince many of the intended conclusion, nevertheless, because others, from variation in their perceptions, also take pleasure in other arguments, I will add six other arguments for the same conclusion, so that it may be more universal and more evident.

[1d. Fourth Argument]

The first is as follows: No good can be attached to anyone in a simply just way unless God provides it to that person by granting it (as is clear from Tract III, *On Divine Lordship*). But God does not provide any of his gifts to anyone while that person is in mortal sin. Therefore, no one in mortal sin has {9} simply justly any good during that time. The minor is clear from this, that prudent persons do not provide anything to enemies they know will only abuse what has been provided and squander the provider's gifts to the provider's own harm; now God is supremely prudent and farsighted; therefore, he does not provide anything to his creatures during the time when they sin mortally.

The argument is confirmed by this, that it is not possible for God to provide anything to anyone except someone worthy. No such person [i.e., no one in mortal sin] is worthy to be God's beneficiary. Therefore, God provides nothing to such persons during the time when they are such. The minor premise is clear from this: Since God cannot provide except voluntarily and rationally, by the very fact of providing something to a creature God makes the creature worthy to be his beneficiary; and since this is a great grace, it seems that when he grants anything to a rational creature God previously or at the same time confers grace on that creature.

It is confirmed, second, by this: Everyone who successfully requests lordship from God must be in grace. But everyone who successfully requests lordship must by that fact obtain it *from God*, since God is the capital lord of everything (as is clear from the third argument of the preceding chapter). Therefore the conclusion. The major premise is clear from this: To request successfully, since it consists in the creature's making himself worthy, is to merit, which cannot be except by grace.

It is confirmed, third, by this: If someone successfully requests something from God, God consents to the request, and consequently it is just for the requester to have it; and since the justice of an accident always presupposes justice in the subject (as is clear from the first argument of the first chapter), it follows that, before it is just for someone to have a gift of God, he must be just in his substance. And Scripture seems to suggest this when it says 'If any of you want wisdom, let him ask of God, who gives to all abundantly and does not upbraid' (James 1:5). Here it is clear that we must make a request to God for whatever we wish to have; second, that God grants only to those who are in grace, because in granting he 'does not upbraid' but he afterwards calls graceless and unbelieving servants to judgment (as is clear in Matthew 25:14 of the man who went abroad after delivering his goods to his servants). This can be confirmed by the text of Psalm 49:16, where he [i.e., God] upbraids the sinner because he tells of his [i.e., God's] justice {10} and takes his covenant into a mouth so unworthy. If, therefore, it is not permissible without grave sin for sinners to preach or treat of the teaching of the divine law, by equal or greater reason it is also not permissible for sinners to receive the use, or rather abuse, of any of God's gifts.

[1d(i). Objections to the Fourth Argument]

The first argument against the above is this. God provides human beings after the fall with both body and soul, and nevertheless they are then in original sin. Therefore, it is sure that God mercifully provides his good things to the unjust. For thus Truth exhorts his disciples to be merciful in imitation of God, who 'makes the rain fall upon the just and the unjust' (Matthew 5:45).

Second, we see that not only Christian sinners but even unbelievers are granted natural goods and goods of fortune, equally with the just. Since therefore 'every perfect gift comes down from the Father of Lights' (James 1:17), it seems that God grants without favoritism to both the just and the unjust.

Third, unless the sinner gained merit by means of his own goods, it would not benefit the sinner to do good, since as such he abuses things that belong to others.

[1d(ii) Replies to 1d(i)]

To the first I say that granting and providing presuppose the existence of the beneficiary, and consequently God does not 'provide' anyone with the substance of his soul. From this it is clear that God does not provide to anyone in original sin any part of his body or any of his gifts. Likewise we ought not to provide or grant anything to sinners while we know them to be such: First, because in that way we would foster a traitor to our lord and would not model our granting in conformity with him [God]. Also, because we are not permitted to alienate goods provided only for us without the permission of our lord. But he does not approve any good to the unjust for the time when they live unjustly. Therefore, neither should we. We ought, nevertheless, to share with them [the unjust], {11} especially in fraternal correction and other goods, so far as these things are means to their conversion and no further. And in that sense we are commanded to love our enemies, that is, wish them good for the sake of God's honor and our advantage. God loves enemies thus, but he does not in the proper sense grant anything to them while they are such.

In support of this it must be noted that 'granting' (*donacio*) means a gracious giving, and 'giving' (*dacio*) can mean equivocally handing over either only for the good of nature (or first being) or for the good of grace (or second perfection): In the first way God gives to all inanimate things and unjust persons whatever they have, but in the second mode of giving, which is granting, he does not give anything except to the just. Thus it is significant that Scripture says that God makes his sun rise on the bad and makes rain fall on the unjust, but it does not say that he *grants* anything to them. And thus we ought to love enemies and share goods of fortune with them in the Lord's name, and not so as to heap up improperly praise or pleasure for ourselves.

To the second argument ([from the granting of goods] of nature [and fortune]): Nothing is properly granted unless God grants it. But God does not grant thus to the unjust. Therefore, neither should any creature (though many distribute to the unworthy things that they do not 'grant' but traitorously usurp, squandering God's good things prodigally and contrary to Aristotle's [virtue of] liberality). To understand this it should be noted that all the natural things of sinners are gifts of God, and thus he grants those things of mere grace. But so that it may be known *to whom* they are granted, according to the sense of Scripture, it must be noted that the whole race of human beings who are to be saved, from our first parent until the last elect, is one church, the bride of Christ, which during the time of active service on earth is mixed with the wicked (as is clear in the Savior's parable of the tares, Matthew 13:24); and the bridegroom loves her equally all the time, giving to her whatever has been imparted to the wicked. Thus when a mortally sinning foreknown person has goods of nature or of fortune, God in imparting them *gives* them to him and wishes him to have such things, but he *grants* them only to his church among human beings. Therefore, he has divided the whole body of the wicked or foreknown, which Truth calls 'the world,' and its ruler, the Devil, along with their things, from the whole body of the predestined, {12} which he often calls 'the kingdom of heaven.' This is clear in John 15:19: 'If,' he says, 'you had been of the world, the world would love what was its own.' And so he 'gives' to the world and 'grants' to the church all the things that are the world's.

This teaching is clear from the Savior's teaching in the parable, Matthew 25:28–29, where, after the goods of the man (Jesus Christ) have been handed over (in baptismal grace and otherwise) to his servants while they are pleasing, the man comes back and when he is about to draw up his account (in the final judgment) condemns the lazy servant because he was unwilling to put the gifts the lord gave him out to usury (spiritually) to obtain an increase (for his advancement and God's service). He speaks to the other servants thus: 'Take the talent away from him, and give it to him who has ten talents.' And the text continues relevantly to our purpose: 'To all those who have it will be given and they will abound, but those who do not have, even what they seem to have will be taken from them.' He says the same in Matthew 13:12. And from the continuation of the parable it is clear, according to the consensus of the learned, that he means it to say two things. The first is that although the sinner may seem in the eyes of the erring church to possess the Lord's gifts, nevertheless he is not truly the grantee but by divine permission unjustly holds these things for the time being. Thus, to indicate this equivocation (in which there is no contradiction), the text of Mark 4:25 and Luke 19:26 has: 'But from those who *do not have*, even what they *have* will be taken away.' And it is clear, second, that he who had the totality of the Lord's goods (symbolized by the fact that the talents number ten) took those goods for himself by the Lord's granting. And thus these goods were taken by the just man actively and from the unjust materially and passively, since the just man took them from him.

And thus the conclusion put forward at the beginning is clear, and it is clear that the minor premise in the second objection and its conclusion are not true – everywhere stipulating, as I suppose has been settled, that God does not grant any good to his creature for the time when it [the creature] is unjust but gives what is needed for natural existence and permits abuse. And thus prelates of the church who think humbly of themselves do not say that they have been put thus in charge by {13} divine ordinance, grant, grace, or will, but 'by divine permission.' They know this to be true by sense and infallible knowledge (and I wish it were not in an equivocal sense!).

To the third objection I say that anyone who is in mortal sin ought to merit and continually use the Lord's good things to do a work good in its kind. It is clear that anyone who is such [i.e., in mortal sin] ought to be in grace and ought accordingly to do the things that befit a faithful servant. Because he does not do this as he ought, he thus sins against God continually.

[1d(iii). A Difficulty]

But the difficulty of the conclusion consists in this: Is it advantageous to the sinner *for the time during which he is in mortal sin* to do an act good in its kind? And the Lincolnian [Robert Grosseteste] explains the affirmative side of this difficulty in Dict. lxviii {14} by a sixfold argument. 'Good works,' he says, 'done without charity, though they do not merit heaven, nevertheless are of value in other ways.' These ways [according to Grosseteste] are as follows.

They excuse the sinner from great evil and damn less the foreknown who exercises himself in them, they submerge him less in sin and consequently distance him less from divine grace, they benefit others in many ways, and they dispose to the first grace. (And these benefits should not be weighed lightly. For just as it is beneficial to a prisoner to be less deeply buried in the prison and less tortured, so we think likewise of the damned; and just as it is beneficial to one who has fallen to be submerged less deeply in the lake and to be less distant from the rescuer, so it is beneficial to the wicked to be enmeshed less deeply in vices and to be closer to someone who will help them toward grace.)

Fifth, a good thing done badly is more beneficial to the church than an act bad in its kind done badly (to such an extent that politicians, judging by appearances, look only on the substance of the good act and do not care whether it has been done well or badly; God, searching hearts, considers this exclusively).

Sixth, just as an exile or someone thrown into prison does not for the time being merit with his lord, from whose presence he is removed, but [may merit with] persons who have free access to the lord, [namely, persons] whom the prisoner separately benefits in part, so a sinner, as such, does not merit for himself blessedness or grace (since no one merits for himself the first grace). It must be that good works that he does for another person who is in grace are an occasion [i.e., an occasional cause having the effect] that the prayer of the grateful recipient of the sinner's alms merits for him the first grace, because under the circumstances he cannot merit in his own person.

And that learned man [Grosseteste] adds a [seventh] good argument, that the physical habituation of the sinner in works that are good in their kind makes it easier for him to act virtuously after he has obtained grace, when he would otherwise act with difficulty even when grace was given.

[1d(iv). Arguments for the Negative]

But it is said that every virtuous person must be in charity (although Aristotle and other pagan philosophers prove that we are made morally virtuous by any action good in its kind developed into a pleasurable habit). {15}

Second, it is said that just as sinners do not for that time merit blessedness, so neither do they for that time merit that someone else should merit for them the first grace or any temporal good. For since in every case for rational creatures to merit is for them to make themselves worthy of reward, it is clear that if someone at some time merits something, he makes himself worthy of it at that time. And since 'to merit' means at once the act of meriting and worthiness to receive the reward, it is clear that if he does not merit now, he does not make himself worthy now of the reward – for otherwise the sinner would undoubtedly merit, for the time when he was in sin, an eternal reward (for there are many who, while they sin, make themselves to be worthy *afterwards* of the kingdom of God).

[1d(v). Solution]

From these points it seems to me that no matter how great a grace the foreknown are in according to present justice, they do not merit the kingdom [of heaven] or the grace of final perseverance but rather some other good. This is because no one merits anything without having a right to it. But the foreknown have no right to the kingdom, since then (in accordance with the conclusion of Tract I [*De mandatis divinis*], chapter 3) they would have, for their own time, a right *in* the kingdom. Therefore, the foreknown do not merit the kingdom, since no one can make himself worthy to have what God wills him not to have, since every created right is drawn from the right that is the divine will. And it follows likewise that the predestined, however gravely they sin in accordance with the injustice in them at the moment, do not deserve an everlasting penalty, because nothing is deserved if its opposite pleases God. Anointing with the grace of predestination, which no one can lose, therefore saves all the predestined even if they sin. But in every case desert of everlasting recompense relates to final perseverance in good or obstinacy in evil, and so no one deserves everlasting recompense except as one or other of these gives completeness of desert. Thus, just as someone hired for a penny for a day's work who works well for the first hour and afterwards loafs continually does not deserve the penny but deserves to lose it, so it is, according to the Savior's parable, with those who earn everlasting recompense.

All the things brought forward for the opposite conclusion assume that a person in grace, or a sinner, has a disposition by which, if it were continued to the end, he would be thus – for example, just as Peter denying Christ had a disposition {16} by which, if continued to the end, he would be damned, so Judas, when he received Christ's gifts, had a disposition in which, if he persevered to the end, he would be saved. And it is clear from this how one should speak in describing mortal sin and grace.

[1d(vi). More Objections to the Fourth Argument]

Chapter 3. Against the doctrine of the last argument [i.e., the fourth argument, p. 597 above] it is argued as follows:

[a] Every sinner is a human being in the same sense as a just person is. Therefore, sinners have body and soul and likewise all the goods of fortune in the same sense as the just have, and consequently sinners are lords in the same sense as the just are.

[b] It is confirmed first by this: Just as it pleases God that they [sinners] are human beings, so it pleases God that they have body and soul and all the accidental instruments and goods, and nothing pleases God unless it is just. Therefore, it is just that sinners have those goods, and consequently they hold those goods by the justest legal title.

[c] Similarly God wills that the unjust dispose themselves to grace by doing acts good in their kind. Therefore, God wills that they have the means of acting thus. The premise is clear from the Lincolnian, above, and from Daniel 4:24, where Daniel advises Nebuchadnezzar, an unbeliever, 'to redeem [his] sins by alms and [his] iniquities by works of mercy to the poor.' But it is certain that so holy a prophet would not give such advice, nor would it be good or pleasing to God that these deeds be done, unless

it would also have been just. Therefore, it is sure that the worst sinners give alms with their property well and justly.

[d] Similarly, the gift of character [in priests, which makes their administration of sacraments valid], the power of the keys [by which penitents may be absolved], and the gift of prophecy can coexist with mortal sin, as is clear from Balaam (Numbers 24). Since, therefore, the power of using temporal goods seems most distant from the gifts of God's grace, it seems that it can coexist with mortal sin; and since that power is a right (from what has been said above), it seems possible for the unjust to hold God's good things justly – especially since the concomitance of grace seems accidental to lordship, and nothing accidental changes the species [of anything]. {17} Therefore, it is not enough to say that God permits such things as he permits sins, since it is by divine approbation that the unjust have both natural goods and goods of fortune.

[1d(vii). Response to 1d(vi)]

[1d(viia) Preliminaries]

Here we must make distinctions concerning 'having' and 'justice.' For although according to Aristotle and the author of *The Six Principles* [Gilbert of La Porée] there are many ways of having, three suffice for the present: natural, civil, and gospel (*evangelica*); and civil possession is subdivided by equivocal senses into true and pretended civil having, as was said in Tract I, chapter 3, concerning right (*De mandatis divinis*, p. 18). In the first way of having sinners have natural goods, and yet not simply justly (as is clear above), but unjustly. In the second way of having, according to both equivocal members, the potentates of this world have goods of fortune. But in the third way of having, which is in its kind the most excellent possible, only those who are in charity or grace 'have' what they have. Hence because of a 'having' that is so equivocal, Truth says (in Luke 19: 26, as above) that 'From those who do *not* have, even what they *have* will be taken away' by the just, where the distinction just stated plainly appears. Hence, just as Peter holding a lordship only tyrannically would be said to 'have' it equivocally, in comparison with Paul who has his own lordship by hereditary right, so the just and the unjust equivocally possess temporal things here in the way [i.e., in this life]. Yet after the fall and the multiplication of sins we must speak thus, since Truth (Matthew 19:22) says of the avaricious young man, 'For he *had* great possessions.'

But for the sake of a complete argument for what is to be laid down, a second distinction must be noted concerning justice: that some things are just [1] actively, others [2] extrinsically or passively. Only what has the virtue of justice {18} formally in itself is just in the first way. This happens in two ways: Either [1.1] this justice is the essence of the just, and only God can be just in this way, or [1.2] this justice is an accident in the category of quality, and only rational creatures who are in grace are just in this way. In [2] the second way of the first distinction, every creature is just, since 'just,' 'being,' and 'good' convert simply. The justice naturally and essentially consequent to the creature is the goodness by which the creature is conformed to the will of the first principle.

This member of the distinction can be based on a threefold argument. First, because God loves nothing except the just. But he loves all things that exist (as is clear from Wisdom 11:25). Therefore, every being is just. Second, every being ordained by God to exist, exists justly (as is clear from Tract I, chapter 1 [*De mandatis divinis*, p. 4]). But every creature is ordained by God to exist. Therefore, every creature exists justly. The inference is clear from the fact that the being of every creature is its essence and vice versa. Third, every work that proceeds from a creature simply just in accordance with the direction of its justice is just, even if it is evil in its kind (as is clear to philosophers, who concede that such works of human beings are virtuous). Therefore, with equal or greater reason, every work of the First Justice, which it does according to the exemplar of his will, will be just. Let whoever knows [of one] give a reason for a difference [between the two cases, of creatures and of God], because in truth I do not know [of one], nor do I believe that God does.

Thus, according to Augustine nothing can be contrary to God in respect of its essence, since all contraries must have limited being in the genus according to which they are formally incompatible with one another (as 'white' and 'black' are two forms that add something to the essence), but in God everything intrinsic is pure being and therefore nothing intrinsic {19} to God can be contrary to anything. The minor premise is clear from Augustine (*On the Trinity*, VII): To be just, good, wise, etc., is not in God something formal superadded to the essence but is to be God, or the divine essence. Since, therefore, nothing, insofar as it is being, is incompatible with another (because thus each would be incompatible with every other), it follows that nothing can be incompatible with the first pure being in respect of what is intrinsic to it, for otherwise the created universe would not adhere to it [i.e., to the first being], as accident to subject.

And so what was said in Tract I, chapter 5 (*De mandatis divinis*, p. 35) [follows], namely, that [some] created laws are incompatible with God's law – that is, with the commands and order God has established for creatures, which the rational creature attempts to break or defect from – but not with the divine essence.

And from this consideration the Philosopher concludes (*Physics*, I [7, 190 b34–5]) that nothing can be contrary to prime matter, since it is not 'such' or 'so great' or any of the other [kinds of] beings (*Metaphysics* VII [3, 1029 a20–22]).

From these points it is clear that no creature can be unjust except *per accidens*, and thus some essence must underlie injustice or sin, by means of which, from its conformity with the divine good pleasure, its existence is just.

[1d(viib) Replies]

[a] From what has been laid down, it is conceded that so far as their essence or nature is concerned the just and the unjust are in the same sense human beings and thus just. Hence, in the same way as every evil nature is good (as is clear from *Enchiridion* 9 [xii.4]), so every unjust nature is just, because what is actively unjust is passively just insofar as it is the work of the first Justice. And thus it is conceded that according to the first existence of a creature both the just {20} and the unjust 'have' both body and soul (along with every other natural [good]) in the same sense. Nevertheless, because the unjust lack second perfection in such things the just and the unjust are therefore not said to 'have' such things according to second perfection except equivocally, since in accordance with what was said above all good things are thus lost to the unjust in respect of their second perfection. And thus, charitable or gospel 'having,' which is the most perfect, is lacking to them. So in the same way as tools or other goods of fortune are lacking to the just when they are lacking as to use (even if they have a civil right in such things), so the things that the unjust 'have' are lacking to them at the time when they are not then using, but abusing, whatever they hold. Thus Jerome (Letter to Paulinus, last chapter) speaks truly and philosophically, when he says, 'Misers lack both what they have and what they do not have.'

It is clear that in the argument at the beginning [above, p. 603] it does not follow that since they have natural goods in the same sense [of 'have'] as the just have them, therefore the unjust are lords in the same sense as the just are. This is because lordship means a second perfection founded in grace, and since this is lacking to the unjust true lordship is also lacking to them. And thus, whenever lordship or kingship over something outside themselves is ascribed to such people, it must be understood that this is usurped, false, and pretended lordship.

[b] To the second, it is conceded that all the unjust have, by divine goodwill, whatever it is just they should have (as is clear in Tract I [*De mandatis divinis*], chapter 1), and thus with all their goods they are just – passively, or by natural justice. But since instead of second perfection they have injustice, it is clear that they hold those goods not 'by the justest title' but by the weakest. And it is clear that this sophistical deceit does not impugn the truth accepted as minor premise at the beginning [i.e., 'nothing pleases God unless it is just,' above, p. 603], since that is limited to first justice without an admixture of injustice instead of second perfection. For since all rational creatures have a power {21} given to them to have whatever they have in the way of having that is best in kind, it is clear that they are much to be blamed if they abuse their power, resting in a purely natural having, as sticks and stones or other senseless creatures have their goods.

Further, if they rest content with a civil having, not obtaining from the Chief Lord the goods of grace and glory to which these [other] goods appertain according to the charter or most secure inscription in the book of life (as Truth says, Luke 10:20), without doubt they should be condemned. Pertinently confirming this teaching, Truth says (Matthew 5:20), 'Unless your justice abounds more than that of the scribes and Pharisees, you will not enter into the kingdom of heaven.' Here it is clear, first, that the Pharisees (though there is no doubt they are unjust) are just naturally or passively; for (as Chrysostom notes) nothing 'abounds *more* than' a justice that does not exist. It is clear, second, against worldly [reasoners], that this natural justice, or civil justice, is not enough for blessedness, but under penalty of everlasting damnation one must add gospel or moral justice. Thus the Lincolnian, commenting on the above text, distinguishes a threefold justice, namely, natural, which follows upon being, political, based upon human traditions (the only justice that was in the Pharisees), and gospel or moral justice, which simply excludes all injustice in its subject.

It must nevertheless be noted that civil lordship is null unless it is based on gospel {22} justice. Therefore, one who sins mortally does not have lordship any more than a perpetual virgin has physical fatherhood, because the foundation upon which such a relation is based is lacking. Thus that lordship is not just, because it does not exist – as, however, body and soul do exist. It is clear that it is just that the unjust should have goods of nature [such as body and soul], which they do not possess but have by simple gift. And if the wild boar of the forest hereupon concludes that he is justly *lord* of the same things, it is clear to any shepherd how, because of its absurdity, the little fox[y argument] is to be caught. For a stone 'has' justly all the things that are its, an unjust person has, by just hire, his neighbor's horse, just as the damned justly has an everlasting penalty, because in all these cases by the good pleasure of his God – and yet none of these is the lord of what has been given him, because for lordship a grant from God is required.

[c] To the next, the first conclusion is conceded, on the supposition made; for God moves and helps sinners to do deeds good in their kind and takes pleasure in every act or positive habit a sinner has, just as every such thing, according to the Lincolnian, is a gift of God. But by the very fact that mortal sin accompanies whatever the sinner does, there is an abuse and a defect, which God does not approve but permits. In this way the following scripture texts should be harmonized: 'They reign, and not by me' (Hosea 8:4) – namely, according to that defect or abuse, and 'He has made a hypocrite reign because of the sins of the people' (Job 34:30) – namely, by approving every first being of a positive external thing but not the second being or defect. The first being is a just punishment or benefit, but God does not approve that someone tyrannizes. And it should be considered that those who through sin abuse the Lord's good things perform acts good in their kind but morally bad in relation to those things, such as eating, clothing oneself, distributing [alms], and the like: and God wills and ordains the substances of all actions, along with the good things that result from them; but he does not will that by savoring abuse you should defect from virtue, as was said in Tract I, chapter 5 (*De mandatis divinis*, p. 36) concerning wicked laws. But all the vicious {23} lack lordship and possession of any distant thing in relation to which they do not perform such positive acts, so that they have nothing of goods of fortune except what is present to them in practice (even if they falsely pretend that they are lords of lands or goods far distant), and in this their lordship differs from full gospel lordship, which because of its spirituality reaches every point in the world.

Concerning Nebuchadnezzar, who the learned believe is probably among those to be saved [cf. *De civili dominio*, II, ch. 6, p. 50, line 37], it is said that his deeds good in their kind caused in him health-giving penitence. And in any person to be saved or damned, they benefit in one of the aforesaid seven ways [see above, p. 601]. And thus God approves the substance of acts sinners perform in relation to goods not their own. But it must not be inferred from this that sinners are lords of such goods or that they perform such acts in a morally just way, since it is possible they are doing the useful good, whose first being God accepts as he does the act of a beast, without meriting [cf. Luke 17:10: 'We are unworthy servants; we have only done what was our duty']. Thus, in accordance with the logic of morals it is conceded that an unjust person who performs deeds good in their kind does *what* he ought to do; indeed, since he has many circumstances good in their kind, he acts in a naturally just way, as he ought to do. But because he lacks moral justice, he therefore does everything he does *as* he ought not do it, because in a morally unjust way. He therefore acts both justly and unjustly in many ways, but because he offends in one [point], he is become guilty of all [cf. James 2:10], though occasionally he greatly benefits himself and others. (Compare the way philosophers speak of vicious people disposing themselves to virtue by means of deeds good in their kind: such people indeed do good deeds, but not virtuously until they have the habit [cf. Aristotle, *Ethics* II 4].)

[d] To the next argument, we concede the minor premise just as we concede the conclusion, that the gift of character, the gift of prophecy, and the power of using the keys can coexist with mortal sin. But it must not be inferred from this that it is simultaneously possible for the unjust to use God's good things with justice, since by the very fact that they are sinners they are involved in a doing or a refraining in which, because of the {24} concomitance of sin, they abuse their power, according to the Apostle's way of speaking in 1 Corinthians 9:18.

But it should be noted that even if one who exercises the power of order or of jurisdiction sins mortally, nevertheless God, in whose name he ministers, supplies what may benefit those able to receive it, just as if a just person were using the power as he ought, except that in the one abusing it the personal merit is withheld [i.e., his ministry earns him no reward]. It is clear that the unjust man should not perform the office in mortal sin but rather, by confessing, ought to minister in grace. If in fault he does a deed good in its kind, it is possible (as was said above) that it will benefit him and that others may merit – though, in acting less well than a just man, he wrongs each of his brothers, whom it is unjust for him to judge, even if the sentence is just.

But to return to the matter in hand, it is conceded that it is possible that the unjust [i.e., those who are predestined, but at this time in sin] should have, despite their injustice, God's eternal will, which is the most efficacious right, to reign in blessedness, a will they cannot lose, just as they cannot lose the grace of predestination, which follows from God's will. And thus it is clear that it is not valid to argue, 'I now have the right to the kingdom or lordship, therefore it is just that I should now be lord or reign,' but it is enough that I should have that lordship in its time. For human beings naturally have a created power, namely, free choice, according to which they can be lords over the whole world; yet a right to reign does not follow from this power. Besides that power, therefore, another power must be added, which is a created right drawn from the eternal right, and it is impossible that someone should have a right to be given this [additional] power together with mortal [sin] and consequently with injustice. Thus, by the advent of mortal sin, God's gift ceases to be the sinner's gift, because a sinner, as such, loses the thing given. Just as those who by human law have a perpetual right for themselves and their [heirs] lose that lordship after forfeiture, even if they have use of it for the moment, so – and much more – do those who are in grace (according to which they can in their own persons enjoy perpetual inheritance of the kingdom and of every part of the world), if they fall into sin (with which the use of every usable {25} is incompatible), lose whatever they had before, even if by imperfect natural having they 'have' (equivocally) many good things. And thus grace is not irrelevant to, but is the basis of, lordship. Just as natural potency and the act of procreating, besides the extremes [i.e., the man and the child], are principles of paternity, so, I say, grace is required for use, and consequently for every true lordship.

[1e. *Fifth Argument*]

Chapter 4. But because few of the worldly agree with this doctrine, being content with human right as commonly accepted, it must accordingly be proved that neither [1] the deposition of witnesses nor [2] the sentencing of a judge nor [3] physical possession, likewise [4] neither inheritance nor exchange nor human grant, nor all of these together, confers on a person without grace lordship or a right to anything.

[1] As to the first, it follows clearly that the duty of witnesses is to testify to the truth of a hidden right. If this right does not preexist, it is certain that the deposition of the witnesses is false, and since nothing false proves

a truth (just as that which has no existence does not cause anything), it follows clearly that the deposition of witnesses does not confer a right but brings to light a right that was previously hidden (supposing, as is possible, that the deposition is true). And this is Augustine's teaching (Letter 37 [Letter 153 in modern editions]), in these words: 'In this life the wickedness of those who possess badly is endured, and certain rights, called civil, are established among them, not with the result that these people become good users, but that their bad use does less harm, until the faithful and god-fearing to whom all things truly belong, [. . .] come to that city where their inheritance is eternity.' This passage establishes that the argument, 'Human laws award a certain usable thing to Peter, therefore [he uses it] not unjustly,' does not follow, since it is not by {26} human law that use is licit.

Again, I ask the politician whether this follows: 'The witnesses depose in favor of Peter's right to some usable, therefore Peter has a right to that usable.' If it is conceded, it must likewise be conceded that if the same witnesses, or others, on another occasion depose the opposite, without relevant change in reality, they extinguish that right and raise a new right. This is impossible, since the origin of right is the divine will, which does not change to follow such inconstant testimony of creatures capable of sin – since indeed the contradiction would then follow that Peter has the right and does not have the right. It is clear that no one who is not blaspheming extols created witnesses to such a height as [to say] that if they depose anything then it is true, since to assert this would be to make a god of a creature capable of sin and would be contrary to sacred Scripture (Matthew 26:60) which says that two false witnesses came against Christ and their testimony did not agree [Mark 14:59]. And the same is clear of the priests who accused Susanna (Daniel 13).

Therefore, since every rational creature except Christ can be deflected from the truth, it seems it should be said that of none of them does it follow: 'That creature making a deposition asserts thus, therefore it is true.' With this established, it is clear that for the deposition or [2] a sentence in favor of the person making the deposition to be just a right must exist before the deposition. However, because that deposition is not enough to provide the basis of a right (as has been shown), it is clear that it is necessary to add another complete cause. None can be imagined, unless we posit the approval and judgment of the chief lord, who is God.

Confirmation: In any such act of deposition or judgment God cannot be neutral, since necessarily in every created action he anticipates any creature. Therefore, if the witness or judge deposes or passes sentence judicially, God first testifies and passes sentence to the same effect. If therefore someone acquires a right by the testimony or judgment of a creature, much more, therefore, {27} by the testimony or judgment of the Creator. Since, therefore, those things must precede in God, and since it is not permissible to imagine that this full right is insufficient unless human beings supplement it, it is clear that, before every right decided by human beings, anyone for whom just judgment is given has full right in relation to God. And it is clear that in pleas, whenever just judgment is delivered the earthly judges are merely instruments of God for promulgating his sentence, and the right of the litigants is not more or less because of what the judges say. Since therefore it is not possible for God to testify or pass sentence in favor of any person's right unless it is just that he have it, it is clear first that by the deposition of witnesses people acquire no right unless they are just. The argument rests on this: Nothing is acquired by human proof unless God justifies first. But God does not justify in favor of the unjust. Therefore, neither does a creature judge justly in favor of the unjust.

Again, no one gives what he does not have. But neither witnesses nor civil judges have a civil right to the good that they judge. Therefore, they do not give a right to him in whose favor they judge. The argument is clear, because God could not give forms for the existence of a creature unless he had in himself the exemplars, which some call ideas and others call the intelligible being of the creature (which is the same essentially with the thing produced). Therefore, much more, a creature cannot give anything to another unless it has it first. That is plain concerning any of the goods of fortune that pertain to but do not inhere in the recipient and [also] concerning any inherent good: Nothing gives another such a form unless it has a similar form or has it virtually in a more excellent way (for example, nothing gives heat to another unless it is itself hot formally or virtually), as the philosophers know − and also the theologians, who concede that Christ's minister does not give grace or the gift of the spirit to another person, although he [the latter] has that gift through his [the former's] ministry, but God alone gives such a person the spiritual gift. The minor of the argument is clear from the fact that the civil right of a lord cannot be proved [to belong] equally to many [*Digest* 13.6.5.15, 49.17.19.3]. Therefore, undoubtedly, if the right rested first in them, witnesses brought forward to testify about the right of another would not [be likely to] testify against themselves. {28} They therefore do not give the right, although they make it known to others. This is confirmed by the doctrine often expressed, that it is not possible for a creature to confer anything justly [on someone] unless it is first naturally just that that person should have it (because, in the absence of the right cause, the creature's conferring is not just), and consequently God fully grants first. Whence it is not without reason that Scripture uses the word 'minister' or 'communicate' in such ministerial giving (as is clear in 2 Corinthians 3:8–9, Galatians 6:6, and elsewhere in many places). It can especially be confirmed, however, from the fact that every power of a rational nature is free for the sake of perfecting the order of the universe; since, therefore, rational nature can have such potency only from God, it is clear that it can have such a power only from God. Who, therefore, could give freedom of choice to the inner self? Undoubtedly, only God, who can penetrate the soul. And this is the conclusion of St Paul, Romans 13:1, who says: 'There is no power except from God.' And it is clear that the earthly judge does not 'warrant' when he sends or gives power to another, any more than a bishop gives a priest the grace of the keys or other gifts appropriated to God, however enemies of the Scripture may have spoken.

From this it is clear that right or justice cannot be sold. For every right is based on a divine volition beyond the power of a creature. Nothing of this kind can be bought with money. Therefore the conclusion. This is why those who buy justice with money or traffic in judges or witnesses seem to sin so greatly, such as Simon who wished to buy the Holy Spirit with money [Acts 8:18–19], because it is everywhere supposed [by such people] that the divine will is carried along in accordance with even illicit contracts. This would follow, however, if human beings gave lordships. Therefore, it is clear that lordship is a special gift of God based upon grace. Thus it is significant that Scripture (Genesis 25:31) says that Jacob said to Esau that he should sell, not the right of primogeniture, but 'the things of primogeniture.'

From these points we gather that, since all power is given by God alone {29} and right, which is the proximate reason of using the grant (since it precedes every use, as is clear from what has been said), is granted by God alone, it follows that ministerial granting by a creature presupposes a granting by God according to those rights which it befits God alone to give. And since God grants only to those who are in grace, it clearly follows that lordship presupposes that the lord is in grace. And since the judge passing sentence presupposes that the sentence to be delivered has been proved by the testimony of the Trinity, it is clear that he does not give a lordship but declares one that is already decided.

[3] And, much more, just possession presupposes that the thing taken possession of belongs to the possessor, because otherwise, without doubt, it would be a usurped intrusion. Thus it is ridiculous to believe that a placing of the feet or other ceremonies performed by the holder in person or by his agent in the sight of the church justifies his use without first grace, and likewise none of the three following [i.e., inheritance, exchange, and human grant].

[4] For if inheritance without preceding grace gave true lordship, then such lordship would be purely natural, not liable to be blocked by forfeiture. The conclusion is against the nature of civil lordship. For if [an act incurring] forfeiture [done] against an earthly lordship (unless amends are made) rules out civil lordship, much more the more serious forfeiture in relation to the Chief Lord. Forfeiture of this kind follows upon every mortal sin, and consequently everyone who sins mortally is unfit for civil lordship. This is clear from what was said in Tract I, chapter 5 (*De mandatis divinis*, p. 38), where it is shown that those who sin mortally are most false conspirators against their God, because they make the servants of their God, to whom they swore fidelity, rise up against him.

This can be confirmed in three other ways. First, because anyone who usurps to himself something that belongs to his king is, as such, a traitor to his king. Therefore, much more, whoever usurps to himself that which can belong only to God is, as such, a traitor to his God. Anyone who is proud does this, and consequently anyone who sins mortally. Therefore, every mortal sinner is a traitor to his God. The minor is clear from the fact that every proud person refuses obedience to his God. Since, therefore, lordship that is not subject to a superior {30} can belong only to God, it follows that every proud person, so far as is in him, usurps royal rights that can belong only to God.

Similarly, every proud person has sin dominating him, as the Apostle says (Romans 5:17, where he says that sin reigns). But no sin is a servant subordinate to God. Therefore, every proud person, in renouncing allegiance to his Lord, subjects himself to a directly opposite lord. And consequently it is not for that time just that he should possess anything by God's right. Rather, as far as is in him, he subjects God to slavery to sin, since undoubtedly God would be a slave to sin in [consequence of] any renunciation of allegiance by which the sinner, withdrawing from God, is joined to the sin opposed to the justice of God, unless God's omnipotence by that fact punished him, making him duly suffer a penalty (for otherwise God would uphold without just vengeance a servant belonging to his enemy and not to him, and if that were so God would undoubtedly be a slave). And it is clear that every proud person is a traitor to his lord. This is despite the fact that God cannot be a slave to sin or forgive any sin unpunished (as is clear in Tract I, chapter 2 [*De mandatis divinis*, p. 7]); because in whatever way he culpably does something by which the lord *would* be betrayed (unless the lord by prudent power blocked it) he is a full traitor, since it is not his doing that that wickedness does not [actually] occur.

Similarly, a person forfeits if he unjustly kills the lord's servant bearing his likeness and representing the lord's person in performing an office thus entrusted to him. It is thus with anyone who sins after being in grace. Therefore, according to God's law he loses any lordship he had while he was in grace. The minor is clear because only too really does the sinner kill *himself*, since sin separates the soul from God, who previously was its life through grace, and he was then in the likeness of his God, cleaving to him by grace and serving him with a ministry most worthy in its kind. Therefore, etc. {31}

Whence let us mark the cases in human law when someone forfeits or should be punished by the ultimate punishment. We will see that the sinner falls into those occasions more really in relation to God – for example, committing, as much as is in him, treason, conspiracy to kill, the deposition of the prince of the kings of the earth, in usurpation of royal rights, in most unjust slaughter, in the most outrageous fornication, and in injury to the whole commonwealth; and similarly of other political occasions [of criminality], of which the original exemplars are in the law of God. Hence those theologians are too much astray who say that such statements are not true by the literal force of the words, because undoubtedly whoever concedes God's lordship over every creature and the servanthood of creatures in relation to God must therefore concede that in one who sins against God the listed crimes are found more really than in those who sin against an earthly lord, to the degree that God is more truly a lord.

Thus politicians, because their minds have been brought up darkened among sensible things, do not consider divine lordship or its service, but immediately upon hearing these words apply them to lordship and service done to human beings; for like beasts they consider only that.

Others say that God's mercy and grace demand [a] that he remit injuries and [b] that he not punish opponents as rigidly as human beings do. Indeed in [a] the first the truth is grasped, since otherwise God would annihilate all sinners by the very fact that they sinned. Undoubtedly, he cannot do this, and therefore he can only punish mercifully – just as he cannot restore sinners to the earlier lordship from which they justly fell through sin except by conferring on them a great grace. Consequently, for the pardoning of a crime or the restitution of lordship a great grace is needed in the forfeiter thus restored; and this is the conclusion aimed at. But as for the second part [b], God undoubtedly punishes traitors most severely, both by the penalty of damnation and by the pain of sense, as is clear in Tract I (*De mandatis divinis*), chapter 2. Therefore in Romans 11:22 the Apostle says against tellers of such tales, 'See the goodness, {32} *and the severity*.' Undoubtedly God cannot forgive any treachery in his kingdom that has not been punished according to rule.

A third fiction [c] in this matter also is of no avail: That it would be just for sinners to be deprived of their lordships, but they must first be convicted by proving the crime. Those who speak thus, however, do not consider that 'The eyes of the Lord are brighter than the sun, seeing round about all the ways of men,' as is said against such persons in Ecclesiasticus 23:28. For he does not need proof by witnesses, since he knows eternally whatever is in a person and inwardly judges the penalty for every delinquent by an eternal judgment that cannot be infringed or revoked by anyone. Earthly lords are deprived of lordship in relation to God by the very acts by which they forfeit, though of his grace he allows them to [continue to] abuse the things granted, in case they will perhaps be willing to be converted. However, God acts much more mercifully toward many, from whom he takes away the abuse of temporal things and inflicts sensible penalties; for it is a sign of divine love that he applies the cure of chastisement and does not permit the desperate to be drowned in a whirlpool of vices, according to the saying of Revelation 3:19, 'Those I love I rebuke and chastise.'

These points, therefore, refute a [d] fourth blindness of worldly people, who think that it is enough to have pretended lordships in the eyes of the church militant, to such an extent, indeed, that [certain] politicians assert, quite heretically, that if the church adjudges to someone some ecclesiastical or temporal good, then it is just that that person should have that good. If this were true, it would without doubt wholly destroy the catholic faith, since it is certain that the church's judgment can co-exist with iniquity on the part of the person in whose favor the judgment is made, also on the part of witnesses or judge, and on all sides because of discord with the first right. It would no more be a right than in someone who held the thing as tyrannically as you please. For example, if the witnesses give false evidence, or the earthly judge gives sentence through a trick hateful to God, or, third, if he gives sentence for someone as being worthy whom God does not approve, no catholic can rightly doubt that by any such judgment an unjust person holds God's good things not lawfully, but damnably. And it is clear how dangerous it is to be involved in secular {33} business. I wish churchmen of our times would purge the eyes of their minds to see the error of this sophistry: 'A secular or ecclesiastical judge has awarded me this good or benefice. Therefore, it is just for me to possess it.' Without doubt a further right must be looked for in respect of God, which cannot exist unless we shun avarice, etc.

Chapter 5. Next in order I will make three other arguments which will satisfy some to prove the conclusion first put forward.

[1f. Sixth Argument]

The first is as follows. By the very fact that a person is in mortal sin, he has the first law against him; and by the very fact that this is so, he does not hold anything except unjustly. Therefore, by the very fact that a person is in mortal sin he does not for that time have just lordship of anything. The major is clear from the Savior's saying (Matthew 5:25), 'Reach agreement quickly with your adversary while you are on the way with him' (as is explained in Tract I, chapter 5 [*De mandatis divinis*, p. 41]). It is clear, therefore, that all sinners have the law that is the first right against them; and since it cannot agree with them in one thing and be against them in another (since it is a wisdom that hates duplicity and only loves or hates wholeheartedly), it follows that the unjust, in all they hold, have the law against them. And since that law is the law simply, upon whose condemnation or approval anything else that is unlawful or lawful ought to depend, it seems that all sinners, having that law everywhere against them, do unlawfully whatever they do.

That is clear to one who knows that God cannot be reconciled with a person for one sin while another sin remains unforgiven, because he does not reconcile or forgive except wholly, because grace is incompatible with each and every mortal sin. Consequently, the learned say that, like the virtues, the vices also are connected. Thus in James 2:10 it is said, 'He who offends in one thing has become guilty of all': because suppose {34} he keeps the commandment about loving God, yet at the same time does not keep the commandment about love of neighbor, or vice versa; if Peter offends in either of these commandments, he sins mortally and consequently wrongs God and every neighbor and consequently does not love anything as he ought to love it (as was explained in Tract I, chapter 2 [*De mandatis divinis*, p. 13]). Indeed, to be specific, it is clear that if anyone offends against *any* commandment, he sins by taking away the goods of a neighbor unjustly and like a thief, even though this connection seems most remote. For anyone who takes another's goods unjustly against the will or without the knowledge of the owner, by that very fact commits theft or robbery. Since, therefore, all the unjust unjustly take the goods of the body and the goods of fortune, which all belong to each of the just (as is shown afterwards), and since it is certain that this is without the agreement of the just (since they would then sin [if they did agree]) and also without their knowledge, therefore the unjust rob or steal every good of this kind. And likewise by desiring while in that sin that all the goods of the world be such as they ought *not* to be, the unjust abuse the goods of every neighbor. Every disordered satisfaction concerning a corporeal nature is abuse. The said volition is a disordered satisfaction concerning every corporeal nature. Therefore, the volition is an abuse. For they ought to take satisfaction in serving God in charity, but instead sinners please themselves, serving sin against God; therefore the satisfaction is inordinate. And it is clear that everything we call an unjust use is really an abuse; but we will speak about this shortly.

[1g. Seventh Argument]

Again, it belongs to the concept of a lord, as such, to be placed over someone or something that serves him. But the unjust, as such, are not placed over temporal things but are subjected to their servants. Therefore, they are not lords of the same. The major is clear from the definition of lordship, since otherwise any creature would be indifferently lord over any other. The minor is clear from the fact that in their love all sinners voluntarily prefer some temporal good to the eternal good, and since this is so they {35} serve this temporal thing, because they subject themselves according to their highest faculty, the will. Therefore, etc. (The argument was explained above, Tract I, chapter 5 [*De mandatis divinis*, p. 37], on the way in which someone is tempted and reduced to sinning, how it is because of adherence to a mutable good and a turning away from an unbendable truth.) From this it plainly appears (since temporal goods damn those who abuse them to such an extent and drag them, according to their highest faculty, to the lowest degree) that then instead of serving human beings temporal things are slaves that would overthrow their lords and drag them by the hair into the lake [of fire].

And thus the learned truly say that whatever we love more we establish as our god and the good to whose worship we chiefly look — and this [a finite good as god] is discord within a single phrase. It is clear how philosophically speaks that divine Philosopher, Truth in the abstract: 'No one can serve,' in the same sense, 'God and mammon' (Luke 16:13). And his disciple lamented that philosophers who turned away from God to the world 'served the creature rather than the Creator' (Romans 1:25). And in this way Augustine must be understood in his Letter 37 quoted above [when he says] of money, 'The good have it more truly when they love it less.' It is also clear how the learned should be understood when they say that idolatry follows upon every sin, because by the very fact that someone sins by a sin of the world, the flesh, or the Devil he prefers in his affection a temporal good, of which he has the idol or image, to the unchangeable good, intelligible above every image, as Augustine shows in *On True Religion* XIV and likewise in his *Confessions*. Thus, because of the connection of sins with one another (mentioned above) and the slavery in which the vanquished sinner serves a creature rather than God, the blessed evangelist says {36} for his final conclusion, adequately summing up the whole Christian rule, 'My little children, keep yourselves from idols' (1 John 5:21). And philosophers do not doubt this judgment if they acknowledge sacred Scripture or philosophical argument without wanton opposition. For all sinners establish as their god the creature they love more than the true God, and this is idolatry. In this it does not matter whether it is silver or gold, which are the miser's idols, or their own body, which is the idol of the carnal, when for the sake of pleasurably cherishing it they offend against the divine commandment: this [i.e., preferring something to God] is an infallible sign of greater love, [even] without an image of worldly honor. All these are connected and undoubtedly poison faith and each of the precepts. It is clear, therefore, that the unjust all lack true lordship of any creature whatever; for they would most of all be lords of their own bodies, but, having been vanquished, they are subjected to the body like slaves. Therefore, etc.

This is confirmed universally by the fact that 'Everyone who commits

sin is a slave of sin,' according to the voice of Truth, John 8:34. But ††
every sin is inferior to slaves, because it has less being than any creature.
Therefore, every sinner degrades himself to the service of something
inferior to any creature. And since 'lord,' as such, signifies superiority, it
follows that the sinner, as such, is not properly lord over any creature; but
the virtuous, dominating every kind of sin, *a fortiori* dominates every
sinner, who is dominated by each sin. Thus Armachanus [Richard Fitz-
Ralph] (who has treated this matter to its foundation) says this in *On the
Savior's Poverty*, IV, chapter 4: 'Since "lord" (*dominus*) is said from the house
(*domus*) over which the lord ought to rule, it is clear that since a sinner
does not thus rule the house but is subjected to it and to the other things
he holds unjustly, truly he should be reckoned {37} a slave and not a lord.'
And the answer is clear to the political question that asks what is needed
for someone to be the lord of another [thing or person], since the existence
of extrinsic things [i.e., the mere coexistence of the extremes of the lord–
servant relationship] is not enough, and (as was proved in the last chapter)
the judgments and ceremonies or opinions of human beings are not relevant. It is therefore necessary and sufficient to add to the extremes the
virtue of the one who dominates by means of which he [the lord] serves
God, and then undoubtedly all created inferiors serve him.

[1h. Eighth Argument]

Again, according to the doctrine we have often touched on every natural
or civil human lordship is principally conferred by God on human beings
for the purpose of continually rendering God due service, according to his
eternally established plan. But all who sin mortally, whether by omission
or commission, by that very fact withdraw that service from their chief
lord and consequently forfeit. Therefore, those who sin mortally should
by that very fact be deprived by right of every lordship. But since God
does not need to wait for proof or conviction (according to what was said
in the last chapter [above, p. 616]), it follows that every sinner is deprived
of true lordship immediately. For if the purpose for which lordship is
conferred, which measures the means, is taken away, then also the means,
which are essentially dependent on it, [are taken away]. For example, if
the *per se* cause of my giving you ten marks is the purpose of obtaining
your service, it is clear that if you withdraw the service and I fully know
and have the power, I will with reason withdraw the lordship conferred
[i.e., over the ten marks]. This is the basis of many of the laws of the

kingdom of England concerning forfeiture, the prior obtaining of permission from the chief lord, and exempt service customarily due to chief lords. A theologian does not doubt the assertion [i.e., the major premise, that every natural or civil human lordship is principally conferred, etc.] in any of its particulars. For God has commanded human beings by natural instinct to serve him in a way that corresponds to his lordship, and he cannot dispense with the debt of this service, since it is based on Scripture and unchangeable law. Otherwise people could be released from the obligation to love God or to do as they ought.

[This argument] is confirmed by the fact that no civil lordship is simply just unless it is based on natural lordship. But no one has natural lordship for the time when he sins mortally. {38} Therefore, neither does he have simply just civil lordship. The minor is clear from the action of the judge who is just most of all, who expelled the first man from paradise after sin (Genesis 3:23, 24); and since he [the man] had previously been lord of Paradise (as is clear in Tract I, chapter 2 [not found; see Tract II, *De statu innocencie*, c. 6]), it is clear that he [God] would have done this unjustly if the man had not lost natural lordship, because God cannot punish except by reason of sin. Therefore, since the same argument applies to anyone who sins mortally, it follows that natural lordship cannot exist with mortal sin. The major of the argument [that no civil lordship is simply just unless it is based on natural lordship] can be made persuasive in three ways.

[1] First, from the action of the highest judge when by reason of sin he expelled Adam from the occupation of Paradise, which he would not have done justly if he [Adam] had then had civil lordship in Paradise. Therefore, since the same argument applies to anyone who sins mortally, the point to be proved follows. For if [as Wyclif denies] conquest or the mere holding of a thing that is not already someone's property makes a civil right (grace being set aside), it cannot be pretended that after sin Adam did not have true lordship of Paradise [a right which, if it existed, expulsion would have violated].

[2] Likewise, after the expulsion Adam or one of his sons had true lordship in this vale of misery. Therefore, something caused true lordship to begin [again]. And since bare holding is not enough, it remains that [the cause of its beginning was] the restoration of natural lordship when grace was given to the penitent (as is touched on in Tract I, chapter 2 [not found]). Therefore, just as every artificial form presupposes a natural one (just as the art of the creature presupposes God's art), so every artificial lordship presupposes natural lordship as its necessary foundation, for oth-

erwise it could not be explained how civil lordships were just originally. So that, when civil lordship was first acquired, since it was not just by human ordinance alone (since the reason why human legislators make an ordinance is that it is [already] just), it remains that God justifies first. But he cannot do this except by giving grace and natural lordship. It remains, therefore, that grace is necessary to human [lordship].

[3] Third, it is confirmed by *reductio ad absurdum*. Suppose that Peter, who is in grace, has only natural lordship of a certain usable, and Paul, who is unjust, has only civil lordship in the same thing; and let it be necessary for both of them at the same time to use this usable by {39} incompatible uses. Then it is asked whether the politician Linus would judge justly in favor of Peter or for Paul in relation to the use in question if he had full knowledge of the right of each. And it seems in three ways that he would decide in Peter's favor. First, because Peter's right is authorized by God and Paul's only by human authority; Peter's right is therefore far fuller. Second, it would be manifest blasphemy to say that the most just judge would withdraw from his pious servant in a situation of extreme necessity the authority or license to use the goods of the Lord he serves so assiduously and give [them] to someone who publicly despises him. Third, it is clear that Linus ought to give judgment in favor of whichever of them has the superior permission in God's eyes if he knows which that is, since every judge who knowingly goes against divine judgment judges unjustly. Therefore, according to the civil law Peter would in this case have a right to the thing and Paul simply none. From these points it is clear that civil right is a right of nature or grace, or something that necessarily presupposes such a right; for in the case supposed, if Linus gave judgment in Paul's favor, he would give judgment unjustly against God's law and against God's judgment. From these points it is clear that civil lordship presupposes grace, because [it presupposes] natural lordship; therefore, etc.

[1i. Ninth Argument]

Chapter 6. Finally, as an epilogue in this matter it is argued as follows. No creature can be lord of anything unless God grants it, as is clear from what has often been said. But God cannot grant anything except in the best manner possible to the capacity of the granter. Therefore, if a creature is a lord, that will be by the title of such a grant. The minor is clear by natural reason and by the testimonies of the saints. For just as God is 'he than whom no greater can be thought,' so he is also he to whom no better

{40} mode of giving can pertain: for since in practicing virtue it is necessary for someone great to give in proportion to his greatness, it is clear that God must grant in the best way possible to the capacity of his lordship, for otherwise defect in the manner of giving would suggest niggardliness on the part of the granter, which cannot be true of God. If God grants anything to a creature, then, he must give [1] most liberally, [2] most securely, and [3] most usefully, in respect of his capacity.

With this established, it is clear, according to the Lincolnian (in Dict. XXVI), that the best manner of granting something usable to a creature is when a gift good in itself is granted and received under the condition that the grantee can use it however and whenever he likes, because if either of these [conditions] is lacking the grant can be made more *liberally* and thus better; second, that no one can take the gift away as long as the grantee wishes to use it, because otherwise it would not be *most secure*, if it could be taken away without fault in the lord; and third, as soon as the grantee wishes to abuse that gift, he thereby loses it, for otherwise it would not be the *most useful* manner of granting, since a gift someone abuses always damages him. Therefore, God will observe this manner of granting usables according to an unbreakable law.

For in this way 'a Son has been given us' in the Incarnation, as is said in Isaiah 9:6, and the Holy Spirit [is given] daily in the best manner possible to a creature, both in respect of the manner of the granter and in respect of the value of the gift. For [1] it is given to us for perpetual enjoyment, [2] in such a way that no one can lose it unless he willingly chooses to transgress; and, [3] undoubtedly, by the very fact that a person sins he loses it. And in these gifts God gives to human beings virtues on the way [i.e., in this life] and consummate glory in heaven (*patria*), and undoubtedly only for enjoyment, in such a way that no one can abuse these goods or lose them without wishing to.

As for goods of nature, it was said above in chapter 2 that [God] always gives them to his spouse or church for use, and no one can lose them unless he wills, since those whose bodies are lacerated by the torturers lay their bodies aside (if {41} charity is not lost) the more gloriously and more securely for blessedness, in accordance with the Apostle's saying (2 Timothy 1:12), 'I know whom I have believed, and I am certain that he is able to preserve what I have laid aside, against that day.' For since it is demonstrable that the just, completing this life, will be beatified in body and soul, and again that the identical essence of the human body is preserved in prime matter, which cannot be annihilated however much it

John Wyclif

may be broken into minute parts and changed in its forms, every Christian ought to be certain with the Apostle that if we lay aside the body for Christ in grace, it is not lost to the interior self but most securely preserved.

As for goods of fortune, it is clear that God cannot give them for abuse but for use only, since he cannot intend or wish human beings to abuse any of his good things. For it is not possible for human beings to use any usable except in accordance with virtue or to abuse except by sinning. Therefore, if God wishes someone to abuse something, in some way he wishes that person to sin [which is impossible].

From these things it is clear, first, that if the unjust receive goods of fortune or other good things of God, they will, because of sin, receive them much more imperfectly than it befits God to grant them, and consequently such possession is not enough to be a foundation of lordship in those who thus possess; rather, whatever the unjust possess in a natural and simple manner God grants to the church. It follows, second, that Adam was created in grace, when God granted him lordship of all sensible things, as is clear in Tract II, chapter – [see *De statu innocencie*, c. 6]; for there would be no reason why God should not give to him in the best manner of giving, since [in Adam as first created] previous sin does not pose an obstacle.

It is clear, therefore, that the unjust all lack lordship: first, because the manner of the divine granting is incompatible with their state; second, because through injustice they lose God's grace and consequently the lordship that follows upon grace. For if people rightly summoned [to court] under human law lose lands and holdings if they fail to appear in person or through a representative, how much {42} more would people rightly summoned to answer for their lordship under God's law lose their lordship if they unlawfully absent themselves? In truth much more reasonably, inasmuch as God is more truly a lord and the crier summoning them more worthy, since it is the Trinity with the saints, who cannot exact anything but what is just. And it is certain that God does summon upon pain of loss of all goods, in respect of the title of grace to continual service; no other mode of possession suffices as a basis for lordship, any more in human beings than in beasts. Third, it is clear because no knowledgeable, able, and prudent head of a family would entrust the charge of his goods to a servant who is a treacherous, wasteful, and most disobedient despiser of his lord – especially while he knows him to be such and, on the one hand, has power to sack him without waiting upon proof by witnesses or the passing of sentence and, on the other hand, has plenty of faithful and prudent servants who love their lord sincerely. No one doubts that to act thus would be the utmost stupidity. It therefore cannot befit the most just judge, all-knowing and all-powerful, who has all the goods of the world to distribute and has at hand those two kinds of servants.

You may object that in fact he has acted thus, since tyrants abound in riches, according to the text of Job 12:6, 'The tents of robbers abound,' and of Jeremiah 12:1, 'You are indeed just, O Lord, if I dispute with you; yet I will speak what is just to you: Why does the way of the wicked prosper? Why is it well with all who transgress and act wickedly?' The solution is clear from what was said before. God allows the unjust to abound in riches, which they 'have' in an equivocal sense, not to their advantage but to their damnation. It is clear, second, that Jeremiah's question implies two things that are false. For it is said in Hosea 8:4, because of such lack of use on the part of tyrants, 'They rule, and not from me' — that is, 'They do not have authority for such bad use.' But God gives to the just the good things that he permits the unjust to subject to abuse, according to the text of Matthew 25:28 quoted above, 'Take the talent from him and give it to him who has ten, for to everyone who has more will be given and he will abound.' To solve the question it should be noted that the finally predestined just possess temporal things in a more excellent manner of possession than the foreknown unjust, who possess them equivocally, {43} abusing them to their own disadvantage. Even if they do not have any sensual urge, yet I marvel how they grow in insatiable anxiety about those things until, with great grief, at the moment of death they lose them, and from then on, because of the deceitful pleasures of abuse, they are everlastingly tormented. On the contrary, the just, truly rich, taking pleasure in such temporal things only in respect of the use appropriate to the state of innocence, grow continually, in the manner of a natural movement, in the pleasant use of possessions, until they enter into the joy of their Lord and reign in blessedness over all his good things. It is clear that these 'havings' are opposite conditions.

But because Jeremiah's question has not yet been resolved, why God permits such abuses, approving in them everything positive, it is said that there are three reasons in general why matters are ordered thus. First, to punish the sins of those who thus abuse God's good things and the sins of the people subject [to them], who for multiple transgressions have deserved to be punished in that way. According to the text of Job 34:30, God 'makes a hypocrite to reign on account of the people's sins.' Thus, in 2 Samuel, last chapter (24:17), David's sin in counting the people was punished by pestilence upon the people and not upon David himself. For a community that poisons the air with pompous words about the deeds of kings and magnates and thus through flatterers provokes them to pride deserves to be punished by a pestilential poisoning of the air – and in proportion to the crime. Thus we do not read in Scripture of the infliction of pestilence unless it is noted that the sin of the tongue poisoning the air has done this.

The second reason is to practice the just in patience against persecutors, which will be rewarded with interest afterwards, when they are blessed, as is clear in Tract I, chapter 2 (*De mandatis divinis*, p. 11). Undoubtedly from these things there follows the beauty of the created universe, adorned with every kind of entity (namely, punishment and reward, jail and kingdom), so that thus it may make known to us the divine severity, justice, and goodness, which ordain these things to just ends – to the punishment of the wicked, the glory of the saints, and the increased extent of the whole; these matters are clear in Tract I (*De mandatis divinis*), chapter {44} 5, and below in chapter 10. Thus it is much better for the whole to be so amply constituted of opposite goods and evils than for it to be more narrowly composed only of goods. And the solution is clear to the question plodding disputants ask, why God, so powerful and foresighted, allows so many evils to come about: for from the just punishments of traitors and the joys of the blessed and the goods thence resulting, God intends to perfect the beauty of the universe. (But let it not be inferred from this that God causes anyone's sin!)

The third reason is to make known to followers of the Gospel that a person's acceptance with God is not proportional to civil lordship or even to just administration of temporal things (as is clear from Luke 12:15 and 21:3), for through this [i.e., seeing the prosperity of the wicked] we would not hope in the uncertainty of riches, or with a pretense of giving alms pile up riches for ourselves, abandoning the gospel life. For it is possible that those who are richest in the world's eyes are ever so much tortured in body, most vicious in soul, and in both soul and body to be punished eternally. And thus we would not prefer goods of fortune to goods of grace, since they are the lowest among the five [namely, goods of glory, grace, reputation, nature and fortune (Poole)]. Hence, according to Augustine (*On the City of God* I 8), if riches were {45} imparted only to the just, the just would not be so free to merit and God would not act so mercifully toward the just, but if the unjust alone had riches, God would be thought not to be the lord of riches, indeed he would fail his faithful servants in the means necessary to the service he requires. And thus it is clear from the manner of 'having' how the prophet's question is resolved.

From these points we gather that if God gives people any good thing whatever, as soon as they abuse it, they lack just claim by title of divine grant; and indeed, if this title is lacking none can be found that will avail. This is proved as follows. God grants these goods only for use, and not at all for abuse. But all sinners abuse God's good things. Therefore, they lack true lordship, because [they lack] the title of divine grant. For example, if I lend you my horse on certain conditions with such-and-such a limit and you without permission everywhere exceed the limit, do you not hold my horse unjustly? Similarly God, stipulating with his servant for continuous service, establishes everywhere limits of use, altogether forbidding abuse; therefore, by the very fact that this servant abuses power, he holds God's goods unjustly, because without any permission given for this: and consequently the Omnipotent by that very fact deprives him of his right; because otherwise God must undoubtedly authorize the unjust person's continuing abuse in whatever he does.

If it is said that then it would be better for God to take their goods from sinners physically or simply – just as anyone who lends a sword to someone of sound mind who afterwards goes mad ought, if possible, to reclaim the sword the madman abuses – it is clear that that way of acting, because of its inappropriateness, cannot be God's. This is clear, first, because thus God would force, not free, a person to merit; second, because then immediately someone sinned in his mind, he would be roughly deprived of every sensible good and consequently exposed to everyone around him, which would be coarse cruelty on God's part. Indeed, if it be well considered, annihilation must then result, and thus the deprivation of goods or penalty would be of no use, for since the first onset of {46} sin is in the power of willing, it is clear that it would be necessary, according to the said law [i.e., that a good abused should be taken away], first to take away the power of willing (along with whatever else is taken away); also, if the will were preserved, there would be present not only ability to sin but, on occasion of the cruelty exercised, an occasion to blaspheme; also, it does not seem reasonable or indifferent that God should take away something that sins or causes action less and preserve what sins more gravely. Therefore, since the essential [the human substance?] cannot exist without the accidental [the will?], it is clear that, according to that law, annihilation [would] follow upon every injustice. It is clear, third, because God, far-sighted governor of his universe, ought, from his intrinsic condition, to have mercy on sinners by taking away their right and lordship, at the same time preserving their nature and permitting the abuse (without perceptible scandal to their neighbor, from whom this [abuse] is hidden). Thus to us, who do not have clear experience of creation, his omnipotence and infinite goodness are made manifest mainly by the divine forbearance and mercy; for he could not †† preserve sin, which alienates a person so far from virtue, together with punishment so obedient and fitting, unless he were of infinite goodness and power; from this infinity on the occasion of sin he perfects his world. And third [sic], he gives us an example how we likewise ought to be merciful to our enemies, not causing scandal by tumultuous contention but, preserving brotherly charity, committing our cause into the hand of the supreme Judge (as was said in Tract I, chapter 2 [*De mandatis divinis*, pp. 9–10]). And it is clear how the law and the manner of giving remain on all sides without blame.

But consider carefully and distinguish subtly that in the rational creature on the occasion of sin God takes away grace and active justice, preserving natural justice. This is true of every positive kind [of natural good] existing in the sinner. But speaking of the disposition that lordship would be, because it does not exist (though to the deceived it seems to exist), it must simply be conceded that the unjust do not have lordship, though, as has been said, in an improper sense they 'have' natural goods. Thus the conclusion concerning the sinner's lack of lordship is plain.

[2. Arguments to Prove that Everything Belongs to the Just]

{47} **Chapter 7.** Next in order after what has been said it remains to show that the just are all lords over the whole sensible world.

[1] First, from the fact that the coexistence of the extremes, the natural superiority of the dominative power, and charity in the dominative power are sufficient for true and natural lordship. But all of these are present in any just person in respect of the whole sensible world – therefore also true lordship over the same. And hence Truth, after speaking about natural solicitude concerning temporals, says, 'Seek first God's Kingdom and his justice, and all these things will be added to you' (Matthew 6:33), meaning that the first of the five goods listed above [above, p. 626] ought to be sought most principally, and by a good means, which is justice, and then upon this, if it is possessed, follows the totality of lower goods. And the just are not troubled that they do not have civil lordship in these goods,

because in truth it would not benefit but harm. Thus Jerome says, in the last chapter of his letter to Paulinus: 'The whole world of riches belongs to the believer, but the unbeliever lacks even a penny, etc.'

[2] Again, everyone who is in the charity of predestination is, whenever he has God's grace, an adoptive son. But by the very fact that he is such he has a right to the whole kingdom, and consequently to any part of it. Therefore, everyone who is just in that way is lord over the whole sensible world. The major is supposed from faith and from the notion of an adoptive son. The minor is clear from this, that if he does not forfeit and does not have a superior whose reign would be incompatible with his, in whatever way a young man is the king's son he is thereby true lord of the kingdom in question. Since, therefore, anyone thus just is the son of the eternal king and does not forfeit or have a reign contrary to him, such a person is thereby truly lord of the kingdom in question. (For because of the spirituality of reigning in the gospel way, any number of reigns {48} are possible together, as is clear by faith and by example; for any number of forms of material qualities are possible together in the same medium [e.g., in a transparent medium of vision], unless those qualities would conflict because of their material coarseness.) Hence the Apostle inculcates the same philosophy in Romans 8:15: 'You have received the spirit of adoption, in which we cry, Abba, father'; and he continues, 'if sons, heirs also.' And thus the Savior says truly (Matthew 5:3, 10), 'Blessed are the poor in spirit' and 'those persecuted for justice's sake, for theirs is the kingdom of heaven.' If, I say, they are blessed, they have whatever good they wish. But it is certain that to be lord over the whole world is a good willable by them, since it would belong to the completion of goods. Therefore, they really have it.

[3] Third, the just all use the whole sensible world. But they use nothing of which they do not have lordship (since they are just). Therefore, the just are all lords over the whole sensible world. The premise is clear from the things said about use and about the lordship of the innocent, for by the very fact that a thing inferior in nature advantages someone, to that extent that person uses it by a lord's use. But the whole world advantages each of the just in many ways. Therefore, etc. It advantages them inasmuch as it terminates [as an object] a meritorious act of contemplation and inasmuch as it makes a whole over which the just are placed, and it helps them as being just in nature. Otherwise the Apostle would not say that the Lord 'gives us abundantly *all things* to enjoy' (1 Timothy 6:17). If the unjust serve the just when they oppose them and torment them with

punishments and other things that seem quite alien to the service of the just, much more also [are they served by] other things that seem less contrary. This seems to be the doctrine of the Apostle: 'For we know that for those who love God *all things* work together to good, for those who according to his purpose have been called to be saints' (Romans 8:28). If, therefore, according to God's eternal purpose all inferior things benefit every predestined person, how will that person not be their lord? – as, if a just man has usufruct of the goods of a miser and with them merits blessedness, whereas they do not serve the miser but hinder by dominating [him], how would the miser be said to be their lord and not the {49} just man, since he can receive their use however and whenever he wishes?

[4] Fourth, God does not give anything to anyone able to accept except in the best manner of giving (as is clear above, chapter 6). But the just are all able to accept the manner of granting that is best in kind. Therefore, for the time in which someone is just, God gives only in that manner. And this cannot be called into question, since, by the very fact that he gives something to someone in charity, he gives him the origin of charity, which is God: in 1 John 4:16 it is written, 'God is charity, and he who dwells in charity dwells in God, and God in him.' And it would not otherwise be possible for the Holy Spirit to be given to human beings unless, by the very fact that grace is given to them, the Spirit itself is given. Whence, just as it is inconsistent with the magnificence of a king of England to give just an atom, especially to the poor or to an enemy, so it conflicts with the magnificent liberality of the King of Kings to grant his servant, who is so needy, the temporal things that Scripture calls dung and dust, except as an accessory to a more complete gift; for then he would remunerate his assiduous servant partly and incompletely. And this seems to me to be the Savior's teaching in Matthew 7:11: 'If you who are evil know how to give good things to your children, how much more will your heavenly Father give the good Spirit to those who seek him?' – as if to say, 'If the gift must be proportioned to the magnificence of the granter, and if you, incomplete fathers who have nothing except by gift, know how to give your children natural goods and goods of fortune, how much more will the heavenly Father, infinitely more loving and more capable, give not only the created good but the uncreated Spirit?' Whence God cannot give creatures any created good unless he has first given them the uncreated. This is clear as follows. God cannot grant anything to a creature unless he gives grace (as is clear above, chapter 2), and he cannot give

grace unless he gives the Holy Spirit (as is clear from what has been said). Therefore, the conclusion. And it is not possible for human beings to receive that gift unless they thereby have the whole world with it; because, since wisdom conquers {50} wickedness (as is clear in Tract I, chapter 5 [*De mandatis divinis*, p. 40]), it is clear that no matter whose wisdom it is, it will take possession of the whole universe, even including sins. And hence, in Romans 8, after the giving of the Spirit to adoptive sons and the mercy of conclusions most beautifully woven together, he adds: 'If God is for us, who is against us?' [v. 31]. And it is certain that we cannot receive a better use of things able to be subjected to lordship than that they should help us fight enemies trying to destroy body and soul and [help us] acquire blessedness. Since to this end every corporeal nature ministers to anyone predestined in grace, it follows that every such person is lord over these things able to be subjected to lordship according to a most fruitful use.

[5] Fifth, by the very fact that someone grants the main thing he grants also anything that essentially results from it. But God grants nothing to human beings unless in the first place he gives himself (as is clear from Romans 8:32 and has been explained in *De divino dominio*, III, chapter 2 [p. 207]). Therefore, God grants everything accessory that results from himself. The major is clear, because it would be a ridiculous grant to give a horse, or any other thing, and not grant a part or an accident resulting from it. And if that conclusion is established, clearly the following argument is sound: Since the intelligible being of any creature absolutely necessarily is in God, but God is granted to someone, therefore also the intelligible being of any creature; and since the highest being of a creature is its intelligible being, it follows that when God is given to someone there is given to that person the highest being of every creature, and consequently much more the being of existence (*esse existere*) of every creature, since that adheres to the intelligible being more essentially than accident to subject, if that is possible. This argument gives full conviction to those trained in the material about ideas, and it is clear from the testimony of the Apostle, Romans 8:32: 'If God did not spare his own son, but gave him up for us all, how will he not {51} also with him grant us all things?' It is quite clear that if someone has uncreated wisdom as his gift, he has also the intellectivity of every intelligible, and consequently the intelligibility of every intelligible, as his gift – and consequently the existence of the intelligible, which is the accessory. And we should understand in this way the text of Wisdom 7:7, 11: 'I called [upon God], and the Spirit of

wisdom came upon me; and I preferred her to kings and thrones, and I thought riches nothing in comparison with her . . . Now there came to me with her likewise all good things.'

There is no doubt that this is the conclusion of Truth, that everyone who leaves all temporal things for Christ's sake, in due affection rightly putting him first, by consequent addition has all those things in a better way than it would be possible to have them by a love in the reverse order [i.e., putting creatures first]. Thus in Mark 10:29, 30 there is testimony as follows: 'Amen, I say to you, there is no one who has left behind home, or brothers, or sisters, or father or mother, or children, or lands, for my sake and for the Gospel, who will not receive a hundred times as much, now in this time − homes and brothers and sisters and mothers and children and lands, with persecutions; and in the world to come eternal life.' A catholic may not deny this in a sense undoubtedly sound by virtue of the meaning of the words. Now these other goods are [1] goods of fortune, [2] goods of worldly friendship, and [3] goods of nature. [1] Inanimate goods of fortune are grand houses, jewels, and other artifacts that are by no means necessary; the relinquishing of those is therefore put first as being easiest. [2] By 'brothers' is meant friendships formed through fleshly kinship, by 'sisters' friendships formed by marriage (since in correspondence with [the female] sex they are weaker). And [3] goods of nature consist in three things, namely, [a] powers of the soul, signified by 'father,' [b] corporeal goods, signified by 'mother' (because in Book IX of the Natural Treatises Aristotle says that in carnal procreation the man gives the form and the woman gives the matter, so those goods are valued in correspondence with the goodnesses of the sexes). [c] The third natural good is the good of offspring, or the {52} growth of body by nutrition, signified by 'sons.' [d] A seventh good more necessary to our life is a temporal good by which we are fed and clothed, and it is signified by the 'land' in which are nourished the things that grow in the earth, such as grain, vines, and animals. The whole range of sins consists in inordinate affection to those seven. Whence, by 'wife' (which Matthew 19:29 adds) is signified pleasure, which, since it is common in all of these, is not put into the count with them.

Therefore, every secular person who abuses the good things of God has some false pretended right to all those things or to some of them. But whoever, for love of Christ and the gospel law, abandons that title, accepting from the chief lord the title of grace, will receive such good things one hundredfold even in this life; and by 'one hundredfold' understand the totality of good things, since it is tenfold multiplied by itself. This is clear as follows. Those who have the title of grace or a gospel right to something then have the whole world and all those good things, since God cannot grant part unless he grants the whole, whereas possession by human title is quite narrow. And this is clear from the value of the transaction in exchanging human title to lordship. Thus in Luke 18:30 it is said that there is no one who makes such an exchange who 'does not receive much more in this time and,' in addition to this, 'in the world to come, eternal life,' as the two gospel writers say in agreement. That Mark's text ought to be understood spiritually is clear from the fact that no one doubts that from such an exchange, by following Christ, the followers of the Gospel do not acquire only hundreds of fleshly brothers, sisters, mothers and children; rather, the whole of the universal church will then [in the world to come] be to him a brother of a higher than fleshly kind, according to bodily nature [in this world] it will be a sister, begetting a man as a son of the church it will be a mother, and by assisting reciprocally, as Christ is formed in them, it will have all as adopted sons. Truth himself teaches this interpretation when, in Matthew 12:50, he says, 'Whoever does the will of my Father who is in heaven is my brother, sister, and mother.' And as for goods of fortune and their appendages, it {53} is certain that, as far as gospel lordship is concerned, all these follow. Thus it seems that the saying of Mark, 'with persecutions' (*persecucionibus*, 'followings'), does not suggest tribulation, but perfect following (*perfectam sequelam*) of anything positive based on the things whose gospel possession is sought (as it is not necessary, if all these things are goods of the just, that the defects in them should also belong to the just, because there is no 'perfect following' (*perfecta secucio*) of sin by a human being). And the truth of every part of Christ's saying is clear; and undoubtedly these goods are preceded in the predestined by the goods of grace and glory and consequently the totality of goods pertains to every just man.

[2a. Implications Regarding True and False Fame]

Chapter 8. From these points it is clear that the good of fame or of friendship presupposes charity or grace in the person who has it. For if a vicious person's fame spreads among human beings as if that person were just, then, since there is underlying falsity, it is not true [fame]. Rather, according to Augustine, when the world praises someone as being such who is not such, they praise not that person but another who is such.

Therefore, just as a creature's lordship presupposes God's grant and consequently the creature's being in grace, so fame or true praise presupposes
God's praise, and consequently grace in the one praised; and this is the
Apostle's conclusion in 2 Corinthians 10:18. He says, 'For it is not those
who commend themselves who are approved, but those whom God commends.' And this ought not to be called into question in the mind of a
philosopher who thinks rightly concerning God's knowledge and inviola-
ble and universal judgment.

[1] From these points it is clear, first, that all the unjust who pretend to
be lords are infamous hypocrites; infamous, because they lack the substance
of good fame, which is virtue; hypocrites, because they pretend to be lords
justly, and consequently to be just, while being nevertheless actually unjust.
Thus it is significant that Scripture says, Job 24:30, that God 'makes a
hypocrite to reign on account of the sins of the people.'

[2] It is clear, second, that all the unjust are hypocrites, and vice versa,
for the unjust all pretend that their possession of the Lord's good things is
not unjust, and since this is false, it is clear that they pretend to be holy
without the underlying truth, which {54} is the characteristic of a hypocrite. For like the virtues, the vices also are connected. Thus it is significant
that the Savior reproves the Pharisees, who abused temporal things according to human traditions, for the sin of hypocrisy, as is clear in Matthew 23.

[3] It is clear, third, that the good of fame is better than the civil lordship
anyone can have. For if someone has true fame, this is because of the
virtue by which that person is commended before God, according to the
Apostle's statement, 2 Corinthians 10:13, 'But we will not glory beyond
measure, but according to the measure of the glory which God has measured out to us.' Since, therefore, commendation before God is superior
to any temporal lordship, the conclusion follows, for the commendation
remains perpetually with the blessed, but every civil lordship must perish,
according to the Apostle, 1 Corinthians 5. Whence it is said in Proverbs
22:1, 'A good name is better than great riches,' and, suggesting that that
name is founded in grace, it adds, 'For good grace is above silver and
gold.'

[4] It is clear, fourth, that no one can take away the fame of the just
unless by sinning they fall from virtue. This is clear as follows. A creature's
fame is always preserved before God in proportion to virtue. But no
creature can take away that fame in God's eyes while the famed person's
worthiness remains. Therefore, the conclusion. Whence it is false that liars
blacken the fame of someone who has constancy, since that fame is written

in the book of life, which is 'a mirror without blemish,' Wisdom 7:26; but, in the characteristic manner of speaking of the Word of Truth, in Matthew 15:12, liars are 'scandalized' by the just, and according to Aristotle, '[The just is] foursquare beyond reproach' (*Ethics* X 10, 1100b21).

If it be said that they blacken their neighbor's fame in the eyes of weighty persons who think ill of a defamed person, it is answered that the fame of the just depends on no such persons, but those persons (and the liars) lose their own fame, if, too credulous, they have suspected what is false. And the fame of the just whose names have been cast out is the brighter, if they bear it with equanimity, since by reason of their patience their names are more approved in the judgment of the three weightiest Persons [i.e., Father, Son and Holy Spirit]. Whence in Matthew 15:12–13, after Truth has reproved the {55} teaching of the Pharisees, calling them hypocrites, the disciples, moved by some blind compassion, said, 'Do you know that the Pharisees were scandalized when they heard that saying?' And he answered, 'Every planting that my heavenly Father did not plant will be uprooted.' This means: The praise or fame of a hypocrite planted in the minds of the deceived will never grow, because it is not written in the book of life, but it will perish completely when the sin of hypocrisy is punished; because in Job 20:5 it is said, 'The joy of a hypocrite is like a moment.' From these things we gather that useful truth should not be left unspoken to avoid scandalizing the reprobate, because anyone who speaks the truth in such a way does not defame. I wish that those who plead for the infamous would kindle to that doctrine, in imitation of Christ, who says, John 8:50, 'But I do not seek my own glory. There is one who seeks and judges.'

And if you object that to slander a brother by lying wrongs him by making other friends hate him and think falsely or evilly of him, the conclusion is conceded. Indeed, it is conceded that we cannot sin in our dealings with someone without injuring every one of our brothers; this is clear in Tract I, chapter 2 (*De mandatis divinis*, pp. 13–14; cf. p. 39). And since we do not proceed against brothers for minor injuries, it is very true that, like hypocrites, we proceed so sharply against them rather on account of fame in the eyes of the church than for brotherly correction. For undoubtedly, as far as we are concerned, our fame would be purer if we entrusted the cause to the supreme Judge, praying charity for the wrongdoer, instead of being zealous for our own vindication. This is clear in Tract I, chapter 3 [not found; see *De mandatis divinis*, c. 2, p. 10]. But under what circumstances such things can be done well appears below, when we discuss whether it is permissible to contend or fight for goods of fortune.

[5] It is clear, fifth, that no man's fame is praiseworthy unless it is promulgated everywhere. This is clear as follows. It is of the nature of fame, as such, that it is a good name, and especially for virtue, published to many. But no one can be widely famed unless the uncreated Trinity shows his {56} name throughout the whole world. Therefore, the conclusion. For a person's fame is not the opinion, true or false, that brothers conceive of him: First, because that opinion is not a good that belongs to the famed person but a good that belongs to those who hold the opinion, quite separate from the famed person, and [true] fame is not proportionally related to such opinions, as is clear to those who compare them. †† Second, because no good inheres [merely on account of the good opinion of brothers] in the person named according to virtue (virtue being a part of the 'name,' which is a collection of properties or accidents in a subject), and thus a good name does not inhere in someone unless it is commonly known everywhere [shown by the Trinity]. For just as God cannot grant his creature lordship unless it extends to every part of the world, so neither can he give a good name to someone unless the Trinity knows that person everywhere. And it is clear how confined is the deceptive fame that is not based on justice, just like such pretended lordship. To explain this, it should be known (according to Boethius, *Consolation* I, prose 12 [II, prose 7]) that the whole sphere of the earth is a mere point in comparison with the greatness of the universe; from this sphere, if you first noted the separate surface of the earth under the torrid zone divided into seven climes and, second, noted the positions of the climes throughout boundless spaces (such as deserts, seas, and open country), and, third, how many places fit for human habitation are not occupied by human beings, and, fourth, [that] however much someone's name may be celebrated in {57} the world it is not therefore wholly known to [even] one province or town (indeed, even if it is, the extent of fame amounts to little or nothing, and it is committed to oblivion even in a moment) – it would then be clear how narrow and empty is human praise. That doctrine is clear in Wisdom, chapter 5. The opposite is true of those who are finally just. Whence Christ, teaching us to flee the world's fame and care about a good name, speaks thus to the seventy-two disciples when they returned with inordinate joy at the fact that the demons were subject to them: 'I saw Satan falling like lightning from heaven. Behold, I gave you power to tread upon snakes. Nevertheless, do not rejoice in the fact that spirits are subject to

you, but rejoice that your names are written in heaven' (Luke 10:18–20). In this statement is clear, first, in relation to the disciples' inordinate joy, an instructive example recalled by [their] empty glory, [namely] when the highest angel, abusing his power in this matter, fell at once from his original lordship; and thus in the lightning are made known the stench of sin, incompatible with heavenly lordship, and the puffed-up inflammation of provoking others to pride. Therefore, Christ's disciples ought not to glory in an empty way in procuring magnificent powers leading to worldly fame and glory, but, being safe, [should glory] in the true, full, and everlasting fame by which they are inscribed in the exemplar reasons and angelic natures. And, second, it is clear what is fame simply or the praiseworthy, that it is only what is accepted with God and everywhere. For although every creature in its intelligible being is famed everywhere, in its being of existence it is, as object of thought and terminatively, in God, and thus in every part of the world, just as lordship is terminatively wherever there is someone or something serving, though fame or lordship is subjectively [i.e., as accident in substance] only in the substance that has lordship or fame.

[6] It is clear, sixth, that nothing can deprive someone of his fame unless he himself freely consents. Proof: By the very fact that he perseveres in grace or virtue, a person's fame remains whole and undamaged (in accordance with the fourth conclusion). But no one can lose virtue without willing to. Therefore, not fame either. The minor is clear in {58} three ways: [first] from the manner of divine granting, which is most liberal (as is clear above, chapter 6). But a granting that is absolute without †† a conflict that would harm the grantee is more liberal than a granting followed by a spoliation without any demerit on the grantee's part. Therefore, only the former can pertain to God. Second, no one can be deprived of virtue without sinning. But no one can sin without consenting. Therefore, etc. For according to Augustine (*Retractations* I 13) every sin is voluntary, to such an extent that if it is not voluntary it is not a sin. Third, if God could despoil his faithful servant of virtue without demerit on the servant's part, he could likewise to any extent damage and wrong someone who more sincerely loves him continually, an inference which is against the faith. Therefore, Chrysostom says that 'We are not wronged unless we are wronged in the first place by ourselves' (as is clear in Tract II, chapter 1 [*De statu innocencie*, p. 480; cf. p. 482]). Since, therefore, God cannot take away the fame of his faithful servant without demerit on the servant's part, and a creature cannot snatch anything from the hand of God

(as Truth says, John 10:28), the conclusion follows. Indeed, a creature cannot do anything unless God approves, using the creature as an instrument; because in John 15:5 it is said, 'Without me you can do nothing.' And, keeping that point in view, it follows concerning any gift of God that no one can lose lordship except by sinning freely; for whoever freely loses such a useful gift of God undoubtedly sins, having become foolish. But the renunciation of civil interests for Christ's sake, even if it seems foolishness to many, is nevertheless very prudent management of one's affairs, {59} since true lordship of the universe is acquired in exchange for a nonexistent deceptive lordship, according to what is written in 1 Corinthians 2:14: 'The sensual man does not perceive things that are of God's spirit; for it is foolishness to him, and he cannot understand, because it is spiritually examined' – for we must examine the will [and] law of God with the substantial truths hidden in it and divest the cogitative power of bodily imaginings and not rely on the following deceptive sophistry: 'No one is lord of any usable in relation to the world unless it is known to the world and he takes possession from the world in accordance with the world's wrongful demands, therefore he is not simply and truly lord in another way.'

That smoke, together with lust for temporal things, blinds many, to such an extent that even professors of sacred Scripture say that such devout matters are fit for sermons but are not true. But in truth sermon points ought to be most thoroughly examined in case they smack of falsity in any respect; first, in case someone who preaches in such a public way perpetrates a lie; second, in case the hearers, if they catch the preacher in any falsehood, regard the whole sermon as suspect and ludicrous. Third, since the preacher's utterances are signs with no or little hortatory effect except to the extent that abstract truth [i.e., truth in itself] truly teaches and incites, it is clear that if truth is lacking, the teacher is lacking, since what does not exist does not teach – hence Augustine says that if some part of sacred Scripture were false he would regard the whole as suspect. Indeed, the hearers would not know when the preacher spoke like a rabble rouser inventing tales and when he preached catholic doctrine. Hence Gregory says that the Savior's parables were true narrations of events, since the Lord of Truth did not need to borrow fables or tell lying jokes to teach the people; in exhortations, certainly, jest, like falsity, ought especially to be put aside. And in truth if I knew that any part of sacred Scripture, and especially a statement of the Lord, was not literally true, I would no longer be a Christian. But I know that heaven and earth would {60} fail sooner, and therefore I adhere by firm faith to Christ's statements. This is clear in [Tract] I, chapter 3 [not found].

[2b. God Will Not Allow the Just to Be Deprived of Anything Without Recompense]

Chapter 9. From these points (if I am not mistaken) it is clear, further, [1] that God cannot grant a person any gift that someone can remove without any damning failing on that person's part, or [2] that someone who perseveres in justice can [not] be deprived of any gift unless God makes some more valuable recompense. The first part is clear from the statements immediately above, that God cannot, by doing damage, wish to remove a grant from a servant who pleases him; and since he can block any creature opposing his law, lest it be substantially dissolved, the conclusion is clear. For since 'removal' implies that what is removed continues to exist, it is clear that if someone removed from a just man a limb or his cloak, then, if he preserves his charity, he has it [i.e., the thing removed, which he still has, since the just have all things] more excellently, because he is in greater grace because his virtue is augmented by his patience, and the greater the grace or love that is the basis of lordship the truer or firmer the lordship, because the more like divine lordship. Augustine therefore says truly, in Letter 37, that temporal things are more truly had the less they are loved, because since love of them draws one away from love of God and vice versa, it is clear that the less they are loved the more intense becomes the love of God. For these loves mutually augment and diminish one another inversely. And it is clear that robbers taking away the temporal property of the just man give him the foundation of a fuller title in them. It is significant, therefore, that in commending the prudence of the Hebrews, the Apostle says that they accept theft of their goods 'with joy' (Hebrews 10:34), not meaning to deny that it is permissible to have temporal things and to be displeased at the injustice of the robber, but that no one should care about them except insofar as he needs them for serving his God, and he will not lose brotherly charity because of some possible wrongdoing of his brother. If injustice occurs, it is clear that the doer of the injustice does no damage, but by an {61} invincible law works to the advantage of God's servant. Thus the first part of the conclusion is clear.

The second part adds ['unless God makes some more valuable recompense'], since it is possible for a person to be deprived of bodily powers, such as sight and other gifts of God, and for these immediately to cease to exist [and therefore he does not still have them], and God can in this way deprive those he loves of goods he had previously granted to them, as is clear in the case of Job, Tobias, and many similar cases. But given, as a false supposition, that Peter, a finally just man, is damaged by being deprived of a gift of God, or that without any failing on his part God does not give back to him a greater value, then I ask whether Peter preserves charitable patience or loses it? If he loses it, he sins mortally; and since no one sins except in something which he can refuse to do (since God's law cannot oblige someone to do what he cannot do), it follows that Peter fails notably – the opposite of what was assumed. If the alternative is given, that Peter perseveres in charitable patience, it is clear that he notably merits, and consequently God grants him a new grace and virtue. And since *each* gift of grace is better than the *totality* of natural goods, goods of body or goods of fortune, it follows that God recompenses him to a much greater value in place of what was taken from him. Consequently, he is made better off and not simply damaged.

From this argument of Christ's law the saints infer that a man can have no tribulation or suffering except what is just. For if he perseveres in the grace of patience, then his suffering is meritorious and thus just, and if he falls pusillanimously from grace, then, because of the sin, it is just that he be thus punished. And I believe that this conclusion, more clearly demonstrable than Pythagoras's theorem, was the faith in which the saints 'conquered kingdoms, etc.' (Hebrews 11:33). The same faith is the New Testament, in which Christ's fatlings are fed and delighted, joyfully bearing for the sake of Christ's Gospel insults and all the penalties that can be inflicted. And that seems to be the Apostle's opinion in 2 Corinthians 4: 16, where, after explaining that tribulations, hardships, and persecutions redound to the glory of the saints, he adds at the end a word of hope: 'For this reason,' he says, 'we do not fail.' And because the body's failings could be {62} objected against him he adds: 'But though our outward man is corrupted, yet the inner is renewed from day to day.' For since the whole personhood of a human being is preserved in the spirit, it is clear that one who lays aside the body on behalf of a faithful Lord who cannot fail is assured of repayment, as has been touched on above in chapter 6. I do not see how a Christian could otherwise believe securely in his God.

[2c. Another Argument to Prove that Everything Belongs to the Just]

From these [points] an argument is formed to prove the conclusion chiefly aimed at. Human beings in the state of innocence had lordship of every part of the sensible world (as is clear in Tract II, chapter – [see *De statu innocencie*, c. 6]); and by virtue of Christ's passion the just have [a] full remission of sins and [b] restored lordship. Therefore, now in the time of grace a just person has full lordship of the totality. And since the same judgment is to be made of every predestined person, the conclusion follows. Now no believer will dissent from the minor in respect of its first part, but in the second part [b] it could be imagined that after the fall he does not have lordship over his body (since when sins are forgiven rebellion remains, according to the Apostle and to very certain experience). In arguing the point proposed I will therefore first remove this proof [against it]. For no one is simply just unless he is free from mortal sin. But by the very fact that he is such, his soul has lordship over his body. Therefore, etc. (For the body does not have lordship over the soul unless it leads it to servitude through sin. Therefore, the Apostle says in 1 Corinthians 9:27, 'I chasten my body and reduce it to servitude, lest after preaching to others I am myself made reprobate.') And it is clear that it is impossible for someone to be morally just unless soul has lordship over the body. The opposite is never experienced, and the Apostle never affirmed it, since the rebelliousness [of the flesh] that is a punishment [for Original Sin] and makes it difficult for us to act meritoriously does not take away lordship.

With these points established, it is proved that lordship is restored to the justified person just as it existed before when he was in grace. For by the very fact that the principal thing is restored to someone, every accessory thing is also restored (and especially if the restoring was done by the Lord). But complete justice is restored to the person who had fallen, therefore also the lordship that follows upon justice as property follows essence. Whence, by virtue of this minor used as a basic principle, worldly philosophers say that irregularity [i.e., incapacity to receive Holy Orders] is taken away in a person who has committed unjust homicide by the power of baptism {63} but not in someone who has killed legally and meritoriously: because, they say, although irregularity is not a sin, it is [in the first case] based on an earlier sin [i.e., the unjust homicide] which, together with its consequences, is blotted out by baptism, and in the other case, since the irregularity is not a consequence of sin, it is not obliterated. The chief conclusion ought not be called into question, since lordship is defined as the relationship by which the lord is described as set over a person or thing that serves him. But the whole sensible world serves the just even after the Fall (as is clear from the statements in chapter 7). Therefore, the conclusion. For otherwise the just would abuse the world, taking for themselves such a useful use of what belongs to another. Therefore, etc.

Thus the Apostle, in 1 Corinthians 3:19, knowing that that wisdom seems doubtful and foolish in the eyes of the worldly-wise, writes thus: 'The wisdom of this world is foolishness in God's eyes.' Hence his statement directed to the Corinthians who were observing charity: 'All things,' he says, 'are yours, whether Paul, or Apollos, or Cephas, or the world, or life, or death, or things present, or things to come; for *all things are yours*' [1 Corinthians 3:21–22]. Truly I do not know how the doctrine could be stated more plainly. If the Corinthians had all those things by the title of charity, then by the argument from equals each of the just has every part of the world. For if the three chief pillars of the church [i.e., Paul, Apollos, and Cephas], indeed even 'all things,' whether life or death, or friends or enemies, and all 'things to come' (of which it seems least likely) redound to the utility of the saints, how [shall this] not [be so of] all the rest of this world?

This is confirmed, first, as follows. God cannot grant what is posterior unless he first grants whatever is essentially prior to it, since he is the first nature and makes grants in the most orderly way – not able to grant anything unless first, by priority of nature, he gives himself, according to the text of the Apostle in Romans 8:9: 'If anyone does not have the spirit of Jesus, he does not belong to him.' Since therefore the transcendent is the first of all the causes, it seems that he could not give a man {64} anything inferior unless, by priority of nature, he gave himself. Consequently, just as he imparts himself to his grantee, so also he imparts his whole ample lordship, according to the text of Matthew 24:47, 'Amen I say to you, he has established him over all his goods.'

Second, since every inferior needs the causality of its superior, it seems that if God grants something inferior, he grants whatever essentially or accidentally causes it. Such is every superior. Therefore, etc. For otherwise the granting would be useless, as if someone granted me the accident and not the substance. Whence by right of the grant that belongs to all the just from God, Ahimelech gave to David and his young men, provided they were pure [1 Samuel 21:4], the holy bread especially consecrated to God, thereby plainly teaching that the just are all permitted in a time of necessity to use by natural lordship God's good things, for otherwise God would fail his servants in their necessities. And it should not be imagined that God gave lordship for the first time in the hour of necessity, because all the foundations of lordship are equal afterwards and before.

Similarly God does not restore or repair anything unless he restores completely and perfectly, because God's works are perfect. But he restores the human race to lost lordship. Therefore, he restores it fully and perfectly. As a sign of this, in Genesis 9:1–3, this is said to the just who had fallen: 'Increase and multiply and fill the earth, and let the fear and dread of you be upon all the animals of the earth and upon all the birds of the sky and all things that move upon the earth. All the fish of the sea are delivered into your hand, and everything that moves and lives will be yours for food. Even as the green herbs, I have delivered them all to you.' We do not read that God granted such full and explicit use to the innocents [before the Fall]; and the same is suggested by any number of the statements of the Scriptures of both Old and New Testaments. Thus in Genesis 4:3–4 it is written: 'It came to pass after many days that Cain offered of the fruits of the earth gifts to the Lord. Abel also offered of the first-born of his flocks.' In this text we thus observe precisely the finger of the Spirit writing in such a nuanced way, that Abel, the just man, offered some of his own things, and the unjust man Cain things from outside [his own], {65} 'of the fruits of the earth.' It is clearly suggested that every simply just man is justly lord over all the things he rules, but the unjust man unjustly holds the things of others, as the lord Armachanus notes and explains (in *On the Poverty of the Savior* II, chapter 3), a useful witness to this doctrine. And the same thing is said by Augustine, Jerome, Hugh of St. Victor, the Lincolnian, and other men of learning, to whom were granted the first-fruits of the senses of the Scriptures. But also in Hebrews 2:8 the Teacher of the Gentiles proves by the text of the Psalm, 'You have subjected all things under his feet,' that as a human being Christ has lordship of the totality. 'In subjecting all things to him,' he says, 'he left nothing not subjected to him.' But since we are Christ's brothers, adopted sons, co-heirs with him, it follows likewise that all things are subject to us, even Christ himself. All things therefore belong to the just; not, however, sins, because they do not †† bestow anything upon creatures, as death and life do [an allusion to 1 Corinthians 3:21–22]. For truth and sin, which are the limits of the created universe, cannot serve anyone, though in some sense they benefit the just.

Further, we must note a certain difference among the just, namely, that some of them are just for a time but soon fall from justice (these are the foreknown), and some are the predestined just who persevere finally. Only the latter are the heirs of the kingdom with a perpetual right 'for themselves and theirs.' The former, however, have as freeholders all the Lord's good things then in their actual possession as long as they serve without forfeiture, but they do not simply have an hereditary, lifelong title to these goods. Their title does not stand because of loss of their lord, since he stipulates with them under pain of forfeiture that all their acts be done in charity (as is clear in 1 Corinthians 16:14), and when they withdraw this due service, they are deprived of his lordship. Therefore, it is not conceded of them that they have 'all things,' but, as far as they merit *de congruo* by means of the goods of grace and nature, [they have] all things *then in their actual possession*. But {66} they do not have their blessedness, since they do not merit it (as is clear above, in chapter 2), and they do not have future goods postdating their condemnation. It is significant that when the Apostle promises the predestined in 1 Corinthians 3:22 that all things are theirs, whether 'things present, or things to come,' he does not mention things past, because, since lordship requires the existence of the extremes [of the lord–servant relationship], it seems that past things that perished before they [the lords] existed are not theirs – as all future things are, since they remain in the perpetual grace of predestination. However, since all past things, which do not now exist, dispositively perfect the present order of the world, it can be said with probability that every predestinate person has all things past or future (and correspondingly that he has everlasting being in second causes), but he does not have them now in their own existence, but rather in effect or in their fruits, in the way in which the deeds of the good 'follow them' (as is said in Revelation 14:13 and we likewise read often elsewhere in Scripture).

[2d. Four Implications Illustrating God's Generosity]

Chapter 10. From these points four truths can be drawn.

[i] First, that because of the Fall human lordship is more extensive and more gracious than it would have been if the whole human race had preserved the state of innocence. This is clear, first, from the fact that by the occasion offered by sin the kingdom of the universe is more extensive – because of the damned and the things connected with them – than it would be if there had been no sin; and over all these all the blessed are lords. Therefore, their lordship is more extensive than it would have been if there had been no sin. In favor of the major premise I suppose for now that the multitude of heavenly citizens is precisely as great as it would have been if sin had not happened. From this it is clear that there will exist as many human beings more than would have existed if the state of innocence had been completely preserved as there are human beings or angels who have been damned. And since the death and life of all these

redound to the glory and service of the saints, according to Paul [1 Corinthians 3:20], it is clear that, by the occasion offered by sin, the lordship of the blessed is more extensive and more glorious.

This is confirmed by the fact that the human race {67} receives many services from Christ, who is 'the angel of great counsel,' and from the other angels that it would not have received if the state of innocence had lasted completely. Therefore the conclusion. The premise is clear from the fact that Christ was a servant to the Hebrews (according to the Apostle, Romans 15:8), and all the others are 'ministering spirits' (as the Apostle says in Hebrews, 1:14); and if sin had not gone before Christ would not have been made flesh and the angels would not have ministered in such a way. From this it seems that both would have been superfluous; rather, assuming that it was so, Christ would not thus have suffered and died, and the angels would not have merited by fighting the Devil. Since all these things serve the blessed for glory, it follows that the lordship of the blessed is now wider than it would have been.

It is confirmed [further] from the fact that by fighting with enemies in the strength of the leader of their army, Jesus Christ, the predestined add one kind of merit that would not have existed in the state of innocence and it [i.e., their merit under other heads] is otherwise equivalent or superabundant in respect of grace. Therefore, the lordship of humanity is simply more gracious and the reward more glorious than it would have been. The inference is clear, both because God allows no praiseworthy triumph to go without reward, even beyond what is condign, and also because by reason of the Fall such grace is purer than it would have been if the adoptive son had remained innocent, simply free from sin. Therefore, joy in the triumph is added to the blessed by the occasion offered by sin, since it is certain that, if there had been no sin, there would have been no rebellion. Thus I have not read that the angels assisted human beings by their ministry before the Fall, since they [i.e., human beings] would have been provided for sufficiently by their own lordship; and it would not have been necessary for the good angels to have opposed the bad, since there would have been no antagonism. Thus, as a sign of this lordship, we read in Revelation, last chapter [22:9], that when John fell at the feet of the angel who had done him service to adore him in worship, the angel said: 'Do not do that; for I am your fellow servant and the servant of your brothers.' We must not think that the angel lied here out of politeness. {68}

It was for this reason, I believe, that in the canticle of the church blessed

Gregory said that Adam's sin — and our own — was 'necessary' and the fault a 'happy' one that merited such and so great a redeemer: happy, I say, by the sign that it can be remitted, as urine is healthy [i.e., a sign of health]. The Apostle seems to allude to this doctrine when he says, 'Where sin abounded, grace superabounded' (Romans 5:20). But (as was said above, in chapter 6) it must not be inferred from this that we should sin so that good may come, because it is not from the occasion given by the crime that good comes but from the Savior's grace. From this it is clear that, because of that doctrine, the Christian would hope in Christ's name, being able to rise up victoriously to fight bravely for a crown, and would more devotedly return special worship to him in whose strength all these things are done. Thus it is clear that the text of the Savior in Luke 15:7 is satisfied literally, that 'There will be more joy in heaven upon one sinner doing penance than over ninety-nine just persons who need not do penance.' To explain this I suppose that in his parable the Savior means by the hundred the totality of the rational creation to be saved, by the lost sheep the human race redeemed by Christ, and by the ninety-nine the totality of nine orders of angels who did not fall. Since, therefore, Christ is one individual of this race, who, though he did not sin, yet did the chief penance for all, it is clear that there should be more rejoicing concerning this race which, in its more numerous part, is a race of sinners, than over all the orders of angels — indeed, over any of those sinners there is matter for greater rejoicing because of the redemption and the life of Christ.

[ii] The second truth is this, that 'the mediator between God and men' redeems the whole human race more completely than it was lost. To explain this I suppose that the whole multitude of the predestined is one generation or race, the head of which is the second, heavenly Adam, and the whole {69} race of the foreknown is the wicked generation, the father or head of which is the Devil. The supposition is clear from the Savior's manner of speaking. The former generation is referred to very often. In 1 John 5:18, 'The generation of God [i.e., Christ] preserves' the predestined. The latter is referred to in Matthew 16:4: 'An evil and adulterous generation seeks a sign.' It is spoken of in Matthew 23:34–36: 'Behold, I send you wise men . . . so that all the just blood may come upon you. Amen, I say to you that all these things will come upon this generation.' There is no doubt he means here the whole multitude of the foreknown, since in Matthew 24:34 he says, 'Amen, I say to you that this generation will not pass until all these things happen.' Thus Chrysostom writes on this text of Matthew 23: 'The generation of all the wicked, the persecutors and the

murderers is one, and if they do not all exist in the one time, they are [nevertheless] all children of persecutors, of Cain himself,' and he explains at length the continuity of this generation from one people to another. Supposing these things, the conclusion is clear concerning the generation of the predestined, which is redeemed as a whole. Since it is redeemed to a greater and better lordship, to a more glorious prize, and according to as great a multitude of the elect as there would have been if innocence had been preserved, it is clear that this generation has been redeemed more completely than it was lost by sin. But whether precisely the same people who would have existed in the state of innocence are now being saved, or whether there would then have been mixedly people of both generations, I do not dare rashly to define. But it can be said with probability that the race saved remains the same as that which was lost through sin (by 'the race' understanding, as before, the generation, excluding the head who is Christ; for none of them wholly did good up to him alone, since he never unlawfully turned aside).

From this it is clear that of the whole human race some are not redeemed, {70} such as the foreknown who have never tasted the charisms of charity; some are redeemed, but not to the inheritance or glory, such as the foreknown who have fallen from grace; and some are redeemed from captivity to glory, such as the generation of the just who persevere finally in grace. But whether more are damned than saved, as the text 'Many are called but few are chosen' (Matthew 22:14) seems to suggest, is not for us to resolve. For it does not follow, 'Many are called, but few are chosen; therefore, more are to be damned than saved,' since the whole generation of those to be saved and the greater part of the adulterous generation are called, and the lesser number [i.e., those who will be saved] is 'few' in respect of the greater [i.e., the saved are fewer than the saved plus the lost who have been called, even if the saved are more numerous than the lost]. Thus, even if [on the contrary] perdition is more general than redemption, it [redemption] is greater because of the final perdition of the foreknown, since it has been carried thence beyond the race of those who would have been saved in the state of innocence, and a price has been paid sufficient to save any number of worlds, if they had existed. And it is clear that the operation of the redeemer remains everywhere superabundant, because he redeems to glory or grace a greater race of human beings than would have been saved in the state of innocence, and beyond this he has created another race which, though lost by its own sin, yet redounds to the glory of those who are to be saved, and a price has been paid sufficient for their redemption if they do not refuse. Hence it is good for Adam, and something eternally ordained to the everlasting perfection of the universe, that he now has more sons, though begotten in an unlawful way, than he would have had if there had been no sin.

[iii] The third truth following from what has been said is this. Just as [a] one who sins after a greater grace sins more seriously, so [b] one who rises again after a fall from grace returns to as great a grace, or greater. The first part seems evident from the fact that sin in the formal sense is a defection. Therefore, where a person ought to be in a greater grace and by his own fault defects, the defection is larger and consequently the sin is greater. This is confirmed by the fact that the ingratitude of one previously in grace, who sins after greater gifts, is to that extent greater; and ingratitude is always a sin or follows inseparably upon sin. Therefore, the sin also is to that extent more serious. It is confirmed by the fact that anyone who is more pleasing to God is to that extent more obliged {71} to him, and consequently by throwing off the obligation is more disobedient and more in debt to the one who obliges him, and these things and sins correspond to one another in seriousness. Therefore, just as one who falls from a higher degree to a situation equally low suffers a loss more serious than that of his equals [i.e., those who are his equals after his fall], so one who falls spiritually from a higher grace to no grace sins simply more. Thus the learned say that our first parent after the state of innocence could not have sinned first venially, because for one so gifted with virtues there would have been no excuse for sinning, by a sin however light in its kind; and since forgivability and excusability from damnation, like their opposites, correspond, the doctrine seems to be clear. Therefore, the first sin was a fault of omission, upon which followed pride, the next actual sin. This is clear in Tract I, on the ordering of temptation, chapter 5 (*De mandatis divinis*, p. 37).

But for the solution of objections it is commonly said that the seriousness of a sin can be looked at in three ways: first intensively, and thus Peter's failing in grace, from which he fell by denying the Lord, was a greater sin than the sin of the betrayer, assuming that Judas was never so full of grace. Second, a sin is said to be more serious than another extensively, and thus any sin of final impenitence is more serious than a sin that is blotted out. Third, a sin is said to be more serious effectively, in that it does more sensible harm to the commonwealth, and thus one who unjustly kills more or better victims sins more than one in more grace who advises or consents to it. And judges take notice only of this [third] seriousness, judging only by appearance; and many err in their opinion of the seriousness of such sensible sin and concerning its penalties, thinking that the pain of sense, because it can be perceived by the senses, will be equal to the pain of damnation.

[b] The second part of the conclusion is clear from the breadth and perfection of the divine work, which cannot repair anything or make it unless it perfects it by increasing it, since he is Joseph, increasing [cf. Genesis 49:22] {72} and not decreasing in any respect or making worse. This is proved by a *reductio ad absurdum*, starting from the false assumption that Peter, falling from grace, for example [from degree of grace] 8, by sinning mortally, is restored only (for example) to degree of grace 6, in which he dies, rewarded in proportion to that grace. Since the graces of the way and the glories of heaven correspond, it is clear that Peter is rewarded more sparingly than he would have been if he had died in the first grace. From this it is clear that he will remain forever deprived of the glory corresponding to the grace, e.g., the eighth degree, to which he had a right before his fall; that, if this loss stands forever, the sin is not fully forgiven. But, because the penalty of the condemned sin, more serious than any pain of sense, remains everlasting, it follows that sin remains forever in one who is blessed. The conclusion is impossible, since God cannot remit part of a sin and forgive the rest unremitted, since he cannot remit a fault unless he pours in grace, which cannot coexist in anyone with mortal sin. And that is the doctrine of the Lincolnian, Armachanus, and other learned men in concord.

[iv] From this it is clear, fourth, that if, without an addition of merit, someone with original sin is baptized, he is restored equally to the lowest degree of grace, which he had lost by the least sin, namely, original sin. But if by attrition or contrition he merits for himself a second grace, then by the common law of divine mercy he is restored to a fuller grace. From this it is clear that, just as God has restored repentant fallen nature to a richer grace than that from which it had fallen, so he has restored it to a more useful lordship, taking away all the evil of fault. From this root the learned infer that Christ did not heal anyone physically without first healing them mentally; because if he healed physically, then he granted such physical health, and consequently grace and whatever else follows. {73} Who, therefore, would not be delighted (with the Apostle, Romans 7:22) in such a law of God?

Emendations

[The Latin text is based on the edition by R.L. Poole, *Ioannis Wycliffe Tractatus de Civili Dominio Liber Primus* (London, Truebner, 1885). We have amended the text of Poole's edition by drawing on variants found in the manuscript used by him (Wien ONB 1341) or in a second manuscript not known to him (Paris, BN, f.l. 15869). A few emendations are conjectural, as indicated. The emendations are listed here by page and line in our translation. Each emendation is preceded by the reading in Poole.]

591.25 primo] primis 591.30 ad] *add* aliquod 591.35 iuste] *add* sic 592.1 videlicet] *add* quod 592.6 Quo supposito . . . propositam] tunc arguo 592.7 de iure] *om.* 592.12 quoad] *add* ad [conjecture] 592.12 iustum] *add* vel iniustum 592.13 erit] est 592.14 in peccato . . . Argumentatur] etc. 592.14 Set . . . deum] minor apparet 592.19 maior] minor 592.31 noscentes quomodo] *om.* 593.5 et] vel 593.5 ac organa] *om.* 593.10 ut dicitur] *om.* 593.11 movet] movit 593.14 nec] vel 593.23 ex . . . quod] quia 593.32 maxime cum] cuius 593.32 sit] esset 593.33 quasi] qua 593.35 de] *om.* 593.37 distribuerit] distribuit 593.37 sed . . . operatur] *om.* 593.37 et] *om.* 594.9 operatur] operetur 594.10 sicut] *add* requirit 594.13 exigitur] exigita 594.29 utatur] *add* eodem 595.9 Iterum tercio] tercio principaliter sic 595.15 adversum] ad verum 595.18 dominaretur] dominatur 595.24 domino mediantem] dominante 595.30 quemquam] quodcunque 596.13 regula] *om.* 596.15 iustum] *add* interesse a quo sine quo consensu non ex [conjecture: est] iustum 596.16 Et patet . . . iustum] *om.* 596.16 patet] *add* quod 596.17 bonum] bona 596.26 auctor] adiutor 596.29 per . . . sic] ita quod ?iste 596.34 nullius] nullus talis 597.17 prestat] *add* quidquam 597.23 quod] *add* oportet omnem impetrantem a deo dominium esse in gratia; sed 597.25 ut] cum 597.26 ultima] tercia 597.27 minor] maior 597.29 inesse] esse 597.34 prioris] primi 598.1 Ecce] ubi apparet 598.10 a maiori vel pari] a pari vel maiori 598.14 Sed obicitur contra illud] contra predicta arguitur primo 598.20 Similiter] secundo 598.20 videmus] *add* quod 598.20 peccatoribus] *add* Christianis 598.25 Similiter] tercio 598.31 et] ex quo 598.31 ad . . . sequitur] *om.* 598.33 deberemus] debemus 599.1 nos] nobis 599.2 approbante] *om.* 599.18 eis] *add* ita et nos debemus diligere inimicos et ?communicare? eis 599.19 accipimus] et 599.26 et per consequens] ?pro ?cuius ? intellectu est notandum quod omnia naturalia ?peccatorum sunt dona dei et ita 599.36 fortune et nature] nature vel fortune 599.36 dat] *add* illa 599.39 ut] vel

600.16 et] *om.* 600.19 dicere] *add* primum 600.21 dotarius] ?donatorius
600.28 hoc] hec 600.30 et] *add* sic 600.30 utraque] *om.* 600.30
consequencia] conclusio 600.31 non] *add* sunt 600.36 perfecti] ?prefecti
600.38 sed] et 601.11 septemplici] sextuplici 601.13 isti] *add* modi 601.14
prosunt] sunt 601.15 micius] minus 601.25 valet] prodest magis ecclesie
quam opus malum de genere male factum 601.34 scit si] meretur sibi
prima gratia oportet; *add* quod [conjecture] 601.37 vel] ut 602.8
difficultate] *add* sed dicitur quod 602.8 enim] *om.* 602.9 mortaliter]
moraliter 602.12 Et patet] Secundo dicitur 602.12 si] sicut 602.13
beatitudinem] *add* sic 602.14 propriam] primam 602.17 id] illud et 602.19
nunc] *add* non 602.19 nunc] non 602.19 esse] *add* nunc 602.25 Et] *om.*
602.28 et] *om.* 602.32 non] nemo 603.5 abstinenciam] obstinanciam
603.10 demerentibus] de merentibus 603.10 propriam] perpetuam 603.28
placet] *add* deo 603.32 per Scripturam] *om.* 604.1 pravissimus]
gravissimus peccator 604.6 utendi] *add* bonis 604.8 stant] stat 604.19
sunt] sint 604.19 modi] *add* habendi 604.19 scilicet habicio] *om.* 604.25
aut fortuita] *om.* 604.28 dicitur] dicit veritas 604.31 tyrannice] *add* solum
604.32 per hoc] *om.* 604.34 multiplicatem] multiplicationem 604.36
divicias] possessiones 605.1 responsionem] rationem 605.2 notanda] *add*
quod 605.8 modo] *add* prime distincionis 605.9 convertuntur]
convertantur 605.15 confirmatur . . . quod] *om.* 605.19 confirmatur . . .
quod] *om.* 605.20 et] *om.* 605.21 concedunt] *add* talia 605.23 continue]
om. 605.24 rogo] quis 605.28 oportet] oporteat 605.31 esse] omne 605.33
quod] *om.* 606.2 leges] *add* create 606.11 et] *add* ita 606.15 Istis premissis
concedo] ex premissis conceditur 606.18 iniusta] *add* est iusta 606.20
concedatur] conceditur 606.28 ad] aliud 606.30 habuit] habuerit 606.32
quis] quod 606.36 iniustus . . . illo] iniuste [conjecture: univoce] est
habens bona naturalia cum iusto, igitur et univoce dominus cum iusto
607.1 set] quia 607.1 distincte] *om.* 607.6 Per . . . consequenciam] Ad
secundum conceditur 607.10 habet] habeat 607.12 ascitam] *om.* 607.12
principio] *add* assumptam 607.13 puram] primam 607.15 habet] habeat
607.26 inplicacio] *om.* 607.27 iusti] *add* naturaliter sive passive qui tamen
non dubie sunt iniusti 607.29 Et] *om.* 607.32 dicit] distinguit 607.33 de
iusticia] *om.* 607.34 cuiusmodi solum] cuius iusticia solummodo 607.35 et
. . . iusticia] *om.* 607.35 expellit] excludit 607.37 Nota] Notandum 608.1
nam] unde 608.2 quod] quia 608.2 sunt tantum] sicut tamen sunt
608.6 quando] quomodo 608.7 nam] *add* lapis 608.8 iniuste] iniustus
608.13 secundum] aliud 608.17 in quocunque quod] quodcunque 608.20
suppone] scilicet 608.20 dicitur . . . facit] ipse fecit regnare 608.22

exterius] exterii 608.22 et . . . est] non autem esse secundum vel defectum
primum est 608.24 hec considera] considerandum 608.28 iustorum] *om.*
608.30 conformiter] *om.* 608.39 esse . . . genere] de numero 609.1 opera]
add de genere 609.13 morum] moralis 609.21 tercium . . . verum] aliud
conceditur assumptum 609.24 hiis] hoc 609.24 iustum] iniustum 609.25
iniusticia] iusticia 609.26 que] quo [conjecture] 609.35 gracia] *add*
ministrare 610.6 et] *add* sic 610.8 tale] illud 610.10 nec] *add* tamen
610.13 et sic est] quam 610.13 inpossibile] *add* est 610.13 habeam] habeat
610.32 sive] nec 610.37 erit] est 611.1 verum] *add* sicut 611.4 conclusio]
sentencia 611.10 et] *om.* 611.10 Ecce] unde habetur 611.16 quod] *om.*
611.16 sequitur] conceditur 611.16 ergo] *om.* 611.17 idem] *add* testes
611.21 contradictorio] contradictio 611.23 quidquam] quidquid deponunt
611.24 ergo] est 611.24 diffinire] ?deificare 611.25 [in]peccabilem]
peccabilem 611.31 deposicio] deponendo 611.32 teneatur] sentenciatur
611.36 alteram] aliam 611.39 Creator] *om.* 612.4 necessario] *om.* 612.4
iudicio et testimonio] testimonio vel iudicio 612.5 ipsum] ista 612.6
sufficiat] *add* plenum 613.10 potencia] *om.* 613.38 dominium] dominum
[conjecture] 614.25 regis sui vel] *om.* [conjecture] 615.34 peccant]
peccanti [conjecture] 620.2 in] inferior [conjecture] 620.12 iuste] iniuste
[conjecture] 620.19 mediate] mediante 622.1 potest] posset 622.13
multipliciter] tripliciter 622.16 similiter] secundo 622.19 Et iterum palam]
Tertio manifestum 622.24 quo] quibus 622.25 supponens] presupponens
622.27 facit sentenciam] sentenciaret 622.28 et] ex quibus 622.28
conclusio] *om.* 622.31 universalis] *om.* 623.9 usibilis] usibilem 623.10
quo] quando 623.11 uti] *add* et quomodocunque et quandocunque
voluerit, ?quod si aliquod istorum ?defecerit possit donatum 623.24 eos]
eum 623.26 illos] illum 623.26 eciam] *om.* 623.30 velit] *add* quo ad bona
creaturae [conjecture: naturae] dictum est supra cap. 2 quod semper dat
illa sumptio [conjecture: sponsae] vel ecclesiae ad utendum nec potest
quis ipsa perdere nisi velit 624.1 minimis micis] minutiis 624.1 vel] et
624.5 abusum] *add* sed ad usum 624.5 potest] possit 624.6 abuti] uti
624.7 usibili] nisi 624.7 virtutem] *add* nec abuti 624.13 habicio] *add* illa
624.13 esset] est 624.15 Ex istis secundo patet] secundo sequitur 624.21
Et] *om.* 624.21 tercio] igitur 624.29 verior] verius 625.12 Et] *om.* 625.12
patet] *add* secundo 625.15 suppone] id est 625.16 promittit] permittit
625.18 habet] *add* omni enim habenti dabitur et habundabit Pro solutione
questionis ?esset notandum quod omnis iustus predestinatus in finem
?excellentiori modo habendi habet hec temporalia quod [conjecture:
quam] iniustus prescitus ipsi enim 625.21 ita equivoce] equivoce habet

ista 625.23 sed miro] miro tamen 625.26 abusum et] abusus 625.27
omnibus] ?talibus 625.27 et . . . usum] solum quo ad usum 625.34 divites]
om. 625.37 se] sic 626.3 adulatorius] adulatoribus 626.19 que rotatur . . .
ore]*om.* 626.19 plebeorum] plebeiorum 626.22 exinde] inde 626.23
peccandum] deus causa peccandi 626.39 eorum] ipsarum 627.1 et] *add*
sic 627.4 deficit] *add* ?sibi 627.5 nescio quis] non est querendum quid
627.6 solum] *om.* 627.6 bona] *add* solum 627.10 pactum et limites]
limitem 627.13 non dubium] *om.* 627.16 oporteret] oportet 627.16 et] *om.*
627.18 Quod si obicitur] si dicatur quod ?tunc 627.18 esse] esset 627.23
sed] *om.* 627.29 oportet] oporteret secundum 627.34 indifferens nec
consonum racioni] consonum racioni vel indifferens 628.1 et . . . iusticie]
om. 628.12 manu] *add* ?summi 628.12 est doctum] dictum est 628.29
sensibilem] *add* igitur 628.31 solicitacionem] sollicitudinem circa
temporalia 628.33 principium] ?primum 628.34 ex] et 629.1 Et] *om.*
629.10 est] foret 629.11 quantumcunque] quomodocunque [conjecture]
629.12 est] sit 629.13 quilibet] *om.* 629.17 moralium] materialium 629.18
ubi] nisi 629.19 moralem] materialem 629.19 unde . . . philosophice] Hinc
philosophiam eandem 629.21 quod summus] si 629.28 Item] tercio 629.30
Argumentum] antecedens 629.35 copulandi] contemplandi 629.36 a] cui
[conjecture] 629.37 tanquam] *add* iustus 630.1 elongari] aliena 630.12
Iterum] quarto 630.15 solum] solummodo 630.28 Veritatis] salvatoris
631.5 patet] *add* quod 631.6 tota universitas] totam universitatem
[conjecture] 631.7 per condonacionem] post donacionem 631.15 Item]
quinto 631.25 possibile creature] creature sit esse suum intelligibile,
sequitur quod dato deo alicui datur sibi supremum esse cuiuslibet creature
632.14 ad sanum sensum vertere in dubium] negare ad sanum sensum
verum indubie 632.20 contracte] *add* cum 632.30 mittuntur] nutriuntur
632.38 centuplum] *add* talium 633.9 sicut dicunt alii] et hoc dicunt 633.21
mihi] *om.* 633.30 etc.] *om.* 634.1 creature] *add* presupponit 634.2
presupponit] *om.* 634.10 infamis] *add* quia deficit sibi substantiam eufamie
quod est virtus, hypocrita 634.13 nostra] *om.* 634.23 personalis] possibilis
634.37 dignitate] *add* famati 635.4 tetragous sive vitupero] tetragonus sine
vituperio 635.5 ipsos] *add* denigrare 635.5 diffimare] *om.* 635.8 sed] ?si
635.14 comparacione] ?compassione 635.23 nunc] *om.* 635.28 falsum] *add*
sive male 635.29 concedo consequenciam] conceditur conclusio 635.30
convivendo] ?communicando 636.3 Ex isto] *om.* 636.13 eciam] *om.*
636.16 vere] *om.* 636.16 nullum] nomen 636.19 nullum] nomen 636.27
quod] quot 636.31 effacio] efflatio 637.11 patet] *add* secundo 637.26
donacioni] donatorio 637.28 Similiter] secundo 637.32 Similiter] ?tertio

638.14 stultis] substantialibus 638.21 nostre] sacre 638.28 subtracta]
abstracta 638.28 veritate] vere 638.32 quomodo] quando 638.32
predicatori] predicator [conjecture] 638.33 quomodo] quando 638.34
dicitur] dicit Gregorius 639.1 de amicicia] *om.* 639.16 excellencius] *add*
quia 640.2 electos] ?dilectos 640.3 da] dato 640.6 et] *add* tunc] 640.12
virtutem] *add* et 640.21 quam ego] *om.* 640.21 demonstrabilem] *add* quam
dulkarnon 640.26 videtur] *add* esse 640.28 redere] ?cedere 640.37 istis] hiis
641.7 lapsus] post lapsum 641.18 vel] nec 641.20 tollit] *add* dominium
641.22 et] ?prius ?existenti in 641.23 restituitur] *add* quodlibet accesorium
et specialiter si restitutio hec fuerit dominica; sed lapso restituitur 641.27
veritate asserti] virtute assumpti 641.27 parte] *om.* 642.11 asserunt quod
quecunque] sed et quelibet 642.13 in] *om.* 642.15 tripliciter] *om.* 642.15
ex hoc quod] sic 642.21 creaturarum] causarum 642.26 Similiter] secundo
642.28 indubie] enim 642.37 equalite] equalia 643.2 alloquitur] dicitur ad
643.15 impius] iniustus 643.15 extranee] extranea 643.30 virtus] veritas
643.31 licet] *add* equivoce iustis proficiant. Ulterius est quaedam iustorum
differentia notanda, ut quod quidam 644.14 sunt] *add* sua 644.20 fruitu]
fructu 644.22 patet] habetur 644.22 ideo etc.] *om.* 644.35 et] *om.* 644.35
fuissent] *add* in 645.4 Secundo confirmatur idem] confirmatur hoc 645.7
Argumentum] Assumptum 645.15 tale] *om.* 645.17 Tertio] *om.* 646.1
confirmasse] dixisse 646.12 illud] *add* salvatoris 646.16 creature] *add*
rationalis 647.7 in] *om.* 647.12 assero] potest dici 647.14 generative]
generationem 647.17 Et] ex quo 647.22 videtur] *add* textus multi sunt
vocati pauci electi Math. 22 647.23 multis scripturam] *om.* 647.23 sapere]
innuere 647.26 pars] *add* generacionis 647.28 minoris] maioris 647.35 dat]
om. 647.35 materiam] ?manet 647.38 gaudium] gloriam [conjecture] 648.8
formaliter] *add* est defectus ubi igitur ?persona debet esse in gratia maiori
et ex culpa propria deficit 648.11 igitur] *om.* 648.14 et tercio] *om.* 648.17
commendent] correspondent 648.21 gradu] gratia 648.21 gradum] gratiam
648.27 submissionis] obmissionis 648.33 fuerat . . . grave] Iudas fuerit ita
gracius 648.34 reliquo] alio 648.35 infinitum . . . doletur] peccato quod
?deletur gravius 649.6 vero] *om.* 649.11 2] 8a 649.15 est premiatus]
premiatur 649.15 foret] fuisset 649.17 secunda] 8a 649.18 dampnacione]
damnificatione 649.21 peccatum] *add* perpetuum 649.21 consequens] *add*
est 649.30 lege] *add* communi

INDEX

Solon, 102, 228, 231

state (*dispositio, complexio, se habens*), 226, 227, 275, 296, 538, 543, 544, 571, 575; best state of a part or whole its virtue, 548–57

state (*status*, condition, status), 83, 126, 137, 183, 197, 267, 324, 394, 414, 458, 546, 552, 624; of innocence, 289, 459, 625, 640, 644, 645, 647, 648; political, 221, 223, 245–46

Stephen Tempier, bishop of Paris, 12, 200, 257, 271

Stephen of Tornai, 154

Stoics, 126

synderesis (*synderesis*), 174, 335; affective or cognitive? 186–91; extinguishable by sin? 191–95; can become depraved through sin? 195–99

Thomas Aquinas, 12, 170, 200, 216, 258, 271, 272, 308, 326, 335, 338, 340, 342, 350, 351, 372–73, 408, 410, 412, 499

Torquemada, Juan de, 418

Tully (Marcus Tullius Cicero), 98, 154, 155, 163, 165, 201, 258, 265, 266, 311, 312, 500, 503, 504, 510, 529, 542

tyrant, tyranny (*tyrannus, tyrannis*), 81, 82, 221, 222, 245, 246, 249, 319, 320, 343, 456, 458, 469, 505, 507, 560, 569, 574, 594, 596, 604, 608, 617, 625

unbelievers (*infideles*), 415, 449, 598, 603, 629; may be used by a Christian king to defend his kingdom? 328–48; pope's authority over, 461–74

undergoing, *see* passion/undergoing/emotion

understanding, *see* intellect/understanding

Vegetius, 201

virtue (*virtus*, excellence, power), 75, 210, 211, 261–63, 275–76, 298–99, 355–56, 364, 543–51, 594, 605; intellectual, 15–17; moral, 15–17, 19, 111–12, 140 (ordered to contemplative happiness, 19, 76, 77–78, 84; civic and military, 99–100; pleasures purer than those of philosophy? 94, 99, 101, 111, 112, 114; needs external goods/activity? 96, 112–13, 114–115, 130; possessed by the gods? 125–26); *see also* perfection

Vitruvius, 81

wanting love (*amor concupiscentiae*), 366, 375, 398, 401; is wanting or desiring something for the sake of another, 352; and amicable love, 289–90; in love of God and self, 291, 292, 293, 297, 299, 300; of God involves using God? 352, 366; *see also* amicable love; love (*amor*); love (*dilectio*)

war, wage war (*bellum, bellare*), 99–100, 125, 262, 265, 315, 317, 320, 326–48 passim, 460, 466, 469

well-being (*bene esse*), 56, 103, 129, 130, 275, 279; *see also* well-being (*salus*)

well-being (*salus*), 260, 261, 262, 266, 269, 298, 299, 310, 311, 312, 313, 446; *see also* salvation; well-being (*bene esse*)

will (*voluntas*): same as intellect? 368, 372, 407, 511–15; acts attributed to, 518–20; enjoyment an act of? 366–73; referring and non-referring acts of, 353; act always preceded by act of intellect, 563, 575; how soul produces its act, 534–39; *see also* freedom of will; intellect/understanding; power (moral/legal/political)

William of Moerbeke, 216, 217

William of Ockham, 170, 349–51, 419, 484–85, 498, 499, 587, 589, 590

William of Ware, 367

woman, old woman (*femina, mulieris; vetula*), 33, 160, 330, 334, 420, 480, 559, 573–74, 632